Mesoamerican Archaeology
New Approaches

Mesoamerican Archaeology
New Approaches

---

edited by
NORMAN HAMMOND

Proceedings of a Symposium on Mesoamerican Archaeology held by the University of Cambridge Centre of Latin American Studies, August 1972

UNIVERSITY OF TEXAS PRESS, AUSTIN

Library of Congress Catalog Card Number 74-2545
International Standard Book Number 0-292-75008-0

Typeset by
Specialised Offset Services Limited, Liverpool,
Printed and bound in Great Britain by
Redwood Burn Limited
Trowbridge & Esher

To the memory of
E. Wyllys Andrews IV
William R. Bullard, Jr.
James C. Gifford

CONTENTS

List of Contributors

R.E.W. Adams, University of Texas, San Antonio.
Gordon Brotherston, University of Essex.
Judith G. Connor, University of Arizona.
George Cowgill, Brandeis University.
Adrian Digby, Stroud, Gloucestershire.
Lawrence H. Feldman, State University of New York at Albany.
David A. Friedl, Harvard University.
Peter T. Furst, State University of New York at Albany.
James C. Gifford, Temple University, Philadelphia.
Gary H. Gossen, University of California, Santa Cruz.
Ronald A. Grennes-Ravitz, Virginia Military College.
David C. Grove, University of Illinois.
Norman Hammond, Cambridge University.
David H. Kelley, University of Calgary.
Thomas A. Lee Jr., New World Archaeological Foundation, Brigham
    Young University.
Alexander Marshack, Peabody Museum, Harvard University.
Arthur G. Miller, Yale University.
René Millon, University of Rochester.
John P. Molloy, University of Arizona.
H.B. Nicholson, University of California, Los Angeles.
Barbara J. Price, New York.
Dennis E. Puleston, University of Minnesota.
Robert L. Rands, University of Southern Illinois.
William L. Rathje, University of Arizona.
Jeremy A. Sabloff, Peabody Museum, Harvard University.
Paula L.W. Sabloff, Brandeis University.
J. Eric S. Thompson, Saffron Walden.
Gordon R. Willey, Peabody Museum, Harvard University.
Glyn Williams, University of Wales, Bangor.

Editor's Preface

The title of this book, though unimaginative, is a valid reflection of the way in which its contents have been received, both when first presented in symposium at Cambridge and by subsequent readers of the manuscript. The majority of the papers were both specifically invited and presented at Cambridge; the remainder are selected from those volunteered: all present the knowledge and opinions of their authors in August 1972, with some slight revisions.

The new approaches are in some cases in the realm of theory, applying new models and techniques to elucidate patterns in archaeological data; in others it is the direction of approach, from iconography or ethnohistory, that is more novel to Mesoamerican archaeology; and in yet others, traditional models and techniques are taken into little-known areas of Mesoamerica.

Gordon Willey's synthesizing Introduction renders a long editorial preface superfluous. My remaining duty is to note that this volume is dedicated, on my sole responsibility, to three scholars in the Maya field, one a contributor to this book, who have all recently died in their prime and with much of their potential still unfulfilled. I did not know any of them well, though I have argued and disagreed with all three. This dedication is a mark of respect which I hope their nearer friends will not find presumptuous.

Norman Hammond

GORDON R. WILLEY

Introduction

The papers of the Cambridge symposium on Mesoamerican archaeology are so disparate and wide-ranging in their subject-matter that
any attempt to integrate them into a summary statement might be
most appropriately titled 'Beyond Synthesis'; but there are various
ways in which an introduction or serial synopsis might be arranged.
The symposium programme, for instance, followed a conventional
arrangement, approximately according to geographical subject
matter. So as to view things from another perspective, in this
introduction I have ordered the papers from the point of view of the
author's approach to the data and his problem-orientation.

By a very general classification, there are two basic approaches to
the data of archaeology in Mesoamerica or elsewhere. One is
essentially descriptive and historical, the other functional or functional-processual. Within this framework, we can further subdivide
and grade. For instance, within the descriptive-historical category
there are papers in the present group which are primarily concerned
with the description of archaeological remains and with the
placement of these in space and in time. Most of these are focused on
specific regions within Mesoamerica, although there is a sliding scale
here from a relatively restricted geographical scope to a larger,
multi-regional one. Continuing along this same geographical scale
there are also some papers where the concern goes beyond
Mesoamerica to take in the possibilities of extra-areal or long-
distance diffusional contacts. Within the functional-processual
category, a good many papers are basically concerned with rather
limited functional explanations (using the word functional very
broadly) of archaeological objects, features or events through
immediate and direct ethnographic and ethnohistoric references.
Such papers operate with the assumption of Mesoamerican cultural-
historical continuity, and they are, in that sense, also historical;
however, it seems to me that the author's fundamental purpose in
such a paper has been the elucidation of objects, features, and
institutions insofar as their workings or functionings can be

identified and explained. In addition, there are articles which are addressed to functional or synchronic comprehensions of the data but in which only the materials of the archaeological past are used or, at least, very heavy emphasis is put upon such materials. Finally, and still continuing in our broad functional-processual category, there are those articles where an attempt has been made to go beyond a working, synchronic picture of the pre-Columbian past to achieve an explanatory or processual understanding of that past. In these studies the diachronic is combined with the synchronic in an attempt to see and isolate the causal forces of culture change.

Of course, no perfect classification of all of our papers into such a scheme is possible, nor is it necessary. There is always overlap between history and function-process. Still, I think it can be agreed upon that there are differences in approach and emphasis. Indeed, much of the argument within modern archaeology over the past ten years has been concerned with these differences and the respective values and limitations of differing approaches. At this juncture, let me say that I am not passing value judgments in this argument now: up to a point, most archaeologists will agree that both approaches are necessary. Let me also emphasize that in this introductory commentary on the papers I am not necessarily labelling the individual contributors as being either committed only to descriptive-historic work or primarily concerned with the search for culture process in prehistory, but am simply commenting upon the papers in hand. I will begin in the order of these observations on the nature of the different approaches to the subject matter, and take up those of a more strictly descriptive-historic vein first.*

Thomas Lee's treatment of Middle Grijalva ceramic chronology and its relationships is a straightforward, sound study of this genre. Over one hundred sites were surveyed; a third of these were test excavated and five dug intensively; from this a long sequence was established; and this stratigraphically constructed sequence was correlated with similar sequences in the Valley of Chiapas and on the Gulf Coast. In ceramic space-time systematics a regional gap had been closed. There remain a good many such gaps in Mesoamerica. In fact, there are more holes than cheese in the overall archaeological picture. Just to name a few, we are still appallingly weak in Guerrero, and there is lots of room for this kind of systematic work in west and northwest Mexico. Glyn Williams has tackled the problem there in his analysis of the Upper Rio Verde drainage, on the Zacatecas-Jalisco border. He was working only with surface or other non-stratigraphic collections, but even with these limitations he was able to draw some positive typological comparisons, especially in figurines, between this northwestern material and Preclassic forms in the Valley of Mexico. The northwestern specimens are probably

* There are no bibliographical citations in this Introduction. My references to authors and works other than papers in this book are covered by the individual bibliographies.

Preclassic chronologically as well as typologically — although we do not really know. The relationships between a Preclassic west Mexican tradition and the more typically Mesoamerican cultural tradition of the Preclassic period remain to be worked out; and, presumably, the Valley of Mexico will be the principal place to do this. I think it was a kind of frontier between the two great zones of Mesoamerica proper and west Mexico at this early time. Later, through a process of progressive 'Mesoamericanization', this frontier was pushed north and west.

Rands on Palenque, while remaining within an essentially historical approach, asks some other kinds of questions after comparing Palenque ceramics and the ceramic sequence there with other Maya regions. Why is Palenque so different? Is it ethnic? Were the ancient inhabitants of the site a different kind of Maya from those of other lowland centres? Or are the differences to be explained by Palenque's relative isolation from trade routes? This last might be a reasonable hypothesis for Early Classic times; but by terminal Late Classic Palenque was probably in the middle of things — including trouble. Rands attempts no firm answers now; the questions remain. They are questions brought up by comparing ceramic sequences, and revealing variability in the record. It is the first step beyond sheerly descriptive space-time systematics.

Gifford's paper is considerably more ambitious than any of the foregoing. It is an attempted cultural-historical synthesis of southern Mesoamerica. He comes out strongly for seeing ceramic horizons as population movements. Thus, Xe and Mamom are linked to pioneering waves of people from Salvador coming into the Peten, while Chicanel is conceived of as essentially Mexican and, in some way, Olmec-related. While it seems reasonable to believe that the first inhabitants of the Peten did migrate there from the highlands to the south, I am skeptical of the Mexicanoid-Olmecoid population as the bringers of the Chicanel ceramic complex to the Maya lowlands. While the main lines of Gifford's arguments are historical, he does ask questions about culture process and change, turning to the always fascinating question of why Classic Maya collapsed; but his answer does not take us anywhere on the road to processual understanding, and his approach could hardly be called that. There was, I am sure, a loss of belief, a disarticulation between the 'Great Tradition' and the 'Little Tradition'; and the people undoubtedly lost faith in their leaders. But why? In just what way did the leadership fail? We are, in effect, left where we were.

Two papers move into the thorny field of Olmec manifestations in the uplands of central and western Mexico. Ronald Grennes, analysing his own work in Morelos, and also taking a look at other Olmec evidences in western and central Mexico, comes up with a strong statement which counters those of archaeologists such as M.D. Coe, Ignacio Bernal, and David Grove, who have all seen Olmec power and influence radiating out of the Veracruz-Tabasco lowlands. Grennes cites radiocarbon dates of about 1200 B.C. on his El Zarco subphase at the Iglesia Vieja site which, in his opinion, invalidate a Gulf Coast to highland movement of Olmec traits. Grove, who contributes the other Olmec paper to this volume, argues out a long and detailed case for the currents of diffusion as running in the more traditionally accepted fashion. It is an enormously complex subject, and an important problem in Mesoamerican prehistory, for the correct formal-spatial-temporal arrangements of Olmec manifest-ations in all parts of the total culture area will have to be laid out before archaeologists will be able to move in on the processes by which such a diffusion or spread took place. Grove indicates here, as he has in several other papers, his deep interest in these processual questions; however, he is primarily concerned in this paper with typological, associative, and chronological matters. In fact, the whole Olmec problem, as raised by these two papers, is an excellent example of the necessity of interrelating processual with more traditional archaeological objectives. In the Grennes-Grove debate, however, I am disposed to favour Grove's arguments. Accepting a 1200 B.C. date for Olmecoid objects in Morelos does not really take us further back than Coe's earlier San Lorenzo levels, in which there are also Olmecoid objects and traits, even though Coe's full Olmec monumental horizon is slightly later than this. There are, of course, many things to clarify and keep straight in any 'Olmec argument'. Grove indicates some of these in his analysis of Olmec manifestations in the Mexican highlands. How will we define what is truly Olmec stylistically from what is merely 'Olmec by association'? There is also another clarification needed: a distinction should be made between Olmec as the earliest highly complex Mesoamerican society or incipient 'civilization', as this is revealed in the great mounds and monuments of San Lorenzo, and Olmec as a style (presumably representative of a mythological or belief system). The histories of the two appear to be very different. Indeed, if Grove is right in his guess that Olmec beliefs originated in tropical South America, and spread to Mesoamerica via the Pacific coast of Guatemala and Chiapas, then it may turn out that some manifestations of Olmec art will prove to be earlier in the west and the highlands than on the Gulf coast; but this would not necessarily mean that the first Mesoamerican achievements of 'civilization' were not at sites such as San Lorenzo and La Venta.

Two papers are strictly historical in that they are concerned with long-range diffusion. The more modest is Feldman's identification of shellfish species from archaeological contexts. Some species, according to Feldman, are as potentially diagnostic of certain archaeological phases as pottery. He notes Oaxacan species in Maya sites, and he also advises archaeologists of the close cognate resemblances between Pacific and Caribbean species, a circumstance that has led to some error in identifications.

David Kelley's long-range connections are of a much more spectacular sort. He points to a number of similarities between Mesoamerican calendars and those of China, India, and southeast Asia — similarities in animal names used to designate periods of the year and in the sequence position of some of these animal names in their respective calendars. These calendrical similarities take on more significance, according to Kelley, when one also takes into account certain Old World-New World parallels in colour direction symbolism, and mythology. Kelley insists that the calendric linkages which he has discovered must date from 350 B.C. or later, and he was unwilling to accept the suggestions made by some members of the symposium group that these resemblances could be residues from much earlier connections — for instance, on a late Palaeolithic level or on a time level of 3000-2000 B.C., a period when some Americanists have seen trans-Pacific diffusion. It is a knotty problem. The data are there in Kelley's paper. The reader is invited to take a look.

Six papers, those by Nicholson, Brotherston, Miller, Furst, Gossen and Marshack, depend on ethnohistoric or ethnographic sources for functional interpretations of the archaeological past. Nicholson writes of Tepepolco and how Sahagún prepared his ethnohistorical account of that Mexican community which gives us a living picture of late sixteenth-century life. Sahagún's account is also a reconstruction of the Postclassic period history of the Chichimecs. Gordon Brotherston has also taken documentary and early historic materials for his study. By showing us how the parvenu Aztecs re-wrote Aztec national history, and refurbished Huitzilopochtli's 'image', he gives a most amusing glimpse into the 'mind of pre-Columbian man' and finds it to have been not unlike that of many other men much closer to us in time.

Arthur Miller takes as his starting point the Temple of the Diving God at Tulum, but he moves quickly from the iconography of this temple to the Mixtec and the Paris and Madrid codices. This is the world of Mayan and wider Mesoamerican cosmography, with a study in the tradition of Eduard Seler. The particular theme of Miller's exercise is what he convincingly defines as the umbilical cord pictorial symbolism of lineage relationships. Going backwards in time, he sees prototypes of the idea as early as Izapan art. It is another paper — and another case — for the underlying unity of Mesoamerican iconography and ideology which, I think, is pretty hard to deny; however, one must always admit the high probabilities that the relationships between meaning and visual symbolism have shifted through time. The question is just how much. Peter Furst's essay is in the same Selerian tradition. He offers a dazzling display of scholarship in making a most probable case for the presence of the morning-glory symbol in Teotihuacan art, and makes the intriguing suggestion that this flower was utilized by the old Mesoamericans as a source of hallucinogens, specifically something very much the same as LSD. His general line of argument — that hallucinogenic plants and drugs have a very ancient worldwide and Mesoamerican history — is further bolstered by ethnographic and archaeological references.

Gossen's and Marshack's use of ethnography as a means of interpreting the past centres on a Chamulan calendar board, recently discovered by Gossen in one of the Chamula hamlets in Chiapas. The board is believed to be about 100 years old, and its owner was a prominent, and highly successful, female shaman. The board, with its simple markings tabulating 20-day units of the year, and the indications that it had been used and re-used for this purpose many times, gives us, perhaps, an insight into how day counting may have been tabulated in the Maya great past, a hint of the kind of 'note-taking' that a Maya priest may have engaged in preparatory to codifying and transferring this information to the more formal records. Marshack, whose own interests are in documenting what he believes to be the very ancient human achievement of time tabulation, is fascinated by the Chamula board as a 'retention' of a simpler calendric mechanism, and he wonders how many 'lost calendars' there may have been among other peoples of the world. This is a justifiable speculation. The board, for instance, may be very much like something that was used in Early Preclassic times in Mesoamerica, or even earlier; the 20-day time-counting unit is the most widespread of any calendrical system in the area. On the other hand, I offer the speculation that the board may be only a 'residue' of a complicated calendrical tradition, that it is something that never could have existed without the rich (and now largely lost) Maya preoccupation with this kind of activity.

A number of other papers are concerned with functional analysis, but largely or wholly from the point of view of the pre-Columbian data, with little or no reference to the ethnohistoric or ethnographic horizon. These essays vary greatly in scope of subject matter and in problem conception. Adrian Digby, in his imaginative paper on the 'crossed trapezes', sets about attacking one small front of astronomical knowledge. He deduced that the pre-Columbian Mesoamericans must have needed, and possessed, a device for giving the position of the sun at points other than those on the horizon. Digby then searched glyphs and sculpture for a representation of such a device and spotted the trapeze-like instrument in the art of Xochicalco and in the year glyphs on the Lapida of Tenango. An actual model of such an instrument was constructed and tested. The whole operation is a minor example of hypothesis formulation and testing, about which we hear a great deal now in archaeology.

Eric Thompson is concerned with recent interpretations of canals in the Candelaria Basin. These have been interpreted variously, but Thompson is of the opinion that they may have been constructed for fishing and the entrapment of fish. He suggests that they may have been constructed by the Putun Maya, a former coastal people who, when they moved inland away from the sea, wanted to continue their fishing activities in a low-lying riverine environment.

Richard Adams ventures into an aspect of settlement pattern — the micro-pattern of residential units in Maya lowland ceremonial centres. To my knowledge this is the first time this has been tried in quite this way. Adams' express purpose is to estimate palace room living-space and by determining its extent to arrive at figures for an upper-class population of a Classic Maya community. The initial assumption is made that palace-type ceremonial centre buildings were, indeed, living and sleeping quarters. Amounts of floor space, numbers of presumed 'sleeping' benches, and other factors are drawn into the equation. Populations of adults and children per building unit are computed. The Uaxactun data are the primary ones employed. Then, total community (sustaining area) populations are computed on the often-used maize cultivation yields per square km., and this total community figure is projected against the relatively small ceremonial centre residential population count. He comes up with a figure of only 1 to 2 percent of the total population residing in the centre proper. This seems an unusually small aristocratic stratum for a society. It would be interesting to compare these proportions with other societies of comparable technological level and general advancement. The whole methodology, as Adams realizes, is jeopardized by pitfalls. In making such computations one is always working from and with variables that are extremely hard to cross-check and control. However, the effort should be encouraged. It is directed toward some very important questions. I should think that other lines of investigation, such as the counting of elite burials within a centre, might serve to support and cross-check the Adams approach.

Dennis Puleston also treats settlement patterns but on wider scale than Adams. He is interested in an intersite area survey of small structures, presumably domestic dwellings. When Maya lowland settlement work began, with the Mayapan and Barton Ramie studies, attention was directed to this general scale of operations, but with an emphasis on the sizes and densities of what came to be called the 'sustaining areas' surrounding ceremonial centres; and the Tikal settlement investigations of Haviland and Puleston have advanced knowledge considerably on this score. Less attention, however, was given to these areas at a considerable distance from major ceremonial centres or more or less equidistantly located between centres. Bullard's 1960 article on Maya lowland settlement was one of the very few writings addressed to this aspect of the subject. Now, Puleston has gone directly to the question. How densely distributed are 'house mounds' in the intersite areas? At one time Bullard and I felt that their density was much the same as it was close to the ceremonial centres. It may be in some regions of the lowlands; however, the new Puleston data, taken together with the Tikal residential area small structure distributions, indicate very clearly that there is a differential in this part of the Peten. In the 120 square km. with the Tikal ceremonial centre at its middle there are an average of 197 small structures per square km. Farther out from Tikal, in the intersite area between Tikal and Uaxactun, Puleston finds an average of only 88 such structures per square km. Puleston also has some interesting observations to make on these settlement data by chronological phase; and one of the surprises is that, after a fairly thin Preclassic intersite occupation, followed by a heavy Early Classic occupation, there is a semi-abandonment of the intersite zones in the Late Classic. In other words, there was a process of centralization and urbanization going on at Tikal in the Late Classic and one that was not entirely related to overall regional population growth. We need many more studies like this one.

If Adams' study could be called a 'micro-pattern' investigation and that of Puleston a 'macro-pattern' settlement concern, then Norman Hammond's essay on the overall distribution of ceremonial centres for the whole of the Maya lowlands could be said to be a kind of 'super-macro-pattern' approach. This broad view of Maya lowland settlement has long been needed; indeed, it is curious that none of us involved in Peten-British Honduras or Yucatecan settlement studies has ever attempted it. Hammond's interests in it have developed from his own researches around Lubaantun where he made a concerted effort to define that centre's immediate sustaining area or 'site exploitation territory' and then its 'realm' or 'region of control', not only as to their extent but as to their environmental diversity and natural resources. Hammond's maps with the present survey study show us a veritable concentration of major ceremonial centres in the northeast Peten; and here, if the sites were of contemporary equal importance, the individual 'regions of control' around each centre were correspondingly smaller than in other parts of the Maya lowlands. One wonders why. Were populations denser here? Were food resources greater? If there were more people in the northeast Peten than in other lowland regions, did this necessitate more centres for socio-political and religious control? And, if so, were these conditions preparing the way for larger territorial states with Tikal, perhaps, emerging as a super-centre, a capital with hegemony over other major centres? These and other questions derive from Hammond's study which, I predict, will be a key article in the development of Maya lowland settlement investigations. One nice thing that Hammond has shown with reference to Lubaantun and some other centres is that these sites are found at locations near junctures of foothills, river plains, and coastal plains, with the implications that they were significantly sustained by multiple resources from these environments.

But to return to archaeological papers which are on the functional rather than the historical side, there are several which I class as being

somewhat more directed toward processual analysis than an explic-
ation of how an ancient society and culture functioned. I admit that
it is difficult to draw the line. Some of those papers which we have
already commented upon, such as Adams's, Puleston's, and Hammond's, reveal an interest in process, in formulating questions and
phrasing hypotheses and examining the data in this light. Some of
those we come to now move still further in this direction.

Millon's long-term project in the mapping and study of Teotihuacan is certainly one which has as its ultimate goal the formulation
and testing of hypotheses about social and cultural growth and
change — about the rise of urbanism from earlier, simpler cultural
levels and just how this came about. He describes data on urban size
and form, on the inferred functions of certain sections or *barrios* in
the great city, on manufacturing centres or 'shops' within the city,
and on the implications of trade in the city's growth. He gives no
simple answers to the question of 'why Teotihuacan'? He is hesitant
to opt for any one cause as the trigger to the processes of urban
growth, and he insists on a systemic consideration of many factors as
being necessary if we are to elucidate the processes of this growth.
Subsistence, demographic, religious, governmental, manufacturing,
and trading factors and functions must all be considered in any such
processual analysis. But, for the present paper, Millon leaves it there.
The very definite intent, however, of providing data for such an
analysis — or many kinds of analyses — is clearly implicit in the
Teotihuacan project; and this is underscored by George Cowgill's
companion paper on the quantification of the Teotihuacan data and
preparing it for computer procedures. Cowgill is always very modest
about his claims for the computer in archaeology, emphasizing that it
is a tool and that the ideas which computer studies are designed to
examine and test must originate with the archaeologist. I have no
computer experience — at first hand, anyhow — but I think there is
some 'feedback' from the computer, certainly, in giving the
archaeologist new leads. Most of us could readily pose some
hypotheses concerning the association, say, of fine ritual objects with
elite residences or ceremonial precincts; but, as Cowgill tells us, there
are all kinds of curious and surprising associations in the archaeological data (particularly in a place such as Teotihuacan) which may
be first discovered by the computer and which may stimulate the
thinking of the archaeologist.

The paper on 'Trade and power in Postclassic Yucatan', by
Sabloff, Rathje, and their colleagues from the Cozumel Island
project, is overtly designed as an attempt to see if certain processes
of pre-industrial trade, which have been examined in Old World
archaeology, also pertain to New World data. They begin with the
concepts of 'ports-of-trade', cities or ports that were maintained by
international agreements and that could only have been maintained
under some kind of a pervasive 'Pax Romana', or 'Pax Teotihuacana'

or 'Tolteca', and 'trading ports', which were maintained by single independent states. They have examined, at least during an initial field season, the archaeology of Cozumel Island, off the Yucatan coast, with these ideas in mind. To date, what they have found would seem to indicate that Late Postclassic Cozumel was a 'trading port', maintained by a local state that had close connections with contemporaneous Mayapan. It now remains to be seen whether or not Early Postclassic Cozumel sustained a 'port-of-trade' under the protection of a Mesoamerica-wide Toltec guidance. To date, the Cozumel work has resulted largely in fundamental descriptive and chronological information, but its *raison d'être* is a study of long-range and large-scale trade and the processes associated with it.

My own paper on the Classic Maya stelae hiatus is spent mostly on describing a pattern in the data — that of the hiatus phenomenon. This is no discovery, but the comparing and contrasting of the hiatus situation, in its various particulars, with the circumstances of the ninth-century 'collapse' is a new slant on the subject; and I hope it may be a productive line of inquiry for others to follow up. To this point what I have had to say in the paper is essentially historical, although with some functional implications; however, I then propose to explain the hiatus as a result of the termination of a Mexican highland-Maya lowland symbiotic relationship, a relationship in which trade had probably been a crucial factor. This is an hypothesis borrowed from Rathje, and from Malcolm Webb, and has been projected by them with reference to the ninth-century 'collapse' events. I make a few 'test' type observations of the data, with reference to this hypothesis, but go no further than this toward a systematic processual study. As a personal aside, I feel somewhat uneasy about, or inhibited in, attempting to explain cause in the archaeological past.

The Molloy-Rathje paper relates to mine in subject matter and historical event in that it sets out to explain why the Maya lowland 'core' zone — the apparent earliest centre of the lowland stelae cult and other civilizational signs in the northeast Peten — was able to recoup its fortunes after the hiatus, at a time when, according to Rathje's earlier arguments, the 'core' centres had lost much of their trading advantage to the 'buffer zone' centres at the peripheries of the southern lowlands. They come up with the very ingenious hypothesis that they managed to do this by 'marrying out' their women of the royal lineages (of 'core' sites such as Tikal) to the rulers of the more *arriviste* centres of the 'buffer zone', who were delighted to enhance their prestige by such unions with the prestigious ancient aristocracy of the Peten. As the reader will see, there is considerable evidence that would seem to support this hypothesis. Although this paper was less formally structured than some others by Rathje on the Classic Maya social scene, it is very much in a processual vein.

The most thorough-going processual paper of the symposium, however, is the one by Barbara Price on Classic Maya *cargo* systems. She begins with a preliminary methodological discussion on ethnographic analogy, distinguishing between those specific-historical analogies that must be restricted, in the main, to documenting specific origins and continuities within a 'genetic model' situation, and those general-comparative analogies that operate out of a cross-cultural reference base and that may be applied to explain persistences or failures of traits or institutions in nomothetic terms. Her specific problem is the Maya *cargo* system, especially as this has been described and analysed by Vogt in the Maya highland community of Zinacantan. According to Price, the ecosystemic function of the *cargo* system is the regulation of inter- and intra-class competition within the society in the transfer of goods and services ('energy') from producers to consumers. She argues that the democratic *cargo* system, as it now exists in present-day Zinacantan, and as it sanctions the draining away of wealth from individuals and families, is a residue or a survival of such a system that once operated among the lower classes of Maya society. Present-day Zinacantan is not a class-structured community, but, to a degree, the Ladino elements from the nearby Mexican towns perform in this role in their selling of goods for rituals and celebrations to the contemporary, and rotating, *cargo* office holders. This differs from an interpretation that attempts to project the present-day egalitarianism of Zinacantan backward in time to the pre-Columbian Maya Classic. That Classic society Price interprets as very definitely class-structured and with an upper class having a very decided interest in preserving class status quo by maintaining such a ritual *cargo* system for what were, in effect, lesser and rotating office holders in the politico-religious establishment. Price is looking for cross-cultural diachronic regularities. She says:

> It must ultimately be asked which circumstances strengthen, and which minimize, the importance of ritual as a socio-economic and environmental regulator.

From the whole line of Price's argument, one could, by extension, offer as a hypothesis the following: uniformity of natural resources, lack of interregional symbiosis, lack of multiple economic niches, and rising population pressures, when taken in concert, *strengthen* ritual as a socio-economic regulator. Thus in the Maya instance the *cargo* system, and an accompanying great elaboration of ritual, was needed both to keep down disruptive rivalry among the peasants and to inhibit the growth of power in that segment of the society which could have been a threat to the established elite. Were these important causes in the development of what, to many observers, has been seen as a 'top-heavy' investment in Maya lowland ceremonial

centres and their elaboration? I do not know if Price would want to
go this far. As I say, I see it as a logical extension of her arguments.
While I have never been comfortable in the projection of the
Zinacantan democratically-maintained *cargo* system as a model for
understanding Classic Maya culture, I am not sure that I agree with
Price or with this extension of her line of reasoning. In any event,
however, her paper is an example, and I think a forceful one, of
combining the data of archaeology, modern ethnography, and more
general cultural analogy into an attack on the citadel of explanation
and process.

I have no generalizations with which to conclude, other than that
all types of investigation are being pursued by modern researchers
within the overall bounds of what we call Mesoamerican archaeology.
Some of these researches, particularly those involving iconographic
interpretation, go back to the tradition of Eduard Seler and before.
Stratigraphers pursue the space-time frames of reference, in the
manner of Gamio and Vaillant. And others of us grope our way along
what appears to me to be an admirable, if not always successful,
course toward functional, and even processual, understanding. Most
encouraging, I think, are the occasional signs of the integration of
'old style' data, iconography, hieroglyphics, stelae calendrics, and
other Mesoamerican 'antiquities', into new problem formulations and
insights.

THOMAS A. LEE Jr.

The Middle Grijalva regional chronology and ceramic relations: a preliminary report

Introduction

The construction of the huge Netzahualcoyotl Dam just below the junction of the La Venta and Grijalva rivers in Chiapas, Mexico (Fig. 1), was the impetus for the Mal Paso Archaeological Salvage Project, realized by the combined forces of the New World Archaeological Foundation of Brigham Young University and the Departamento de Monumentos Prehispánicos of the Instituto Nacional de Antropología e Historia of Mexico.

The short term Mal Paso project was a desperate attempt to save at least a small sample of the cultural history that was to be lost in the projected lake basin. The field work was begun in the fall of 1965 and ended abruptly in May, 1966 as the engulfing waters behind the completed dam entered the last upriver site. A total of six months were spent in the same basin pursuing simultaneously three aspects of the field work phase of the project. While the reconnaissance was still being carried out some of the sites were selected for limited testing while at the same time others were receiving an intensive investigation. At the end of the field operation a total of 105 sites had been located and sketch-mapped. Where available, a ceramic sample was collected. Some 35 sites were tested by excavations and at five of these the excavations were more extensive.

The laboratory phase of this project has been carried on by members of the Foundation with the close cooperation of Carlos Navarrete of the Sección de Antropología of the Universidad Nacional Autónoma de México.

To date four articles (Agrinier 1964; Matos Moctezuma 1966a and 1966b; Navarrete 1966a) have appeared which are either introductory notices of the project or preliminary studies of special archaeological features such as a sweat bath and a double ballcourt. One site monograph has been published on San Antonio (Agrinier 1969) and another on excavations in San Isidro is due out soon (Lee, in press; a). Six other monographs are in an advanced state of

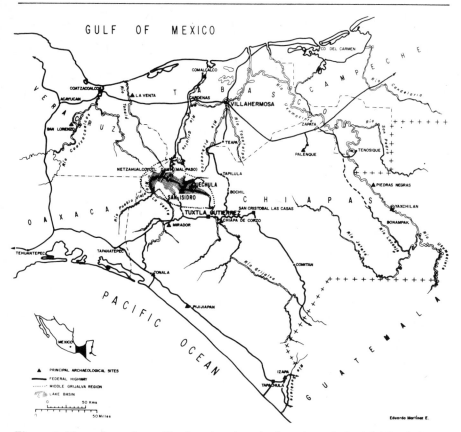

Figure 1 Map of southern Mexico showing the location of the Middle Grijalva region.

preparation and will all go to press by the end of 1973.

The now long-filled lake basin is located in what we have called the Middle Grijalva region, which is physiographically separate from both the Central Depression of Chiapas upstream and the Tabasco coastal lowlands downstream. The region is surrounded by mountains, which greatly constrict the course of the river and limit the size of the adjacent river terraces on which both the ancient and modern human population chose to establish themselves.

With regard to the natural environment, since time and space limitations prohibit a complete description here and since adequate publications on the area are available, only a short summary will be given. (References on the area to the following subjects are, for geology, Mullerried 1957; Echeagaray Bablot 1957, vol. 1, Fig. 19, and vol. 2, 351-2; for the hydrology and climatology, Echeagaray Bablot 1957, vol. 1, 37-54; for the vegetation, Miranda 1952, 1953; and for the fauna, Alvarez del Toro 1952, 1960.)

The climate is hot humid tropical forest with exuberant vegetation. The area receives between 1500 and 3000 mm. of rainfall annually and there are from 120 to 150 days each year with rain and the same number of days with cloud cover (Tamayo 1953: 118, 126). The temperature maxima through the year range from 44° C. to 6° C. The high mean annual temperature and the high annual rainfall are the most significant factors in the environment. In the Koeppen system of classification the area has a Afw'g type, or a tropical forest climate with the heaviest rains in the Fall and the maximum temperature before the summer solstice (21 June).

The Grijalva river is the major watercourse in the region and is navigable, with one short portage, from Quechula to the sea, a distance over 200 km. I have argued elsewhere that this route, from the time it was first described or mentioned in 1523 (Diaz del Castillo 1964) until the beginning of this century, may have been the principal route of communication between the lowlands of Tabasco and southern Veracruz and the Central Depression of Chiapas (Lee n. d.). Archaeological evidence is presented in the same paper which suggests that this route began to function at least by 1200 B.C. with the Olmec culture, if not long before.

During and after the Mal Paso project I collected ethnographic data on the canoe transport system on the Middle and Lower Grijalva River as it functioned up until about 1920, which demonstrate the river's importance as a route of communication between the lowlands of Veracruz and Tabasco, and the interior of Chiapas. Several old *bogas* or canoemen are still alive who earned their living in hauling cargo between Quechula and Huimanguillo, Tabasco.

The description of this transportation system will appear soon in Spanish as one part of a larger monograph on the Postclassic Zoque occupation of the lake basin (Navarrete and Lee, in press).

Chronology

The Middle Grijalva regional chronology is the result of the collaboration of Gareth W. Lowe and myself (Fig. 2). In 1969 Lowe (n.d., Fig. 4) ordered the materials of the Preclassic and Protoclassic periods from Mound 20 at San Isidro in cultural horizons which were in turn related to the ceramic sequences of the 'Greater Isthmus' area and the Maya lowlands. The Mound 4 materials from the same site were studied in 1970 (Lee, in press *a*). The collections of cache and burial offerings from Mound 4 overlapped those found in Mound 20 during the Late Preclassic and Protoclassic periods and extended in good stratigraphical order into the Early, Middle and Late Classic. Mounds 1 and 2 also produced an excellent series of Late Classic and Early Postclassic burial lots which were studied at the same time (Matos Moctezuma, in preparation). It has been possible to construct a local phase sequence based on refuse lots and cached vessels compared to other established sequences in the Greater Isthmus area

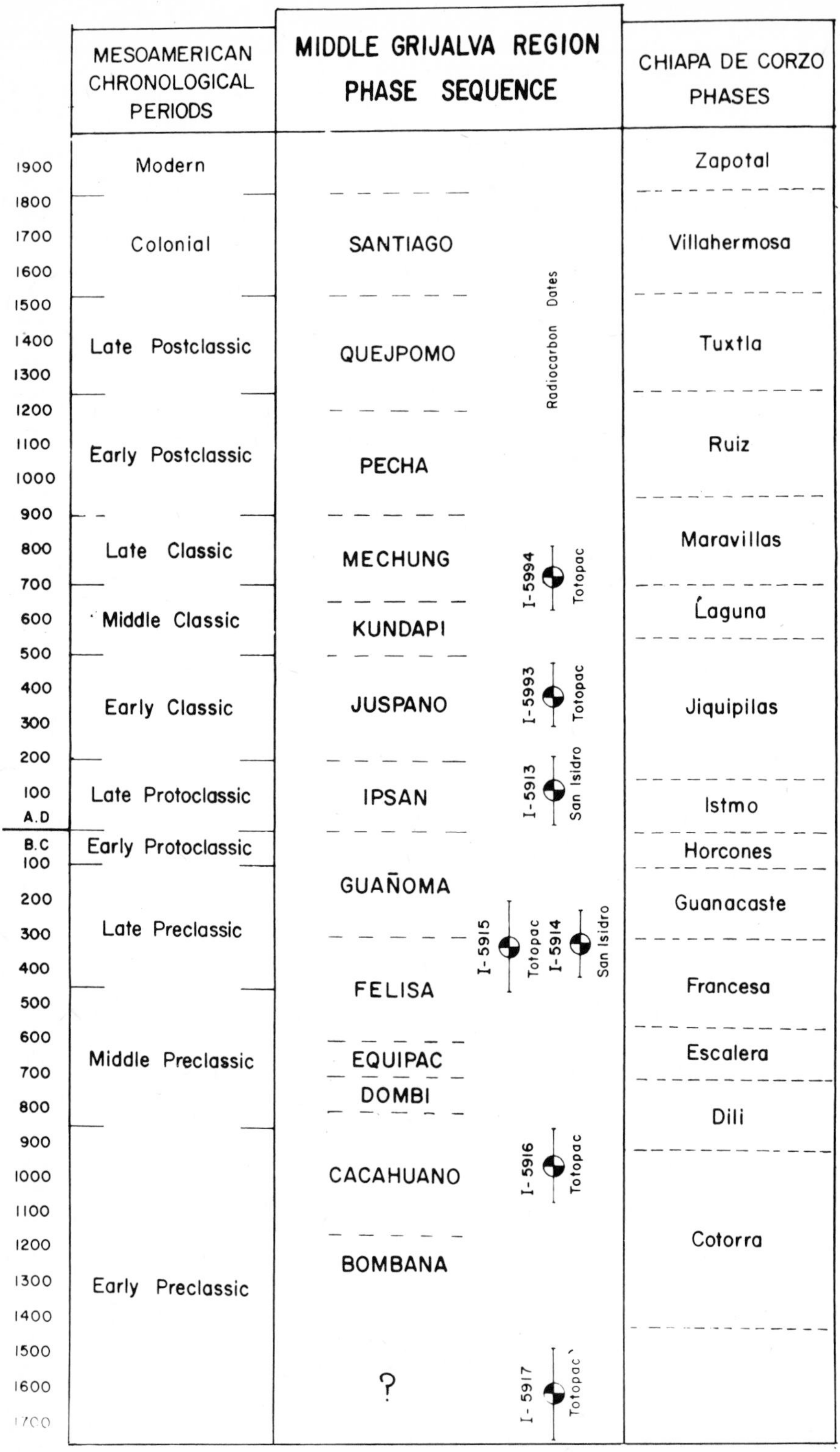

Years	MESOAMERICAN CHRONOLOGICAL PERIODS	MIDDLE GRIJALVA REGION PHASE SEQUENCE	Radiocarbon Dates	CHIAPA DE CORZO PHASES
1900	Modern			Zapotal
1800				
1700	Colonial	SANTIAGO		Villahermosa
1600				
1500				
1400	Late Postclassic	QUEJPOMO		Tuxtla
1300				
1200				
1100	Early Postclassic	PECHA		Ruiz
1000				
900				
800	Late Classic	MECHUNG		Maravillas
700			I-5994 Totopac	
600	Middle Classic	KUNDAPI		Laguna
500				
400	Early Classic	JUSPANO	I-5993 Totopac	Jiquipilas
300				
200				
100 A.D	Late Protoclassic	IPSAN	I-5913 San Isidro	Istmo
B.C 100	Early Protoclassic			Horcones
200	Late Preclassic	GUAÑOMA		Guanacaste
300			I-5915 Totopac I-5914 San Isidro	
400				
500		FELISA		Francesa
600	Middle Preclassic	EQUIPAC		Escalera
700		DOMBI		
800				Dili
900	Early Preclassic	CACAHUANO		
1000			I-5916 Totopac	
1100				
1200		BOMBANA		Cotorra
1300				
1400				
1500				
1600		?	I-5917 Totopac	
1700				

Figure 2 A chronological chart correlating the Middle Grijalva regional phase sequence with the general Mesoamerican chronological periods and the more specific Chiapa de Corzo phase sequence.

without resorting to statistical manipulation of sherd lots.

The phase sequence terminology is patterned after that of Chiapa de Corzo (Lowe and Agrinier 1960: 4-6). The phase names are local Zoque and Spanish words in loose alphabetical order, leaving space for possible future subdivisions or additions.

The proposed Middle Grijalva regional chronology covers a span of about 3000 years divided into thirteen phases (Fig. 2), beginning around 1500 B.C. and ending in 1821 with the Independence of Mexico and the end of the Colonial period. The dating of the individual phases is based mainly on the correlation of ceramic attributes with established sequence data from sites in the surrounding regions. This relative dating is supported by 7 viable radiocarbon dates. The age, provenance and fit with the associated archaeological material of all dates are discussed in Lee (in press, *a*).

San Isidro, the largest site in the project area, provided the basis for the chronology. Only the last two Postclassic phases were not located in the excavations at this great site.

Before beginning a description of the ceramic complexes of the phase sequence and their relationships, a word of caution must be said. Since the ceramics from the reconnaissance and several sites briefly tested have not been completely analysed this description cannot be considered final. It is expected that inclusion of the unstudied material will make no changes in the phase chronology but certainly will amplify the content of the ceramic complexes.

The ceramic study is theoretically based on the Type Variety system of classification (Smith, Willey and Gifford 1960; Willey, Culbert and Adams 1967; Gifford, n.d.). The final names have still not been given to the various ceramic units of the first four phases nor the last three, so they are presented by description only. The ceramic continuum will be published in several parts, in individual site and period reports as well as in a final summary volume.

Bombana phase

The Bombana phase is the earliest evidence of man found in the lake basin and is tentatively dated on comparative ceramic attributes and modes with the San Lorenzo Bajio phase from 1350-1250 B.C. (Coe 1970: 22). It has only been identified at San Isidro in refuse dumps in the bottom of a few of the deepest excavations in front of Mound 20 (Lowe, n.d., 37).

The content of the Bombana ceramic complex is limited in quantity, but rather diverse in form, surface colour and decoration. The most common pottery is a thick paste ware slipped white, highly burnished and decorated with specular haematite paint in zones or covering the complete exterior or interior of the vessel. The forms of this ware include a flat-bottomed cylinder, a flat-bottomed, low, flaring-walled bowl, an exteriorly thickened rim bowl, and a fluted jar or bottle made in the form of a squash. A small tecomate form with a slightly raised rim is slipped with the specular paint all over. Tecomates also occur in a light tan-coloured paste and are decorated by either brushing or pattern burnishing with a widely-spaced parallel-lined design and zoned punctation. The differential firing technique is present with finely polished black and white surfaces in straight-walled cylinder and thick, flaring-walled bowl forms.

The presence of at least one hollow fat figurine leg with white slip reminds one of the hollow spraddle-legged infant figurines so common in typical Olmec material.

The Bombana ceramic complex appears related to the Bajio ceramic complex at San Lorenzo (Coe 1970: 22-5). The shared forms of these two complexes are 'squash-bottles', flat-bottomed bowls with out-flaring rims, and tecomates. Wares and slips common to both ceramic complexes include black and white differential fired pottery, white-slipped pottery (although Coe 1970: 24 is not specific on the latter mode), and all-over burnished specular haematite painted pottery. Mutual decorative techniques of these two ceramic complexes include brushing, patterned burnishing, zone punctation, zoned painting in specular red paint, and fluting.

In short, it seems abundantly clear that Bombana and Bajio are closely related. I suggest that they are part of a single ceramic sphere as defined by Willey, Culbert and Adams (1967: 306-7; Willey 1970: 316), although the type descriptions are not completed for either phase. In spite of the paucity of material from San Isidro I think that this will be found to be the case. Certainly the close similarity appears indicative of more than just participation in the same cultural horizon. Both of these ceramic complexes may be earlier than any known ceramic complex in the Central Depression of Chiapas except the Ocos complex recently identified on the Upper Grijalva (Angostura Basin).

Cacahuano phase

Stratigraphically the Cacahuano complex sherds were directly on top of the Bombana phase materials. Like the earlier phase, the Cacahuano is dated relatively to the San Lorenzo phase at San Lorenzo on the basis of similar ceramic modes which are thought to occur between 1150-900 B.C. (Coe 1970: 26). The Cacahuano phase is known at San Isidro and from at least one site in the Totopac River drainage (Lee, in preparation).

The Cacahuano ceramic complex is characterized by white wares, white-rimmed black pottery, a highly-polished red type which may be Tatagapa Red of San Lorenzo, a polished tan ware, a plain and brushed brown ware and a polished black type. The two most important vessel forms are the tecomate and the flat-bottomed bowl with vertical, or occasionally slightly out-slanting walls, and heavy everted or exteriorly bolstered rims. Deep flat-bottomed cylinders also are frequent. The decoration ranges from red-on-white painted zones, usually rim edges, to brushed surfaces, coarse incising, and a combination of incising and excising.

The key diagnostic pottery of the Cacahuano ceramic complex is the incised and excised polished black types which appear to parallel closely the Calzadas Carved and Limon Carved-Incised types at San Lorenzo. The former is characterized by 'familiar Olmec elements like cross bands, jaguar paw-wing, flame brows, and fire-serpent jaws' (Coe 1970: 26) which are rare motifs at San Isidro (Lowe n.d., 57). The polished incised-excised black pottery of San Isidro is more like Limon Carved-Incised which has the same shape, colour and firing. The incised designs are nearly restricted to the opposed rotated scrolls or *ilhuitl* motif (Coe 1970: 26).

Coe (1970: 26-7) has pointed out the occurrence of the Calzada Carved Olmec motifs in the core area of the Olmecs as well as in the Cuadros phase on the Pacific Coast, in the San José phase of Oaxaca and at Tlatilco and Las Bocas well away from this area.

The other types of the Cacahuano ceramic complex in general seem to parallel the pottery units described for the Chicharras phase at San Lorenzo, which continue on with only minor changes in the San Lorenzo phase. A ceramic complex directly comparable to Chicharras has not been identifiable at San Isidro. Perhaps Chicharras is a local development at San Lorenzo and did not reach San Isidro. Its similarity to the later San Lorenzo ceramic complex would support this. It is possible, however, that both are present at San Isidro in mixed deposits which we have been unable to separate. The presence of the Chicharras ceramic complex at San Isidro is supported by the possible occurrence of a type very similar to Tatagapa Red, mentioned earlier.

There is no doubt that the Cacahuano ceramic complex is closely allied to that of the San Lorenzo. I suggest that they are, as during the previous Bombana and Bajio phases, part of the same ceramic sphere.

The basic similarity between the Cacahuano and San Lorenzo ceramic complexes is obvious, but the relative lack of Calzadas Carved, with its typical Olmec motifs, and the complete lack of Olmec stone monumental sculpture at San Isidro indicates that San Isidro did not participate fully in the elaborate and sophisticated nature of the Olmec climax area. San Isidro was undoubtly an important provincial centre.

Dombi phase

The early part of the Middle Preclassic period is represented in the

Middle Grijalva region by the Dombi phase, which is dated from about 900 to 700 B.C. (Fig. 2). It is one of the poorest-defined phases in the Middle Grijalva region. Pottery of this ceramic complex was found in a few excavations at San Isidro, in at least one site in the Totopac river drainage and in San Antonio on the La Venta river. It has not been possible to separate this phase satisfactorily from the Equipac phase.

Far more important than the ceramics to the Dombi ceremonial life were the massive celt and pseudocelt offerings found dating to this and/or the following phase. A few of the celts from these offerings were well made and of a very high quality hard grey or greenish stone, but most of them were hurriedly made of a very soft greenish-grey silt-stone. These celt offerings accompanied all burials, all ceramic vessel offerings, and a very special large jade earspool and celt axial and directional offering. The celt offerings also occurred unaccompanied by other artifacts, and included from 2 to 45 celts. A total of 219 celts and pseudocelts were recovered.

The Dombi ceramic complex as defined to date contains only two types of pottery. One type is made up of flat-bottomed bowls, greyish-black in colour with straight out-slanting walls and an exteriorly thickened rim. The other type consists of reddish-brown paste tecomates or neckless jars decorated with a single incised line about the mouth and two lug handles not far from the mouth. The tecomate paste appears to have been tempered with finely crushed limestone or organic material which has subsequently leached out, leaving a finely pock-marked porous surface.

We are handicapped in relating the little-known Dombi ceramic complex to other contemporary complexes nearby, such as Chiapa de Corzo, Mirador, Vistahermosa and San Lorenzo where the complexes are much better known. The lack of better knowledge of the ceramic complex for this time period at La Venta, where the massive celt axial offerings indicate a close tie with San Isidro, further hinders the alignment of the Dombi ceramic complex. Lowe (n.d., 134) has pointed out the elaborate and extensive development of the Dili phase in the Central Depression, closely allied to La Venta, during this approximate time period and stated that it is not known who was influencing whom. Coe (1970: 28-9, 32) believes that his contemporary Nacaste phase at San Lorenzo represents the arrival of new peoples with different pottery, possible from Chiapas. Without more excavations this remains as only a viable hypothesis.

An important idea which Lowe (n.d., 135) has presented is that:

> It is possible to see in the Dili and Vistahermosa ceramic complex variation (ceramic spheres) a beginning of the Zoque-Maya split . . . from a parent Mixe-Popoluca population. This differentiation continued for a thousand years and is reflected in the constant ceramic distinctions noted between Chiapa de Corzo and

not-very-distant Mirador . . . San Isidro was in an intermediate position (along with La Venta) and after the Escalera (the Equipac phase) horizon seems to have remained entirely within the Zoque regime with its external relationships maintained most closely with Mirador.

This division between Maya and Zoque can be inferred from the early historical documents, dated between 1530 and 1533, in which Francisco de Montejo claimed the Maya lowlands' western boundary was the Rio Cupilco in Tabasco, probably somewhere near Comalcalco (Scholes and Roys 1948: 96). It can be demonstrated from another series of documents that at least 12 towns of the Ahualulco area west of the Rio Cupilco were Zoque-speaking at the end of the sixteenth century (Solis 1945). It is, then, with no little interest that we find Sisson's (1970: 46) Chontalpa and Ahualulco reconnaissance establishing a possible boundary between ceramic spheres in this area during the Late Preclassic. Lowe (n.d., 138) has suggested that this boundary, based on the polished red waxy wares, must exist at least one phase earlier during the Middle Classic just after the La Venta abandonment.

It is important to point out here that a rather large (5.8 m. high) Dombi phase pyramid within Mound 20 was exposed by the excavations in that mound. This early San Isidro pyramid ranks along with a similar construction 10 m. high inside Mound 30*a* at Izapa as one of the earliest known pyramid structures in Mesoamerica (Ekhom 1969; Lowe n.d., 64). Perhaps the great pyramid at La Venta is contemporaneous with these structures or even earlier, but until someone excavates it, current speculation concerning it is purely academic.

Equipac phase

The Equipac phase is contemporary with the Escalera phase at Chiapa de Corzo, which is dated from 700 to 550 B.C. The Equipac appears to be a relatively short phase when compared to the following Felisa phase.

The most characteristic pottery of the Equipac ceramic complex belongs to the Hama Red ware and the Shitu Black-and-White ware. The Pason group of the Hama Red ware is a red-slipped, highly polished monochrome pottery occurring in low open bowls with large diameters. The bottoms are flat or slightly concave, with either a composite profile or a simple out-slanting wall, and a narrow flaring rim or thick everted rim. Decoration is limited to the double line break on the upper surface of the bowl interior, just below the rim.

The Hugguitz group of the Shitu Black-and-White ware has only been found in a frog-effigy bowl form modelled in the round.

The Equipac ceramic complex may be the missing complex between the Nacasta and Palangana phases at San Lorenzo where Coe (1970: 29) has proposed a hiatus in his sequence. The Escalera ceramic complex at Chiapa de Corzo is clearly related to the Equipac complex, but it is either later or simply better known, as it has considerably more complex forms than are present at San Isidro. Certain Complex A offerings at La Venta contain pottery vessels with modes similar to those in the Equipac ceramic complex, such as effigy composite vessels probably in polished red (Drucker, Heizer and Squire 1959, Fig. 52; Drucker 1952: 109-10, Fig. 34, *a-b*).

I have already mentioned Lowe's (n.d., 135) belief that the Maya-Zoque split was intensified during this phase and that San Isidro was in an intermediate position along with La Venta. After this phase both were part of the general Zoque development. It is widely argued that the widespread development of related red-orange ceramic wares during the early Middle Preclassic from Veracruz throughout Tabasco and Chiapas and in the general Isthmus area suggests that part of the homeland of the predecessors of the Mamom ceramic horizon was in this area, well to the northwest and southwest of the lowland Maya area proper.

Felisa phase

The Felisa phase represents the late part of the Middle Preclassic and the early half of the Late Preclassic, overlapping both periods (600-300 B.C.).

The Felisa ceramic complex is dominated by Hama Red ware and Nas White ware. The Aguaima group represents a direct continuation into the Felisa complex of the Hama Red ware of the previous phase. This highly-polished, often cloudy, red ware is found in small and large everted-rim bowls, tall-necked jars, and cylinders. Decoration is limited to broad and shallow parallel grooves on the everted rims. The Nas White ware is an innovation of the Felisa phase. It tends to be cruder than the Hama Red ware and is slipped with a thin watery white slip. Some of the forms are common to the Hama Red ware. New shapes include large burial urns, deep flat-bottomed bowls, and bird-effigy everted-rim bowls. Decoration includes grooving, incising, modelling, and rarely painting in red.

Another ware of the Felisa complex is the Poiya Polished Brown which occurs in the form of plates, shell-effigy bowls, and deep bowls. This brown pottery is well polished and decorated by modelling, incising, painting, and stuccoing. Both Hama Red ware and Poiya Polished Brown seem related to the Palangana phase at San Lorenzo and the Mamom ceramic horizon of the Maya lowlands, as well as to the Early Francesa phase of Central Chiapas.

Guañoma phase

The sixth identified phase in the Middle Grijalva region, the Guañoma, dates from 300 B.C. to the birth of Christ. The Guañoma ceramic complex is one of the most diversified and well-represented complexes in the Middle Grijalva Region. There are three paste colour classes, each forming one ware. These wares are white-rimmed black, polished brown, and rough tan. There are five red paste wares in the Guañoma complex.

The Mactucan White-rimmed Black ware is found in the form of straight flaring-walled bowls, hemispherical bowls and standing wall jars. Most have a white painted band about the exterior.

The Poiya Polished Brown ware is represented in the complex by the Masapac group whose form range includes low standing-wall bowls, cylinders, vases, jars, and shallow bowls. Decoration is limited to infrequent use of low parallel grooves on the standing walls of this form of bowl, and rarely a three-colour stucco.

The tan-coloured Metzan Rough ware is undecorated and occurs in out-flaring wall bowls, pedestal incense burners, cylinders and urns.

At least four locally made red wares and a possible imported ware, Sierra Red, make up the diversified group which carry on the polished red ware tradition begun in the Equipac ceramic complex. Mesanduk Polished Red and Pomo Orange wares are limited in form to everted-rim bowls only, but the Tucan Thick Red and Masan Red-Brown wares have greatly expanded form inventories. The forms include cylinders, hemispherical bowls, everted-rim bowls, flat-bottomed bowls with straight out-slanting walls and vases. The decoration is limited and only painting and incising are known.

The Sierra Red ware examples are probably imported since they are rare — only four specimens are known. The everted-rim bowl and the tall, typical constricted and fluted cylinder shapes are the only ones present at San Isidro. The important cuspidor shape known at Chiapa de Corzo and Tikal is not found at San Isidro.

The Guañoma phase maintained contact with a very wide area, as is evidenced by the similarities seen in contemporaneous ceramics both near to and far away from the Middle Grijalva region.

The Masapac group is related closest to similar brown ware shapes at Mirador. At other sites such as those reported by Piña Chan and Navarrete (1967, Figs. 9, 27, 54, 66) along the Lower Grijalva, and at Tres Zapotes, brown wares are common, but they usually occur in more complex forms and styles of incised decoration which are not found in the Masapac ceramic complex. It is possible that they are later developments of the Poiya Polished Brown ware or evolved from a common ancestor.

It is the red wares which show such far-reaching parallels in the continuation of the highly polished red ware tradition, represented in earlier ceramic complexes at San Isidro by the Hama Red ware. Wares from areas as far apart as Trinidad, Tabasco; Mirador, Chiapas; and the Tehuantepec area of the Isthmus have been shown to have a similarity in form, colour, surface finish and lack of decoration with this ware. These comparisons can be extended over much of eastern Meso-america also in the development of the 'Mamom' horizon style.

The presence of the widely traded Sierra Red ware in an elaborate tomb burial offering which also contained a bridge-spouted anthro-pomorphic grey ware jar from Oaxaca demonstrates that San Isidro was in contact with the same group which was supplying Sierra Red vessels to such widely scattered sites as Altun Ha, Belize; Tikal, Guatemala; and Chiapa de Corzo, Chiapas.

Contact with the valley of Oaxaca directly or through inter-mediaries was also established. During the Guañoma phase San Isidro and Mirador belonged to the same ceramic sphere.

Ipsan phase

This phase corresponds to the Late Protoclassic period dated in the Middle Grijalva region from about the birth of Christ until A.D. 250. A radiocarbon date of 115 ± 95 (I-5913) is associated with an architectural unit of this phase at San Isidro and falls about in the middle of this phase. A hiatus is suggested between the Guañoma and Ipsan phases by the lack of correspondence and the lack of other Protoclassic manifestations such as Monte Alban II and Holmul I. It is also possible that the Middle Grijalva region did not participate in the more general Protoclassic period.

The Ipsan ceramic complex in the Middle Grijalva region appears to be intrusive. Some of the wares and groups which represent it are completely new and are only in a very general way related to the Metzan Rough Ware of the Guañoma complex.

In both the brownish-tan Yatsipo Sandy ware and the reddish brown Yahama Rough ware the most common vessel form is a flat-bottomed bowl with widely out-flaring walls. Cylinders, low bowls, hemispherical bowls, and jars do occur but they are by far in the minority. Decoration is unknown.

The vessels, particularly the flaring-walled bowls, which make up the cache offerings, are often in pairs in a mouth to mouth relationship. Similar vessels in the same type of offering were found at Media Luna, a dry cave in the La Venta river not far to the south. These offerings contained folded pieces of spotted and stained amate and palm 'cloth', human hair, small balls of copal, and short cords tied off neatly at each end (Lee, in press, *b*). The stains on these 'cloths' have not been analysed but are thought to be blood, a common form of offering throughout Mesoamerica generally.

The ceramic vessels containing these offerings are so similar in shape, size, colour, and unslipped and unpolished surface finish to the Yahama Rough ware that they are undoubtly of the same ceramic sphere.

Although similar ceramic vessels are found contemporaneous at Aguacatal and Monte Alban, the stylistic relations of the Ipsan ceramic complex are principally southern and perhaps western. There seems little doubt that Media Luna and San Isidro are parts of a single ceramic sphere during the Ipsan phase, and that this sphere overlaps Mirador and Chiapa de Corzo and most of southwestern Chiapas.

Juspano phase

The Juspano phase is dated from A.D. 250 to 500. The beginning date coincides with the terminal date of the preceding Ipsan phase which is based on the late end of the one-sigma range of a radiocarbon date which falls at A.D. 210. For convenience this figure has been rounded off at A.D. 200. The end of the Juspano phase is drawn at A.D. 500 in order to leave a small lapse of time for a Middle Classic period. This A.D. 500 dividing line between Early and Middle Classic in this region closely approximates to the late end of the one-sigma range of another radiocarbon date of A.D. 385 ± 90 (I-5993).

The Juspano ceramic complex is in part a continuation out of the preceding ceramic complex, as is demonstrated by the presence of the Yahama Rough ware. The form is the same as earlier, but there are greater extremes in individual size.

The Kombe Black-and-White ware of the differential firing tradition is the diagnostic of the Juspano ceramic complex. Forms are limited to flat-bottomed bowls with out-slanting wall, tetrapod cylinders, and large open-mouthed flat-bottomed jars with slightly constricted waists. Decoration consists of shallow parallel grooving on the interior just below the rim of bowls, incising of hatched triangles and/or 'wave-design' on the exterior, and small appliquéd nobs evenly spaced about the rim.

The Juspano ceramic complex spatial relationships are based entirely on the distribution of differentially fired pottery, which is very extensive. It has been found as far north as Panuco and as far south as Kaminaljuyu, but the centre of highest concentration is apparently in the Los Tuxtlas region of southern Veracruz or in western Chiapas. The closest similarities are with sites in these last two named areas. A secondary area in which similar ceramics can be seen is along the western Campeche coast.

The beginnings of differential firing have been described by Coe (1970: 24) in the Bajio phase (1350-1250 B.C.) at San Lorenzo, Veracruz, and its latest occurrence is apparently in Chiapas in the caves of the Municipalities of Ocosocoautla, Jiquipilas, and Cintalapa during the Late Classic (*c.* A.D. 770-900). One of the most pressing ceramic problems in southern Mesoamerica is the elucidation of the relationship of this differential firing tradition to the grey-black pottery tradition of Oaxaca. Whether the Isthmus or the Oaxaca Valley is the point of origin of these similar traditions is not known, but surely the spread must have been via a group of Zoquean or Mixean speakers, some of whom still live on the very edge of the Valley of Oaxaca (Longacre 1967, Fig. 15; Wallrath 1967: 15).

Kundapi phase

In the Middle Grijalva region, the Middle Classic period is represented by the Kundapi phase. The A.D. 500 to 650 dates given for the beginning and ending of the phase are arbitrary, but they both approximate the beginning and the end of the one-sigma range of two radiocarbon dates. The first has already been mentioned in reference to the end of the Juspano phase and the other occurs associated with material of the Mechung phase (720 ± 90, I-5994).

The Kundapi ceramic complex is poorly known at San Isidro and its extra-regional relations are limited.

Four wares with one ceramic group each make up the Kundapi complex. The Tzuhi Orange and Pokho Smoothed wares are rather crudely made brownish pottery vessels and occur in three forms, large and small out-slanting walled bowls and tall straight in-slanting necked jars. None of the vessels are decorated. The Kombe Black-and-White ware is represented by a single pedestal-based tecomate, with fine incised decoration about its mouth.

The Tuma Orange ware form range includes collared bowls, flat-bottomed flaring-walled bowls and similar flat-bottomed flaring-walled bowls with hollow round-nob tripod vessel supports. One type-variety of this ware is plain and undecorated; the other has an all-over slip of specular haematite.

Only two of the Tzuhi Orange ware vessels were found in a mouth to mouth relation, but it is still indicative of the continuation of this early offering style. Most of the vessels of this ware were placed together in unstructured offerings. The nearest parallels in function and ceramic attributes are found in Chiapa de Corzo, where many similar crude vessels were placed together in offerings, but the Chiapa de Corzo examples are dated to the earlier Jiquipilas phase.

In the Central Depression, Turi Coarse/Turi Variety parallels the Pokho Smoothed ware of the Middle Grijalva, mirroring a widespread Protoclassic and Classic period tradition of simple offering vessels.

The most common decorated pottery of the greater Zoque area is in the black and white ceramic tradition. The presence of a single example of the Kombe Black-and-White ware is not indicative of its importance in the Middle Grijalva. The established type-variety is closely related to Painagua Recessed/Painagua Variety found at Mirador, Chiapa de Corzo and Santa Cruz, and in innumerable caves of western Chiapas. One important centre of production of black-and-white ware has to be in western Chiapas. Why the Middle Grijalva region should appear to lack the quantity of this pottery that could be expected in view of its position within the area of maximum distribution is not easy to explain, but it may very well be a matter of sample size.

Mechung phase

One of the better-defined phases in the Middle Grijalva region is the Late Classic period, called the Mechung phase. The temporal boundaries of this phase have been placed at A.D. 650 and 900. One raiocarbon date of A.D. 720 ± 90 (I-5994) has been derived from carbon associated with Mechung materials at a Totopac river site. The assigned end date of 900 for this phase is about 50 years earlier than generally accepted for the end of the Late Classic and the beginning of the Postclassic and is based on our experience at Izapa where Tohil Plumbate ware, the hallmark for the later phase, is thought to begin earlier than generally accepted.

The Mechung ceramic complex is by far the most extensive known of any of the complexes in the region. Large quantities of whole vessels were excavated at San Isidro in Mounds 1 and 4, at sites in the Totopac drainage and at San Antonio on the La Venta river. It is therefore to be expected that the ceramic relationships seen in this complex will be more numerous and intense than those recognized in other Middle Grijalva complexes.

Two wares are found in the Mechung complex which have had a long history. One, Kombe Black-and-White ware of the differential firing tradition, was first picked up in the Juspano complex; the other, Tzuhi Orange ware, began in the Kundapi phase. In the Mechung complex the black-and-white pottery occurs in a simple bowl form with appliquéd flat pellets spaced evenly about its rim. The Tzuhi Orange ware form is a small flat-bottomed cylinder with evidence of white painted decoration. The Canoaa Coarse ware forms include a comal and an incense burner cover shaped like a round, upside-down dishpan with a centrally located tubular chimney.

The most common shape of the thick creamy slipped Tuma Orange Ware is a deep flat-bottomed bowl with vertical walls. Many other shapes also occur, including a plain flat-bottomed flared-walled bowl, a bridge-spouted effigy jar, a pedestal base bowl, a round-sided bowl, a tripod cylinder, and a tripod bowl. Another very important form is the standing-collar bowl.

Decoration on the types and varieties of the Tuma Orange ware

are the most diverse in any ceramic complex known in the Middle Grijalva. The diversification comes from the use of incising and painting, either alone or combined, and the fact that paint comes in two colours, red and a watery black. Painting further complicates the decoration range in that the design may be either positive or negative.

There is no complete mixing of techniques, however, as red is never the background for incision, nor is it used to produce negative design motifs. Negative designs are rarely the background for incised elements.

The motif content includes incised cartouches or glyph-like elements and painted geometric, animal and anthropomorphic figures sometimes in a negative style. Both red and black are used in plain painted zones and occasionally red specular haematite paint is used to fill the incised design, but red never occurs with black.

Of the four wares of the Mechung ceramic complex three, Tuma Orange, Tzuhi Orange and Kombe White-and-Black demonstrate a local continuity from the preceding Kundapi complex, but it is the diversity of the sophisticated Zuleapa group of the Tuma Orange ware which provides the basis for the most important and far reaching relationships. Sites with demonstrable relationships at the varietal level occur generally toward the Gulf Coast at least as far as Huimango, Tabasco.

At broader typological levels the distribution of related orange wares includes the Gulf Coast as far north as Jaina, Campeche. The lack of excavation in the Central Depression precludes the possibility of tracing relationships there. The presence of Santa Cruz orange with white slip on thin-walled bowls as at Santa Cruz, on the Grijalva in the same area, suggests that eventually this area will be seen to participate in this general ceramic development to a greater extent than is believed at present.

Modes common to the Zuleapa group such as the deep bowl shape and negative-style painted decoration on a cream or white slip also show relationships to sites much further away, in the highlands of Chiapas and Guatemala, and in El Salvador and Honduras. These modes appear to be part of a still not generally recognized Late Classic horizon style.

Pecha phase

The Early Postclassic period in the Middle Grijalva regional chronology is called the Pecha phase. Its temporal limits are assigned arbitrarily at A.D. 900 and 1200. Beyond the end date of the preceeding Mechung phase already mentioned there is no internal basis for these dates, other than those generally accepted for this developmental period.

The Pecha ceramic complex is basically composed of the continuation of most of the Tuma Orange ware of the preceding complex, with the addition of new, even more directly related Gulf Coast wares. These ceramics will be published by Matos Moctezuma (in preparation), and Lee, Lowe and Navarrete (in preparation).

The newly added ceramics consist basically of two wares, a fine orange ware and a polished brown ware, known mainly from the late tomb burials at San Isidro and sites close by in the Totopac river drainage. The orange ware is thin with a soft paste but a hard slip. The forms are the simpler ones normally associated with X Fine Orange (Smith 1958, Figs. 3 and 4), but include an exotic round-sided bowl with three flat areas spaced evenly about the maximum circumference and supported by round hollow rattle tripods. The polished brown ware forms are low bowls with stepped-slab tripod supports like those in U Fine Orange (Smith 1958, Fig. 6). No decoration is found on either of these wares.

These new ceramic components of the Pecha complex suggest the continuation and intensification of contact with the Lower Grijalva area and beyond to include the entire Tabasco riverean area and most of the Campeche coast. The lack of comparative material from the Central Depression prohibits placing the Middle Grijalva area in proper perspective, but it probably was a connecting link between the lowlands of Tabasco and the higher lands of central Chiapas.

Quejpomo phase

In the Middle Grijalva, the Late Postclassic period is represented by the Quejpomo phase, dated from the end of the Early Postclassic at A.D. 1200 and ending with the first known Spanish attempt to conquer Chiapas in 1523 (Diaz del Castillo 1964: 387-396). This first *entrada* passed through the Middle Grijalva region from one end to the other, the most direct route from the Veracruz-Tabasco lowlands to central Chiapas. Quechula, not far above San Isidro on the Grijalva river, is mentioned in the account. Naturally, traditional Zoque culture did not change immediately, but the Spanish set in motion a cultural process which was to eliminate, slowly but surely, most of Zoque culture, both material and non-material.

The Quejpomo ceramic complex is not too different from that generally known elsewhere in Chiapas during this time period. It is made up of five basically brown wares. Three wares, Kowi, Yomone and Witum, are crudely made, and only the latter is polished. Yomone is highly fire-clouded and has a fillet decoration. The forms common to these wares are deep bowls with large mouths, jars with three loop handles, hemispherical bowls and *comales*. The shapes present in the remaining two wares, Kopun and Tusqu, are shallow bowls with zoomorphic tripod supports or semi-globular rattle tripod feet, and large water jars with three loop handles. Both of these wares are decorated in polychrome painting. Kopun ware, related to Nucatili polychrome of Chiapa de Corzo (Navarrete 1966*a*: 58-9), is painted in red, black and white. The Tusqu ware has decorative elements in black and fugitive white while the neck is a highly polished painted red.

More material is necessary before even a tentative statement can be made as to the inter-regional relationships of the Late Postclassic ceramics.

Santiago phase

The Santiago phase represents the Colonial period, beginning with the 1523 *entrada* of Luis Marin and Bernal Diaz del Castillo (1964) and ending with the date of Mexican independence from Spanish rule. This phase encompasses the mixing of two cultures, the indigenous Zoque and the imperial Spanish. It covers the long and painful process of complete Zoque acculturation and partial Spanish accommodation to a new situation.

Only the site of Quechula, a Zoque capital during the Late Postclassic and the site of a large Dominican church with its congregation by the mid-sixteenth century, contained cultural material which shows the fusion of the two cultures.

The Santiago ceramic complex is composed of three wares. The Bernal ware, the only one which was definitely made on a wheel, is limited to a single shape: a flat-bottomed, flaring-walled bowl or *borcelana* as it is called today. This orange wheel-made ware is of a very fine paste, and is apparently without temper.

Godoy ware consists of *aceteras* or pointed-bottomed oil vessels with a short neck and heavily thickened rim exterior. These vessels are glazed, but were not made on a wheel.

Crude brown ware deep bowls and *comales* form the Marin ware. This ware appears to be very similar to that commonly found in the locally-made ceramics of Tuxtla Gutierrez and Ocosocoautla.

It would be premature, on the basis of these limited data, to try to interrelate the ceramics of the Colonial period to the ceramics of other regions at this time.

Acknowledgments

I would like to thank the directors of the New World Archaeological Foundation of Brigham Young University, and the Departmento de Monumentos Prehispánicos of the Instituto Nacional de Antropología e Historia of Mexico, for their support in this work, particularly Gareth W. Lowe (Field Director, N.W.A.F.), José Luis

Lorenzo, then Director (Mon. Prehis. of I.N.A.H.), and Carlos Navarrete, Project Field Director. The Comisión Federal de Electricidad, through the good offices of Ingeniero Enrique Marrón V., supported the project with lodging, transportation, food, and part of the labour, all of which is gratefully acknowledged.

REFERENCES

Agrinier, P. (1964) La casa de banos de vapor de San Antonio, Chiapas. *Boletín de Instituto Nacional de Antropología e Historia*, 25, 27-32.

Agrinier, P. (1969) *Excavations at San Antonio, Chiapas, Mexico.* Papers of the New World Archaeological Foundation, no. 24.

Alvarez del Toro, M. (1952) *Los animales silvestres de Chiapas.* Publicaciones del Departmento de Prensa y Turismo del Gobierno del Estado. Tuxtla Gutierrez, Chiapas.

Alvarez del Toro, M. (1960) *Los reptiles de Chiapas.* Instituto Zoológico del Estado. Tuxtla Gutierrez, Chiapas.

Coe, M.D. (1970) The archaeological sequence at San Lorenzo Tenochtitlan, Veracruz, Mexico. In *Magnetometer Survey of the La Venta Pyramid and Other Papers on Mexican Archaeology*, Contributions of the University of California Archaeological Research Facility, no. 8.

Diaz del Castillo, B. (1964) *Historia verdadera de la conquista de la Nueva España.* Mexico.

Drucker, P. (1952) *La Venta, Tabasco: a Study of Olmec Ceramics and Art.* Bureau of American Ethnology, Bulletin no. 153.

Drucker, P., R.F. Heizer and R.J. Squire (1959) *Excavations at La Venta, Tabasco, 1955.* Bulletin of the Bureau of American Ethnology, No. 170.

Echeagaray Bablot, L. et al. (1957) *Lo que ha sido y lo que puede ser el sureste.* 3 vols. Secretaria de Recursos Hidraulicos, Mexico.

Ekholm, S.M. (1969) *Mound 30a and the Early Preclassic Ceramic Sequence of Izapa, Chiapas, Mexico.* Papers of the New World Archaeological Foundation, no. 25.

Gifford, J.C. n.d. A conceptual approach to the analysis of prehistoric pottery. Unpublished thesis presented in 1963 to the Department of Anthropology, Harvard University, Cambridge, Mass.

Lee, T.A., Jr. (in press, *a*) *Mound 4 Excavations at San Isidro, Chiapas, Mexico.* Papers of the New World Archaeological Foundation, no. 31.

Lee, T.A., Jr. (in press, *b*) Cuevas secas del Rio La Venta. *Antropología e Historia de Guatemala*, 22, no. 2.

Lee, T.A., Jr. (in preparation) *Excavations along the Totopac and Grijalva Rivers, Chiapas, Mexico.* Papers of the New World Archaeological Foundation.

Lee, T.A., Jr. (n.d.) The historic communication routes of Northern Chiapas and Tabasco. Paper read at the Routes of Communication and Cultural Contact Symposium of the 40th International Congress of Americanists, Rome, September 3-9, 1972.

Lee, T.A., Jr., A.W. Lowe and C. Navarrete (in preparation) *The Middle Grijalva Ceramics.*

Longacre, R. (1967) Systemic comparison and reconstruction. In *Handbook of Middle American Indians*, vol. 5, 117-59. Austin, Texas.

Lowe, G.W. n.d. The Olmec Horizon occupation of Mound 20 at San Isidro in the Middle Grijalva region of Chiapas. Unpublished thesis, University of the Americas, 1969.

Lowe, G.W. and P. Agrinier (1960) *Mound 1, Chiapa de Corzo, Chiapas, Mexico.* Papers of the New World Archaeological Foundation, no. 8.

Matos Moctezuma, E. (1966*a*) Un juego de pelota doble en San Isidro, Chiapas.

Boletín de Instituto Nacional de Antropología e Historia, 25, 36-7.

Matos Moctezuma, E. (1966*b*) Arqueología de rescate en Mal Paso, Chiapas, *C.F.E. Sirviendo a Mexico*, 1, no. 2, 32-7. Comisión Federal de Electricidad, Mexico.

Matos Moctezuma, E. (in preparation) *The Excavations of Mound 1 and 2, San Isidro, Chiapas, Mexico*. Papers of the New World Archaeological Foundation.

Miranda, F. (1952) *La vegetación de Chiapas*. 2 vols. Departamento de Prensa y Turismo, Tuxtla Gutierrez, Chiapas.

Mullerried, F.K.G. (1957) *La geología de Chiapas*. Gobierno Constitucional del Estado de Chiapas, 1952-1958. Mexico.

Navarrete, C. (1966*a*) Excavaciones en la presa Netzahualcoytl, Mal Paso, Chiapas. *Boletín de Instituto Nacional de Antropología e Historia*, 24, 36-40.

Navarrete, C. (1966*b*) *The Chiapanec History and Culture*. Papers of the New World Archaeological Foundation, no. 21.

Navarrete, C. and T.A. Lee, Jr. (in preparation) *Quechula: una introduction al arqueologia Zoque*.

Piña Chan, R. and C. Navarrete (1967) *Archaeological researches in the Lower Grijalva region, Tabasco and Chiapas*. Papers of the New World Archaeological Foundation, no. 22.

Scholes, F.V. and R.L. Roys (1948) *The Maya Chontal Indians of Acalan-Tixchel*. Carnegie Institution of Washington, Publication no. 560.

Sisson, E.B. (1970) Settlement patterns and land use in the northwestern Chontalpa, Tabasco, Mexico: a progress report. *Cerámica de Cultura Maya*, 6, 41-54.

Solis, J. (1945) Estado en que se hallaba la provincia de Coatzacoalcos en el año de 1599. *Boletín del Archivo General de la Nación*, 16, no. 2, 195-246; no. 3, 429-79. Mexico.

Smith, R.E. (1958) The place of Fine Orange pottery in Mesoamerican archaeology. *American Antiquity*, 24, no. 2, 151-60.

Smith, R.E., G.R. Willey and J.C. Gifford (1960) The type-variety concept as a basis for the analysis of Maya pottery. *American Antiquity*, 25, no.3, 330-40.

Tamayo, J.L. (1953) *Geografía moderno de México*. Mexico.

Wallrath, M. (1967) Excavations in the Tehuantepec region, Mexico. *Transactions of the American Philosophical Society*, n.s., 57, part 2.

Willey, G.R. (1970) Type descriptions of the ceramics of the Real Xe complex, Seibal, Peten, Guatemala. In W.R. Bullard, Jr. (ed.), *Monographs and Papers in Maya Archaeology*, Papers of the Peabody Museum of Archaeology and Ethnology, vol. 61, 313-55.

Willey, G.R., P. Culbert and R.E.W. Adams (1967) Maya lowland ceramics: a report from the 1965 Guatemala city conference. *American Antiquity*, 32, no. 3, 289-315.

GLYN WILLIAMS

External influences and the upper Rio Verde drainage basin at Los Altos, West Mexico

Until recently West Mexico was treated as a relatively impoverished
archaeological region of Mesoamerica. Since no state-like formation
of the stature of those in Southern Mesoamerica and the Central
Valley of Mexico had been encountered in the region it was felt that
West Mexico was not only late in developing the traits generally
associated with the High cultures, but was believed to have had only
minimum contact with such cultures. In many respects the entire
West Mexican region was held to be populated by rudimentary,
warlike, Chichimecan groups. This attitude was to a great extent
responsible for the conservative approach to West Mexican chronology which in turn resulted in a reluctance to relate the region to
other Mesoamerican archaeological regions. Even when material with
a clear influence from the High cultures was discovered it was
invariably explained in terms of culture lag. Yet such material kept
turning up, and with the advent of radiocarbon dating it finally
became acceptable to think in terms of a Preclassic phase for parts of
West Mexico. An exception to all of this, of course, was the
Chupicuaro site. From the time of its excavation in the 1940s (Porter
1956) its relationship to the Central Valley was recognized, and this
site has become accepted as a key site in terms of West Mexican
chronology.

As a result of the above attitude, the literature includes such
statements as 'the whole complex of social and religious ideas which
went into the formation of the theocratic Classic period appears to
have by-passed them [West Mexican areas]' (Emmerich 1963: 30).
Even at the beginning of the 1960s we learn that ' . . . none of the
[West Mexican] sites show definite evidence of considerable antiquity' (Armillas 1964: 318) and that ' . . . clearly defined horizon
style links with Central Mexico are demonstrable only at the end of
the first millennium' (ibid.: 319). Two influential authors writing at
this time similarly claimed that the Early Classic in West Mexico was
unrelated to the Valley of Mexico and that it was not until the Late
Classic that West Mexico was influenced by Central Mexico (Taylor

and Long 1966: 457). However, they do admit that 'West Mexico, while definitely peripheral to the cultural developments in the Valley of Mexico, is an area of considerable importance to an understanding of Mesoamerica' (ibid.: 459).

The past few years have seen something of a different attitude among some workers. The acceptance of radiocarbon dates that firmly establish a Classic and Preclassic horizon in West Mexico has prompted a reappraisal not only of individual items but also of the culture history of the entire region, while new discoveries tend to be increasingly evaluated from a new temporal-spatial framework (Taylor et al. 1970). Not least among this new attitude is the willingness to reconsider the relationship of West Mexico to other culture areas. The work of J. Charles Kelley in Durango and Zacatecas (Kelley 1971) has shed considerable light upon the relationship of this area both to Mesoamerica and the southwest of the U.S.A. His work has established that a Central Mexican influence was felt either directly or indirectly in this area during the Late Preclassic (ibid.: 800). In addition further light has been shed upon Preclassic sites such as that at Infernillo (Litvak King 1968). Furthermore, the dating of the large hollow figurines generally held to be characteristic of West Mexico has been established at Tequilita, Nayarit (Taylor et al.: 22) and Etzatlan, Jalisco (Long and Taylor 1966), shaft tombs have been dated (Furst, personal communication), and the work of Isabel Kelly at Colima (Bell 1971: 742) promises to extend our knowledge of the West Mexican Preclassic. Similarly, workers (McBride 1969) are now also more willing to consider Classic contacts between West and Central Mexico.

The aim of this paper is to expand this discussion by referring to external contacts for one corner of West Mexico, thereby answering the call for 'more work . . . to answer questions concerning the extent, duration and internal and external relationships' (Bell 1971: 752). Since the evidence drawn upon consists of unexcavated materials which exist in large local, private collections or which were encountered in the possession of local peasant farmers who had found them in the process of their agricultural work, the seriation is by necessity tentative. However, painstaking efforts were made to establish the site provenance of all material and where any doubt exists concerning such provenance the material is excluded from the following discussion.[1] What in effect I am doing is studying type pieces and relating them to positive site attributions and local pottery associations. The bulk of the material consists of figurines which, as Vaillant (1930, 1931, 1935) recognized, are excellent time markers, despite the fact that as McBride has noted (1969: 49) the emphasis placed upon architecture and ceramics has relegated the use of figurines to a secondary role.[2]

An attempt is made to place the figurines according to local type before relating them to established types in other locations. The process involves grouping the figurines into types and subtypes on the basis of shape, physical features, decoration, material, method of composition and proportion. By type is meant only that these traits are employed to distinguish between one specimen or group of specimens and another. Where the broad traits are similar but the specimens still reveal variations along minor traits these will constitute subtypes. Once the types have been determined they will be related to figurines from other areas on the basis of the same aspects involved in the initial typing. This comparison with the classifications of other workers should serve as a validation of my own typology. Finally, the conclusions drawn by the above method will be validated by ceramic and other material drawn from local private collections. In this context it is held that 'the pursuit of a general feature or outstanding element frequently clarifies a general problem' (Cook de Leonard 1971: 195).

There is of course no substitute for controlled excavations with acceptable concrete dating, and in presenting the following ideas it is perhaps not necessary to emphasize their tentativeness. In studies of this kind one can seldom 'prove' anything, but one may hope to indicate new approaches to a problem and new channels through which still further research may be pursued. Much of the archaeological work thus far undertaken in West Mexico has been of what might be called the 'pit and run' variety, involving a minimum of preliminary reconnaissance and theoretical construction. On the contrary, what is discussed in this paper stems from the belief that

Figure 1 Mesoamerica, showing area of study.

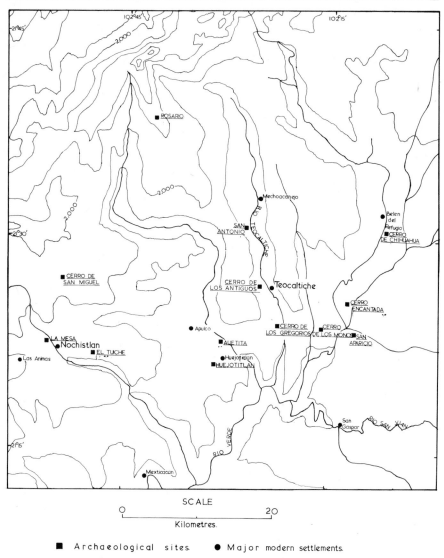

Figure 2 Archaeological sites of the Upper Rio Verde drainage basin.

such problem-orientation is possible and that preliminary reconnaissance provides the basis for theoretical insights which can be tested by subsequent excavations.

The area in question consists of the Upper Rio Verde drainage basin along the border of Zacatecas and Jalisco (Fig. 1). The Rio Verde is a tributary of the Rio Grande de Santiago, and its headwaters lie in an area of contrasting ecological niches, varying between elevated forested areas which lie at an altitude of up to

2,500 m., and the alluvial plains at an elevation of about 1,850 m. (Fig. 2). It is conceivable that this local diversity could have served to provide a variety of adaptive economic postures, varying from hunting to agriculture. At present the river is dry during four months of the year, the growing season coinciding with the onset of rains during June to January. However, a fairly high water table makes the use of irrigation possible in some localities, as also do perennial springs.

Within the area thirteen sites have been identified (Fig. 2). These sites vary in size and architectural complexity, this accounting for the diversity in the amount of archaeological material associated with each site, although other factors such as the degree of looting and the extent of ploughed land at the site are equally important in this respect. All the sites lie near the river and one suspects that the settlement pattern conforms to an as yet unidentified spatial hierarchy.

Figurines

The figurines can be categorized into four types.

Type I

Figurines of type I are characterized by a variety of features typical of Central Mexican Late Preclassic figurines (Fig. 3). The head, which varies in length from 3.5 cm. to 6.5 cm. and from 2.3 cm. to 4.0 cm. in width, is squarish in shape and is moulded into a concave form, with the upper head being straight and the lower face revealing a pronounced prognathism. This prognathism is negated somewhat by a circular appliqué noseplug which tends to obscure the mouth, which, when visible, consists of a broad horizontal slash. The nose is generally concave and has a pointed tip created by an angular cut which serves to form the area of the mouth. The eyes are oval and double gouged, and the forehead is long and curved at the edges, but with a simple appliqué headdress which may or may not be decorated by line incisions, serving to counteract the impression of forehead tallness. The ears are not always present, and when they are, they may represent a lateral extension of the head or may be of an appliqué form. An earplug is usually apparent and can take the form of a simple hole, a circular appliqué or appliqué and line decoration.

At the neck is a sectioned necklace which can assume a variety of decorations, and most of the bodies are covered with a simple garment that extends to knee level. The body is often about as long as the head and the posture is invariably the same, being a forward

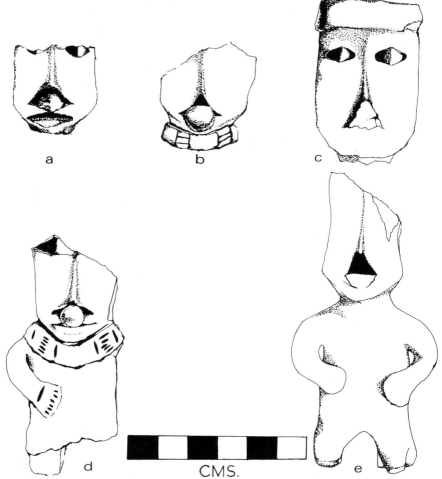

Figure 3 Figurines of type I.

facing standing figure with arms placed on the hips. Sometimes plain appliqué pieces are placed across the garment. The hands are either plain or they may show fingers by simple line incisions. The feet are simple arched forms, extending to the back and front and serving as supports for the figurines which are unpainted or unslipped.

While these are the main characteristics of this type of figurine, they do reveal significant variation. For example, some have no eyes, while others have painted eyes or a double gouged eye and holes punched into the nose to represent nostrils. Only one case of an appliqué mouth was encountered. Painted decoration consists of red and blue paint and white stucco.

Type I: subtypes

Four figurines, while belonging to this basic type, are different

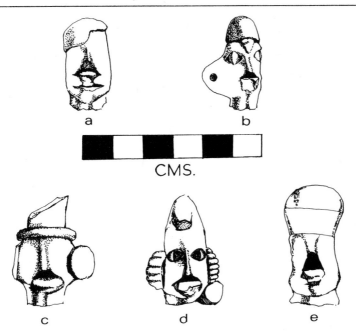

CMS.

Figure 4 Figurines of type I: sub-types.

enough from the norm to justify being regarded as a subtype (Fig. 4). All of them have a long narrow head and two of them are almost identical. These two have concave sallow cheeks and a tall rounded forehead with headdress. They also have round noseplugs and earplugs. Apart from the narrowness of the heads of the other two figurines the main deviation is in the forehead, one having a pointed peak to the head and the other a head adorned with a cap-like application.

Taken as a composite form this type resembles Late Preclassic types, and yet it is impossible to place them definitely in any of Vaillant's definitive groups. By and large they consist of traits associated with a variety of Central Valley types. The double gouged eyes are typical of types B and E, while the prognathism together with this eye form is typical of type E. the cutting away of the base of the nose, which gives it a pointed, upturned effect, is found in B and E II types, while the semicircular noseplug is reminiscent of H III types. Similarly the body form is suggestive of HIV or HV types. Thus despite the fact that there are similarities with Middle Preclassic types (B and even C) the main stylistic association appears to be with Late Preclassic types (E and H). The overall impression is suggestive of a derivation from the Early Zacatenco and Arbolillo phases, as described by Noguera for Cholula (Noguera 1954). As we shall see, this explanation is tempting. Yet some bodies (3d) as well as the arched feet reflect West Mexican features while at least one of the subtypes (4e) suggests a Nayarit influence.

This type of figurine does not appear to have been restricted to this location alone for Seler has an illustration of the same type for La Quemada (Seler 1960, vol. 3, 556, Fig. 17) while Saenz (1966: 47-9) has described, with illustration, similar types for Ixtepte, Jalisco.

I have also encountered two others deriving from Guanajuato and Zacatecas in the Museo Nacional de México. Bearing in mind the paucity of small solid figurines of definite provenance in West Mexico the limited number thus far encountered is not surprising. Within the Upper Rio Verde this type is associated with the following sites: San Aparicio, San Antonio, Tequesquite, and Cerro de los Monos. Significantly these sites are both large and small.

Type II

Three figurines only of type II have been encountered in the area, all of them associated with San Aparicio, and all of them being incomplete fragments (Fig. 5). The head is elongated horizontally, being twice as wide as it is long. They are flat and have been pressure moulded. It is quite possible that they were part of effigy vessels.

The most significant feature of these heads is their mouse-like features, which result from the protrusion of the nose and mouth to convey a snout-like effect. The flat forehead is adorned with a wide red painted band representing a headdress. Immediately below this band are the eyes, which in two cases consist of circular depressions, while in the third case they are double gouged. The mouth is either a horizontal slash into the protruding area of the face or two down-turning slashes on either side of this protrusion. One head has nostrils represented by simple slashes above the mouth. The ears are modelled extensions of the head and in one case are represented by a circular indentation and peripheral line decoration. One of the heads has the remnants of white stucco decoration over a polished red finish.

The literature does contain reference to this type of figurine in Central Mexico, the most significant being that described by Gamio (1922: vol. 6, 196) as an 'Archaic' type and which has recently been associated with the Teotihuacan II period (Cook de Leonard 1971: 191). The other reference of significance is ascribed to Noguera (1965) who discusses figurines designated as G2 which are not unlike the three associated with San Aparicio. If this last explanation is accepted it suggests that this small group might have evolved from type I which we associated with Vaillant's type E. However, the only feature in common is the single pair of double gouged eyes. Gamio claimed that the example he described came from inside the Pyramid of the Sun at Teotihuacan and Tezayuca figurines are often polished red and carry a slit mouth.

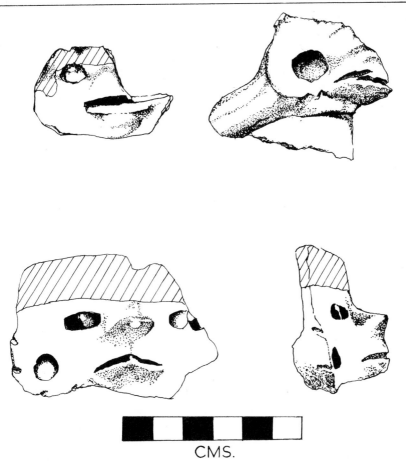

Figure 5 Figurines of type II.

Type III

Type III (Fig. 6) is very common in the area, and yet very little is known about some parts of the figurine. It differs from types I and II in having a gloss finish and having been fired black, although there are many buff-coloured forms with signs that this resulted from mis-firing.

The head has an elongated appearance resulting from a long flat forehead which is square in shape, except in some examples which have a slightly concave top giving the head a horned appearance. The overall shape of the head is triangular, with the bottom half ending in a prognathous jaw. The technique of modelling is far superior to that of types I and II. The eyes consist of rectangular slits gouged to an even depth, which are generally horizontal, although some are slanted. The mouth consists of a simple slash across the prognathous lower face, while the nose is pinched and rounded at the tip. Ears are oversimplified, being no more than projections from the side of the

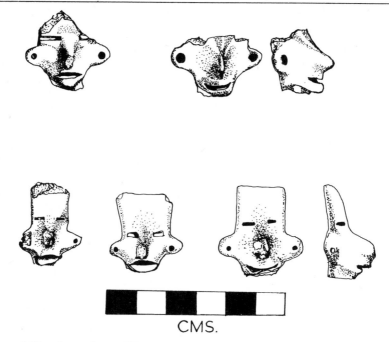

CMS.

Figure 6 Figurines of type III.

head that have been pierced with a circular hole. There are signs that the elongated forehead was tempered by a headdress, but apart from one case no evidence about the nature of the adornment has been discovered. This single figurine carried a simple headdress with simple vertical line incisions as decoration similar to a type that does appear early at Teotihuacan (Noguera 1965: 29). The headdress was applied at the top of the forehead, whereas other pieces suggest a mid-forehead position. In form the figurine bears a slight resemblance to the terminal Preclassic in the Central Valley, but again, traits such as the squarish head suggest a relationship with some West Mexican shaft tomb figurines (Furst, personal communication) as well as some Chupicuaro forms (Frierman (ed.) 1969: 60-1).

Thus far these figurines have been associated with only two sites, Cerro de Chihuahua at Belen and at San Aparicio. It is significant that these are the two largest sites in the area. Furthermore, apart from that cited by Seler (1960 vol. 3: 556) as being related to La Quemada no other case is known to the writer. However there are similarities between this type of figurine and terminal Preclassic figurines in the Central Valley. Most conspicuous of the traits of course is the pronounced prognathism. The mouth and ear forms are also not unknown among such forms and the narrow, pointed modelled nose is common. However, the nose tends to be straight and jutting over the upper lip unlike most Protoclassic forms. Since the similarities are limited one must conclude that the figurine type in question, if it does bear a resemblance to Central Valley forms of the Protoclassic, is a local adaptation of the Southern form distinctly modified.

Type IV

a   b

c   d

e   f

CMS.

Figure 7 Figurines of type IV.

TYPE I (a) Headdress

(b) Collar

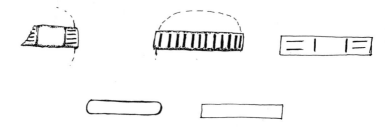

(c) Ear

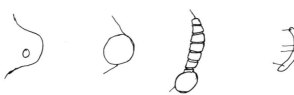

TYPE IV (a) Headdress

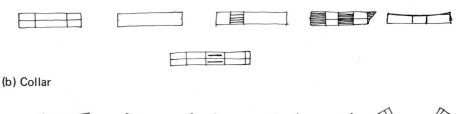

(b) Collar

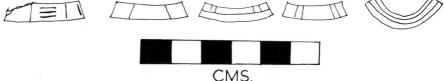

CMS.

Figure 8 Variations of headdress, collar and ear in types I and IV.

The final type of figurine, type IV, differs from the other three types in that prognathism is absent (Fig. 7). The head tends to create an impression of being round even though it is in effect elongated, the length being counteracted by the simple lateral extension of the head to form the ears. The ears themselves are represented by simple perforations which, because of the lack of detail of the ear area, give an impression that the face has a hole in each cheek. The nose is generally straight or slightly concave, beginning slightly above the level of the eyes. The base of the nose is cut away much in the style of type I, and the body ornamentation of the two types (Fig. 8)· suggests an evolution of type IV from type I. Into the area cut away below the nose an oval mouth has been punched, being identical to the form of the eyes. The headdress varies from a simple appliqué band with shaded decoration around the forehead to a complex formation which includes a decorated protruding piece off the left side of the head. Many of these figurines reveal a double line over the top of the head and, almost as if these lines served as a centre parting, two appliqué strands of hair extending below the headdress on either side of the face. Only one of the figurines of this type thus far encountered had a noseplug, this being a circular appliqué disc. It is significant that this head, the largest of this type, was also the only one to be adorned with round appliqué earplugs. The overall impression is one of a realistic portraiture.

The neck is adorned with a collar represented by line incisions or by an appliqué necklace, the difference quite possibly representing sex distinction. The body tends to be somewhat larger than the head although the latter dominates the figurine. The posture is either one in which the figure is seated with knees raised and the hands resting on the knees, an upright stance with hands on hips, or a seated position with child in arms. The hands are represented by line incisions and the legs, which tend to be stocky and held together, have feet which may or may not have toes showing. Some of the unadorned bodies have breasts, although as stated above clothing may be a more definite sex distinction. This adornment is most highly developed on one figurine which has appliqué bands with line incisions which represent a *quexquemetl* (Fig. 9a). Below this is a full-length skirt with a vertical design at the base. Above this decoration and lying on the hips is a wide appliqué band, the skirt flaring below this point. The only other body adornment consists of a breech cloth similar to that ascribed to ball players (Sejourne 1969: 223).

Within this type is an interesting group of miniatures whose composition is as described above apart from the following additional information that can be gleaned from these figurines. The smallest figurines measure about 2 cm. in height and may be buff or black with a gloss finish like that of the larger buff figurines. (Fig. 10). They may also be decorated with paint. The arms and legs are part of the body mass, being distinguished by lines or limited moulding. Where there is no headdress there is invariably a hole in the top of the head. One other of these figurines is different in

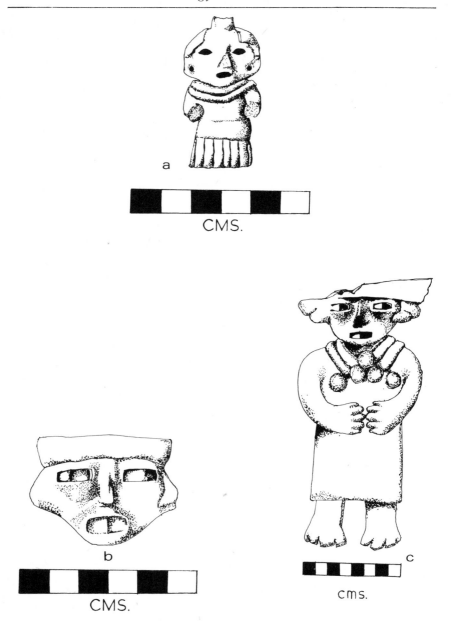

Figure 9 Figurines of type IV(*a*) and type K(*b* and *c*).

having long flowing hair. Also of interest are three anthropomorphic forms, one having a dog-like head with appliqué circles on the head and a human body, another a sharp snouted head with long flowing hair on a pregnant human body in crouched position, and the third a dog-headed figure holding a shield in front of the body. This shield is divided into four quadrants which, as we shall see, is a common

Figure 10 Figurines of type IV: miniatures.

ceramic motif. The most interesting of this group of figurines is an almost complete figure elaborately clothed with a sleeveless, decorated, three quarter length garment which is divided into an upper and lower section by a line at the waist (Fig. 10*b*). These two sections are decorated on the front and the back by a motif that resembles the upper half of the butterfly motif. The garment is further decorated by diagonal lines at the shoulder. The head carries a single ear plug which is concentrically decorated and what appears to be a circular shell pendant hangs at the neck. Finally at the top of the head is what appears to be a tall hat decorated with cross-hatching and appliqué decorations.

To my knowledge only two figurines of this type are ascribed to areas outside the locality in question. One is in the National Museum and is held to derive from Michoacan (Kelemen 1969: Plate 113*a*), while the other is in the Albers collection (Albers 1970: 63). In the Upper Rio Verde area this type is associated with the sites at San Aparicio, Cerro de Chihuahua and San Antonio. Dr M. Coe has described the Albers figurine as a depiction of Xipe Totec and has assigned it to Teotihuacan III. Certainly the portrait nature of the face is suggestive of Teotihuacan forms as are the oval eyes and mouth, the prominent earplug features, the elaborate headdress, especially the protruding section on the left of the head, and the hair framing the face. Furthermore, the dress and *quexquemetl* described above, with its tendency to give the figurine a triangular form, is characteristic of the Tzacualli phase in the Central Valley, as is the overall configuration (e.g. Fig. 7*a*) (Millon, personal communication). However, this type may bear a stronger relationship to Chupicuaro forms, or more specifically to the Michoacan branch of the Chupicuaro culture.

Other figurines

While the above figurines are the most typical of the local made figurines, others which have non-local spatial identification are also found in the area. It is these more than anything that serve to identify concretely the temporal and spatial relationship between the Upper Rio Verde and other regions. Although they are only seven in number their importance as a foundation for the argument of this paper can not be denied. This being the case it depends upon the secure provenance of each figurine, this having been carefully checked in the field.

The first two figurines (Fig. 9*b*, *c*) are of the K type which are generally ascribed to the Middle or Late Preclassic (Gendrop 1970: 268; Vaillant 1934). Although this type of figurine has been found in association with Tlatilco D and Gualupita figurines, Vaillant insisted that they were of a West Mexican source, and they have been associated with Ixtepete (Saenz 1966) of Jalisco, and La Quemada (Seler 1960: VIII, Figs. 17-19). These figurines were found at San Aparicio and Cerro de los Gregorios. The other five figurines are unmistakably Classic Teotihuacan or Teotihuacanoid types. Two are similar, being very similar, although not identical, to Teotihuacan IV forms, and derive from Cerro de los Antiguos and San Antonio (Figs. 11*a*, *b*). Another is a Teotihuacan III type from Cerro de los Antiguos (Fig. 11*e*), which is also the source of the other two figurines which are of the old Fire God Huehueateotl (Teotihuacan III) (Fig. 11*d*) and the negroid figure (Teotihuacan IIA) (Fig. 11*e*) respectively.

Perhaps this area is best known as the source of the horned hollow figurines whose provenance appears to have puzzled archaeologists while they were being purchased by North American collectors during the 1960s (Kan, Meighan and Nicholson 1970: 50-1). These figurines emanated from Cerro Encantada de Tequesquite, which now resembles a battlefield as a result of the looting. Careful cross-checking has established that thus far this type of figurine is not associated with any site other than Tequesquite. A limited number of pits were dug at the site by Betty Bell in 1968 and we are fortunate in having at least some archaeological knowledge of these figurines and their associations (Bell, personal communication). Her preliminary conclusions were that 'the site had but one occupation, possibly a fairly brief one'. She has obtained a radio-carbon date of 1800 ± 80 years B.P., but this is a single date,[3] although Diego Delgado is also alleged to have obtained similar dates from shell material at the same site (Bell 1971: 734). Furst (reported in Scott and Easby 1970: 118) has suggested a movement from Nayarit to this area during the Classic, and certainly the leg forms, body posture

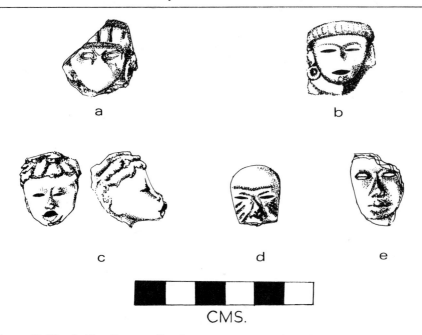

a   b

c   d   e

CMS.

Figure 11 Classic Teotihuacan figurines.

and some of the adornments are characteristic of Nayarit figurines.

Apart from the horned figurines two specimens of hollow figurines, both with negative painting and a pose with hands pointing palms outwards which is characteristic of Antonio Escobado (Bell 1971: 726, Fig. 26; Parres Arias 1962), are associated with this site. The facial characteristics are different for each figurine, one resembling figurines of the Sayula area and the Antonio Escobado figurines to a lesser extent, and the other having eyebrows and eyes and mouth punched with a hollow circular object.

Apart from the hollow figurines, Bell's work produced very few others. Of the four solid figurine fragments that she recovered, only one, a portion of the head of a figurine type I, was in any way reminiscent of the above-mentioned types. The others were more reminiscent of northern types (Culiacan) having appliqué coffee-bean eyes and a beak-like nose. One fragment is not unlike some of the figurines of the southwest, while the other two are the equivalent of the large hollow figurines.

Three other figurines, all carved from shell (a characteristic of the southwest) are also associated with the Tequesquite site. Two of them appear to have served as pendants since the head is perforated. The characteristic feature of these figurines is the nose, which dominates the face and, with the eyes on either side of the nose, suggests a northern association. The third figurine was in all likelihood also a pendant, since there is a hole through the forehead.

This figurine also has a long prominent nose, dividing the eyes which are diamond-shaped, a characteristic West Mexican trait. The mouth is double gouged, this being the only feature that breaks the line consisting of the nose and a line that divides the body in two. It certainly suggests that shell carving was a highly developed skill at this site. Among the shell material associated with this site are the large conch shells (*Turbinella angulatus*, Solander 1786) usually associated with West Mexican shaft tombs and assumed to be contemporary with the Late Preclassic-Early Classic in West Mexico (Taylor et al. 1970: 22); *Laericardium elatum* (Sowerby 1833) which Feldman claims is 'a clam shell often found at archaeological sites from northern Sinaloa to the American South West. It is quite uncommon south of a line running from Guasave, Sinaloa to Durango, Durango, and might therefore be considered as indicative of a cultural zone of northern Mexico'; *Patella mexicana* (Broderip and Sowerby 1829) which has a 'highly restricted natural distribution, being found particularly on rocky headlands. The only known coastal West Mexican site where it is relatively common is Morett, Colima. However, its use at your site is better suggested by the *P. mexicana* pectorals widely known elsewhere in Mesoamerica'; and *Fasciolaria princeps* (Sowerby 1825) in the form of the *atlatl* rings which ' . . . are becoming common in West Mexican sites on the North Western periphery of Tarascan Michoacan'.[4]

Other evidence

Since the Tequesquite site has been so extensively looted it is inevitable that most of our knowledge of the area derives from this site. However, local farmers in the area tend to put aside surface material encountered during their work, this material generally taking the form of the unusual. In addition, surface collections of sherds do exist in local private collections, although one suspects again that such collections are based upon the unusual rather than any acceptable systematic collection.

Perhaps the most interesting of the material to be considered under this heading is a limestone slab measuring 7.5 by 12.8 cm. carved on both sides (Fig. 12). The depiction is of a highly stylized Fire God complete with such general characteristics as the speech scroll, face mask and headdress. Interestingly the feet resemble claws, suggesting some association or confusion with Quetzalcoatl. Since this piece was carved from limestone derived from a quarry five km. to the north of the San Aparicio site where it was discovered, it suggests that a fully developed Fire God cult, or at least a person or personages sufficiently versed in religious imagery to be able to depict one of the main deities of the Teotihuacan religious complex, existed at the site. If this assumption is correct it is reasonable to

CMS.

Figure 12 Limestone slab with Tlaloc sculpture.

assume that similar symbolism and relationships should be associated with other plastic forms, e.g. ceramics, but it should be recognized that the figure deviates from the customary Fire God forms, e.g. the eyes, while large, are not of the 'goggle' form, and the lower body is particularly confused.[5]

Sherd material from various sites suggest that a variety of vessel forms are associated with the area. Particularly interesting are vessel supports which are summarized in Table 1.

Table 1 Vessel supports

	Spider	Mummary	Nubbin	Slab	Claw + Face	Pointed	Bulbous Hollow	Ring Base	Tall
Tequesquite	X	X			X	X	X	X	X
San Aparicio	X	X	X	X	X		X	X	X
San Antonio	X						X		X
El Tuiche	X	X			X	X	X	X	X
Huejotitlan							X		
Teocaltiche					X		X		

Since there is a tendency for many Preclassic ceramic traits to reappear in the Postclassic (Tolstoy 1958: 67) it is virtually impossible to associate this range of vessel supports with any satisfactory chronology without supporting evidence. Certainly most of the above supports are associated with both the Preclassic and Postclassic. However, all the mummary supports appear to conform to the Chupicuaro types as also do the tall, solid types.

Furthermore, if as Bell suspects Tequesquite had a limited occupation, the spider, pointed and hollow bulbous would also conform to Preclassic forms. The claw and face type of support are reminiscent of the knee and foot supports of the Cantillo phase of the Suchil B ranch of the Chalchuites culture (Kelley 1971: 780) except that the leg has 'eyes' and a 'nose'. Ring based vessels have a low ring base. Little can be said about the comparative-temporal nature of this support nor of the other three types.

A few more obvious pottery correspondences can be considered, although it should be emphasized that they can not be placed stratigraphically. Firstly, a basal ring vessel with stepped fret cloisonné designs would appear to point to Classic associations, possibly with the Early Classic cloisonné of the Suchil phase to the north, although it is of course possible that it relates to the Early Postclassic (Bell 1971: 727). The same is true of the stucco painted sherds from Cerro de Chihuahua, a single champlevé sherd from San Aparicio and sherds with Alta Vista designs, while the numerous miniature black ollas associated with San Aparicio are identical with those found in funerary offerings at Teotihuacan.

Beyond this, the ceramic inventory consists of variations on the following colours: red, orange, black, cream, brown, buff and polychrome-bichrome variations. Among the wares thus far encountered are the following: orange, red on brown, red-rimmed, red on black, black on red, black on red with negative design, polished red, polished brown and polished black, orange on brown, red on orange, red on cream, cream on red, red and cream on black; red and buff with negative design, and red, buff, black and white polychrome. Of these it would appear that the wares with negative design, as well as the cream on red, black on red, red on orange, black incised and polished monochrome wares, are equivalent to the Chupicuaro related types to be discussed below with reference to Cerro Encantada de Tequesquite. It is of course possible that they persist beyond the assumed occupation of this site.

Some of the other types bear a general relationship to West Mexican sites. For example, red-rimmed wares are characteristic of Chametla (Kelly 1938), Peñitas (Bordaz 1964), Amapa (Bell 1960), and Morett (Susia 1961) as well as the Zacatecas/Durango region (Kelley 1971: 793) during the Middle and Late Classic and may well have derived from Chupicuaro red rimmed wares. Similarly red on brown ceramics are found in Nayarit, Jalisco, Colima, Sinaloa, Zacatecas, Durango, Michoacan, and Guerrero (Lister 1955:106-7) during the early Postclassic while of course being characteristic of Toltec horizons in Central Mexico. Red on black ceramics are found in Central Mexico during the Late Preclassic but are rare (Piña Chan 1971: 165), while the white on red forms are associated with Central Mexico during Late Preclassic and Classic (Vaillant 1930; Piña Chan 1971: 162) and with the north during the Late Postclassic (Lister

1955: 27). Similarly red on cream forms are associated with the Protoclassic at Totoate (Kelley 1971: 770) and Los Ortices (Kelly 1948: 65-6) and with Central Mexico (Acosta 1957) during the Early Postclassic. Orange wares are found at Morett (Susia 1961) and Amapa (Bell 1960) and the several black polished minature ollas are found at Teotihuacan during the Classic. The general assemblage of ceramics is not unlike that at Totoate (Kelley 1971: 770-3) but in the absence of satisfactory evidence about decoration or vessel form nothing but a tentative comparison can be made.

The relationship between the Tequesquite site and several of the other Upper Rio Verde sites is attested by a diagnostic ware, a deep buff bowl with two rows of nested horizontal chevrons around the outside below the rim, as well as by the thin black ware. An early association for at least one site is also attested by a single punctuate-incised sherd. Furthermore, San Aparicio black and red and negative sherds carry identical motifs to some Tequesquite wares. Yet despite these cross-ties it is surprising that no evidence of the hollow figurines has turned up.

As stated above, a large amount of material has been looted from the Tequesquite site, and since most of our knowledge pertains to this site it is appropriate to discuss its significance in terms of surrounding sites in the hope that this will help to shed light upon the cultural history of the Upper Rio Verde area. The most conspicuous feature is that the vessel forms, while being deviant in relation to Mesoamerican forms as a whole, are in accordance with the range associated with Chupicuaro. Among them are *patojos*, duck shapes, oval bowls, effigy ollas, tripods with tall mummary supports, bowls in the form of a squash, bowls with loop-like handles set around the rim, cylinder vessels, containers with human faces near the rim, and barrel rectangular shapes. Yet despite all these similarities the characteristic Chupicuaro hollow and solid figurines have yet to be encountered in the area. However, some of the hollow horned figurines are, in many respects, similar to the Chocker, Fine Ivory variants. The body, and especially the legs, are almost identical, the only difference being in the arms and hands, which resemble the Hollow Thin variety. Body colouring consists of red pigment on a white slip, while the head is typical of the horned figurines. Furthermore, type I carries a vague relationship to the prognathous figurines of Late Chupicuaro phases.

Several plain wares are associated with the site. One is a polished grey ware with tripod legs and three concentric body breaks. Associated with this type is a handled lid. Another consists of plain bowls with a repeated incised pattern of interlocking horizontal Vs below the external rim, while another incised ware is a polished black ware in which the incisions were filled with white paint. In addition polished thin black ware and polished red wares are present.

In addition to the above types another five types have been

identified: black on red; black, red and negative; cream on red; white on red; and red on buff. By far the most prominent type involves negative painting. It consists essentially of plates, tripods with vertical sides or with flared rims, and ollas. The interior base of the tripods and plates is frequently decorated with negative filled circles, which may or may not cover the entire basal area. The upper areas often carry designs in red and black paint. The designs tend to be quite complex, often involving a composite of star, stepped fret, triangle, squiggly lines, circling lines and nested diamond motifs. The ollas tend to have the middle portion decorated with triangles suspended from a plane line circling the vessel or by a wavy or fret design circling the vessel. The upper portion of the ollas may have a series of interlocking wavy lines, nested five-pointed stars, a series of nested diamonds, or a composite design of vertical lines dividing the vessel into sections which have repeated designs. Also present is the repeated nested triangle pendant to the rim that has been associated with both Zacatenco and the southwest (Sayles 1945).

The interiors of many of the tripods are characterized by designs which involve a quadrate design formed by intersecting triangles. Each quadrant contains some form of design and the entire area is surrounded by concentric straight or wavy lines or a stepped fret design.

The plates also carry complex design variation, varying from a quadrate divided in the centre and surrounded by concentric stepped fret, straight and wavy lines, to a centre with a circle surrounded by nested five-pointed stars which are in turn surrounded by red-filled stepped frets framed by a negative buff. The rims of the plates are often painted red. Other motifs include nested pentagons, a circle with six stepped fret projections emanating off it in a circle, and dots and lines arranged in a circle almost like the spokes of a wheel.

The cream on red forms consist essentially of tripods, small ollas painted with vertical white lines to resemble pumpkins, and larger ollas. The latter carry a stepped fret and straight line design around the vessel and a simple stylized step fret design around the neck. The interiors of the tripods carry the most complex designs. These include red five-pointed stars with a hollow centre and cream-bordered wavy-edged arms. Alternatively the stars may vary in number and may carry a stepped fret rather than a wavy line shape. The lips of the tripods are also heavily decorated, carrying straight lines in groups of three, four or five, between which might be a three-legged animal or bird (road runner?) motif. Other tripods carry concentric wavy lines on the interior, although this is the customary design on the underside of the tripods. Sometimes the underside carries negative dots.

What is interesting about the Tequesquite ceramics is that they appear to bear a relationship not only to the Chupicuaro style but also to Northern styles. This is apparent from a survey of the motifs.

The animal forms on the rim of the cream on red tripods are also found on Chupicuaro wares, while they are not unlike those found in the Ayala phase of the Guadiana branch of Chalchuites culture (Kelley 1971: 802). Similarly, the series of triangular motifs surrounding many of the ollas is also found at Chupicuaro, while the wavy line divisions associated with it are typical of the Alta Vista phase of the Suchil Branch at Rio Colorado (Kelley 1971: 801). The alligator monster which is found on the Michila red-filled engraved of the Alta Vista phase is represented on the single ring vessel from Tequesquite (not discussed above). Furthermore, this motif may also appear in stylized form on the white on red forms. Perhaps more significant is the relationship between the characteristic Chupicuaro stepped fret design and the nested diamonds, star motifs and quadrant designs that are characteristic of the Alta Vista phase. If, as Kelley (1971: 795) suspects, some of these motifs and designs represent a symbolic expression of an involved religious ceremony, associated with an astronomical-religious complex involving Quetzalcoatl and related star and sun symbols, which emanates from a Mesoamerican source, its association at Tequesquite with Chupicuaro symbolism is certainly significant. Certainly the animal motifs found at Chupicuaro, Tequesquite and in the Zacatecas-Durango area are likely to represent a religious depiction. If this supposition is correct it suggests that a religious form, most likely emanating from the Chupicuaro culture, moved north and persisted for several centuries after the occupation of Chupicuaro itself has ceased.

Conclusion

Having considered all the above material evidence, what conclusions can be drawn? One thing is clear; whatever conclusions are derived must by necessity be tentative in nature, and in reality will serve as no more than a basis for a working hypothesis to be tested in the field with the assistance of controlled excavations. It is felt that in an area where considerable material is available for study, and where such work is not likely to promote any further looting, such a preliminary theoretical consideration should serve as an invaluable basis for deriving hypotheses that can subsequently be tested under controlled excavationary conditions.

It would appear from the preceding discussion that a Central Valley influence can be accepted for this portion of West Mexico. The local figurines bear a substantial similarity to Central Mexican forms of the terminal Preclassic and the limited number of Teotihuacan figurines lends further credence to this southern influence. This is substantiated by evidence of what may be a Fire God cult and also by the existence of paint cloisonné and stucco pottery, even though most of the pottery appears to relate to West

Mexico. A Mesoamerican influence can also be argued from the nature and extent of some of the sites. Certainly Cerro de los Antiguos, San Aparicio and Cerro de Chihuahua reveal abundant evidence of involved ceremonial complexes which more than likely include a ball court, and certainly involved construction employing cut limestone blocks. Furthermore, the spatial extent of San Aparicio suggests not only a considerable resident population but also one that could support an involved ceremonialism. What of course cannot be ascertained at this juncture is the temporal relationship between these factors. The extensive construction may be later than is suggested by the ceramic evidence.

In addition, there is a clear relationship with Chupicuaro for one site if not for more. The involved complexity of the Chupicuaro ceramic tradition is certainly in evidence at Tequesquite, although it would appear that thus far the brown polychrome which is now thought to be early at Chupicuaro (Frierman (ed.) 1969: xii) is not in evidence and most evidence suggests a relationship with transitional and late Chupicuaro. The high incidence of negative painting is interesting in that, as Porter has recently stated, this type of decoration was rare at Chupicuaro, but as Bennyhoff (1966) has recently shown it was emphasized in the contemporary 'Cholula' complex in the Valley of Mexico. The Chupicuaro influence is modified by the local tradition, and may even represent a selective acceptance of the Chupicuaro influence, as is suggested by ceramic motifs and specific figurine traits drawn from specific figurine types. Intermingled with the Chupicuaro influence is a Western influence associated with the shaft tombs complex of the Magdalena Basin and Nayarit. It is interesting that these two traditions (shaft tomb and Chupicuaro) intermingle, in that it suggests that they may have been contemporaneous, although the nature of the interrelationship is not clear. Despite such influences it is clear that the Upper Rio Verde had a character of its own during the Late Postclassic, and if it was part of an integrated Chupicuaro culture it may have existed as a subculture, or even a cult area, as is suggested by the profusion of horned figurines which Furst has suggested may refer to a cult which involved the use of hallucinogenic mushrooms.

A northern influence is also evident. Certainly there is evidence of a close relationship between Tequesquite and the Zacatecas-Durango area, and further ties with Culiacan and even the southwest are also suggested. Figurines from the site which resemble Culiacan figurines present a problem, in that this site is regarded as being of the Postclassic period, although Morss (1949) has suggested a similar type at Cuicuilco. On the other hand these figurines may relate to the Sedentary Period of the Hohokam, which has many motif similarities with Tequesquite, including the shell symbol (Willey 1966: Fig. 4.44) which is found representing earplugs on the horned figurines.

How can all this material, which appears to derive from so many diverse sources, making this locality an apparent 'crossroads of culture', be placed in a meaningful context? What is there in the culture history of these diverse contact areas that may help to explain, or a least to suggest, the construction of a coherent history for the Upper Rio Verde?

McBride (1970) has recently suggested a considerable sphere of influence for the Chupicuaro culture, which is now judged to have extended between La Quemada and San Jeronimo. His essay certainly made it clear that the Chupicuaro stylistic tradition was far more than a local phenomenon, since he suggests a Chupicuaro influence for areas as widely separated as Tulancingo, Hidalgo; the Guerrero coast; Ixtlan del Rio, Nayarit; La Quemada, Zacatecas; and Cuernavaca, Morelos. Furthermore, Chupicuaro type traits have been suggested for many parts of West Mexico in Lister's (1955) important synthesis. Kelley (1966) has gone even further in suggesting substantial similarities between Chupicuaro ceramics and those of early Mogollan and Hohokam pottery. Certainly he is not alone in suggesting that the source of this influence lies in an area that would include the Upper Rio Verde (Kelly 1944; Woodward 1950; Vaillant 1932; Jennings 1955). He suggests that, together with the introduction of the painted wares into the southwest, this area was responsible for introducing cosmological and ceremonial concepts.

Bennyhoff (1966) has recently summarized the conclusions of the extensive work undertaken by Millon and associates at Teotihuacan. What is suggested is that the Teotihuacan ceramic tradition is a result of a reformulation of the Cuicuilco ceramic tradition, which was subjected to extreme pressure from the north by a group of the 'Chupicuaro' tradition and from the south by the 'Cholula' tradition. It would appear that during the Tezayuca (200-100 B.C.) phase the northern influence was rejected in favour of the southern complex, gradually transforming the Cuicuilco (and the coextensive Tlatilco culture) tradition into what became the Teotihuacan culture. The Tzacualli (A.D. 100-150) and Miccaotli (A.D. 150-200) phases are regarded as transitional, the Teotihuacan culture not being fully developed until Early Tlamimilolpa (A.D. 250-375) phase. He further claims that there is no evidence of 'the persistence of Chupicuaro until Teotihuacan since extensive negative paintings, architectural complexes, and the prognathic figurine traditions are held to emanate from the Southern influence'. Characteristic of early Teotihuacan are traits that include nubbin supports and slit-eyed figurines.

In the north we have, if we follow Kelley's argument, a situation in which the Preclassic frontier of Mesoamerica extended as far as Jalisco and Guanajuato but with its influence being felt in the southwest. By A.D. 100 there appears to be more direct influence with the southwest, the suggestion being that the influence emanated from 'some northern outpost of the Chupicuaro culture'. The full Classic traits from Central Mexico are judged to have reached the Suchil area by A.D. 300, its influence spreading subsequently from this area as early as the Late Preclassic.

How then does this apparent sequence of events relate to the Upper Rio Verde? Although the K type figurines suggest a Middle Preclassic occupation related to the Central Valley of Mexico and West Mexico in general, it is the Chupicuaro-related culture of the Late Preclassic that is most apparent in the area. Furthermore it appears that the early Chupicuaro culture was not apparent in the area. It is possible that this influence was replaced during the second century A.D. by a terminal Preclassic influence from the Central Valley of Mexico represented by type I figurines. The most convincing of the possible explanations for this suggested process is that when the Chupicuaro influence in the Central Valley faded during the Late Preclassic, the southern (Cholula) Central Valley influence spread northwards. In time the fusion of Chupicuaro, shaft-tomb and Central Valley influence was pushed further north,[6] possibly in the form of a semi-assimilated group, to be replaced by a full-blown Teotihuacan influence, which included ceremonial architecture with stone facings arranged around plazas and a distinctive religious art. Thus it appears that sites such as Tequesquite, whose drainage and agricultural potential is limited, were abandoned and growth was concentrated upon more richly endowed sites with fairly wide flood plains such as San Aparicio, Cerro de los Antiguos and Cerro de Chihuahua. It is further suggested that this nuclear Mesoamerican influence or control extended as far as the northern line of forts of which La Quemada is one. Yet that the ceramic evidence suggests a West Mexican influence may imply that this influence was selective in nature. It is however, unlikely that such a cultural system could have been superimposed upon a rudimentary socio-cultural framework; the preceding culture must have been of a fairly complex nature.

The above argument is based upon a predominant influence and a relative absence of effective ideological and material intrusion from the North. This is certainly logical, not only in view of the traits but also in view of the influential effectiveness of diffusion from an urban or proto-urban source. It is reasonable to assume that a city of the size and complexity of Teotihuacan which controlled an extensive hinterland was capable of creating a peasantry of the rural population under its control. Such a situation involves, among other aspects, what Redfield (1960) termed the 'Great Tradition' of the urban centre and the 'Little Tradition' of the majority of the peasants. This involves a rephrasing of such elements of the 'Great Tradition' as religious structure into a context that is meaningful to the peasantry, this process thereby becoming part of the 'Little

Tradition'. It is therefore not unrealistic to expect that side by side with full-blown Teotihuacan religious imagery is a modified symbolism created locally. What I am suggesting here is that with an effective Teotihuacan influx we are witnessing a change from a local agricultural society to a peasant society. However, it would appear that the forces promoting such a change existed in the area from the Late Preclassic, but that it was not effective in gaining ascendancy over a synthesized Chupicuaro-Nayarit influence until the socio-political structure was sufficiently developed to promote territorial expansion.

If Betty Bell's preliminary observations that Tequesquite had a limited occupation focusing upon the second century A.D. are correct, it suggests that there was a sequential movement north of a Chupicuaro influence, or possibly of a Chupicuaro culture which ceased to exist at Chupicuaro at about A.D. 200, i.e. shortly after the expansion north. By A.D. 300 the influence was felt in the Zacatecas-Durango area and possibly as far as the southwest. Thus within a period of about a hundred years the Chupicuaro tradition had been pushed to the limits of Mesoamerica. The question remains of whether this progressive spatial advancement of a culture involved an entire population or simply a movement of culture traits. Kelley (1971: 801) suggests that the Alta Vista Phase of Zacatecas was one of pronounced population growth, which suggests that the flow of ideas and traits involved the movement of people. If such was the case, it is possible that what has been discussed for the Upper Rio Verde involved a pioneer fringe during the Late Preclassic, and the expansion of Teotihuacan culture into this region involved a selective replacement in which the cultural style with a superior adaptive response in terms of the local environment replaced the less effective 'cultural style'.

In conclusion I would like to paraphrase a recent statement of McBride's (1969: 47):

> To consider this great region as part of a single tradition at a time level as early as the Late Preclassic may help a great deal in reconstructing events of this period. We must consider how such a region, somewhat culturally unified to some extent in the regions where the tradition was most intense, would affect the neighbouring regions by direct and indirect influences such as conquest, migrations and extensive trade. We should abandon the idea that the region, at the time, was in a simple 'development' or 'formative' stage of socio-political structure and consisted of culturally isolated areas of small rural villages.

This paper has been an exercise in presenting the existing evidence in exactly such a framework so that subsequent archaeological work can be undertaken with something more than a simple excavationary process that precedes the process of analysis. The evidence thus far considered certainly suggests that this area should reveal information that will be invaluable in answering questions concerning not only the local culture history during the Late Preclassic, Classic, and Postclassic but also that of areas such as the Central Valley and the arid southwest.

NOTES

1 I am grateful to John M. Howe, U.C.L.A., for his participation in the field work in connection with this research, and to Aled Evans for the line drawings.

2 There have been exceptions in West Mexican work, for example Grosscup 1961, McBride 1969 and Saenz 1966.

3 This single date was obtained from a burnt antler (Betty Bell, personal communication). Other dates are expected from material currently being analysed.

4 I am indebted to Dr Lawrence Feldman for identifying the shell material. In addition to those mentioned in the text he has also identified the following:— *Pyrene major* (Sowerby 1832) 'a pacific coast shell that is uncommon archaeologically'; *Moruum tuberculosum* (Reeve 1852, ex Sowerby MS) which is 'also known from Apatzingan'; *Oliva* cf. *spicata* (Rosing 1798) 'also known from San Gregorio, Michoacan, Culiacan, Sinaloa and Portrero del Calichal, Zacatecas'; *Oliva* cf. *incrassata* (Solander 1786) 'also known from Guasave, Sinaloa, Cojumatlan, Michoacan, and San Sebastian Etzatlan, Jalisco'; *Olivella valutella* (Lamarck 1811) 'also known from Tula, Hidalgo'; *Marquella apicina* (Menke 1828) 'also known from Cerro Portosuelo Mexico, Santa Ana Zape, quite common in lowland Maya sites'; *Glysymeris maculata* (Broderip 1832) 'common in Hohokam sites and sites between US border and Culiacan, Sinaloa'; and *Aequipectan circularis* (Sowerby 1835) 'a few found in almost every site with marine shells'.

5 It may well be that this figure represents a depiction of a Postclassic Tlaloc; it is hoped to discuss the carving in a future publication.

6 The Chupicuaro culture may have pioneered an area as far north as the arid southwest at an early date since an association with Hohokam has been suggested for as early as 300 B.C.

REFERENCES

Acosta, J.R. (1957) Resumen de los informes de las exploraciones arqueológicas en Tula, Hidalgo durante las IX y X temporadas 1953-1954. *Annales de Instituto Nacional de Antropología e Historia*, 9, 119-69.

Albers, A. (1970) *Pre-Columbian Mexican Miniatures.* New York.

Armillas, P. (1964) Northern Mesoamerica. In J.D. Jennings and E. Norbeck (eds), *Prehistoric Man in the New World.* Chicago.

Bell, B. (1960) *Analysis of Ceramic Style: A West Mexican Collection.* Unpublished Ph.D. thesis, University of California.

Bernal, I. and G.F. Ekholm (eds) (1971a) *Archaeology of Northern Mesoamerica, Part One. Handbook of Middle American Indians*, vol. 10. Austin, Texas.

Bernal, I. and G.F. Ekholm (eds) (1971b) *Archaeology of Northern Mesoamerica, Part Two. Handbook of Middle American Indians*, vol. 11. Austin, Texas.

Bennyhoff, J. (1966) Chronology and periodization: continuity and change in the Teotihuacan ceramic tradition. Sociedad Mexicana de Antropología, *Teotihuacan: XI Mesa Redonda.* Mexico.

Bordaz, J. (1964) *Pre-Columbian Ceramic Kilns at Peñitas, a Postclassic Site in Coastal Nayarit.* Unpublished Ph.D. thesis, Columbia University.

Cook de Leonard, C. (1971) Ceramics of the Classic period in Central Mexico. In I. Bernal and G.F. Ekholm, 1971a.

Emmerich, A. (1963) *Art Before Columbus: The Art of Ancient Mexico, from* the Archaic Villages of the Second Millennium B.C. to the Splendour of the Aztecs. New York.

Frierman, J.D. (ed.) (1969) *The Natalie Wood Collection of Pre-Columbian Ceramics from Chupicuaro, Guanajuato, Mexico at UCLA.* Occasional papers of the Museum and Laboratories of Ethnic Arts and Technology, no. 1.

Gamio, M. (1922) *La población del valle de Teotihuacan.* Secretaria de Agricultura y Fomento, vol. 1. Mexico.

Gendrop, P. (1970) *Arte prehispanico en Mesoamerica.* Mexico.

Grosscup, G.L. (1961) A sequence of figurines from West Mexico. *American Antiquity,* 26, 390-406.

Jennings, J.D. (1956) The American southwest: a problem in cultural isolation. In R. Wauchope (ed.), *Seminars in Archaeology,* Memoirs of the Society of American Anthropology, no. 11.

Kan, M., C. Meighan and H.B. Nicholson (1970) *Sculptures of Ancient West Mexico: Nayarit, Jalisco, Colima.* The Proctor Stafford Collection, Los Angeles County Museum.

Kelemen, P. (1969) *Mediaeval American Art,* 3rd ed. New York.

Kelley, J.C. (1966) Mesoamerica and the American southwest. In R. Wauchope (ed.), *Handbook of Middle American Indians,* vol. 4. Texas.

Kelley, J.C. (1971) Archaeology of the northern frontier: Zacatecas and Durango. In I. Bernal and G.F. Ekholm (eds), 1971*b*.

Kelly, I.T. (1938) Excavations at Chametla, Sinaloa. *Ibero-Americana.*

Kelly, I.T. (1944) West Mexico and Hohokam. In *El Norte de Mexico, Mesa Redonda,* 206-22.

Kelly, I.T. (1948) Ceramic provinces of northwestern Mexico. In *El Occidente de Mexico, Mesa Redonda,* 55-71.

Kelly, I.T. (1949) The archaeology of the Autlan-Tuxcacuesco area of Jalisco II: the Tuxcacuesco-Zapotitlan zone. *Ibero-Americana,* 27.

Lister, R.H. (1955) *The Present Status of the Archaeology of Western Mexico: A Distributional Study.* University of California, Series in Anthroplogy, no. 5.

Litvak King, J. (1968) Excavationes de rescate en la presa de la villita. *Boletín de Instituto Nacional de Antropología e Historia,* 31, 28-30.

McBride, H. (1969*a*) Teotihuacan style pottery and figurines from Colima. *Katunob,* 7, no. 3, 86-91.

McBride, H., (1969*b*) The extent of the Chupicuaro tradition. In J.D. Frierman (ed.), 1969.

Morss, N. (1949) *Clay Figurines of the American Southwest.* Papers of the Peabody Museum of Archaeology and Ethnology, Harvard University, 49, no. 1.

Noguera, E. (1954) *La ceramica arqueológica de Cholula.* Mexico.

Noguera, E. (1962) Nueva clasificación de figurillas del horizonte clásico. *Cuadernas Americas,* 5.

Parres Arias, J. (1962) Nuevas adquisiones del Museo de Arqueologia. *Instituto Jaliscense de Antropología e Historia,* 12.

Piña Chan, R. (1971) Preclassic or formative pottery and minor arts of the Valley of Mexico. In I. Bernal and G.F. Ekholm, 1971*a*.

Porter, M.N. (1956) Excavations at Chupicuaro, Guanajuato, Mexico. *Transactions of the American Philosophical Society,* 46, part 5.

Rattray, E.C. (1966) An archaeological and stylistic study of Coyotlatelco pottery. *Mesoamerican Notes,* 7-8, 187-211.

Redfield, R. (1960) *The Little Community and Peasant Society and Culture.* Chicago.

Saenz, C. (1966) Cabecitas y figurillas de barro del Ixtepete, Jalisco. *Boletín de Instituto Nacional de Antropología e Historia,* 24, 47-9.

Sayles, E.B. (1945) *The San Simeon Branch*. Medallion Papers, no. 34.

Scott, J.F. and E.K. Easby (1970) *Before Cortes: Sculpture of Middle America*, Metropolitan Museum of Art, New York Catalogue, New York Graphic Society.

Sejourne, L. (1969) *Teotihuacan, métropole de l'amérique*. Paris.

Seler, E. (1960) *Gesammelte Abhandlungen zur Amerikanischen Sprach und Altertumskunde*, vols. 3 and 5. Graz.

Susia, M. (1961) The Morett sequence. Mimeographed. Dept. of Anthropology, UCLA.

Taylor, R.E. and S.V. Long (1966) Suggested revision for West Mexican archaeological sequences. *Science*, 154, no. 3755, 1458-9.

Taylor, R.E. et al. (1969) West Mexican radiocarbon dates of archaeological significance. In J.D. Frierman (ed.), 1969.

Tolstoy, P. (1958) Surface survey of the northern Valley of Mexico: the Classic and Postclassic periods. *Transactions of the American Philosphical Society*, 48, part 5.

Vaillant, G.C. (1930) *Excavations at Zacatenco*. American Museum of Natural History, Anthropological Papers, vol. 32, part 1.

Vaillant, G.C. (1931) *Excavations at Ticoman*. American Museum of Natural History, Anthropological Papers, vol. 32, part 2.

Vaillant, G.C. (1932) *Some Resemblances in the Ceramics of Central and North America*. Medallion Papers, no. 12.

Vaillant, G.C. (1935) *Excavations at El Arbolillo*. American Museum of Natural History, Anthropological Papers, vol. 35, part 2.

Vaillant, G.C. and S.B. Vaillant (1934) *Excavations at Gualupita*. American Museum of Natural History, Anthropological Papers, vol. 35, part 1.

Willey, G. (1966) *An Introduction to American Archaeology*. Vol. 1, *North and Middle America*. Englewood Cliffs, N.J.

Woodward, A. (1950) Excavations at Snaketown, IV: reviews and conclusions. *American Antiquity*, 16, no. 2, 172-3.

ROBERT L. RANDS

The ceramic sequence at Palenque, Chiapas

The investigation of ceramics at Palenque was first undertaken by my
wife and me as part of the programme of archaeological explorations
by the Instituto Nacional de Antropología e Historia of Mexico
under the direction of Alberto Ruz Lhuillier. Initial fieldwork dates,
therefore, from the early 1950s, and although preliminary reports
appeared fairly rapidly (Rands 1954; Rands and Rands 1957), a
comprehensive monograph is still in preparation. Such slow publication of 'final' results is not without its parallels in Middle American
archaeology. Massive ceramic collections are typical but more often
than not consist of redeposited materials. Clear-cut stratigraphy is
the exception rather than the rule for a culture such as the Maya,
given to repeated demolition and rebuilding, with the result that
sherds were incorporated in the fill of plazas, substructures, and
sometimes floors and walls, having undergone a varied history with
the inevitable mixing of pottery of differing age. In such cases,
ceramic sequences must result from the techniques of seriation,
guided by generalized stratigraphic trends, and exceptional circumstances illuminated by those highly-prized occurrences of two
sequentially superimposed ceramic complexes.

Yet these reasons, although important, are not the primary ones
why a well-rounded monograph on Palenque pottery has been so
slow in preparation. It was obvious, during the first season's work in
1951, that Palenque did not fit well with other Mayan sequences
known at that time. I well recall the conversation with Bob Smith, at
the close of our first season, when he questioned me as to the
ceramic types we had located at Palenque. Consistently, he received a
negative reply: we did not have that type or ware. Finally, in
desperation, Smith asked, 'Well, what in God's name *did* you find?'
When finally Smith had a chance to look over our collection,
he — and other members of the Carnegie Institution of Washington
staff — walked around the sherd tables, shaking their heads, and
concluding something to the effect that each new excavation doesn't
solve old problems; it merely creates new ones.

It quickly became apparent that for the vast bulk of the material, only generalized tradition trends and modal similarities would link Palenque ceramics with those of the better-known Maya sites. Field work in the environs of Palenque — especially in the strategic area to the east — was necessary in order to establish firm chronological connections with extant Maya sequences. Palenque ceramics, clearly, were peripheral to those of major Maya centres. Following the terminology of the Guatemala City Ceramic Conference in 1965 (Willey, Culbert and Adams 1967), we would now say that, subsequent to the sparse Preclassic occupation, Palenque was in a ceramic sphere marginal to those of the Peten and, for that matter, showed far fewer specific ceramic connections with Central Mexico than did sites located in the Maya heartland such as Uaxactun and Tikal.

Perhaps all this may not be too surprising. On an elite level, Palenque is a highly unusual Maya site. Wall tablets substitute for stelae; caches of eccentric flints or obsidians are unknown; the ratio of room width to wall thickness is exceptionally great, suggesting somewhat later Yucatecan architecture such as that of Uxmal and Chichen Itza rather than contemporaneous sites in the southern Maya lowlands. Seen in this perspective, the aberrant pottery of Palenque may not be too strange. Nevertheless, it was a headache to those of us who were attempting to establish meaningful time-space relationships.

Furthermore, the extreme weathering and the highly fragmentary nature of the pottery are partially responsible for difficulties in establishing firm cross-ties with other Maya sites. At least two factors appear to account for this. One is the extraordinarily heavy rainfall at Palenque, which is located on the first escarpment overlooking the Chiapas-Tabasco Plains. Also, the pottery of the Palenque area tends to be unusually thin-walled; vessels shatter into small fragments, and soil acids are presented the opportunity of a many-faceted attack. Moreover, as will be seen, slips in use at Palenque during the Late Classic period appear to be far less resistant to weathering than the Preclassic 'Waxy' ware or the Tzakol-like 'Gloss' ware. The latter was apparently imported to Palenque from Peten sources in the latter part of the Early Classic. Even relatively well-protected tomb and cache furniture is severely affected. In short, the archaeologically sensitive attributes of slip and painted design are so poorly preserved as to vitiate standard archaeological typology, at least as a means of systematic quantification.

Under these circumstances, my wife and I had two essential choices. We could toss in the towel, so to speak, come out with a highly generalized, even superficial, report and move on to more lucrative diggings. Or we could gird our loins and attempt to make sense of this recalcitrant material. In view of the importance of Palenque — its classic refinement and elegance in an outpost situation — we chose the latter course. Placing unusual emphasis on the time-consuming reconstruction of vessel shapes and on paste characteristics, we have attempted to extract maximal information about the characteristics of the Palenque pottery. This was supplemented by my reconnaissance and excavations in the surrounding region of northeast Chiapas and adjacent Tabasco, as well as by undertaking a detailed study of pottery from Piedras Negras. Applied to the ceramics of Palenque and neighbouring sites, the technological approach presented new opportunities and challenges, leading to the investigation of trade wares, to problems of manufacturing and redistribution centres, and, inevitably, to the socio-economic implications of these data (Rands 1967a). By using these approaches, I fear we opened not just one of Pandora's boxes but a number of them. Because of the long delay in detailed publication, with the certainty of more time-consuming analysis to come, an outline of ceramic sequences at Palenque appears appropriate at the present time. This will deal only with major trends. Specialized ceramics, such as censers and figurines, will not be considered beyond noting the high degree of their elaboration in the late ceramic complexes. In order to do justice to changes in other vessel classes, it has been necessary largely to ignore the long-sustained tradition of Red-Brown ware utility bowls and basins, which underwent an exceptionally large number of elaborative modifications.

Sources of ceramic data at Palenque

Information about the ceramics of Palenque comes from several sources. We have made test pits at various parts of the site. Surface survey has been carried out in *milpas* at Palenque and adjacent to the site. A series of superimposed burials has been excavated by my wife and me from the plaza in group IV, an architectural unit best known as the provenance of the Tablet of the Slaves. Unfortunately for our ceramic studies, burials from the lowermost levels were unaccompanied by pots.

In addition, much of the pottery recovered in the course of archaeological investigations at Palenque by the Instituto Nacional de Antropología e Historia has kindly been made available to us for study. Such ceramics include materials, mostly of late date, which were obtained when clearing architectural features, as well as sherd lots from limited but highly important investigations into earlier structures. Rarely, ceramic materials come from deposits underlying a major structure. Pottery used in apparently dedicatory caches and burials provides a more direct basis for dating a building ceramically.

Ceramic sequences at Palenque are pieced together from such data.

The ceramic sequence at Palenque

At the present time, five named ceramic complexes are recognized during the Early and Late Classic periods at Palenque. Occupation of the site apparently extended as far back as the Middle Preclassic, although a full ceramic complex cannot as yet be described for any of the Preclassic materials. Likewise, a sparse terminal occupation is indicated by Fine Orange ware of the Silho (X) Group but is so poorly represented as to render almost meaningless a formalized complex designation.

The identifiable ceramic complexes are named after *arroyos* at Palenque and so consist of both Spanish and Chol Maya words. From late to early, the complexes are:

Balunte (divisable into early and late facets, the latter apparently post-dating the collapse of elite culture at Palenque. In time, Balunte approximates late Tepeu 2 and the beginning of Tepeu 3, *c.* A.D. 770-850).

Murcielagos (temporally, the equivalent of early and middle Tepeu 2, *c.* A.D. 700-70).

Otolum (generally equivalent in time with Tepeu 1, perhaps A.D. 600-700. Provisionally, Otolum is divided into early and late facets).

Motiepa (lacking association with Long Count dates, Motiepa is much less securely dated but apparently falls on a middle to late Tzakol level).

Picota (post-Chicanel but prior to Motiepa, Picota falls somewhere in the early or middle part of the Early Classic period, perhaps extending back to a Protoclassic base).

The equivalents which have been suggested are temporal only, the characteristics of Palenque's ceramic complexes being far different from those of Uaxactun or other well-known Maya sites.

Preclassic

Preclassic pottery is poorly represented at Palenque, especially in the major ceremonial precinct. A relatively large proportion of Preclassic sherds comes from the site's western periphery or from nearby smaller sites. An excavation in the western part of Palenque yielded sparse Preclassic remains, directly overlain by Picota refuse. However, Preclassic ceramics have usually been found out of context in mixed, if somewhat early, deposits.

It appears possible to recognize the existence of at least two Preclassic manifestations.

Middle Preclassic sherds are extremely sparse. Identifying modes, distinguishing them from Late Preclassic pottery, apparently include

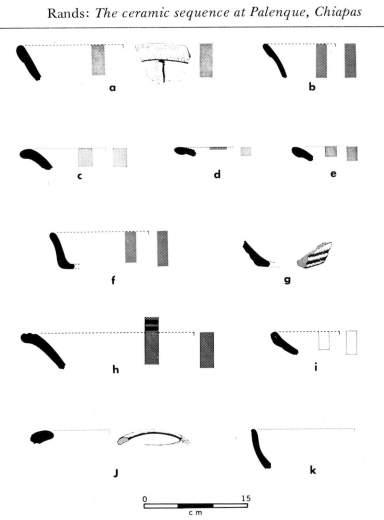

Figure 1 Preclassic. *a*, Late Preclassic, transitional to Picota(?); *b-h*, Late Preclassic; *i*(?), *j*, *k*, Middle Preclassic. *a-i*, *k*, miscellaneous bowls and dishes; *j*, tecomate. *a-f*, *h*, waxy red slip; *i*, white slip; *g*, weathered; *j*, *k*, unslipped. *a*, *g*, *h*, vertical, horizontal and rim grooving. *a-h*, volcanic ash temper; *i*, fine paste or lightly tempered; *j*, *k*, carbonate temper.

tecomates, unslipped bowls, carbonate temper, and perhaps a white slip (Fig. 1*i-k*). The outcurved bowl in Fig. 1*k* resembles materials from the Palangana phase at San Lorenzo (M.D. Coe, personal communication).

Late Preclassic sherds generally similar to Chicanel are better represented, although still infrequent (Fig. 1*b-h*). A dark red slip is characteristic, its distinctive feel — which has given rise to the name 'Waxy Ware' — being especially pronounced. Volcanic ash temper is usual, and several sherds are highly micaceous. Affiliations exist with the Sierra Red type and with Matheny's recently-named Xicalango Red type on the Campeche coast (Matheny 1970). The labial flange

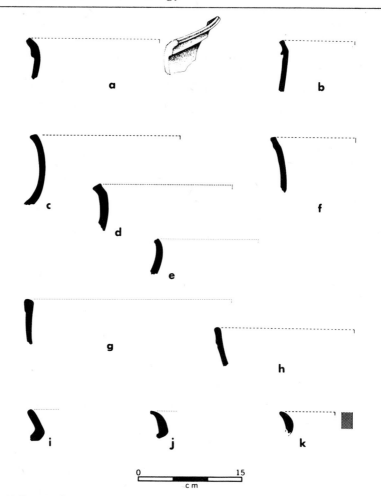

Figure 2 Preclassic and possible Preclassic. *a-h*, temporal position uncertain; *i-k*, terminal Middle Preclassic or early Late Preclassic. *a-e*, high-necked jars; *g, h*, bowls or basins; *i-k*, short-necked jars (*j, k*, tapered rims). *a-j*, unslipped or weathered, *k*, red slip. *a, b, f, g, h*, folded rims and rim mouldings. *a-e, j, k*, carbonate temper; *g, h*, quartz sand temper; *i*, pumice temper.

and Usulutan pottery are notable for their extreme rarity or absence at Palenque.

The atypical sherd in Figure 1*a* may date from the close of the Preclassic period. It is vertically grooved, in a style reminiscent of the Early Classic Picota complex.

A short, flaring-neck jar, with thickened rim which tapers to a blunt or stubby lip, is occasionally found at Palenque (Fig. 2*i-k*). The form constitutes an important marker for the terminal Middle Preclassic or beginning Late Preclassic at Trinidad (the Chacibcan Complex). It is known from other Preclassic sites on the Usumacinta near Emiliano Zapata (Rands 1967*b*), and, farther to the north, occurs in the Late Preclassic Pinzon complex of Aguacatal (Matheny 1970). To the south, it is known at various sites in the Low Sierras close to Palenque. The jar rim is sometimes red-slipped. Temper is carbonate, volcanic ash, or pumice.

Unslipped, high-neck jars, often with folded rims, may also date from the Preclassic period (Fig. 2*a-f*). This is an infrequent form at Palenque, known only from mixed although consistently early contexts. Wide-mouth bowls with somewhat similar rim moulding also occur in early but 'floating' contexts (Fig. 2*g*, *h*). Modal resemblances exist with bowls of the Middle Preclassic Bacha complex at Trinidad (Rands 1969) and with bowls and jars of the Early Classic Peninsula complex at Aguacatal (Matheny 1970).

Picota ceramic complex

Appropriately, the Picota complex is named after the Arroyo Picota, being most fully represented in house-mound refuse a short distance to the west of that stream. Near the centre of Palenque, Picota pottery and sherds of the subsequent Motiepa complex were present in the fill of the plaza which underlies the Pyramid of the Conde. Picota sherds have been recovered in mixed lots elsewhere at the site.

Although placed on an Early Classic and perhaps Protoclassic level, Picota has little in common with the Floral Park sphere and only modal connections with Tzakol. Absences are notable, including such hallmarks as polychrome painting and tetrapod or mammiform supports. Orange-slipped ceramics are absent or nearly so. Sherds from basal-flange bowls, although present, are very rare.

The Picota ceramics are almost exclusively monochrome. Red-slipped pottery is well represented, but this is not the 'waxy', Preclassic red.

Vertical grooving, incising, and resist painting are the three principal decorative modes in Picota pottery. Grooves may be widely spaced or appear in restricted zones, separated by extensive plain areas (Fig. 3*d*, *j*). Incised lines occasionally appear on the rims of everted-rim bowls — a Preclassic-like treatment (Fig. 3*g*) — or on the interior of shallow vessels. Resist dark-red on light-red decoration occurs, incorporating circles, scrolls, and other linear patterns (Fig. 3*b, c, e*).

Flaring-wall bowls and dishes take two major forms in the Picota complex. (1) Tripod bowls with moderately everted rim, basal moulding, and solid rectangular slab feet are most distinctive. The low slab feet are often massive, measuring up to 12 cm. in length. The everted-rim bowls are most frequently decorated with vertical grooving (Fig. 3). (2) A direct-rim or, rarely, everted-rim bowl, with flat or ring-stand base, tends to be more shallow and less subject to plastic decoration. Red slip is common (Fig. 4*f-h*).

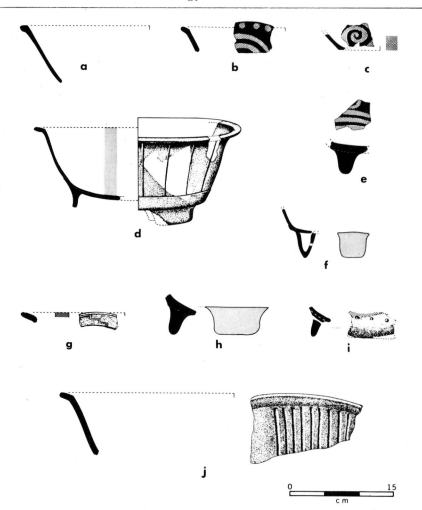

Figure 3 Picota ceramic complex, everted-rim tripod bowls. *d, h*, solid slab feet; *e*, solid subconical foot; *f*, hollow slab foot; *i*, solid slab foot with perforations. *a, d, f, h-j*, unslipped or weathered; *b, c, e*, resist-painted (dark-red on light-red); *g*, red lip. *d, j*, vertically grooved; *g*, incised. *a*(?), *d, i*, fine paste; *b, c-h, j*, quartz sand temper.

Jars are mostly unslipped with short, flaring necks and exterior-thickened rims (Fig. 4*a-c*). It is possible that the high-neck jars with folded rims (Fig. 2*a-f*) are intrusive items in the Picota complex rather than dating from the Preclassic period.

Except for the jars, most Picota pottery is sand-tempered. However, a significant amount is fine-textured, probably un-tempered. The fine paste pottery (e.g. Figs. 3*a, d*, 4*f*) does not differ notably in slip, shape or decoration from tempered examples.

In summary, the content of the Picota complex is strange for an Early Classic Maya site. Several important Early Classic diagnostics

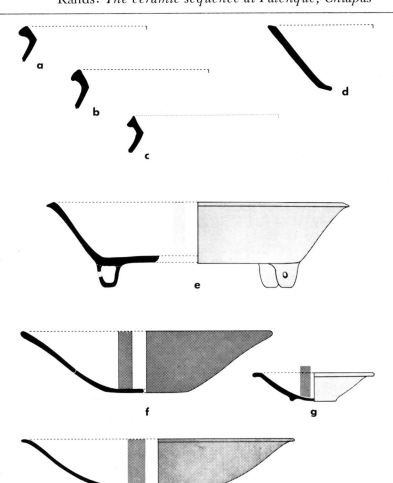

Figure 4 Picota ceramic complex. *a-c*, short flaring-necked jars with exterior-thickened rims; *d, e*, interior- and exterior-bevelled-rim flaring-wall bowls (*e*, hollow-foot tripod); *f*, direct-rim flaring-wall bowl; *g, h*, ring-base flaring-wall bowls with wide- and slightly-everted rims. *a-e*, unslipped; *f-h*, red slip. *a, d, e, g, h*, quartz sand temper; *b, c*, carbonate temper; *f*, fine paste.

are absent, such as polychrome painting, while some of the characteristic Picota modes are reminiscent of Preclassic ceramics (e.g. monochrome red-slipped and wide everted-rim bowls). That some continuity existed with the Preclassic is also indicated by the combination of Picota-like vertical grooving with Preclassic features (Fig. 1a). Nevertheless, Sierra Red and other 'waxy' slip types had, apparently, completely died out by full Picota times. The rare occurrence of the basal flange, together with abundant ring-stand bases, points to an Early Classic horizon. The many solid, rectangular slab feet suggest a level prior to strong Teotihuacan influence in the

Maya area, although such contacts, or a drift toward the Teotihuacan-Early Classic norm, may be indicated by a single hollow slab foot (Fig. 3*f*). Relationships to the west may be reflected in low, rectangular slab feet, sometimes solid and sometimes hollow, at Tres Zapotes. As is regularly the case in the Picota Complex, the Tres Zapotes examples occasionally appear on flaring-walled, everted-rim bowls (Weiant 1943: 24, Figs. 21, 35; Drucker 1943: 56, Fig. 20). In Coe's reformulation of southern Veracruz and Tabasco ceramic sequences, at least some of the slab feet are provisionally placed in 'Tres Zapotes II', i.e., on a Protoclassic horizon (Coe 1965: 700).

Motiepa ceramic complex

The Early Classic Motiepa complex is characterized by the introduction of carbonate-tempered 'Gloss Ware' imports, by the imitation of Tzakol types in more localized pottery, and by the incorporation of modes, having apparently greater strength or antiquity in the Peten, in the locally-produced ceramics. Pottery showing these Peten-based influences is, however, rare. Side by side with these ceramics, and much more abundantly represented, was an ongoing local tradition of polished, sand-tempered, red-brown bowls and plates. Curiously, ring-stand bases, which had been fairly strongly developed in Picota times and which were highly characteristic of Peten pottery, declined markedly during Motiepa. Slab feet took on a characteristic Teotihuacan-Early Classic form but declined almost to the point of extinction.

Unlike earlier ceramic developments, Motiepa pottery is better represented at the major precinct of Palenque than in the western portion of the site. Motiepa ceramics appear in mixed fill at various locations, including the plaza underlying the Conde and in the nucleus of the Pyramid of the Inscriptions. Motiepa remains are clearly sealed off from overlying Otolum deposits in a plaza excavation to the north of Temple XI. Motiepa pottery is present in the oldest burial known at Palenque, Tomb 3, in a partially dismantled structure under Temple XVIII-A (Fig. 5*d-g*; Ruz Lhuillier 1962: Figs. 5, 9*a-f*).

Most of the vessels from this burial show relations to Picota pottery (cf. especially Figs. 4*f*, *h* and 5*f*). However, two black, round-sided bowls have affiliations with the Peten-based Balanza Black group (Fig. 5*g*).

Rare examples of polychrome with preserved design are known in the Motiepa complex (Fig. 5*a, b*). These are red and black on orange, classifiable as distinct varieties of Dos Arroyos Polychrome in a taxonomy in which types and wares are independent, free to cross-cut one another (Willey, Culbert and Adams 1967: 304). Figure 5*c* is Picota-like in shape but, with matt red on orange

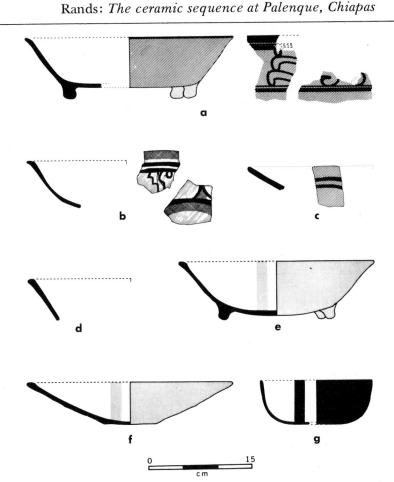

Figure 5 Motiepa ceramic complex. *a-f,* flaring-wall bowls or dishes, *g,* round-sided bowl. *a, b*(?), Dos Arroyos Polychrome type; *c,* red on orange; *d-f,* unslipped; *g,* Lucha Incised type(?). *a,* carbonate temper; *b-g,* quartz sand temper. *e-g,* Temple XVIII-A, Tomb 3.

surface, participates in the general tradition trend of Motiepa, substituting an orange slip for the red slip of Picota.

Pottery of the orange-slipped Aguila ceramic group is carbonate-tempered with the hard, glossy slip characteristic of Classic Peten ceramics (Fig. 6*d-f, h*). There seems no doubt that it was imported to Palenque. Simple silhouette bowls as well as a tripod basal-flange bowl have close counterparts in vessel shape at Piedras Negras.

Black-surfaced pottery forms another unit, wholly or partially imported, in the Motiepa complex. At least one handsome example of the Paradero Fluted type is present (Fig. 6*i*). Modes of vessel shape are shared with the Aguila ceramic group (Fig. 6*d, f, h, j, k*). Cross-hatched triangles and bold, cursive incising are important decorative modes (Fig. 6*j, k*). Much of the black Motiepa pottery is carbonate-tempered (Fig. 6*i, k*), although sand is also present as a tempering material (Fig. 6*j*).

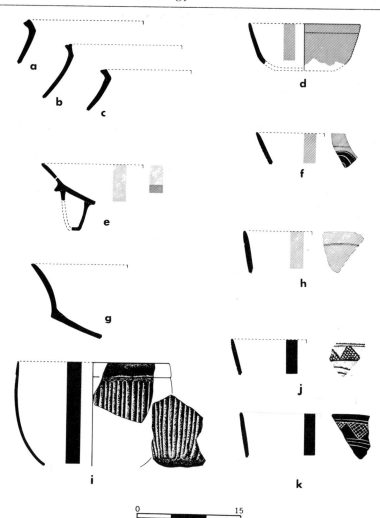

Figure 6 Motiepa ceramic complex. *a-c*, short flaring-necked jars angling steeply
to shoulder; *d, f, h, i-k*, round-sided bowls; *e*, tripod basal-flange bowl; *g*,
composite silhouette bowl; *d-j*, tapered rims; *d, f, i*, rim mouldings. *a-c, g*,
unslipped or weathered; *f*, variegated and incised; *d-f, h*, Aguila ceramic
group; *i*, Paradero Fluted type; *j, k*, Lucha Incised type(?). *a-f, h, i, k*,
carbonate temper; *g, j*, quartz sand temper.

Essential continuity with Picota is to be seen in the unslipped
Motiepa jars (Fig. 6*a-c*). Rim treatments are simpler, however, and
below the short neck the wall tends to angle even more steeply
toward the shoulder. As in Picota and subsequent ceramic complexes, jars were normally thin-walled, unslipped and without
striations.

Otolum ceramic complex

Otolum pottery is well represented in construction fill at Palenque. Sherds of this complex occur, as an unmixed lot, atop a floor of Motiepa date, subsequently being sealed by mixed Murcielagos and finally pure Balunte deposits. Otolum pots are associated with one of the stratified burials in Group IV. Significantly, vessels of this complex occur as burial furniture or dedicatory caches in several of the major structures at the site. Apparently Otolum may be subdivided into early and late facets. If so, all of these structures — the Inscriptions, Cross and Conde — would date from the late facet. Palenque, a comparatively small and unimportant site until this time, had finally come into its own.

Developmental trends in a principal Otolum diagnostic, the everted-rim tripod plate, are suggested in Fig. 7. Trends are from strongly convex to gently convex bases, from tilted to almost flat rims, and from relatively deep vessels to more shallow examples. Throughout Otolum, most of the plates had unslipped exteriors, slip or painting, if any, being confined to the vessel lip and interior. Decoration usually consisted of red and black painting and an orange ground, although cream slip, anticipating Murcielagos developments, is also known. Linear painted designs prevail to the exclusion of naturalistic subjects so far as we can tell, although heavy weathering is frequent, limiting understanding of the nature of the compositions. The failure of the slip to withstand weathering, even under the relative protection of tomb conditions, is in contrast to 'Gloss Ware' slips of Motiepa and to Preclassic 'Waxy' slips. The plates are usually sand-tempered with a red-brown paste. Apparently many, perhaps all, are indigenous to Palenque and closely neighbouring sites.

Unslipped cylindrical vases have been recovered from sub-floor tombs in the Temple of the Conde (Fig. 7d, i), being associated with a polychrome plate (Fig. 7c), and are apparently contemporaneous with the erection of the structure (Ruz Lhuillier 1958c: Figs. 3, 14). Plates and vases were associated in the Inscriptions tomb (Fig. 7a, b; Ruz Lhuillier 1955: 90, Fig. 7), being approximately coeval with the temple-pyramid (c. A.D. 690, in the Goodman-Martínez-Thompson correlation). Of the five vessels in this tomb, only one is polychrome. The poverty of ceramics in the tomb, so richly adorned with stone sculpture and stucco and so lavishly stocked with jade, presents a notable difference from what one would normally expect in an important Maya burial. The contrast with the almost contemporaneous tomb under Temple I at Tikal (Burial 116), which contained large numbers of polychrome vessels of the early Imix ceramic complex (Coe 1967), is overwhelming. Yet the perfunctory inclusion of vessels in the Inscriptions tomb is quite in accordance with burial practices at Palenque.

Returning to ceramic developments of Otolum, short, flared-neck

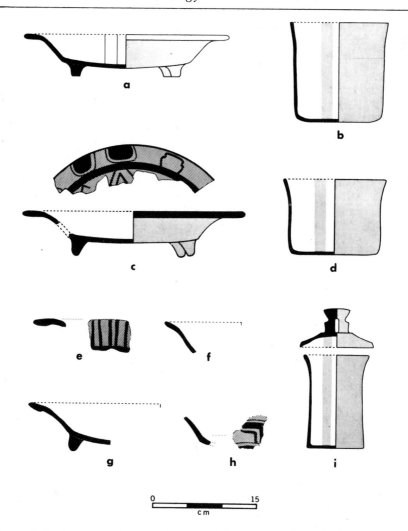

Figure 7 Otolum ceramic complex. *a-d, i,* late-facet; *e-h,* early-facet. *a, c, e, g,*
wide everted-rim tripod plates. *b, d, i,* cylindrical vases. *a,* cream slip; *c, e*(?),
h, red-black-orange; *b, d, f, g, i,* unslipped or weathered (*f* has traces of
painting). *a, b, d*(?), *e-h,* quartz sand temper; *c, i*(?), fine paste. *a, b,*
Inscriptions Tomb; *c,* Temple of the Conde, Tomb 2; *d,* Conde, Tomb 3; *i,*
Conde, Tomb 1.

jars are placed in the early facet (Fig. 8*f-h*). The traditional Picota
and Motiepa jar form is carried forward, although the wall curves or
angles less steeply to the shoulder. An early-facet carbonate-
tempered jar (Fig. 8*f*) from Group IV is directly associated with a
convex-based, wide everted-rim Otolum plate (early-facet), resting
directly on the stones covering Burial 9 and overlain by the wall of a
Balunte burial (Rands and Rands 1961: Figs. 10, 11).

Jars of the provisional late facet underwent abrupt changes in

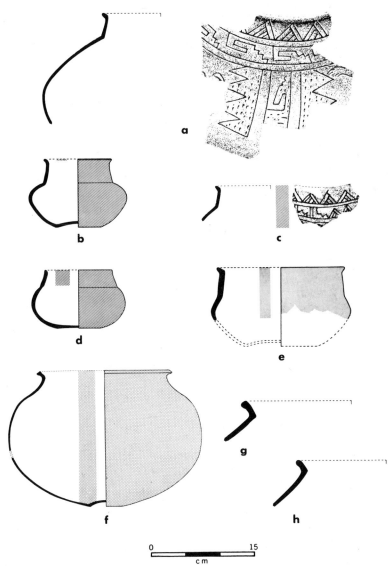

Figure 8 Otolum ceramic complex, jars. *a-e*, late-facet; *f-h*, early-facet. *a-e*, high-necked jars with interior-bevelled rims (*a-c, e*, rims slightly everted); *f-h*, short flaring-necked jars curving or angling to shoulder at an intermediate pitch relative to jars of Motiepa and Balunte. *a, c*, incised (cf. Choc Incised); *b-d*, orange slip; *e-h*, unslipped. *a-e, g, h*, quartz sand temper; *f*, carbonate temper. *b, d*, cache (Ofrenda I), Temple of the Cross; *f*, Group IV, in apparent association with Burial 9. (Scale of *f* is one-half that of other specimens.)

shape and surface treatment, although the shift, which had already begun, was carried out from carbonate to sand temper. Necks are high, almost vertical. Rims are interior-bevelled and slightly everted.

The shoulder, although well-defined, is sometimes little greater in diameter than the orifice (Fig. 8*b, d, e*). Orange slip is occasionally present (Fig. 8*b-d*). Elaborate incising occurs, featuring hachured triangles, rectilinear designs such as frets, and zoned punctation (Fig. 8*a, c*). Two of the late-facet jars are from an apparently dedicatory sub-floor cache in the Temple of the Cross (*c.* A.D. 690) (Fig. 8*b, d*; Ruz Lhuillier 1968*a*; Figs. 2-4).

Murcielagos ceramic complex

The period of late Otolum and early Murcielagos ceramic developments apparently coincided with the zenith of Palenque's monumental architecture and other hierarchical works. A probable dedicatory cache vessel from the Temple of the Foliated Cross (Fig. 9*i*; Ruz Lhuillier 1958*a*: Figs. 7, 10, 11) appears to date the construction of this temple as Murcielagos. Nevertheless, the interval between building the Cross and the Foliated Cross cannot have been great. Some interdigitation of late-facet Otolum and the Murcielagos complex is to be expected. In terms of the Maya Long Count, it seems appropriate to place the beginning of Murcielagos at approximately 9.13.0.0.0.

Elsewhere at Palenque, Murcielagos ceramics are best known from within the walls and surrounding fill of Group IV burials of early Balunte date, from some late plaza construction, and near the group of structures on the northern part of the site known popularly as the Murcielagos.

Two major ceramic developments characterize the Murcielagos complex. Locally-produced polychrome and its major vessel form, the wide everted-rim plate, largely disappear at Palenque. More or less synchronously, slipped and painted fine paste pottery was imported in significant quantities. A wide range of slip colours — orange, red, and cream — was commonly used, and a strong development took place in resist decoration (Fig. 9*i*).

Significantly represented in the fine paste pottery of the Murcielagos complex is a cream-buff paste containing minute, microscopically-observable particles of volcanic dust and opal phytoliths, the latter derived from silica-accumulator plants such as grasses and sedges. These inclusions probably occurred naturally in the clay rather than being purposely added as tempering materials. Similar pottery is best known from the Naab complex of Trinidad and other sites on the Usumacinta river near Emiliano Zapata, Tabasco (Rands 1969).

Additional ceramic relationships clearly exist between the Naab and Murcielagos complexes. Available evidence does not permit us to isolate precise centres of production, innovation or trade, although the intrusive nature of many ceramic elements in Murcielagos

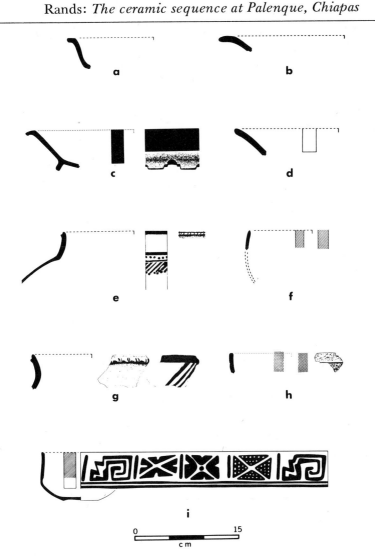

Figure 9 Murcielagos ceramic complex. *a-c*, everted-rim bowls, dishes or plates; *d*, direct rim; *e*, *g*, beaded-rim high-neck jars; *f*, *h*, *i*, round-sided bowls (*i*, vertical upper wall and concave base). *c*, notched basal flange; *e*, *g*, notched rim; *h*, incised. *c*, smudged; *d*, cream, *e*, *g*, red painted; *f*, orange, *h*, red slip, *i*, resist exterior (black and cream), orange on cream interior. *a*, *e*, *i*, quartz sand temper (volcanic dust present in *e*); *b-d*, *h*, fine paste with volcanic dust (opal phytoliths usually present); *f*, fine paste with phytoliths; *g*, volcanic ash temper. *i*, cache, Temple of the Foliated Cross.

suggests that Palenque's sphere of commercial and perhaps socio-political influence had enlarged to incorporate new ceramic traditions. Alternatively, intrusion can be viewed as evidence of a growing socio-cultural weakness at Palenque — a vacuum into which expanding, commercially aggressive units on the Classic Maya frontier were quick to move. However, at the beginning of the

Murcielagos complex, the elite culture of Palenque gives every indication of exceptional innovative vigour.

Balunte ceramic complex

The Balunte complex is divided into early and late facets. The latter, which we originally regarded as a separate complex, 'Huipale' (Rands 1967b, 1969), has proved impossible to separate consistently from early Balunte. Yet the distinction is an important one in the history of the site, for elite culture at Palenque appears to have gone into eclipse at the close of early Balunte. This was accompanied by severe population loss.

Diagnostics of the late facet are: (1) fairly large ceramic assemblages having high percentages of Fine Grey ware, and (2) the presence of Fine Orange ware, mostly of the Balancan (Z) ceramic group. 'Pure' late-facet refuse is best known in the western part of the site, toward and beyond Picota. In addition, a number of surface deposits may represent mixing of early- and late-facet materials.

Early Balunte is known from controlled stratigraphic contexts, especially those which are concerned with large-scale activities of a nature which presupposes a functioning 'Classic' rather than shattered society. Pottery associated with a major rebuilding of the north stairway of the Palace is a case in point (Ruz Lhuillier 1958d: Fig. 1), as well as caches in several parts of the Palace (e.g., Ruz Lhuillier 1958b: Fig. 1, Pl. 63b). The early facet is also known from shallow refuse behind the Pyramid of the Inscriptions and elsewhere. Apparently dating from the beginning of Balunte are upper level burials in the Group IV plaza (Rands and Rands 1961) and others in small, sub-floor tombs in the twin temples, XVIII and XVIII-A (Ruz Lhuillier 1958b: Figs. 15, 32; 1958d: Figs. 9, 10). Correspondences in pottery associated with these burials are striking, suggesting near-contemporaneity for the Group IV burials and the construction of Temples XVIII and XVIII-A in their latest form (cf. matching pots in Fig. 10 *e, f* and in Fig. 11*f* and *h, g* and *i*, and *j* and *k*).

The basic ceramic patterns of Balunte will be sketched only briefly. These include reduction not only in the amount of polychrome but of any pottery with a contrasting slip; surfaces, however, were often well polished. Moreover, the early facet witnessed a strong development of evenly-fired smudged pottery — a lustrous black in the few unweathered examples. Vessel walls, always tending to be thin at Palenque, became even more delicate. Correlated with this was an increase in untempered pottery. Whereas fine paste ceramics in the Murcielagos complex were frequently made of a cream to buff firing clay with abundant particles of volcanic dust and opal phytoliths, this source became less important in Balunte, most of the fine paste wares oxidizing to brown or buff

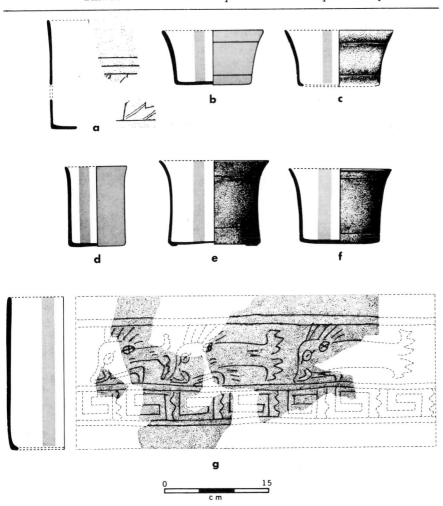

Figure 10 Balunte ceramic complex. *b-f*, early-facet contexts. *a, d, g*, cylindrical vases; *b, c, e, f*, outcurved bowls (beakers). *a*, weathered; *b-g*, unslipped. *a*, incised and dentate-stamped; *b, c, e, f*, groove-incised; *g*, incised. *a, b, d*, quartz sand temper; *e, g*, fine paste (with phytoliths). *b*, Group IV, Burial 14; *c*, Palace cache, Northwest Patio; *d*, Temple XVIII, Burial 2; *e*, Group IV, Burial 6; *f*, Temple XVIII, Tomb 1.

and lacking volcanic dust, although rich in opal. New trading relationships, probably emphasizing resources closer to Palenque, are indicated. There was, however, a basic continuity in sand-tempered Red-Brown ware. Fine paste pottery was primarily utilized in beaker-bowls and cylinders (Fig. 10), the local Red-Brown ware in plates, dishes and basins (Figs. 11a-i, 13e). Plates were flat-based throughout Balunte, the earlier examples tending to have solid, subconical feet and the later large, hollow supports. Sharp basal Z-angles and greater rim elaboration tended to correlate with the hollow-foot tripods (Fig. 11a, c).

Figure 11 Balunte ceramic complex, miscellaneous bowls and plates. *a, b, d-i, k,*
early-facet contexts. *a, c,* flat-base Z-angle tripod plates, large cascabel feet
and downturned everted rims; *b,* convex-base tripod bowl, solid feet and
direct rim; *d, e,* small flaring, convex-base plates; *f, h,* flat-base tripod plates,
solid feet and flaring wall (*h,* slight everted rim); *g, i,* flat-base, direct-rim
bowls; *j, k,* deep, flat-base bowls, outcurved or slightly flaring rims (*j,* nubbin
tripod feet, *k,* labial and basal mouldings). *a, c, g-i,* unslipped (polished); *b, d,*
f, cream slip; *e, j, k,* smudged-black. *a,* fine paste; *b-i,* quartz sand temper; *j, k,*
fine paste with accessory minerals of volcanic derivation. *b,* Group IV, Burial
1; *d, e,* Palace cache, Northwest Patio; *f,* Group IV, Burial 4; *g,* Group IV,
Burial 7; *h,* Temple XVIII, Burial 2; *i,* Temple XVIII-A, Tomb 2; *j,* Temple
XVIII-A, Tomb 1 (non-contemporaneous?); *k,* Group IV, Burial 4.

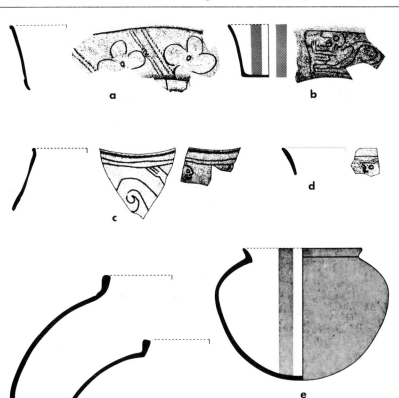

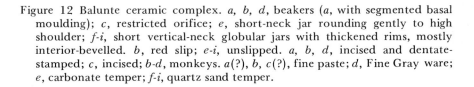

Figure 12 Balunte ceramic complex. *a, b, d*, beakers (*a*, with segmented basal moulding); *c*, restricted orifice; *e*, short-neck jar rounding gently to high shoulder; *f-i*, short vertical-neck globular jars with thickened rims, mostly interior-bevelled. *b*, red slip; *e-i*, unslipped. *a, b, d*, incised and dentate-stamped; *c*, incised; *b-d*, monkeys. *a*(?), *b, c*(?), fine paste; *d*, Fine Gray ware; *e*, carbonate temper; *f-i*, quartz sand temper.

Unslipped, globular jars with short, vertical necks and thickened rims are a Balunte diagnostic (Fig. 12*f-i*). Heavily tempered with quartz sand, these, like much of the fine paste Balunte pottery, were made of an opal-rich clay. This is also true of a newly-introduced utilitarian form, a buff basin with wide everted rim and slightly rounded upper wall, rounding to a convex base (Fig. 13*a, b*). This basin contrasts, in details of shape as well as ware, with a form which was apparently made locally, at or near Palenque — a bolstered-rim basin with vertical upper wall which angles sharply to a flat base

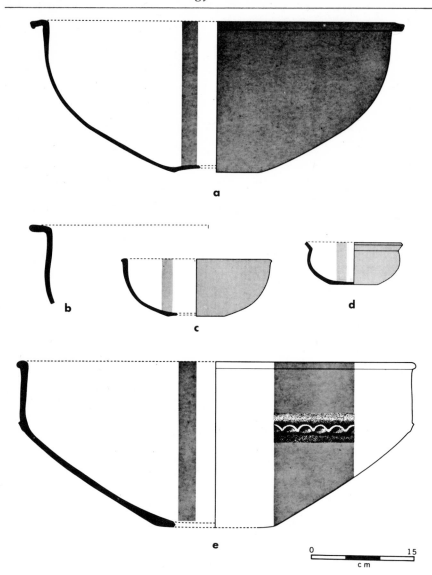

Figure 13 Balunte ceramic complex, utility bowls and basins. *a, b,* wide
   everted-rim basins with vertical upper walls, rounding toward concave base; *c,*
   slight everted-rim bowl rounding toward slightly concave base; *d,* recurved
   bowl with flaring rim; *e,* bolstered-rim basin with vertical upper wall, angling
   sharply toward flat base. *a-e,* unslipped (*e,* polished). *e,* thumb-impressed. *a,*
   b, quartz sand temper with opal phytoliths in clay, buff paste; *c, d,* carbonate
   temper (bowl class in *c* usually has paste characteristics of *a, b*); *e,* quartz sand
   temper without appreciable phytoliths in clay, red-brown paste.

(Fig. 13*e*). The latter was, apparently, the end-point of a long
developmental sequence which is represented at Palenque. In
contrast, the former appears suddenly at the site in quantity,
virtually without known antecedents.

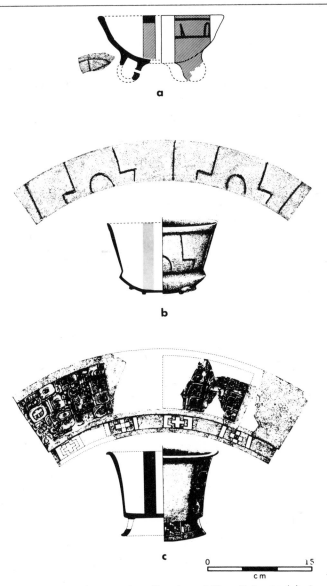

Figure 14 Balunte ceramic complex (*b*, *c*) and Post-Balunte (*a*). *b*, early facet context, Palace cache; *c*, inferentially early-facet because of functional hieroglyphic text. *a*, Yalton black-on-orange type; *b*, Gray Chablekal group; *c*, carved, fine paste black.

Simple to complex incising is an important feature of Balunte (Fig. 10). Incised monkeys and/or dentate stamping form a sub-complex of the sort normally associated with Fine Grey ware of the Grey Chablekal group. Yet of the examples shown here (Figs. 10*a*, 12*a-d*), only one (Fig.12*d*) has typical Fine Grey characteristics, in surface or paste. One of the monkeys is incised in what may be an untempered version of the local Red-Brown pottery (Fig. 12*c*). A typical member of the Grey Chablekal group, an incised vessel from a sub-floor Palace cache appears, from its stratigraphic context, to be early Balunte in date (Fig. 14*b*).

The classic nature of a handsome black bowl, correctly carved with an Initial Series and a base in the 819-day count, is a strong argument that the specimen, which records a date equivalent to A.D. 799, belongs to the early facet of Balunte (Fig. 14*c*). Therefore, the collapse of elite culture at Palenque must have occurred later than the carving of the vessel. But the collapse could not have been much later, as the late facet of Balunte was probably under way prior to the explosive spread of Fine Orange ware from its homeland, presumably in Tabasco, by approximately A.D. 830.

Post-Balunte

Fine Orange pottery is sparse at Palenque, and most is badly weathered. It appears, however, that the Balancan (Z) Group is best represented and belongs to the late facet of Balunte. In addition, a few specimens of the Silho (X) Group are known (Fig. 14*a*). Unless this group of Fine Orange ware is considerably earlier than has generally been supposed, it would appear that a small scale reoccupation of the site took place following its effective abandonment at the close of Balunte.

Acknowledgments

The Palenque ceramic project has been made possible by the cooperation of the Instituto Nacional de Antropología e Historia, Mexico. Field work at Palenque and neighbouring sites has been supported by the Institute of Andean Research, the Wenner-Gren Foundation for Anthropological Research, the John Simon Guggenheim Memorial Foundation, the American Philosophical Society, and the National Science Foundation. Special thanks are owed the long-term director of archaeological work at Palenque, Professor Alberto Ruz Lhuillier, for his patient and unflagging support of the ceramic investigations, and are also due to Robert E. Smith for sharing with us his unrivalled knowledge of lowland Maya ceramics.

REFERENCES

Coe, M.D. (1965) Archaeological synthesis of southern Veracruz and Tabasco. In R. Wauchope and G.R. Willey (eds), *Archaeology of Southern Mesoamerica*, part 2. *Handbook of Middle American Indians*, vol. 3. Austin, Texas.
Coe, W.R. (1967) *Tikal: A Handbook of the Ancient Maya Ruins*. Philadelphia.
Drucker, P. (1943) *Ceramic sequences at Tres Zapotes, Veracruz, Mexico*. Smithsonian Institution, Bureau of American Ethnology, Bulletin no. 140.

Matheny, R.T. (1970) *The Ceramics of Aguacatal, Campeche, Mexico.* Papers of the New World Archaeological Foundation, no. 27.

Rands, B.C. (1954) *Ceramics of the Temple of the Inscriptions, Palenque, Chiapas, Mexico.* M.A. Thesis, University of New Mexico.

Rands, B.C., and R.L. Rands (1961) Excavations in a cemetery at Palenque. *Estudios de Cultura Maya*, 1, 87-106.

Rands, R.L. (1967a) Ceramic technology and trade in the Palenque region, Mexico. In C.L. Riley and W.W. Taylor (eds), *American Historical Anthropology: Essays in Honor of Leslie Spier*, 137-51. Carbondale and Edwardsville.

Rands, R.L. (1967b) Cerámica de la región de Palenque, México. *Estudios de Cultura Maya*, 6, 111-47.

Rands, R.L. (1969) *Mayan ecology and trade 1967-1968.* Mesoamerican Studies, Research Records, University Museum, Southern Illinois University, Series '69M(2)A.

Rands, R.L., and B.C. Rands (1957) The ceramic position of Palenque, Chiapas. *American Antiquity*, 23, 140-50.

Ruz Lhuillier, A. (1952) Exploraciones en Palenque: 1950. *Anales del Instituto Nacional de Antropología e Historia*, 5, 25-45.

Ruz Lhuillier, A. (1955) Exploraciones en Palenque: 1952. *Anales del Instituto Nacional de Antropología e Historia*, 6, part 1, 79-110.

Ruz Lhuillier, A. (1958a) Exploraciones arqueológicas en Palenque: 1953. *Anales del Instituto Nacional de Antropología e Historia*, 10, 69-116.

Ruz Lhuillier, A. (1958b) Exploraciones arqueológicas en Palenque: 1954. *Anales del Instituto Nacional de Antropología e Historia*, 10, 117-84.

Ruz Lhuillier, A. (1958c) Exploraciones arqueológicas en Palenque: 1955. *Anales del Instituto Nacional de Antropología e Historia*, 10, 185-240.

Ruz Lhuillier, A. (1958d) Exploraciones arqueológicas en Palenque: 1956. *Anales del Instituto Nacional de Antropología e Historia*, 10, 241-99.

Ruz Lhuillier, A. (1962) Exploraciones arqueológicas en Palenque: 1957. *Anales del Instituto Nacional de Antropología e Historia*, 14, 35-90.

Weiant, C.W. (1943) *An Introduction to the Ceramics of Tres Zapotes, Veracruz, Mexico.* Smithsonian Institution, Bureau of American Ethnology, Bulletin no. 139.

Willey, G.R., T.P. Culbert and R.E.W. Adams (1967) Maya lowland ceramics: a report from the 1965 Guatemala City conference. *American Antiquity*, 32, 289-315.

JAMES C. GIFFORD

Recent thought concerning the interpretation of Maya prehistory

Preclassic Maya populations

The first farming population units for which we have evidence in the southern Maya lowlands had simple social attainments. They made unslipped pottery with fillet appliqué decoration, called Jocote Orange-Brown at the site of Barton Ramie (Willey, Bullard, Glass and Gifford 1965), where it is characteristic of the Jenney Creek ceramic complex. These Xe people (Gifford 1970a, b) were the first to settle the Belize Valley in British Honduras, and their house mound debris lies stratigraphically at the bottom of the deposits where it occurs. Pottery of this kind, so close in its typological relationships as to suggest common population unit derivations, is also found at Altar de Sacrificios (Adams 1971) and at Seibal (Willey 1970: 315-55) on the western frontier of the Maya territories. Age is comparable both in the east and west and extends from 900 to 600 B.C. Farther west during this time interval typological comparisons are not close, and suggest no more than contacts and trade.

For the pre-Mamom complexes, Willey, Culbert and Adams (1967: 293) wrote: 'Such linkages as there are between the Pasión River sites and Chiapa de Corzo are modal and not based on high content similarities.' The central Peten where Tikal became located does not contain pottery of this time value, according to Patrick Culbert's analysis, and population units do not seem to be present.

The Xe people came to the southern Maya lowlands about 900 B.C., and settled along important river ways that subsequently became the east and west borders of the lowland Maya realm. During recent years Robert Sharer has conducted extensive testing at Chalchuapa in El Salvador. His important work has produced a continuity of ceramic development going back in time beyond 900 B.C. In his collections he has been able to recognize the pottery types from which Jocote Orange-Brown derived, and he also finds Jocote contemporaneously with its appearance at Barton Ramie. Because the identities are so close in a utilitarian pottery that probably had no trade value, we suggest common population unit derivation, and believe the Xe people of the Peten peripheries came from Central America and such site-zones as Chalchuapa, following coastal and major river drainage patterns as routes of migration (Sharer and Gifford 1970).

At Chalchuapa there were other lines of ceramic development that gave rise to the much more refined and skilfully executed pottery called Savana Orange (Smith and Gifford 1966) or Mars Orange ware (Smith 1955) in the southern Maya lowlands, where it is accompanied by Palma (red) Daub. These two kinds of pottery are keys to the Mamom horizon (Willey, Culbert and Adams 1967: 293-5). Sharer has been able to show that with both Savana Orange and Palma Daub earlier prototypes exist in the El Salvador Chalchuapa sequence, and probably the Peten Mamom phenomenon is Xe magnified, consolidated, and added to by Central American leadership contingents as well as population increments. Xe people were pioneers; Mamom people were consolidators (leaders, traders, specialists of rudimentary character).

Stanley Boggs (1950) has documented an Olmec presence in El Salvador. Although I would not contend that either Xe or Mamom peoples were Olmec or had Olmec leaders, I would suggest that in Central America under Olmec influence, slash-and-burn agricultural knowledge could have been transferred, so that when particular Mamom peoples encountered the Peten terrain they were able to take advantage of it and spread from the riverine Xe habitats into the deep jungles of the Peten, where we find their deposits lowermost in the great sites such as Tikal and Uaxactun (Willey, Culbert and Adams 1967: 293-95).

The Chicanel horizon appears in all of the Peten ceramic sequences. It is massive in bulk of deposit and in the character of its pottery. Sierra Red is its diagnostic pottery type and the geographic range of this single pottery is enormous, covering more square km. in quantity of deposition than any pottery type I know of in Middle America. The entire territorial extent of the lowland Maya domain is outlined by this pottery type, and forever afterwards things change within that range but not very much beyond it — it seems to set the perimeter for all of Maya time.

In ceramic character, Chicanel has always reminded me of the great Olmec heads, when they are considered within their own medium of stone sculpture. Once again, however, I would not want to say Chicanel people were Olmec people, but the appearance of Sierra Red in the Maya ceramic sequences coincides with a really abrupt end to previous close population ties with Central America. It is as if a new leadership had arrived with Sierra Red and a whole new leadership structure was developed that formed a stubborn, tenacious, rigidly conservative, rocklike foundation for the Maya cultural continuum. Sierra Red seems related to a powerful chiefdom kind of social structure.

Other than the pottery we know far too little of the Chicanel people. There are suspicions that as we approach the time of Christ their ceremonial activities assumed grand proportions, especially in Yucatan where E. Wyllys Andrews IV and others note the possibility of very large Chicanel mounds (Willey 1964: 150). The same is true at certain sites in Chiapas.

I feel Chicanel is primarily of Mexican inspiration or origin. It came to the lowland Maya territories both as a third and relatively large population increment, and as an extremely important leadership faction that in turn, perhaps, had been influenced by an Olmec model in the territories of its origin. We see in this beginning, that the Olmec indirectly may have had much to do with Maya, first by way of agricultural techniques especially suited to a lowland ecological setting, and secondly, by way of political leadership and organization. The sources and mechanisms were different in each instance, but the thread of distant Olmec ideologies is quite possible.

So the stage is set for final advancement to the Classic position and the advent of lowland Maya civilization in the form of the Old Empire. The uniqueness of Maya civilization is undisputed. There are many elements such as an inordinate interest in jade, cranial deformation, astronomical observation, calendrics, ceremonial centre features, to mention but a few, that remind us once again of the now vanished Olmec. It is not their agricultural teachings or their political expertise, but Olmec ceremonial traits that now emerge in the Classic Maya, complete with extremely vigorous trade consummated for ritualistic and spiritual reasons.

Maya Classic, though, was composed of still another element. And just as Chicanel terminated Central American influences when it took hold, Chicanel itself was ended by a new Protoclassic population pulsation from Central America hundreds of years later. This new intrusion is apparent at Barton Ramie (Willey and Gifford 1961) and we have called it Floral Park. The diagnostic pottery is called Aguacate Orange. It is especially abundant in the eastern portion of the southern Maya lowlands and Sharer has traced it to El Salvador and the general area of Chalchuapa (Sharer and Gifford 1970). Of equal importance also at this time is the appearance among the Maya of polychrome pottery. For some reason the Chicanel people were not receptive to polychrome decorated pottery. In my opinion it is no accident that Ixcanrio Orange-Polychrome made its appearance in the Protoclassic phases of the Maya cultural continuum when the other elements of Classic Maya ritual arts also started. Something takes place that breaks the Chicanel hammerlock, and art of Maya character begins. One of the first indications of this that survives is Ixcanrio Orange-Polychrome (Willey and Gifford 1961: Fig. 5). The artistic conception to its design configuration is the beginning of the Maya art style, and that is not of Olmec inspiration.

Once the Protoclassic hold was secure, the spread and fulfilment was rapid, and lowland Maya became a civilization in the blaze of spiritual, ritualistic, and artistic opulence so carefully documented for us by many scholars. Until the end of the Maya continuum, after A.D. 900, a serious case for military invasion cannot be made. The ceramic sequence argues again and again for various kinds of population increments, and the impingements of important influences on a selective basis. But no matter how profound the influences were, and no matter how changed thinking became as a result of those encroachments, all but the very final one (heavily involved with the actual collapse of the Empire) were absorbed. What was before absorbed what came in, and this can be seen in the pottery sequences — periods of stability and slow or little change, impingements mixing, all with new results but not of a kind so as to leave behind all that went before. Never is the ceramic slate wiped clean until very near the end.

Despite the fact that I believe Olmec influences weighed in upon the Maya for a lengthy portion of their early continuum, I do not believe any of the Maya people were, strictly speaking, Olmec people. The Olmec phenomenon (M.D. Coe 1968), in my thinking, is a separate one, centering in other places. On the other hand, Olmec influences from possibly before 1500 B.C. up to near the time of Christ may have been enormous. Regarding Middle America as a whole, no people may have been more fundamentally influential than the Olmec. They possessed certain specialized skills and knowledge concerning elements leading to power control that were unparalleled in their effectiveness and survival value. They also travelled widely. We do not know exactly how all that was Olmec articulated, but I believe they were more a rulership and that their people were a wide variety of population units, some under far more direct Olmec influence than others. And because of their obvious success and extended travel, parts of their configuration may well have been emulated in different places and in different ways, thus leading to different Olmec-inspired developmental trends that eventually cross-cut and cross-fertilized one another through southern and central Middle America well after Olmec proper had terminated.

As to Olmec origins, it is difficult to determine a source that satisfies all the evidence. Sarma has spoken with clarity concerning Harappan civilization of the Indus Valley. New developments in Indus Valley chronology, the kinds of specialized knowledge and the particular elements capitalized upon by the Olmec, their physical type, and the known Harappan skills in navigation, lead me to think Olmec leadership might have derived from the Indian subcontinent and been related to the fall of the Harappan kind of high civilization.

The Old Empire Maya Classic distinguishes itself as a nation

A person born and raised in Florence cannot help being conditioned by churches, palaces and parks, their sights, sounds and smells. Even if the Florentine is not consciously aware of these experiences, they become, nevertheless, part of his being and make him lastingly different from what he would have become in London, Paris, Barcelona or New York . . . Human behavior would be a chaos of pointless acts and exploding emotions if it were not that even the most fundamental aspects of life are shaped by culture . . . The resistance to change of social entities probably accounts for the origin and continued existence of nations . . . Nations do not exist as geological, climatic or racial entities, but as human experiences . . . Modern historical knowledge has confirmed that groups of people whom circumstances force to live together in a certain place tend to develop a body of shared ideas, values and beliefs, which progressively becomes their ideal and guide. The culture they develop constitutes a whole which shapes itself as a continuously evolving national spirit . . . In this light, national characteristics are expressions of human choices based on the collective acceptance of certain conventions and traditions — and, perhaps, especially of myths. (Dubos 1972: 62-3)

Willey and Phillips (1958) define this in prehistory through the conceptual mechanism called the 'stage'. The Classic Stage reflects that interval in a cultural continuum during which 'expressions of human choices based on the collective acceptance of certain conventions and traditions' (Dubos 1972) have reached high points of attainment and have thus become shared ideas, values, and beliefs, serving as ideals and cultural guides.

Among many other appropriate observations, Willey and Phillips' definition consequently mentions that the Classic Stage is marked by 'superlative performance in many lines of cultural endeavor. There is evidence not only of mastery of technologies and arts but of their conjunction in single cultures and societies. The various and scattered inventions and innovations of the Formative are now drawn together into rich, diverse and yet unified patterns' (Willey and Phillips 1958: 184).

Among the ancient Maya, these descriptions are especially applicable to the Old Empire Early Classic. Certainly the Early Classic Maya were a nation distinct from all others by this time (A.D. 300-600), and their distinctiveness as the Maya nation must have stood out in the ways Dubos mentions. The Maya Early Classic gradually reached a climax, then turned on a swift-moving hinge to the Late Classic, moving with ever accelerating momentum toward

Empire hierarchic dissolution in the Postclassic Stage.

> Even now most Americans believe, as did their predecessors, that they must 'conquer' nature rather than adapt themselves to the natural environment; they tend to put their faith in machines and technological fixes rather than in the complexities of ecological systems and in the slow process of nature. This conquering attitude, which has dominated man's relationship to nature from the beginning of American history, has contributed to material progress and to the technological and economic supremacy of the United States, but it has also been responsible for enormous damage to the environment. (Dubos 1972: 65)

Similarly the Maya undertook and stressed (ultimately to an inordinate degree), certain preoccupations that were founded in their 'national outlook', their ways of doing things, that were basic ingredients of their value orientation. Because of the extent to which they were stressed, these evidently became seriously deleterious to the Old Empire. Attention also should be given to the genetic effect of mass population inbreeding within a matrix that did not encourage the incorporation or absorption of 'outsiders' on the local level. Certainly the idea 'that kinship and marriage rules regulate a fourth type of communication, that of genes between phenotypes' (Lévi-Strauss 1962: 333) had validity among the Maya.

In my view the Maya nation contrasted sharply with neighbouring and other cultural configurations throughout the New World. They seemingly developed in great measure from within (Rathje 1969, 1971) and their reliance on internal trade for internal purposes was probably quite crucial. In so doing they came to manifest an unusual amount of cultural homogeneity and internal cultural integrity which intensified through time until the obvious hierarchic disintegration of the Old Empire began to take place (Willey and Shimkin 1971). I do not believe the lowland Maya were an offshoot of Mexico or a variant of the Mexican theme. Much in the way one describes Japanese versus Chinese people, I think the lowland Maya valued their cultural integrity both highly and tenaciously. Their way of looking at things, including death, was never that of Mexico, idealistically or philosophically. The Maya were a nation unto themselves.

The derivation of ethnographic data from the Maya art style

One of the most unique and distinctive features of the Old Empire Maya in their Classic Stage of development was their art style. It was expressed as pictorial and representational art in paintings on walls and on the exterior of pottery cylinder vessels. The extraordinary uniqueness but at the same time 'trueness to the Maya' of their art style may be a consequence of its lacking a specific forerunner. It probably owes its real inception to the Maya Classic crystallization. Old Empire Maya religious and spiritual leadership may well have Olmec derivations, but these seem concentrated more in the areas of jade values, class- and cult-oriented cranial deformation, calendrics, possibly numerology, and the concept of the ceremonial centre, as mentioned earlier. It is difficult to see the roots of any pictorial and representational art, as expressed in Olmec painting, that is exactly equivalent to Classic Maya artistry, despite the occurrence of certain cave paintings (Gay 1967, Wicke 1971) and the presence of a monumental sculptural component (Bernal 1969, Gay 1971). I feel the Izapa artistic expression, or style (M.D. Coe 1966: 60-2) is a late Olmec derivational offshoot of Mexican blending and that it is not the prototype to the Classic Maya art style. Olmec representations are strong, tough, large, and almost harsh. Where the Olmec combined working skill with power, the Old Empire Maya blended artistic skill with beauty — resulting in aesthetic harmony that served them poetically and philosophically as a dimension of their language and communication.

Elsewhere I have presented a view of ancient Maya society as one that was composed of two real worlds — that of the village homeland and that of the ceremonial centre (Gifford 1971*a*, in press). It is to the second of these, that of the ceremonial centres and the 'Great Ones', that we associate and attribute the Maya art style. There in that world the art style was executed with great fidelity and impressive accuracy by expert craftsmen who were glued to the reality of their ceremonial centre world but who worked regularly with a medium that everyone in that world could understand. Their art expressed reality as well as abstractions — reality in the wonderful portrayals that show us mortal Maya ceremonial centre beings in their ceremonial context and abstract elements that symbolize the Maya spiritual realm through images of immortal divinities. In between was much that was partly real and partly supernatural, and this occurred wherever there was Maya pictorial art (see Fig. 1, series *a-o*).

Of the most influential works to appear recently we can include those of Evon Vogt (1969, 1970). For me there is a fascination about what Vogt tells us of the Zinacantecos. It would seem that the roles and duties attributed to their ancestors by present-day Zinacantecos, were probably those carried out by the living Great Ones of the Old Empire and their associates of high rank within their once real ceremonial centre world. The painted pictures executed on some cylinder vessels are probably accurate, detailed scenes of important Old Empire persons carrying out the behavioural manifestations related to the roles they occupied (Gifford 1971*b*). In the same way that we see the Bonampak murals spread before us (Tejeda 1955), they represent the duties and activities Old Empire personages of import pursued as a given situation took place at a particular instant (historic moment) during the ancient Maya continuum. Looking at certain cylinder vases is like opening a Zinacanteco sacred mountain for a dramatic look inside — there is the ceremonial centre world as it once was. As it is with the ethnographer, by patient study of the activity patterns we may come to understand what is happening in those views so faithfully portrayed by the Maya artists. We have before us, in these archaeological evidences, ethnographic vignettes of what was once a living life-way (see Fig. 1, series *a-o*).

Michael Coe (1972: 79-88) has recently made a series of fine observations concerning Maya Late Classic cylinder vases. Many of the points Coe makes merit serious attention, but I do not, at this time, agree that only the Maya world-after-death is depicted by the cylinder vessel artists. I tend to think in terms of individual explanations for individual cylinder vessels and admire, for example, Adams' interpretation of the Altar Vase (1963: 90-92, 1971: 68-75). When considering all the evidences and all cylinder vessels besides those of Chama, it is my feeling that the representations shown on cylinder vessels vary from living persons dressed in normal garb to individuals dressed in full ceremonial regalia and clothed partly or entirely in costumes and masks indicative of ceremonial, mythical, or spiritual phenomena (see Fig. 1, series *a-o*). All kinds of ceremonial centre scenes are shown, but they do seem to be restricted to that world and frequently to moments in Maya history involving living persons. Although often impersonators, the persons shown seem to be alive and actively participating in some real event. And of course, in some examples the artist does portray mythological creatures and gods.

Figure 1*a-o* A series of Classic Maya cylinder vessels indicating the life-like renditions executed by cylinder vessel artists and showing the range of variation encountered in their illustrations. Portrayals of events seem often shown as they actually took place, with important personages reposing on seats of authority and engaging in gesture-supported conversations with persons of lesser station. What seem to be living persons are similarly shown partially or fully costumed in accord with belief pattern identities of a spiritual nature, and still others portray life-like scenes in the world of mythology.

a, after W.R. Coe, 1965: 42, upper left; *b*, after W.R. Coe 1967: 30; *c*, after W.R. Coe 1965: 42 upper right; *d*, after Merrin 1971: Fig. 7; *e, f*, after Merrin 1971: Fig. 15; *g-j*, photographs (by the author) taken at the Museum of the American Indian, Heye Foundation (special exhibit for the 70th Annual Meeting of the American Anthropological Association in New York City, 1971); *k, l*, after W.R. Coe 1967: 52, upper and middle; *m*, after W.R. Coe 1965: 42, lower; *n*, after Ekholm 1970: 114, upper right; *o*, after Jones 1969: item 616.

a

b

c

d

e

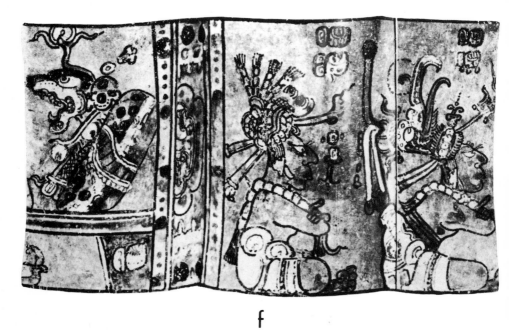

f

g

h

i

j

l

k

m

n   o

These paintings emphasize only partially what there is to see in Maya representational art. To me they are ethnography in prehistory. In addition to portraying ceremonial centre activity patterns, when combined with the intricate sculptural efforts of the Old Empire Maya, I believe that the representational art of the Maya graphically indicated a segment of their philosophic orientation and from it also can be discerned some of their basic belief principles.

The village homeland world is neglected. The farmers and their important activities are scarcely, if ever, shown. It was as if the gods should see and be pleased by all that was portrayed, and some subjects (village settings, for instance) could never be shown because the gods derived no pleasure in viewing them.

There are observations in Vogt's inclusive work that with sufficient study might help explain what the ancient artists have drawn. There is a rhythmic consistency to Maya logic that persists regardless of circumstances, so that nothing is shown out of sheer fantasy. Because Maya representational art was simply pictorial logic, a Zinacanteco shaman's thoughts are the same Maya philosphical logic stripped of its artisan conveyors, and one will partly explain the other in the abstract. What the Zinacantan believe today does not seem all that different from what the Old Empire Maya reveal through their art work as their beliefs. The real world of the ceremonial centre crumbled to bits and vanished to the touch, but in the minds of Zinacantan Maya today it still exists as an image inside sacred mountains into which their shamans can see and go. It is as if at the Old Empire collapse the ceremonial centre world melted back into the village from which it originally arose, transforming itself from a thing the Maya could see with their eyes to a thing of mental images most appropriate to a shaman.

The possible use of a model in the interpretation of the Maya cultural continuum

I have tried to appreciate the ancient Maya by looking not only at archaeological evidences that reflect their prehistoric life-style, but by attempting to look at all that surrounded them. With sufficient attention the enormous quantity of information about these people, both past and present, can be posed as a model in the way cultural and other anthropologists have proposed (Lévi-Strauss 1962).

In thinking about the model we do not undertake a whole at once, but a thing of pieces that eventually will fit together as a whole. We want to know what governed the internal mechanisms of Maya society not at one point in their prehistory, but through the time-scope of their continuum. And among the major areas of question, we want to know how and why the Maya social structure changed through time; what were the underlying causalities for culture change.

> When the structure of a certain type of phenomena does not lie at a great depth, it is more likely that some kind of model, standing as a screen to hide it, will exist in the collective consciousness. For conscious models, which are usually known as 'norms', are by definition very poor ones, since they are not intended to explain the phenomena but to perpetuate them. Therefore, structural analysis is confronted with a strange paradox well known to the linguist, that is: the more obvious structural organization is, the more difficult it becomes to reach it because of the inaccurate conscious models lying across the path which leads to it. (Lévi-Strauss 1962: 321-50)

Thus we may have at least two levels of inaccuracy to think about: our own recovery of the evidence may be inaccurate (or incomplete), and the Maya themselves may have been misleading in the manner in which they unconsciously projected their material culture as a dimension of a conscious model of themselves. The Maya were not trying to *explain* themselves, but rather to *project* themselves as they would have their image seen by others and, very importantly to them, to perpetuate themselves.

If a model is developed by the archaeologist, it will be one that is constructed from the material remains which the Maya unconsciously left, but certainly intended, as a dimension of the model of themselves by which they wished others to know them, including their own all-embracing gods. This model, then, will not of itself necessarily tell us of causalities; it may well be simply a screen stationed between the analyst and the true cultural causalities.

Perhaps the nature of this screen (the archaeological evidence) will serve to instruct the viewer how to see through it. The Maya continuum had a massively powerful undercurrent, and I believe historical events were not the triggers to causalities but followed in the wake of them, and became indicative of them. Most certainly the Maya architected the splendours of their age for all who came to them to see. Possibly they relied on visual impressions as a compelling force in their society more than any of the other high civilizations, and much of their visual magnificence survives as archaeological evidence. Finally, because much in archaeology does come to us as reflections of what once constituted norms, we must remember 'that the cultural norms are not of themselves structures. Rather, they furnish an important contribution to an understanding of the structures, either as factual documents or as theoretical contributions . . . ' (Lévi-Strauss 1962: 324).

I have relied heavily on various of Vogt's works for the interpretive impressions in this paper. I place these impressions as a series of suggestions for which we as archaeologists seek ways of verification. They represent serious questions that can be asked of ancient Maya culture, not only because of the way Maya Old Empire evidences present themselves but equally because of statements that Vogt and his associates have made about a segment of contemporary Maya society. I accept as a basic premise Vogt's statement that 'Highland Chiapas is probably one of the crucial regions for the discovery of ancient Maya patterns in relatively undisturbed form' (Vogt 1966: 177).

To verify or increase the accuracy of these suggestions may require new ethnological and cultural ways of looking at the archaeological data — possibly ways not usually contemplated by archaeologists. We want to work toward methods concerning how you work with the *mind* of man through archaeological materials.

It is not sufficient merely to note what the ethnographer has said of his work. We must ask what it means with respect to the prehistoric evidence. To cite an example, we find Vogt (1966: 181) observing for Zinacantecos: 'While the priestly hierarchy is function-ing in the ceremonial center with its complex annual round of rituals, the religious life of the outlying hamlets is essentially in the hands of the *b'iloletik*. The term *b'ilol* means literally "seer", the belief being that while in ancient mythological times all Zinacantecos could "see" into the mountain and observe their ancestral gods directly, now only the *b'iloletik* can accomplish this miracle.' This seems to be a direct reference to the idea that at one time all village homeland people could visit the great ceremonial centres (such as Tikal and Yaxchilan) and see living there the Great Ones.

A second basic premise regarding Maya study is that ancient Maya Old Empire Classic society was a stratified social phenomenon. This is well documented in the recent summary article by Willey and Shimkin (1971: 1-18; see also the many outstanding contributions to our knowledge of this aspect by Tatiana Proskouriakoff and Rathje 1970). Zinacantan society is not stratified as was Maya society in the Old Empire; *that* stratification was lost when the underlying components of the Old Empire ceremonial world disarticulated and caused the rapid disintegration of the Empire.

Every high civilization known had its preoccupations — elements that were emphasized above all others and that at times in its history became obsessions. Among those emphasized by the Old Empire Maya, communication with the gods, and social stratification as a means of achieving and maintaining this essential line of communication, were paramount. The stratified nature of Old Empire society was one of the foundation pillars holding up the entire structure. To recast Zinacanteco thought and mind into a semblance of the Old Empire, one of the many things to be worked with is the reintroduction of stratification and other tribal component variables into the model.

The hierarchic dissolution of the Maya Old Empire

By Vogt's account the Zinacantan are lineage-oriented. It is possible that the ancient Zinacantecos had specific defined functions in the Old Empire ceremonial centre world because considering the entire tribal whole of the Old Empire, the Zinacantan would have had certain lineages. Unlike the present, the situation then might well have involved severe *lineage* stratification, which included job specialization. Representational art in the Old Empire Late Classic implies that in the ceremonial centre world, lineages and their animal spirits were ranked, and that this ranking was most applicable, or operative, in the ceremonial centre world. So where the lineages became stratified, so followed the specialities (or perhaps the other way around in point of developmental origins). It is important to state that these interpretations refer to the Late Classic of the Old Empire rather than to the Early Classic, Protoclassic, or Formative aspects.

Also in Late Classic Old Empire archaeological manifestations, there is an emphasis within the Empire on geographical districts. I believe these accorded with the tribal units of the Empire and have previously suggested that the Zinacantan as a distinct population of today is, in fact, a disarticulated remnant of the Lowland Maya civilization, relocated and reconstituted as a tribal entity. The lowland Empire provided them with special roles and status which were theirs alone and a particular geographical reference that we might call their tribal homeland. In the days of lowland Maya civilization there were two kinds of Zinacantan men — those who in fact occupied positions in accord with the special roles and status niche that were theirs and who permanently resided in or immediately adjacent to the ceremonial centres and gave of their special theological services to the Empire on a full-time basis, and then there were those who remained in the tribal 'homeland' district and resided in the villages and could be counted among the basic food producers. (Gifford 1970: 15)

Today the Empire world is gone; it disappeared with the collapse and attendant societal decapitation associated with the abrupt termination of the Empire by approximately A.D. 900. But the homeland world persists and the Zinacantecos maintain the spiritual essence of the Empire in their religion and ritual, and in the depths of the belief system they still tenaciously retain.

To effect the collapse of the Empire, crucial component population units could 'have completely disengaged themselves, disarticulated themselves from the whole that was the "Old Empire" '. If so, what they did for the Empire, their particular job specialization,

might no longer be done, and under such circumstances the Empire could no longer possibly maintain itself. Its primary hierarchic social elements would have become disengaged, separated, each gone its own way — the articulation of peoples and their services so vital to the lowland Maya Empire would no longer exist . . . so the 'Empire' would cease to be almost overnight as the populations disassociated themselves in a permanent sense from the societal framework that itself was the Empire. Not all Maya population elements would necessarily have moved as the Tzeltal-speakers did, or as the ancient Zinacantan did, if we can equate the two. Various segments of the lower echelons of the 'Empire' might well have remained where they were, Empire-less but *in situ* Maya remnants. If so, these could well be what we see as New Town at Barton Ramie and Caban at Tikal — the lowland post-Civilization Maya manifestations known to have lived on in the lowlands after A.D. 900 and after their 'Empire' had vanished. (Gifford 1970b: 18)

Regardless of what changes took place within the Maya continuum, back and forth communication between the people and the gods, the gods and the people, was a major concern. On behalf of the village homeland districts, such as the Belize River valley, Old Empire *b'ilols* may well have communicated with the ceremonial centre world and been in close spiritual touch 'with the ancestral deities of the lineages making up the *sna*' (Vogt 1966: 183) who, in fact, were real occupants of the ceremonial centre world during the Old Empire. This basic need for a particular kind of communication was a main reason and certainly a primary philosophical and moral justification for the existence of the second world of the Old Empire, its ceremonial centre world. Maya life, existence itself, could not and would not be unless communication was maintained. Zinacantecos still believe this, but manage without the elaborations and complexities of their lost civilization.

Sabloff and Willey (1967: 311-36) and Willey and Shimkin (1971: 1-18) assess the collapse of Classic Maya civilization in the southern lowlands. They deal with its many possible and probable causalities and evaluate the empirical evidence in the following statements: 'The Maya collapse was a complex phenomenon combining a variety of internal and external events, still imperfectly understood, into an intensifying disaster', which was exacerbated because

> Classic Maya exposure to, contacts with, and pressures from non-Classic Maya groups at its western frontier set in motion a series of events that resulted in the collapse and eventual extinction of the old Maya way of life ... All of these manifestations speak against theories of large-scale military conquests or of violent and general 'peasant revolts'. Nor do they fit well with the idea of a major agricultural failure which, it seems more likely, would have begun in the drier eastern regions than in the west. They are, however, consistent with the disruptions that a delicately balanced socio-economic system might undergo from small bands of intruders expert in violence yet ignorant of management or indigenous values. (Willey and Shimkin 1971: 10-12)

Especially does this seem probable in the case of an Empire that was overextended and disillusioned in many different ways and had no real professional military component (army) with which to protect itself.

To this I would add the idea of the disarticulation of the Old Empire tribal units in such ways as to disconnect the two real worlds of the Old Empire from one another, resulting in a disintegration of the civilization by virtue of the severance of the village homeland world from the ceremonial centre world. So many specific ills in so many aspects of the Empire, including astronomical miscalculations or omissions, led them to feel the vital communication system with the gods had failed and was no longer operative. Its only real purpose was to facilitate communication with the gods, and since it no longer functioned properly, it was no longer needed.

I believe the Maya people and their leadership perhaps jointly determined that communication with the gods in the fashion they had built for so many hundreds of years was somehow no longer operative. The many unfavourable dimensions coalescing together could have made it appear to Maya minds on all levels of society that the leaders had lost touch with the gods. The Great Ones had no armies. The force of the gods was the power of the Great Ones. Without that power, the power of speaking to the gods directly, the people would not give to them of their strength.

To the village homeland world there would no longer be any justification for the ceremonial centre world so expensive and now, in its final days, so frenetically draining for those people. Here is a reason for the 'collapse' that can be equally applied to every part of the Empire and that demands no physical destruction of the centres. If the centres were not needed any more and the Maya people terminated their maintenance and there was no societal force at hand to coerce the resumption of that maintenance, they would simply die as human individuals would without food; an aspect of society no longer useful in the face of a multitude of demonstrable malfunctions.

The vast middle echelon of persons living in the ceremonial centres held lineage relationships that in some way tied them to a village context in their tribal homeland part of the Empire, and so they returned to their kin. Even though their surrounding elaborations and complexities had become a special way of life to them, their magnificent services were to no avail — the gods could not hear the Maya people by this means. The ceremonial centre populations had worked for the ability of a Great One to communicate with the gods, but the Great Ones had lost their voices. The wondrous belief bond — the civilization that was motivated by an idea that among them there were Great Ones who could speak to the gods — was gone. The structure crumbled that once sustained a communication system underpinned during the Early Classic by an absolute faith in the need for man to talk continuously with the gods.

Today on the local level we still see remnants of the tribal units that survived after the collapse of the Old Empire. Of these the Zinacanteco *b'iloletik* concept is quite striking. Many of the people probably did abandon the Peten also, in the belief that the land itself had been deserted by the gods, because food and productivity did not match population size. In many key places the land was haunted by Mexican marauders against whom no army could be raised. Over-population in itself would have seriously bothered the Maya psychological orientation and been yet another underlying reason for return to villages and movements of tribal units to new terrain, such as Highland Chiapas.

The final conclusion that the gods could not hear them may have been reached by the Great Ones themselves, sensing their people as great leaders often do, for the abandonment of the centres was accomplished without turmoil, as the archaeology suggests. Each ceremonial centre was quietly foresaken when the last Great One himself, for whom it served as a home, actually died in the normal course of events, his tomb and its temple having already been constructed. If you look archaeologically at the great ceremonial centres, you see that they did not stop all of them at once, but seem to have quietly shut down one after another over the time space of a generation or so, as for each in its turn the last Great One really died forever with no thought to a successor. For each it was *his* centre, so when he died, it died with him. The Maya peoples' faith and trust in their gods did *not* perish, so probably the people were instructed to return to their homeland and their shamans. Perhaps this plan was predestined by the Great Ones amidst impressive ceremony and all the splendour that would slowly, bit by bit, die with them, never to be resurrected.

REFERENCES

Adams, R.E.W. (1963) A polychrome vessel from Altar de Sacrificios, Guatemala. *Archaeology*, 16, 90-2.
Adams, R.E.W. (1971) *The ceramics of Altar de Sacrificios.* Papers of the Peabody Museum of Archaeology and Ethnology, vol. 63, no. 1.
Bernal, I. (1969) *The Olmec World.* Berkeley.
Boggs, S. (1950) 'Olmec' pictographs in the Las Victorias group, Chalchuapa archaeological zone, El Salvador. *Notes on Middle American Archaeology and Ethnology*, 99. Carnegie Institution of Washington.
Coe, M.D. (1966) *The Maya.* New York.
Coe, M.D. (1968) *America's First Civilization: Discovering the Olmec.* New York.
Coe, M.D. (1972) The Maya 'Book of the Dead.' *Discovery*, 7, 79-88. Peabody Museum of Natural History, Yale University.
Coe, W.R. (1965) Tikal: ten years of study of a Maya ruin in the lowlands of Guatemala. *Expedition*, 8, no. 1.
Coe, W.R. (1967) *Tikal: A Handbook of the Ancient Maya Ruins.* Philadelphia.
Dubos, R. (1972) We are all shaped by environment, people and nations. *Smithsonian*, (From *A God Within*, to be published in 1973) vol. 3, no. 4.1.
Ekholm, G.F. et al. (1970) *Ancient Mexico and Central America.* American Museum of Natural History, New York.
Gay, C.T.E. (1967) Oldest paintings of the New World. *Natural History*, 76, no. 4, 28-35.
Gay, C.T.E. (1971) Chalcacingo. *American Rock Paintings and Petroglyphs*, 1. Portland, Oregon.
Gifford, J.C. (1970*a*) The earliest and other intrusive population elements at Barton Ramie may have come from Central America. *Cerámica de Cultura Maya*, 6.
Gifford, J.C. (1970*b*) Residual social consequences of societal stratification in ancient Maya society. *Cerámica de Cultura Maya*, 6.
Gifford, J.C. (1971*a*) Ideas concerning Maya concepts of the future. In *1971 American Anthropological Association Experimental Symposium of Cultural Futurology*, pre-conference volume. Office for Applied Social

Science and the Future, University of Minnesota.

Gifford, J.C. (1971*b*) Elements of abstract thought within ancient Maya 'Old Empire' society. Paper presented at the 70th Annual Meeting of the American Anthropological Association, November 19, 1971, New York.

Gifford, J.C. (in press) A consideration of the southern lowland Maya cultural continuum through two thousand years. In A.V.N. Sarma and E.P. Lanning (eds), *Late Pleistocene and Holocene Climatic Changes and Their Human Ecological Implications: A Symposium Volume.* Westport, Conn.

Jones, J. (1969) The Americas. In *Art of Oceania, Africa, and the Americas from the Museum of Primitive Art.* The Metropolitan Museum of Art, New York.

Lévi-Strauss, C. (1962) Social structure. In S. Tax (ed.), *Anthropology Today: Selections.* Chicago.

Merrin, E.H. (1971) *Works of Art from Pre-Columbian Mexico and Guatemala.* Edward H. Merrin Gallery, New York.

Rathje, W.J. (1969) The daily grind. Paper read at the Annual Meeting, Society for American Archaeology, Mexico City.

Rathje, W.J. (1970) Socio-political implications of lowland Maya burials: methodology and tentative hypotheses. *World Archaeology* 1, no. 3.

Rathje, W.J. (1971) The origin and development of Lowland Classic Maya civilization. *American Antiquity,* 36, no. 3, 275-85.

Sabloff, J.A. and G.R. Willey (1967) The collapse of Maya civilization in the southern lowlands: A consideration of history and process. *Southwestern Journal of Anthropology,* 23, no. 4, 311-36.

Sharer, R.J. and J.C. Gifford (1970) Preclassic ceramics from Chalchuapa, El Salvador, and their relationships with the Maya lowlands. *American Antiquity,* 35, no. 4, 441-62.

Smith, R.E. (1955) *Ceramic Sequence at Uaxactun, Guatemala.* 2 vols. Middle American Research Institute, Publication no. 20, Tulane University, New Orleans.

Smith, R.E. and J.C. Gifford (1966) *Maya Ceramic Varieties, Types and Wares at Uaxactun.* Supplement to *Ceramic Sequence at Uaxactun, Guatemala.* Middle American Research Institute, Publication no. 28.

Tejeda, A. (1955) *Ancient Maya Paintings of Bonampak, Mexico.* Carnegie Institution of Washington, Supplementary Publication no. 46.

Vogt, E.Z. (1964) Some implications of Zinacantan social structure for the study of the Ancient Maya. *Actas y memorias del XXXV congreso internacional de Americanistas,* 1, 307-19.

Vogt, E.Z. (1969) *Zinacantan: A Maya Community in the Highlands of Chiapas.* Cambridge, Mass.

Vogt, E.Z. (1970) *The Zinacantecos of Mexico: A Modern Maya Way of Life.* New York.

Wicke, C.R. (1971) *Olmec: An Early Art Style of Pre-Columbian Mexico.* Tucson, Arizona.

Willey, G.R. (1964) An archaeological frame of reference for Maya culture history. In E.Z. Vogt and A. Ruz Lhuillier (eds), *Desarrollo cultural de los Mayas.* Centro de Estudios Mayas, Universidad Nacional Autónoma de México.

Willey, G.R. (1970) Type descriptions of the ceramics of the Real and Xe complex, Seibal, Peten, Guatemala. In W. R. Bullard, Jr. (ed.), *Monographs and Papers in Maya Archaeology,* part 4, no. 1. Papers of the Peabody Museum of Archaeology and Ethnology, no. 61.

Willey, G.R. and J.C. Gifford (1961) Pottery of the Holmul I style from Barton Ramie. In S.K. Lothrop et al., *Essays in Pre-Columbian Art and Archaeology,* Cambridge, Mass.

Willey, G.R. and P. Phillips (1958) *Method and Theory in American Archaeology.* Chicago.

Willey, G.R. and D.B. Shimkin (1971) The collapse of Classic Maya civilization in the southern lowlands: a symposium summary statement. *Southwestern Journal of Anthropology*, 27, no. 1, 1-18.

Willey, G.R., T.P. Culbert and R.E.W. Adams (1967) Maya lowland ceramics: a report from the 1965 Guatemala City Conference. *American Antiquity*, 32, no. 3, 289-315.

Willey, G.R., W.R. Bullard, Jr., J.B. Glass and J.C. Gifford (1965) *Prehistoric Maya Settlements in the Belize Valley*. Papers of the Peabody Museum of Archaeology and Ethnology, no. 54.

RONALD A. GRENNES - RAVITZ

The Olmec presence at Iglesia Vieja, Morelos

While constructing the Yautepec-Tlaltizapan Morelos highway in 1951, a road-crew razed a group of low mounds containing Preclassic burials, 1.6 km. south of the former Hacienda de Atlihuayan. During the subsequent period of rapacious looting, the Museo Nacional de México aquired the well-known 'Atlihuayan figure' (Bernal 1969: Plate 59), a hollow figurine depicting a kneeling Olmec deity covered with a cape fashioned from what seems to be a stylized jaguar skin. This figure and other fine pieces unearthed at the time, some of them stylistically Olmec, were taken in non-stratigraphical context. With the singular exception of the 'Atlihuayan figure', all of the large ceramic figurines looted from the burial mounds eventually found their way into prestigious private collections. A few tentative test pits were dug in the immediate area (Piña Chan and Lopez Gomez 1952) but there were no serious attempts to excavate the site.

While conducting an archaeological survey of the Yautepec Valley in 1968, I was pleased to note that although sporadic looting in the Atlihuayan area had continued over the years, the primary Preclassic zone of occupation, which I have called Iglesia Vieja, situated on the sloping terrace east of the road, was relatively undisturbed. It was decided to make an intensive stratigraphical study of Iglesia Vieja with the purpose of establishing the relative place of the highland Olmec within the Morelos sequence.

During the 1969-70 field seasons, in the El Terror phase, which marks the Early and Middle Preclassic occupations of Iglesia Vieja, a multi-component ceramic assemblage showing a marked affinity to the Tlatilco burials was encountered. One of the components of this assemblage is Olmec and is characterized by solid and hollow baby-faced figurines, cylindrical roller stamps with paw-wing motif, kaolin ware, white-rimmed black ware, excised black ware, and flat-bottomed cylindrical *vasos* decorated with such motifs as the St Andrews cross, the U element, and zoned cross-hatching.

The second component is characterized by a preponderance of D and K series figurines, especially D2, almost to the exclusion of other types, brown *cajetes* decorated with exterior incising in triangular zoned panels often rubbed with specular haematite, small clay masks, tripod vessels with long solid supports, and stem stamps in the shape of the human foot. The D figurines, incised *cajetes,* and stem stamps from Gualupita, the Tlatilco burials, Tlapacoya, and the El Terror Phase of Iglesia Vieja are typologically identical. Similarities between individual pieces from these four sites are so pronounced that they are virtually interchangeable.

The enigmatic nature of the Tlatilco burials, in which at least three components are present, is well known. One is Olmec and is mirrored in the material excavated at Iglesia Vieja. Another is related to the later 'Zacatenco' communities. From the El Terror evidence, it is obvious that the third component found in the Tlatilco burials, the previously unidentifiable *tertium quid,* is a unit of Morelos origin closely related to the initial phase of Iglesia Vieja.

The rare and fortunate discovery of an extant Olmec burial at Iglesia Vieja presents a unique opportunity for dating the Olmec presence in the central highlands. The radiocarbon date for the burial is especially significant considering that it comes directly from specific burial material in which incontestable Olmec elements are present, rather than from random samples of material gathered at arbitrary levels. Most important, it establishes a minimal date for the Olmec presence in the central highlands.

The burial was found in a matrix of soil permeated by a yellowish crust of human skeletal remnants in an extremely poor state of preservation, the only readily identifiable parts of the skeleton being some mandible fragments, an incisor and two molars, parts of the lumbar vertebrae, a tibia, and some metatarsus. The interred was in a supine position, extended, with head oriented northwest. The rectangular gravepit, which measured 1.73 m. by 0.78 m., had been dug to a depth of 1.33 m. and lined with a layer of very fine, grey, volcanic sand approximately 8 cm. thick which served as a pallet for the body. A flat-bottomed, differentially fired, white-rimmed black plate and an effigy whistle in the form of a bird with head crest were found at the feet. The humic acid in the soil had destroyed any traces of slip or design on the whistle.

A hollow Olmec head was encountered at 1.04 m. in a position directly above the facial plane of the interred. The helmet and face were found as two separate pieces, in a prone position, 12 cm. apart. A considerable number of very small fragments from the back of the head and shoulders of the figurine were found with the face and helmet. Unfortunately, the fragments were so small in size, and their fracture lines such, that they could not be utilized in a reconstruction. No evidence of the torso of the figurine was found.

Among the head and shoulder fragments, remnants of a highly polished haematite mirror were found. The largest piece measures 2.4 x 1.8 cm. and is perforated. It is probable that the mirror was

Figure 1 Olmec burial figurine dated 1190 B.C. ± 120.

placed around the neck of the figurine, in the manner of those from Tlatilco (Porter 1953: Plate 4*b*) and La Venta (Drucker, Heizer and Squier 1959: Plate 461), and was broken at the same time as the figurine.

Solid charcoal scraped from the inside rim of the white-rimmed black funerary plate resulted in a radiocarbon date of 1190 B.C. ± 120 based on the Libby half-life of 5570 years for C14, and referenced to the year A.D. 1950 (Geochron Laboratories Inc., Cambridge, Mass., GX-1678).

In Trench R, adjacent to the burial, at 1.23 m., a ceremonial cache covered by large pieces of black excised pottery was encountered. The cache contained five figurine heads, two of them of the Olmec baby-face type, and three D2, a stem stamp with dragon-serpent motif, and a large green partially worked rhyolitic stone. It is probable that the burial and the cache were related.

The El Terror phase

The following sequence for the El Terror phase of Iglesia Vieja, spanning the Early and part of the Middle Preclassic occupation of the site, is based on the 53 stratigraphic pits and trenches dug during the 1969 and 1970 field seasons, and emphasizes figurine typology, which since Vaillant's initial excavations in the Basin of Mexico has been extensively utilized as a chronological and cultural index. I have adopted to a great extent the nomenclature found in the recent study of Preclassic figurine types by Rosa Reyna de Covarrubias, whose revision and amplification of the original Vaillant classification is based on the analysis of more than 15,000 Preclassic figurines, hundreds of which were previously unpublished. While it is obvious that no system can successfully deal with the morphological nuances and subtle gradations of style which inevitably leads to the creation of never-ending figurine subtypes and equivocal classification, the approach taken by Reyna de Covarrubias, stressing the larger taxonomical unit of the tradition, is valid and extremely useful.

> El Zarco subphase 1200-850 B.C.   ⎰   El Terror phase
> La Manuela subphase 1400-1200 B.C. ⎱   1400-850 B.C.

The deepest stratum of the La Manuela subphase, marking the initial occupation of Iglesia Vieja, is dominated by the presence of female D2 figurines with heads that are usually excessively large in proportion to bodies modelled with bulbous thighs, wide hips, flaring buttocks, and occasionally exhibiting an advanced state of pregnancy. Also present are D3 figurines, a larger, hollow variant of the D2, sometimes showing fading vestiges of a red slip, and the type of K figurine which MacNeish, Peterson and Flannery (1970: Fig. 14, 15) call Spherical and Flat-Punched Feature Heads and assign to the Early Ajalpan phase of Tehuacan (1500-1100 B.C.). Brown *cajetes* decorated with exterior incising in triangular zoned panels identical to those found at Tlatilco (Porter 1953: Plate 11D), Gualupita (Vaillant and Vaillant 1936), and in the Roche Collection from Tlapacoya, comprise the most common service ware, while large, thick-walled ochre ollas were utilized for storage. Brown and red-on-brown globular bottles decorated with vertical incising shading into light gadrooning are present both in the midden debris and as burial offerings, frequently accompanied by D2 figurines. Animal effigy whistles, cylindrical roller stamps with geometric motifs, and stem stamps, most commonly in the shape of the human foot, occur in the La Manuela strata.

By 1200 B.C., this ceramic complex, the oldest known in Morelos, is modified by the appearance of the Olmec elements previously cited. This perceptible Olmec ingression, *c.* 1200 B.C., signals the beginning of the El Zarco subphase during which two new figurine types, the C9 Fino and D1, appear, and are found with relative frequency by middle El Zarco, which is marked by a demographic surge and subsequent expansion of the site to the southeast. The C figurine tradition of the Basin and corresponding ceramic wares are extremely scarce throughout the El Terror phase, with the exception of the terminal part of El Zarco, when the only significant intrusion of Basin ceramics occurs. The existence of D1 and D2 figurines in early Zacatenco (Vaillant 1930) and El Arbolillo (Vaillant 1935) strata most probably reflects this terminal El Zarco temporal span.

Although the Olmec presence during the whole of El Zarco is clearly evident, fully 92 percent of the identifiable figurine fragments and vessel rims excavated within this subphase belong to the pre-Olmec La Manuela unit which I will refer to as the Morelos component of the El Zarco ceramic assemblage. The term Morelos does not imply place of origin, but merely indicates the geographical area of greatest concentration during the Early and Middle Preclassic. The D2 figurine, the hallmark of the Morelos component, fully developed from the inception of La Manuela, and continuing as the dominant feature of Iglesia Vieja through the end of El Zarco, exhibits no immediately perceptible stylistic evolution from something more archaic in Morelos-Puebla, nor for that matter from known figurine types from other areas in the same temporal range. The K series, consistently encountered with the D2 in Morelos as well as in the Basin, although much less frequent proportionally, seems to be focused in an area extending from the Rio Cuautla-Chinameca south into Guerrero.

It is evident that El Zarco is part of a regional phase which is widely distributed temporally and spacially over the Basin of Mexico, much of Morelos, western Puebla, and portions of eastern Guerrero, an area circumscribed by Sander's (1968) Central Mexican Symbiotic Region (CMSR). Within the boundaries roughly conforming to the CMSR, c.1200-900 B.C., a ceramic assemblage very similar to the Morelos and Olmec components of El Zarco has been found in a very early context at sites such as Tlatilco, Tlapacoya, Gualupita, Las Bocas, Oaxtepec and many lesser known places, underscoring the essential unity and interdependence of the microgeographical areas within the CMSR, even in Early Preclassic times, ranging from the Tierra Fria of the Basin of Mexico to the Tierra Caliente of the Rio Balsas Depression.

The Olmec component of this assemblage, thought to reflect the grandeur and sophistication of the great ceremonial centres of the Gulf Coast heartland, has been attributed by some as the bearer of civilization to the nether regions of much of Mesoamerica, including the CMSR, by the transmission of superior heartland culture through a resident elite. However, many traits previously accepted as characteristically Olmec, such as roller stamps, hollow figurines, rocker-stamping, and metallic mirrors, are already present in the La Manuela pre-Olmec occupational refuse. Bernal (1969) ascribes the invention of the hollow ceramic figurine to Olmec ingenuity, yet the hollow D3 clearly preceeds the Olmec baby-face variety in the El Terror statigraphy and is encountered in the lower La Manuela deposits along with roller stamps, another alleged Olmec import, rocker-stamped sherds, and the depiction of concave mirrors hanging from the necks of D2 figurines. The later appearance of roller stamps with paw-wing motif, and of hollow baby-face figurines, seems primarily to reflect the accommodation of Olmec iconography to existing Morelos ceramic types. This intrusive Olmec iconography, which ushers in the beginning of El Zarco, does not replace the older geometrical designs on roller stamps, nor does it curtail the production of the D2, D3, and K figurines, which continue to be manufactured in increasing numbers. Instead, the new Olmec motifs are integrated into the highly sophisticated regional ceramic tradition, where, although readily visible, they remain relatively scarce.

The belief in the quintessential nature of the Olmec in the CMSR is fallacious. Within the El Zarco subphase of El Terror, there is no suggestion of status attached to the Olmec material as both units, Morelos and Olmec, are encountered in the same midden debris, as well as together in burials, the only real distinction being the overwhelming quantitative predominance of the Morelos component represented by the D and K series figurines and associated ceramics. Qualitatively, there is no evidence to suggest that the Olmec material is the product of an aristocratic sub-culture whether military, civil, or sacerdotal, and thus the proportional scarcity of Olmec ceramics during El Zarco should not be interpreted as an indication of exclusiveness, nor of elitism, but more correctly underscores the secondary nature of this component within the assemblage. Indeed, most of the opulent burial material from Tlatilco that originally suggested intense social stratification to Miguel Covarrubias (1957) is in the final analysis decidedly non-Olmec, belonging instead to the Morelos unit. If we equate Olmec with San Lorenzo and La Venta-like material, and then take away all of the Morelos and later Zacatenco ceramic material from Tlatilco, only an infinitesimal part of the burial furniture can be classified as Olmec. Consequently, it would be a gross distortion to continue to refer to Tlatilco as an 'Olmec' or 'Olmecoid' site, which carries the stigma of tendentious phraseology that incorrectly implies the existence of a pan-Mesoamerican state under the aegis of the Gulf Coast Olmec. Instead, the term 'D Assemblage' will be used to define the admixture of Morelos and Olmec components present in the El Zarco strata and widely distributed over the CMSR, *c.*1200-900 B.C., to accentuate the true essential character of that multi-component assemblage which has as its salient cultural diagnostic the ubiquitous D2 and closely related figurines, emphasizing the condition to which all available evidence overwhelmingly points, that within the D Assemblage the Morelos unit is regional and pre-eminent while the Olmec is intrusive and demonstrably secondary.

A seriation of Tlatilco figurines in the storerooms of the Museo Nacional de Antropología, and those from the Roche Collection in the Universidad Nacional Autónoma de México, based on the vertical stratigraphy of El Terror, indicates that the Morelos component of the D Assemblage was the predominant feature at both of these sites. The Tlatilco burials date from c.1300-850 B.C., and as previously cited, consist of three components, of which the Morelos, running the entire time span, is overwhelmingly represented. In the compilation of the contents of 120 Temporada II burials made by Luis Covarrubias, only 16 of the graves contain offerings which are indisputably Olmec, and in almost every case they are accompanied by Morelos material, a common pattern at Iglesia Vieja also. The burials with the most elaborate funerary material, nos. 42, 60, 123, 160, 161, 162, are characterized almost exclusively by the presence of D figurines and associated vessels, and date from approximately 1100-950 B.C.

A very large quantity of early D2 and K figurines, as well as brown cajetes with the distinctive incised triangular panels and most of the other elements common in the La Manuela strata, have been recovered from Tlapacoya both before and after the destruction of that site by bulldozers during the construction of the Puebla highway and rather conclusively indicate a substantial pre-Ayotla occupation. This contradicts the contention (Tolstoy and Paradis 1970) that Ayotla, most of which equates with middle El Zarco, is the earliest ceramic complex in the Basin, which is characterized as being essentially a vacuum prior to the Olmec arrival. The failure to isolate the individual components of the D Assemblage has led to the erroneous assertion that the Ayotla subphase is essentially Olmec, which it is not.

Apart from Tlatilco and Tlapacoya, there are several other sites in the Basin which are probably pre-Ayotla, the most noteworthy being Peña Pobre, adjacent to Cuicuilco, where in 1965, early La Manuela D2 and K figurines were found in the lowest levels of several stratigraphic shafts sunk by I.N.A.H. students.

The early D2, D3 and K figurines (R. de Covarrubias 1971: 265), along with human foot stamps, animal effigy whistles, and fluted red-on-brown bottles recovered at La Bocas, Puebla, indicate the participation of this site in the same early regional culture which characterized much of Tlatilco and Tlapacoya, early Gualupita and the El Terror Phase of Iglesia Vieja.

The D2 figurine, probably the oldest of the D series, has been viewed by some as an Olmec manifestation; however, the stratigraphy of El Terror clearly demonstrates that the D2 was being produced in Morelos prior to the Olmec intrusion into the CMSR, and before the beginning of the San Lorenzo heartland phase. In addition, D2 figurines are conspicuously absent from heartland sites during the Early and Middle Preclassic and their origin can hardly be attributed to a region in which they are non-existent. What Weiant (1943: Plates 20-21) calls the 'Morelos Type' at Tres Zapotes, is basically the C9 Fino which Reyna de Covarrubias attributes to the fusion of the Morelos and Olmec traditions. This thesis, based on stylistic analysis, is supported by the stratigraphy of El Terror, in which the C9 Fino occurs for the first time in the middle El Zarco deposits.

Extensive, long-term excavations at major heartland sites like Tres Zapotes, La Venta, and San Lorenzo have established the San Lorenzo phase (Coe, Diehl and Stuiver 1967), 1150-900 B.C., corresponding to Bernal's (1970) Olmec II, as the earliest discernible, characteristically Olmec phase on the Gulf Coast, and inexplicably it appears full-blown without antecedents (Coe 1969). Recent radiocarbon dates from a number of sites in the CMSR have illuminated the existence of a well-defined Olmec presence in that area which is as old as or older than the first manifestations of the San Lorenzo phase, and raises the question of the validity of the basal premise of the 'Colonial Olmec' theory which explains the existence of the Olmec component in the CMSR in terms of imperialistic egress from the heartland during the apogee of San Lorenzo and La Venta.

Recent radiocarbon dates from three CMSR sites include:

Ayotla (Tlapacoya)	1070 B.C. ± 80	(Tolstoy and Paradis 1970)
Burial 74 (Tlatilco)	1230 B.C. ± 120	(Tolstoy and Paradis 1970)
Burial 14 (Iglesia Vieja)	1190 B.C. ± 120	(Grennes-Ravitz)

The five radiocarbon dates establishing the San Lorenzo Phase (Coe, Diehl and Stuiver 1967) are:

Y-1797	1060 B.C. ± 80
Y-1798	1050 B.C. ± 140
Y-1800	1100 B.C. ± 100
Y-1801	1140 B.C. ± 80
Y-1802	920 B.C. ± 140

There appear to have been two distinct periods of Olmec diffusion into the CMSR. The first took place, *c.*1200 B.C., when Olmec elements, primarily distinctive design motifs and a new figurine type, appear for the first time in many Mesoamerican areas, introduced from an as yet unknown region. An interpretation of the ideology symbolized in this iconography is at best speculative, but it seems probable that in the CMSR the jaguar-epicene deity was absorbed into the regional pantheon to become one of several already existing tutelary deities in the same manner that later alien gods were accommodated into the highly syncretic religions of the Postclassic period. Contemporaneously, in Veracruz-Tabasco, the religious configuration represented by Olmec iconographic elements became the 'primary impetus' (Coe 1969) for the construction and maintenance of the great ceremonial centres of the heartland which became the focus of Olmec civilization where the jaguar cult attained entelechy. It follows that a certain degree of underlying ideological unity was present in these two regions during this period, but due to diverse sociocultural patterns and environmental factors, there also existed a very pronounced disparity in terms of acceptance, implementation, and emphasis given to the new religious stimulus.

The initial widespread diffusion of Olmec elements was followed later by a second period which corresponds to the florescence of San Lorenzo and La Venta. Much of the Olmec presence attributable to this second stage of diffusion into the CMSR can perhaps best be explained in terms of a pilgrimage-market model which is congruent with the ceremonial nature of both San Lorenzo and La Venta. The first period of diffusion, rather than the second, seems to have been primarily responsible for the distinct aura of unity found in diverse areas of Mesoamerica during the Early Preclassic.

The Olmec presence is protean in nature and varies greatly in degree of emphasis and importance according to region. The reaction to the nexus of Olmec iconography, *c.* 1200 B.C., in many parts of Mesoamerica, has led some to endow the Gulf Coast Olmec with a kind of procrustean influence, based on the assumption that an essential structural matrix of culture was first developed in the heartland and diffused to regions like the CMSR, where it became the indispensible genesis for the development of the following Classic period. The metaphorical usage of the terms 'Colonial Olmec' and 'Olmecoid' to connote civilization is clear, and seems to be a recurrence of the 'Mother of Civilization' syndrome succinctly alluded to by Proskouriakoff (1967), in which the significance of regional development and interaction is overlooked in favour of a more facile view of civilization as rising and moving out from a single focus, in this case Veracruz-Tabasco, and Olmec has become the new metaphor, replacing Maya. This thesis is untenable in the light of recent evidence, and it overstates the importance of Olmec, especially in the CMSR where radical permutations attributed to coercive heartland ingress are illusory, and where Olmec influence on the ontogeny of Preclassic regional culture, which culminates in the emergence of Teotihuacan, is decidedly minimal.

Acknowledgments

The excavation of Iglesia Vieja, Morelos was authorized by the I.N.A.H. and supported by the Virginia Military Institute Foundation through the efforts of General James Morgan and Colonel Albert L. Lancaster. The laboratory analysis of Iglesia Vieja burial material was done by Dr Samuel Treves, Chairman, Department of Geology, University of Nebraska, and the photography by Lois Pierce, Department of Art History, University of Nebraska. I would like to thank cadet John D. Biggs for his valuable assistance during the difficult 1970 field season.

REFERENCES

Bernal, I (1969) *The Olmec World.* Berkeley.

Coe, M.D. (1965) *The Jaguar's Children.* Museum of Primitive Art, New York.

Coe, M.D. (1969) *The Archaeological Sequence at San Lorenzo Tenochtitlan, Veracruz, Mexico.* Paper read at annual meeting of the Society for American Archaeology, Milwaukee.

Coe, M., R.A. Diehl and M. Stuiver (1967) Olmec Civilization, Veracruz, Mexico: dating of the San Lorenzo phase. *Science,* 155, no. 3768, 1399-401.

Covarrubias, M. (1957) *Indian Art of Mexico and Central America.* New York.

Covarrubias, R.M. Reyna de (1971) *Las figurillas preclasiscas.* Tesis Profesional, Instituto Nacional de Antropología e Historia, Mexico.

Drucker, P., R.F. Heizer, and R.J. Squier (1959) *Excavations at La Venta, Tabasco, 1955.* Bureau of American Ethnology, Washington, Bulletin no. 170.

MacNeish, R., F. Peterson, and K.V. Flannery (1970) *The Prehistory of the Tehuacan Valley.* Vol. 3, *Ceramics.* Austin, Texas.

Noguera, E. (1965) *La cerámica arqueológica de Mesoamerica.* Instituto de Investigaciones Históricas, U.N.A.M., Mexico.

Piña Chan, R. (1955) *Las culturas preclásicas de la cuenca de Mexico.* Fondo de Cultural Económica, México.

Piña Chan, R., and V. López Gomez (1952) Excavaciones en Atlihuayan, Morelos. *Tlatcani,* 1, no. 1.

Piña Chan, R., and L. Covarrubias (1964) *El pueblo del jaguar.* Museo Nacional de Antropologia, Mexico.

Porter, M. (1953) *Tlatilco and the Preclassic Cultures of the New World.* Viking Fund Publications in Anthropology, no. 19, New York.

Proskouriakoff, T. (1968) Olmec and Maya art: problems of their stylistic relations. In E.P. Benson (ed.), *Dumbarton Oaks Conference on the Olmec,* 119-30. Washington.

Sanders, W.T. and B.J. Price, (1948) *Mesoamerica: The Evolution of a Civilization.* New York.

Tolstoy, P. and L.I. Paradis (1970) Early and Middle Preclassic cultures in the Valley of Mexico. *Science,* 167.

Vaillant, G. (1930) *Excavations at Zacatenco.* Anthropological Papers of the American Museum of Natural History, 32, no. 1.

Vaillant, G. (1935) *Excavations at El Arbolillo.* Anthropological Papers of the American Museum of Natural History, 35, no. 2.

Vaillant, G. and S. Vaillant (1934) *Excavations at Gualupita.* Anthropological Papers of the American Museum of Natural History, 35, no. 1.

Weiant, C.W. (1943) *An introduction to the ceramics of Tres Zapotes, Veracruz, Mexico.* Smithsonian Institution, Bureau of American Ethnology, Bulletin no. 139.

Wicke, C. (1969) *Olmec: An Early Art Style of Precolumbian Mexico.* Tucson, Arizona.

DAVID C. GROVE

The Highland Olmec manifestation: a consideration of what it is and isn't

Because the Early and Middle Formative archaeological manifestation of Mesoamerica's Gulf Coast, Olmec culture, seems to represent the beginnings of complex culture in Mesoamerica, Olmec studies today draw an unusual amount of archaeological interest. Recent investigations in the Gulf Coast region (Coe 1968, 1970; Coe, Diehl, and Stuiver 1967; Heizer 1968; Heizer, Drucker and Graham 1968; Heizer, Graham and Napton 1968; Sisson 1970) have done much to clarify the nature of the Formative period in that region and have presented new insights into the antiquity, nature, and diversity of the archaeological culture we call Olmec. There seems little doubt, whatever the ultimate origins of Olmec culture, that the tropical lowlands of Veracruz and Tabasco represent the heartland of Olmec culture; therefore in this paper I shall utilize the term Olmec to refer specifically to this Gulf Coast archaeological culture. Nevertheless, artifacts and art identified as within the Olmec style are not restricted to ceremonial centres within this tropical riverine eco- logical setting, but are found in far different geographical and ecological settings throughout Mesoamerica, from the mountainous Pacific slopes of Guerrero to the piedmont zone of El Salvador. Sites yielding artifacts within the Olmec style seem particularly abundant in the central Mexican states of Morelos, Guerrero, Mexico, Puebla, and the Federal District, where the archaeological manifestation has received the term 'highland Olmec'. In fact, in sheer percentages, there are more Olmec style artifacts known from this highland region than from the Gulf Coast, although unfortunately the large majority of pieces are from illicit excavations, thus yielding little in the way of archaeological data. The quantity of Olmec style artifacts in the highlands has led some persons to suggest that Olmec origins may actually lie in this highland context (Covarrubias 1957: 76; Piña Chan 1955a: 26-7, 1955b: 106-7). Recent non-archaeological dis- coveries of apparently Formative period figurines from the region of Xochipala, Guerrero (Gay 1972b) have again raised the suggestion of Olmec origins from the highlands. This highland origin hypothesis is not however in agreement with the archaeological data from the Gulf Coast (Coe 1970; Grove n.d., *a*), but still there remains some confusion among archaeologists as to just what 'highland Olmec' is or isn't, and so in the pages which follow I would like to present my analysis of the situation, utilizing recent data gathered primarily from my excavations since 1966 at a number of Formative period, 'highland Olmec' sites in Morelos. These data I believe are applicable to central Mexico as a whole.

Several major points must be considered in our discussion of the relationship between Gulf Coast Olmec culture and the Formative period cultures of highland central Mexico. The first of these points is chronology. In general, the Olmec manifestation in Mesoamerica has until recently been considered a Middle Formative archaeological horizon, thus suggesting contemporaniety among major Olmec centres. For the Gulf Coast at least this viewpoint is no longer held, for Coe's excavations at San Lorenzo indicate a greater time depth to Olmec culture there than previously suspected (Coe 1970; Coe, Diehl and Stuiver 1967). There now appears to be an Early Formative Olmec culture represented by sites such as San Lorenzo, and a Middle Formative Olmec culture represented by sites such as La Venta (e.g., Berger, Graham and Heizer 1967). Thus we are considering a temporal span of c.700 years, or c.1300-600 B.C. (although based upon radiocarbon dates, these dates are not corrected for bristlecone pine correlations, etc.), and in viewing the great differences between the cultural assemblages of San Lorenzo and La Venta, it becomes obvious that in the Gulf Coast we are viewing a constantly evolving cultural tradition. This means that in areas outside of the Gulf Coast, where Olmec style artifacts are present, they can no longer be viewed as simply evidence of an Olmec archaeological horizon, for obviously just as Olmec culture changes through time on the Gulf Coast, so too will its external influences and manifestations undergo change. The chronology of central Mexico's Formative and the position and nature of Olmec manifestations within this framework must be properly understood in order to understand further the nature of 'highland Olmec'.

A second point to consider is the cultural nature of 'highland Olmec'. Olmec style artifacts occur in quantity in the highlands, or so a review of the literature would imply. The 'Olmecness' of the 'highland Olmec' manifestation is seldom seriously questioned, however, and few would dispute the similarity between a white-slipped hollow baby-face figure from Tlapacoya when compared to another with a provenance from the Gulf Coast. Nevertheless, that is but one example from a rather large inventory of 'highland Olmec' artifacts, and I for one am skeptical over how much of 'highland Olmec' is truly representative in any way of Gulf Coast influences or relationships. I further believe that there has been an overreaction to the identification of some Olmec style artifacts in the highlands with a subsequent trend toward identifying many non-Olmec artifacts as 'highland Olmec', a trend which has distorted and biased our archaeological perspective. A basic contention I would like to explore in this paper is that much of 'highland Olmec' is not Olmec at all, even when linguistic modifiers such as 'Colonial Olmec' or 'Olmecoid' are added (e.g., Bernal 1969: 12). The problem basically resolves to this: what attributes in an artifact make it Olmec? Is it an artifact such as a figurine, vessel, or carved jade, which includes design motifs common also in the art of Gulf Coast sites? Is there any implication in the term 'highland Olmec' of contact with or manufacture of an artifact by a person from the Gulf Coast (e.g. 'Colonial Olmec', Bernal 1969: 12)? Or does a 'highland Olmec' artifact include one which although lacking specific identifying attributes was found at a highland site yielding other artifacts with Olmec stylistic attributes (what I wish to term, 'Olmec by association')? Perhaps the answers to these questions appear obvious, but apparently it is not as obvious as one might think. While I believe that the majority of archaeologists today primarily use various stylistic attributes as criteria for identifying Olmec manifestations outside the Gulf Coast heartland, the other criteria have also been implied or utilized in the literature, and will be discussed below.

Unquestionably the most difficult point to discuss in this paper will be cultural process, due unfortunately to our relative lack of archaeological knowledge at present. Cultural processes must be considered not only in analysing the diffusion of the Olmec manifestation, but also in analysing the contributions of 'Olmec influences' to highland Formative cultures including evolutionary changes within those cultures, as well as possible highland contributions to Gulf Coast culture.

Chronology

In the literature and text books it is the rule rather than the exception to find the 'highland Olmec' manifestation (and/or Tlatilco culture — Tlatilco generally being considered as a major 'highland Olmec' site) considered as contemporaneous with the Middle Formative Zacatenco culture. Thus Olmec influences in the highlands are considered as a distinct entity of relatively limited temporal duration. Sites in the central highlands yielding stylistically Olmec materials such as Las Bocas, Tlatilco, and Chalcatzingo, to name only a few, are thus considered as coeval. The implications of this were discussed by Covarrubias (1957: 30-3) who suggested that the sophisticated Olmec-Tlatilco culture was living side by side with the peasant Zacatenco culture in the Valley of Mexico. However, as previously noted, Gulf Coast Olmec culture represents an evolving archaeological tradition with many distinctive changes in the archaeological record through time. The question to be considered is therefore whether such an evolving Olmec tradition exists or at least is reflected in the highlands, or whether Olmec influences in the highlands are present only once, for a short duration?

A recent article by Tolstoy and Paradis (1970) has done much to clarify the time depth to Olmec influences in the highlands. Their investigations at Tlapacoya in the Valley of Mexico place the Olmec manifestation at that site within their Early Formative Ixtapaluca phase, *c.*1250-950 B.C. The Ixtapaluca phase correlates in time with San Lorenzo on the Gulf Coast and there are stylistic similarities between San Lorenzo phase ceramics and those of the Ixtapaluca phase at Tlapacoya. It should be noted that the Ixtapaluca phase occurs before the Zacatenco phase. In their article (1970: 349) they find it difficult to place Tlatilco ceramics within their chronological framework.

Sites identical to Tlatilco in artifact content (and obviously contemporaneous) are quite abundant throughout the Valley of Mexico, Morelos, western Puebla, and northeast Guerrero, and I believe that for the sake of discussion we can speak of a common 'Tlatilco culture' in this region. It is this Tlatilco culture which includes many Olmec style artifacts. The chronological placement of this Tlatilco culture in Morelos is clear, for my excavations have yielded good stratigraphic records and associated radiocarbon dates (Grove n.d., *b*). There is little doubt that the Tlatilco culture in the highlands is Early Formative and occurs generally within the Valley of Mexico's Ixtapaluca phase, (c.1350-900 B.C. in Morelos).

Within the Morelos Early Formative I have presently defined two phases (Grove n.d., *b*: 41-2). The earliest, the La Juana phase, I tentatively date at *c.*1350-1250 B.C. This phase, which predates Tolstoy and Paradis's Ayotla subphase (of the Ixtapaluca phase), is characterized primarily by brown ware globular bottles with wide line incision and flaring-walled flat-bottomed bowls with slightly bolstered or everted rims. Zoned rocker stamping, some differentially fired grey wares, roller seals, and D2 figurines also occur.

Our second phase, the San Pablo phase, I have subdivided into San Pablo A and B subphases (see Fig. 1) on the basis of several important changes in the ceramics and lithics of the San Pablo phase. The San Pablo A phase, tentatively dated 1250-1050 B.C. is marked by the appearance of red-slipped ceramics (often specular red slip) in our stratigraphic sample. Three types of red-slipped vessels occur: flat-bottomed flaring-walled bowls with red-slipped interiors, slightly incurved rim bowls with the red rims bordered by an incised line paralleling the rim, and Red-on-Brown bottles. These latter, in which the red-slipped areas are often delimited by incision, are common as burial furniture at Tlatilco sites throughout central Mexico. D2 figurines continue and hollow red-slipped figures appear. The San Pablo B subphase, *c.*1050-900 B.C., is simply a continuation of San

Pablo A, but is distinguished by a marked increase in cylindrical bowls, kaolin wares, Olmec stylistic attributes (for example, 'carved wares', see Coe 1970: 26), and the appearance of unusual Red-on-Brown vessel forms including belted bottles and stirrup-spout bottles (Grove 1970a: 67-8). Tolstoy (personal communication) feels that these latter vessel forms may actually appear later in the sequence than the strongly Olmec style ceramics, which would tend to support an observation I made in 1970 (1970a: 71; chronologies in the article are now revised in this paper and in several previous publications) but is not strongly apparent in our Morelos stratigraphic sequence, which can neither confirm or deny such placements. One further interesting feature of the San Pablo B subphase is that at the site from which the majority of our stratigraphic data is gathered, San Pablo and Nexpa, obsidian blades do not occur in the stratigraphic sequence until this subphase. In our stratigraphic records, only obsidian chips occur in the La Juana phase and San Pablo A subphase samples.

At both San Pablo and Nexpa, the levels immediately overlying the San Pablo B subphase levels contain white wares decorated with the incised double-line-break on the rim. Ceramics of this nature were absent throughout the La Juana and San Pablo phases. This aids in dating these phases as Early Formative, for the double-line-break is commonly associated with the Middle Formative, although it begins in the Valley of Mexico, in small quantities in the Justo subphase (Tolstoy and Paradis 1970: 347; Tolstoy: personal communication).

The Morelos data offer substantive data for the chronological placement of Tlatilco within the highland Mexican Early Formative, demonstrating that Tlatilco predates rather than being contemporaneous with the far more peasant-like Zacatenco culture. Our San Pablo B subphase ceramics appear to correlate well with the Ayotla subphase of the Valley of Mexico, while the La Juana and San Pablo A subphase appear to predate the Ayotla. Exact correlations between the Tlapacoya and Morelos Early Formative data are difficult to make for apparently (on the basis of available data) the Red-on-Brown ceramics common at Early Formative highland sites are uncommon at Tlapacoya.

A question remains to be answered. Does the presence of differential firing, zoned rocker stamping, and roller seals in the La Juana phase in Morelos represent Olmec influences? Are these attributes to be considered as Olmec or simply as derived from a general source in southern Mesoamerica? The 1350 B.C. date for the beginning of the La Juana phase, if correct, would make this highland phase contemporaneous with the Bajio phase at San Lorenzo, a phase which Coe (1970: 22-4) does not identify as Olmec culturally. It must be noted, in a discussion of 'origins', that the Gulf Coast archaeological material seems to be far more strongly in the evolutionary line to Gulf Coast Olmec than any of the early ceramics in the highlands (see Grove n.d., a: 15-19).

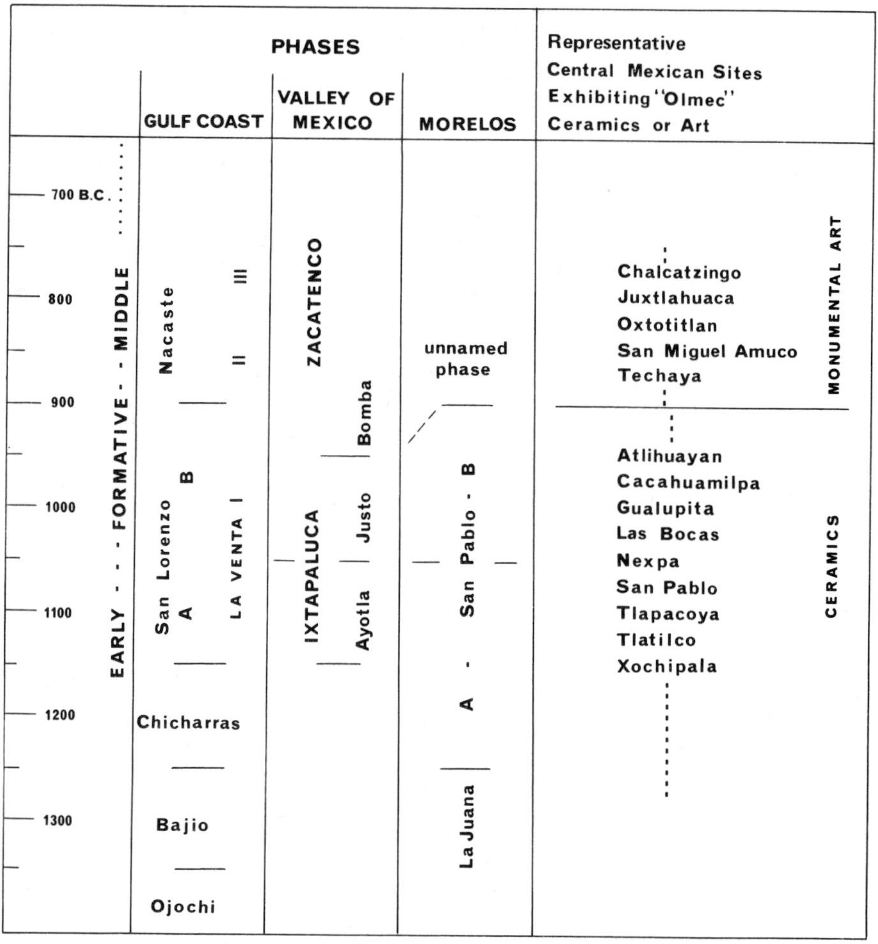

	PHASES			Representative Central Mexican Sites Exhibiting "Olmec" Ceramics or Art
	GULF COAST	VALLEY OF MEXICO	MORELOS	

Chronological chart (left axis: 700 B.C., 800, 900, 1000, 1100, 1200, 1300; left margin label: EARLY - - FORMATIVE - - MIDDLE)

Date	Gulf Coast	La Venta	Valley of Mexico	Morelos	Central Mexican Sites
700 B.C.			ZACATENCO		
800	Nacaste	III / II		unnamed phase	Chalcatzingo, Juxtlahuaca, Oxtotitlan, San Miguel Amuco, Techaya (MONUMENTAL ART)
900			Bomba		
1000	San Lorenzo B	LA VENTA I	IXTAPALUCA — Justo	San Pablo - B	Atlihuayan, Cacahuamilpa, Gualupita, Las Bocas, Nexpa, San Pablo, Tlapacoya, Tlatilco, Xochipala (CERAMICS)
1100	San Lorenzo A		Ayotla	San Pablo - A	
1200	Chicharras				
1300	Bajio			La Juana	
	Ojochi				

Figure 1 Chronological chart for the Early and Middle Formative.

By 1250 B.C. new ceramic types appear in the highland sequence: Red-on-Brown bottles, appearing primarily as burial furniture rather than as utilitarian ceramics (the same context can be said to be true of Olmec style ceramics). In complexity the Red-on-Brown bottles reach a peak apparently c. 1000 B.C. with a great diversity of bottle forms, many of which appear to represent skeuomorphs of bottle gourd containers (Grove n.d., *a*: 35). It is at this same approximate time that Olmec style ceramics reach their peak (if by Olmec we refer to kaolin ceramics and vessels decorated with design motifs generally attributable to Olmec culture). It is important to note that 'highland Olmec' ceramics are similar to Early Formative Gulf Coast ceramics primarily in decorative attributes rather than in vessel form. A vessel form common in the Gulf Coast Early Formative, the tecomate, is quite rare in highland assemblages.

In the highlands, the majority of sites identified as 'highland Olmec' (because they yield Olmec style ceramics) can be dated as Early Formative and are probably primarily contemporaneous to the Ayotla and San Pablo phase. If Olmec influences truly did penetrate the highlands from the Gulf Coast in the Early Formative, the influences must then have derived from Early Formative centres such as San Lorenzo.

As the reader will note, several sites considered as 'highland Olmec', such as Chalcatzingo, Oxtotitlan, and Juxtlahuaca, are omitted from the list of Early Formative highland sites. It will also occur to the reader that these sites are identified as Olmec not through their ceramic inventory but because they are noted for their monumental art in the Olmec style. Where do these sites belong chronologically? I have noted on several occasions (1968a: 490; 1970b: 33) that the monumental art at these sites appears to have the closest stylistic affinities with the monumental art of La Venta. There are a number of important stylistic differences between the monumental art of La Venta and San Lorenzo, as would be suspected of an evolving cultural tradition. Do highland sites with monumental art then post-date Early Formative highland sites such as Tlatilco, Tlapacoya, San Pablo, etc.? Our 1972 field season data from Chalcatzingo indicate that the answer to that question is unequivocally yes. There is no doubt that the major occupation and site use at Chalcatzingo is related to the early Middle Formative. Our 1972 Chalcatzingo ceramic assemblage contains a high percentage of white wares decorated with the incised double-line-break on the rims, plus *laca* wares. Figurines were nearly entirely C1, C2, B and C8 varieties (Fig. 2 *e-i*). The Chalcatzingo ceramics seem to correlate stylistically with Bomba subphase ceramics from Tlapacoya (Tolstoy and Paradis 1970: 347) and are essentially similar to Zacatenco and El Arbolillo ceramics. In other words, there is nothing Olmec at all about Chalcatzingo's ceramics! If anything must be considered 'Olmec' within the ceramics than I would have to nominate the C8 figurines which are quite distinctive, receive surface treatments not found on other figurines, and which occur in restricted areas and ceremonial contexts in our excavations. There is good reason to believe that the Chalcatzingo bas-relief carvings are also datable to the same approximate time span, or c. 900-800 B.C. I believe too that Oxtotitlan (Grove 1970b), Juxtlahuaca (Gay 1967; Grove 1970b: 29-31), and San Miguel Amuco (Grove and Paradis 1971) are also early Middle Formative sites. In fact the same is probably true of the other scattered examples of Olmec monumental art such as Pijijiapan, Las Victorias, Techaya, etc.

The Morelos data strongly suggest that just as on the Gulf Coast we can note a series of important changes in the archaeological record through time, so too are changes present in the 'highland Olmec' archaeological record. Chalcatzingo as a site differs in its ceramic assemblage from earlier 'Olmec' sites. In fact it is distinctive in a number of ways. The majority of Early Formative highland sites (Tlatilco, San Pablo, Nexpa, Las Bocas, Atlihuayan, Gualupita, etc.) are located near important water sources. Such sites contain little in the way of elaborate architecture, although architecture is present in many cases (e.g. Grove 1970a; n.d., b). At this time however we have little data on the internal settlement patterns of these sites. Site location suggests that incipient water control systems might have been utilized during the Early Formative. An Early Formative area exists at Chalcatzingo too and differs little from the description above of other Early Formative sites. Where associated with the major Middle Formative zone at Chalcatzingo, the Early Formative San Pablo B subphase ceramics underlie four metres of the site's typical Middle Formative stratigraphy. The Middle Formative site at Chalcatzingo is quite different, for the settlement at Chalcatzingo is on the heavily terraced hillside away from the spring waters in the valley below (location of most of the Early Formative materials). We believe that the shift to the hillside and the concomitant terracing is a probable reflection of improved water control systems. Two such systems, apparently Middle Formative, were found by our 1972 field season, although only one was excavated. The Middle Formative settlement is, surprisingly, dispersed. Each large agricultural terrace at Chalcatzingo has, at its upper edge, a Middle Formative house area. By comparison, however, the site's uppermost terrace, adjacent to the mountain and carvings (Piña Chan's 'Plaza': Piña Chan 1955a) appears to represent the Middle Formative ceremonial zone. Although few Middle Formative architectural features exist on the surface, our 1972 excavations uncovered a series of completely buried stone architectural features. Thus, it seems likely that a small but elaborate ceremonial precinct existed at Chalcatzingo during the Middle Formative and included at least one long platform mound, ceremonial (non-domestic) rooms and a possible ballcourt. At this time, Chalcatzingo represents a site quite distinct from other highland Middle Formative sites, not only in its presence of monumental art but also as an early ceremonial centre with definite ceremonial architecture. However, I must reiterate that in the ceramic assemblage, there is little at the moment which would distinguish Chalcatzingo from other Middle Formative sites, and nothing that looks particularly Olmec. The ceramics follow a general pattern common to Mesoamerica at this time (white wares with double-line break decorations). Unfortunately, La Venta's ceramics are not well known. Perhaps they too have nothing that distinctive, thus making it difficult to identify Middle Formative Olmec influences in anything but monumental art.

What is Olmec in the highlands?

As noted above, the Olmec influences in central Mexico's Early Formative appear in ceramics, while such influences are far more difficult to determine in Middle Formative ceramics and the Olmec influences are primarily known through monumental art and in some instances small portable jade, jadeite and serpentine carvings (axes, figurines, etc.). Though unknown stratigraphically in highland contexts, I place these small portable stone carvings in the Middle Formative for several reasons including their general absence at Tlatilco and other highland Early Formative sites (they may appear with some double-line-break ceramics in the final gasp of Tlatilco) and the fact that no jade objects were found until the Nacaste phase (Middle Formative) at San Lorenzo (Coe 1970: 27-9).

The question must now be asked, how many of the artifacts in the highlands identified as 'Olmec' are in actuality Olmec? In other words, how many are derived or related in some significant manner to the Gulf Coast Olmec culture? I previously mentioned different ways in which the term 'highland Olmec' was utilized in the literature: containing Olmec stylistic attributes; contact with or manufacture by a Gulf Coast person; and 'Olmec by association'. The second point, contact with a Gulf Coast person (presumed well versed in Olmec belief systems) would be hard to prove at any archaeological site without detailed burial and skeletal analysis of, for instance, a statistically reliable sample of Tlatilco burials, to determine if the 'Olmec' ceramics associated with some Tlatilco burials occur as burial furniture with a skeletal population which differs significantly from skeletal populations in the same cemetery lacking Olmec burial ceramics. Although I feel such data may prove quite inconclusive in Early Formative Tlatilco sites, we will be attempting to make such tests in future field seasons at Chalcatzingo, where stratification patterns appear more visible. As one possible instance of direct Gulf Coast contacts, the reliefs at Chalcatzingo, and in particular two of the four newly discovered during our 1972 field season, are so similar to La Venta monumental art that a strong possibility exists that at least some of the reliefs were executed by Gulf Coast artisans. Returning to the first point, the identification of 'highland Olmec' simply as artifacts containing Olmec stylistic attributes seems the only real way in which to approach the question at this time, until further data are available archaeologically. However, two further questions must be asked of artifacts in the highlands bearing motifs which are stylistically Olmec: are the motifs indeed Olmec? Even if the motifs are Olmec, does this make the site at which they were found Olmec? This will be further discussed below. The final point, 'Olmec by association' at a site yielding other artifacts which are stylistically Olmec, seems obviously the weakest reasoning, and yet just such reasoning pervades the published data on

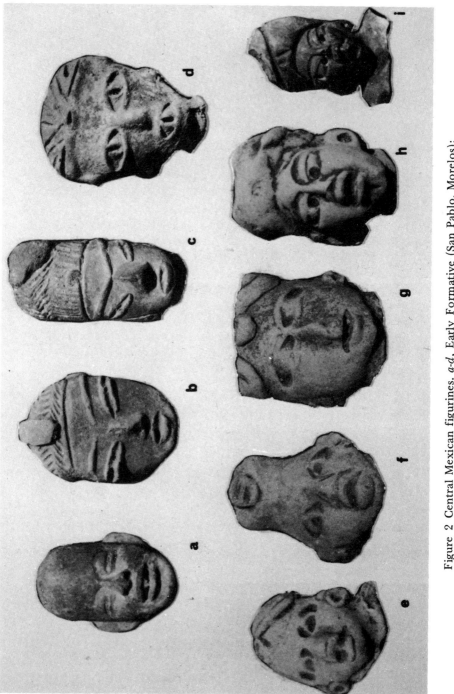

Figure 2 Central Mexican figurines. *a-d*, Early Formative (San Pablo, Morelos); *e-i*, Middle Formative (Chalcatzingo). Figurine *a* is Olmec, *h* and *i* are type C8. Note the difference in eye treatments.

Figure 3 Early Formative 'Tlatilco culture' ceramic vessels from Central Mexico. *a*, Olmec; *b-h*, non-Olmec Red-on-Brown bottle forms. Bottles *b-d* include resist painting.

the highland Formative. The major case in point is the site of
Tlatilco, for this site has long been considered as an Olmec site and
from the published data it would be hard to dispute this contention.
However, my excavations at Early Formative Tlatilco sites in Morelos
led to several important observations in the field which I subsequently checked with available data on Tlatilco burials. Paul
Tolstoy (personal communication) has been conducting a similar and
even more thorough analysis with quite similar results. In the burials
at Tlatilco sites both Olmec ceramics and Red-on-Brown bottles
occur. The very fact that Olmec ceramics were found at Tlatilco has
caused that site to be identified as a highland Olmec site and all
Tlatilco ceramics as representative of highland Olmec (e.g. Coe 1965;
Porter 1953). Thus, Red-on-Brown bottles were considered as part of
the highland Olmec manifestation, and because stirrup spout bottles
occur as part of the Red-on-Brown bottle complex at Tlatilco and are
also found in the Chavin culture of Peru, several authors took that to
mean some sort of Olmec-Chavin relationship (Porter 1953: 76;
Wicke 1971: 155). However, as I have previously pointed out
(1970a: 67-72) excavation data from Tlatilco sites indicate that the
majority of burials at these sites have Red-on-Brown bottles as burial
furniture and at the same time lack Olmec style ceramics. Conversely, burials at the same sites with Olmec style vessels as offerings
lack associated Red-on-Brown bottles. While hypothesizing once that
this was chronological (1970a: 71-2; also discussed earlier in this
paper) I now believe that much of the difference may be the result of
some pattern of social stratification (although temporal differences
may too play a role). My point nevertheless is that Red-on-Brown
bottles and Olmec style ceramics represent in general two separate
entities within the same local highland cultural (burial) pattern. In
actuality the quantity of identifiable Olmec ceramics at Tlatilco
sites is quite small: an estimate would place the *maximum* percentage
of 'Olmec' ceramics at 10%, the Red-on-Brown bottle complex being
four or five times more numerous *minimally*. Because nothing like
the sophisticated and abundant Red-on-Brown bottle complex is yet
known from the Gulf Coast, and because it is quite unique and lacks
diagnostic Olmec attributes, there is no reason to consider this
complex as Olmec at all. It is apparently representative of the local
Early Formative culture in the highlands and appears to have its
origins in West Mexico (Grove n.d., a; Tolstoy 1971: 26). Since these
ceramics are non-Olmec there is no connection between stirrup spout
bottles in Chavin and those in the Olmec culture, for they do not
occur in Olmec culture! South American influences in West Mexico
are another matter (Grove n.d., a).

Other equally tenuous 'Olmec' traits in the highlands can likewise
be questioned. Some highland sites, such as Las Bocas, appear to
yield a high quantity of 'Olmec' ceramic materials, far greater than
the 10 percent estimated here for Tlatilco sites (of which Las Bocas

is probably one). A number of reasons may explain this phenomenon. Obviously, because 'Olmec' pieces are in demand by
collectors, a bias will be present on which pieces reach the
'profitable' antiquities market and come to the view of collectors and
some professionals; the complete range of artifacts from a looted site
is never seen. Secondly, Las Bocas was long ago exhausted as a source
of supply but materials from other sites in the same region arrive on
the market with the provenance of 'Las Bocas', again biasing the
data. But equally important to consider is, how many of the pieces
sold as 'Olmec' are actually Olmec? The hollow baby-face figurines
from Las Bocas certainly are, but what of the numerous D2
figurines? These are not Olmec but again appear to represent the
local culture. D2 figurines do not occur on the Gulf Coast. In fact a
large majority of the published 'Olmec' vessels from Las Bocas are
unlike any yet found on the Gulf Coast. While it must be understood
that no Gulf Coast cemetery areas of comparable age have been
archaeologically excavated, many of the very elaborate and sophisticated ceramics at Las Bocas, Tlatilco, Tlapacoya, and in fact all the
highland Early Formative sites seem to represent the intermixing of a
highly sophisticated local ceramic tradition with introduced Olmec
stylistic motifs. While these vessels can be called 'highland Olmec',
this term distorts their true cultural significance and detracts from
our understanding of the cultural level, abilities, and processes in the
highlands.

Roller seals occur at Tlatilco, Las Bocas, Nexpa, and many other
Early Formative highland sites (see Fields 1967). They are generally
considered as an Olmec diagnostic and Fields (1967: 32) speaks of an
'Olmec sello tradition'. However, a glance through the archaeological
literature will show that roller seals occur in quantity only in the
highlands and are rare in archaeological contexts in the Gulf Coast.
They may in fact occur at an earlier date in the highlands (c.1250
B.C.) than in the Gulf Coast. At this moment, even though some
incorporate Olmec stylistic designs, it would be better to consider
them as a highland artifact. In fact, a large number of the designs on
roller seals have nothing diagnostically Olmec to them, and one
wonders if even many of the 'Olmec' designs on these seals, if fully
investigated, would be found to have Gulf Coast counterparts?
Again, these must be considered as much a part of the sophisticated
highland culture which certainly appears capable of having developed
its own set of stylized design elements.

With the advent of the Middle Formative, ceramics as a whole
become more homogeneous, and Chalcatzingo's ceramics and
figurines in general are indistinguishable from those of Zacatenco, El
Arbolillo, or other Middle Formative highland sites. No definite
Olmec influences appear in the ceramics (future field seasons at
Chalcatzingo will continue investigating this phenomenon). Does the
lack of identifiable ceramic influences imply that the nature of

Figure 4 Chalcatzingo Relief XII, the 'Flying Olmec', discovered in 1972.

Olmec influences in the highlands has significantly changed?

Several bas-relief carvings at Chalcatzingo show such strong similarities to La Venta monumental art that I suspect some form of direct contact. Other Chalcatzingo reliefs contain motifs within the scope of Gulf Coast iconography, but still to be discovered in Gulf Coast monumental art. An example of this latter is the series of reliefs, some long known, some newly discovered, adjacent to Relief I high on the hillside. This group consists of five small creatures with iguana-like characteristics, shown crouched above scrolls (Reliefs VI-VII, VIII, XI, XIV, XV). Occasionally they are represented as 'spitting another scroll from their mouth, over which hangs a jaguar-mouth-shaped rain-cloud from which rain-drops fall' (see Relief XIV, Fig. 5). James Schoenwetter has suggested to me that the scroll they 'spit' from their mouths could represent, due to its morphology, a germinating seed. In three cases, below these animals are carved squash plants. While apparently unique to carved art, these small creatures, which are probably equivalent to the Maya concept of *Itzamna* (see too Grove 1970*b*: 16-17), are also known from several highland Formative period ceramics. Finally, there are Middle Formative motifs, including the goggle-eyed rain diety (*Tlaloc* to the Aztecs) which may have highland roots rather than diffusing

Figure 5 Chalcatzingo Relief XIV, an iguana-like animal, above which is a rain cloud and falling raindrops, below which is a scroll and carved squash plant. This creature is probably equivalent to the *Itzamna* of the Maya. Relief discovered in 1972.

from the Gulf Coast. An apparently Middle Formative goggle-eyed rain deity appears as a painting at Oxtotitlan cave (Grove 1970b: Fig. 27) and several other possible Middle Formative examples (including a possible but tenuous Chalcatzingo carved example) are known from the highlands (Gay 1972a: 66; Parsons, personal communication; Grove and Angulo: 1972 Chalcatzingo field notes). No examples are known from the Gulf Coast, although the evolution of the goggle-eyed deity from the Olmec were-jaguar was implied by Covarrubias (1957: Fig. 22). Thus, while for many motifs (jaguars, harpy eagles, *Itzamna*, etc.) it seems proper to assume diffusion to the highlands from the lowland Gulf Coast, for some other motifs perhaps there are highland priorities.

The nature of 'highland Olmec'

It became obvious in viewing the archaeological data that there is not simply one archaeological manifestation which can be termed 'highland Olmec', for the nature of the manifestation varies regionally and chronologically. It in fact seems doubtful that there is any highland archaeological complex of such significance that it warrents the designation *Olmec* in the same manner as the Formative culture of the Gulf Coast. During the Early Formative the highland manifestation appears to be composed of a local 'Tlatilco' culture or sub-culture which adopts and/or adapts from the Gulf Coast, in some manner, a series of iconographic motifs. A number of hypotheses have been published to account for the penetration of Olmec influences into the highlands, from religious diffusion, to military conquest, to colonization, to simple trade relationships. Because the Early Formative manifestation appears to be present to some degree in *all* highland Early Formative sites, both large villages and small hamlets, and because such sites occur in quantity throughout the highlands, factors such as wholesale migrations, colonization, etc. seem to be ruled out. The spread of iconographic symbols through the highland population would be better ascribed to the spread of a belief system. This belief system may have related to religion, status, or both, but I believe that the majority of the highland population had no contacts with actual persons from the Gulf Coast Olmec culture. That the influences were in the nature of borrowed beliefs (see Flannery 1968) I believe is evident in the fact that Gulf Coast ideas and ideology are not alone influencing the highlands. The highland appearance of West Mexican influences throughout the Early Formative, and in far greater quantity than Olmec influences apparently, indicates a fusion of various ideas in the highlands.

I personally have favoured trade as a major vehicle for the diffusion of Olmec ideas within Mesoamerica, and believe that Flannery's suggestion (1968: 98-108) of status borrowing from more complex cultures (in this case the Gulf Coast Olmec) is particularly applicable to the situation in the highlands during the Early Formative. While I now feel that my original statements (Grove

1968*b*) are no longer completely valid because of today's more refined chronology, I still believe that certain highland sites were probably important commercial centres as well as religious centres. The most reasonable current explanation as to the substance involved in this trade network is obsidian, an item found in the archaeological record and capable of being traced to its source. Other items such as cotton, food plants, cacao, etc., while possibly also quite important, are none the less harder to discern in the archaeological record. There is good evidence that obsidian from the Teotihuacan valley was being exploited and traded to the Gulf Coast during the Early Formative. Interestingly, recent data (Peres-Ferreira: personal communication) indicate that San Lorenzo obtained 62 percent of its obsidian from the Guadalupe Victoria source in eastern Puebla and 5 percent from a source in the Teotihuacan Valley (Barranca de los Estetes). The same data indicate that between 90-100 percent of the obsidian utilized by the Early Formative Tlatilco culture sites came from the Teotihuacan valley source and none from Guadalupe Victoria. This, plus other data, leads Peres-Ferreira to believe that San Lorenzo must have been in control of the Guadalupe Victoria source. I believe that the implications of this data are quite interesting, for if San Lorenzo did indeed control Guadalupe Victoria as a source of obsidian, then the absence of this same obsidian in the central highlands is significant. The Teotihuacan valley obsidian source occurs within the probable boundaries of Tlatilco culture, and the fact that they exploited this source so heavily suggests to me that they probably were controlling it too. This implies to me that Tlatilco culture in the central highlands was autonomous and culturally independent from the Gulf Coast, and not under the control of San Lorenzo. In the Middle Formative the Chalcatzingo obsidian appears still to derive from the Teotihuacan valley source, and obsidian distribution patterns at Chalcatzingo suggest that the site may have served as an important obsidian manufacturing centre. However, in addition to obsidian, it is also possible that worked jade passed through Morelos and Chalcatzingo on its way from stone-working centres in Guerrero to the Gulf Coast, in what Michael Coe has called the 'jade route' (Coe 1965). Trade of course can be conducted with minimal contacts, and during the Middle Formative the nature of the monumental art at Chalcatzingo, Oxtotitlan, etc. leads me to suspect that some Gulf Coast persons were probably present in small numbers in the highlands. The same situation may have prevailed also during the Early Formative, but such presence at either time does not make the highland cultures 'Olmec'.

As far as cultural processes are concerned, we lack data at the moment to consider the possible reasons for the apparent shift from a wide spread manifestation of Olmec traits during the Early Formative to a restricted distribution during the Middle Formative. Did such drastic changes in reality occur, or are we simply witnessing an incomplete and biased archaeological record? Ceramically there appears to be a degeneration from the sophisticated vessels and figurines of the Early Formative to the far more peasant-like Middle Formative ceramics. The cultural process responsible for such a degeneration, which appears to have occurred throughout much of central and southern Mesoamerica, remains to be analysed. Was it somehow linked to the apparent shift in Olmec power centres from San Lorenzo to La Venta? If so, why? Do trade and exploitation patterns change? Are there no Gulf Coast status symbols to be borrowed any more? Does the decline of sophisticated ceramics in the highlands imply a decline in intensive contacts with the Gulf Coast or simply a change in the nature of the contacts? Why do the West Mexican influences also appear to decline at the end of the Early Formative? Is it possible that what we are witnessing in the shift from Early to Middle Formative culture in both the highlands and Gulf Coast (the latter in particular) is simply a shift from the utilization of ceramics as a means of status expression to an emphasis in monumental art and elaborate ceremonial architecture? Perhaps the limited distribution of Middle Formative highland sites with monumental art (and architecture at Chalcatzingo) present us with a truer perspective of the number of highland sites, in either the Early or Middle Formative, which were actively participating in some form of significant cultural contacts with the Gulf Coast. In the beginning of the paper I briefly touched upon the notion of the possible highland origins of Olmec culture. Recent looting activities in Guerrero, particularly at the site of Xochipala, have brought a flood of highly sophisticated ceramics onto the market, none of course with known provenance or stratigraphic context or association. None the less, Olmec stylistic attributes occur on some ceramic vessels and figurines from Xochipala, and at least one author has labelled Xochipala as the 'beginnings of Olmec art' (Gay 1972*b*). Here again we find the same problems encountered earlier with Tlatilco and 'Olmec by association'. I believe that in the case of Xochipala we find simply another sophisticated Early Formative regional style, perhaps stimulated by trade contacts with the Gulf Coast, adopting some of the Gulf Coast symbolism. That it is the 'beginnings of Olmec art' seems improbable. I believe that the archaeological data today strongly suggest that the origin of Olmec culture is southern Mesoamerican and strongly related to early cultures on the Pacific Coast of Chiapas and Guatemala, with many of the basic ideas probably derived ultimately from a tropical forest hearth in South America (Grove n.d., *a*).

REFERENCES

Benson, E. (1968) (ed.) *Dumbarton Oaks Conference on the Olmec*. Washington.
Berger, R., J.A. Graham and R.F. Heizer (1967) A reconsideration of the age of the

La Venta site. *Contributions of the University of California Archaeological Research Facility*, 3, 1-14.

Bernal, I. (1969) *The Olmec World*. Berkeley.

Coe, M.D. (1965) *The Jaguar's Children*. Museum of Primitive Art, New York.

Coe, M.D. (1968) San Lorenzo and the Olmec civilization. In E. Benson (ed.), 1968, 41-78.

Coe, M.D. (1970) The archaeological sequence at San Lorenzo Tenochtitlan, Veracruz, Mexico. *Contributions of the University of California Archaeological Research Facility*, 8, 21-34.

Coe, M.D., R.A. Diehl and M. Stuiver (1967) Olmec civilization, Veracruz, Mexico: dating of the San Lorenzo phase. *Science*, 155, no. 3768, 1399-401. Washington.

Covarrubias, M. (1957) *Indian Art of Mexico and Central America*. New York.

Field, F.V. (1967) Thoughts on the meaning and use of pre-Hispanic Mexican sellos. *Studies in Pre-Columbian Art and Archaeology*, 3.

Flannery, K.V. (1968) The Olmec and the valley of Oaxaca: a model for interregional interaction in Formative times. In E. Benson (ed.), 1968, 79-110.

Gay, C.T.E. (1967) Oldest paintings of the New World. *Natural History*, 76, no. 4, 28-35.

Gay, C.T.E. (1972a) *Chalcatzingo*. Portland, Oregon.

Gay, C.T.E. (1972b) *Xochipala, the Beginnings of Olmec Art*. Princeton, N.J.

Grove, D.C. (1968a) Chalcatzingo, Morelos, Mexico: a re-appraisal of the Olmec rock carvings. *American Antiquity*, 33, no. 4, 486-91.

Grove, D.C. (1968b) The Preclassic Olmec in central Mexico: site distribution and inferences. In Benson (ed.) 1968, 179-85.

Grove, D.C. (1970a The San Pablo pantheon mound: a Middle Preclassic site in Morelos, Mexico. *American Antiquity*, 35, no. 1, 62-73.

Grove, D.C. (1970b) The Olmec paintings of Oxtotitlan cave, Guerrero, Mexico. *Studies in Pre-Columbian Art and Archaeology*, 6. Washington.

Grove, D.C. (1972) Preclassic religious beliefs in Mexico's Altiplano Central. *Religión en Mesoamerica*, XII Mesa Redonda, Sociedad Mexicana de Antropología, 55-9. Mexico.

Grove, D.C. (n.d., a) The Mesoamerican Formative and South American influences. In, *Primer Simposio de Correlaciones Antropológicos Andino-Mesoamericana*, in press. Ecuador.

Grove, D.C. (n.d., b) *Archaeological Investigations along the Rio Cuautla, Morelos, 1969 and 1970*. Submitted in 1972 to I.N.A.H., Mexico. Mimeographed.

Grove, D.C. and L.I. Paradis (1971) An Olmec stela from San Miguel Amuco, Guerrero. *American Antiquity*, 36, no. 1, 95-102.

Heizer, R.F. (1968) New observations on La Venta. In Benson (ed.), 1968, 9-40.

Heizer, R.F., P. Drucker and J.A. Graham (1968) Investigations at La Venta, 1967. *Contributions of the University of California Archaeological Research Facility*, 5, 1-34.

Heizer, R.F., J.A. Graham and L.K. Napton (1968) The 1968 investigations at La Venta. *Contributions of the University of California Archaeological Research Facility*, 5, 101-203.

Piña Chan, R. (1955a) Chalcatzingo, Morelos. *Informes*, 4. Instituto Nacional de Antropología e Historia, Mexico.

Piña Chan, R. (1955b) *Las culturas preclásicas de la cuenca de Mexico*. Fonda de Cultura Económica. Mexico.

Porter, M.N. (1953) *Tlatilco and the Preclassic Cultures of the New World*. Viking Fund Publications in Anthroplogy, no. 19. New York.

Sisson, E.B. (1970) Settlement patterns and land use in the northwestern Chontalpa, Tabasco, Mexico: a progress report. *Cerámica de Cultura Maya*, 6, 41-55.

Tolstoy, P. (1971) Recent research into the Early Preclassic of the Central Highlands. *Contributions of the University of California Archaeological Research Facility.* 11, 25-28.

Tolstoy, P. and L.I. Paradis (1970) Early and Middle Preclassic culture in the Basin of Mexico. *Science,* 167, 344-51. Washington.

Wicke, C.R. (1971) *Olmec, an Early Art Style of Pre-Columbian Mexico.* Tucson, Arizona.

LAWRENCE H. FELDMAN

Shells from afar: 'Panamic' molluscs in Mayan sites

The shores of Mesoamerica are divided between two molluscan faunal provinces, the Panamic and the Caribbean. Each of these, the Panamic in the Pacific Ocean and the Caribbean in the Atlantic Ocean, have characteristic species found nowhere else on this earth.[1] The archaeologist finds their shells, has their species identified, ocean of origin determined and postulates contact with the inhabitants of the shores of that ocean. At this time I would like to take a closer look at some of these archaeological shells, those that live on the Pacific coast of Mesoamerica (the Panamic province), in order to obtain further information about the Mayan inhabitants of Central America who utilized them.

First a word about those molluscs that live in *both* the Caribbean and Panamic faunal provinces. Before the late Miocene epoch the Isthmus of Panama did not exist and there was free passage of animals from one ocean to another (Keen 1971: 2). Since this passage disappeared, marine animals on either coast of Central America have evolved away from their common ancestors. This change is often not great among molluscs. Some species remain identical in every respect in both oceans. Others remain very similar; these unfortunately quite common molluscs pose the problem of telling cognate species apart when the specimens in question are not those of living animals but only less well preserved archaeological shells. Therefore, in order to avoid possible confusion, the only Panamic shells discussed here are those without close Caribbean cognates.

Eighteen of these Panamic species were found in Mayan sites (Table 1). Six lived on sandy beaches, eight lived on a rocky shoreline, two were in association with mangrove swamps and the others in either a rocky or sandy habitat. The animals, when living, did not all inhabit the same environment; and this fact is important for archaeologists. These differences are significant because these habitats are not uniformly distributed along the Pacific coast. Between Puerto Angel (west of Tehuantepec) on the Oaxacan coast and Acajutla in El Salvador, there are no localities where the eight rocky shore animals live today or could have lived in the past 50 centuries. This means that the shores of Chiapas and Guatemala, so close to the Mayan lands, were not the source of these shells.

The same may be true for the sandy shore molluscs. Here the evidence is more circumstantial. Although the range of one species (*Polinices reclusianus*) does not go further south than the coast of Nayarit, the others do live in southern Central America as well as western Mexico. However, the literature and modern collections do not provide evidence for the presence of these animals along the coast of Chiapas or Guatemala. This absence is confirmed by the archaeological data. Of the thirty-six midden species known from this coast, *not one* is a sandy shore Panamic shell known from inland Maya sites. Thus between the coast of Oaxaca and the coast of Costa Rica, there is no evidence for their existence as live animals. The only inland Maya molluscan species found on this coast are the two mangrove swamp species alluded to previously.

Finally a few words on the temporal distribution of molluscs in archaeological sites. To the inhabitants of the Mesoamerican coast most of these molluscs were as available fifty centuries ago as they are today. Yet their usage has not persisted uniformly from those days to the present. *Polinices reclusianus* obtains a widely spread distribution only in the Early Postclassic. *Spondylus calcifer* is associated with typical Early Classic period (Miccaotli) offerings in Belize (Pendergast 1971: 455-461) and wares of equivalent age at Monte Alban (Acosta 1958: 27). The same species is again widespread in the Early Postclassic (see Table 1); but it is not found in deposits of other time periods.[2] While some breaks in temporal usage are due to the absence of samples, I strongly suspect that usage is subject to short-lived cultural changes, and thus, in conclusion, that shells are potentially just as diagnostic of archaeological phases as pottery.

Table 1 Panamic Mayan archaeomolluscan species[3]

Capital letters signify the following time periods: A(1200 to 900 B.C.), B(900 to 600 B.C.), C(600 to 100 B.C.), D(100 B.C. to A.D. 300), E(A.D. 300 to 600), F(A.D. 600 to 900), G(A.D. 900 to 1200) and H(A.D. 1200 to 1600).

Rocky Shore Molluscs

GENUS – SPECIES	SITES AND PERIOD
Ancistromesus mexicana	Kaminaljuyu(E), Mixco Viejo(H), Iximche(H), Uaxactun(n.d.)
Crucibulum spinosum	Piedras Negras(n.d.)
Jenneria pustulata	Altar de Sacrificios(?F)
Leucozonia cerata	Tikal, Kaminaljuyu(E)
Pinctada mazatlanica	Zaculeu(?G)
Spondylus calcifer	Piedras Negras(n.d.), Altun Ha(D), Jaina(G), Copan(n.d.)

Spondylus princeps	Amatitlan(F), Uaxactun(D-F), Tikal(D-F), San Jose(F), Guaytan(F)
Trivia radians	Altun Ha(n.d.)

Intertidal Sand Beaches and Sand Flats to 10 metres Molluscs

GENUS – SPECIES	SITES AND PERIOD
Hexaplex regius	Guaytan (F) Kaminaljuyu (E)
Lyropecten subnodosus	Tikal(?E), Uaxactun(D-E)
Malea ringens	Kaminaljuyu(E)
Melongena patula	Kaminaljuyu(E)
Oliva porphyria	Chichen Itza(n.d.), Loltun(n.d.), Copan(n.d.), Asuncion Mita(n.d.), Bay Islands Honduras(n.d.), Tikal(?E)
Oliva spicata	Còpan(n.d.)
Polinices reclusianus	Zaculeu(G)

Low-Salinity Lagoon and Mangrove Environment Molluscs

GENUS – SPECIES	SITES AND PERIOD
Anadara grandis	Copan(F)
Geloina inflata[4]	Jaina(G)

Other Molluscs (Sandy Shore or Rocky Shore)

GENUS – SPECIES	SITES AND PERIOD
Cerithium adustum	Tikal(n.d.)

Table 2   A comparative listing for some Mayan archaeomolluscs[5]

Capital letters signify the same periods as in Table 1.

GENUS – SPECIES	SITES AND PERIOD
Ancistromesus mexicana	Xico Valley of Mexico(?H), Monte Alban(n.d.)
Leucozonia cerata	Teotihuacan(E)
Pinctada mazatlanica	Puerto Marquez Guerrero(A), Nexpa Morelos(B), Tlatilco Valley of Mexico(B), Ticoman Valley of Mexico(C), Teotihuacan(E), Mexico City(H), Tlacuache Oaxaca(n.d.)
Spondylus calcifer	Monte Alban (D), Teotihuacan (G), Tlatelolco Valley of Mexico(H)
Spondylus princeps	Teotihuacan(E&G), Mexico City(H)
Trivia radians	Mexico City(?H)
Lyropecten subnodosus	Puerto Marquez Guerrero(A&B), Teotihuacan(E)
Malea ringens	Puerto Marquez Guerrero(C)
Melongena patula	Puerto Marquez Guerrero(B-C), Boca del Rio Oaxaca(?C), Teotihuacan(E), Mexico City(H)
Oliva porphyria	Monte Alban(D), Cerro Portesuelo Valley of Mexico(F&G), Teotihuacan(G), Tula(n.d.)
Oliva spicata	Teotihuacan(n.d.)
Polinices reclusianus	Culiacan Sinaloa(G), San Gregorio Michoacan(n.d.), Teotihuacan(E), Cerro Portesuelo Valley of Mexico(n.d.)

Anadara grandis	Salinas La Blanca Guatemala(B), Teotihuacan(G)
Geloina inflata	Ocos Guatemala (modern)
Jenneria pustulata	Tula(n.d.)

NOTES

[1] The Panamic faunal province is also known as the 'Tropical West American' (Keen 1971). It extends from the head of the Gulf of California (about lat. $30°30'$ N.) south to Cabo Blanco in northwestern Peru (lat. $4°15'$ S.). This tropical zone has average surface temperatures of between 80 to 85 degrees Fahrenheit except where modified by upwellings of cooler waters (Olsson 1961: 24).

2 Other species of special interest include *Spondylus princeps*, which occurs earlier in the Maya area than in central Mexico, and *Ancistromesus mexicana*, a species restricted to the Middle Classic and Late Postclassic. It is one of the very few marine species known from highland Guatemalan Late Postclassic sites.

3 Dr Ignacio Bernal made it possible for me to examine Jaina shells in storage at the Musco Nacional de Antropología of Mexico. Drs David Pendergast (for the site of Altun Ha) and Gordon Willey (for Altar de Sacrificios) kindly made available lists of previously identified species. Other references for this table are: Andrews 1969, Coe 1959, Moholy-Nagy 1963, Longyear 1952, Woodbury and Trik 1953, Kidder 1947, Stromsvik 1941, Strong 1935, Ricketson and Ricketson 1937, Kidder, Jennings and Shook 1947, Smith and Kidder 1943, Guillemin 1965, Stromsvik 1950 and Pendergast 1971.

4 This species is often called *Polymesoda inflata*. In all other species names this paper follows Keen (1971).

5 I wish to express my debt again to Ignacio Bernal for making available shells from Teotihuacan, Tlatilco, Monte Alban and Tlaquache Oaxaca. Others who made this table possible by allowing access to unpublished material are Dr Henry B. Nicolson (for the site of Cerro Portesuelo), Dr Richard Diehl (for the site of Tula), Dr Charles F. Brush (for the site of Puerto Marquez) and the staff of the Departamento de Prehistoria of the Instituto Nacional de Antropologia e Historia (for various sites in Mexico City). Other references for this table are: Batres 1902, Kelly 1945, Meighan and Foote 1968, Linne 1942, Vaillant 1931, Borbolla 1947, Noguera 1955, Grove 1972, Ekholm 1961, Coe and Flannery 1967, and Acosta 1968.

REFERENCES

Acosta, J.R. (1958) Exploraciones arqueológicas en Monte Albán XVIII*a* temporada, 1958. *Revista Mexicana de Estudios Antropológicos*, 15, 7-50.

Andrews, E.W. IV (1969) *The Archaeological Use and Distribution of Mollusca in the Maya Lowlands*. Middle American Research Institute, New Orleans.

Batres, L. (1902) *Archaeological Explorations on Escalerillas Street, City of Mexico*. Mexico.

Borbolla, D.F. R. de (1947) Teotihuacan: ofrendas de los templos de Quetzalcoatl. *Anales de Instituto Nacional de Antropología e Historia*, 2, 61-72.

Coe, M.D. and K.V. Flannery (1967) *Early Cultures and Human Ecology in South Coastal Guatemala*. Washington.

Coe, W.R. (1959) *Piedras Negras Archaeology: Artifacts, Caches, and Burials*. University Museum Monographs, University of Pennsylvania.

Ekholm, G.F. (1961) Some collar-shaped shell pendants from Mesoamerica. In *Homenaje a Pablo Martinez del Rio*, 287-93. Instituto Nacional de Antropología e Historia, Mexico.

Grove, D.C. (1972) *Archaeological Investigations Along the Rio Cuautla, Morelos, 1969 and 1970*. Submitted to the Instituto Nacional de Antropología e Historia, Mexico.

Guillemin, J.F. (1965) *Iximche, capital del antiguo reino Cakchiquel*. Publicación del Instituto de Antropología e Historia de Guatemala.

Kean, A.M. (1971) *Sea Shells of Tropical West America.* 2nd. ed. Stanford, California.

Kelly, I. (1945) Excavations at Culiacan, Sinaloa. *Ibero-Americana*, 25.

Kidder, A.V. (1947) *The Artifacts of Uaxactun, Guatemala.* Carnegie Institution of Washington, Publication no. 576.

Kidder, A.V., J.D. Jennings and E.M. Shook (1946) *Excavations at Kaminaljuyu, Guatemala.* Carnegie Institution of Washington.

Linne, S. (1942) *Mexican Highland Cultures: Archaeological Researches at Teotihuacan, Calpulalpan and Chalchicomula in 1934-1935.* Stockholm.

Longyear, J.M. III (1952) *Copan Ceramics: A Study of Southeastern Maya Pottery.* Carnegie Institution of Washington, Publication no. 597.

Meighan, C.W. and L.J. Foote (1968) Excavations at Tizapan El Alto, Jalisco. *Latin American Studies*, 11. University of California.

Moholy-Nagy, H. (1963) Shells and other marine material from Tikal. *Estudios de Cultura Maya*, 3, 65-83.

Noguera, E. (1955) Extraordinario hallazgo en Teotihuacan. *El México Antiguo*, 8, 43-56.

Olsson, A.A. (1961) Molluscs of the tropical Eastern Pacific particularly from the southern half of the Panamic-Pacific faunal province (Panama to Peru). *Panamic-Pacific Pelecypoda.* Palaeontological Research Institution, Ithaca, New York.

Pendergast, D.M. (1971) Evidence of early Teotihuacan-lowland Maya contact at Altun Ha. *American Antiquity*, 36, no. 4, 455-9.

Ricketson, O.G., Jr. and Ricketson, E.B. et al. (1937) *Uaxactun, Guatemala: Group E, 1926-1931.* Carnegie Institution of Washington, Publication no. 477.

Smith, A.L. and A.V. Kidder (1943) Explorations in the Motagua Valley, Guatemala. *Contributions to American Anthropology and History*, 8, no. 41, 109-84.

Stromsvik, G. (1941) Substela caches and stela foundations at Copan and Quirigua. *Contributions to American Anthropology and History*, 7, 63-96.

Stromsvik, G. (1950) Las ruinas de Asuncion Mita: informe de su reconocimiento. *Antropología e Historia de Guatemala*, 2, no. 1, 21-9.

Strong, W.D. (1935) *Archaeological Investigations in the Bay Islands, Spanish Honduras.* Smithsonian Miscellaneous Collections, vol. 92. Washington.

Vaillant, George C. (1931) Excavations at Ticoman. *Anthropological Papers of the American Museum of Natural History*, 32, no. 2, 199-439.

Woodbury, R.B. and A.S. Trik (1953) *The Ruins of Zaculeu, Guatemala.* Richmond, Virginia.

DAVID H. KELLEY

Eurasian evidence and the Mayan calendar correlation problem

I have previously argued that the Mesoamerican calendar system was an invention based on a thorough knowledge of Hellenistic science in its Indo-Greek variant. I have also argued that there are elements in Mayan astronomy which strongly suggest that no attempted correlation of the Mayan calendar known to me is correct. With these views, I have felt that it was desirable to summarize what limits could be placed upon the correlation problem from a knowledge of the history of Eurasian characteristics involved in the Mesoamerican calendar.

Since the movement of people and ideas from India to Mesoamerica is presumed, for purposes of the present paper, it seems desirable to mention briefly certain key theoretical elements of my own position. In the first place, I think that sporadic contacts between almost any two cultures are quite likely, but I would expect that any record-keeping area of the Old World would have preserved the memory of any sustained and repeated contacts between the Old World and the New World. A classic example is provided by the records of the Norse community in Greenland.

In attempting to understand the cause of similarities between cultures in different parts of the world, I think that it is important to know whether the particular similarities are the results of partial divergence from a common historical original or whether they represent normal developmental processes occurring independently. In either case, many of the processes involved will be identical. I think that there are important differences between cultures in the degree to which innovations are acceptable. Most markedly innovative cultures seem to accept new ideas with readiness, whether they are from within their own culture or from other cultures. I would not deny that there may be occasional differences of importance produced by this effect alone. In my own judgment, rate of cultural change is much more closely tied to willingness to accept innovation than it is to inventive capacity. However, adoption of a foreign trait involves re-modelling to make it acceptable in the society, and the more important the item is to the borrowing culture, the more apt it is to be substantially modified. This process involves a substantial amount of local innovation and I think that extensive diffusion generally produces substantial local invention and is unlikely to occur except within a society which is already making important innovations. I would also argue that effective diffusion can only occur when a society has reached a socio-economic level where it is probable that a more complex level might be independently reached. The two major differences between my position and those of scholars who emphasize economic factors as a major determinant of social progress are that I do not think that cultural advance to a more complex level will always occur when a society has reached the capacity for it, and that I believe that the specific past history of particular borrowed items severely restricts further variation, so that contacts do have a theoretically important place in cultural development.

The purpose of the present paper is neither to argue these theoretical problems nor to present the detailed similarities which suggest the derivation of the developed Mesoamerican calendar from India, but rather to show what relevance the history of these items has to the Mesoamerican correlation problem.

The principal Asian traits which provide parallels to elements of the Mesoamerican calendar are the following:

(a) the Eurasian animal cycle
(b) the Hindu deity cycle
(c) the system of four world ages and their associations with colours
(d) Hindu and Greek four-element theory and relationship to the world ages
(e) the use of an astronomical and cosmological era base
(f) the association of cataclysmic catastrophes with the era base, with planetary revolutions and with eclipse calculations
(g) the use of a zero in calculating the era base
(h) the use of the nine-day planetary week
(i) iconographic items such as the *makara/cipactli* parallel and the *makara* tree.

Most of these have complex histories behind them in Eurasia, often known through very sketchy evidence. However, even this is much more than we have for most of the data in the New World and it provides some valuable clues.

(a) Although a 12-animal cycle is attested from the first century B.C. in Egypt and a different one from slightly earlier in China, direct evidence of 27- or 28-animal lists is substantially later. The earliest 27-animal list known to me is in B.M. pap. 121 of the fourth century A.D. (Weinstock 1950: 60). It is a very good example of the part played by vagaries of transmission in our knowledge of this material, for no other Greek version is known. A T'ang dynasty series of representations, of not earlier than the seventh century A.D., is the earliest Chinese evidence known to me; there are many later Chinese lists.

No other list is known to me prior to the seventeenth century A.D. The Hindu-Tamil 27- or 28-animal list is structurally and geographically intermediate between the Chinese and Egyptian 12-animal lists and may be their prototype (as my student, Joe Steward, MS, 1971, has noted), but direct evidence of this is completely lacking. Hence the lists could furnish evidence for the correlation problem only by very roundabout arguments.

(b)   The Hindu deities of the lunar mansions are already attested in the *Atharvaveda*, perhaps in the eighth century B.C. The particular form of the list used by Kirchhoff in his comparisons showed similarities which Dr Budruss, of Tubingen, thought could not antedate the first century A.D. (Kirchhoff 1964). However, I am by no means sure that any of the valid comparisons contain elements which can be dated with this degree of assurance.

(c)   The system of four or five world ages is attested in Greece in Hesiod's *Works and Days*, where an age of heroes is interpolated in a series of four metal ages. The first attested occurrence in India is in the *Mahabhārata*, which dates, in general, from about the second century B.C. Here the fourth age is, in an incidental remark, identified as the iron age, which suggests familiarity with the Greek system, if not derivation from it. Two passages associate the world ages with colours, which is the earliest suggestion of colour symbolism known to me from India. Colours, directions and astronomical animals are associated much earlier in China, where there is no clear doctrine of world ages, and there are colours associated with directions by Empedocles in Greece, but the details are in both cases markedly distinct from India and Mesoamerica. Stimulus diffusion from China seems to me quite possible but difficult to demonstrate. The particular colours used by the Indians and the Mayas are the 'primary' colours of Democritus of Abdera (about 420 B.C.).

(d)   India seems to have a priority of several centuries in the theory of the four 'elements', air, fire, earth and water, apparently present by about the seventh century B.C. In Greece, the set was formalized in this way by Empedocles in the fifth century B.C. His contemporary, Herodotus, in describing the customs of the Persians, says that they give sacrifices to the whole firmament, to sun, moon, earth, fire, water and winds, and that these are their only ancient gods. Although Greek writers gave credit to Empedocles for formulating the idea of the four elements, slightly variant versions were known both earlier and later. The Chinese series of five elements, metal, wood, fire, earth and water is attested early in Han times. Although I think there is some evidence of a historical relationship with the Greek series, the differences help to eliminate China from serious consideration as the source of the Mesoamerican ideas.

Fire and water were associated with periodic cataclysms at the solstices of the 'great year', defined astronomically by Aristotle; and Melito, much later, suggested destructions by air, fire and water. Lucretius mentioned previous destructions by fire and water and a forthcoming destruction by earthquakes. Nonetheless, no single Greek or Roman source formally associates the four world ages with destructions, in turn, by each of the four elements. In India, the Buddhists developed a very elaborate system of world ages with 64 major divisions, of which 56 were destroyed by fire, seven by flood and one by wind. Perhaps earth was omitted as the subject of all this destruction. I do not know the date at which this system appeared. The *Mahabhārata* shows that in the second century B.C. the ordinary view was that several different kinds of destruction entered into the end of each world age.

At present, I am uncertain as to whether the formal association of the four elements in their destructive aspects with the four ages had already been developed in India or whether it was a new idea in Mesoamerica. In either case, the ideas likely to lead to this pattern do not seem to have been present before Aristotle in Greece and the cataclysmic emphasis was probably still later in India.

(e)   The earliest use of a constant era from a fixed base, attested by contemporary documents, is the Seleucid era of 312 B.C. which came into existence shortly after that date. Many local eras were used in India, counting from allegedly historical dates earlier than this, but these may be due to back calculation and none is directly attested earlier than the Seleucid era. Since northern India was a part of the Seleucid empire, it has often been assumed that the native eras of India represent stimulus diffusion of the concept of an era base from the Seleucids.

As far as I know, the earliest attested use of an astronomically based era is the era of Nabonassar, counting from 747 B.C. and first known to us in the works of Ptolemy in the second century A.D. The Kaliyuga era base of 3102 B.C., representing the beginning of the present world age and used by Indian astronomers, is not explicitly attested before the fifth century A.D. but a passage in the *Mahabhārata* suggests that it may have been in use as early as the second century B.C.

(f)   There is no evidence known to me that the world ages were originally associated with cataclysmic destructions, and no early evidence for periodically conceived destructions, but Aristotle gives an account of a 'great year' which was determined by the return of all the planets to their places; a flood destroyed the earth at the 'winter solstice' of this year and a destruction by fire occurred at the 'summer solstice'.

In the developed Hindu system of the four world ages, the fourth age, or Kaliyuga, began with a conjunction of all the planets at the spring equinox; apparently this was also calculated as a solar eclipse (Gleadow 1968: 143; my own calculations do not quite agree but would allow this result with a small shift in the value used for node passage by the moon). This date was then used as an era base in astronomical calculation. The system was in use by the fifth century A.D. in astronomical writings, abounding in Babylonian astronomical ideas and values which Neugebauer thinks were passed through the Greeks in northern India. Although not directly attested earlier than the fifth century A.D., this suggests a considerably earlier development of this era. A passage in the *Mahabhārata* puts the cataclysmic end of a preceding world age in the lunar station Revati, where the vernal equinox fell at the time of the *Mahabhārata*. If not a later interpolation, this strongly suggests that the astronomical associations of the world ages and probably the use of the Kaliyuga as an era base had already come into existence.

The second century B.C. is a reasonable date both for the planetary calculations and for the use of imperfect eclipse cycles. Neugebauer (1957-62: 142) stresses the 'very unsatisfactory situation' with respect to eclipse prediction even at 200 B.C. and the fact that no fully valid Babylonian theory was ever developed. The Babylonian method was not cyclical.

(g) The use of place value notation and of a symbol for zero is first attested in Babylon, clearly before 300 B.C. (Neugebauer 1957-62: 27); the symbol used by the Babylonians was a simple separation mark, and this seems to be the case also with the symbol used in Graeco-Egyptian papyri (Neugebauer 1957-62: 14), which resembles the later Hindu zero. Place value was used in China much earlier but without a zero symbol. Place value is clearly attested in India by the fifth century A.D. but direct epigraphic evidence for the use of any sort of zero symbol does not antedate the eighth century A.D. (Needham 1959, 3: 10-11); however, a zero symbol appears in Cambodia and Sumatra in 683 A.D. The fact that the first attested use of place value notation in India is in the same astronomical texts which have the first attested use of an astronomical era base and employ largely Babylonian astronomical contexts suggests that the ideas came together out of Babylon, during the time when it was part of the Seleucid empire.

(h) The nine-day planetary week of India is composed of the normal Hellenistic seven-day planetary week, with the addition at the end of two invisible planets, Rahu and Ketu, which were believed to

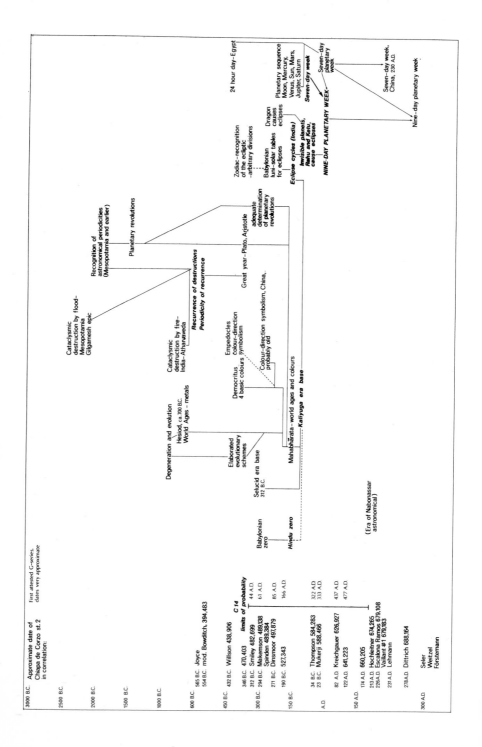

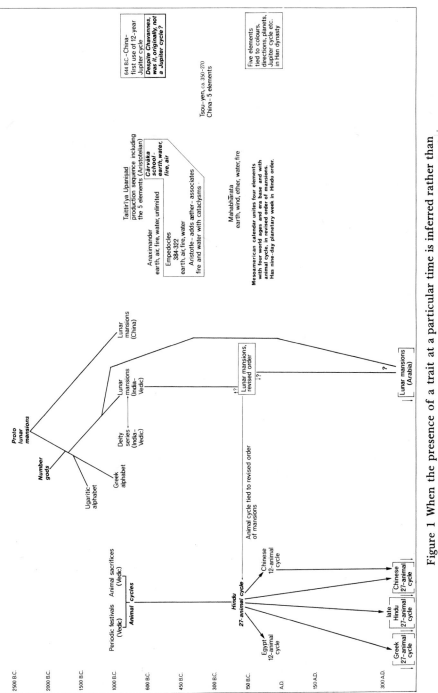

Figure 1 When the presence of a trait at a particular time is inferred rather than attested, the trait is italicized. This chart was prepared for me by Mary Beth Stokes.

3000 B.C.

2500 B.C.

2000 B.C.

1500 B.C.

1000 B.C.

600 B.C.

450 B.C.

300 B.C.

150 B.C.

A.D.

150 A.D.

300 A.D.

Proto lunar mansions

Lunar mansions (China)

Number gods

Ugaritic alphabet

Greek alphabet

Deity series (India-Vedic)

Lunar mansions (India-Vedic)

Lunar mansions, revised order

Lunar mansions (Arabia)

Periodic festivals (Vedic)

Animal sacrifices (Vedic)

Animal cycles

Animal cycle tied to revised order of mansions

Hindu 27-animal cycle

Chinese 12-animal cycle

Egypt 12-animal cycle

late Hindu 27-animal cycle

Chinese 27-animal cycle

Greek 27-animal cycle

Taittirīya Upaniṣad production sequence including the 5 elements (Aristotelian)

Cārvāka school – earth, water, fire, air

Anaximander earth, air, fire, water, unlimited

Empedocles 384–322 earth, air, fire, water

Aristotle – adds aether – associates fire and water with cataclysms

Mahābhārata earth, wind, ether, water, fire

Mesoamerican calendar unites four elements with four world ages and era base and with animal cycle, in revised order of mansions. Has nine-day planetary week in Hindu order.

644 B.C.–China– first use of 12-year Jupiter cycle

Despite Chavannes, was it, originally, not a Jupiter cycle?

Tsou-yen, ca. 350–270 China – 5 elements

Five elements tied to colours, directions, planets, Jupiter cycle etc. in Han dynasty cause eclipses. The order of the planets in the week is based on their assumed distance order from earth, coupled with the assumption that each ruled in succession over the hours of a 24-hour day. The distance order used was first generally accepted in Greece in the second century B.C. The planetary week itself is not certainly attested before the first century B.C. Between 40 and 60 A.D., Apollonius of Tyana is said to have been given, in India, a set of seven rings bearing the names of the seven planets, which he wore according to the names of the days (Colson 1926: 23). Recent evidence has shown that the reliability of the life of Apollonius is quite high and the story suggests that the seven-day week was known in India at that time. It is usually held that the seven-day week was not introduced into India until the third century A.D. and that the nine-day week was a later development.

With respect to the Mesoamerican comparisons, the G series of glyphs is not attested earlier than the Leyden Plate, and if one were to assume a separate introduction from India, there would be an additional 360 years of leeway. However, I am reluctant to assume more than one introduction. If the Nine Lords of the Night were introduced into Mesoamerica at the same time as the other calendrical traits considered, I do not believe that it is possible to find a correlation which will fit Mesoamerican evidence and allow the introduction of the seven day planetary week into India as late as the third century A.D.

(ii) I am here considering only iconographic evidence directly associated with the calendar. Of this, the comparison of *cipactli* with *makara* is most striking and Mesoamerican forms most closely resemble Indian forms of the first century B.C. or slightly later. I do not find iconographic comparisons of *cipactli* with Olmec or Chavin crocodilians as convincing. However, later Mesoamerican representations might depend in part on both sources. The incorporation of the crocodile head as the base of a tree is attested from Izapan times in Mesoamerica, but I have not found it until much later in Hindu areas.

The turtle with a snake wound around it is one of the four major calendar animals of China, attested from Han times, about the first century A.D. Iconographic evidence in India and the Hindu colonies is substantially later (as it is in Mesoamerica) but Hindu myths suggest that the basis for it is much earlier in India.

A similar situation exists for the rabbit in the moon, generally believed to have been introduced into China from India during the Han period, although iconographic evidence of the idea in India at that date is not known to me. Mythology suggests that the concept was well established in India much earlier.

The elephant-headed gods of India are first attested iconographically substantially later than their mythological prototypes, although even in mythology clear evidence for the elephant-headed gods does not seem to antedate the second century B.C. in sources known to me.

If one looks at these ideas together, they suggest a fixed limit not earlier than the time of Aristotle (say about 350 B.C.) and probably substantially later. In terms of the hypothesis of derivation from the Old World, all correlation constants smaller than 470,000 are extremely unlikely and those under 525,000 are quite unlikely. If the Nine Lords of the Night are accepted as coming with the other traits, I think that 525,000 can be accepted as a nearly absolute limit on correlations. In terms of suggested correlations, this would eliminate Spinden, Smiley, Makemson, Dinsmoor and the constant 507,994, which I have thought fitted my own ideas of the Mayan astronomy. Both the Thompson and Mukerji correlations handily pass this criterion, as do the many late correlations, which I think can be rejected on general Mesoamerican evidence.

REFERENCES

Bogue, P. (1967) The world directions in Greece, India and Mesoamerica. *Wisconsin Sociologist*, 5, nos. 1-2, 1-10.

Colson, F.H. (1962) *The Week*. London.

Gleadow, R. (1968) *The Origin of the Zodiac*.

Kelley, D.H. (1960) Calendar animals and deities. *Southwestern Journal of Anthropology*, 16, no. 3, 317-37.

Kelley, D.H. (1970) Indo-Greek cosmology and science in ancient Mesoamerica. Presented at the Symposium on New World Writing Systems in New York, July 1970. To be published.

Kelley, D.H. (1972) The nine lords of the night. University of California.

Kirchhoff, P. (1964) The diffusion of a great religious system from India to Mexico. *Proceedings of the 35th International Congress of America*, 1, 73-100.

Moran, H.A. and D.H. Kelley (1969) (Revised edition of Moran 1953) *The Alphabet and the Ancient Calendar Signs*. California.

Needham, J. (1959) *Science and Civilization in China*.

Neugebauer, O. (1957) Reprinted 1962. *The Exact Sciences in Antiquity*. New York.

Stewart, J.D. (1971) Graeco-Egyptian, Indian and Chinese animal cycles. Unpublished.

Weinstock, S. (1950) Lunar mansions and early calendars. *Journal of Hellenic Studies*, 69, 48-69.

H.B. NICHOLSON

Tepepolco, the locale of the first stage of Fr. Bernardino de Sahagún's great ethnographic project: historical and cultural notes

It has long been recognized that the single most valuable ethno-graphic source for any pre-Hispanic Mesoamerican high culture is the encyclopaedic compilation of Fr. Bernardino de Sahagún. His project was pursued over a long period (apparently c.1547-1585), primarily in three communities of the Basin of Mexico, Tepepolco, Tlatelolco, and Tenochtitlan. The identification, description, and analysis of the surviving Sahaguntine documentation and the reconstruction of the various stages in his complex endeavour have been challenging tasks for modern scholarship — in which the names of Ramírez, Chavero, García Icazbalceta, Brinton, Seler, Paso y Troncoso, Toro, Jiménez Moreno, Nicolau d'Olwer, Garibay, León-Portilla, Ballesteros and associates, Dibble and Anderson, Robertson, Baudot, and Cline perhaps stand out most prominently. As a result of the investigations of these and other students our understanding of Sahagún's com-plicated bibliography has been considerably clarified, and the evolution of his monumental undertaking has been well blocked out in general. However, many obscurities remain. Above all, more analysis is needed to establish the precise relationships of the various data collected in different places at different times.

Recently the author (Nicholson, in press) analysed the first comprehensive compilation of data gathered under the direction of 'the father of modern ethnography', that obtained from informants in a large but somewhat peripheral community located near the northeast edge of the Basin of Mexico, Tepepolco. By means of a detailed, section by section comparison (summarized in a series of charts) between the material collected in Tepepolco — which Paso y Troncoso dubbed the *Primeros Memoriales* (PM) — and the final *Historia General (Universal) de las Cosas de la Nueva España* (HG), I was able to demonstrate that, contrary to often expressed views, most of the PM does not appear, intact or modified, in the final HG.

As I concluded my analysis in the article cited:

Very little of the ethnographic information collected by Sahagún in Tepepolco at the outset of his ambitious project actually ended up, as such, in the final 12 Books of the HG. It amounts to only five full paragraphs and parts of two others, out of a total of 47 (excluding 1 and 8). And all, with only one exception (Tetzcoco and Huexotla dynasties in Chapter III, par. 1), are confined to HG, II, Appendix. Even the fairly extensive illustrative material was virtually ignored in the final work, the only certain exceptions being the 20 deity representations derived from those in Chapter I, par. 5, which illustrate the *Florentine Codex* version of HG, I, and the Tetzcoco and Huexotla dynastic lists of the *Florentine Codex* version of HG, VIII, 3, 4, derived from the pictures of Chapter III, par. 1. Whatever the reasons — perhaps because his Tlatelolco information was generally more copious than that compiled in Tepepolco, because he knew the former community more intimately, or because some of his best native informants originated there — when drawing up the HG Sahagún consistently preferred his Tlatelolco to his Tepepolco data, especially when they covered about the same ground. This fact has not been sufficiently appreciated. One reason, perhaps, is that Sahagún's own phrasing of the relation of his Tepepolco to his Tlatelolco information in his prologue to HG, II, is somewhat ambiguous and appears to place greater emphasis on the Tepepolco materials than on those from Tlatelolco, when the exact opposite was clearly the case. Sahagún thus did not just revise and expand his Tepepolco data in Tlatelolco. Although obviously still guided by his Tepepolco *minuta*, he gathered a great amount of new and independent information, most of which passed into the final HG while most of the PM did not. The full implication of this circumstance is that the PM can generally stand on its own as a separate document and should be handled as such rather than merely as a brief, preparatory stage in the compilation of the HG. Certainly the publication of palaeographies of all its texts and their translations in a current major language, as a unit, with notes, indices, and all other normal apparatus of modern critical scholarship, would seem to be one of the most obvious needs of Sahaguntine studies. Although the Tables show that most of the PM has been palaeographized and translated, they also indicate that such publications are widely scattered throughout the literature and in different languages — aside from being somewhat uneven in quality. Merely to assemble in one place all of the significant PM translations requires the acquisition of a great number of separate, often scarce publications. The great desirability, therefore, of the unitary publication of the palaeography and translation of the *Primeros Memoriales* is evident.

Sahagún (1956, I: 27-31, 105-7; Cline 1971: 242-44, 247-9) himself, in his general prologue and, above all, in that to Book II of his HG, tells us most of what we know about the initial, Tepepolco phase of his great project. After receiving an order from his Provincial, Fray Francisco de Toral, to compile in Nahuatl what would be useful in furthering the Christianizing of the natives, Sahagún moved to Tepepolco. There, with the aid of a 'minuta o memoria', he began a systematic interrogation of a group of informants consisting of the 'señor del pueblo', Don Diego de Mendoza, and ten or twelve 'principales ancianos'. He was aided by four of his trilingual ex-students of the Tlatelolco Colegio de Santa Cruz, also *principales*. For close to two years he pursued his questioning, following the order of his *minuta*. His informants supplied him with pictorial materials in response to his queries, and the trilingual students wrote the explanations below them. Sahagún mentions no dates, but there is compelling evidence (Nicolau d'Olwer 1952: 51, 55) that this Tepepolco investigation took place between 5 January 1558 and 6 September 1561, most probably during 1559-1561. Luckily, much of this priceless Tepepolco *corpus*, the *Primeros Memoriales*, has survived, divided between two Madrid libraries (Real Academia de la Historia and Real Palacio). It is virtually all in Nahuatl and contains many native tradition pictorial representations. Photographic reproductions of all of the relevant manuscript pages of the PM were published in 1905 by Paso y Troncoso, and many of its sections have been palaeographized and translated in modern times directly into German, Spanish, or English (see Tables in Nicholson, in press).

One of the most significant aspects of the PM is that most of its data were supplied by informants hailing not from one of the great native power centres of central Mexico but from a populous but relatively obscure community. Aside from the invaluable *relaciones geográficas* of the 1579-85 series, the lesser communities of Mesoamerica are rarely well represented in the sixteenth-century sources. The fact that the PM provides a view of late pre-Hispanic culture from the standpoint of a subordinate community lends it special ethnographic value.

In spite of the obvious importance of knowing as much as possible about the pueblo where so much priceless information was collected by the greatest of the Spanish missionary-ethnographers, Tepepolco has received little systematic archaeological or ethnohistorical investigation.[1] A fair amount of documentation is extant concerning this community and others in its vicinity. At Contact, this whole area, a rolling, semi-arid steppe particularly well-suited for maguey cultivation and studded with medium-sized hills (among them 'Tepepul', seat of a noted Tlaloc shrine (Torquemada 1943-44, II: 46), which gave its name to the town, 'Place of the Large Hill' was known as 'las provincias de la campiña' (Alva Ixtlilxochitl 1952, II: 168) and

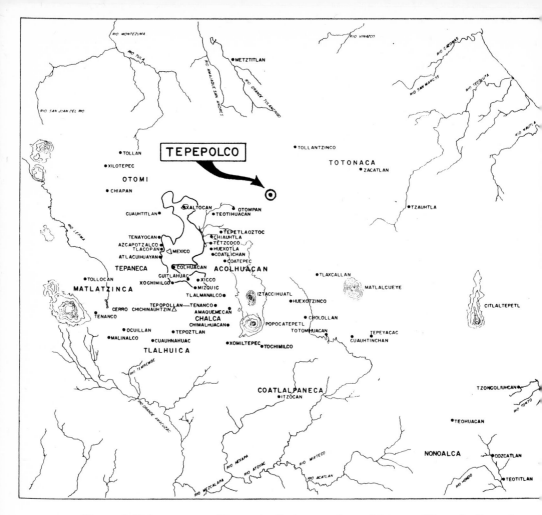

Figure 1 Major communities and ethnic groupings of late pre-Hispanic Central Mexico, specifying location of Tepepolco (base map after Carrasco 1971: Fig. 1).

belonged to northern Acolhuacan, the super-province ruled from Tetzcoco (see Gibson 1956).[2] Four large communities located in this region, Acolman, Teotihuacan, Otompan, and Tollantzinco, boasted rulers who were counted among the 'catorce grandes del reino'. They were members of powerful *tlatoani* lineages in their own right, although in Triple Alliance times they rendered fealty to the *huey tlatoani* of Tetzcoco. All four must have exerted strong influence on Tepepolco and its immediate neighbours, which lacked *tlatoani* rule and were administered by stewards appointed by the Tetzcoco ruler (Alva Ixtlilxochitl 1952, I: 167-71, 176).

Although nominally all part of Acolhuacan, some of Tepepolco's closest neighbours (Cempoallan, Tlaquilpan, Tecpilpan, Epazoyocan, Itzihuinquilocan, Tezontepec, Temazcalapan, Teacalco, Maquizco, Aztaquemecan, et al.) were directly tributary to Tenochtitlan as well (Barlow 1949: 64-72, who cites primary sources). Whether Tepepolco also paid a portion of its tribute to Tenochtitlan is not clear. Apan, one of its dependencies, along with four other unnamed towns, was apparently a Tenochca *calpixqui* headquarters (Scholes and Adams 1957: 44). Consequently, it is possible that Tepepolco was included in this tribute jurisdiction in spite of López Cacho's (1905: 297-8) informants' claim of an autonomous, tribute-free status for the community (which, as far as Tetzcoco at least is concerned, seems patently false). Certainly the strong Mexica influence in this region is abundantly evident in the PM, particularly in the religious sphere. Underlying and undoubtedly providing a fertile seedbed for this late (post-Itzcoatl) Tenochca influence was an earlier wave of Colhuaque movement into the area (the Tenochca can also be considered, in some sense, a Colhuaque branch), probably sometime in the second half of the fourteenth century or near the start of the next (Dibble 1951: Sheet 5; Alva Ixtlilxochitl 1952, I: 139-40; Obregón 1949: 31, 36; Torquemada 1943-4: 89). And it was probably at this time that most of the religious-ritual system, so importantly recorded by Sahagún in the PM, must have become established. However, the Huitzilopochtli emphasis was undoubtedly much intensified by the later imposition of direct Tenochca political control over part of the Tepepolco area.[3]

The Tepepolco zone at Contact was trilingual, Nahuatl, Otomi, and 'Chichimeca', with the former clearly dominant (e.g., López Cacho 1905: 294). The survival of 'Popoloca' in neighbouring Teotihuacan (Castañeda 1905: 220) and the tradition of a former Totonac occupation of next-door Cempoallan (Obregón 1949: 30; one form of the place sign is the head of a Totonac on a hill (Obregón 1949: Lám. VI; Beyer 1923-24)) provide some tantalizing clues to the pre-Chichimec linguistic picture — which is of particular interest because of the challenging problem of the speech of Classic Teotihuacan. Most of the communities of the area, including Tepepolco (López Cacho 1905: 292: 'Tlecolistle, Chalote [Techalote?], Epcoatle, Tespotle [Tezcapoctle?]') boasted of valiant 'Chichimec' founders. Remnants of this original element, therefore, apparently survived into the sixteenth century.

According to the *Códice Xolotl* (Dibble 1951: Sheet 1; cf. Alva Ixtlilxochitl 1952, I: 84; Torquemada 1943-44, I: 42), Tepepolco was apparently already established when Xolotl entered the Basin of Mexico (5. Tecpatl, 1120, in accordance with the most likely reconstruction of the internal chronology of this source) — or perhaps its place sign here only indicates a reconnaissance of the region where the community was later founded. In any case, according to the same source (Dibble 1951: Sheets 1-2; cf. Alva Ixtlilxochitl 1952, I: 89-90, II: 38; Torquemada 1943-4, I: 46-7), a Chichimec chief, Zacatitechcochi, who with five others entered the Basin of Mexico between 1129 and 1134, was established there by Xolotl a few years later. Tepepolco is next (1. Tecpatl, 1168) mentioned (Dibble 1951: Sheet 2; cf. Alva Ixtlilxochitl 1952, I: 95-7, II: 46, 49) as participating in the Xolotl-directed construction of a large game enclosure east of Tetzcotzinco, along with four other communities of the area including Cempoallan and Tollantzinco. A few years later (1. Acatl, 1207) this whole northern region, ruled by the six Chichimec chiefs now led by Yacanex (Yacatzotzoloc) of Tepetlaoztoc, was given in fief by Xolotl to Huetzin of Coatlinchan, the original Acolhuaque *cabecera*. Soon after, Tepepolco became involved in the two 'Chichimeca Wars' (1220 and 1324?, 1350?; Dibble 1951: Sheets 3-4) centred in this area during the reign at Tetzcoco of Quinatzin (*Códice Xolotl*: 1220 (1272?)-1357).[4] According to Alva Ixtlilxochitl (1952, I: 99-100, 124-8, II: 50-2, 65-7; cf. Torquemada 1943-4, I: 65, 85-6), these involved the struggle of the 'unreconstructed' northern Chichimeca against the civilizing influences flowing northward through the more southerly portion of Acolhuacan, from Colhuacan and Chalco. As a consequence of the defeat of Yacanex and his barbarous hosts, Zacatitechcochi was either put to flight (Alva Ixtlilxochitl 1952, I: 288) or killed by Quinatzin of Tetzcoco (Torquemada 1943-4, I: 84) and Cuauhtlatzin substituted as governor in his place (Alva Ixtlilxochitl 1952, I: 127.

A Xaltocan source (Paso y Troncoso 1939-42, X: 105; see Carrasco 1950) includes Tepepolco in the fairly extensive fourteenth-century empire of this great Otomi centre. The Colhuaque migration to the area, which had such transcendent cultural effects, probably occurred near the end of this period. Some Otomi movements might also have taken place at this time, but perhaps most of the Otomi colonization of the region occurred in the wake of the Tepanec conquest of Xaltocan (Alva Ixtlilxochitl 1952, I: 137-8, II: 77-8; cf. Torquemada 1943-4, I: 87-8). After the fall of Xaltocan around the close of the fourteenth century, Tepepolco might have briefly passed under the hegemony of Teotihuacan (Castañeda 1905: 219), but the *Códice Xolotl* (Dibble 1951: Sheets 5, 7; cf. Alva Ixtlilxochitl 1952, I: 141, II: 83, 158) indicates that Techotlalatzin (1357-1409) and his son and successor, Ixtlilxochitl (1409-18), controlled Tepepolco and other towns of this area. The latter's nurse, Zacaquimiltzin, in fact came from Tepepolco.[5] Tepepolco's ruler of this period is shown on *Códice Xolotl* Sheet 5, but the interpretation of the name sign was not given by either Alva Ixtlilxochitl or Torquemada and is defaced.

Tepepolco almost certainly became part of the Azcapotzalco empire of Tezozomoc after the Tepanec conquest of all of 'core Acolhuacan', including Tetzcoco, in 1416-18, despite the disclaimers of López Cacho's informants in 1581 (López Cacho 1905: 297-8). Now ruled by a Huehueilpicatzin (Dibble 1951: Sheet 9; Alva Ixtlilxochitl 1952, II: 104), Tepepolco favoured the restoration movement of Nezahualcoyotl, the exiled heir to the throne of Tetzcoco, and aided his successful cause (Alva Ixtlilxochitl 1952, I: 217, II: 135). With the downfall of Azcapotzalco in 1428, Tetzcoco — and, increasingly, Tenochtitlan — dominated the region politically until the Conquest, and its Nahuatization and, to a much less extent, its Otomization, must have proceeded apace. In the 1430s, after his assumption of power at Tetzcoco, Nezahualcoyotl made Tepepolco, with thirteen dependencies, the head of a tributary province ruled by a steward named Coxcoch (Alva Ixtlilxochitl 1952, II: 169). Its basic political-administrative status probably did not change appreciably until the Conquest, although, as mentioned, at some point some of its tribute might have been also assigned to Tenochtitlan.[6]

Table 1   Pre-Hispanic rulers of Tepepolco
(after *Códice Xolotl* and Alva Ixtlilxochitl)

Names	Approximate Dates
Coxcoch (steward appointed by Nezahualcoyotl)	1435—?
Huehueilpicatzin	1400—1435
Cuauhtlatzin (illegible name sign, *Códice Xolotl* Sheet 5)	1375—1400
Cuauhtlatzin	1350—1375
Zacatitechcochi	1130—1350 (series of leaders symbolized by most prominent member?)

Certainly the Tepepolco zone shared in the great rise to power and prosperity of all of Acolhuacan after the establishment of the Tenochtitlan-Tetzcoco-Tlacopan Triple Alliance in this same decade. The town was obviously thriving and populous at Contact. Cook and Borah (1960: 65) have estimated the population of Tepepolco (*cabecera* and dependencies) in 1568 at 17,408. It was certainly much higher than this at the time of the Conquest. Motolinia (1971: 119) remarks on the size and importance of its principal temple. As late as 1581 it was being referred to as 'el grande pueblo de Tepepulco' (Obregón 1949: 34-5). In a march location, with the great autonomous and hostile super-province of Tlaxcallan just to the east, Tepepolco seems to have exercised dominion over a fairly extensive area (29 dependencies are listed in one mid-sixteenth century source (Paso y Troncoso 1905-7, I: 84-5), 39 in another (López Cacho 1905: 303-5) of somewhat later date), which included some fairly sizable sub-*cabeceras* such as Tlalanapan, Apan, and others. Apparently exceptional opportunities existed for military activity on the part of Tepepolcan manhood. One of the *xochiyao-yotl*, 'flowery war', fields was located on its eastern boundary (Alva Ixtlilxochitl 1952, II: 207; Durán 1967, I: 34, II: 290). The great importance of the Huitzilopochtli cult here might have owed something to this fact — in addition to the obvious strong Mexica influence already noted.

Kirchhoff (1955) has suggested that Tepepolco had become a major culture centre as well and that this played a part in Sahagún's selection of it as the place to initiate his systematic ethnographic investigations, but this seems quite speculative. Certainly, if this had been the leading criterion, Tetzcoco would have appeared to have been a more logical choice. Sahagún was probably assigned to the Franciscan establishment in Tepepolco for other reasons in addition to the facilitating of his ethnographic project. It could perhaps be argued that any major Basin of Mexico native community where the Franciscans had founded a convent probably would have served as well for his purposes. In any case, Tepepolco must have been a representative carrier of the dominant culture patterns current in all of the major communities of the Basin of Mexico at the advent of Cortés. Whatever the reason it was chosen, this particular Central Mexican Indian community, otherwise not particularly prominent in the annals of this region during the late pre-Hispanic period, will always enjoy a special fame because the dedicated Spanish ecclesiastic who was perhaps the greatest ethnographer until modern times happened to begin his systematic investigations there.

NOTES

1 Paso y Troncoso, in his notes to López Cacho 1905, provides a sketchy but very useful summary of information concerning the pre-Hispanic and early colonial community. First taken as an *encomienda* by Cortés, Tepepolco was placed in the Crown by the Second Audiencia in 1531 (Archivo General de la Nación 1952: 400). Although Nicolau d'Olwer (1952: 52) states that the Franciscans established themselves there in the same year as that in which Sahagún began his investigations, López Cacho (1905: 302-3) indicates that the convent was founded by another famous missionary-ethnographer, Fr. Andrés de Olmos, within a period which Paso y Troncoso calculated as 1530-33 (cf. Kubler 1948, II: 475-6; Gorbea Trueba 1957: 8-9; Vázquez Vázquez 1965: 62). At any rate, as we know from Motolinia (1971: 118-119), Tepepolco was one of the first native communities to respond favourably to Franciscan proselytization efforts. Subordinated to a former dependency, Apan, in the later colonial period (its size had fallen to 64 families in the mid-eighteenth century (Villaseñor y Sanchez 1946: 381), in 1917 the community (population 1,330 in 1950), now known as Tepeapulco, became the *cabecera* of a *municipio* of the state of Hidalgo.

A well-documented summary of the post-Conquest administrative, ecclesiastical, and demographic history of Tepepolco is included in Peter Gerhard's recent (1972) *A Guide to the Historical Geography of New Spain* (Cambridge Latin American Studies, 14), pp. 52-4.

2 Apparently the Tepepolco area was located just to the southeast of the famous 'Teotlalpan' (Cook 1949), although some sources (e.g., López de Velasco 1894: 195) include it in a 'Provincia de la Teotlalpan'.

3 Following the fall of Tollan, one group of Toltec emigrants, led by Nauhyotl (who died in the area), apparently moved through this region en route to Colhuacan. Some Toltec-Colhuaque settlement, therefore, might have been made at this much earlier time (see Kirchhoff 1955). The presence of *estancias* and *barrios* named Tlailotlacan in this area (e.g., Castañeda 1905: 221 (Teotihuacan); Ledesma 1905: 88 (between Epazoyocan and Itzihuinquilocan)) might suggest that an even earlier civilized wave, the Tlailotlaque from the Chalco region, reached this Chichimec area before (first half of the fourteenth century?) the Colhuaque groups moved in (Dibble 1951: Sheet 4; Alva Ixtlilxochitl 1952, I: 123-4, 289, II: 69-70). According to Alva Ixtlilxochitl, the Tlailotlaque were particular devotees of Tezcatlipoca, and the PM indicates that his cult was well developed in the Tepepolco area.

4 The dates of the two 'Yacanex Wars' present a considerable chronologic problem. The first is clearly dated at 1. Tecpatl on *Códice Xolotl* Sheet 3, probably A.D. 1220, following the 'dead reckoning' system (departing from 1. Acatl = 1519) of correlating native and Christian dates in this pictorial (see discussion in Nicholson 1972: 193-5, where the variant Jiménez Moreno-Kirchhoff system (Mexica 1. Acatl = 'Chichimec' or 'Tetzcocano' 7. Acatl), which consistently correlates *Códice Xolotl* dates 20 years later — i.e., 1. Tecpatl, 1220, becomes 1240 — is also recognized). Probably the same year, 1. Tecpatl, is also specified as that of Quinatzin's accession as Tetzcoco ruler. The second conflict, which also occurred during Quinatzin's reign, is not dated in the *Códice Xolotl* (Sheet 4). Alva Ixtlilxochitl in one place (1952, I: 287-8) appeared to date it at 1. Tecpatl (1324), in another (1952, I: 124-31), explicitly with 1. Tochtli (1350) — in any case, in all his accounts, between the death of Tlotzin Pochotl, Quinatzin's father (1. Tochtli, 1298), and the latter's own demise (8. Calli, 1357). Even if the date of the first conflict (and Quinatzin's accession — as Alva Ixtlilxochitl did in one place (1952, I: 109-110)) is shifted forward one 52 year cycle, to 1272, we are confronted here with obviously impossible time spans, as with many of the reigns of the earlier 'Chichimec' rulers in the *Códice Xolotl* — and also in the works of its chief interpreter, Alva Ixtlilxochitl. To attempt to harmonize the *Códice Xolotl* dates with 'logically possible' reign and life lengths, as prectically all modern students have tried to do, is, in my view, a questionable procedure since we seem to be dealing here with traditional accounts later adjusted to somewhat artificial chronologic schemes (cf. Nicholson 1971: 64-70).

5 This purported Teotihuacan political control over Otompan and Tepepolco might be based on a dim recollection of the period of the apogee of Classic Teotihuacan, but this seems doubtful.

6 Tepepolco was supposedly involved in the 'revolt' of Ixtlilxochitl against his half brother, Cacama, c. 1516-17, favouring 'ò por miedo, o por amor' his cause (Torquemada 1943-4, I: 224-5; cf. Alva Ixtlilxochitl 1952, II: 330-2). For Tepepolco's administrative status within the imperial system of Acolhuacan at the time of the Conquest and in the early colonial period, see Gibson 1956, who cites all relevant primary sources.

REFERENCES

Alva Ixtlilxochitl, F. de (1952) *Obras Históricas de Don Fernando de Alva Ixtlilxochitl.* 2 vols. 2nd (offset) edition. Mexico.

Archivo General de la Nación (1952) *El Libro de las tasaciones de pueblos de la Nueva España, siglo XVI.* Mexico.

Barlow, R. (1949) The extent of the empire of the Culhua Mexica. *Ibero-Americana,* 28.

Beyer, H. (1923-24) Sobre algunas representaciones de antiguos Totonacos. *Anthropos,* 18-19, 253-7.

Carrasco, P. (1950) *Los Otomies; cultura e historia prehispánicas de los pueblos Mesoamericanos de habla Otomiana.* Universidad Nacional Autónoma de México, Instituto de Historia, Publicaciones, Primera Serie, no. 15.

Carrasco, P. (1971) The peoples of central Mexico and their historical traditions. In R. Wauchope, G. Ekholm and I. Bernal (eds.), *Handbook of Middle American Indians,* 10, 459-73.

Castañeda, F. de (1905) Relación de Tecciztlan y su partido. In F. del Paso y Troncoso (ed.), *Papeles de Nueva España,* 6, 209-30.

Cline, H.F. (1971) Missing and variant prologues and dedications in Sahagún's *Historia General*: texts and English translations. *Estudios de Cultura Nahuatl,* 9, 237-51.

Cook, S.F. (1949) The historical demography and ecology of the Teotlalpan. *Ibero-Americana,* 33.

Cook, S.F. and W. Borah (1960) The Indian population of central Mexico, 1531-1610. *Ibero-Americana,* 44.

Dibble, C.E. (1951) (ed.) *Códice Xolotl.* Universidad Nacional Autónoma de México, Instituto de Historia, Publicaciones, Primera Serie, no. 22.

Durán, Fr. Diego de (1967) *Historia de las Indias de Nueva España e Islas de la Tierra Firme,* ed. A.M. Garibay K. 2 vols. Mexico.

Gibson, C. (1956) Llamamiento general, repartimiento, and the empire of

Acolhuacan. *Hispanic American Historical Review*, 36, 1, 1-27.

Gorbea Trueba, J. (1957) *Tepeapulco*. Instituto Nacional de Antropología e Historia, Mexico, Dirección de Monumentos Coloniales.

Kirchhoff, P. (1959) Las dos rutas de los Colhua entre Tula y Culhuacán. *Mitteilungen aus dem Museum für Völkerkunde in Hamburg*, 25 (Festband Franz Termer: Amerikanistische Miszellen), 75-81.

Kubler, G. (1948) *Mexican Architecture of the Sixteenth Century*. 2 vols. New Haven, Yale Historical Publications, History of Art, V.

Ledesma, Fr. Bartolomé de (1905) Descripción del Arzobispado de México sacada de las memorias originales hechas por los doctrineros ó capellanes y compiladas por . . . O.S.D., administrador del mismo arzobispado. In F. del Paso y Troncoso (ed.), *Papeles de Nueva Espana*, 3.

López Cacho, J. (1905) Relación de Tepepulco. In F. del Paso y Troncoso (ed.), *Papeles de Nueva España*, 6, 291-305.

López de Velasco, J. (1894) *Geografía y descripción universal de las Indias*, ed. J. Zaragoza. Madrid.

Motolinia (Fr. Toribio de Benavente) (1971) *Memoriales o libro de las cosas de la Nueva España y de los naturales de ella*. Universidad Nacional Autónoma de México, Instituto de Investigaciones Históricas, Serie de Historiadores y Cronistas de Indias, 2.

Nicholson, H.B. (1971) Pre-Hispanic central Mexican historiography. In *Investigaciones contemporáneas sobre historia de Mexico. Memorias de la Tercera Reunión de Historiadores Mexicanos y Norteamericanos, Oaxtepec, Morelos, 4-7 de Noviembre de 1969*, 38-81.

Nicholson, H.B. (1972) The problem of the historical identification of the Cerro Portezuelo/San Antonio archaeological site: an hypothesis. In *Teotihuacan: XI Mesa Redonda* (Sociedad Mexicana de Antropología), 157-200.

Nicholson, H.B. (in press) Sahagún's *Primeros Memoriales*, Tepepolco, 1559-1561. *Handbook of Middle American Indians*, Austin, Texas.

Nicolau d'Olwer, L. (1952) Fr. Bernardino de Sahagún (1499-1590). Mexico, Instituto Panamericano de Geografía e Historia, Publicación 142 (Comisión de Historia, 40; Historiadores de America, 9).

Obregón, L. (1949) Relación de Zempoala y su Partido, 1580. Tlalocan III, 1, 29-41.

Paso y Troncoso, F. del (ed.) (1905) *Historia general de las cosas de Nueva España* por Fr. Bernardino de Sahagún. Madrid.

Paso y Troncoso, F. del (ed.) (1905-7) *Papeles de Nueva España*. 6 vols. Madrid.

Paso y Troncoso, F. del (ed.) (1939-42) *Epistolario de Nueva España, 1505-1818*. 16 vols. Biblioteca Histórica Mexicana de Obras Inéditas, Segunda Serie, 1-16. Mexico.

Sahagún, Fr. Bernardino de (1956) *Historia general de las cosas de Nueva España*, ed. A.M. Garibay K. 4 vols. Mexico.

Scholes, F.V. and E.B. Adams (eds.) (1957) *Información sobre los tributos que los Indios pagaban a Moctezuma: año de 1554*. Mexico.

Torquemada, Fr. Juan de (1943-44) *Monarquía Indiana*. 3 vols. Mexico.

Vázquez Vázquez, E. (1965) *Distribución geográfica y organización de las ordenes religiosas en la Nueva España (siglo XVI)*. Universidad Nacional Autónoma de México, Instituto de Geografía.

Villaseñor y Sánchez, J.A. (1746) *Theatro americano: descripción general de los reynos, y provincias de la Nueva España, y sus jurisdicciones*. Mexico.

GORDON BROTHERSTON

Huitzilopochtli and what was made of him

The Aztecs left no-one in doubt about how much Huitzilopochtli mattered to them. His temple, with Tlaloc's, crowned the largest pyramid in the largest living city encountered by Europeans in America. Those who traded, fought or dealt in any way with the Aztecs could not and did not fail to register his presence, hundreds of thousands of them mortally. The Spanish sensed him at the heart of all that threatened them. In the eyes of Sahagún he waxed so great that from being simply a major god in the Nahuatl of his Informants he became 'el principal dios que adoraban ... los mexicanos' (Anderson and Dibble 1950).

If prominent, Huitzilopochtli was also complex, notably so even in a religion as intricate as that of the ancient Mexicans. He has been seen as a solar, but also a lunar god; god of fire and war, yet son of Tlaloc; only a common man yet omnipotent. Sometimes he is born once, sometimes twice; sometimes he is a sacrificer, sometimes a victim. His name links him with the hummingbird, the agave, the south, left-handedness, and a range of proper names. In some texts he leads his people from Aztlan; elsewhere he turns up later on the journey to Tenochtitlan, if at all.

Efforts to make sense of all this were made already in the sixteenth century in Spanish texts like the *Códice Ramírez*; but little of value was done before Eduard Seler began his researches 300 years later. In fact Seler devoted only one essay specifically to 'Uitzilopochtli, der sprechende Kolibri' (1923) and it is certainly elliptical even by his standards. But this piece, together with other oblique commentaries in 'Eine Liste der mexikanischer Monatsfeste' (1902), 'Wo lag Aztlan?' (1904), 'Einiges über die natürlichen Grundlagen mexikanischer Mythen' (1908) and other studies bring into sharp focus the fundamental difficulty of Huitzilopochtli: his dual nature. On the one hand Seler registers exhaustively Huitzilopochtli's divine qualities and celestial nature as they are displayed in the Borbonicus and Telleriano-Remensis codexes, and in the myth and Sacred Hymns gathered by Sahagún's Informants, and links them definitively with the fifteenth-century carvings and statuary known to archaeologists of his day. On the other hand he allows free rein to an uncharacteristic euhemerism and detects many local, human and 'personal' features in Huitzilopochtli's make-up. The sources he used to support this second line of thought were not always as good as they might have been, however. Tezozomoc's Spanish chronicle is preferred to his Nahuatl one, and to more intelligent and less Europeanized works in Nahuatl like Castillo's fragments and Chimal-pahin's *Rélations*; also Durán and Torquemada are quoted too fondly, and to the exclusion of primary texts like the *Unos annales históricos de la nación mexicana*. This partly explains why he left his main essay open-ended ('Vielleicht war Uitzilopochtli nur ein Mensch') and in tacit contradiction with arguments advanced elsewhere in his *Gesammelte Abhandlungen*.

Acknowledging Seler's start, Lewis Spence (1923) then added theories of his own, emphasizing Huitzilopochtli's fetishist origins as a humming-bird warrior and then the spirit of the agave. This led both to some brilliant (though finally unprovable) insights into his involvement in the *pulque* ceremonies as reported by Sahagún, and to the unequivocal statement that from such humble beginnings Huitzilopochtli's status was abruptly raised to that of a solar god at a late stage, he being then provided with an appropriate hymnology and a myth which was 'obviously aetiological and exhibits the influence of priestly contrivance and popular imagination'. After this have come the consolidating, though decidedly less disenchanted, references in the work of Alfonso Caso (1936 and 1953), and more recently Miguel León-Portilla (1959). We have also Ignacio Bernal's 'Huitzilopochtli vivo' (1957), a valuable summary and collation of first sources, and R.C. Padden's *The Hummingbird and the Hawk* (1967), with its overtly anti-*indigenista* bias. Padden explains Huitzilopochtli's name in terms of the fascination of the Aztecs as 'palaeolithic barbarians' for the hummingbird (*huitzilin*) crests fashioned to the south (*opochtli*) in Michoacan, and his role as a sacrificer by an incorrect reading of Seler. And while he may be right in contending that Huitzilopochtli the oracle promising riches could not have been part of the Aztecs' original experience or oral literature, he is patently not so in claiming that 'we have no alternative but to assume' that this role can have been assigned to him only by the 'conquering Mexica' from 'a position of imperial prominence'. His neo-historical advice that we should 'look more closely into the affairs of the men who created Huitzilopochtli' is refreshing; it is a pity he didn't first consider other alternatives and then take it himself.

A fact of what Bernal has helpfully called 'el complejo Huitzilo-pochtli' which has been generally agreed on or at least not disallowed is that unlike both ancient Mesoamerican gods like Tlaloc and astral deities of the invading Chichimeca such as Tezcatlipoca, Huitzilopochtli has an indelible secular streak, a not wholly suppressed biography as an earthly being. The most powerful indication of his humanness is of course that of Sahagún's Informants, in the famous phrase 'çan maceoalli çan tlacatl catca' (Anderson and Dibble 1950: he was only a common man, a human being). Chimalpahin and Castillo both speak of him as a real hero of early Aztec history and, though independent as sources, coincide in giving him a proper name from which his divine one was later derived. For the former he was Huitzilton (1889: 269) and for the latter Uitçitl, a 'macehual' indeed and a warrior who was also simply left-handed: 'auh yece opochmaye, uei tiaquaul' (1908: 82). *Unos annales históricos* also present him as an earth-bound creature, and Tezozomoc's *Nahuatl* (1949) elaborates this, saying he once lived among his people and was their friend: 'yhuan oyntlanne oquin mocniuhtiaya in yehuantin Azteca'. No less important is the fact that there is not a graphic depiction of him which does not indicate earthly origin. In the Boturini Codex we find the most prosaic drawing of the hummingbird 'disguise' which was characteristic of him; here he is helping the journeying Aztecs as a dead warrior's soul, the hummingbird guise being perhaps preferred to the alternative of the butterfly because of the phonetic association with his name. In the Borbonicus Codex he appears, in addition, with the eye-adornment (*mixcitlal-huiticac moteneua tlayoualli*) which according to Seler (1923: 164) was worn specifically by a 'toter Häuptling'. The sources quoted above may otherwise differ greatly from one another, but they have the common message that at one point at least Huitzilopochtli was a human being.

Beside this residually historical character stands Huitzilopochtli the celestial, the divine. This is the being who rises as the sun to the zenith, celebrated in Aztec carvings, sacred hymns and myths. These sources (Seler 1904: 767ff and 965ff; Garibay 1958) are consistent in telling of his miraculous conception in the womb of the earth-mother Coatlicue and of his birth on his shield ('chimalpanecatl' as the 5th Sacred Hymn puts it) on the mountain Coatepec. Bearing his shield (*teueuel*), and his *xiuhatatl* or *xiuhcoatl* (his standard weapons as a deity in all sources), he pursues and slays his elder sister Coyolxauhqui, the moon, and his half-brothers the Centzon-Uitznaua, the 400 or countless stars of the southern sky. His might enables the sun to rise and is itself solar: 'quen ya noca o ya tonac' (for through me the sun rises).

The poetic force of surviving compositions which celebrate the solar Huitzilopochtli, together with the fact that he appears as a god in certain Mesoamerican sagas of undeniable antiquity, could suggest that the Aztec tribal chief, Huitzilopochtli the man, took his name from a famous god, in his honour, in the way, for example, that the historical Quetzalcoatl attached himself to an ancient and illustrious plumed serpent deity. For according to the *Historia de los mexicanos por sus pinturas* (León-Portilla 1959: 93-5) he was the fourth son of the original dual creator Ometeotl, and shared responsibility with Quetzalcoatl (the third divine son) for establishing order on earth and for making the first man and woman. In *Una historia de los reinos* (Seler 1923: 63) he is found again among the first gods, sacrificing himself with Tezcatlipoca to give the sun life, an act arguably alluded to in the First Sacred Hymn. With Tezcatlipoca as a companion once more, he was the devilish dancer who helped to wreck Tula, according to Sahagún (1938: 275).

References like these are very rare, however, and cannot resist close examination. In the last case Sahagún in fact hedges with the phrase 'dicen que era Huitzilopochtli'. As for the more imposing creator god enshrined in the *Historia de los mexicanos*, his shape is far from pristine, as much else in that Spanish document. Indeed 'Uchilobi' turns out to be but a second name of the fourth son 'Ometecitl', further known as 'Maquezcoatl', and as a name is expressly reported to be the one the Mexicans decided to use for this deity. This still leaves the joint sacrifice with Tezcatlipoca in a document as substantial as *Una historia de los reinos*, and there is no simple explanation for it, although another source no less substantial (Sahagún 1938) has Xolotl perform the act singly and instead.

Huitzilopochtli the god is unlikely to have preceded the man first of all because of the absence of any carving and statuary of, or relating closely to, the god which is older than the fifteenth century. For all their fervour the Spanish could hardly have removed every such trace had his cult been deeply embedded and ancient. All records of the man on the other hand indicate that he lived before the fifteenth century, and certainly no leader named after the god Huitzilopochtli could have existed in this or the following century without being mentioned in the many detailed histories (*xiuhpohualli*) of the period.

Nearly all the extant stonework in fact derives specifically from the great pyramid in Tenochtitlan, which was inspired by Tlacaelel and finally completed in the 1480s, and on which Huitzilopochtli's temple stood beside Tlaloc's (this arrangement incidentally explaining the hindsighted report that Tlaloc called Huitzilopochtli his son, *nopiltzin*, when imagining their future pyramid in the *Historia de la nación mexicana*, Dibble 1963: 46). Many of the pieces were found in this vicinity and correspond to descriptions of the temple before its destruction: Coatlicue; Coyolxauhqui's head, carved on the base to show it was severed; the so-called *Indio triste*, the banner-holder; Huitzilopochtli sacrificing opposite Moctezuma; arguably as a warrior-victim on the 'Quauhxicalli del tigre' (Seler 1904: 767ff; Caso 1953: 46). Given their late date, the fact that they consubstantiate the solar myth summarized earlier is of first importance. Indeed the newly-constructed temple itself was intended to be Coatepec, and was choreographically essential in scale and situation to the hymns which celebrated Huitzilopochtli's bellicose birth. The solar myth itself gives details of the approach of Huitzilopochtli's enemies to the temple-steps over the 'Snake-sand' (*Couaxalpan*) and the terrace Apetlac, and of the paper and other clothing worn by those acting out the Sacred Hymns while travelling the route through Tlaxotlan and Popotlan (places mentioned in them) and back to the temple during the Panquetzaliztli festival (Sahagún 1938: 192-200; Garibay 1958: 39). Further there is much internal evidence in the Sacred Hymns themselves to suggest that they were largely re-shaped, if not expressly composed for these mass imperial ceremonies: the Tlaloc *icuic* for example refers to the statue of the god newly-erected on the pyramid (Seler 1904: 984). This is worth emphasizing because the hymns feature Huitzilopochtli so prominently and have often been tacitly assumed to be much older, evidently by Brinton (1890), for example, when he dubbed them collectively *Rig Veda Americanus*. In short, unlike our information about Huitzilopochtli the man, evidence we have of his divine being is markedly coherent and points strongly to the deliberate imperial campaign of Tlacaelel's which Léon-Portilla (1959) has described in detail, even if with too much sympathy for the 'great man' view of history. In other words it comes to confirm Chimalpahin's laconic but resonant phrase for Tlacaelel's activities in the year 1440: 'yhuan huel no yehuatl oquichiuhtinen yn tlacatecolotl Huitzilopochtli yn inteouh Mexica, yn oquinnotztinen' (1890: 107; and he was the one who was always busy demonstrating that the devilish Huitzilopochtli was the god of the Mexicans).

The task of transforming Huitzilopochtli, a local hero or an obscure tribal deity, into what he became, one of the great gods of Mexico, cannot have been easy, indeed was never fully accomplished. Seler (1923: 89, 164) has pointed up minutely the astrological discrepancies in the birth myth and referred them to recent earthly origins. He explains thus that the '400' slain by Huitzilopochtli come from the south sky, and not the north, their proper home as male warriors: they must be seen as real enemies defeated by the Aztecs made into retainers of Coyolxauhqui, subordinate to the moon and her part of the sky, approximating but not fully becoming true astral creatures. He further remarks that as a solar myth Huitzilopochtli's birth is still more about him than the sun as such. No such myth was necessary to Mesoamerican religion: it was as gratuitous as Huitzilopochtli's intrusion into the pantheon itself. For Huitzilopochtli never enjoyed the status of a lord of the day or night hours, was *de trop* among the calendar gods. The Telleriano and the Vaticanus A codexes, it is true, show him with his own month (the 15th) and his festival (the Panquetzaliztli). But these very depictions reveal how such modest elevation was at all possible. His face-painting (*ixtlan tlatlaan*) and adornment strongly resemble Tezcatlipoca's. Indeed, it was on the day of this God's coming, in the Teotleco festival, that an official birthday was found for him. The imperial Huitzilopochtli certainly had similarities with other gods, of fire and the moon (Spence 1923: 66, Seler 1908: 340); but he flourished chiefly in a solar guise under Tezcatlipoca (as Castillo put it) as an associate, an aspect even of that equally northern but long established and 'real' god (*uel teotl*). And this can account for his joint appearance with him, retrospectively written in, in *Una historia de los reinos.*

The technical elevation of Huitzilopochtli to divine and celestial status, as a feat and an event, was intimately connected with the burning of Aztec tribal records demanded by Tlacaelel when it all began. Itzcoatl's incendiarism is recorded clearly enough by Sahagún's Informants (León-Portilla 1959: 251). And so are the motives for it: that the paintings, *in tlilli in tlapalli*, could undermine authority. That is, the sons of an oppressed tribe wandering towards and around the Valley of Mexico, poorly clad and insignificant, had become conscious now of their new status after the political and military successes of the 1430s. But just because these records were burned it is harder to be sure of the status of surviving information about Huitzilopochtli the man. How much is genuinely ancient having survived the destruction of the codexes at a folkloric, or (following Castillo) an overtly plebeian level? How much is entirely apochryphal or stems after the conquest from dim memories or wilful late interpretations of the 'official' myth? The suggestion has been made for example that Huitzilopochtli's standard hummingbird guise may have been prompted by phonetic association with an original proper name, and that the stars he slew were once real enemies of the Aztecs. Similarly, the Coyolxauhqui of the official myth might well derive from a sister Huitzilopochtli really had, Malinalxochitl, who was ugly and whom he detested according to *Unos annales históricos.* For his part, Garibay (1953: 322) speaks confidently of a large 'pre-Homeric' oral tradition of ballads and sagas celebrating the deeds of the hero and episodes of his life, which as such survived Itzcoatl's bonfires. In turn this literature, fragmentarily recorded in the earliest post-Conquest documents, *Unos annales históricos,* the Boturini Codex, became the imaginative springboard for certain later writers, as they did for the Europeanized artists of what Robertson (1959) calls the '2nd stage' codexes.

There seems to be much sense in this if we compare, say Tezozomoc's chronicles of c.1600 with *Unos annales históricos,* having previously asked where else the authors of the annals could have got their material in 1524. As for Tezozomoc, as Huitzilopochtli's biographer he leaves no-one in doubt about his methods and motives. He gathered material indiscriminately, freely supplementing old sources with hearsay (from the *mestizo* Alonso Franco for example) when not his own fancy, linking and re-shaping episodes initially unrelated in *Unos annales históricos,* putting pieces together according to Western norms, like the Europeanized artists of the Boban Atlas and the *Historia de la nación mexicana*: all in a pathetic

attempt to make for himself a coherent national hero out of
Huitzilopochtli, through whom to vaunt the lost glories of his past.
His encomium of Huitzilopochtli as the one who led the Aztecs
through thick and thin, the oracle who promised them wealth and
luxury and the warrior who climactically founded Tenochtitlan by
planting the heart of Copil (Malinalxochitl's son) on the site, is all
too transparent and undeserving of confidence. It is worth insisting
on this because Seler (1908: 324-30) devoted perhaps his six most
labyrinthine pages to proving the worth of this late fable and to
integrating it into the purest structures of Mesoamerican religion and
astrology. His exercise is in fact inexplicable in view of his general
scepticism towards Huitzilopochtli and of his specific insinuation
elsewhere that this figure was a 'Stammheros' of the literally most
trivial kind. Indeed, viewing the Aztec migration hero with as little
belief as the geography of the route he enjoined, Seler (1923: 167)
once actually proposed that Huitzilopochtli truly had the crossroads
of Tlaxotlan as a 'Heimstätte', as could be arguably suggested by the
1st Sacred Hymn, which he identifies in turn (1904: 969) with the
'cuicatl . . . itoca tlaxotecayotl' mentioned by Sahagún: in other
words, that Huitzilopochtli helped and inspired the Aztecs only after
they had reached the Valley of Mexico.

   Garibay's heroic oral tradition may or may not have existed;
maybe we can be certain of no more than that Huitzilopochtli was a
leader important to the Aztecs at one point in their history who was
idolized after his death, but who achieved grand apotheosis only less
than a century before the conquest. But carefully considered, this in
itself is an astounding situation. The very confusion and variety of
surviving histories and biographies point to one quite precise fact:
that while they devoted intelligence and energy to the making of
Huitzilopochtli the solar god, son of Coatlicue, Tlacaelel and his
contemporaries neglected entirely to foster and attribute to him an
historical role, even though their own ambitions and concerns were
in part manifestly secular. For example, in a fine '1st stage' codex
like the Boturini, Huitzilopochtli is not even credited with having
started the Aztecs on their way from Aztlan (we have to wait for the
Historia de la nación mexicana for this), but joins them only later in
Colhuacan-Chicomoztoc. He is their guide here and in *Unos annales
históricos* more by default than anything else, no-one's father and
no-one's son. As Bernal (1957) has noted, his historical role as a man
goes unmentioned in all non-Aztec chronicles, while Sahagún's
neutral Informants, who had so much to say about his divine
functions, do not at any point whatsoever associate him with the
Mexican migrations.

   Such an evident lack of concern, on the part of the imperial
Aztecs, with history as apologia or national justification effectively
left their survivors and descendants strangely denuded after the
conquest. In lawsuits they found themselves without a credible

patron *abogado*, and were in an unenviable position when proving a *titulo* or substantiating a claim to land or tribute, that is, when playing the Europeans at their own game. They were notably worse off in this respect than other peoples of Mesoamerica, the Texcocans for example, or the Tlaxcala with their Camaxtli (a relative of Huitzilopochtli's), or the Quiché, who in Balam Quitze rooted their historical claims no less deeply than the Jews did theirs in the Old Testament. Even the chauvinist Tezozomoc, intolerant as he was even of the claims of neighbouring Tlatelolco, found no better recourse than to affirm Tenochtitlan's greatness in a standard reference to Quetzalcoatl and Tula, leaving to Huitzilopochtli no more than a supporting role as the one who strengthened the throne Quetzalcoatl had founded, and in the older god's name (Seler 1923: 104).

There could be a simple explanation for this. All accounts of the Aztecs' arrival in the Valley and their rise to power not written by the Aztecs themselves spare no pains to present them as upstarts, with whom the very notion of pedigree would be grotesque. The Chalcan Chimalpahin amusedly recalls the newly arrived Aztecs' excitement on seeing Popocatepetl erupt when for everyone else around it was a familiar event: jokes at the expense of their *parvenu* rulers spiced Nahuatl poetry during the Triple Alliance (Schultze Jena 1957). For them to have tried to make an imperial father out of a tribal leader like Huitzilopochtli would have been a mistake; to have forged an Aeneas, or more modestly even the kind of Quetzalcoatl the Texcocans shaped dynastically for themselves, could hardly have been practicable.

If the same embarrassment which led to the codex burning in the first place was in fact responsible for the absence of an authorized version, an epic history of Huitzilopochtli, then the Aztecs can be seen to have got a most genial idea from that apparent disadvantage. For to 'authorize' a hero-god means ultimately to guarantee and hence limit him: to insert him into a national dynasty and design, however grand, will be to restrain him. This the makers of the imperial Huitzilopochtli seem to have understood very well. Indeed their awareness of what they were doing comes through in little-noticed qualities of the solar birth myth itself. Huitzilopochtli's horrendous energy derives after all precisely from mention of his illegitimacy, of his uncertain authorship or fatherhood. In Coatlicue's womb he hears his half-brother plotting against him, they being disgusted at the dishonour implied by his conception: this is more than enough reason for him to kill them all mercilessly as soon as he is born, establishing his position through courage and strength. Nowhere is it said why the brothers might have been mistaken. The contrast here with parthenogenesis in other American Indian myths could not be greater: the Incas, with Coniraya's son by Cauillaca, and the Quiché, with Hunahpu and Xbalanque, most carefully and subtly resolved the genealogical and family problems inherent in such births (indeed the Aztecs are if anything closer to those Christians who sacrificed Jesus's brothers by writing them out of the Bible, in honour of the divine Child and as if to compensate for their normal intolerance of adultery, a sin which was of course punishable by death among the Aztecs).

Huitzilopochtli's extreme touchiness and the absent paternal explanation are at the antipodes of the desire to *warrant* power. He is a child terror, Hercules as Sahagún said, Oskar of *Die Blechtrommel*, who scares his way towards it. And more than one source explicitly identified that terrific strength with his fatherlessness in the epithet *tetzahuitl*, which according to Molina (1571) means both scandalous and frightening:

> Auh yn uitzilopochtli no mitouaya tetzauitl ye yca ca çan iutl yn temoc yn ic otztic yn innan ycouacue cayac nez yn itá (Sahagún's informants in Seler 1904: 1100: and Huitzilopochtli was also called *tetzahuitl* for his mother became pregnant just from a falling feather and no-one came forward as his father).

An idea of what the Aztecs believed such a terror institutionalized on a large scale could bring is well expressed in the violent cadences of the speeches Castillo attributes to Huitzilopochtli. For serving the sun, for becoming his people and terrifying others, Huitzilopochtli promised not just the luxury Padden found so important, but an ever-widening limit to their desires: 'atle inquaxoch, atle quin tlacauaĺtiçque' (nothing will be their bound, nothing will they have to do without) — a moral programme worthy indeed of a 'great' power.

In this way Huitzilopochtli rapidly became a dominant force in Mesoamerica, the embodiment of Aztec religious and military aspiration. He was the devil openly feared by hardy conquistadors like Bernal Díaz (1939), and the centre at which attempts at organized resistance, Cuauhtemoc's for example, originated and found sustenance. Heine was no more frivolous in making him the only American opponent of the Virgin Mary in her league (in the poem 'Uitzliputzli') than Sahagún was misguided in endeavouring to destroy principally him, of all the gods he encountered. As soon as the struggle was over, however, fear came to seem undignified and the long attrition of Huitzilopochtli, still continuing, began. Urbane historians like Durán (1867) soon cut him down to size: that story of his about Moctezuma and those feckless advisers who sent envoys to Coatlicue to find out more about her son, and to tell her he was doing well, may anticipate Cervantes in sophistication and irony (Sancho's visit to Dulcinea) but clearly contradicts the whole spirit of the imperial age. The forgers of Aztec religions had no need to make such enquiries of anyone, and their people absorbed the myths and hymns they composed so deeply that they were remembered in every detail long after Sahagún began his work in 1548. A far better impression of what was made of Huitzilopochtli, of how his presence came to be felt, can be gained from Chimalpahin's account (1890: 180) of how a small rebellion in Chalco was suppressed in 1509. The offending Itzcahua and Nequametl were thus addressed by Moctezuma's envoys:

> Otechhualmihualli yn amotlatocauh yn Tetzahuitl yn Huitzilopochtli yn tolihtic yn acatlihtic in ihiyotl yn quimati conmihtalhuia: xiquilhuican ynocol yn Itzcahua yhuan yn Nequametl ca ocachi ye noconcui yn Mexica yn Tenuchca, mach çan nel cana ceuh yyaoyotl, ca nalquiz (We are sent here by your lord Tetzahuitl Huitzilopochtli whose breath is in the rushes and in the reeds and who has let this be known: 'Say to Nequametl and his uncle Itzcahua that I will take over this little bit more for Mexico Tenochtitlan; war is certainly said somehow to be dying out now, altogether'.)

The rebels surrendered and were well treated, a victory far removed from those early run-rounds in the lake marshes. But while, to be feasible, such politics may have presupposed Aztec military might, the conscious exploitation of the *idea* of unlimited ambition is something altogether remarkable. The quoted speech is in fact a psychological masterpiece, worthy of our century, for the way it intimidates while remaining agreeable and remote. As Chimalpahin noted, Tlacaelel and his fellows well understood the techniques of persuasion. Their genial creation was 'yn Tetzahuitl yn Huitzilopochtli', who was unplaced in sexual and secular history only to be the better able to intervene in secular affairs and further their cause.

Huitzilopochtli's creators were interested in his maximum presence, not his past deeds. While his solar myth may now seem to us 'operose', as it did to Lewis Spence, and while his hymns and insignia have become irrelevant and partly opaque, in imperial Tenochtitlan he enlivened all that was associated with him. As the solar entity of the First Sacred Hymn he dispels night and anarchy (identical in the Nahuatl metaphor), just as, the victim of godly flesh (*teoqualo*), he is at the heart of a mass ritual which seemed like a diabolical parody of Holy Communion to the Spanish invaders. Above all he was the protagonist, the actor who actually embodied the truth of literary claims made for him; a person wholly absorbed into persona. Garibay (1958: 37) has rightly pointed out (though mistranslated!) a phase in the First Sacred Hymn: 'noteouh tepanquizqui mitoa' (my god is called *tepanquizqui*), where *tepanquizqui* means 'the one who comes over you' in the sense of overwhelming in battle, and of coming across as a performer or actor.

The fact that no coherent literature relating to Huitzilopochtli has survived, except these fragments from his rituals, indicates that Aztec imperial leaders well knew how to cater for their people's mytho- poeic demands and that they had a yet more refined motive for destroying their early historical records. For those scripts, like any elevated new version of them, as literature, could act only as diversion from the task in hand, and would ultimately serve the interests of the apologians and the defenders better than those of the choreographers of mass enthusiasm. This is why in our age, for example, Artaud the dramatist felt so drawn to Huitzilopochtli, and why D.H. Lawrence, caught in the paradox of his primitivism and discovering in the end his own literariness, avoided him as best he could.

REFERENCES

Anderson, A.J.O. and C.E. Dibble (1950) *Florentine Codex.* Book I, *The Gods.* School of American Research, Santa Fe.

Bernal, I. (1957) Huitzilopochtli vivo. *Cuadernos americanos*, 96, 127-52. Mexico.

Brinton, D.G. (1890) *Rig Veda Americanus.* Library of Aboriginal American Literature, vol. 8. Philadelphia.

Caso, A. (1936) *La religión de los Aztecas.* Enciclopedia ilustrada mexicana. Mexico.

Caso, A. (1935) *El pueblo del sol.* Fondo de cultura económica. Mexico.

Castillo, C. de (1908) *Fragmentos de la obra general sobre historia de los Mexicanos.* Ed. F. del Paso y Troncoso. Florence.

Chimalpahin Quauhtlehuanitzin, D. (1889) *Annales de . . . 6ᵉ et 7ᵉ Rélations (1258-1612).* Ed. R. Siméon. Bibliothèque Linguistique Américaine, vol. 12. Paris.

Díaz del Castillo, B. (1939) *Historia verdadera de la conquista de la Nueva España.* 3 vols. Mexico.

Dibble, C.E. (ed.) (1963) *Historia de la nación Mexicana.* Reproducción a todo color del Códice de 1576 (*Códice Aubin*). Madrid.

Durán, Fr. D. (1867) *Historia de las Indias de Nueva España y islas de tierra firme.* 2 vols. and Atlas. Mexico.

Garibay K., A.M. (1953) *Historia de la literatura Nahuatl.* Vol. 1. Mexico.

Garibay K., A.M. (1958) (ed) *Veinte himnos sacros de los Nahuas.* Mexico.

Léon-Portilla, M. (1959) *La filosofía Nahuatl estudiada en sus fuentes.* 2nd ed. Mexico.

Molina, Fr. A. de (1571) *Vocabulario en lengua Castellana y Mexicana.* Mexico.

Padden, R.C. (1967) *The Hummingbird and the Hawk: Conquest and Sovereignty in the Valley of Mexico, 1503-1541.* Columbus, Ohio.

Robertson, D. (1959) *Mexican Manuscript Painting of the early Colonial Period: The Metropolitan Schools.* New Haven.

Sahagún, Fr. B. de (1938) *Historia general de las cosas de Nueva España*, vol. 1. Mexico.

Schultze Jena, L. (1957) *Alt-aztekische Gesänge.* Quellenwerke zur alten Geschichte Amerikas, vol. 6, Stuttgart.

Seler, E. (1902) *Gesammelte Abhandlungen*, vol. 1. Berlin.

Seler, E. (1904) *Gesammelte Abhandlungen*, vol. 2. Berlin.

Seler, E. (1908) *Gesammelte Abhandlungen*, vol. 3. Berlin.

Seler, E. (1923) *Gesammelte Abhandlungen*, vol. 4. Berlin.

Spence, L. (1923) *The Gods of Mexico.* New York.

Tezozomoc, F.A. (1944) *Crónica Mexicana.* Mexico.

Tezozomoc, F.A. (1949) *Crónica Mexicáyotl.* Ed. A. León. Mexico.

Torquemada, Fr. J. de (1615) *Los veintiun libros rituales y Monarquia Indiana.* 3 vols. Madrid.

Unos Annales Históricos de la Nación Mexicana. (1945) Facsimile edition by E. Menguin. Corpus Codicum Americanorum Medii Aevi, vol. 2. Copenhagen.

ARTHUR G. MILLER

The iconograpy of the painting in the Temple of the Diving God, Tulum, Quintana Roo, Mexico: the twisted cords

During the 1971-2 field season of the Tulum Mural Project sponsored by the Center for Pre-Columbian Studies, Dumbarton Oaks, part of the painting on the east wall of the interior of the so-called Temple of the Diving God (Structure 5) was carefully recorded by means of photography and drawing (Fig. 1). The results show a far more complex design than recorded by Fernández (1945, Lám. 18). The interior painting of Structure 5 is organized into three horizontal registers: the upper register shows mat motifs and a celestial band painted a most impressive Maya blue directly on a black background; the middle register, painted black on white with a blue background, shows two ceremonial scenes of confronting figures dressed in ritual or god costume transferring from one to the other enormous vertically oriented objects. The lower register, also painted black on white with a blue background, between the north and south benches of the room and beneath the painted horizontal jaguar pelt band, shows underworld scenes of serpents and earth monsters. As of now we have carefully recorded only the central portion of the middle register and the entire lower register (Fig. 1). We plan to complete our reconstruction of this important and masterfully painted wall during our 1972-3 field season.

The twisted cords

I will consider here one prominent motif in the iconography of the painting on the east wall of Structure 5: the twisted cordlike borders enframing the two pairs of confronting figures of the middle register and the twisted cord enframing the floating fishlike creature of the lower register.

The twisted cords are shown only in a vertical position, three times in the middle register and twice in the lower register. There is

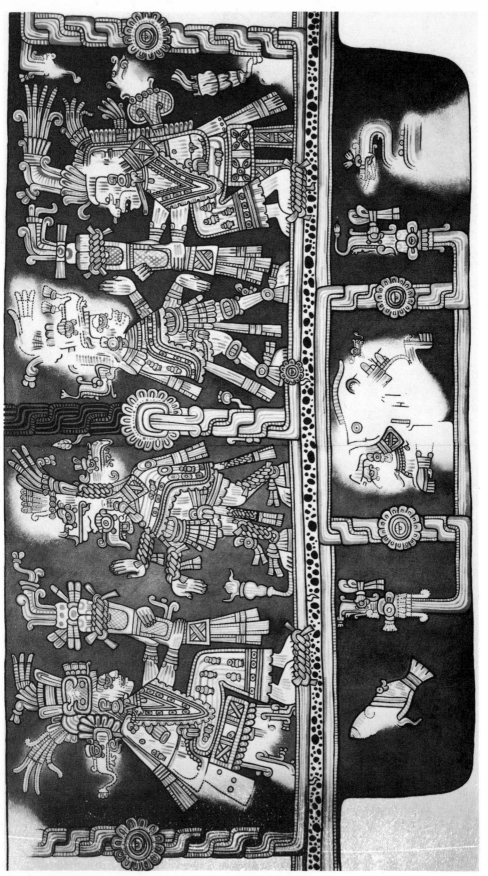

Figure 1 The central section of the painting on the east wall of the interior of Tulum Structure 5 in Quintana Roo. Rendering by Felipe Davalos G.

an untwisted horizontal lower frame for the middle register which probably eventually ends in a serpent head on the left and a serpent tail or another serpent head on the right (Lothrop 1924: 54, 86), although this remains to be demonstrated when we carefully study and reconstruct the two end panels.

Large circular forms with eyes in the centres are located at the mid-sections of the vertical twisted cords in the middle and lower registers; the circular motif on the central twisted cord is conspicuous in being located at the exact centre of the wall and in having a parallel double line element suspended from it and bifurcated at its lower end.[1]

The central and south vertical twisted cords of the middle register have associated with them, as if growing out of the cords, leaf and flower motifs.

Twisted cords in the Codex Paris

There are uses of twisted cords in one of the extant Postclassic Maya codices which may relate to the use of the twisted cord in this interior mural of Structure 5 at Tulum.

Twisted cords are used as enframing devices on pages 21 and 22 of the Codex Paris (Villacorta 1930: 216, 218). Page 21 of the Paris shows the twisted cord enframing calendrical tables. Page 22 of the Paris (Fig. 2) shows the cord motif enframing two profile figures which confront each other while seated upon a serpent sky band. The ends of the twisted cord enframing the two confronting figures of the upper register are joined together in a crude knot hanging between the figures; it connects with two confronting figures in a lower register by attaching to the top of the head of each figure. These two lower register confronting figures wear 'death collars' around their necks (the figure on the left is marked on the cheek with a death sign) and are each positioned over the open gaping mouth of a serpent deity (Itzam-Cab?), all suggesting underworld associations. As in the register above, this lower pair of confronting seated figures has between them a crude knot joining the twisted cords which descend from the register above.

There is a cord used more specifically in the partially damaged page 19 of the Codex Paris (Fig. 3). The cord is clearly a depiction of an umbilical cord suspended from a lost section above and attached to the belly of a figure which is shown naked except for jewelry.[2] The figure appears to be seated upon a serpentine motif. The shape of the eye and unnatural position of the body suggest that a dead figure is shown.

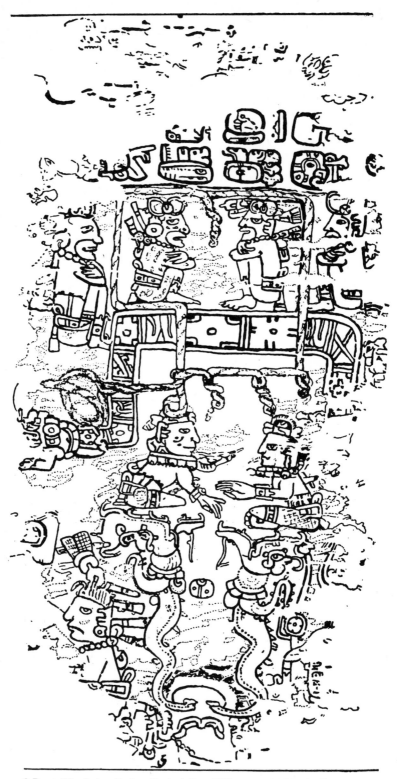

Figure 2 Page 22 of the Codex Paris (after Villacorta 1930: 218).

Figure 3 Page 19 of the Codex Paris (after Villacorta 1930: 212).

The Kusansum myth

A Maya belief recorded by Tozzer (1907: 153) and mentioned by Thompson (1970: 341) may also be pertinent to a discussion of this Tulum mural. Recounting information obtained from the Maya, Tozzer discusses the ethnographic Maya belief that the world is now in the fourth period of its existence. It was in the first period, a mythical and glorious period, that there

> was a road suspended in the sky, stretching from Tuloom and Coba to Chichen Itza and Uxmal. This pathway was called *kusansum* or *sabke* [sic] (white road). It was in the nature of a large rope (*sum*) supposed to be living (*kusan*) and in the middle flowed blood. It was by this rope that the food was sent to the ancient rulers who lived in the structures now in ruins. For some reason this rope was cut, the blood flowed out, and the rope vanished forever (Tozzer 1907: 153).

At the time the Maya Kusansum myth was recorded by Tozzer, the people of the Peninsula of Yucatan had experienced a series of catastrophic social upheavals generally referred to as the Caste War of Yucatan. One of the many complex issues of the struggle involved the reassertion of what were thought to be ancient Maya traditions. In the second half of the nineteenth century, the Cruzob Maya of the eastern forests of the Peninsula re-established social, political, and religious structures which paralleled those Maya social structures known to have existed at the time of European contact early in the sixteenth century (Reed 1964: 212, 220). The Kusansum myth was recorded by Tozzer in the vicinity of Valladolid, a city which is on the edge of this eastern forest area, now called the territory of Quintana Roo.[3]

The Kusansum myth compares a mythical pathway in the sky with a *sacbe* (*sabke*), which is the term used to describe the artificially raised limestone causeways which connect certain Maya centres, the best known of which is the sacbe connecting Coba in Quintana Roo with Yaxuna in Yucatan. The myth also implies that the pathway in the sky which once connected the land of the gods with the earth is like a giant umbilical cord containing blood. The cord was cut and the earth was no longer joined with the sky, the supernatural and the natural were no longer one. Such a myth must have something to do with the human experience at birth when the cord containing blood, the umbilical cord, is cut, severing the infant from its mother. In the Maya Kusansum myth, the common human experience of cutting the umbilical cord is projected on a cosmic scale to express the formation of two contrasting and once connected worlds: the natural world and the supernatural world.

There is a possible reference to the Kusansum myth in the *Popol*

Vuh. According to Edmonson's (1971) new translation of the *The Book of Counsel*, on pages 7 and 8 (manuscript lines 50-70), a section of The First Creation describes that there was once a manuscript of the Book of Counsel written in the remote past. The manuscript referred to is clearly an ancient book of origins, an early statement of Maya cosmogony. The text reads:

> there is no longer A sight of the Book of Counsel . . . There was once the manuscript of it, And it was written long ago, . . . Great was its account And its description . . . Of when there was finished The birth Of all of heaven And earth: The four creations, The four humiliations, The knowledge Of the four punishments, *The rope of tying together, The line of tying together, The womb of heaven, The womb of earth* . . . [italics mine].

Edmonson's footnote (1971: 6, MS 67-8) referring to the italicized lines above states: 'The reference here is probably to the "tying of the years" at the end of the 52-year cycle; see Sahagún, 1938; 2: 269.'

Is it possible that these lines referring to Maya cosmogony in the *Popol Vuh* ('The rope of tying together, The line of tying together, The womb of heaven, The womb of earth') refer to a concept of a glorious period in the past when heaven and earth were connected as expressed in the Kusansum myth recorded by Tozzer near Quintana Roo?

Some umbilical cord representations: ethnographic explanations

Among the representations of twisted cords in the codices which possibly refer to the umbilical cord are the above-mentioned twisted cord motif enframing the calendrical tables of page 21 and the confronting figures of page 22 of the Codex Paris (Fig. 2).

Does the tied umbilical cord shown on page 22 of the Codex Paris refer to a joining together of the mythical umbilical cord described in the Kusansum myth? If so, is it possible that the interior painting of Structure 5 at Tulum depicts an unrecorded aspect of the Kusansum myth? Is it possible that the severed cord containing blood of the myth is reconnected through the ritual ceremony depicted and that joining is indicated by the circular knotlike motif at the exact centre of the mural? Such an interpretation is strengthened by the fact that the upper half of the central vertical twisted cord is painted blue on black — the dominant colour of the sky band — (the supernatural half of the severed umbilical cord?). The lower half of the twisted cord is painted black on white (the earthly half of the severed umbilical cord?). The vegetal forms growing out of the 'umbilical cord' may refer to a pictorial metaphor for a cord containing blood (i.e. *kusansum*) and generating life.[4]

Is the twisted cord shown in the interior painting of Structure 5 at Tulum an umbilical cord, 'The rope of tying together, The line of tying together, The womb of heaven, The womb of earth . . .'?

In addition to the Codex Paris, there are Postclassic codices from southern Mexico which also represent the umbilical cord in metaphorical contexts. I think that it is generally agreed that the Postclassic manuscript painting from southern Mexico is related in style to the Codex Paris; and to some Tulum wall paintings. I mention southern Mexico in the context of the Postclassic Maya because they are probably contemporaneous and certainly the iconography overlaps (Robertson 1970).

In the Codex Borgia, page 15, five representations of seated deities each hold in one hand an umbilical cord descending from above attached to an infant kneeling below. Similar scenes are shown in the Codex Vaticanus 3773B, on pages 38-40, and in the Codex Féjerváry-Mayer, on pages 24, 26 and 27. The Codex Vaticanus shows five scenes of deities (two seated, three standing) each holding up an umbilical cord with infant attached to it below. On page 40 of the Vaticanus and on page 27 of the Féjerváry-Mayer, a standing deity is shown holding the vertically oriented umbilical cord in one hand and a cutting axe in the other. On page 26 of the Féjerváry-Mayer, two priests are shown, legs flexed, holding umbilical cords attached at the upper end to sky elements and to the infant on the lower end. In both cases the deity holds a flint knife in one hand. Seler (1963) thought these scenes referred to the Venus cycle. I wonder if they may instead, or perhaps also, refer to a ritual cutting of the umbilical cord on a propitious day. In each of the codices mentioned there are five deities shown each associated with four day signs: a twenty-day cycle is shown here. It is known that the Maya held the choice of the day upon which the cutting of the umbilical cord took place as very important and as a religious event with the significance of ritually commencing a human life cycle.

In his translation of the *Popol Vuh*, Edmonson relates Ximénez's comments on the ritual significance of cutting the umbilical cord. Referring to the passage of the *Popol Vuh* which says, 'Each of us shall plant this cornstalk for you; In the middle of our house we shall plant it then. It will be the sign of our death If it should dry up' (Edmonson 1971: 108), Ximénez notes (Edmonson 1971: 121-22):

> They cast lots to see which day would be good for cutting the umbilical cord, and when the day was found they placed the cord over an ear of corn (and) with a (shell) blade that had not been used, they cut it and the blade was thrown in a fountain as something blessed. The ear of corn they stripped of its seeds and planted it if it were time, and if not they kept it until its time and

planted and cultivated it as a sacred thing; and shucked and ground they made of it the first *pap* which they gave to the child; the rest that the grain produced was for the priest, and they even kept some from that grain for the child to plant when he grew up.

Girard (1952: 182) reports the survival of the ceremonial planting of corn in courtyards among the twentieth-century Quiche (mentioned in Edmonson 1971: 108, footnote 3436).

Is the cutting of the umbilical cord over a special ear of corn and then planting the corn a metaphorical expression of the beginning of a human life cycle, i.e., as the cutting of the umbilical cord begins a human life cycle, the planting of corn begins another kind of life cycle? In this regard it is interesting to note an observation by a Mexican scholar, Luis Azcue y Mancera, who states (1967: 109) that page 19 of the Codex Paris is about 'Producción'. He argues for two meanings for the page in the Maya codex: 'Producción del Maíz' and 'Producción Humana'. Is it possible that the additional meaning given in the note by Ximénez in his translation of the *Popol Vuh* (Edmonson 1971: 108, footnote 3436) relating the cutting of the umbilical cord with the planting of corn is here referred to on page 19 of the Codex Paris?[5]

The umbilical cord as representing lineage

Lineage is certainly one of the most important preoccupations of the ethnographic Maya, and I think that most scholars would agree that it was an ancient one as well (Vogt 1971: 32; Roys 1957). Indeed a preoccupation with lineage was not only a Maya trait but it was a pronounced trait in all of the civilizations of Mesoamerica. What better way to represent a family lineage than by means of an umbilical cord, the twisted cord containing life-giving blood which literally connects one generation to another? In this context it should be pointed out that the human umbilical cord is actually made up of two parts — a vein and an artery — which are twisted and that the cord is characterized by its extraordinary length, about 20-30 inches.

The genealogical use of the umbilical cord is present in the Codex Vindobonensis Mexicanus and in the Codex Laud. There is a pictorial genealogy of unknown provenance in the collection of codices of the National Museum of Anthropology in Mexico which pictorially expresses lineage by means of twisted cords and which is called the Genealogy of Nexmoyotla, Ateno, Zoyatitlan and Hueytetla (Glass 1964: 136, Fig. 87). Shown are four horizontal lines of figures connected to each other by twisted cords, probably representing umbilical cords.

An interesting sixteenth-century genealogy of the Xiu family

Figure 4 The Xiu genealogical tree (after Gates 1937: 120).

which shows a European 'Tree of Jesse' theme to express a native Maya family genealogy may include a representation of the umbilical cord (Fig. 4). European and pre-Columbian artistic representations are mixed. A figure dressed 'Indian style', wearing an Aztec *xihuitzolli*, is shown leaning on his right elbow and holding an elaborate fan in his left hand fashioned in the shape of a serpent at its handle end. Out of the figure's loins a tree emerges in the manner of European representations of the Tree of Jesse, known to be quite common in northern Europe during the sixteenth century. In addition, the genealogical tree was a favoured pictorial means of representing the 'spiritual genealogies' of such religious orders as the Augustinian friars and appears in the wall painting of sixteenth-century Mexican churches (e.g. San Miguel, Charo, Michoacan).

Of importance to our consideration of umbilical cords among the Maya is the possible representation of the umbilical cord to express lineage in this Xiu genealogical tree. Along the back of the Maya

'Jesse' figure, the founder of his lineage (whose name was Hun Uitzil Chac Tutul Xiu), extended from the neck to the waist, is a twisted cord, one line of the twist unshaded, the other shaded, very much resembling an actual umbilical cord. This motif, or anything like it, never appears in European representations of the Tree of Jesse theme. It could of course be braided hair that is represented, but the light and dark alternating twists make the motif look more like the intertwined artery and vein of the human umbilical cord which have slightly different colouring.

Is the twisted cord shown along the back of this 'Jesse' figure a reference to a Maya pictorial metaphor for lineage? Certainly its context in an incontrovertible genealogy supports this hypothesis.

In terms of the painting on the interior of Structure 5, is the possible umbilical cord representation a kind of visual genealogical tree describing Maya cosmogony, when the earth was once connected with the sky, as implied in the Kusansum myth and in the *Popol Vuh*: 'The rope of tying together, The line of tying together, The womb of heaven, The womb of earth . . .'?

Diving gods

Important to our consideration of the iconography of the painting of the Interior of Structure 5 at Tulum is the descending figure associated with Structure 5.

The meaning of representations of the diving god at Tulum and among the ancient Maya in general is not clear. (The most informative discussion of various possible interpretations of descending gods as representing falling rain and the bee can be found in Tozzer 1941: 143, note 686.)

Structure 5 at Tulum is named 'The Temple of the Diving God' because a winged descending figure appears in a prominent central position over the entrance of the structure. The diving god of Structure 5 was so extensively restored by Fernández (1941: 166) in the late 1930s on the basis of Lothrop's dubious reconstruction of 1924 (Lothrop 1924, Fig. 22), that it cannot be considered seriously as visual data here. The identification of the diving god of Structure 5 as God D – the Maya Sun God Yun-kin (Lothrop 1924, 47; Fernández 1941: 163, 166) – on the basis of Seler's theory that descending figures represent Tonatiuh (Seler 1902-3: 11) does not take into account the iconography of the paintings in Structure 5.

Fortunately, there is one surviving example of the representations of the diving god at Tulum which is neither extensively destroyed nor restored and which can be taken to represent what probably originally appeared in the central niche over the doorway of Structure 5; this is the diving god on Structure 25 (Lothrop 1924, Pl. 23). The iconography of this well-preserved stucco figure relates to the

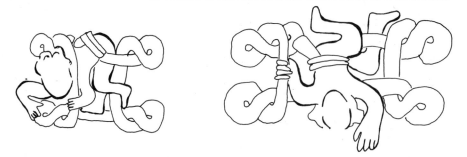

Figure 5 Stucco reliefs from the upper facade of Tulum Structure 16 (after Fernández 1941, Fig. 56).

iconography of the murals of Structure 5. The winged descending figure with thrown back (and therefore upright) head, carries with him in his descent twisted cords and elaborate knots or mat motifs like those in the mural under discussion (Fig. 1). Also two descending naked figures in low relief stucco decorating the upper facade of Structure 16 at Tulum (Fig. 5) are clearly attached to their elongated and intertwined umbilical cords (Fernández 1941: 166). The diving figure associated with umbilical cord at Tulum also recalls the images of two diving gods shown descending over a pyramid on page 35a of the Codex Madrid (the New Year rites for the Kan years; Villacorta 1930: 294). The uppermost of these figures has knotted appendages on the sides of his arms. The lower diving figure has twisted cords attached to his wrists and ankles; this lower diving figure also has conspicuously associated with him representations of the mat motif. Both the pyramid form and mat motif shown on page 35a of the Codex Madrid appear painted on the lower cornice facade of Structure 5 at Tulum (Fernández 1941, Fig. 53a).

In considering descending deities associated with ropes or umbilical cords, it is significant to recall a scene in a codex from Postclassic southern Mexico, an area whose book illustration and mural painting is related in style and iconography to late mural painting at Tulum (Robertson 1970). In the Codex Vindobonensis Mexicanus (page 48), there is a sky band with a rope descending from a break in the sky: two deities descend along twisted cords from the sky band. In the wall paintings at Mitla there are also deities shown hanging on twisted cords (Seler 1895, Tafel 1).

It should be noted that the flanking figures at the extreme ends of the middle register of the Tulum Structure 5 mural (Fernández 1945, Lám. 18) are conspicuous in the feather appendages on their arms. Are these mural figures profile views of the diving gods? Is the diving or descending god at Tulum the bearer of the supernatural portion of the severed umbilical cord referred to in the Kusansum myth? Further reconstruction of this mural may help to answer these questions.

In the meantime I would like to consider the possible represent-ation of umbilical cords and descending deities in an art style removed in time and area from Tulum but nevertheless perhaps related in iconography. I am referring to the remarkable carved sculpture at Izapa which has the unique distinction of being the only Late Preclassic sculpture which has escaped intentional destruction by later peoples. In fact Izapa monuments may be the only sculpture of Mesoamerica venerated enough by later peoples to be reused continuously in a ceremonial context.[6] At Izapa there is clear archaeological evidence that monuments at the site (probably made during the Late Preclassic and Protoclassic periods) were used in the Late Classic and Postclassic periods. They were used ritually, not as fill or intentionally destroyed in the manner which has been the historical fate of so much of Mesoamerican monumental sculpture. The reasons for the obvious veneration of Izapa monuments probably have to do with the fact that their subject matter was allegorical[7] and religious rather than political and had sacred meaning to later peoples. I think it is valid to consider the iconography of the Izapa monuments as related to that of Tulum.

Umbilical cords and diving gods at Izapa

There are a number of descending deities shown on Izapa monuments and some of them have associated with them umbilical cords such as we have seen in the diving god of Tulum Structure 25 and in the figures on the facade of Tulum Structure 16 (Fig. 5). Stela 23 at Izapa is a possible example of a diving figure associated with umblical cord. Others have been noted by V. Garth Norman, in his recent commentary on the Izapa monuments.

Stela 50 at Izapa (Fig. 6) is particularly interesting because it shows a very clear umbilical cord representation. A skeleton is attached to his umbilical cord which is also a serpent motif. That the umbilical cord is also a serpent will be discussed more fully in the next section. Of particular interest is that above the skeleton is a possibly winged figure holding the umbilical-serpent cord.

For those who doubt the continuity between the Izapa icono-graphy of the Late Preclassic and the iconography of Postclassic Tulum and Tulum related codices such as the Codex Paris, I would like to point out that the position of the skeleton in Izapa Stela 50 is almost identical to that of the dead figure on page 19 of the Codex Paris (Fig. 3) from whose belly an umbilical cord extends upward. Is this mere coincidence, or is this an example of iconographic continuity in Mesoamerica from Preclassic to Postclassic times?

Is the winged figure holding the umbilical-serpent cord in Izapa Stela 50 related to the descending deities of Tulum, some of which are shown associated with umbilical cord?

Figure 6 Izapa Stela 50. Photograph and line tracing by V. Garth Norman.

There are figures in upper registers of Izapa monuments which have very clear umbilical cords attached to them. The upper register of Izapa Stela 1 (Fig. 7) shows a figure attached to his umbilical cord and the placenta with four dots and a glyph cartouche, possibly referring to a date; perhaps this is a reference to the importance of the day upon which the cutting of the umbilical cord takes place as mentioned in the *Popol Vuh* (Edmonson 1971: 108, footnote 3436) and portrayed in Codices Borgia, Vaticanus B, and Féjerváry-Mayer.

Entwined cord, entwined serpent or umbilical cord?

Anyone trying to solve the problem of the identity and significance of what is represented in the intertwined borders of the painting in Tulum Structure 5 must consider the many examples of intertwined borders in Mesoamerican art, from the Postclassic period and from earlier periods as well.[9] Obviously, intertwined borders most commonly represent serpents, especially borders of late Teotihuacan mural painting where a serpent head is shown at one end of the intertwined border and serpent rattlers are shown at the other end. Facades of many Maya structures of the Classic period feature the intertwined serpent border motif.

Sometimes a simple intertwined cord (probably made of henequen fibre) is shown, as in the borders of the Mitla murals where there are deities shown hanging from twisted cords.

I think we must consider the possibility that the Maya and other peoples in Mesoamerica used the twisted cord to mean various things at once. That the twisted cord represented at Tulum is also an intertwined serpent *as well as* umbilical cord is not inconsistent with Maya patterns of thought. Multiplicity of meaning is common in almost every aspect of Maya thought.[10] The twisted cord border at Tulum can mean *both* intertwined serpent and umbilical cord. In fact, there is ethnohistoric evidence that the Maya thought of the umbilical cord as a serpent. For example, in the *Ritual of the Bacabs* (Roys 1965: 42, MS 123), a reference is made to four snakes which form the world. These snakes are in the next paragraph compared to (among other things) 'arbors' and to umbilical cords: 'He would be beheaded by his mother, by his progenitress . . .' Here is a reference to snake, i.e. personified umbilical cord, being cut by the mother, the cutting a necessary concomitant of every childbirth. There is, again in the *Ritual of the Bacabs* (Roys 1965: 58-60, MS 174-80), a direct reference to childbirth: 'Incantation for the placenta.' The umbilical cord as part of the placenta still attached to the unborn child and the mother is metaphorically compared to a biting snake, thereby expressing the pain attending childbirth and, by metaphorical extension, the creation of the world: 'Great movement, great

Figure 7 Izapa Stela 1. Photograph and line tracing by V. Garth Norman.

pain . . . The great causer of pain are you, the great biter . . .' (Roys 1965: 59, MS 175-8).

A good example in Izapa of visual simultaneity of meaning is the skeleton of Stela 50 (Fig. 6) described in the previous section as being in the identical position as the dead figure to which an umbilical cord is attached shown on page 19 of the Codex Paris (Fig. 3). Here the cord emerges from beneath the rib cage of the skeleton, extends horizontally for a short distance, forms a loop, and continues in a vertical direction until it passes through the left hand of the winged figure described previously. The cord curves out of the hand downward and then upward to the slightly upraised right hand of the winged figure. Just above this hand the cord ends where another serpent head appears on the cord (Norman, in press). Here on Izapa Stela 50 the umbilical cord has the meaning of both umbilical cord and serpent.

Does the evidence described above admit the possibility that the twisted cord enframing borders of Tulum Mural 5 are both umbilical cord and intertwined serpent?

Conclusions

I would like to conclude this essay by stating that there is an impressive list of evidence that suggests that umbilical cord may be what is represented in the twisted cord enframing borders of the interior painting of Structure 5 at Tulum:

1. The Kusansum myth recorded by Tozzer in 1907 near Quintana Roo possibly gives an explanation of the iconography of Structure 5.
2. The passage in the *Popol Vuh* referring to Maya cosmogony is possibly a reference to the Kusansum myth: 'The rope of tying together, The line of tying together, The womb of heaven, The womb of earth . . .' (Edmonson 1971: 8, MS 50-70).
3. The Mixtec codices iconographically related to Tulum paintings which have representations of umbilical cords demonstrate the preoccupation with a propitious day for its cutting.
4. Ximénez's note in the *Popol Vuh* about the cutting of the umbilical cord and planting of corn may be an example of Vogt's 'conceptual replication' among the Maya; this supports the idea that the ritual cutting of the umbilical cord may have its cosmic replication in the Kusansum myth.
5. Lineage was cited as a possible meaning for the archaeological Maya use of umbilical cord symbolism; the genealogical use of the umbilical cord was cited in the Mixtec codices and in the sixteenth-century Xiu genealogical tree.
6. Diving gods were seen to have an important role in the umbilical

cord symbolism of the Maya. Descending deities may have been the 'Mercury gods' for the Maya and in some cases had the function of carrying down the supernatural part of the severed umbilical cord in the Kusansum myth. The iconography of the monumental carving at Izapa was cited as being supportive evidence of the association of descending deities and umbilical cords among the Maya.

7. The hypothesis that the borders of the interior painting of Tulum Structure 5 could represent *both* twisted snake and umbilical cord is supported by ethnohistoric evidence in the *Ritual of the Bacabs* and by the principle of multiplicity of meaning so common in Maya thought.

8. The Codex Paris, with its umbilical cord iconography and style is clearly related to the Tulum paintings (Lothrop 1924: 50-3; Robertson 1970; Ruz 1971: 222) and may have been the native document that Cortes acquired near Tulum on the island of Cozumel.[11]

9. The hypothesis that the iconography of Structure 5 at Tulum refers to the Kusansum myth and its cosmic extension of the experience of childbirth also finds support in the geographic position of Tulum, because the location of Tulum may have made it a centre for activities related to umbilical cord symbolism, i.e. those concepts inherent in the Kusansum myth. Located on the eastern shore of the Yucatan Peninsula, Tulum is in a position to have been one of the Postclassic embarkation points for pilgrimages to Cozumel and the Postclassic shrine of Ix Chel, one of most important aspects was that of goddess of childbirth.

Acknowledgments

The typescript of a paper written by Johannes Wilbert discussing umbilical cord concepts among the Warao of Venezuela initially stimulated my investigation of umbilical cord imagery at Tulum. I would like to thank Floyd Lounsbury, Michael Coe, Gareth Lowe, George Kubler, and Susanna Ekholm-Miller for their ideas pertaining to the iconography of the mural discussed in this paper, a condensed version of which was presented at the Mesa Redonda on 'Religion in Mesoamerica' held in Cholula, Mexico, in June 1972.

NOTES

1 Fernández (1945, Lám. 18) mistakenly rendered all of the circular motifs of the middle register as having the bifurcated double line element.

2 In his book *Códice Peresiano*, Luis Azcue y Mancera comments (1967: 109) that the naked figure on page 19 of the Codex Paris is a representation of a woman with an open stomach from which an umbilical cord extends upwards.

3 Another reference to a cord containing blood was recently pointed out to me by G.W. Lowe. In an article which appeared in the Merida newspaper *Novedades de Yucatán, Suplemento Cultural*, of July 2, 1972, Prof. José A. Xiu related a legend told him by a Maya of Chunhuaz and Chunhuhub, Quintana Roo. The story is a varient of the legend of the dwarf of Uxmal; in it there is reference to 'the marvellous rope . . . the *Cuxaan-zuum*': 'I carry here the marvellous rope . . . the *Cuxaan-zuum* . . . which when joined to its twin which is jealously guarded in Mani, at the command 'Moc-te-zumaa', will be strung up like an immense suspension bridge between the turbulent Caribbean Sea and this sacred city of Ichanzihó.'

Cuxaan can be translated as 'living' (Swadesh 1970: 41); *zuum* can be translated as 'cord' (Swadesh 1970: 96). Thus, the meaning of *Cuxaan-zuum* is 'living cord'.

'Moc' can be translated as 'knot'/'to tie' (Swadesh 1970: 65); 'zum' is a variant of 'zuum' and can be translated as cord (Swadesh 1970: 96). Thus 'Moc-te-zumaa' has the significance of 'tie together the cord'.

4 Laughlin (1962) suggests that flower among the Maya of Zinacantan, Chiapas signifies blood.

5 Among the ethnographic highland Maya, Vogt (1971: 42-4) has pointed out that there is 'a process of conceptual and structural replication whereby the same concepts are replicated at various levels of culture . . .' He cites as an example of conceptual replication 'the similarities in the manner in which the Zinacanteco father and mother (called *tot* and *me'*) care for, or "embrace" as the Indians put it, a child; the manner in which an *h'ilol* (also called *tot*) cares for, or "embraces", a patient during a curing ceremony; and the manner in which the ancestral gods (called *totilme'iletik*) care for, or "embrace", the *chanuls* in *bankilal muk'ta vits* (older brother large mountain) . . . Infant, patient, and *chanul* are all being treated properly and affectionately at various levels in the system: childhood, adulthood and supernatural world.' The ritual of cutting the umbilical cord and planting corn cited by Ximénez can be seen as examples of Vogt's process of 'conceptual replication' among the Maya. The ritual of cutting the umbilical cord may have its cosmic replication in the Kusansum myth.

6 The only exception to this observation may be the monuments at Seibal in the Peten, Guatemala. But these Seibal monuments are late Late Classic in date and remained in good condition probably because there was no significant occupation at Seibal after the erection and use of the monuments there.

7 The statement that the subject matter of Izapa monuments is allegorical is derived from an important observation concerning the nature of Mesoamerican symbolism made by Tatiana Proskouriakoff: 'In studying symbolism, you take into consideration not only the meaning of it, which you derive ethnographically, but its use. For instance, whether it is used emblematically, allegorically, or realistically.' (Proskouriakoff 1969: 176).

8 Norman's work on Izapa will be published soon as Paper 30 of the New World Archaeological Foundation.

9 That intertwined borders in Mesoamerican painting can be merely and only decorative with no meaning (Toscano 1944) is rejected as a possibility because I do not believe in the existence of meaningless forms in Precolumbian art.

10 See Edmonson, 1971: xi-xvii for a discussion of multiplicity of meaning in the *Popol Vuh*. See also Edmonson 1970: 37-50.

11 Suggested by H.B. Nicholson at the Mesa Redonda on 'Religion in Mesoamerica', Cholula, Mexico, June 1972.

REFERENCES

Azcue y Mancera, L. (1967) *Códice Peresiano*. Mexico.

Codex Fejérváry-Mayer (1901) M 12014 Des Free Public Museums de Liverpool. Paris.

Codex Laud (1966) MS. Laud Misc. 678, Bodleian Library, Oxford. *Codices Selecti*, vol. 11. Graz.

Codex Vindobonensis Mexicanus 1 (1963) *Codices Selecti*, vol. 5. Graz.

Edmonson, M.S. (1970) Metáfora Maya en literatura y en arte. In *Verhandlungen des XXXVIII Internationalen Amerikanistenkongresses*, band 2, 37-50. Munich.

Edmonson, M.S. (1971) *The Book of Counsel: The Popol Vuh of the Quiche*

Maya of Guatemala. Middle American Research Institute, Tulane University, Publication no. 25. New Orleans.

Fernández, M.A. (1941) El templo núm. 5 de Tulum, Quintana Roo. In *Los Mayas antiguos*, 155-80. Fondo de Cultura Economica, Mexico.

Fernández, M.A. (1945) Las ruinas de Tulum, II. *Anales del Instituto Nacional de Antropología e Historia* I (1939-40), 95-105. Mexico.

Gates, W. (1937) *Yucatan Before and After the Conquest by Friar Diego de Landa.* The Maya Society, Baltimore.

Girard, R. (1952) *El Popol-Vuh: fuente histórica.* Editorial del Ministerio de Educación Pública, Guatemala.

Glass, J.B. (1964) *Catálogo de la colección de códices.* Museo Nacional de Antropología, Mexico.

Laughlin, R.M. (1962) El símbolo de la flor en la religión de Zinacantan. *Estudios de cultura Maya*, 2, 123-39. Universidad Nacional Autónoma de México.

Lothrop, S.K. (1924) *Tulum; An Archaeological Study of the East Coast of Yucatan.* Carnegie Institution of Washington, Publication no. 335.

Norman, V.G. (1973) *Izapa Sculpture*, Part 1: Album. Papers of the New World Archaeological Foundation, no. 31. Provo.

Norman, V.G. (in press) *Izapa Sculpture*; Part 2: Text. Papers of the New World Archaeological Foundation, no. 31. Provo.

Proskouriakoff, T. (1968) cited in P.T. Furst, Discussion of the Olmec Were-Jaguar motif. In *Dumbarton Oaks Conference on the Olmec,* 176.

Reed, N. (1964) *The Caste War of Yucatan.* Stanford.

Robertson, D. (1970) The international style of the Late Postclassic. In *Verhandlungen des XXXVIII Internationalen Amerikanistenkongresses*, band 2, 77-88. Munich.

Roys, R.L. (1957) *The Political Geography of the Yucatan Maya.* Carnegie Institution of Washington, Publication no. 613.

Roys, R.L. (1965) *Ritual of the Bacabs.* Norman, Oklahoma.

Ruz Lhuillier, A. (1971) Influencias Mexicanas sobre los Mayas. In *Desarrollo cultural de los Mayas*, 203-41. Centro de Estudios Mayas, Universidad Nacional Autónoma de México.

Sahagún, Fr. B. de (1938) *Historia general de las cosas de Nueva España.* Mexico.

Seler, E. (1895) *Wandmalereien von Mitla.* Berlin.

Seler, E. (1902-3) *Codex Vaticanus 3773.* Berlin.

Seler, E. (1963) *Comentarios al Códice Borgia.* 3 vols. Mexico.

Swadesh, M., M.C. Alvarez and J.R. Bastarrachea (1970) *Diccionario de elementos del Maya Yucateco colonial.* Centro de Estudios Mayas, Cuaderno 3. Mexico.

Thompson, J.E.S. (1970) *Maya History and Religion.* Norman, Oklahoma.

Toscano, S. (1944) *Arte precolombino de México y de la América Central.* Mexico.

Tozzer, A.M. (1907) *A Comparative Study of the Mayas and the Lacandones.* New York.

Tozzer, A.M. (1941) *Landa's Relación de Las Cosas de Yucatán.* Papers of the Peabody Museum of American Archaeology and Ethnology, Harvard University, vol. 18.

Wilbert, J. n.d. Tobacco and shamanistic ecstasy among the Warao Indians of Venezuela. MS. University of Southern California.

Villacorta, A.J. and C.A. Villacorta (1930) *Códices Mayas.* Guatemala.

Vogt, E.Z. (1971) The genetic model and Maya cultural development. In *Desarrollo cultural de los Mayas*, 9-48. Mexico.

Xiu, J.A. (1972) Una variante de la leyenda del emano de Uxmal. In *Novedades de Yucatán*, Suplemento Cultural, July 2. Merida.

PETER T. FURST

Morning glory and mother goddess at Tepantitla, Teotihuacan : iconography and analogy in pre-Columbian art

1. Ecstatic-visionary shamanism and hallucinogens

From Fr. Ramon Pané on Columbus' second voyage of discovery in the Caribbean (1493-6), to the father of Mesoamerican ethnography, Fr. Bernadino de Sahagún, and his contemporaries and successors in colonial Mexico, the early European chroniclers of Indian beliefs and customs were fascinated and puzzled at least as much as they were outraged by the widespread ritual use of botanical hallucinogens and intoxicants by native peoples of the Americas. Ethnobotanist Richard Evans Schultes (1972: 3-54), foremost authority on New World hallucinogens, estimates that the Indians of North and South America discovered and utilized the potent chemical properties of between eighty and one hundred different hallucinogenic plant species to trigger what they experienced as ecstatic confrontation with the supernatural. In central Mexico alone, the clergy tried in vain over several centuries to uproot a wide variety of religious and divinatory ritual practices that involved the use of such potent botanical hallucinogens — all considered sacred — as tobacco; the peyote cactus; morning glory seeds or *ololiuhqui*; *datura*; psycho-tropic mint; and several species of divine mushrooms known to the Aztecs by such revealing names as *teonanacatl*, 'flesh of the gods'. All these, and more, are still employed today.

Inevitably, the question arises how much older than the sixteenth century such practices might be — indeed, how much older even than the earliest 'mushroom stones' from highland Guatemala, which have been dated *c.*1000 B.C. and which are now generally believed to have been connected with a Preclassic cult of hallucinogenic mushrooms.

In a recent paper on hallucinogens and their possible role in the shamanistic origins of religion, Weston La Barre (1972: 261-78) went so far as to propose Palaeolithic and Mesolithic roots for the prominent role psychotropic substances have long played in the religious beliefs and rituals of the aboriginal New World.

In essence, La Barre based his argument on the fact, well documented by ethnologists from Boas on, that the base religion of American Indians from Alaska to Patagonia was, like that of palaeo-Siberian hunters and reindeer herders — indeed, of hunting peoples, ancient and modern, everywhere — ecstatic-visionary sham-anism. In this respect, he writes (1972: 270): 'Aboriginal religion in the whole New World represents a kind of mesolithic fossil, little changed except in high cultures founded on agriculture, and the religion even in these cultures still shows shamanic origins.'

One area in which these ancient shamanistic survivals manifest themselves especially forcefully is in the ritual use of hallucinogenic intoxicants. Palaeo-Siberian shamans until very recently employed a psychotropic mushroom, *Amanita muscaria*, or fly agaric; American Indians, whose big-game ancestors drifted across the Bering land bridge from Siberia into Alaska in the Late Pleistocene, were to discover a great variety of plant species with which to bring about the kinds of ecstatic trances their Siberian cousins experienced with the fly agaric. La Barre attributes this phenomenon to the funda-mental nature of ecstatic-visionary shamanism, which is, 'so to speak, culturally programmed for an interest in hallucinogens and other psychoactive drugs' (1972: 272). The suggestion that right from the beginning palaeo-Indian shamans might have consciously explored their new environment for hallucinogenic plants, rather than dis-covering them accidentally in the course of the food quest, is an intriguing one that finds some support in the ethnographic present.

From his argument, it would follow that the pervasive narcotic complex which so astonished the early European explorers (but whose true significance and extent most anthropologists have only just begun to appreciate), may already have been part and parcel of the ideological baggage carried into the New World from northern Asia by palaeo-Mongoloid big-game hunters toward the end of the Pleistocene, when, as most prehistorians agree, the peopling of the Americas on any considerable scale had its beginnings.

Unfortunately, delicate organic materials are preserved only under the most favourable circumstances, and, in the absence of securely dated and chemically tested early archaeological evidence, La Barre's hypothesis was unproven, however logical and attractive. True, Junius Bird's excavations at Huaca Prieta had turned up a whalebone snuffing tablet and associated birdbone snuffing tube, suggesting that in coastal Peru hallucinogenic snuff was used at least three millennia earlier than the first Spanish accounts of this practice among the Taino Indians of Hispaniola in the late fifteenth century. Since the mescaline-containing San Pedro (*Trichocereus pachanoi*) cactus figures prominently on ritual vases of the Cupisnique or Chavin style, and on painted textiles of the same period, we may assume that the twentieth century use of this hallucinogenic species in Peruvian folk therapy (Sharon 1972: 114-35) has a history of at least three thousand years. The early mushroom effigy sculptures from southern Mesoamerica, mentioned above, suggest an equal antiquity for the modern Mexican mushroom cult. West Mexican mushroom effigies are somewhat more recent, dating between 1600 and 2000 years ago. Peyote is depicted on West Mexican funerary ceramics of the first century A.D. or thereabouts, while snuffing pipes from Guerrero, Oaxaca, Colima, and Nayarit attest to a widespread Mesoamerican snuffing complex that endured, at a minimum, from c.1200-1100 B.C. into the first centuries after Christ (Furst 1972a: 61-8). No snuffing was reported from Mexico by the early chroniclers.

These are all respectable ages. But since they are associated with a more or less sedentary agricultural life (or, in the case of Huaca Priesta, a coastal fishing culture with the beginnings of cultivation), rather than nomadic or semi-nomadic hunting and gathering, a Pleistocene origin for the hallucinogenic phenomenon among Palaeo-Indians had to remain largely conjectural, however persuasive the circumstantial evidence marshalled by Schultes, La Barre, and others concerned with this important culture-historical problem.

In fact, however, for some time there has been reasonably good evidence, from sites in northern Mexico and Texas, suggesting an ecstatic cult of considerably greater antiquity than anything found elsewhere in Mesoamerica in sedentary, pottery-making and food-producing village contexts. This evidence, in the form of caches of the red bean-like seeds of the *Sophora secundiflora* shrub, came from rock shelter sites of the Western Archaic, or Desert Culture, which archaeologists like W.W. Taylor (1956; 1966) have recognized as a widespread and extraordinarily conservative cultural continuum, extending over much of arid north-central Mexico and Texas, and enduring, with its basic way of life and many of its artifacts virtually unchanged, for some ten thousand years. The nature of this remarkably long-lived cultural phenomenon, and its various sub-phases, has been discussed in some detail by Taylor (1966: 59-94), based on his own excavations in well-preserved stratigraphic cave sites in arid Coahuila, especially at Frightful Cave in the Cuatro Cienegas basin of the Sierra Madre Occidental.

Trade in hallucinogenic *Sophora secundiflora* seeds among the Indians of Texas was mentioned by Cabeza de Vaca in 1539 (Schultes, 1972: 31-2). In historic times — indeed, until the latter half of the last century — the powerfully psychotropic red 'bean' was the focus of a widespread complex of ecstatic-visionary shamanistic cults or medicine societies, especially among the numerous tribes of the southern Plains. These hallucinogenic cults were known among Whites by various names, among them Red Bean or Red Medicine Society, Red Bean Cult, Deer Dance, Wichita Dance, or Mescal Bean

Cult (Troike 1962: 946-63). The last-named was, of course, wholly in error, since mescal is a distilled liquor made from the agave cactus and not from a leguminous shrub like *Sophora secundiflora.*

Quantities of these narcotic seeds were found in a dozen or so Desert Culture sites in Texas and Coahuila, Mexico. In rock shelter sites on the Lower Pecos River in Texas, the narcotic seeds are associated with a remarkable complex of pictographs of which the earliest, belonging to the Pecos River style, are estimated to date to the earliest Desert Culture in this region, prior to 6000 B.C.

In his recent monograph on Pecos River art, Newcomb (1967: 65-80) favours a shamanistic interpretation of many of the paintings and relates their content to hallucinogenic and divinatory red bean rites, as these are known from historic times. Remarkably, the iconography of the painted prehistoric anthropomorphic figures is very similar to that of participants in historic red bean cults, so much so that, as Newcomb (1967: 75) writes:

> If members of mescal bean societies had been portrayed on rock surfaces they would undoubtedly look amazingly like the anthropomorphic beings depicted in the Pecos River style pictographs. Animals, particularly deer, are important to both, and the animal pelts, bird feathers, rattles, and other paraphernalia used in the modern cult have close counterparts in the lower Pecos pictographs. Even the purpose of rodent jaws, included with mescal beans and other objects in a basket in a lower Pecos River archaeological site, is suggested by the usage of garfish jaws in the modern cult.[1]

The earliest radiocarbon dates from Frightful Cave (where *Sophora secundiflora* beans occur throughout all of the cultural deposits, from the earliest to the most recent) published by Taylor ranged from 7585 to 7345 B.C. However, these computations, made some years ago, when radiocarbon dating had not yet attained its present state of sophistication, carried a plus or minus factor of from 400 to 550 years. Hence these dates could be read as either older or younger by as much as half a millennium.

Recently, the cultural materials from Frightful Cave and related sites excavated by Taylor have been restudied at the Smithsonian Institution by James M. Adovasio and his colleagues and a new series of some fifty C14 dates computed by the Smithsonian's Radiation Biology Laboratory, under Robert Stuckenrath. As might be expected, these dates carried a far smaller margin of error.[2] According to the new computations, *Sophora secundiflora* seeds occur at 7265 ± 85 B.C. in the lowest deposits, and at A.D. 750 ± 50 in the uppermost, as well as in all of the intermediate levels. It should be noted that the seeds are found in what appear to be ceremonial contexts.

Comparable ages were reported for Desert Culture sites in the Amistad Reservoir area of Trans-Pecos Texas. At Fate Bell Shelter, for example, the psychoactive seeds of *Sophora secundiflora* and of another plant, *Ungnadia speciosa*, were found in all levels spanning the well-dated Trans-Pecos archaeological Periods II through VI (7000 B.C. to A.D. 1000). Similarly, Eagle Cave, which has also been well-dated, yielded the two species in association in occupation levels dating from 7000 B.C. to the eleventh century A.D.

There is thus no doubt of a well-developed shamanistic, ecstatic-visionary complex involving *Sophora secundiflora*, and perhaps other psychotropic species, in the period immediately following the decline and extinction of Late Pleistocene big game.

Of even greater interest are new radiocarbon dates for Bonfire Shelter. According to Adovasio, this well-dated and important archaeological site has yielded *Sophora secundiflora* remains from its lowest occupational stratum, Bone Bed II, now dated at 8440 to 8120 B.C., well into the Late Pleistocene big game hunting era. Indeed, the narcotic seeds were found with Folsom and Plainview points and the bones of extinct *Bison antiquus*. They also occur in all of the subsequent levels, up to A.D. 1040, when the site had its final occupation.

It is therefore reasonable to assume that the historic red bean cult of northern Mexico and the Southern Plains of the United States has a time depth reaching back beyond the Archaic precisely into the Mesolithic-Palaeolithic horizon postulated by La Barre. While migrations of small hunting bands from Asia into Alaska almost certainly began as early as 20-30,000 years ago, if not earlier, they probably did not cease at least until about 10-12,000 years ago, when the rising seas finally submerged the Asian-American overland connection (the ancestors of the modern Eskimos, whose culture continued to be wholly Mesolithic until modern times, arrived later, probably between 4000 and 2000 B.C.). Thus, at a time when new groups were still crossing the Bering land bridge, palaeo-Indian hunters of bison, mammoth and other Pleistocene big game had already discovered and were utilizing the psychoactive properties of various New World plants, a phenomenon which lends credence to La Barre's suggestion that such knowledge and skills were directly derived from the traditions and practices of ecstatic-visionary Eurasian shamanism.

Likewise, the survival of these ecstatic practices, not only into early food cultivation but also into the urbanized, highly complex manifestations of Postclassic Mesoamerican civilization, supports La Barre's characterization of much of pre-Christian American Indian religion as a kind of Mesolithic-Palaeolithic fossil, in which the basic precepts of the ecstatic shamanism of earlier hunting cultures continued to play a major role. Needless to say, this is not meant as a value judgment; on the contrary, the 'archaic' forms survived because they had proved themselves to be eminently satisfying and adaptive, and because, in contrast to the Old World, with its often bloody religious upheavals and reformations, they were not generally subjected to violent repression and radical transformation but, as a rule, to far gentler, 'natural' or evolutionary modifications.[3]

From the writings of Sahagún and other sixteenth-century chroniclers, it is clear that the sacred hallucinogens played an important part not only in divinatory or curing practices on the 'folk level' of religion and ceremonial, but also in the far more complex beliefs and rituals of the priestly hierarchies that served the demanding gods of Aztec Tenochtitlan and its allies and tributaries. The priesthood, of course, was eliminated with the Conquest, so that by the time of Hernando Ruíz de Alarcón or Jacinto de la Serna, to mention two seventeenth-century churchmen most concerned with native beliefs and customs, especially those involving hallucinogens, as these had survived the first hundred years of acculturation and repression, the cults of the divine hallucinogens were almost wholly in the care of Indian village shamans, diviners, and curers. These are still the guardians of the ancient traditions, however modified or syncretic. We may assume a parallel development in the Maya area, for which, unfortunately, we lack detailed documentation on the use of psychoactive plants comparable to the rich data compiled for central Mexico by the early chroniclers. But, as the noted Maya scholar J. Eric S. Thompson (1970: 185) pointed out, notwithstanding the silence of the colonial sources on this topic, 'it is hard to believe that the lowland Maya had nothing of that sort in view of the widespread use of toxic aids in other parts of Middle America', and also in consideration of the many ancient representations of mushrooms in the Maya highlands, and some in the lowlands as well. (Since the publication of Thompson's recent book on Maya religions and history, what appears to be a cult of hallucinogenic mushrooms has come to light in the Maya lowlands among the Lacandon Maya in the Usumacinta region (Merle Greene Robertson, personal communication).)

By extension, the rich store of information that Sahagún, Fr. Diego de Durán, and their fellow sixteenth-century chroniclers compiled on the complex religion of Aztec Tenochtitlan helps us to understand something of the beliefs of its civilized predecessors, especially Teotihuacan, from whom it took, directly or indirectly, much of its ultimate inspiration. The folk cults of rural Mexico, as described by Ruíz de Alarcón, above all constitute a primary source for rural Indian religion as it persisted beyond the trauma of the Conquest. Almost certainly, however, these seventeenth-century folk beliefs reflect a good deal of the common ideology not only of the preceding pre-Conquest era in central Mesoamerica but also of far earlier times. It seems to me that we are justified in making this assumption in light of the fact that much of what Ruíz de Alarcón wrote in 1629 is almost equally applicable today, especially where it concerns the role of the divine hallucinogens. Such a high degree of ideological conservatism, in a time when native religion was subjected to its greatest stresses and its most powerful pressures for radical change, allows us to suppose at least as little fundamental modification as we move backward in time from the early colonial period and the Conquest into the Postclassic and Classic.

In any event, the following pages will, hopefully, demonstrate the great potential value of the legacy of Ruíz de Alarcón and, among his predecessors, especially Durán, for the analysis and understanding of certain well-defined areas of pre-Columbian art and iconography.

2. The Tepantitla mural

In an earlier paper (1970) I tentatively proposed a reinterpretation of the great 'tree' above the frontal deity in the so-called Tlalocan, or Paradise of Tlaloc, mural at Tepantitla, Teotihuacan, as a metaphysical conception of the morning glory vine, *Rivea corymbosa*. In Aztec times, the potent hallucinogenic seeds of this plant, whose active principles have been identified as lysergic acid derivatives, were worshipped as the divine *ololiuhqui*. Like peyote, the sacred mushrooms, and other traditional hallucinogens to which god-like qualities were attributed, *ololiuhqui* survived the Conquest, and to this day is widely employed in curing and divinatory ritual to induce ecstatic intoxication, or 'altered states of consciousness'. Mestizos and Indians know it under such names as *ololuc, badoh, semilla de la Virgen, semilla de la Santa Maria*, etc.

At the time I also suggested that notwithstanding the Tlaloc-like nose bar or mouth mask with its characteristic row of fang-like teeth, the Tepantitla deity was not in fact Tlaloc, nor even male, as it is identified in most of the Mesoamerican literature, but rather an earth and fertility goddess, who might be called Mother of Water. This was not actually a wholly new idea, since Kubler (1962: 37) had already referred to her briefly as a water goddess,[4] without, however, attempting to identify her further or linking her with any of the well-known earth and fertility goddesses of the late Postclassic period. Kubler, as we know, rejects the concept of continuity between Teotihuacan and the Aztecs, and with it also the validity of calling the gods of Teotihuacan by Aztec names.

On the contrary, I felt then, as I do now, that conceptually, iconographically, and by ethnohistoric and ethnographic analogy, the Tepantitla goddess can be identified with one or more of her Puebla-Mixteca-Aztec counterparts, and also with the Huichol earth and fertility goddesses, especially the Mothers (or All-Mother) of Water. In the absence from the complex Huichol pantheon of a

Figure 1 Detail from the reconstruction painting by Agustin Villagra of the socalled 'Tlalocan' mural at Tepantitla, Teotihuacan, showing the central deity flanked by attendant priestesses (or priests in female clothing), with the 'tree' — actually a twining flower vine — rising from the great *quetzal* headdress of the goddess. Museo Nacional de Antropología, Mexico City.

Tlaloc-like male rain deity, these Mothers are goddesses both of terrestrial water (springs, waterfalls, streams, rivers, lakes, water holes, etc.) and of rain. This is because rain is seen as the child of the earth, in that it has its ultimate origin not in the celestial regions but in the terrestrial water, from which the Mothers make it rise in the form of clouds at the beginning of the rainy season. This fundamental Huichol conceptualization of the earth as the mother of rain may be significant to our understanding of the nature of Tlaloc, and of his curious synthesis with the Earth Goddess at Teotihuacan and subsequently in Aztec art.

Notwithstanding the fact that the frontal deity is not the Aztec god of rain, there is obviously a close conceptual and iconographic relationship between the earth mother and Tlaloc, whose full name is Tlalocatecuhtli, Lord of Tlalocan. Etymologically the name is unrelated to rain; Thelma Sullivan (personal communication) instead connects it with *tlalli*, earth, and derivations of this word that have to do with the earth and its natural or supernatural manifestations.[5]

Figure 2 Detail from the 'Tlalocan' mural. Along with other evidence discussed in the text, the characteristically morning-glory-like structure of the flowers in profile suggests identification of the 'tree' as *Rivea corymbosa*, whose hallucinogenic seeds, worshipped as divine in Aztec times, are still widely employed in Mexico to induce ecstatic vision states in ritual curing and divination.

A conceptual and iconographic (and perhaps etymological) relationship between Tlaloc and the Earth Goddess is unmistakable especially in the latter's animal aspect — the monstrous toad Tlaltecuhtli, meaning Lord, Owner, or Master of the Earth. In Aztec art these two conceptions — Tlaltecuhtli and Tlalocatecuhtli — are sometimes synthetized into a single being, with the body of the monstrous toad with jaguar claws and the characteristic goggle-eyed face of Tlaloc. If Tlaloc is male, however, Tlaltecuhtli seems to leave no doubt of her essential femininity, in that she is invariably depicted in the characteristic squatting, or *hocker*, position in which Indian women traditionally give birth. If there were any question of the meaning of Tlaltecuhtli's *hocker* or childbirth position as symbol of regeneration and rebirth, it is dispelled by the well-known painting of the goddess Tlazolteotl in the act of giving birth in the pages of the Codex Borbonicus. Tlazolteotl is another aspect of the old Earth Mother Toci, Our Grandmother, who is also worshipped variously as Tonantzin, Our Mother; Teteoinan, Mother of the Gods; and Coatlicue, Lady of the Serpent Skirt, and whose animal aspect is the earth toad as genetrix of all life, who alternately devours and regenerates the Sun and light and whose womb receives the bones and souls of the dead. In a creation tradition the monstrous toad is closely connected with the origin not only of the land but of terrestrial water and of the useful plants that sustain man. All this

Figure 3 Cast of the underside of the Colossal Coatlicue in the Museo Nacional de Antropología, with relief of Tlaltecuhtli, the deified Earth in her form as a monstrous squatting toad in the *hocker*, or birth-giving position, but with the goggle-eyed face of the male earth and rain god Tlaloc. Similar reliefs, with or without the head of Tlaloc, are found on the underside of other Aztec monuments, including sacrificial vessels, idols of the Mother of the Gods, and even of Quetzalcoatl.

bears significantly on the iconography of the Tepantitla deity, as on the problem of continuity or discontinuity between the Aztecs and their central Mexican predecessors.

At the time of my earlier paper I did not have the benefit of a scholarly and insightful art historical analysis of the Tepantitla fresco complex which Esther Pasztory (1971) was then preparing, and which she has since presented as her doctoral thesis. Nor had I had the chance to discuss the murals with Doris Heyden of the Museo Nacional de Antropología, who has long been concerned with the application of ethnohistory to central Mexican iconography.

Figure 4 The earth as Tlaltecuhtli, redrawn from the Codex Borbonicus. Note flint knife emerging from her fanged jaws, as symbol of light and Sun, which she alternately devours and regurgitates. Tlaltecuntli's squatting, or *hocker*, position, is that assumed by Indian women when giving birth and so presumably symbolizes the dualistic life-death role of the Earth Mother as genetrix as well as destroyer. Tlazolteotl, Goddess of Sustenance, herself another aspect of the basic Earth Mother Goddess of the Aztecs, is depicted in the same position as she gives birth to the young Maize God Centeotl.

Hence my initial identification of the frontal deity was somewhat impressionistic, lacking the meticulous analytical and detailed approach Pasztory was to bring to the problem.

Essentially, my identification was based on a comparison of the two profile attendant figures with that of the frontal deity, herself only a half-figure, or bust, as Huichol deities often are in ceremonial art. Of the frontal deity, only the upper part — face, quetzal bird headdress, shoulders, and arms — are wholly visible, the rest of the abbreviated figure being hidden under the bifurcating stream that gushes from beneath the Tlaloc-like mask, and by other water and vegetation symbols.

The profile figures wear headdresses, jade jewelry and some other accoutrements identical to those of the frontal deity, but unlike her face, which appears to be masked, their faces are human. We may assume them to be priests or priestesses impersonating the deity. Their attire, however, is feminine, distinguished especially by the *quechquemitl*, the triangular, poncho-like upper garment which in Aztec times was worn exclusively by women of noble status and which also served to identify certain earth goddesses in the codices (Doris Heyden, personal communication). It follows that the deity being impersonated had also to be essentially female, notwithstanding certain male characteristics, such as the Tlaloc-like mouth and the fire band eyes, which are associated with the male fire deity.

Over the past two years, Pasztory, Heyden, Arthur Miller (whose own monograph on the murals of Teotihuacan appeared in 1973), and I have had occasion to discuss the complex Tepantitla iconography in some detail. The present paper has benefited greatly from these conversations, and I would like to take this opportunity to thank these colleagues for freely sharing their many helpful and stimulating ideas.

We are generally agreed that the frontal deity is indeed female and that she seems to represent the earth mother in a youthful and bountiful aspect. Pasztory believes that she comes closest in character to Xochiquetzal (Precious, or Quetzal, Flower), the young Earth Mother and creator goddess of fertility and vegetation in the pantheon of the Aztecs. As fountainhead of terrestrial water, which pours from the area of her nose and mouth, she seemed to me to embody primarily the characteristics of Chalchiuhtlicue, Lady of the Jade Skirt, goddess of water that flows over and under the earth, mother of springs, streams, lakes and water holes, and, according to some traditions, wife, or sister, of Tlaloc. Heyden understands her more fundamentally as the all-encompassing Earth Mother Goddess as genetrix of all life. This more generalized interpretation is perhaps the most useful one. It carries a most important inference — that perhaps the principal, or at least fundamental, deity of Teotihuacan was the universal Mother Goddess.

In a sense, of course, we are all talking about the same thing, inasmuch as Xochiquetzal and Chalchiuhtlicue are not wholly distinct and separate deities but, along with a number of other earth and fertility goddesses, closely related aspects of the same basic creative female principle, personified in the Earth as *Urmutter*. By this I do not mean to deny them the well-defined personalities which they obviously possess and which are reflected in their distinctive accoutrements and the rituals specifically dedicated to them. Nevertheless, in essence they are the youthful and fertile aspects of the old goddess of the earth and of life, the Mother of all — as are Cihuacoatl, Snake Woman, goddess of female fertility and parturition and divine patronness of those who died in childbirth;[6] Xilonen, an earth goddess apparently of Huaxtecan origin; Ixcuina, goddess of filthy things (especially sexual transgressions) to whom one confessed; Iztaccihuatl, Sleeping Woman; Chicomecoatl, Seven Serpent, whom the chroniclers called the Goddess of Sustenance, and others. Notwithstanding their distinctive names, attributes, functions, and ceremonies, to dichotomize too rigidly between them would be to misunderstand the fundamental nature of Mesoamerican religion, where few such sharp distinctions prevail.

Much the same phenomenon can still be observed today among

the Huichol of western Mexico. The multiplicity of deities in the Huichol pantheon, that so bewilders the ethnographer when he first encounters this most traditional of remaining Indian cultures in Mexico, becomes more comprehensible as soon as he realizes that the numerous goddesses of the earth, rain, terrestrial water, flowers, fertility, childbirth, maize, etc., are essentially only different, youthful and fecund, aspects of the old Earth Mother Goddess Nakawe. Lumholtz (1900: 13) recognized this long ago, when he noted that such earth goddesses as Tatei (Our Mother) 'Utuanaka and Tatei Yurianaka were not separate and distinct but different attributes of their own mother, whom he called Grandmother Growth. 'Utuanaka is the Earth Mother of maize and sustenance, Yurianaka the Earth Mother who has been prepared by rain and moisture for the planting season. Zingg (1938) rejected the identification of these earth goddesses with the old Creator Goddess, insisting that the different youthful earth mothers were in fact entirely separate rather than only different aspects of the old goddess. My own research fully supports the insight of Lumholtz as essentially correct.

Another major point on which Heyden, Pasztory, Miller and I are agreed is that the 'tree' rising behind and above the frontal deity (or, perhaps, growing directly out of her image?) is not just a symbol of vegetation and fertility, but embodies several layers of meaning, which go beyond natural history and ethnobotany.

Thirdly, we feel that there is a sufficient degree of ideological continuity not only between all the different local and temporal manifestations of Mesoamerican civilization, to justify attempts at interpretation by ethnographic and ethnohistoric analogy, especially, but by no means exclusively, to Aztec cosmology and ritual, as these have come down to us from the early Colonial sources and from some of the prehispanic codices.

Where some of us diverge (at least as of this writing), is in the more specific botanical identification of the flowers on the ends of the twining branches of the 'tree' as those of *Rivea corymbosa*.[7]

Pasztory (147-9) believes this determination to be too specific. She prefers to interpret the stylized, funnel-shaped blossoms, whose form is very common in the art of Teotihuacan, as symbols for flowers in general, especially inasmuch as the same conventionalized flower in profile is also used on plants that are unequivocally creeping or climbing vines[8] without the clearly supernatural or mythic attributes of the Tepantitla 'tree'.

Pasztory agrees, however, that while the central plant at Tepantitla has never in the past been called anything but a tree, it does in fact more closely resemble a twisting vine, perhaps one that is filled with water or sap; its form, she writes, suggests a cross between spouting streams of water and plant. On the whole, she views the plant as embodying the widespread concept of a Cosmic Tree at the centre of the world, symbolizing with its associated images the interrelationship of all nature and life.

I have no fundamental quarrel with such an interpretation, especially since it does not really conflict with a more specific botanical identification as *Rivea corymbosa*. As we know from ethnography and ethnohistory, the sacred hallucinogens provided the means by which man could transcend the limitations of the human condition and achieve direct confrontation and intercourse with the supernatural in ecstatic trances. 'Pillar-of-the-World', 'Mainstay-of-the-Sky', is how the Rig-Veda of ancient India addresses the divine Soma, identified by R. Gordon Wasson (1968) as the hallucinogenic *Amanita muscaria,* or fly agaric, mushroom. The neophyte shamans of the Carib Indians of South America climbed to the sky along hallucinogenic vines on their celestial trance journeys.

I have heard Huichol shamans refer to the tobacco plant as the 'special tree of shamans', and to the little peyote cactus, *Lophophora williamsii,* whose crown barely projects above ground, as 'tree of our life'. Vine, tree, bush, fungus, or cactus, they are conceived as magical stairways to the Upper- and Underworld, and so tend to merge with the *axis mundi* and Cosmic Tree that connects heaven and earth at the centre of the world.[9]

Be that as it may, notwithstanding the degree to which the natural features of the Tepantitla plant are overlaid with metaphysical symbolism, the botanical determination is supported by the following:

1. Total configuration as a twining plant with twisted flowering branches, rather than as a typical tree with central trunk and lateral limbs (of which there are examples in the same mural).
2. Funnel-shape of the flowers in profile; characteristically metachlamydeous (united), rather than separate and overlapping, petals, and typically morning-glory-like relationship of calyx to corolla.
3. Seed pods and/or unopened buds which, in contrast to the synthesis of botanical and metaphysical characters that marks the plant as a whole, appear surprisingly faithful to the natural model.
4. The morning glory's preference for wet places, such as the banks of streams, rivers, drainage ditches or canals, and the coincidence of its flowering season in central Mexico with the onset of the rains in early summer, all of which might have served as validation for the metaphysical and pictorial association of *Rivea corymbosa* (or the other hallucinogenic morning glory species, *Ipomoea violacea*) with a Mother Goddess of Water.

In light of the above, I venture that, were it not for the greatly exaggerated diameter of the interlacing, double-outlined branches, which give an x-ray-like impression of transparent, hollow tubes, filled with liquid, and containing spiders, butterflies, deposits of insect or spider eggs (?), and, here and there, small quatrefoil rosettes, the supposed 'tree' might long ago have been identified as a morning glory, even in the absence of any knowledge of the profound role the morning glory played in prehistoric and in historic times.

This is not to say that the flowers in profile are wholly natural-istic — only that they may be recognized botanically with a high degree of probability. Aside from general stylization in accordance with Teotihuacan tradition, the flowers are fraught with symbolism: for example, the rim of the corolla is set with a row of three eyes, which are repeated also on the streamers that fall, water-like, from quatrefoil disks in front of each blossom. Much has been written of this eye motif in the art of Teotihuacan; unfortunately, its meaning continues to elude us.

There is another curious iconographic association in the Tepantitla mural that should be considered in this context. Wasson (personal communication) has long believed that sacred mushrooms of the species *Psilocybe* are represented on the edges of the 'streams' of seeds falling from the hands of the two attendant priests. These edges are set with alternating plant symbols of which one appears to be a seed or seed pod and the other resembles a slender-stemmed mushroom with the cap seen from below. Whether or not these are in fact mushrooms, the seeds within the streams, and below the cave mouth symbol at the base of the central deity, can be identified botanically as the narcotic *Rhynchosia pyramidalis*, known in Oaxaca as *piule*.[10] *Piule* is taken with the sacred mushrooms on the slopes of Popocatepetl. It is interesting that the term *piule* is also sometimes applied to the hallucinogenic morning glories (Schultes 1972: 51).

The quatrefoil, or cruciform, rosettes are very curious and require consideration. First, we find a similar juxtaposition of profile and *en face* flowers in the centre of the figure, above what appears to be a symbol for cave, or the entrance to the underworld. Funnel-shaped morning-glory-like flowers alternating with frontal, cruciform rosettes can also be seen on some painted vessels. The presence of both forms on the same plant would suggest (as does Pasztory) that they are indeed meant to represent the same flower, seen from different angles, despite their unmistakably dissimilar configurations.

While this may well be the case, there is an alternative, or perhaps only supplementary, explanation. It may be that while the profile view identifies the specific flower, its conventionalization into a cruciform or quatrefoil — which is botanically comparatively rare — stands for something more — perhaps a mythic or cosmological attribute in some way related to the four sacred world directions and the vital centre.

It could hardly be considered coincidental that the same quatrefoil motif occurs at Teotihuacan also in other iconographic contexts, where it is obviously not part of a flowering plant — for example, on *incensarios*, of the headdresses of figurines, and very prominently on the facade of the Temple of the Plumed Conch Shells, where large cruciform rosettes are juxtaposed with conch shell trumpets decorated with quetzal feathers.

It was Seler (1915: vol. 5, 462-9) who long ago interpreted the quatrefoil flower at Teotihuacan as symbol of the Sun God, by analogy to the very similar Maya *kin* sign, glyph for Sun or day, and sign of the Sun God, who is also the god of number 4. Seler noted that some of the mould-made Teotihuacan figurines identified by him as idols of the Sun God on the basis of the quatrefoil symbol also share with the Maya Sun God the characteristic filing of the incisor teeth to a T-shape.

Assuming, then, that the botanical identification of the 'tree' as the *Rivea corymbosa*, source of the divine *ololiuhqui*, is correct, the above would suggest solar attributes for the morning glory, or at least some sort of symbolic association with the Sun. Considering the heliotropic, or phototropic, behaviour of the morning glory, such a connection would be hardly surprising. While there is almost certainly a deeper meaning that escapes us, the morning glory might well have been regarded as herald or companion of the diurnal Sun God, in that its blossoms typically open with the first rays in the morning and close again at dusk. (Notwithstanding the apparent 'logic' of the above, it may be that the quatrefoil 'flower' in Teotihuacan art — especially those associated with the large conch shell trumpets on the facade of the Templo de los Carcoles Emplumadas — has additional or even different meanings. It could, for example, symbolize a kind of quatripartite or four-directional underworld as place of ultimate origins and home of the great Earth Mother Goddess. This concept of an underworld with four quarters persists to this day among some of the Pueblo Indians of the southwest.)

3. The divine ololiuhqui

Ololiuhqui is a powerful hallucinogen, containing, as Albert Hofmann, the discoverer of LSD-25, was to determine in 1960, d-lysergic acid amide (ergine) and d-isolysergic amide. These, writes Hofmann (1963: 352),

> are closely related to d-lysergic acid diethylamide (LSD) . . . which we had produced synthetically and investigated many years previously whilst working on LSD. From the phytochemical point of view this finding was unexpected and of particular interest because lysergic acid alkaloids, which had hitherto only been found in the lower fungi of the genus *Claviceps*, were now for the first time

found to be present in higher plants, in the plant family of *Convolvulaceae*.[11]

According to Francisco Hernández (1651), the learned and observant physician to the King of Spain who spent some eight years in sixteeth-century Mexico studying the medicinal lore of the Aztecs,

> when the priests wanted to communicate with their gods, and to receive messages from them, they ate this plant (*ololiuhqui*) to induce a delirium. A thousand visions and satanic hallucinations appeared to them.

Actually, as the Spanish clergy quickly recognized, *ololiuhqui*, like other sacred psychotomimetic plants, was more than just the agent of communication with the supernatural. It was itself supernatural, indeed a god. It would almost have had to be to account for its powerful presence in the Tepantitla mural.

In fact, even in the Colonial era, in the face of the most ruthless persecution by the ecclesiastical authorities, *ololiuhqui* retained its divine character as a deity, revered in secret domestic oratories and shrines, addressed with prayers, petitions, and incense, and presented with sacrificial offerings and bouquets of flowers. *Ololiuhqui* could also manifest himself in human shape to those who drank the hallucinogenic infusion. Accounts of the worship of *ololiuhqui* and other hallucinogens as divinities are too specific and occur too often in the colonial literature to be dismissed as mere ethnocentric misconstruction of indigenous beliefs.[12]

Far and away the best source on the subject of *ololiuhqui*, as on seventeenth-century survivals of Indian beliefs and practices in general, is the treatise on the 'idolatries and superstitions' of the Indians of Morelos and Guerrero authored by Ruíz de Alarcón (1629). This work was the result of a wide-ranging investigation of native religious beliefs and rites, as these had survived the first century of Spanish rule. It was commissioned by the Church to serve as a manual of instruction for the clergy in the recognition and extirpation of 'idolatrous and superstitious' behaviour. The manuscript covers a wide range of indigenous customs, especially with respect to curing, divination and magic, much of it deeply rooted in pre-Hispanic religion and ritual.

Its greatest value lies in its numerous original Nahuatl texts of magical incantations and invocations, employed by native shamans, curers and diviners in a variety of contexts, from therapy to agriculture, hunting and fishing, and artisanry. These were evidently dictated to the author, who spoke Nahuatl fluently, by professional shamans, many of them women, detained and interrogated by him in his role of investigator for the Holy Office (Inquisition). Some of these magical incantations exhibit Christian influence, but the majority show little or no acculturation. Apparently at least some of these chants were 'acquired' by their owners in ecstatic trances induced by *ololiuhqui*. Acquisition of chants and other magical formulae in ecstatic trance or dream states is of course a well-known phenomenon in shamanism.

Several chapters are devoted to what their author calls 'the superstition of the *ololiuhqui*', to which, he complains, the Indians continued to attribute divinity in the face of his most vehement denunciation and severest punishment. Worse, the same 'superstition' was wont to infect 'base persons' among the Colonials, including, he writes, Negroes, Mulattoes and even Spaniards. For this reason, he said, he would refrain from identifying the precise botanical source of *ololiuhqui*, other than that it was a vine that grew especially profusely along the banks of the rivers and streams in his native Guerrero and neighbouring Morelos (as it still does).

There are repeated complaints that no matter how diligently one tried to discover and suppress the old customs, the Indians seemed always to find new ways to thwart one's best efforts, hiding the consecrated *ololiuhqui* baskets and pottery bowls in secret places, lest contamination by alien hands so anger the deity that he might punish the Indians for allowing such sacrilege. And the Indians, he says, seemed always to be far more concerned with the good will of *ololiuhqui* than the displeasure and penalties of the clergy. Since this important work has not previously appeared in English,[13] the following account of one of his investigations, involving a woman whom a relative had denounced as an idolater following a family quarrel, is cited *in extenso*:

So that it can be warned with what care one should handle these affairs, I refer to another case: In the town of Cuetaxxochitla, an Indian woman had a little basket that had this *ololiuhqui* superstition, and she had I know not what kind of dissension with those of her household, and shortly afterward I arrived in that town, which being of my *beneficio*, would enable the Indian woman to overcome her fears.

When I arrived I got news of the basket, which was given me by one of her relatives; so that I wouldn't miss my chance I sent him to check the house again, and he asked if he could do it alone since he was from the same house, and he would see if the basket and the *ololiuhqui* and all the other things which he had denounced were still there. With this, he went to the house and returned to me saying that the basket was not in the same place as before, nor anywhere in the oratory.

Therefore, with all diligence, I had the Indian woman, owner of the basket, brought before me, and placed some guards in the house of a sister of hers in the town. And then I interrogated the criminals so carefully and with such detailed and careful descriptions of the basket that she couldn't deny it, but she said that she didn't have inside (it) that which we were looking for, nor any other thing of interest, and that the basket had not been removed from her house. I then sent for it, and they found it where she said it was, but now emptied of its treasure, because, to her way of thinking, all the *ololiuhqui* had been taken out, and a cloth (bag) of those which they offer (in sacrifice), which the denouncer had set aside; so that there was a very little *ololiuhqui* in the basket. Seeing the quantity of *ololiuhqui* and the cloth that was missing, I had the sister of the criminal detained, and although I confronted her with the truth, and a well-informed description, as good as the owner could testify herself, I spent the whole day in questions and answers to find out what she had taken out of the basket, because in the brief amount of time that it had taken me to call the sister and to send guards to her house, she had time to remove all the *ololiuhqui* from the basket and return it to her sister's oratory, and to divide the *ololiuhqui* up into many parts, which added to the superstition of the cloth and the basket.

When she was asked why she had denied it so perversely she answered, as they always do, 'Oninomauhtiaya', which means, out of fear I did not dare. It is important to indicate that this is not the same fear which they have for the ministers of justice for the punishment that they deserve, rather (it is) the fear that they have for this same *ololiuhqui*, or the deity they believe that resides in it, and in this respect they have their reverence so confused that it is necessary to have the help of God to remove it; so that the fear and terror that impedes their confession, is not one which will annoy that false deity that they think they have in the *ololiuhqui*, so as not to fall under his ire and indignation. And thus they say, 'Aconechtlahuelis', 'may I not arouse your ire or anger against me'.

The investigation completed, the good friar arrived in Atenango, seat of his benefice in what is now the state of Guerrero (he himself was born in Taxco). Here,

knowing the blindness of these unfortunate souls, to remove from them such a heavy burden and such a strong impediment to their salvation,

he began at once to preach vigorously against *ololiuhqui*, ordering the vines that grew along the river banks to be cleared away, and casting prodigious quantities of the confiscated seed into the fire in the presence of its owners. With this, he writes, 'Our Lord was served'.

Immediately afterwards he fell ill, which he attributed to the unfamiliar climate of the hotlands, but which his Indian parishioners promptly credited to the displeasure of the *ololiuhqui*, 'for not having revered it, it being earlier angered by what I had done to it: this is how blind these people are'. He recovered, and to prove them wrong, chose a solemn feast day to assemble the entire *beneficio* for another, more impressive burning of confiscated *ololiuhqui*. He ordered a huge bonfire built,

> and into it, with all of them watching, I had almost the totality of the said seed which I had collected burned, and I ordered burned and cleared again the kind of bushes where they are found.

Alas, the old ways persisted:

> Such is the diligence of the devil that it works against us, for by his cunning we find each day new damage in this work, and thus it is good if the ministers of each jurisdiction are diligent in investigating, extirpating and punishing these consequences of the old idolatry and cult of the devil . . .

While Ruíz de Alarcón credits the devil with encouraging idolatry, it is not unlikely that he himself unwittingly helped reinforce the old belief in the divine nature of the *ololiuhqui* and the power of the ancient gods. Far from destroyer, fire in Indian Mexico was divine purifier and transformer, god of the sacred centre — as indeed it remains to this day among the Huichol. Hence the burning of the divine seed is likely to have had profoundly different meanings for the Indians and for the Spaniards. Burnt offerings to the gods are a common feature of Huichol ritual. On ceremonial occasions nothing is eaten, drunk or smoked that is not first shared with the fire, deified as Tatewari, Our Grandfather, First Shaman and tutelary deity of Huichol shamans, who put the universe in order in primordial times at the behest of his progenitress, the old Earth Goddess. If the Nahuatl-speakers of Guerrero and Morelos were anything like the Huichol in their reverence for fire — and the mystical references to fire in the magical incantations suggest that they were — the casting of *ololiuhqui* into the flames was more probably regarded as a proper, if somewhat wasteful, offering to the gods than as ignominious destruction — especially when the occasion was a solemn religious holiday.

Like other Colonial clergy of his day, Ruíz de Alarcón seems to have had a sneaking suspicion that the 'superstition of the *ololiuhqui*' and other hallucinogenic plants had some basis in fact, and that the Indians who employed it to foretell the future, find strayed animals, spouses, property, etc., and, above all, to ascertain the causes and proper cures of fevers and sicknesses, really were able to do so — at least on occasion. If so, however, then it had to be the work of the Devil, acting through the *ololiuhqui*, and not some property of the plant itself. To some degree the Indians thought along the same lines — except that to them the power of the *ololiuhqui* was a native god rather than the Christian Devil.

While most of the best Colonial data for the use of hallucinogens pertain to central Mexico, even without the Tepantitla evidence we would not assume the Aztecs to have been the first to discover the potent hallucinogenic principles of *Rivea corymbosa*, or the first to attribute divinity to the plant. In fact, only very long tradition can account for its pervasive mystical and ritual role at contact time, or its wholly successful resistance against the most determined efforts by the clergy to eradicate it as divine vehicle of ecstatic confrontation with the supernatural. As noted above, there is ample evidence that apart from *Sophora secundiflora*, which appears to have been restricted mainly to the arid north, the major hallucinogens of the sixteenth century had a very long history and a wide distribution in Mesoamerica. Some, like peyote, were ritually employed hundreds of miles from their native habitat, as they still are. This suggests long-distance trade in psychotropic substances in prehistoric times, and/or arduous religious pilgrimages on the order of the peyote quest of the contemporary Huichol Indians (Furst 1972: 136-84). (To obtain peyote, which is central to their ideology and to many of their ceremonies, small groups of Huichol, under the leadership of full-fledged or aspiring shamans, make annual treks from their present homeland in the Sierra Madre mountains of western Mexico to the scrub desert of San Luis Potosi, in north-central Mexico, to which the divine hallucinogenic cactus is native — published statements that peyote occurs naturally in Western Mexico are in error.)

As for *ololiuhqui* itself, the iconography of the seventy-metre-long Early Classic (*c.* A.D. 2-300) mural of the *bebedores* (drinkers) recently unearthed at Cholula, Puebla, suggests that the alcoholic beverage, whose intoxicating, and even transforming, effects are graphically depicted in the paintings, may have been fortified with morning glory seeds. The ritual practice of adding *ololiuhqui* or another hallucinogen to fermented or distilled liquours still survives in present-day Mexico.

Everything considered, it is reasonable to assume that *ololiuhqui* was well-known to the people of Teotihuacan, along with other sacred hallucinogens in cultic use within its considerable sphere of influence, and even beyond. Indeed, in light of the profusion with which morning glories grow in the valley of Cuernavaca and elsewhere in the state of Morelos and adjacent Guerrero, one cannot help but speculate on the role *ololiuhqui* might have played in trade relations between these more tropical regions and the Valley of Mexico in Teotihuacan times — as well as later.

In any event, only about seven centuries separate Tepantitla, which dates to the seventh or eighth century A.D., from the Aztecs — a healthy interval, to be sure, but, considering the cumulative evidence for continuity in Mesoamerican culture history, probably characterized less by any fundamental dislocation or transformation than by different levels of elaboration of basic common themes. Whatever their ultimate origins as 'rude barbarians' from the north, the Aztecs were the inheritors of the Mixteca-Puebla tradition. And this tradition, in turn, owes much to Teotihuacan.

Without doubt, many of the gods of Teotihuacan and its contemporaries reappear in the Aztec pantheon, having first passed through the filter of Teotihuacan's major and minor successors in the central basin. This sort of continuity should apply even more to the 'folk' level of belief and ritual, where the various cults, such as those of the divine hallucinogens, survived long after the organized priesthood, which once shared in these cults and presumably greatly elaborated them, had ceased to exist. And, as we saw, the cults themselves also had their origins long before there were priests — in the family and band shamanism of hunting and gathering cultures more than ten thousand years ago.

4. The 'Mother of Water' and ololiuhqui

Elsewhere in these pages I raised the possibility that the divine morning glory 'tree' of Tepantitla might be read as an organic part of the mother goddess, growing directly from her own body. There is, in fact, some ethnohistoric and folkloric evidence to support such an interpretation of a close, indeed consanguineal, kinship between the divine Mother and the divine *ololiuhqui.*

A hint of this relationship may be contained in the various hispanicized names for the sacred seed — *semilla de la Virgen, semilla de la Pastora, semilla de la Santa Maria, semilla de la Madre Santissima*, etc. — which reflect the characteristic syncretism of Mexican folk religion, in which the pre-Hispanic Earth or Mother Goddess has become merged with the Virgin Mary. These names suggest that regardless of the sexual identification of the divinity inherent in *ololiuhqui* as male (according to Ruíz de Alarcón), the seed, and the plant from which it comes, are considered to be the child of the Virgin as Mother Goddess. It might be noted in this connection that in contemporary folk ritual there is a close association between *ololiuhqui* and other traditional hallucinogens (among them not only mushrooms but also another morning glory, the purplish-blue *Ipomoea violacea*) and a kind of suprasexual female principle, symbolized by the requirement that these substances should always be prepared by a *doncella*, or untouched maiden. This aspect of the ritual use of hallucinogens in modern Mexico has been well documented for Oaxaca by Wasson (1963, 1966).

The identification of the morning glory with the Mother Goddess is reflected also in a curious sweeping ritual in honour of the deified morning glory plant and its divine hallucinogenic seeds which, as described by Ruíz de Alarcón, calls to mind a similar sweeping ritual in honour of Toci, Grandmother, the Aztec Mother of the Gods and Heart of the Earth, sometimes simply called Woman (Durán, 1971: 229-37). Toci's ceremony was called *Ochpaniztli*, Feast of Sweeping or Sweeping of the Paths, celebrated in the middle of the month of the same name (September in the European calendar). Significantly, the Feast of Sweeping for Toci was conducted, with elaborate impersonations of the goddess and sacrifices in her honour, immediately following, and indeed concurrently with, that for Chicomecoatl, Seven Serpent, Goddess of Sustenance, who, as Durán explicitly notes, was identical with Chalchiuhtlicue, Divine Mistress of terrestrial water, vegetation and fertility — that is, Toci herself in a youthful guise.

As initial act of this important ceremony for the Earth Mother and Mother of the Gods, Durán (1971: 448) tells us,

> everyone had to sweep his possessions, his house, and all its corners, leaving nothing without diligent sweeping and cleaning.

Likewise, the shrine of Toci had to be swept clean and adorned by her priests and attendants. Fittingly, a broom was one of the principal insigniae of the goddess, as were unspun and spun cotton, spindles, weaving implements and cloth woven of maguey fibres — accoutrements that link her not only to the Huichol Earth Mother Goddess Nakawe but also to Spider Grandmother, Earth Goddess of the Pueblo Indians of the southwest and patroness of weavers.

Ritual sweeping in honour of the 'Mothers', goddesses of the earth, fertility and sustenance, is still an important part of Huichol ceremonial. And, of course, no one who has ever visited Mexico could fail to be impressed with the diligence with which women sweep around their houses and in the streets, not only on feast days but in the early hours of each day — a secularized survival of the sweeping ritual for the pre-Hispanic Earth Mother.

(In this connection it is also of interest that the potsherd altars on which the Quiche-Maya of Momostenango, in highland Guatemala, make their offerings to the earth deity are called *mesabal*, Place of the Sweeping (Robert M. Carmack, personal communication), surely denoting a prehistoric connection with the ceremony of *Ochpaniztli*.)

According to Chapter 29 of Ruíz de Alarcón's *Tratado*, the *ololiuhqui* deity was likewise honoured with ritual sweeping, not only in and around the oratories in which the sacred containers with their stores of hallucinogenic seeds were kept, but also the dwellings and even the places in the countryside where the morning glory grew. There were also special 'conjurations' addressed to the *ololiuhqui* which made reference to the sweeping rite. For example:

Isabel Luisa of the Mazatec nation, among others, used this remedy and she applied it diluted as a drink, and the conjuration that she accompanied it with is in the form of an entreaty, or prayer, to the *ololiuhqui*, and it goes like this: 'Come hither, cold spirit, for you must remove this heat, and you must console your servant, who will serve you perhaps one, perhaps two days, and who will *sweep clean the place where you are worshipped*' (my italics).

This conjuration in its entirety is so accepted by the Indians that almost all of them hold that the *ololiuhqui* is a divine thing, in consequence of which . . . this conjuration accounts for the custom of veneration of it by the Indians, which is to have it on their altars and in the best containers or baskets that they have, and there to offer it incense and bouquets of flowers, to sweep and water the house very carefully, and for this reason the conjuration says: '. . . who will sweep (for) you or serve you one or two days more.' And with the same veneration they drink the said seed, shutting themselves in those places like one who was in the *Sancta Sanctorum*, with many other superstitions, and the veneration with which these barbarous people revere the seed is so excessive that part of their devotions including washing and sweeping (even) those places where the bushes are found which produce them, which are some heavy vines, even though they are in the wildernesses and thickets.

One may question whether the shared sweeping ritual in and of itself necessarily reflects a direct relationship between morning glory and the Mother Goddess. However, there is other evidence in the early colonial sources that also suggests such connections.

An intricate symbolic network relating the morning glory, water, fecundity, maize and the Mother Goddess is suggested by Aguirre Beltrán (1963: 130-37) in his discussion of the effects of religious acculturation on the prehispanic *ololiuhqui* complex in early post-Hispanic times. He draws attention to the several names by which the sacred morning glory was known in Aztec times and in the Colonial era; one of these was *coatl xoxouhqui*, Green Snake. Another, mentioned by Hernández, was [*ololiuhqui*] *coaxihuitl*, which can be translated as '[ololiuhqui]herb of the serpent'. These terms, which may have been inspired by the plant's twining and creeping qualities, remind one of the snake motif in the Tepantitla mural. In addition, we should note that the names of several Aztec goddesses contain the term *coatl*, serpent, and that there was a close identification of snakes with the Mother Goddess. This is still the case among the Huichol.

Yet another name, according to Ruíz de Alarcón, was *cuezpalli*, which he also renders as *cuexpalzi* and *cuetzpalli*. The correct spelling, as Aguirre Beltrán points out, is *cuetzpaltzin* or *cuetzpallin*, the day sign Sacred Lizard, fourteenth day in the 20-day month of the Aztec calendar. *Cuetzpaltzin* stood for abundance of water, fecundity, and pleasure without pain. It also had sexual connotations: in early manuscripts in which the day signs refer to the parts of the human body, the Sacred Lizard is the symbol sometimes of the penis, sometimes of the uterus.

Aguirre Beltrán connects the water-fecundity-abundance symbolism of the *cuetzpaltzin* to the belief, 'still extant in our times, that the ponds where the lizard lives never dry up, even during the severest drought'.[14] In ancient Mexico, he notes, plentiful water and prosperity in general were equivalent concepts, which in turn explains why on the mystical level *cuetzpaltzin* and maize, the sacred and basic food and symbol of well-being, should have become synonymous, to the extent that *cuetzpaltzin* was also another name for Centeotl Itztlacoliuhqui, the god of ripe maize and son of the Earth Goddess in her aspect as Tlazolteotl. Centeotl's fiesta, like the ceremonies for his mother, the Earth Goddess, in her different aspects, was celebrated in the month Ochpaniztli.

These associations, writes Aguirre Beltrán, demonstrate the intimate connection in Indian thought between the supernatural herb (morning glory), the divine food with which the gods formed men (maize), and the animal (lizard) which binds them together on the mystical plane into a kind of sacred triad — rather in the manner in which deer, maize and peyote form a divine triad in Huichol symbolism.

As to a synthesis between the divine morning glory and the Mother Goddess — in her pre-Hispanic aspects or in her post-Hispanic form as the Virgin — we have the testimony, cited by Aguirre Beltrán (1963: 133), of Father Alonso Ponce, who reported in the 1580s that *El Ololiuhqui* was merged by the Indians with *Nuestro Senor*, i.e. Jesus Christ, with the angels, and most significantly, with *Maria Santissima*, that is, the Virgin Mary.

Since *ololiuhqui* was considered to be male, such a synthesis with the Christian Virgin would be especially noteworthy. On the other hand, Aguirre Beltrán writes, Father Ponce might have misunderstood his informants, to the degree that it was not the male *ololiuhqui* that was merged with the Virgin but rather its counterpart, with which it was frequently combined in the narcotic potions. This plant, not otherwise botanically identified, was known as *atl ynan*, Mother of Water. According to de la Serna, writing in the mid-1700s, *atl ynan* was thought to be 'the sister of *ololiuhqui*'. Intimately related to the male morning glory, this female plant might well have come to be syncretized with the Virgin Mary, who thereby assumed a Christo-pagan identity as 'Mother of Water' or 'Lady of the Waters' — names by which she is still called in some parts of rural central Mexico.

On the other hand, in the light of the sexually dualistic character that emerges from the iconography of the Earth Mother in both Aztec and earlier ceremonial art, a more direct post-Hispanic synthesis between the male *ololiuhqui* and the Mother Goddess is hardly inconceivable, especially inasmuch as the very concept of a Virgin Mother is itself an expression of sexual ambiguity.

To carry this a step further, one wonders to what degree these seventeenth century folk traditions, especially that of the female *atl ynan*, Mother of Water, and her brother, the divine *ololiuhqui*, might actually reflect much older traditions — beliefs that long ago might have inspired the iconography of Tepantitla.

Clearly, none of the above conflicts with Pasztory's conclusion that the real significance of the plant at Tepantitla 'has to be sought in mythology and not in natural history' (1971: 149). On the contrary, natural history — or, more precisely, ethnobotany — provides additional means by which to look into the complex mythological world embodied in such iconographic associations as that of flowering vine and Mother Goddess in the Tepantitla mural.

NOTES

1 For ritual scarification of initiates into the ecstatic-visionary shamanistic medicine societies. According to Newcomb (1961: 311-312), neophyte shamans were given a beverage containing the hallucinogenic seeds, which was so potent that the initiates lost consciousness for as much as twenty-four hours. When aroused they 'related the dream experiences they had had — the journeys their souls had taken. Their experiences were cast in songs'. The description fits any number of shamanic initiations in North and South America.

2 I am greatly indebted to Dr J.M. Adovasio, recently of the Smithsonian Institution and presently at the University of Pittsburgh, for permission to cite these as yet unpublished radiocarbon dates. A summary of sites in Trans-Pecos Texas that have yielded a variety of psychotropic plant remains, with a discussion of chronology, is being prepared for early publication by J.M. Adovasio and G.F. Fry.

3 It can be argued that even the religions of the Old World carry recognizable vestiges of shamanistic antecedents. This applies especially, but by no means exclusively, to folk beliefs and practices.

4 Since the above was written, I have been informed by Doris Heyden that Eulalia Guzmán many years ago identified the same deity as female and that she also identified her as the goddess of terrestrial water, Chalchiuhtlicue.

5 One is reminded of Vogt's description of the shamanistic rituals for the *Yahval Balamil*, Lord of the Earth, in Zinacantan, Chiapas (Vogt, 1969: 456-461). According to one of his informants, the ceremonies and offerings for the Earth God are intended to persuade him to 'order the clouds to come out of the earth, clouds to rain on our corn, so our corn should not die . . . and if we did not pray thus, he would strike us dead with his snake of lightning . . . We do not see the Lord of the Earth, but he is there under the earth . . .' (459). The similarity to Tlaloc with his lightning snake is unmistakable, as is the parallel to the Huichol belief that clouds and rain are ultimately a function of the earth, not the sky.

6 In Mexican folklore and song this goddess evolved into *La Llorona*, the 'Weeping Woman', who is said to carry a cradle or the body of a dead child in her arms and to weep at night at crossroads, where travellers encounter her (Caso 1958: 54).

7 I am indebted to Dr Richard Evans Schultes, Director, Botanical Museum of Harvard University, for pointing out those features of the Tepantitla mural and other floral motifs at Teotihuacan that suggest *Rivea corymbosa*, rather than some other flowering plant or flowers generically.

8 This is also one of the reasons why we concluded that the profiled flower motif at Teotihuacan might have been derived from the morning glory. Pasztory (148) was also struck by the fact that most flower designs at Teotihuacan bore a strong resemblance to one

another, and asked, 'Are we to assume that most Teotihuacan flower representations derive from or refer to the *ololiuhqui* narcotic and its cult?' Not necessarily, of course, but it does suggest a profound role for the morning glory in the beliefs and ritual practices of Teotihuacan as well as respectable antiquity for the widespread celebration of the *ololiuhqui* cult as we know it from Aztec and Colonial times, not to mention the present.

9 Wasson recently made the interesting suggestion that the very idea of the Tree of Life and Magical Herb may ultimately derive from the mycorrhizal relationship between the hallucinogenic fly agaric mushroom and the towering Siberian birch and certain conifers, whose trunk the shaman climbs in his trance 'to go on his travels to the land of departed spirits' (Wasson, 1972: 210-213). He points out that the birch especially is the shaman's tree *par excellence*, object of a widespread Eurasian cult. The reason may be that the birch is the preferred host for the mushroom which played an important role in ecstatic shamanism, perhaps as far back as the Mesolithic and Palaeolithic.

10 Wasson (personal communication) points out that the red and black seeds shown in the Tepantitla mural have the hylum in the red area, which is characteristic of *Rhyncosa pyramidalis*, or *piule*. Were the hylum in the black field the species would be *Abrus precatorius*, which is highly toxic and potentially damaging to the liver.

11 Hofmann notes further that the isolation of lysergic acid derivatives in two morning glories, *Rivea corymbosa* and *Ipomoea violacea*, closed a long research series 'like a magic circle'. It was his synthesis of LSD-25 that led to subsequent investigations of the hallucinogenic mushrooms and the isolation, in his laboratory in Switzerland, of their active compounds, psilocybin and psilocin. These studies, in turn, resulted in collaboration with the French mycologist Roger Heim and the American ethnomycologist R. Gordon Wasson. It was the latter who in 1959 sent Hofmann the first samples of morning glory seeds for laboratory testing. These tests proved so promising that additional quantities of seeds were sought. Wasson enlisted the aid of the late Mexican ethnologist Roberto Weitlaner and his daughter, Irmgard Weitlaner-Johnson, in obtaining 12 kg. of *Rivea corymbosa* seeds and another 14 kg. of *Ipomoea violacea*, from which Hofmann isolated lysergic acid derivatives. The Weitlaners' interest in the ritual use of hallucinogens in Mesoamerica goes back to the nineteen-thirties, when they first observed the divinatory use of *teonanacatl* – the 'God's flesh' of the Aztecs – on a field trip in the mountains of Oaxaca. Wasson, with his late wife, Valentina P. Wasson, is credited with the rediscovery and, in collaboration with Professor Heim, the serious ethnographic and ethnomycological investigation of these survivals of the pre-Hispanic cult of divine mushrooms. Richard Evans Schultes also played a key role in the history of *ololiuhqui* research, in that it was he and B.P. Reko who in 1939 collected the first unquestionable voucher specimen of the seeds of *Rivea corymbosa* from a Zapotec *curandera* in Oaxaca, who grew the plant in her courtyard and who used its seeds in her divinatory curing rites. Until then a claim by the botanist William Safford (1917) that the early sources were all wrong, and that *ololiuhqui* pertained to Datura rather than a morning glory, was widely accepted, at least outside Mexico. The key paper on the correct botanical identification of *ololiuhqui* was that of Schultes (1941). After that it remained only for *ololiuhqui* to be experimentally tested for hallucinogenic effects (e.g. Osmond, 1955) and its active principles to be identified in the laboratory (Schultes, 1972).

12 The sacred hallucinogenic mushrooms and other hallucinogenic plants are to this day personified as divine beings. To the Huichol peyote is the divine deer or supernatural master of the deer species, who merges with some of their most important deities. Personification of the divine power believed to reside in the sacred mushrooms also explains the representation of animals and human figures or faces on the stipes of many archaeological mushroom stones, some dating to 1000 B.C.

13 A translation of the complete text is in preparation.

14 According to Aguirre Beltrán (1963: 133), it was its connection with water that gave *ololiuhqui* its mystical 'cold' condition, alluded to in the conjuration or incantation addressed to the divine seeds by the Mazatec *curandera* and diviner Maria Luisa. The condition of 'cold' with which it was imbued by the Indians made it efficacious as a cure for fevers. In contrast, the Spaniards, who employed the Hellenistic system of classification into four states, endowed *ololiuhqui* with a 'hot' quality: Hernandez, for example, called it 'a hot plant of the fourth (i.e. highest) order'.

REFERENCES

Aguirre Beltrán, G. (1963) *Medicina y magia: el processo de acculturación en la estructura colonial.* Instituto Nacional Indigenista, Colección de Antropología Social, no. 1. Mexico.

Caso, A. (1958) *The Aztecs: People of the Sun.* Trans. Lowell Dunham. Norman, Oklahoma.

Durán, Fr. D. (1971) *Book of the Gods and Rites and The Ancient Calendar.* Trans. and ed. F. Horcasitas and D. Heyden. Norman, Oklahoma.

Furst, P.T. (1970) The *Tsité (Erythrina* spp.) of the *Popol Vuh* and other psychotropic plants in pre-Columbian art. Annual Meeting of the Society for American Archaeology, April 29-May 2, Mexico.

Furst, P.T. (1972*a*) Ritual use of hallucinogens in Mesoamerica: new evidence for snuffing from the Preclassic and Early Classic. In *Religión en Mesoamerica, XII Mesa Redonda,* 61-8. Sociedad Mexicana de Antropología, Mexico.

Furst, P.T. (1972*b*) To find our life: peyote among the Huichol Indians of Mexico. In P.T. Furst. (ed.), *Flesh of the Gods: The Ritual Use of Hallucinogens,* 136-84. New York.

Hernández, F. (1651) *Nova Plantarum, Animalium et Mineralium Mexicanorum Historia.* Rome.

Hofmann, A. (1966) The active principles of the seeds of *Rivea corymbosa* (L.) Hall F. (*Ololiuhqui, Badoh*) and *Ipomoea tricolor* Cav. (*Badoh negro*). In *Summa anthropológica en homenaje a Roberto J. Weitlaner.* Instituto Nacional de Antropología e Historia, Mexico.

Kubler, G. (1962) *The Art and Architecture of Ancient America.* Baltimore.

La Barre, W. (1972) Hallucinogens and the shamanic origins of religion. In P.T. Furst (ed.), *Flesh of the Gods: The Ritual Use of Hallucinogens,* 261-78. New York.

Lumholtz, C. (1900) *Symbolism of the Huichol Indians.* Memoirs of the American Museum of Natural History, vol. 3. New York.

Newcomb, W.W., Jr. (1961) *The Indians of Texas, from Prehistoric to Modern Times.* Austin, Texas.

Newcomb, W.W., Jr. (1967) *The Rock Art of Texas Indians.* Austin, Texas.

Osmond, H. (1955) *Ololiuhqui,* the ancient Aztec narcotic. *Journal of Mental Science,* 101, 526-27.

Pasztory, E. (1971) The mural paintings of Tepantitla, Teotihuacan. Ph.D. Dissertation, Department of Art History and Archaeology, Columbia University.

Ruiz de Alarcón, H. (1892) Tratado de las supersticiones y costumbres gentilicas que oy viuen entre los Indios naturales desta Nueua Espana (1629). F. del Paso y Troncoso (ed.), *Anales del Museo Nacional de Mexico* ep. 36, 123-223.

Safford, W.E. (1917) Narcotic plants and stimulants of the ancient Americans. *Annual Report of the Smithsonian Institution for 1916,* 387-424. Washington.

Schultes, R.E. (1941) *A Contribution to Our Knowledge of Rivea corymbosa, the Narcotic Ololiuhqui of the Aztecs.* Botanical Museum of Harvard University, Cambridge, Mass.

Schultes, R.E. (1972) An overview of hallucinogens in the Western hemisphere. In P.T. Furst (ed.), *Flesh of the Gods; The Ritual Use of Hallucinogens,* 3-54. New York.

Seler, E. (1915) *Gesammelte Abhandlungen zur Amerikanischen Sprach-und Altertumskunde,* vol. 5. Reprinted 1961. Graz.

Sharon, D. (1972) The San Pedro cactus in Peruvian folk healing. In P.T. Frust (ed.), *Flesh of the Gods: The Ritual Use of Hallucinogens,* 114-35. New York.

Taylor, W.W. (1956) Some implications of the Carbon-14 dates from a cave in Coahuila, Mexico. *Bulletin of the Texas Archaeological Society*, 27, 215-34.

Taylor, W.W. (1966) Archaic cultures adjacent to the northeastern frontiers of Mesoamerica. In R. Wanchope (ed.), *Handbook of Middle American Indians*, vol. 4, 59-94. Austin, Texas.

Thompson, J.E.S. (1970) *Maya History and Religion.* Norman, Oklahoma.

Troike, R.C. (1962) The origins of plains mescalism. *American Anthropologist*, 64, 946-72.

Vogt, E.Z. *Zinacantan: A Maya Community in the Highlands of Chiapas.* Cambridge, Mass.

Wasson, R.G. (1963) Notes on the present status of *Ololiuhqui* and the other hallucinogens of Mexico. *Botanical Museum Leaflets*, Harvard University, 20, 161-93.

Wasson, R.G. (1966) *Ololiuhqui* and the other hallucinogens of Mexico. In *Summa antropológica en homenaje a Roberto J. Weitlaner*, 329-48. Instituto Nacional de Antropologia e Historia, Mexico.

Wasson, R.G. (1968) *Soma, Divine Mushroom of Immortality.* New York.

Wasson, R.G. (1972) What was the Soma of the Aryans? In P.T. Furst (ed.), *Flesh of the Gods: The Ritual Use of Hallucinogens*, 201-13. New York.

Zingg, R. (1938) *The Huichols: Primitive Artists.* New York.

GARY H. GOSSEN

A Chamula solar calendar board from Chiapas, Mexico

Introduction

This paper is intended as a preliminary report of what seems to be the first occurrence in the modern ethnographic record of a graphic representation of the Ancient Maya solar year, or *haab*.[1] This cycle consists of eighteen 'months' of twenty days, plus a five-day special period. In the pre-Columbian period (and in some modern Guatemalan communities as well), this cycle was used in permutating fashion with the *tzolkin*, the 260-day ritual cycle representing the intermeshing sequence of twenty named days with the numbers one to thirteen. Together, the vague solar year and the *tzolkin* intermeshed to form the 52-year Calendar Round, which was present among all the Mesoamericans and presumably is of very great age. It certainly antedates the beginning of the famous Maya Long Count in the first centuries B.C. (Coe 1966: 54-60). In the solar calendar, therefore, we are dealing with a piece of Mesoamerican intellectual equipment which was probably invented some time in the Middle Formative Period (800 to 300 B.C.) and possibly before. One of the earliest computative schemes devised by Mesoamerican civilization, it has remained viable in Maya communities 'through the spasm of the conquest and colonial periods and even into the modern period. In sum, it is a remarkably conservative Mesoamerican culture trait.

As of 1952, there were eighty-two known Mesoamerican communities, mostly speaking languages of the Maya family, which retained some form of the ancient calendar, ranging from minimal retention of the twenty named days, to maximum conservation of the Calendar Round. Fifty-six of these Indian communities retained the solar calendar, either alone or in combination with the 260-day cycle. The others retained some form of the *tzolkin* cycle (Miles 1952). The last two decades of ethnographic research in the Maya area have added to this list. Chamula, a conservative Tzotzil-speaking community in the Chiapas highlands of southern Mexico, is a significant addition to Miles' survey, for it not only retains the solar calendar as a popular form of reckoning time, but also retains a graphic form of it. This calendar board, which I obtained in 1969 while doing ethnographic field work in the community, is to my knowledge the first such artifact to be reported from the Maya area. Western reports of the existence of the *concept* of the solar calendar in the oral tradition and in ritual observance of the Maya date from Landa's account of a Yucatec version, of the year 1553, reported in his *Relación* (Tozzer 1941: 149-67). In the dozens of reports of the Maya calendar since that time, it has apparently been assumed that no written references or graphic patterns exist for it; that is, it has been assumed to be popular knowledge in the oral tradition, or esoteric knowledge kept by specialists (see Berlin 1951: 156). It is my hope, therefore, that this description of the Chamula *?otol k'ak'al* ('counter of days') will contribute another dimension to our knowledge of Maya calendrics.

Before presenting a description of the calendar board, a brief description of the community, with emphasis on temporal concepts and cosmology, will be given. This background information is necessary for an understanding of the special function that the solar calendar has in Chamula. After the description of the board, I shall present brief comparative data from other Maya communities, particularly those in the Tzotzil-Tzeltal-speaking area of Chiapas. Finally, I shall attempt to explore some of the possible implications of the Chamula 'counter of days' for Maya calendrics and religion, ancient and modern.

The community

Chamula is a Tzotzil-speaking *municipio* of approximately 40,000 Maya Indians which lies at the top of the central Chiapas highlands of southern Mexico. Perhaps five percent of the population is bilingual in Spanish and Tzotzil. All Chamulas engage to a greater or lesser extent in subsistence maize, squash and bean agriculture, with supplementary income coming from day labour, the sale of produce and from dozens of specialized cottage industries such as pottery, furniture, charcoal and sandals.

Chamula is among the largest, most conservative and most self-conscious of the Indian communities of highland Chiapas, and has apparently been a discrete cultural entity since before the time of the Spanish conquest and Dominican missionization. At present it permits no Spanish-speaking Mexicans to live permanently or to hold property within its boundaries except for one family, that of the Mexican secretary who helps the Chamulas in their dealings with the state and national governments. Chamula is one of the most rapidly growing communities in the highlands and the population explosion is forcing people to use whatever means they can to acquire additional land outside the *municipio* boundaries. They take maximum advantage of agrarian reform laws and are relocating in large and small colonies throughout the state of Chiapas. These relocated groups, however, do not generally become acculturated nor do they cease to speak Tzotzil, for they generally move in units large enough to maintain a microcosm of 'normal' Chamula life. Their ties to their home *municipio* remain very strong and they continue to regard it as 'the navel of the earth', the centre of the moral universe.

Chamulas live virilocally in dispersed hamlets which belong to one or more of the three subdivisions or *barrios* of the *municipio*. The three *barrios* converge on the ceremonial centre, which has virtually no permanent population. Rental houses there provide homes for political and religious officials while they serve their term in office, usually for one year. The centre serves as the symbolic focus for nearly all public ritual and administrative activity. Most public ritual life in Chamula follows the Mexican Catholic version of the Gregorian calendar. This is not to say that content and meaning of their ritual cycle are Catholic. This is far from the case. However, at first glance, it would seem an unlikely place to find an Ancient Maya calendar board still in use. Chamulas are governed by a civil hierarchy of over sixty positions or *cargos*. This political organization is partly traditional and partly prescribed by Mexican law. A religious hierarchy consisting of sixty-one major *cargos* supervises ceremonial activities and cults to the saints and to the sun and moon deities. It also coordinates its activities with those of the political organization. Political and religious authority at the local hamlet level lie in the hands of past *cargo*-holders, heads of patrilineages, and shamans. Chamula shamans are independent specialists in curing and divination who work on a fee basis. They do not participate in the formal, public ritual organization of the community. However, they are active on the local level, where they take charge of many domestic rituals, including waterhole-, field- and house-blessing ceremonies as well as the treatment of illness and other supernaturally-caused maladies. Some shamans also specialize in traditional calendrical information and keep track of the date, using the old calendar board. This will be described at greater length below.

Although the public *cargo*-holders do not have responsibility for calendrical knowledge, they do participate actively and metaphorically in maintaining order in the solar year. All *cargos*, both political and religious (with the exception of those prescribed by Mexican national law) are held for one year and require relatively enormous expenditures of money and time. This forces most officials to give up their ordinary economic activities during this time. Hence, holding a *cargo* is conceived of as 'bearing a burden for a year', in a way not unlike the concept of year-bearer deities of Ancient Maya religion and calendrics (Bricker 1966, Vogt 1969: 246). It is also worth noting that the majority of *cargo*-holders enter and leave office in a period of about ten days which cluster around the beginning of the Chamula solar year, 1 *ȼ'un*, equivalent to December 26 or 27. Ritual officials, therefore, follow the solar cycle very closely in the term and spirit of their tasks. As one of the oath-of-office prayers says, referring to the image of the Sun/Christ deity, whom he will serve:

> I shall lift you,
> I shall carry you,
> For one year,
> As for one day.

(For more ethnographic information on Chamula, see Gossen, 1972 and 1974, and Pozas 1959.)

For a further appreciation of the importance of the solar year (*ʔavil* in Tzotzil, related to *haab* in Yucatec Maya) to Chamulas, it is important to remember that the sun, who is synonymous with Christ in their syncretistic belief system, is the primary deity in the Chamula pantheon. This is a conservative trait which is no doubt related to the primacy of the sun (*k'inh*) in pre-Columbian Maya religion, cosmology and philosophy (see León-Portilla 1968). At once in the Chamula concept of the sun, most units of lineal, cyclical and generational time are implied, as well as the spatial limits and subdivisions of the universe, vertical and horizontal. Most of the other deities and all men are related lineally or spiritually to the sun-creator, who is the son of the moon, the same as the Virgin Mary and also a major deity. Day and night, the yearly agricultural and religious cycles, the seasons, the divisions of the day, most plants and animals, the stars and the constellations, are all the work of the creator, Our Father the Sun, the life-force itself. Only the demons, monkeys and Jews are logically prior to and hostile to the coming of order. These forces killed the sun and forced him to ascend into the heavens, thus providing the beginning of heat, life, light and order (see Gossen 1972). Hence, the Tzotzil words for day (*k'ak'al*) and fiesta (*k'in*) are related to the Tzotzil word for fire (*k'ok'*), and to the Proto-Maya word for sun, time and deity (*k'inh*), respectively. It is also relevant that one of the several names for the sun-creator is *htotik k'ak'al*, or 'Our Father Heat (Day)'.

The fundamental spatial divisions of the universe, the cardinal directions, are also derived from the relative positions of the sun on his east-west path across the heavens:

East: *lok'eb k'ak'al*, 'emergent heat (or day)'
West: *maleb k'ak'al*, 'waning heat (or day)'
North: *šokon vinahel ta baȼ'i k'ob*, 'The side of heaven on the right hand'
South: *šokon vinahel ta ȼ'et k'ob*, 'The side of heaven on the left hand'.

Following from this, Chamula cosmological and ritual symbolism has as its primary orientation the point of view of the sun as he emerges on the eastern horizon each day, facing his universe, north on his right hand, south on his left hand. The principal temporal divisions of the day are also described in terms of the relative position of the sun on his path across the heavens. For example, 'in the afternoon' is expressed in Tzotzil as *ta šmal k'ak'al*, 'the heat is waning'. 'In the mid-morning' is expressed as *štoy ša k'ak'al*, 'the heat (day) is rising now'. Space and time are thus constantly referred to as aspects of, or in relation to, the sun. In all these references to the sun deity, his influence is both cyclical and cumulative, a factor closely related to the solar calendar. Nowhere in Chamula cosmology is this more clearly revealed than in their view of linear time. It was the sun who set up order on the earth as Chamulas know it. He did this in progressive stages, separately creating the first three worlds, or creations, and then destroying them, when people behaved improperly. It is only the Fourth Creation, which includes the present, which has been successful.

The four creations provide the largest cyclical temporal units which the Chamulas recognize. There is no evidence for survival of the Ancient Maya Long Count. However, the four-part creation was solidly entrenched in Ancient Maya belief. (See, for example, the Quiché Maya *Popol Vuh* (Edmonson 1971), the whole of which is organized according to the Four Creations.) The four creations as they exist in Chamula, though cyclical, can also be said to succeed each other in a linear sense, for the events of later creations are not mere repetitions of earlier creations. These units seem to have an orthogenetic, cumulative development. In this sense, the four-part creation cycle forms a whole concept which is greater than the sum of its parts. In each of the first three creations of the universe, the creator failed to achieve his ideal for mankind and destroyed his abortive efforts. Although Chamulas believe the present Fourth Creation to be his most successful effort so far, they also know that it is full of evil and ever in danger of destruction. The length of the four creations is not known; nor is it guessed with any consistency from one person to the next. Among my informants, opinions regarding the antiquity of the First Creation vary from 300 to 80,000 years. The Fourth Creation never begins more than 400 years ago and may, according to some, have begun a mere 120 years ago, which is the maximum limit of genealogical memory. Variation is similar for the Second and Third Creations. Therefore, even an average of the opinions of all informants would not yield a significant figure for the absolute age of the creations. The point is that they succeed each other chronologically as relative levels of time.

Within the present, Fourth Creation, several other sets of temporal categories are operative. The life cycle is usually marked by ritual observances of birth, baptism, marriage and death. Between birth and baptism, a period varying from one month to two years, a child is

called a *maš* ('monkey'), for he has no name. The monkey association with the unbaptized child is explained by the presence of
monkeys on earth in the First Creation, before human society in its
correct form had appeared. The monkey people did asocial things
such as eating their unnamed children at puberty. Hence, the giving
of a name at baptism has considerable symbolic significance in
bringing the child closer to the realm of social behaviour. From
baptism to death, the individual completes a cycle of heat. From
cold at birth to hot in ripe old age, a person symbolizes the progress
of the generations of ancestors toward the present. It can be said
with accuracy that many symbolic aspects of ontogeny — the individual life cycle — recapitulate mythological phylogeny. This perspective helps to explain the deference given to elders in this society,
for they have absorbed much of the respected knowledge — and
heat — of past generations. The successful and complete human life is
therefore like a solar cycle.

Although past generations are respected, genealogical memory is
relatively shallow, reaching a maximum of four or five generations in
powerful descent lines and two generations in ordinary descent lines.
An old man may remember events and kinsmen covering sixty or
eighty years of his own lifetime, and by hearsay, perhaps sixty to
eighty years of his father's, grandfathers', and great grandfathers'
times. That total, 120 to 150 years, is the very upper limit of
Chamula generational and historical memory. Formal records are
kept in the ceremonial centre by years in the Gregorian calendar, but
these data are known by only a handful of prominent Chamulas and
affect the lives of average men in no significant way. Past time is
most meaningful if it is treated in relation to generations of known
lineages, or in relation to significant natural and human events. The
future is important only in that important *cargo* positions may be
requested as many as fifteen years in advance, but no more. There is
some fear of millennial destruction of the Fourth Creation by
earthquakes in the year 2000, but this, for Chamulas, is properly a
matter of cyclical time and not linear time.

The most commonly used markers of chronological time in the
Fourth Creation are not units at all, but natural and historical points
of reference. A typical example is a time called *yora pale mikel*,
which refers to Father Miguel Hidalgo, and the Wars of Independence
(1812-1825). There are at least ten such historical landmarks in the
Fourth Creation. This is not unlike the Ancient Maya custom of
erecting calendrical stelae to mark major events in political and
dynastic history. Unlike the Ancient Maya, however, the Chamulas
have no vestige of the Long Count and are able to subdivide no more
than about 150 years by these historical landmarks. Beyond this
level, Chamulas claim that they have no reason to talk about the
chronology of the past; the four creations suffice. This boundary of
approximately 150 years appears to mark the borderline between

events of human (i.e. Chamula) experience and those of their early ancestors and the gods. The landmarks of the Fourth Creation are more or less standard in that they have a consistent relation to one another for most Chamulas with whom I worked. The dates *per se* have little meaning; it is the relative order of events that counts.

Another important temporal scheme within the Fourth Creation is of course the Mexican Catholic version of the Gregorian calendar. This is published annually as a kind of almanac pamphlet in Mexico City and is called the *Calendario del más antiguo Galván.* It is sold in Ladino trade centres for one or two pesos. Political officials and religious officials, together with their literate scribes, use the *Galván* to set up the correct public ceremonial schedule. The *Galván,* however, is not every man's calendar; it is for specialists. The great majority of the people know the dates of the saints' festivals in the ancient solar calendar rather than in the Spanish months and days of the *Galván.* The old calendar, of course, does not determine the days of celebration of the saints' festivals in any way. The only regular ritual function pertaining to *cargo* activity which still seems to be controlled by the old calendar is the flower-changing ceremony (*k'eš ničim*). This is not a public affair. It involves changing flowers and greenery on the *cargo*-holder's home shrine and offering incense to the saints' objects, kept in a coffer. This ritual should be performed every twenty days, at the end of each of the eighteen regular ancient Maya months. This should be done by all religious *cargo*-holders, yet I have no data which would allow an estimate of the percentage of compliance. With the exception of this flower-changing ritual, all of the rest of the ceremonial year for *cargo*-holders is built around the *Galván* calendar.[2]

The public festival cycle is the annual round which is used with greatest frequency as a popular reference to time. All adult Chamulas can locate precisely or generally any day of the year with reference to days before, during, or after a festival. This is possible because so many of these are celebrated — an average of two or three per month. All Chamulas know the relative order of the festivals (called *k'in,* related to Proto-Maya *k'inh,* meaning heat, time, deity and sun), and most know the dates of major festivals in the old solar calendar. This is so even though the dates of celebration are determined by the Catholic calendar. These events mark the high points of recreation for the laity and the time of most intense ritual activity for the religious *cargo*-holders. Although each festival is associated with a specific saint or saints and is the principal responsibility of certain *cargo*-holders, all Alféreces and Mayordomos are expected to partici-pate each time. The major festivals last three days (*čuk ničim,* 'tying of flowers'; *yišpereš,* 'the eve of', from the Spanish *víspera*; and *sk'ak'al k'in,* 'the day (heat) of the festival'), reaching a climax on the final day with a procession of the images of the saints. Minor festivals follow the same time schedule, but are not accompanied by as much public ritual. The principal exception to this schedule is Carnaval, in February, which lasts five days and appears to be related to the five-day special month (*č'ay k'in*) in the old solar calendar. Metaphorically speaking, each festival to Chamulas is like a cycle of heat, like the day, or year, or human life, beginning cold, reaching a climax of heat, and dying.

The seasonal cycle provides still another important temporal and symbolic reference for Chamulas. The reasons for this are strong ones. First, there is a striking difference between the rainy season and the dry season. Second, these differences control the annual agricultural cycle. Since the old solar calendar is used primarily as a guide to agricultural activity, I have prepared a table (Table 1) which shows the old Maya months together with Christian ones and associated terminology for weather and agricultural activity. This will be referred to in the discussion of the calendar board (below).

Many other minor cycles are used to refer to time. The parts of the growing cycle for nearly all highland crops and edible wild plants can be used as annual temporal markers (e.g., *yora yuytik*, 'the time of mushrooms', throughout June). The most important of these is of course the maize cycle, whose major divisions are given in Table 1. There are also nearly thirty terms for referring to the time of day. These are descriptive terms relating to the sun, and not numerical terms. At least ten terms refer to the phases of the moon. Knowledge of the lunar cycle is necessary for proper use of the solar calendar, for auspicious days given by the solar calendar for agricultural activity must be checked with lunar phases before going ahead with work. For example, even if the solar calendar indicates that 10 *sisak* is a proper day for planting maize, one cannot plant on this day if it falls in the dark of the moon. To do so would cause the seeds to rot and not to germinate; those few that sprouted would soon yellow and die. Chamulas also recognize regular cycles of several constellations and separate planets. The qualities of brightness and predictable movement separate these heavenly bodies from other celestial phenomena.

The counter of days or solar calendar board

It will be evident from the discussion above that (1) Chamulas, like the Ancient Maya, are seriously concerned with the measurement of time; (2) that the sun is both the primary deity and the creator of nearly all temporal and spatial categories; and (3) that the old solar calendar, though important, occupies only a specialized niche in Chamula time reckoning. It is primarily concerned with regulations of agricultural activity. It is also used by nearly all adult Chamulas to give the dates of festivals and other annual events when asked, yet this is not its main task. All adults know the relative position of

Table 1 The seasonal cycle in Chamula

MONTH		WEATHER		AGRICULTURAL ACTIVITY
Christian	Maya	Precipitation	General	Maize Cycle
November	*pom* *yašk'in*			Harvest
December	*muš* *¢'un*	*yora ta?ivtik* Time of Frost		Clearing and Ground-breaking
January	*ba¢'ul* *sisak*	and	*yora* *k'epelaltik* Time of Clearness	Planting
February	*č'ayk'in* *muk'tasak*	*yora k'inobal vo?* Time of Winter Wind and Drizzle		
March	*mok*			
April	*?o?lal ti?*			
May	*?ulol* *?ok'en kahval*			First Weeding
June	*?uč*	*yora čakilvo?* Time of Thundershowers	*yora vo?* Time of Rain	Second Weeding
July	*h?eleč* *hničk'in*	*bik'it korišma* Little Dry season		
August	*sba vinkil*			Third Weeding
September	*sčibal vinkil* *yošibal vinkil*	*yora čakilvo?* Time of Thundershowers		Doubling Over of Stalks
October	*sčanibal vinkil*			

festivals in the annual cycle; precise dates are important to none but those responsible for sponsoring them and making advance preparations. Oral transmission of information suffices to let people know when the big ritual affairs in the ceremonial centre are to be held. The Gregorian calendar determines the annual round of public ritual life, with a few exceptions which I shall note below. Other temporal cycles have their special functions, as discussed above. The whole effect must bear a vague resemblance to the world of the Maya before the conquest – a people deeply concerned with time, for whom many cycles concerned with different aspects of life, some in the hands of specialists, were operative.

Location and description

The calendar board described in this paper comes from a hamlet called Milpoleta. This hamlet is one of over 100 which lie in the *municipio*. Milpoleta belongs to Barrio San Juan and is, relatively speaking, a very poor hamlet. Its lands are badly eroded and it does not produce nearly enough food for its population. Its economic specialities are cane liquor manufacture, pottery-making and sandal-making. Although Chamula is generally a very conservative community, Milpoleta is not among the more conservative hamlets. It lies very close to the ceremonial centre, accessible by truck, and thus experiences considerable contact with the people and goods of the modern world. Furthermore, Milpoleta men must spend many months a year working outside the *municipio* – mostly on the lowland coffee plantations. Like the rest of the *municipio*, however, it is overwhelmingly monolingual in Tzotzil and hostile to the Spanish-speaking world. In sum, the place of origin of the calendar board suggests to me that there are probably many, many more in regular use in the community. The reason is that there are dozens of hamlets which are more closed to the ways of the outside world than Milpoleta.

I had worked for more than a year on calendrical concepts and time-reckoning before having the good fortune of being presented with the calendar board one frosty morning in January, 1969. Salvador Guzmán Bakbolom, who obtained it for me, assured me all along that some shamans (*h?iloletik* or 'seers') still kept track of the traditional solar year by marking its days and months with charcoal on a wooden tablet. I was excited by the prospect, but not too optimistic. Salvador finally obtained one (for twenty pesos) from a woman shaman in Milpoleta, his home hamlet, after much bargaining and begging. She said that her father had had it as long as she could remember and that it had belonged to her paternal grandfather before that. I would estimate her age at around 70. This gives the board a very approximate age of at least 100 years. It has not been dated by any other means. The owner of the board asked not to be identified, but it is not a betrayal of her confidence to say that she is very prominent as a shaman, very expensive, and, by hearsay, very effective. I shall call her Loša for reference in this paper. I attended a cornfield-blessing ceremony performed by her in Salvador's house and was much impressed by her bearing and magnificent chanting. Loša would not speak to me and barely tolerated my wife's and my presence during the ceremony. Gossip reported that she thought we were earth lords (*?anheletik*). Some also advised us to avoid her because she was a witch and did not like us. So, for various reasons, I was never able to talk to her about the calendar. Salvador, however, prepared an extensive text about the board which is based on two informal discussions with Loša. Much of what follows in this section is based on his text. Other assistants also wrote down and discussed with me what they knew of the old calendar.

Fig. 1 is a line drawing of the calendar. The photographs which accompany Alexander Marshack's infra-red analysis of charcoal series on the board will give a much better general impression of the board than the drawing in Fig. 1. It is intended simply as a reference for discussion in the present paper. As Marshack's photos reveal, a minor misfortune happened before Salvador gave it to me. Salvador took the trouble to do me the favour of writing in pencil the names of each month by the appropriate charcoal series on the board. This, of course, mars the overall effect, but it could not be helped and was done with the best intentions. It *does* provide evidence that the series represents what we think it does, for Salvador checked each identification with Loša and wrote it down on the board in her presence.

Loša, a widow, lives with her son and his family and helps with household tasks when she is not away on curing and other ritual missions. The board was hanging from a nail at the foot of Loša's sleeping platform. She said she could make another after selling the old one to Salvador. She reportedly marks each day with charcoal as soon as she gets up in the morning. (Chamula days, however, begin at midnight, which is the time when the sun passes the nadir of his orbit in the underworld to begin his upswing to the eastern horizon; see Gossen 1972.) When she is away overnight or for several days on curing business, she marks the days when she returns. No one does it for her. She wipes the slate clean at the end of each year and starts a new series of marks. As far as Salvador was able to find out, she performs no ritual which relates to use of or maintenance of the board. (This of course must be checked on a future field trip.) Asked why she marked the days on the calendar, she said that it was important to her in various aspects of her work to know the exact date in the old calendar. In particular, she apparently offers 'consulting' services, for a fee, about propitious days for various agricultural tasks such as planting, cultivating, harvesting, etc. She also says that it is important to know the date in the old calendar in order to determine auspicious times to perform domestic rituals such as new house-blessing ceremonies, cornfield-blessing ceremonies, petitions to earth gods (for rain) and wind gods (to cease wind damage to corn fields). She claims that not all shamans keep track of the date in the old calendar, but that the better and more effective ones do. She said nothing about whether the calendar was used in relation to curing ritual, which is the major activity of most Chamula shamans. This special use of the solar calendar in regulating agricultural and other mundane activity concurs with reports of its function as an agricultural almanac among the Ancient Maya (Thompson 1950: 104) and in some modern Mesoamerican communities (Thompson 1950: 104-5; La Farge 1947; 165-9).

The calendar board itself is made from what appears to be a discarded piece of door panel, possibly from the rubbish of a burned house. The non-calendar side of the board is badly scarred with charred patches and has decorative grooved patterns which are still used for door panels. This side also has four wooden pegs in each corner of the style that prevent splitting by allowing contraction and expansion. The side which serves as the calendar slate appears to be the reverse side of the door. It is irregularly planed, but very smooth, as though it had been wiped clean hundreds of times. (See Marshack's paper for identification of older series of marks, not visible to the naked eye, which have been revealed by infrared photographic examination.) The exact dimensions of the board and the arrangement of the current series of charcoal marks are given in Fig. 1.

The tally marks are to be read from left to right, top to bottom. It may be significant that this order of information follows closely the arrangement of glyphs in Ancient Maya calendrical and other inscriptions (Spinden 1924: 30). Note furthermore that the *ends* of the months (*ʔuʔetik*, in Tzotzil) are marked by a thickened charcoal mark. The beginning mark of the month receives no special treatment. This suggests the presence of a concept also important among the Ancient Maya, that the end of a cycle has more significance than the beginning because it represents not only completion of one cycle, but the 'seating' of the next cycle and the beginning of its influence (Thompson 1950: 59-61, 181-207). Conceived spatially, the marks give the same message in the Chamula calendar representation: they seem to pile up as a burden during the progression of the month until they 'rest' on the final day, allowing the next cycle to take over. This concept of time as a cumulative burden has many analogues in Ancient Maya art, religion and philosophy and certainly exists among the modern Maya as well (Bricker 1966; Thompson 1950: 59). For example, as noted above, Chamula *cargo*-holders express in their ritual formulae that they are carrying the burden of public service for a specified period of time.

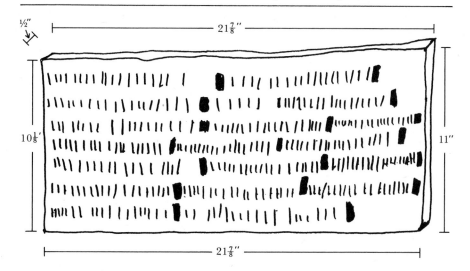

Figure 1 The Chamula *ʔotalk'ak'al*, 'Counter of Days' or solar calendar.

The months are (1) *ȼ'un* (1 *ȼ'un* corresponds to December 26 or 27); (2) *baȼ'ul*; (3) *sisak*; (4) *č'ayk'in*; (5) *muk'ta sak*; (6) *mok*; (7) *ʔoʔlal tiʔ*; (8) *ʔulol*; (9) *ʔok'en kahval*; (10) *ʔuč*; (11) *hʔeleč*; (12) *hničk'in*; (13) *sbavinkil*; (14) *sčibal vinkil*; (15) *yošibal vinkil*; (16) *sčanibal vinkil*; (17) *pom*; (18) *yašk'in*; (19) *muš*.

The calendar is to be read from left to right; top to bottom. All months (*ʔu*) have twenty days except *č'ayk'in*, which has five days. Note that the heaviest and thickest marks (all done with charcoal) correspond with the last day of each month and *not* with the first day. The exception to this pattern is the month of *č'ayk'in*, which has no heavy mark at all. The drawing attempts to represent the arrangement of marks on the actual calendar, which is apparently made from a discarded door.

This is not unlike the Ancient Maya gods who carried the burden of time for their respective cycles. The metaphor of cumulative time as a burden finds expression in the Chamula calendar not only in the thickened charcoal mark at the end of the month, but also in the fact that the calendar is renewed each year with another layer of charcoal marks, thus increasing its burden.

It is of some significance, I think, that the only month on the calendar which does not receive a heavy charcoal mark at completion is the five-day month of *č'ayk'in* ('lost fiesta' or 'lost period'). This is the nineteenth special month (*ʔu*) which completes the solar year (18 x 20 plus 5 = 365). It obviously corresponds to the five-day special period which occurs in all Maya solar calendars. Best known as Uayeb from the Yucatec versions of the calendar, it was a period of ritual chaos at the end of the year, an imperfect, incomplete cycle, fraught with bad omens and evil, and was greatly feared by all (Thompson 1950: 117-18). In Chamula a similar feeling about the imperfection and ritual danger of *č'ayk'in* exists. This is reinforced by the fact that it usually falls on or close to the time of the five-day festival called *k'in tahimoltik* — 'festival of play and games'. This is celebrated every year in the five days preceding and including Ash Wednesday in the Gregorian calendar. It is perhaps the biggest festival of the year and includes, among other unique events in the annual ritual cycle, a massive cult to the Sun-Christ deity, climaxed by ritual officials running through a long east-west path of flaming grass which represents the sun's path across the sky. The festival also includes numerous ritual observances, costumed characters and games which symbolize reversal. Ritual officials fast and observe sexual abstinence. Ritual sequences include male transvestites, monkeys (associated with the First Creation and hostile to the sun), Ladino soldiers, mock battles with horse manure, etc. This is similar to the kind of ritual of inversion which Landa describes in association with Uayeb among the sixteenth-century Yucatec Maya (Thompson 1950: 118). Thus, the Ancient Maya five-day month, a year-end time of ritual reversal, has become solidly identified with the five-day fiesta of Carnaval in Chamula. This holds true even though, in the majority of cases, the Gregorian Easter cycle does not place the five days preceding Lent so that they correspond with the true date of *č'ayk'in* in the Chamula solar calendar. I suspect that all of this represents a kind of victory for the Dominican missionaries, who forbade public heathen ritual during all of the ritual year *except* during Carnaval, preceding Lent, a time when all of Catholic Europe observes quasi-pagan rituals of inversion and excess. Perhaps they forced the Indians to pour all of their pagan ritual, if they had to retain some of it, into Carnaval observance, where it would be fitting. Little did they know that straightforward worship of the Ancient Maya sun god would continue in this fashion until the twentieth century. This is speculation, of course. Nevertheless, the absence of a heavy charcoal mark at the end of *c'ayk'in* begs for interpretation, and its status as a special month certainly becomes intelligible to me in the terms just stated.

Month names

I shall now give the month names, with meanings and/or folk etymologies. The order given is the order in which they fall in the Chamula calendar. There is remarkable consistency in the order of the months in all of the Tzotzil-Tzeltal area, with the exception of the month of *č'ayk'in*, which occasionally is placed after *muk'ta sak* rather than before *muk'ta sak*. This exception, however, is recorded only rarely in the entire Tzotzil-Tzeltal area and seldom in Chamula (Whelan 1967; Berlin 1951). Consistency in the month names and their sequential order has been remarkable across time as well. With a few differences in phonetic transcription of the month names, and a one-month discrepancy in the beginning of the year, the Chamula list collected in 1968 is a virtual duplicate of a Tzotzil list compiled in 1688 by a Franciscan Friar, Juan de Rodaz, in a manuscript entitled *Arte de la lengua Tzotzlem ó Tzinacanteca con explicación de Año Solar y un Tratado de las quentas de los Indios en Lengua Tzotzlem* (Charency 1885; Berlin 1951). In sum, there seems to have been a distinctive Tzotzil-Tzeltal solar calendar, with month names which were different from the highland Guatemalan and Yucatec versions, since the time of the Conquest (Thompson 1950: 107-19; Berlin 1951). The problem of correlation with the Gregorian year will be considered in the next section.

1. ¢'un

This is the first month of the Chamula *?otol k'ak'al*. One *¢'un* usually correlates with December 26 in the Gregorian calendar, but December 27 and 28 are common variant correlations. (See the next section for details of correlation problems.) It literally means 'to sow'. This has little meaning as such in the Chamula agricultural cycle, for this time of year is the beginning of the dry season and also a time of frost in the central Chiapas highlands. No highland crops are sown at this time. However, some hamlets which lie in the northern part of Chamula are actually in a more moderate temperature zone and *do* sow some important crops at this time (see Appendix A). For the majority of people with whom I have talked *¢'un* has a more metaphorical than a literal sense; it is the beginning of the cycle, the 'sowing of the year'. They observe that December 26 (or December 27, the most common variant correlation) comes immediately after the ritual birth of Christ on December 25. This for Chamulas is the same as the birth of the sun, and as such it makes excellent astronomical sense to them. It was clear to a few of my informants that the sun's apparent position at sunrise has moved ever so slightly to the north (a direction of good omen) on the eastern horizon by 1 *¢'un*. It reached the extreme southerly position (a direction of bad omen, see Gossen 1972) shortly before Christmas festivities. Thus, these few careful observers see the beginning of *¢'un* as the passing of the winter solstice (known in Tzotzil as *skomil k'ak'al*, 'the day's shortness or shortening'). I want to emphasize, however, that the majority of Chamulas with whom I talked about this prefer the metaphorical interpretation relating to the ritual birth of the Christ/Sun on 20 *muš* or December 25.

The most important festival of this month is the installation of new *cargo* officials on December 31 and January 1 (6 and 7 *¢'un*). All civil and many religious officials prepare themselves ritually on the first day and finally take the oath of office on the second day, equivalent to January 1. Although the date of this office-changing ritual is surely the product of Spanish civil and religious custom, it nevertheless makes good functional sense to traditional Chamulas. As noted above, the *cargo*-holders actually 'help' the sun to maintain order during his annual cycle; this in fact is stated in almost all ritual speeches and prayers pertaining to the office-changing ritual. A sample segment follows from the 'blessing' offered the incoming First Alcalde of Barrio San Juan by his outgoing counterpart on 6 ¢'*un*.

> May your body emerge, may your flesh emerge,
> Like unto the young god, like unto the young Jesus,
> As he burst forth, as he was born,
> So with your body, so with your flesh,
> So it was considered, so it was chosen,
> Your body, your flesh,
> At the armoury of God, at the armoury of Jesus Christ,
> At the changing of tasks, at the crossing of the wall.

Thompson notes that the Tzotzil-Tzeltal ¢'*un* corresponds to the ninth month, Ch'en (meaning well, hole or cave) of the Yucatec Maya year (1950: 111). This yields little insight into the meaning of the month in Chamula, but does emphasize that both month names and position in the year are significantly different in the Tzotzil and Yucatecan calendars.

2. *ba¢'ul*

This is the second Tzotzil month. It is not distinguished in any way except for the fact that a major festival, that of San Sebastián, occurs on 4-6 *ba¢'ul*.[3] It is not an active month for agricultural activity, but it is considered to be a good month, for food is abundant (harvest is just completed). The only important agricultural labour in the Highlands is that of breaking the soil and preparing the ground for sowing several months later. (See Appendix A and Table 1 for more data on agricultural activity and weather related to the Chamula months.)

Interpretation of the meaning of *ba¢'ul* is not too rewarding, perhaps about like our wondering about the meaning of January. However, the Chamulas, being fond of language, offered some interesting thoughts on the matter. Two interpretations emerged. The first, and to me the most plausible, is that *ba¢'ul* means 'monkey atole'. *Ba¢'* refers to the lowland howler monkey, which is much feared and is associated with the chaos of the First Creation. Skin from this animal is used on conical caps which are worn by hundreds of monkey characters (*maš*) at the 'Festival of Games' or Carnaval, just before Lent in the Catholic calendar. Preliminary Carnaval activity, which includes these monkey personages, begins in this month and could very well be related to the month name. *?ul* is a thick, sweet maize gruel or *atole*; hence the 'monkey *atole*'. It is highly prized and is served as part of a ritual meal at Carnaval. Thus, both monkeys and *atole* figure prominently in the ritual symbolism of this season, and I think such an interpretation of the month makes functional sense. The second interpretation which I heard with some frequency was that it meant 'the true *atole*', deriving from *baȼ'i*, which means 'true' or 'genuine', and, again, *ʔul*, meaning maize gruel.

Thompson correlates this month with the tenth (Yax) of the Yucatec calendar, but there is no overlap whatsoever in meaning (1950: 111). He quotes Vicente Pineda (1888), who says that Batzol means first amaranth. However, Thompson finds this interpretation dubious; so do I.

3. *sisak*

This, the third month in the Chamula calendar and the eleventh (Zac) in the Yucatec calendar, is mysterious as far as meaning is concerned. When pressed, informants say that it means 'white firewood' (derived from *siʔ*, firewood, and *sak*, which means white in nearly all Maya languages). Following up this interpretation, one Chamula suggested that during this month firewood (and indeed everything) that stays outside overnight will be white with frost in the morning. This purely descriptive interpretation seems adequate to me, but Thompson believes that *sisak* means 'little Zac', contrasting with *muk'ta sak*, 'Great Zac', which is a month which follows it in some Tzotzil/Tzeltal month series (but seldom does so in Chamula). I know of no similar-sounding Tzotzil root meaning 'small' or 'little' which would support this interpretation, but it may be an archaic word of which I am unaware. At any rate, most Chamulas with whom I talked favoured the 'white firewood' interpretation. It certainly presents a vivid picture of frosty mornings in *sisak*, but this will probably qualify as folk etymology more than it will as proper linguistic interpretation.

The major festival of *sisak* is *sometimes* Carnaval, depending upon when the Gregorian year places the Easter cycle each year. However, Carnaval is overwhelmingly identified in the popular mind with *č'ayk'in*, the five-day month which follows.

4. *č'ayk'in*

I have discussed the fascinating background of this five-day month above and will not repeat much of it here. It suffices to say that it definitely represents the Tzotzil equivalent of the Uayeb, the five-day period of chaos and reversal which occurred in the Yucatec calendar as the nineteenth and final month. Of all the months in the Ancient Maya calendar, it seems to have been subject to the most wandering and instability since the Conquest, but it is inextricably bound to pre-Lenten activities in Chamula. It makes excellent functional sense in this position, since it involves a veritable orgy of inverted beings, ritual reversals, as well as the major annual cult to the Sun/Christ deity. If Christmas is the birth of the sun, Carnaval is his ritual maturation and ascent into the sky, to begin the long cycle of heat needed for the agricultural cycle.

Although Carnaval often does not actually fall in *č'ayk'in*, the five-day length and special qualities of each make them synonymous in the popular mind. Some informants even said that the orderly progress of *sisak* or *muk'ta sak* (the other alternative times for Carnaval) were interrupted to insert *c'ayk'in* to correspond with the celebration of Carnaval. Others (the majority) laughed at this interpretation, saying that you cannot meddle with the progression of the 'count of the days'.

5. muk'ta sak

This, the fifth month, means 'great whiteness'. This is the consensus of all of my informants. They differ in their interpretations of 'great whiteness'. Some say that it refers to morning frost, which still can occur in this month, although rarely so. Others say that it refers to *sbe ta?iv*, 'the path of frost', which is equivalent to what we call the Milky Way. The latter interpretation is supported by the fact that the Milky Way *is* unusually visible in the clear night skies of *muk'ta sak*. However, I must be content with the literal description here, for I do not know of any supernatural or other symbolic significance which 'the path of frost' has — other than being a sign of a winter storm. Perhaps that is all that is implied. Thompson reads no more into it, although he is inclined to pair it with *sisak*. He correlates it with the twelfth month of Ceh or Chac in the Yucatec calendar (1950: 111-12).

Although Easter can sometimes fall in *muk'ta sak*, this spectacular though less well-attended festival usually comes in the following month of *mok*. As far as Chamulas are concerned, the major event of *muk'ta sak* is the beginning of maize-sowing season for the highlands. The first days prescribed by *all* readings of the 'counter of days' as propitious for sowing are in *muk'ta sak*. Some say that sowing can begin in *č'ayk'in*, but on this there is not agreement. There is conflict here because of the very special and sometimes negative symbolic associations of Carnaval. Furthermore, one could not plant during a prescribed planting day if it fell in the dark of the moon. Carnaval should always fall in the dark of the moon; hence the ambivalence about planting in *č'ayk'in*. *Muk'ta sak* offers the first truly safe dates for planting.

6. mok

This, the sixth month, means wall, fence or barrier. In Thompson's reading it correlates with the thirteenth month — Mac — in the Yucatec calendar. Mac, which is cognate with the Tzotzil *mok*, implies closure. In particular, he believes that its completion marks a segment in the solar year at which 260 days would have been counted (Thompson 1950: 113), thus closing a sort of compartment in the solar year. Two hundred and sixty days is the length of the sacred ritual almanac, the *tzolkin*. This interpretation certainly is plausible for the Yucatec calendar, but is not particularly illuminating for the Chamula equivalent, since Chamula does not have the *tzolkin* and since different beginning dates are operative in the two systems.

To Chamulas the wall or fence implied by this month name means something mundane, but absolutely critical to this season in the agricultural cycle. After planting, the maize seeds are threatened by raccoons and birds while still in the ground, and by rabbits and many other creatures once they have come up. Furthermore, once the maize plants are a few inches high, sheep pose an added threat. Thus, as soon as planting is completed, Chamulas construct barriers around their fields. They make them sheep-proof, but keeping birds, rabbits and raccoons out is next to impossible (see Appendix A). Hence *mok* suggests one of the major agricultural problems of this period. Related of course is the fact that this month is a prime time for sowing; it has at least eight prescribed days for sowing (see Appendix A).

Mok has no major festivals identified with it, perhaps because this is such a busy agricultrual season.

7. ?o ?lal ti?

The seventh Chamula month, correlated with the fourteenth month — Kankin — in the Yucatec calendar, is nearly impossible for Chamulas to decipher. In Tzotzil it literally means 'half-bite'; in this informants are in agreement. But no one can imagine what it is a half-bite *of*. This is illuminated somewhat by Thompson's suggestion that the patron of this month in the Ancient Maya calendar was probably a canine deity of some sort. He relates this deity to the dog that is associated with the underworld in most Maya cosmologies (1950: 114). In Chamula, such a dog exists, but he is more related to the Day of the Dead (All Saints and All Souls Day in early November) than to this part of the year. Thompson also notes that fangs and other canine traits appear in Ancient Maya glyphic representations of this month. I am convinced of the possible canine association, but this in no way occurs in Chamula interpretations. Perhaps it is as alien to them as the etymological relationship between the English Thursday and the Nordic god Thor, for whom it was supposedly named.

ʔoʔlal tiʔ contains the last large group of propitious days for planting according to the 'counter of days'. No major festivals occur regularly this month, although Easter may occur as late as this.

8. *ʔulol*

This is another difficult one for Chamulas to interpret. It is the eighth month for them, and the fifteenth month for the Yucatec Maya; Thompson associates it with a bird deity, the Moan bird (1950: 114). Nothing in Chamula interpretation suggests this. Their most frequent speculation about its meaning was that it meant Zinacanteco. *ʔuloʔ* is the most common term which Chamulas use in reference to their neighbours, the Tzotzil-speaking Zinacantecos. However, they cannot make sense of why it is a month name — if this is its meaning. One can speculate that it may commemorate some political event preceding the Conquest, for the Zinacantecos were an influential people at that time. Others suggested that it might mean 'Lorenzo's month', since *ʔu* means month and *lol* is a common rendering of Tzotzil of the Spanish Lorenzo. *Lol* is probably also a given name which existed before the Conquest; it may have referred to a deity or a powerful dynastic figure. In sum, speculation is all that can be offered here.

Practically speaking, *ʔulol* offers the very last days when one may plant highland maize (see Appendix A), for the first big storm of the rainy season nearly always comes during this month. It is considered foolish to wait until *ʔulol* to sow, for one risks the onset of the rainy season and a serious delay in the growing cycle for one's crops. *ʔulol* also marks a major domestic festival, *kʔin kurus*, or the festival of Santa Cruz (May 3). This is a time of major waterhole rituals, imploring the earthlords to send abundant rain for the oncoming growing season. I have been told that shamans who know the old calendar are nearly always recruited to participate in these waterhole activities, but I cannot say whether this is so from my own observation. There are no other major festivals in this month.

9. *ʔokʔen kahval*

This, the ninth month, is the first full month of the rainy season in the Chiapas highlands. The storms are often spectacular ones, complete with hail and lightning bolts. These storms and all precipitation are believed to be sent by the earthlords in cooperation with the Sun/Christ deity. Hence the interpretation of the month name is fairly certain. It means 'the crying of Our Lord'. *ʔokʔ* means 'to cry' and *kahval* means 'my lord' or 'my patron'. The Yucatecan equivalent is Pax, the sixteenth month, and has a symbol γ which suggests a vegetal origin. This is helpful here, for the Chamulas were in complete agreement that the month implied the beginning of the rainy season and growing cycle. It is possible, following Thompson (1950: 115), that the month name might mean 'time of sowing', or, by my extension of it, 'festival of sowing'. These derive from *k'in*, meaning 'time, season or festival', and *?aual* (Yucatec; Tzotzil, *?ovol*), meaning to sow'. Both interpretations fit into the context of this period in the Chamula agricultural and ritual year, but I feel that the first rests on sounder linguistic and ethnographic data than the second.

There are no major festivals in this month, but it marks a crucial time in the agricultural cycle, called the 'first weeding'. The young maize, bean and squash plants have sprouted and grown to a three-to-six inch height now and must be carefully cultivated to assure a successful crop. This is the most important of three weedings which are done throughout the growing season.

10. (mol) h?uč

This is the tenth Chamula month and correlates with Kayab, the seventeenth month in the Yucatecan calendar. *H?uč* alone means 'male opossum'. *Mol h?uč* yields 'old man opossum' and is an optional form of the month name. Sometimes the preceding month of *?ok'en kahval* is called *me?el ?uč*, meaning 'old woman opossum'. Thus, these may at one time have been a related pair of months. None of my informants could give more of an explanation than the literal meaning 'opossum'. Some ventured to say that the opossum was more often seen at this time of year. Others said that the danger of opossums killing chickens and turkeys was great at this time of year. In sum, I fail to come up with any supernatural or natural interpretation for this month, beyond the most obvious.

This month is the end of the time for the 'first weeding'. Its most important event is the festival of the patron saint of Chamula, San Juan. This festival falls on 15 or 16 *uč*, or June 24; the two dates in the Chamula calendar derive from the alternate beginning dates of 1 *¢'un* as December 26 or 27. This festival and Carnaval are the highest points in the ritual year for the laity if attendance is an index.

11. h?eleč

The eleventh month of the Chamula calendar refers to a small mammal which lives in dry logs. I was not able to identify the animal; nor did I ever see one. Informants were generally in agreement that it was a small animal. but they could not go beyond this level. The glyph for the corresponding Yucatec month of Cumku has the sign for ripe maize together with a serpent or other dragon-like creature. Thompson speculates that this might have been the god of stored maize (1950: 117), but the relation of this to the Chamula month is not at all clear.

If people wish to sponsor it, this is the month for the *h?olol ?avil* (half-year) ceremony. This, however, is an optional domestic ritual in Chamula. Its date, when celebrated, is apparently determined by the old calendar. Although I have not attended one of these rituals, I have been told that their content involves thanks to the saints, the Sun/Christ and to the earthlords for the year so far, and a petition for continued good fortune and good crops for the remainder of the year. Shamans are in charge of the *h?olol ?avil* ceremony,

There are no major festivals in *h?eleč*. The major agricultural activity is the beginning of 'the second weeding'. There are apparently no specified days in the Chamula 'counter of days' for weeding and cultivation. However, planting and harvest require close attention to the schedule dictated by the old calendar.

12. hničk'in

The twelfth Chamula month means 'festival of the flowers' or 'flower festival'. Thompson believes that this may have been the first month in the pre-Columbian Tzotzil calendar (1950: 107), corresponding to the month of Pop in the Yucatecan calendar. I shall not enter this debate, for I find Chamula interpretation of this month as mid-way in the growing season for maize to be convincing. My informants observed that this is the month when the maize flowers or tassels and begins to produce small ears; hence the month name. Maize-flowering time gives farmers pleasure, for it means that the plants are strong and will probably make it through a productive cycle if adequate rains continue. There may have been a 'festival of the tasselling' to mark this stage in the maize cycle in the past, but I know of no equivalent in the present.

Hničk'in is time for continuation of the second weeding in the agricultural cycle. There are no major festivals during this month.

13-16. sbavinkil, sčibal vinkil, yošibal vinkil, sčanibal vinkil

These four months obviously form a series and they are so conceived by the Chamulas, so I shall discuss them together. They mean First, Second, Third and Fourth Man or Companion. *Vinkil* is related to the word *vinik*, which means man. *Vinik* is also the root for the number 20, which is the base unit of the Tzotzil number system. The reference is to the twenty fingers and toes of a man. Thus, the four month names may refer simply to the unit of twenty days. However, my Chamula informants felt that more personification was involved. In particular, they suggested that the four men mentioned in the month names might refer to the four earthbearers (*hkučlumetik*) who, according to some Chamulas, are believed to carry the earth on their shoulders at the intercardinal points. There are no rituals observed during this period which would support this interpretation;

nor are there any myth texts which illuminate this interpretation. Thompson believes that these four Tzotzil months form an interrupted series of what was once a longer series of months counted from the beginning of the year (1950: 107-9), assuming that *hničk'in* was the first month. If one must speculate, I would go with the Chamulas' own interpretation. I find it convincing because the second half of the solar year (summer solstice to winter solstice) in their cosmological symbolism is generally associated with the earth, underworld, and the female principle, for the days have begun to grow shorter; hence the influence of the sun is less. This would make the earthbearers likely candidates as patrons of this period (see Gossen 1972). It may be worth mentioning that all four of the major festivals in honour of the female saints and the moon occur in the period between the summer solstice and the winter solstice. Two of the major festivals of the *vinkil* months illustrate this: Santa Rosa on August 28-30 (20 *sbavinkil* and 1 and 2 *sčibal vinkil*) and the Virgen del Rosario on October 5-7 (18-20 *yošibal vinkil*). The other major festival of the period is in honour of San Mateo, September 19-21 (2-4 *yošibal vinkil*).

The major agricultural activities of the period are the 'third weeding' in *sbavinkil*, and the doubling over of the corn stalks in the remaining three months of *vinkil*, as this is necessary. The doubling over is a process which allows the grain to ripen and harden while being protected from possible rot and insects brought by the heavy rains of this period; since the top of the ear points down after doubling, moisture cannot enter the ear from the top.

17. pom

The seventeenth month is *pom*, which means incense. Informants were in complete agreement on this meaning, although Thompson suggests that the Tzotzil-Tzeltal word *pom* may also mean pus. He uses this association to interpret the meaning of the month as similar to the sixth month (Xul) in the Yucatecan calendar; the tie is with a sore ear (hence the pus) which is found on the canine motif of a Mexican variant of the Xul glyph. He believes that this is the canine deity who conducts the sun through the underworld at night in most Mesoamerican cosmologies (Thompson 1950: 109). I find this a bit far-fetched, for *pom*, if it means pus at all in Tzotzil, is surely an archaic form; it is certainly not in everyday use. However, this *is* the month of the Feast of the Dead (5 and 6 *pom*), corresponding to All Saints' and All Souls' Days (November 1 and 2) in the Catholic calendar. I remember that when we attended the meal for the dead at the home of a Chamula friend, our black dog was explicitly invited. This was most unusual, for Chamulas customarily treat dogs very badly. They even gave her a tortilla, telling us jokingly that we had to be good to her so that she would help us in the underworld after death. Thus, associations of this month with the underworld are strong, and Thompson's dog thesis may be correct.

Another plausible interpretation suggested by my informants is that the dead, who return at around 2:00 a.m. on the morning of 5 *pom*, need incense as food for their journey from the underworld. Incense was certainly abundant when we witnessed this ritual; we were told that the dead needed it to guide them home and that they also needed it as food for the road. In sum, this month is clearly identified, among Chamulas, with incense, the underworld and the dead. This is emphasized by the fact that the only major festival in this month is the Feast of the Dead, *k'in santo*.

Immediately after the Feast of the Dead, the dry season and the harvest begin in the Chiapas highlands. The term *šlah santo*, 'at the end of the Feast of the Dead' is the most common term for stating the time for the beginning of the harvest. Specific days are given by the Chamula calendar for harvesting (see Appendix A). It is most important to *start* on a propitious day specified by the calendar. In other words, in practical use, the calendar specifies propitious starting days; continuation may or may not follow the calendar. I should note that such casualness regarding the calendar seems to be much more common at harvest than at sowing time. Reasons for this are not clear.

18. yašk'in

This, the eighteenth month of the Chamula calendar, is the same (with a difference of one glottalized consonant) as the seventh month, Yaxkin, of the Yucatecan calendar. Of all the months, this is the one which has cognate forms in the calendars of nearly all of the Maya linguistic family. In Tzotzil, it means 'new, fresh or green festival'. In Yucatec the meaning is very similar, 'new sun, green sun, first sun or dry season' (Thompson 1950: 110). In both cases there is clear overlap of meaning, for the month marks the time of abundant harvest, the reappearance of the bright sunny days of the dry season and a time of general optimism in the annual cycle. People have time to relax even though they must complete the harvest. Most households have a ritual of gratitude after the harvest is completed, but this is definitely a domestic and not public affair.

The month is mostly absorbed in harvest activity and there are no major festivals. The traditional calendar is in active use during this month, as people must be careful to begin harvesting fields on propitious days which do not fall in the dark of the moon.

19. muš

The last month in the Chamula calendar corresponds to the eighth month (Mol) in the Yucatec calendar (Thompson 1950: 110). The meaning of neither is very clear. Chamulas could agree on only one interpretation: that *muš* simply meant negation. It is a variant form of the negative particle *mu*, which is a root used to make negative statements of many kinds. It is also an adjective meaning bad or evil. *Muš* may also be an archaic form of *maš*, meaning 'monkey'. All of these interpretations are intelligible in terms of Chamula cosmology, for this month has the shortest days in relation to nights and also the most southerly apparent position of the rising sun. These cosmological facts bode ill, for they imply decreasing influence of the sun on earth. He spends more time in the underworld than he does in the sky. The underworld is believed to be the home of the dead, monkeys, demons and other beings hostile to the sun and the terrestrial social order. Hence, both negation and monkeys (who appear as ritual personnel at Carnaval in the special five-day month of *č'ayk'in*) express important cosmological facts about the last month of the solar year. It is fitting that the next month, which begins a new annual cycle, is *¢'un*, meaning 'to plant'.

Two major festivals in honour of female deities occur in this month: La Virgen de Guadalupe (5 or 6 *muš*, or December 12) and Santa María, identified with the moon (19 or 20 *muš*, or December 25). The dominance of the female principle in this, the last month, is resonant with the fact that it has the least influence of the sun, who symbolizes the male principle, of all the months. Harvest is completed in this month, according to specified days in the traditional calendar. Thus the fruit of harvest, the earth, the moon and femininity, as well as ritual danger prevail as important associations with *muš*.

To summarize, we have seen that the names of the nineteen months of the Chamula 'counter of days' express significant facts about the parts of the solar year. Implied in the month names and their activities are an impressive number of facts and symbols about Chamula seasons, agriculture, ritual and cosmology. The month names, with few exceptions, mean something to Chamulas and make sense in their position in the solar year. Although some meanings are lost to time, the majority go together to form a whole meaningful cycle.

Correlation with the Gregorian year

The most common correlations which I found in Chamula were: 1 *¢'un* equals December 26 or 27, in that order of preference. It will be obvious from the discussion of the individual months above that these variant correlations make for some confusion about fiesta dates. This is more complicated by the fact that all fiestas have three days and one, Carnaval, has five. More potential confusion is introduced by the fact that the 'counter of days' does not account for a leap year. The same was apparently true of the Ancient Maya *haab* (Thompson 1950: 121). Presumably, people are able to rectify their counts every four years as they find key festivals, controlled by the *Galván* Gregorian calendar almanac, being celebrated one day out of phase with their own counts. Certainly, no Chamula with whom I talked considers this to be a serious problem. Only a few are even aware that it is a problem at all.

For comparative purposes, I shall give in summary form an annual monthly correlation chart. Key festival dates which most Chamulas know by heart are given above in the discussion of the month names.

1 *¢'un*	—	26 or 27 December
1 *ba¢'ul*	—	15 or 16 January
1 *sisak*	—	4 or 5 February
1 *č'ayk'in*	—	24 or 25 February
1 *muk'ta sak*	—	1 or 2 March
1 *mok*	—	21 or 22 March
1 *ʔoʔlal tiʔ*	—	10 or 11 April
1 *ʔulol*	—	30 April or 1 May
1 *ʔok'en kahval*	—	20 or 21 May
1 *ʔuč*	—	9 or 10 June
1 *ʔeleč*	—	29 or 30 June
1 *hničk'in*	—	19 or 20 July
1 *sbavinkil*	—	8 or 9 August
1 *sčibal vinkil*	—	28 or 29 August
1 *yošibal vinkil*	—	17 or 18 September
1 *sčanibal vinkil*	—	7 or 8 October
1 *pom*	—	27 or 28 October
1 *yašk'in*	—	17 or 18 November
1 *muš*	—	6 or 7 December

There are abundant comparative calendrical data from over a dozen Tzotzil- and Tzeltal-speaking communities in the Chiapas Highlands: Berlin (1951), Becerra (1933), Schulz (1953), Guiteras-Holmes (1961), and Whelan (1967). Many of these are integrated into Miles' excellent comparative study (1952). Nearly all of these reports deal only with lists and correlation dates and not with function and cognitive significance. Nevertheless, they are useful for comparative purposes in the rather tedious and unrewarding correlation problem.

There seems to be considerable variation in the Tzotzil-Tzeltal area about the beginning month of the year. The first data reported from the Chiapas highlands (in 1688) show *ba¢'ul* as the first month (Berlin 1951). The next reports, from 1845, from six communities, show *muk'ta sak* as the first month in five of these and *ʔoʔlal tiʔ* as the first month in one (Becerra 1933). These data are interesting in that they place *č'ayk'in*, the month of five days, at the end of the year, where it presumably belonged in the Ancient Maya calendar. The next material, from 1917, includes one Tzotzil community which begins its calendar with *¢'un*, as the present Chamula calendar does. The other 1917 report is of a Tzeltal calendar which begins with *baȼ'ul* (Schulz 1953). Becerra (1933) indicates, after consideration of data from several communities, that the 'normal' versions of both the Tzotzil and Tzeltal calendars begin with the month of *?o?lal ti?*. His argument rests on the fact that *mok*, which would be the final full month if *?o?lal ti?* were first, means 'closure' or 'end'. I am not convinced by his argument, for, as I have discussed above, *mok* (also meaning wall or fence) can refer to a mundane but important task *within* the agricultural cycle, falling neither at the beginning nor the end. Schulz's Tzeltal data (1953), collected in 1941 and 1953, show *baȼ'ul* as the first month, while Guiteras-Holmes' Chenalho material (1961) is very similar to my Chamula material and that of Whelan (1967) and Pozas (1959), with *ȼ'un* as the first month in all of these cases. Berlin (1951) reports data from three Tzotzil communities in which *baȼ'ul* is the first month. It has been argued (Whelan 1967) that researchers simply line up the beginning dates of the Tzotzil months with the Gregorian months as closely as possible and report them that way. It could also be argued that the Spanish missionaries successfully changed the beginning dates of the old calendar so as to bring popular calendrics more into phase with their own religious calendar. However, in most cases, the Tzotzil-Tzeltal calendar has been a distinctive system based on the solar year as a cycle running roughly from winter solstice to winter solstice. *Baȼ'ul* and *ȼ'un* seem to be the most common beginning months across the past three centuries, and these fall relatively close to the winter solstice. Furthermore, I am convinced that the year beginning with *ȼ'un* and ending with *muš* makes excellent functional sense to Chamulas. In this order, the meanings of the names of months fall strikingly close to specific agricultural, weather, cosmological and ritual facts about their respective periods. However, the position of *č'ayk'in* has certainly been manipulated by anxious missionaries.

In this exercise in speculation it should be remembered that the absolute time of year to which each month pertains does not vary much throughout the Maya area. Beginning and ending dates of the year certainly do. Among the ancient Yucatec Maya, for example, the month of Pop (corresponding to the twelfth Tzotzil month, *hnič k'in*) was the *first* month of the year, falling sometime between our July 4 and July 25, with July 14-16 being the most probably correlation date (Thompson 1950: 304-307). It is of course possible that the Tzotzil-Tzeltal calendar was so organized at the time of the Conquest, but, if so, the Chamulas have shown a remarkable ability to rationalize and accommodate the Dominican missionaries' forced changes to their own belief system. As stated above, I feel that there is good reason to believe that the Tzotzil-Tzeltal calendar has been distinctive since before the Conquest and that it has been a winter solstice to winter solstice cycle since that time as well.

Taking the month of *ȼ'un* as an example, I should now like to review briefly the variation in absolute data correlation in the Maya area. The 26 or 27 December correlation with 1 *ȼ'un* lies around midway in a range of variation throughout the highland Chiapas area. The 1688 Tzotzil calendar reported 1 *ȼ'un* as equivalent to December 28 (Berlin 1951: 157). The 1845 data reported by Becerra (1933) show a variation from December 25 to 28 for 1 *ȼ'un*. Most Tzotzil-Tzeltal reports from this century show the same variation, with the exception of some Tzeltal communities which vary by as much as a 20-day month. In this comparative study, Becerra (1933) shows the regular Tzeltal correlation of 1 *ȼ'un* to be December 12. In sum, the Tzotzil correlation varies between December 20 and December 28. The Tzeltal correlation varies between December 3 and December 28.

Summary of function and use

It can be seen that the basic organization of the Chamula 'counter of days' is typical of those solar calendars that survive throughout the northern Maya area. It is atypical, and perhaps unique, in that a graphic form of it is still used. It is also unusual in that it is widely used and understood by the laity and shamans as well. Many other reports from the Maya area suggest that the solar calendar is dead or dying, a vestige of Ancient Maya culture that does not retain meaning or significance in the present. (There are of course exciting exceptions to this statement, such as Santa Eulalia in northwestern Guatemala, where an old calendrical system vastly more complex than Chamula's exists (La Farge 1947).) In Chamula, much as among the Ancient Maya, I would speculate, the solar calendar has its appointed function, that of regulation of agricultural and other mundane activity. Chamulas understand it as such, and are well aware of the natural and supernatural associations of the month names throughout the annual cycle. Nearly all adult males know the propitious days for planting and harvesting. These they use together with the lunar cycle to schedule their agricultural labour (see Appendix A for a typical lay interpretation of the 'counter of days'). Shamans, some with calendar boards, are available for consultation when in doubt. Many other temporal cycles are operative and have their specialized tasks. For example, the solar calendar does not serve primarily as a ritual guide, except for domestic rituals pertaining to agriculture. There is good evidence that Chamula *cargo*-holders' flower changing ceremonies at their home altars follow a strict twenty-day cycle which has the old calendar as its referent, but this is not documented to my satisfaction. The Gregorian calendar determines the vast majority of public ritual, perhaps filling the slot occupied by the old 260-day ritual cycle in the pre-Columbian period. As a long chronicle of time, the Four Creation cycle is available to Chamulas, and they use it frequently; they are able to place nearly every narrative event in their folklore in one of the four creations (see Gossen 1974). As a short count of recent events in the Fourth Creation, they have a system of natural and historical 'landmarks' whose order in a relative time sequence is known to all. Many other minor temporal cycles, discussed above, fill specialized niches in their time reckoning. In sum, Chamulas, like the Ancient Maya, are obsessed with time; the 'counter of days' is but one cycle among many which they use daily to live in the world of the sun.

Conclusions and implications for Maya calendrics

1. Possible insight offered for interpretation of calendrical texts in Ancient Maya Codices. While the Chamula solar calendar is but one of over fifty which have been discovered in contemporary Maya and other Mesoamerican communities, the graphic representation of it in the form of the calendar board is at present unique and offers promise that more will be discovered. This provides evidence that contradicts the long-held belief that no written form or pattern of the calendar existed (see Berlin 1951: 156, 161). The organization, order and conceptual factors involved in the tally of months on the calendar board are fundamentally pre-Columbian in origin. The names, number and meaning of the months, the graphic emphasis upon completion rather than beginning of periods, the concept of 'burden' implied by annual application of a new layer of charcoal, the function of regulating agricultural activity and some agricultural ritual, the left-to-right, up-to-down organization of information, the role of shaman in maintenance and interpretation — all of these may be assumed to be very conservative traits of Mesoamerican calendrics. The fact that these ancient traits are still part of a vital living tradition may offer some important insights into the interpretation of calendrical texts in the Ancient Maya inscriptions and codices. For example, it seems reasonable to speculate on the basis of the Chamula data that the solar calendar was always known and at least partially understood by the peasant laity. It was that important for regulation of everyday agricultural activity. Priest specialists need not be assumed to have been the sole bearers of the tradition. In other words, it was probably not esoteric information. Furthermore, its probable vitality in the domestic lay sector of Maya culture at the time of the conquest is perhaps the reason that it survives so vigorously in so many modern Maya communities. I would also speculate that the graphic form of the calendar in the hands of a few specialists has probably contributed to its survival as a detailed agricultural almanac in non-literate communities such as Chamula, for its partially removes the necessity of preserving that information only in the oral tradition.

2. *The solar calendar need not be in the hands of institutionalized specialists in order to survive.* This conclusion, which follows from the discussion just above, challenges a hypothesis offered by Manning Nash (1957). He suggests that the solar calendar and other true chronological cycles (as opposed to divinatory cycles such as the 260-day *tzolkin*) survive only in those Mesoamerican communities where the calendar expert is part of the formal religious and civil organization. On the other hand, he suggests that in those communities in which the shaman or other calendar expert is *not* a part of the formal religious and civil organization, only divinatory and ritual cycles, primarily the 260-day *tzolkin*, will survive (1957: 152). The Chamula data clearly do not substantiate this hypothesis. In the first place, both shamans and the laity possess detailed information about the solar year. In the second place, Chamula shamans work independently and are in no way tied to the formal religious and civil organization. This would imply that they would have only the *tzolkin* if they had any calendar. Such is not the case. This discussion and challenge of Nash's hypothesis lead me to believe that our future research strategies on calendrics in Mesoamerican communities should emphasize the domestic, private or lay sectors of the community as well as the formal, public sectors. The Chamula data offer promise in this direction, and the historical facts of Spanish missionization in Mesoamerica certainly indicate that it was public rather than domestic customs which were the friars' first and easiest targets for Christian 'reform'. Shamanistic ritual and practice are among the most conservative traits in all Mesoamerican communities, as are calendrics. Surely the reason is that they have stayed 'underground' in the domestic sector since the time of the Conquest.

3. *The Chamula solar calendar, like the Ancient Maya haab, is but one of many operative temporal cycles.* This has been discussed extensively in the body of the paper. I should only like to emphasize that the Chamulas preserve the Ancient Maya preoccupation with time, such that the solar calendar occupies but one small niche in the mesh of temporal cycles which they require to live properly in the world of the sun. Because the Sun/Christ created all temporal and spatial order, the solar calendar and all other cycles, whether concerned with mundane or religious life, are imbued with latent sacred significance. The pervasive sacred qualities of time can be observed in the striking number of aspects of Chamula life which share metaphorically or actually follow the pattern of the solar cycle: the life cycle, the day, ritual sequences, the four-part creation, the agricultural cycle, the festival cycle, even the seasons — and of course the solar calendar.

4. *The Tzotzil-Tzeltal area of Chiapas preserves a distinctive form of the Ancient Maya solar calendar which is a winter solstice to winter*

solstice cycle. For at least three centuries both the names of months, their order and their correlation with the Gregorian year have remained strikingly constant in the Tzotzil and Tzeltal communities of highland Chiapas. I agree with Berlin (1951) that it is not simply a degenerate or marginal form of the Yucatecan calendar, but a distinctive variant of the Ancient Maya *haab*. Thompson and others notwithstanding, there is good reason to believe that the only significant change which the Spanish missionaries brought to the superficial features of the calendar was the manipulation of the five-day *č'ayk'in* to correspond with pre-Lenten Carnaval (see above). My primary reason for believing that the Tzotzil-Tzeltal calendar has been a winter solstice to winter solstice cycle since the Conquest is that the highland maize cycle follows this same cycle so closely. Furthermore, contemporary Chamula interpretation of month names is resonant with the idea that the sequence deals with aspects of the slow waxing and waning of solar intensity. It is also interesting that most symbolic domains of Chamula life (e.g., fiestas and the lifecycle) which are isomorphic with the solar cycle begin with cold, rise to heat, and return to cold (see Gossen 1972). Although the matter remains open to speculation, I find the suggestion that the old Tzotzil solar count began in *hničk'in*, in the midst of the maize cycle, and after the summer solstice, to be implausible when considered in the light of Chamula cosmology and agricultural practice. Then, again, we may be dealing with a syncretistic phenomenon that is even more complex than the ancient Maya *haab*.

Appendix A

The following is a free translation of a Tzotzil text written by a Chamula, Manuel López Calixto, who was about thirty-five years old in 1968. He had never held a *cargo* and had never been to school. His brother and I taught him to write. Manuel wrote the text in response to the question: what do you know about the 'counter of days'? Manuel's text reveals typical lay knowledge of the calendar and related activities. In no way is this esoteric knowledge. It is divided into two sections. The first part refers to warmer areas outside Chamula where many Chamulas have rental fields. The second part refers to conditions in the colder home *municipio*. Most Chamulas must have knowledge about both climatic zones. The two-part text is therefore an accurate reflection of typical calendrical knowledge. I have retained the antiphonal, seemingly redundant style in the text because this is so characteristic of Maya speech and narrative.

(For Hot Country)

In the month of *¢'un*, what do the people do?
They sow their fields.
On what dates in *¢'un*?
On 5 *¢'un* and 10 *¢'un*.
They sow black beans and fava beans.
This is for those who live on the road to San Andrés Larrainzar,
For those who live on the road to San Miguel Mitontic.
These people sow their fields before we do.
In *¢'un* they also break ground for their cornfields.
For the twenty days of *¢'un* they break the ground, until *¢'un* is
    over.
What do they do then?
Nothing yet.
On 4 *ba¢'ul* they begin sowing.
They begin their first sowing (of corn).
On 5 *ba¢'ul* they are at work sowing their fields.
On 7 *ba¢'ul*, 10 *ba¢'ul* and 15 *ba¢'ul* they work sowing their fields.
They are sowing black beans as well as corn.
So the people work.
So they only sow the fields in *ba¢'ul*,
So it is until the twenty days of *ba¢'ul* are over,
They are in the labour of sowing.
When this round of sowing is over, what do they do?
They break the ground once again, so the people do.
When *sisak* is almost upon them, what do they do?
They break ground until 5 *sisak*.
Then, on 5 *sisak*, the people begin to sow their fields again.
So once more, the people do.
In solid labour of sowing the people spend the twenty days of *sisak*.
Do they sow their fields each day?
No, not at all.
Don't you see that it is not proper to sow fields all the time.
Only on 7, 10, 15, 17 and 19 or 20 *sisak*.
So it is with everyone,
So they sow their fields where the frost does not fall upon their
    houses.
That is why they sow their fields early,
The frost no longer falls.
That is why those who live where the land is a bit warmer are the
    ones who sow their fields first.
It is because frost does not fall upon their lands.
Don't you see?
For us, *¢'un* is time of frost,
ba¢'ul is time of frost,
sisak is time of frost.

It is different where the land is warmer.
The frost does not come where the land is warmer.
That is why they are the first to sow their fields.
It is because frost does not come.
But not everywhere can one sow at this time.
Only those who live where the land is warmer.
That is why all that they plant grows well.
Their sugar cane grows well,
Their red potatoes grow well,
Their green tomatoes grow well,
Their avocados grow well,
Their red tomatoes grow well,
Their chiles grow well,
Their onions grow well,
All grows well for those who live where the land is warm.
Do you know when they plant their wheat?
Toward the end of the time of the 'Feast of the Dead'.
On 2 *pom* and 3 *pom* they sow their wheat,
They also sow peas, fava beans and onions at this time.
These they sow after the time of the 'Feast of the Dead'.
They sow garlic in *pom* also.
This they sow on 9 *pom*.
When do they sow chiles and tomatoes, do you know?
After the time of the 'Feast of the Dead'.
On 10 *pom* and 15 *pom*.
This is when they sow their chiles and tomatoes.
All has its time of sowing.
The red potato is sowed toward the very end of *pom*.
19 *pom* and 20 *pom* are the days to sow red potatoes.
All has its time of sowing (in Hot Country).
It is after the time the 'Feast of the Dead'.
So my father said.

(For Cold Country)

It is different with us in Cold Country.
We do not sow anything until *č'ayk'in*.
Not until then do we begin to sow our cornfields.
Not until *č'ayk'in* do we begin this work.
What work do they do?
They work at sowing their cornfields.
On what days do they sow their cornfields in *č'ayk'in*?
On 2, 3, 4 and 5 *č'ayk'in* they may sow.
When *č'ayk'in* is over and *muk'tasak* comes,
This too is sowing time.
On what days in *muk'tasak* do people sow their corn?
On 3, 6, 10, 13, 15, 17, 19 and 20 *muk'tasak*.

On these days, it is time of sowing.
Throughout *muk'tasak* people do nothing but sow their fields.
mok is also time of sowing.
Throughout *mok* people sow their fields.
They work at sowing their fields.
On what days in *mok* do they begin sowing?
On 3 *mok*, 5, 7, 10, 12, 15, 17, 20 *mok*,
On these days people can sow.
In *ʔulol* one can still sow corn,
But no longer does everybody sow.
Only those who must hurry because they are behind.
So it is that one can sow in *ʔulol*,
But it is for those who must hurry to get their crop in.
So it is with those who wait until *ʔulol* to sow.
On what days in *ʔulol* do the people do their sowing?
On 5, 7, 10, 12, 15 and 20 *ʔulol* they sow their cornfields,
Those who wait to sow until *ʔulol.*
When they have sowed their fields, what do they do?
They begin closing in their fields.
On what days?
There are no particular days.
The Counter of Days does not apply to mending fences.
Fencing fields need not be done on a particular day.
But when the corn is up, it is immediately time for fencing in the
    fields.
So it is that there are no particular days for fence-building.
It is done whenever it is necessary.

Do you know when the people begin to break the soil?
The people begin in *muš* to break the soil.
In *muš* it is time to prepare their seedbeds.
In *muš*, in *¢'un*, in *ba¢'ul*,
This is ground-breaking time for the people.
The people work most of these months at this labour.
So it is year after year,
The people begin the work of preparing the soil.
They wait until later to sow their fields.
Even though the ground is dry on the surface, it is moist underneath.
Even though it hasn't rained, the moisture in the earth allows the
    corn to sprout.
So it is that corn first comes up where the ground has not dried out
    so rapidly.
So it is best to prepare the soil early,
So that the earth will remain moist.
So it is best to break the ground as early as possible.
There is good reason to prepare the soil early.
Then, when the rain falls, the crops will grow rapidly,

For it is still moist deep down in the earth.

After the second shower, the rabbits come out.

They come out to eat the corn.

It is when the shoots are still small that the rabbits come out to eat the corn.

When the showers fall heavily, that is when the rabbits come out to find food.

The armadillo behaves differently at sowing time.

The armadillo comes out, but only digs the seeds right after sowing.

The rabbit eats the leaves.

But he does it when they are still small.

In *ʔuč* it is time to weed.

In *ʔok'en kahval*, it is time to weed,

The weeding of the cornfields,

This is the first cultivation.

In *ʔeleč* it is time for the second cultivation of corn.

So it is year after year that the people work.

It is this way because the first people showed them how to do it this way.

The first people showed (us) how to sow and care for our cornfields.

But this was very long ago,

At the time of the first people.

The Counter of Days was left to us long ago, by that name.

That is why it is called that to this day, the Counter of Days.

So that the people will know how to keep track of the days.

So it was that it remained that way for the people . . .

So said my father.

It was given by our ancestors.

For this reason we don't know how many thousand years ago it was.

Don't you see that it was given by the first people, very very long ago?

In *hničk'in* people do more weeding of their fields.

They dig out the grass to help at the time of sowing their fields in *muk'ta sak*.

By the time they sow, the grass will be well rooted.

This is why they dig the grass out early too,

So that the ground will benefit from the rotten grass.

So it is that they weed the grass out in *hničk'in*.

This has its secret and its reason for the people.

So it is that they do weeding in *hničk'in*,

For it is the time of grass in the cornfields.

They do this each year wherever the grass is growing.

In *hničk'in*, thus, the people are in the labour of weeding.

In the months of *vinkiltik* people also do the weeding.

The months of *vinkiltik* are also the time of bending the stalks.

Vinkiltik are also the months for planting black beans in Hot Country,

For those who have cornfields in Hot Country.
They go to sow black beans in *sčibal vinkil.*
They also bend the stalks of corn when they sow the beans.
They leave their cornstalks bent over, whoever has a cornfield in Hot
    Country.
In *vinkiltik* they bend the stalks, for it is time for this in Hot
    Country.
Not until the moon is full do they begin doubling over the corn in
    Hot Country.

After the Feast of the Dead,
The people in Cold Country begin the harvest.
They harvest in 10 *pom*, 15 *pom*, 17 *pom* and 20 *pom.*
All the people harvest their fields in *pom.*
They harvest when the moon is full;
Not until that time do the people harvest.
If the frost comes early,
The leaves will dry up even if they were still green.
But if the beans are still green, they rot after frost.
So with all that is immature,
It quickly rots after the frost.
So everything dies after frost.
In this way, we can harvest everything together (corn, beans and
    squash),
That which is dried up by the frost.

NOTES

1 My thanks are due to Professor Evon Z. Vogt, whose Harvard Chiapas Project provided my first introduction to Tzotzil communities in 1965. His assistance and encouragement throughout my field work (1968-9) and thesis preparation are gratefully acknowledged. The National Science Foundation and the National Institutes of Mental Health provided maintenance and research funds throughout my predoctoral training and field work. Dozens of participants in the Harvard Project, particularly Victoria R. Bricker, Robert Laughlin and Frederick Whelan, provided important insights into the complex view of time which characterizes Tzotzil communities. My special thanks are due Salvador Guzmán Bakbolom, a constant Chamula friend and assistant, who found and secured the calendar board for me.

I have called this a preliminary report in all honesty, for Salvador located the board for me only ten days before we were scheduled to leave Chamula. Crash interviewing during the final days of my field stay, followed by correspondence with Salvador about the calendar, provided my limited acquaintance with its mysteries. Frederick Whelan's excellent summer field report (1967) was also valuable to me in preparation of this report. I hope it will be understood, therefore, that much remains to be investigated about the lore and function of the Chamula solar calendar. The present paper is but a beginning.

2 In nearby Tzotzil-speaking Zinacantan, public year-beginning, half-year and year-end ceremonies are held. They are handled by shamans, with the cooperation of *cargo*-holders. High-ranking shamans determine the dates, yet they do not, so far as I know, depend on the old calendar for this information. The old calendar is not widely known or used in that community (cf. Vogt 1969: 603; Whelan 1967). The only similar festivals in Chamula are held in the homes of private individuals who wish to sponsor them, for they are not a part of the public ceremonial year and are not obligatory.

3 Note that festival dates in the Chamula calendar are often very confusing, for all festivals consist of three days, only one of which is the official date of that saint's commemoration according to the *Galván* Catholic almanac.

REFERENCES

Becerra, M.E. (1933) *El antiguo calendario Chiapaneco.* Mexico.

Berlin, H. (1951) The calendar of the Tzotzil Indians. In S. Tax (ed.), *The Civilization of Ancient America: Selected papers of the XXIXth International Congress of Americanists*, 155-61. Reprinted in 1967.

Bricker, V.R. (1966) El hombre, la carga y el camino: antiguos conceptos Mayas sobre tiempo y espacio e el sistema Zinacanteca de cargos. In E.Z. Vogt (ed.), *Los Zinacantecos.* Mexico.

Charencey, L.F.H.G. de (1885) Recherches sur le calendrier zotzil. *Revue d'ethnographie* (Paris), 3, 398-401.

Coe, M.D. (1966) *The Maya.* New York.

Edmonson, M.S. (1971) *The Book of Counsel: the 'Popol Vuh' of the Quiche Maya of Guatemala.* Middle American Research Institute, Publication no. 35, New Orleans.

Gossen, G.H. (1972) Temporal and spatial equivalents in Chamula ritual symbolism. In W. Lessa and E.Z. Vogt (eds.), *Reader in Comparative Religion: an Anthropological Approach.* New York.

Gossen, G.H. (1974) *Chamulas in the World of the Sun: Time and Space in a Maya Oral Tradition.* Cambridge, Mass.

Guiteras-Holmes, C. (1961) *Perils of the Soul.* Glencoe, Ill.

La Farge, O. (1947) *Santa Eulalia: the Religion of a Cuchumatan Indian Town.* Chicago.

León-Portilla, M. (1968) *Tiempo e realidad en el pensamiento Maya.* Instituto de Investigaciones Históricas, Universidad Nacional Autónoma de México.

Miles, S. (1952) An analysis of modern Middle American calendars. In S. Tax (ed.), *Acculturation in the Americas: Proceedings and Selected Papers of the XXIXth International Congress of Americanists*, 273-284. Reprinted in 1967.

Nash, M. (1957) Cultural persistences and social structure: the Mesoamerican calendar survivals. *Southwestern Journal of Anthropology*, 13, 149-55.

Pineda, V. (1888) *Historia de las sublevaciones indígenas habidas en el estado de Chiapas. Gramática de la lengua Tzeltal y diccionario de la misma.* Chiapas.

Pozas, R. (1959) *Chamula: un pueblo Indio de los altos de Chiapas.* Memorias del Instituto Nacional Indigenista, no. 8, Mexico.

Schulz, R. (1953) *Nuevos datos sobre el calendario Tzotzil-Tzeltal de Chiapas.* Mexico.

Spinden, H.J. (1924) *The Reduction of Mayan dates.* Papers of the Peabody Museum of Archaeology and Ethnology, 6, no. 4.

Thompson, J.E.S. (1950) *Maya Hieroglyphic Writing: Introduction.* Carnegie Institution of Washington, Publication no. 589.

Tozzer, A.M. (1941) *Landa's relación de las cosas de Yucatán.* Papers of the Peabody Museum of Archaeology and Ethnology, 18.

Vogt, E.A. (1969) *Zinacantan: A Maya Community in the Highlands of Chiapas.* Cambridge, Mass.

Whelan, F. (1967) *The Passing of the Years.* Unpublished summer field report, Harvard Chiapas Project.

ALEXANDER MARSHACK

The Chamula calendar board: an internal and comparative analysis

Analysis of the Chamula calendar board was conducted before I had read Gossen's ethnographic paper which arrived shortly before its presentation at the symposium. The analysis that follows is, therefore, based primarily on the internal evidence, the data derived from a study of the board. One of the queries presented by Gossen in supplying the board was whether my methods of analysis, developed for study of Upper Palaeolithic notation, could determine and document the fact that the board had been used and reused over a long period. My own interest lay in the cognitive contents and strategies that might have been employed in the notation.

The analysis is divided into four parts. The first concerns the board as a notational device with a discussion of calendric notation in general. The second deals with the particular breakdown of sets. The third, more inferential and deductive, attempts to read certain phylogenetic and semantic contents into the tradition. The fourth refers back to the Gossen paper and to the relevance of the ethnographic materials to the quite specialized notational analysis.

The paper thus offers a unique opportunity to explore the possibilities and limitations of different analytic methods and types of data. It is hoped that the paper will be of value, therefore, to Americanists and to those interested in the developing subdisciplines of cognitive archaeology and anthropology.

1. The board as a notational device

Fig. 1 is a photograph of the Chamula board. Fig. 2 is a schematic rendition of the visible notation in Fig. 1, indicating its structure and form.

It is possible to note in these two illustrations a complexity in the variability, stroking, intensity and thickness of the charcoal marks, a

Figure 1   The Chamula calendar board with wire holder and charcoal marking for 365 days. The darkening and discoloration of the board is due to burning of the reverse face.

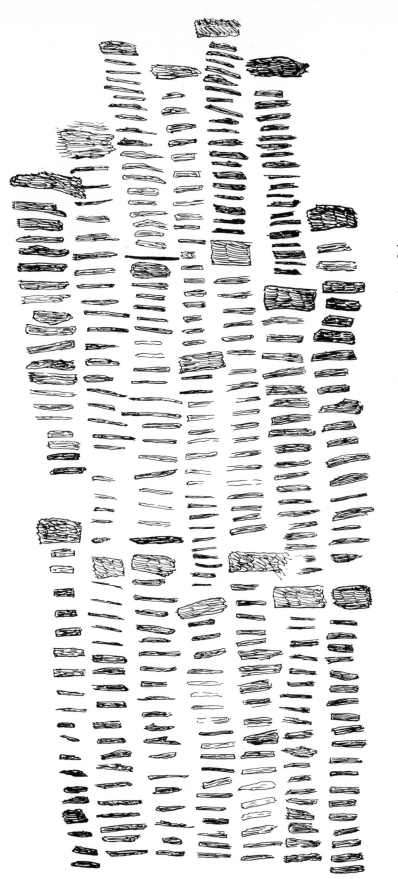

Figure 2 Schematic rendition of all the marks of the last notation and use of the board indicating the difference in intensity of the marking and spacing of the sets.

variability that is hardly evidenced in the sketch of the board supplied by Gossen (his Fig. 1) which indicates the 'design' pattern of the composition to scale. His Fig. 1 is made in the traditional manner of rendering such compositions; and the Upper Palaeolithic engraved notational materials, for instance, had until recently been published in this manner, as linear representations of the apparent 'design' of a composition. The analysis that follows will attempt a cognitive re-creation of the design.

Before beginning, it should be noted immediately that the Chamula board could not, except under the most unusual circumstances, survive as an archaeological artifact. The marking is so fragile that the charcoal of some of the thicker marks can be blown away with a strong breath and the wood would not survive in the soil context of a habitation site. This raises questions concerning the accidental and selective nature of those symbolic and cultural materials of stone, bone, ceramic and metal that have survived archaeologically. It poses a more pertinent question concerning the age and origin of the Mesoamerican tradition of marking sets with charcoal, a tradition for which the archaeological evidence may never be obtained.

In the Upper Palaeolithic, because of a large industry in worked bone, a body of engraved notational sequences has survived, due in part, at least, to the availability of the herbivore herds and protection of the habitation sites by the *abris* or rock shelters. In eastern Spain the huge herds were absent and limestone slabs were used for marking and these, too, have survived; in the East Gravettian cultures of Czechoslovakia large chunks of mammoth ivory were used and an occasional piece has survived. By the time of the Mesolithic the great herds had disappeared from Europe but engraving on the regionally available amber has preserved evidence of the continuing notational tradition in the north.

The Chamula board hints at the possibility that, despite the body of engraved evidence, the primary notational tradition in the Upper Palaeolithic and Mesolithic may have been on perishable materials. In North America the few notational devices that have been collected ethnographically are painted on skins or are engraved on wood. Among the Australian aboriginals there is a rich contemporaneous tradition of symbolic and notational painting and engraving on wood and bark and rarely on bone. There is absolutely no archaeological trace of this obviously ancient, abundant tradition. In the Museum of Archaeology and Ethnology at Cambridge University there are two engraved Nicobar Island lunar calendars on soft tropical wood. They are so fragile they could not become archaeological artifacts and, in fact, they have deteriorated seriously since I first examined them.

There are indications that perishable notations comparable in that respect to the Chamula board existed in the Upper Palaeolithic. A painted fragment of bone with descending rows of marks, roughly similar to those on the Chamula board, was found by Movius in an Upper Perigordian level of the Abri Pataud, Les Eyzies (Dordogne), c. 20,000 B.C. The marks had been made by a finger dipped into a red ochre solution. A rare group of Upper Palaeolithic bones with painted sets of marks and symbols comes from the Soviet site of Mezin. That the painting of sets did represent a basic tradition in the Upper Palaeolithic is also evidenced by their survival on the walls of many limestone caves in the Franco-Cantabrian region. Charcoal marking, if it existed, has disappeared.

When the engraved sets were first found in Upper Palaeolithic levels they were described as decorations or as hunting tallies. Microscopic analyses of these sequences, however, have shown that the cognitive complexities in the sequences cannot be explained by these theories (Marshack 1970; 1972 *a, b, c*). The analysis of the Chamula board reveals comparable cognitive strategies and solutions to specifically notational problems, and these verify the notational and calendric nature of the marking.

The first set of 20 marks on the Chamula board is made with a wide, free use of space, creating a large rhythm or spacing. The next sets are tighter. The third to sixth rows, each of which has three sets, are spaced more closely. This is particularly true when the first set at left is relatively large. The smallest set at left, the fourth row down, makes it possible to have the largest of the sets at right. The third sets in a row often look squeezed as though by the realization that too much space had already been used.

The final set on the Chamula board, the second in the seventh row at bottom right, is made with a wide free use of space as though with the knowledge that no following set would fill that row. This final set has the largest spread of any on the board. This is not the kind of accumulation or patterning that one finds in decoration where a pattern and its rhythms are usually roughed out in mind in advance of the marking and where, despite variations, the composition achieves a balance. Here it is obviously the full and complete set of 20 marks that is the necessary and determining element rather than any visual balancing of the design.

Note also the vertical alignment at the left along the board's edge, arranging the beginning of all the rows. This, with the irregularity at the right, helps us determine the place of beginning, the direction of marking and the place of ending.

What we have, then, is a sequence of non-verbalized, perceptual, cognitive strategies and solutions which arose in the process of marking. These are separate from the cultural patterns which provide the basis of the notation. Such problems and solutions relating to the accumulation of sets are typical in notation but occur seldom in decoration or art. In the Upper Palaeolithic long narrow bones were often used for the accumulation of sets; when space ran out and another set was needed, it would sometimes be engraved over the

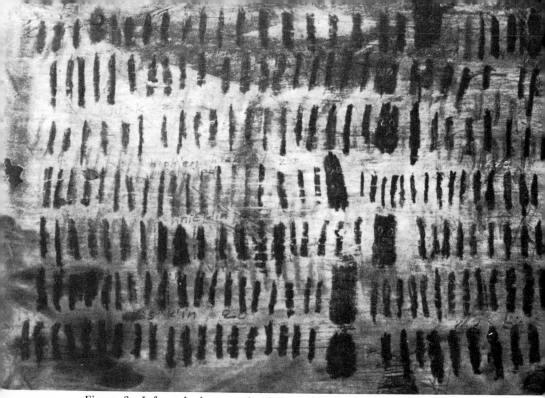

Figure 3a Infra-red photograph of the left half of the Chamula calendar board indicating the presence of underlying sets of marks which had been wiped away. Note that their placement does not correspond to the present marking.

Figure 3b Infra-red photograph of the right half of the Chamula calendar board indicating the underlying marking. Note that at top right the place of a previously heavy 20th day mark is far from the more recent mark. The present mark for day 20 partially covers still another, previous day 20 on that same row. Few of the underlying rows are in the place of present rows.

final set, creating a hatch effect, or within the final set, creating a sense of disorganization. The same cognitive solution is found in modern historic calendric notation (Marshack 1972 *a*: 141). These are not diffused techniques so much as the solutions to notational problems.

The second analysis was conducted by infra-red photography and microscopy. Infra-red photography of the board revealed the presence of many barely discernable underlying sets of marks which had been wiped away in order to make a clean slate of the board (Fig. 3 *a, b*). These underlying sets do not match the current sets of charcoal marks, either in their placement, rhythm or size of marking. It is obvious, therefore, that while the board was used and reused the prior sets did not serve as reference for the latter. Calendar boards which do serve as continuous references occur in the historic pegboard calendars of Europe, Africa and Asia. Here, apparently, the model was in the mind of the maker and the notation was put down mark by mark and set by set following a conceptual rather than a visual, graphic model. This is important since a conceptual model of this complexity implies a linguistically and semantically supported tradition whose full range will not be evident in the abstracted notational structure.

Microscopic examination indicated that the marking surface of the board had been polished by repeated rubbings and wipings, though a gloss was not everywhere apparent because the board had been burned through and so was inherently incapable of showing polish in some areas.

In Upper Palaeolithic and Mesolithic engraved notation such wipings, of course, do not occur; however, cognitively similar techniques can occur with engraving. Among the incised non-calendric tally bones excavated from the historical period in Europe one finds that after a surface had been completely marked it was shaved with a metal knife and the 'cleaned' surface was again notated. The continued shaving created a squared bone. Microscopy revealed the remnants of prior engraved rows of notation among the current markings. In the Upper Palaeolithic roughly comparable data are obtained from the use and reuse of a single bone or surface. There is often evidence for differential wear and hand polish among sets engraved at different times, and there is also evidence for the intentional reshaping and reworking of bone artifacts in order to produce a notational surface after termination of the primary use of the bone (Marshack 1970, 1972 *c*). Such data indicate notational intent, and the Chamula data are of this class.

Microscopy also revealed that the charcoal marks on the Chamula board were made by many charcoals with different intensities of black and of varying hardness and thickness (Fig. 4 *a, b*). At times the charcoal seemed to have been changed for every stroke, at other times one piece seems to have been used for many strokes. There is a

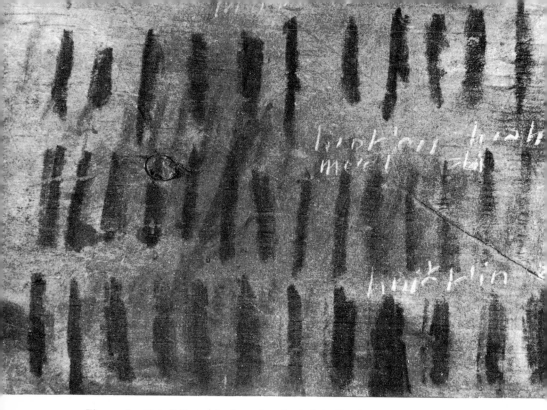

Figure 4a Detail from the board at far left indicating the differences in stroking and charcoals of the different sets.

Figure 4b Detail from the board at far right to same scale as Fig. 4a, indicating the differences in rhythm of stroking and intensity of the charcoal. Fingerprint is visible at bottom right.

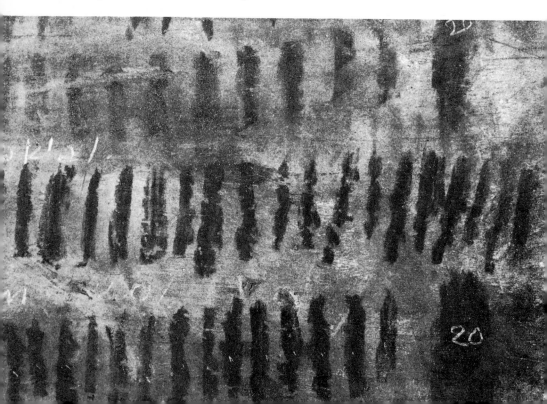

randomness in this sequence of changes which seems to indicate that a piece of charcoal could be kept at hand for a number of days to serve as a marking tool, or a piece might be picked up, used and discarded. Since it is possible to hold and use a piece of charcoal in a number of positions, there is the possibility that a single piece, with a general intensity and hardness, was held differently through many uses. This could account for some of the changes apparent in the pattern or print among close marks. In addition, the effects of the grain and surface of the board are apparent in adjacent marks. Despite these facts, the evidence for a continuous change in the marking tool is clear.[1]

The charcoal data, then, also suggest a sequential and cumulative complexity which would not usually be present in decorative marking. Comparable but different data are found among the Upper Palaeolithic engraved notations. Long sequences of unit marks reveal that different engraving tools, gravers or burins, were used to make different sets and subsets. A stone point will last longer than a piece of charcoal, particularly in very fine, shallow engraving, and a stone tool will usually be gripped in the same position each time for use of the same engraving edge or point. The result is that Upper Palaeolithic engraved sets and subsets often indicate retention of the same tool for a considerable period (Marshack 1972 *c*). Still, as many as twenty or more tools have been documented as having performed the engraving on a single notational surface.

It is also interesting that on the Chamula board each set of 20 marks maintains its own internal rhythm and spacing, different from that of the neighbouring sets, though made cumulatively and by the use of many charcoals. This, again, suggests a conceptual ordering by set, though the marking of the set was broken up over a period of time. A comparable set or subset spacing and rhythm is apparent in the Upper Palaeolithic notations. In these earlier sequences we have the additional factor that many sets were engraved by the same tool. Markings made by one stone point seem to have a rhythm often based on the size and shape of the tool and the engraving point. A sharp point and a wide point are used differently, and a large tool will be gripped and handled differently from a small. Despite differences due to the varying instruments and materials used in these different cultures, the analytic data are comparable and help us establish notational intent and an accumulation in time.

Analysis of the board also reveals that three fingerprints appear on the marking surface (Fig. 4*b*). By their casual and accidental placement it would seem that they were made by later handlers of the board. It is apparent that the person marking the board handled it with great care and that concern was exercised not to smudge or destroy the markings. The board, however, hung from a wire so that some of the visible variation in intensity among certain sets may be due to an occasional accidental brushing by clothes.

A final analytic note. Since the board, as described by Gossen, represents the full year and since the notation and count are complete, it would seem that it was obtained on the day of completion, a rather fortuitous circumstance unless planned for. Normally a board of this type would stand completed only to the day in the year of its most recent marking. It would therefore almost always be incomplete. The full sum of 365 marks, as here documented, would not ordinarily appear on a board that was ethnographically obtained and it would almost certainly not appear on a board that was accidentally preserved archaeologically.[2] If the last marks on the Chamula board were put down before the year's true end in order to complete it in the tradition of its marking there would be no essential difference in its analytic content. The Chamula board is cumulative and notational. It is possible, therefore, that the essential pattern, breakdown and count might have been symbolized in permanent form on stone. However I know of no such published artifact.[3]

2. The sets

The basic count of 20 is divided into 19 plus 1, with the anomalous exception of the set of 5. Whether the final, heavy 20th mark is a notational cue sign indicating for the marker the end of a set, or whether it has symbolic or storied meaning in the tradition, cannot be determined from the one example. It would be difficult, for instance, to achieve this precise thickening effect in an engraved sequence. A different kind of notational solution would have to be found.

Other notational calendric traditions may be of interest here. The use of cue marks, reference signs, images and other visual differentiations such as space separations and change of angle in marking sets is quite common (Marshack 1972 *a, b, c*). Sometimes the cue marks are storied and symbolic, sometimes they are counted and sometimes not. In the Nicobar calendar system a single long engraved line might indicate the end of the month; this line would also be counted as a day. Or there might be a deep, small pockmark at the end of the month; this would be a month indicator and would not be counted as a day (Marshack 1972 *a*: 141-4). If the heavy 20th mark on the Chamula board was a cueing device, the person making these marks had a simple visual system for differentiating the accumulating sets of 20. This kind of notational cueing would perhaps be comparable to the Classic Mayan method of arithmetic notation in which the 5th mark in a set of 5 unit marks was heavier and as a bar could stand for the set or sum of 5. The Chamula board may represent a vigesimal form of this abstractional, notational way of thinking. If so, one need not seek profound meanings in the heavier 20th mark.

If this 20th mark is a form of cueing and summing, we may have a cognitive clue to some of the more evolved developments in Classic Mayan calendrics. The problem will be more fully discussed in another paper and with other documents.

We thus have one aspect of the Chamula marking of sets. There is another. The persistent 'count' of 20 might suggest an ability on the part of the marker to count or a use of counting in the marking. This could be an analytic illusion. It is possible to maintain a sequence of matched sets of marks without numeration merely by naming. We do this with our own sequences of named days of the weeks and months. The naming of the days in a month or week and the naming of the months is common in Asia and the Pacific. The notation of such named lunar sequences would, analytically, look like counting.

One type of naming sequence exists in the Nicobar Islands which is put down notationally. It consists of the breakdown 4-10-6-10 for the lunar month. This sum of thirty is 'observational' and is occasionally adjusted. The four irregular subsets represent storied periods: dark (4), waxing (10), light (6) and waning (10). There is no way of determining a lunar reference from the subsets. One can do so only from the sequence of sets representing 29 or 30 marks. The lunar month is also broken down by the Nicobarese into subsets of 10-10-10, the 30 being adjustable, with no storied reference to the phases in these numbered subsets.

It is therefore difficult to determine from an analysis of the Chamula board whether we have a named or numbered sequence for the marker. The board does, however, present data which suggest that there was an ability to count in the underlying tradition though, again, it need not have been applied by the person making the notation.[4]

Eighteen sets of 20 plus one of 5 gives a sum of 365, a sum that must have been derived from observation and a count of notated days in the tropical year. Analytically the artificial sets of 20 structuring a superordinate sum of 360, plus 5 days representing an observational adjustment of the count, are comparable to the artificial subsets of the Nicobar calendar which structure a 30 day lunar month, but with the subsets and therefore the sum being adjustable on the basis of observation.

In the Upper Palaeolithic one does not find evidence of a structured, traditional count or frame, either for the month or for the year. Instead there is evidence for lunar observation and notation, for the sequencing of lunar quarter phases, their accumulation and grouping. In this stage, apparently, there was no concern for a count of the days in a month or of the lunar months in a year. This does not mean that a form of counting did not exist, merely that it is not evidenced in the notations. The Upper Palaeolithic notations seem to have been a means of keeping track of the sequence of named seasonal 'moons', each of which had its specialized phenomena, activities and rites. At whatever level, then, calendric observations and notations serve the purpose of defining essential phenomenological and related cultural periodicities.

The count of 365 in a Mesoamerican context poses a number of questions. It presumes a solstitial or equinoctial observation and notation. Whether this was done originally by the peoples or cultures now making the board cannot, of course, be determined from the board. Such determination requires other forms of archaeological and ethnographic evidence. One can, however, assay certain inferences from the tradition as it is represented on the board.

Neither counting nor notation are necessary for observation of the equinoctial or solstitial days. Such simple observations may be sufficient for an agriculture with a limited number of crops and a simple sequence of ritual needs. Observations of this type were common among many American Indian groups. It is also possible to utilize a non-arithmetic lunar naming sequence to mark off the months of the year in conjunction with equinoctial or solstitial observation, and such usage was also common in the Americas. The base of calendric lore was therefore present in the New World, available for possible indigenous local developments.

But at what stage would arithmetic day counting and the detailed notational structuring of a lunar or solar year become viable and practicable? I suggest, briefly, certain cognitive and cultural prerequisites for achieving or adopting such structured calendars, including the tropical year sum of 365.

One can assume, theoretically, that the observational determination of the sum of 365 days requires temporal and geometric-positional stability. Whether one is measuring the seasonal change in the length of the sun's shadow from a stick in the ground or the changing position of the sun's rise along the horizon or its changing angle of elevation in the sky, the observational position must remain frozen for at least one year and most likely for a series of years. This presupposes that the economic and cultural activities of the observer will proceed around the observational fulcrum. With the observational point static, however, we must presume an increasingly precise and differentiated sequence of territorial and seasonal activities, economic and cultural. To achieve the arithmetic sum of 365 days and to confirm it requires notation, record keeping and counting, and these combined technologies argue also for an original fixed habitation or ritual-ceremonial storing centre.

Just as a culture will probably not develop counting unless there are many classes of items needing often to be counted, so one can presume, almost tautologically, that calendric counting will not develop until there are many periodic sequences, cultural and economic, that require calendric sequencing and sorting. These are the probable prerequisites for indigenous developments or for the adoption of arithmetic calendric methodologies.

It is therefore possible to assume that long-term, increasingly intensive agricultural developments within one region or valley offer the preconditions for the potential development of a structured, arithmetic, solar or tropical year calendar. The fact is that any valley or terrain, ringed by a horizon of hills and differentially exploited over a considerable period of time, becomes an 'astronomical' observatory. If one accepts the MacNeish evidence for an early indigenous development of agriculture in Mesoamerica, with the evidence for increasingly complex exploitation of diverse micro-environments and terrains and an increasing diversity of crops, then one must also accept the necessary skill, lore and precision required for the sequence of exploitation. Where developments of this type occur in one region over a period of thousands of years, the presence of a structured calendar of some type would be no more surprising than the highly structured complexities and sequences of the agricultural lore. These are generalizations and simplifications. They do not consider in such a development the simultaneous specialization of roles and persons and the politicalization of the social and economic process. These too would increasingly contribute to the inter-relational complexity and the need for calendric sequencing and precision.

But, as stated earlier, this is the same point at which the adoption or incorporation of other calendric methodologies would be feasible, particularly if they had relevance for already known and utilized sequences.

If we turn to the Chamula board we can begin to explore what may be the indigenous contents and discuss tentatively their possible relevance for the development of Mesoamerican calendrics.

3. The tradition

The tradition of notating with charcoal may be ancient, earlier in Mesoamerica than the artificial frame on the Chamula board. It is certain that the tradition would not have originated or been used in its present form.

For one thing, the technique of wiping a calendar board clean each year and of replacing it with a fixed, artificial structure is functional only with an already established, traditional calendar frame.

The board also contains internal evidence that there was probably no solar observation employed by the maker of the marks, though the original count was established on the basis of solar observation. The evidence is in the placement of the anomalous 5. In astronomical notation one normally begins just before, at or just after a periodic observation. In lunar observation these points occur around the crescents or the new or full moon. In solar observation they occur at the solstitial or equinoctial points, and the only place in the sequence where one can determine any inconsistency or difference between the full counting frame and the observation is at the end. The anomalous 5, therefore, is a terminal counting and notational phenomenon. It does not exist astronomically. If solstitial or equinoctial observation alone are employed there is no anomalous period. That the 5 appears in mid-board argues for a non-observational readjustment of the original notational frame. This also suggests that for the marker there was no solar observation and no counting of the sum of 365. Everything, then, points to the fact that the board represents a late, evolved and subsequently devolved tradition. Though originally arithmetic the whole structure could now be maintained by naming. If the board was maintained by a naming sequence, the heavy 20th mark could in its present context also serve as a cueing and notational device within a storied sequence, signifying by its stress some storied aspect of the 20th day name.

If we try to re-create certain aspects of the original counting and notational tradition utilizing the limited evidence of the Chamula board we are faced with the normal analytic and inferential difficulties of working with calendric notation.

We can probably assume, as stated, that the count of 365 was based on equinoctial or solstitial observation. We can also assume that the tradition of solar observation was of necessity older than the notational and arithmetic frame which was developed or acquired to structure the sequence. It is of interest here that a lunar month and tropical year count can be combined in a linear notational sequence or they can be run separately. In the Mayan tradition separate notational sequences were maintained.

It is probable that before the structuring of the tropical year an earlier lunar year was maintained, at first named and then notated and counted. The assumption is based on the fact that all the evolved calendar systems or traditions of which we have record, including the non-lunar Egyptian Sothic year and our own non-lunar tropical year, are derived from earlier lunar calendars and years.

The 20-day 'month' in this frame probably indicates that it was arithmetic and non-lunar from its inception and I take this as evidence of a relatively late introduction.

I also assume that the particular notating and counting form of the Chamula board was an indigenous Mesoamerican development. It seems to consist of an original system in which sets were accumulated, in which the *terminated* set could then be abstracted by a sign and in which these signs could then be accumulated in similar sets, which sets then could also be abstracted by a sign and collected. This is a strictly notational procedure and in an early notational form could have looked like the Chamula board. If the sum of the tropical year, 360 (plus 5), or the sum of an artificial lunar year of 360 (12 months of 30 days) was symbolized as the terminated sum of 20 was, and if a separate notational sequence was kept of the signs of these terminated years, we would have a possible notational and methodo-logical beginning for certain aspects of Mayan calendrics.

I also assume that before development or acquisition of arithmet-ical notation both the lunar and solar sequences were mythologized. When notation and counting did develop or were introduced they represented a means of abstracting and structuring established narra-tive sequences as well as observed phenomenological units and periodicities. These symbolized contents cannot be found analytic-ally in a calendar frame such as the Chamula board, but their presence can be inferred since they are the necessary correlates of an agricultural calendar.

Any notation of a mythological sequence can develop toward a use of image and sign. One can see the tendency at work as early as the Upper Palaeolithic for one already finds in this period that the image can stand for the set and vice versa.

These few thoughts, based on an analysis of the Chamula board and on a comparison of its cognitive and calendric contents with other calendric notations and traditions, are introductory. They do not explain the complexities of classical Mayan calendrics but they may offer certain insights to the study. An analysis of particular cognitive elements in the evolved classical Mayan calendric tradition will be presented at another time.

4. Remarks on Gossen's paper

On reading Gossen's paper I add these thoughts:

1. His description of the use of the calendar board by the shaman would indicate that despite the so-called 'conservatism' of the Chamula we have a degenerated, remnant aspect both of the shamanistic specialization and the calendar's use.
2. The extraordinary complexity of the semantic systems support-ing the board's use is significant. Without such ethnographic evidence one nevertheless has to deduce comparable complex-ities.
3. The presence of a traditional lunar lore in the agricultural sequence suggests again that a lunar calendar was both ancient and indigenous and may have preceded the present solar construct.
4. Appendix A may be the most significant for the inferences I have assayed since it documents precisely those aspects of agricultural specialization and differentiation which would re-quire adoption of a solar calendar and day count, a phenomeno-logical precision that could not be met by a lunar calendar or a lunar naming sequence.

NOTES

1 Gossen (personal communication, 1972) states: 'Ideally the board is marked every day. However, when she (the shaman) was away, she would mark the elapsed days all at once when she returned.'

2 ibid. 'The calendar was in fact delivered to me in early January ... Negotiations preceded the date of delivery, so I presume that it was left fully marked from the previous year, in anticipation of removal ... my friend who obtained the board started talking to the owner sometime after Christmas. It was delivered to me on January 5.'

3 After delivery of the above paper Furst suggested analysis of a pyrite Olmec mosaic from Las Bocas, Puebla, c. 1000 B.C., as an artifact which may have symbolized and summed the calendar year. Analysis, based on the sequential, cognitive method devised for the Chamula board, found no evidence of a solar count but did find arithmetic patterning and a possible lunar count. The analysis was presented at the *Symposium on Archeo-astronomy*, A.A.A.S. meeting on 'Science and Man in the Americas', Mexico, 1973. It will appear in the proceedings of the symposium.

4 Gossen, ibid., writes: 'All adult Chamulas can count ... even though they are non-literate. I presume that all days were named throughout the Maya area in the pre-Columbian period. This survives today only in Guatemalan communities of the northwest Highlands.'

REFERENCES

Marshack, A. (1970) *Notation dans les gravures du paléolithique supèrieur.* Mémoire 8, Institut de Préhistoire, Université de Bordeaux.

Marshack, A. (1972a) *The Roots of Civilization*, London and New York.

Marshack, A. (1972b) Cognitive aspects of Upper Palaeolithic engraving. *Current Anthropology*, 13, no. 3-4, 445-77.

Marshack, A. (1972c) Upper Palaeolithic notation and symbol. *Science*, 178, 817-28.

ADRIAN DIGBY

Crossed trapezes : a pre-Columbian astronomical instrument

Nevertheless it is more than probable that the day and night were divided into parts. In truth some such division would have been indispensable for astronomical computations.

These words of Eric Thompson turned the author's mind to the possibility of finding some instrument which would give the position of the sun, and possibly of the moon, at times other than sunrise and sunset which is all that can be obtained by the well known line of sight methods to points on the horizon, or between monuments set in line to give bearings to the rising or setting of heavenly bodies at particular seasons. Any such instruments would probably have been made of wood, a perishable material, so our best chance of finding any indication of their existence would be in representations of them in geometrical designs in glyphs and on sculpture — for any such instrument would of necessity be of a geometrical shape.

A search on these lines showed, in two examples of the year glyph, one at Xochicalco combined with Caso's turquoise glyph, and in four almost identical year glyphs on the Lapida de Tenango, two trapezes crossing each other. Ignoring for a moment both Caso's interpretation of turquoise, and Thompson's of the two trapezes as a water symbol, we can see in the Xochicalco glyph (Fig. 1) the elevation and plan of two trapezes set on a ring base. The four year glyphs on the Lapida de Tenango illustrated by Caso in his *Glifos Teotihuacanos* show with extreme clarity two trapezes crossing each other, though they give no indication of the shape of the base or the angle at which they cross. In Fig. 2, a drawing from Marquina's *Arquitectura Prehispánica* and a drawing of the glyph on the Lapida de Tenango are compared with perspective drawings, seen from slightly above, of the author's reconstruction of them. Such an instrument would combine some of the properties of a sundial with those of an astrolabe. If the instrument were oriented to the points of the compass, the shadow of the north-south trapeze would move daily from west to east reflecting the apparent east-west movement of the

Figure 1 The year glyph and turquoise glyph on the Temple of the Plumed
Serpent at Xochicalco. Photograph kindly supplied by Mrs Doris Heyden,
taken by Dr Otto Schondube.

sun. Simultaneously the shadow of the east-west trapeze, reflecting
as well the changing altitude (angle of elevation) and azimuth
(bearing) of it, would creep up towards the central east-west axis of
the instrument until noon, after which it would fall away. The
position reached at noon would depend on the declination of the
sun, which varies as a result of the tilt of the earth's axis in relation
to the plane of its orbit round the sun. The distance therefore of this
shadow from the axis at noon would change with the daily variation
of the declination and so give an indication of the time of year.

The purpose of this paper is to make a theoretical study of the
way of using the instrument, to consider the possible connection of
the game of Patolli with it, to give an account of experiments which
suggest its probable size, and show that it would have been sufficiently accurate to show the change of declination between any two
consecutive days except for a period of between twenty and thirty
days before and after the solstices. To justify this exercise I must give
in summary form some of the arguments developed in a paper read at
the Americanists Congress meeting in Rome, entitled 'Evidence in
Mexican glyphs and sculpture for a hitherto unrecognized astronomical instrument'. The argument is briefly as follows. Thompson's and
Caso's interpretations of the respective elements in the glyph from
Xochicalco are not inconsistent with the *derivation* of the glyphs we

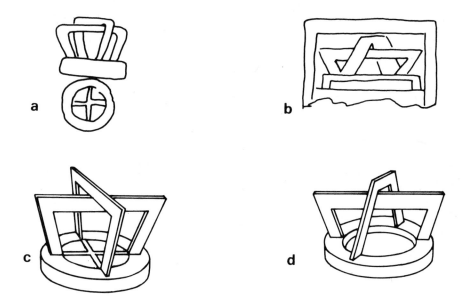

Figure 2 Two year glyphs compared with perspective reconstructions. *a* On the pyramid of the Plumed Serpent, Xochicalco. *b* On the Lapida at Tenango. *c* Perspective reconstruction of *a*. *d* Perspective reconstruction of *b*.

have suggested. Several examples of recognisable objects form the subject of glyphs which have a meaning only indirectly associated with their shape. Moreover the ideas of turquoise in the sense of blue, and water or rain, having an intimate relationship with meteorology or rather with the Mexican equivalent, calendrics or astronomy, make an astronomical instrument a suitable ideograph for such concepts. Secondly, the principle of using the shadow of a horizontal bar instead of the radially moving shadow on the more familiar circular sundial is known outside Mexico. Thirdly, it was found that several glyphs and diagrams representing time periods were derived either from the instrument itself or from parts of it combined with the shadows it cast (Figs. 3, 4, 5). One of these designs is not confined to Tlaloc, but also occurs on the Moon goddess, and on a Mixtec gold figurine, wearing a beard, and the design in question as ear ornaments. The author believes this figurine to represent a Sun God.

Turning from this bald summary to the instrument itself, the first problem which confronts us is whether it was arranged horizontally, which would be the most natural position, or whether it was tilted to face the sun at the equinox. There is apparently no evidence to show which position was adopted, but the latter position presents overwhelming advantages. The instrument would then be elevated to a plane parallel with the earth's axis of rotation, and the effect of latitude on the local altitude of the sun would be eliminated and the

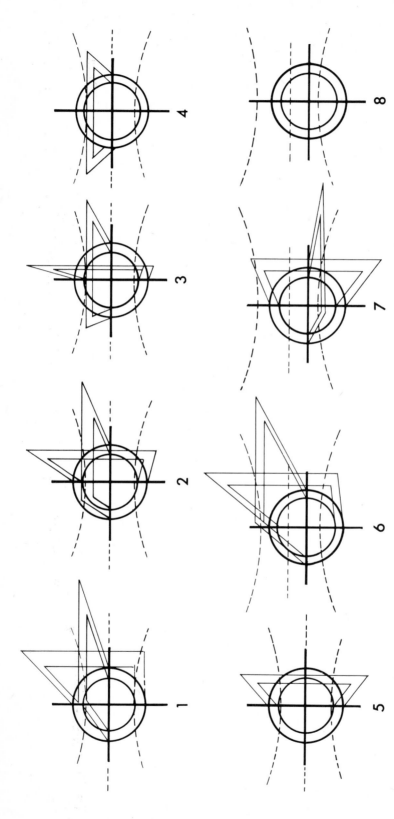

Figure 3 Shadows obtained from trapeze instrument. 1-5: with the instrument tilted to latitude, (1) at 3 p.m.; (2) at 2 p.m.; (3) at 1 p.m.; (4) at noon, all at the winter solstice; (5) at 2 p.m., at the equinoxes. 6-8: with the instrument horizontal near Copan, (6) at 3 p.m., winter solstice; (7) at 2 p.m., summer solstice; (8) with the sun overhead at noon.

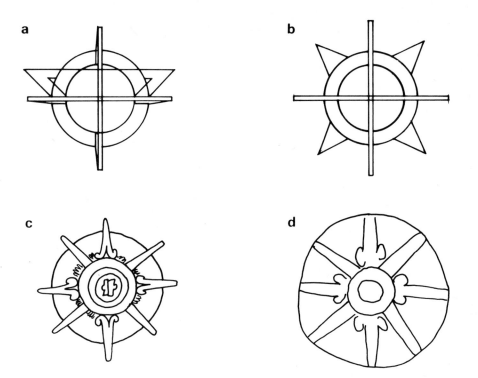

Figure 4 Derivation of the Mixtec sun symbol for the trapeze dial. *a* Looking down on the instrument, with the shadow of the east-west trapeze showing noon at winter solstice. *b* Showing the shadow of both winter and summer solstices conventionalized into points. *c* Carefully drawn sun symbol from the Codex Zouche Nuttall. *d* Carelessly drawn symbol from the Codex Selden.

scale for winter and summer would be of equal length. Fortunately for the possibility there are features inherent in the instrument itself which almost cry out for such an elevation and provide the means by which this could be done very easily. Fig. 6 compares the path of the point of intersection of the shadows of the two trapezes as they wax and wane across the instrument. In both drawings the paths of the shadow follow a curved locus at the two solstices and a straight line at the equinoxes.

The upper drawing, *a*, drawn from a graph kindly supplied to the author by B. Hellyer of the Science Museum, shows what would happen if the instrument were horizontal in latitude 20° N, which is practically the latitude of Tula. The lower one, *b*, shows the position of these same shadow paths in relation to the instrument if it were elevated to face the sun at noon at the equinoxes. Anybody observing the displacement of the shadow path at the equator over a number of years would be tempted to play with it, tilting it this way and that to see the effect of different degrees of tilt on the shadows, the ever changing patterns of which are, as the author has found with

a

b

c

d

e

Figure 5   Designs derived from shadows of the trapeze instrument which have
affinities with the diagram for the Tonalpohualli. *a* Vase from Teotihuacan
(Caso, *Glifos Teotihuacanos*). *b* Body stamp from Teotihuacan (after
Sejourne, *Teotihuacan: metropole de l'Amérique*). *c* God of agriculture (Diaz
Solis, *La flor calendárica de los Mayas*). *d* From a vase from Chupicuaro in
the Museo Nacional de Antropologia, México. *e* Completion glyph, Palenque
(after Maudslay, *Biologia Centrali Americana*).

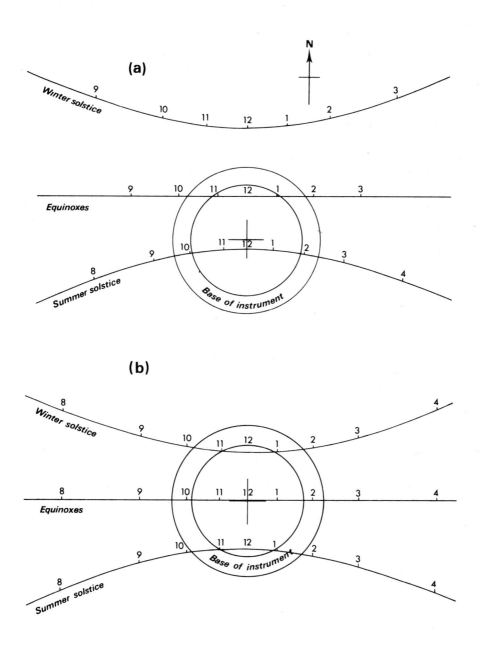

Figure 6 Paths of the intersection of the shadows of the trapezes at the solstices and equinoxes compared. *a* Instrument level at 20° N (approximate latitude of Tula), from a graph kindly supplied by B. Hellyer of the Science Museum. *b* Instrument tilted to face the sun at the equinoxes.

models, a matter of great fascination. There would have been no difficulty in tilting the instrument, because as we have already said it would be made of wood, and as will be shown below not much more than 20 cm. high, and therefore very light. Given the urge to point the instrument at the sun when the shadows traced a straight line between the paths traced at the solstices (the time, incidentally, when the sun rose due east and set due west), the outward spread of the arms supporting the top bar of the trapeze would form a very simple self-aligning device. At all angles other than when the instrument was directly in line with the sun the shadow cast by these elements would be an acute angle, varying in its sharpness with the amount it was out of alignment. This was an interesting discovery which explained the supports of the trapeze being spread outwards. A similar principle was employed by the Alexandrian astronomer Hipparchus, who set up a ring parallel to the equator, which is of course the same angle of elevation as the trapezes would assume when pointed towards the sun at the equinoxes. With Hipparchus's ring the shadow cast would only be a straight line when the rays of the sun were directly in line with it. At other times than the equinoxes the ring would have cast a shadow in the form of an ellipse of greater or less thickness, according to the declination of the sun. With this simple device he was able to discover the precession of the equinoxes. In passing we may wonder what calculations and astronomical discoveries the ancient Mesoamerican astronomers were able to make with their rather more advanced counterpart to Hipparchus's ring, and what calculations based on observations with a device like this may not still remain hidden in the Maya inscriptions.

For our immediate purpose we can say that the pre-Columbian astronomers had both the inducement and the means to tilt their instrument to the angle of the latitude. This leaves us free to postulate scales on the north-south axis of the instrument showing scales of equal length between each solstice and the equinoxes. The scales on the east-west axis present problems of a different kind, and will not be discussed in this paper, partly for lack of space and partly because we lack the crucial evidence of the relative heights of the two trapezes. If we look for some design which might suggest a scale on each axis, the board for the game of Patolli is the obvious choice. It has various calendrical connections. It has been suggested that both Patolli and the ball game are symbolic of the movement of the heavenly bodies. Caso believed that it represented the fifty-two-year cycle, and Sahagún, describing the game, says it was stopped because of suspicions of its being connected with 'superstitious' practices. If, as is possible, the board was used as a kind of abacus on which the movement of the sun and moon were represented by the movement of beans, he may well have been right. In the drawing in the Codex Magliabecchiano, there are seven divisions on each arm of the cross working outward from their intersection (except on the top arm where the last graduation seems to have been omitted through carelessness by the draftsman). There are diagonal crosses on the penultimate divisions which are crucial to our argument, but we first must discuss the accuracy of the instrument. Meanwhile it is interesting to note that there are, to the nearest day, ninety-one days between solstice and equinox, about a quarter of a day being lost at each stage. If we assume that the seven divisions represent thirteen days, we find that the ninety-one days from the winter solstice, represented by the missing division at the top of the drawing, to the equinox at the centre, and a further ninety-one days from the equinox to the summer solstice, make 182 days, and with a similar time for the return journey we arrive at a total of 364 days, which is the length of the computing year described by Thompson. We could consider that the traverse of the shadow was divided into seven units of thirteen, which would give us the same divisions on the instrument as appear on the Patolli board. We can very easily calculate the position of the shadow of the east-west trapeze at noon for any day in the year by looking up the declination of the sun in any nautical almanac, subtracting the declination from 90 degrees to find the altitude of the sun at the equator (which will be the same as that for any instrument anywhere provided it was tilted to the latitude), and multiplying the cotangent of the altitude by the height of the instrument. The same figures can be obtained even more simply by the tangent of the declination. The Mexican astronomers, so far as we are aware, did not have the advantages of any trigonometrical system and would have had to make their scale empirically, marking the point where the shadow seems to fall at, we believe, thirteen-day intervals.

The traverse of the scale from solstice to solstice would of course take approximately 365 days and a quarter. However it is very doubtful if the difference in declination of a quarter of a day would be noticeable on an empirical scale made by marking observed positions. One would perhaps be a minute distance too far from the centre; the next just a little too near. By and large our astronomers would expect the shadow to fall either exactly on the line or a minute fraction off. They would therefore not expect a more accurate reading than to the nearest day. Of course after a year the count of 364 days would lag one day and an unmeasurable quarter of a day behind the shadow, whose position would be governed by the sun but the Mexican astronomers would continue doggedly with their count. After a number of years the accumulated lag, including the quarter day in each year, would become noticeable. When this would be is hard to say without knowing the accuracy of the instrument under Mexican conditions; possibly a gap of approximately five days might be visible after four years. Experiments were carried out to determine both the probable size of the instrument and the degree of accuracy with which a shadow could be read, not only to settle this point, but also to show whether the accuracy would be fine enough for any kind of readings. These experiments will be described in some detail, because they revealed a rather surprising degree of accuracy, and an optical phenomenon which not only gave an almost artificial degree of accuracy but also explained why in all the later instruments a trapeze was used instead of a point, as might be deduced from several of the glyphs.

At first sight we might expect that the indeterminate penumbra of a long shadow might make it impossible to detect very small movements. In fact this proved not to be the case. A sliding panel was constructed, a thick black line was drawn across it at right angles to the direction of motion, and a rectangular bar about a centimetre thick was supported above it so that the shadow fell parallel to the black line. The panel was then moved by a micrometer screw until the line merged into the shadow, the reading on the micrometer was noted and then it was unscrewed until a line of light appeared between the black line and the shadow and the reading taken again. This gave the minimum movement which could be detected. Naturally the nearer the bar was to the panel the smaller was the penumbra, and vice versa. Of course a bigger throw of the shadow would give a reading, other things being equal, of a smaller movement of arc. One factor tended to cancel the other out. After a number of trials with the bar at various heights, the best results were obtained when the bar was about 20 or 25 cm. above the sliding panel. This gave a probable size for the instrument and agrees with a number of sculptures showing gods or priests wearing the device as a headdress. To fit over the head, the ring of the instrument would have to be about 20 cm. in diameter, and the proportions which may be inferred from sculpture and glyphs would suggest that the height of the taller trapeze was about the same size as the diameter of the ring.

Taking 20 cm. as a standard, a number of readings by different observers were taken. The abnormally bad summer, and variation in the quality of the sunlight from weak to, on one or two rare occasions, bright and strong, together with natural differences in the eyesight of the observers, made the results less reliable than would be desirable, but there has been no opportunity of repeating them. The results from 94 observations converted to metric units gave a mean measurement of .29 mm. with a standard deviation of .09 mm. Under pre-Columbian Mexican conditions we would expect a greater degree of accuracy, but imperfections in the straightness of the lines on the scale and possibly of the bar of the trapeze might reduce the accuracy of observations. We can probably regard .5 mm. as the minimum movement likely to be observed in practice, but ideally we should repeat the experiment in Mexico with a fairly crudely made instrument. The figure of .5 mm. is however near enough for our hypothesis. Mention must be made of an optical phenomenon noticed during the experiments. The black line appeared to create a bright thin area of light between itself and what may be termed the edge of the true shadow, after it had passed over the edge of the penumbra, and it was this which made the small readings possible. Obviously the black line could have no effect on the nature of the light impinging on the panel, so the effect must have been in the eye of the observers. The author is indebted to Arthur Hopkins of Reading University for an explanation of the nature of the penumbra. So far as the author, who is not a physicist, understands it, the more solid part of a shadow is caused by the obstruction of rays of light coming from the part of the sphere of the sun directly opposite, but light coming from any other part of the sphere is only seen at an angle to its radial direction from the centre of the sphere, and the intensity of the light diminishes with the angle. Owing to the subtended angle of the sun's disc, any light radiating from the sun's edge will be very weak, but it will impinge on the unilluminated area of the shadow, creating a graduation of the illumination at the edge of the shadow which becomes clearly differentiated only when the black line produces a contrasting effect which can be detected by the human eye. There is also the effect of the phenomenon known as Fresnil diffraction, which might have some bearing on the line of light, though Professor Hopkins does not think so. Whatever the explanation may be the phenomenon is there.

After this diversion into a subject about which the author is not really qualified to speak, we still have a probable figure of about half a millimetre. As the variation of the shadow on the scale will vary from day to day as a function of the declination, it will be very small in days near the solstices and comparatively large at other times of the year. The following table gives the day-to-day change in the position of the shadow, with an instrument with a trapeze 20 cm. above the scale, at thirteen-day intervals.

Table 1 Variation from day to day in the position of an instrument 20 cm. high at thirteen-day intervals, from solstice to equinox

Number of days from solstice	Difference in position of the shadow on consecutive days
0	negligible
13	.34 mm
26	.69 mm
39	1.01 mm
52	1.24 mm
65	1.31 mm
78	1.42 mm
91 (equinox)	1.40 mm

Applying our accuracy factor of about half a millimetre to these, we can say that for all except the two thirteen day intervals before and the two after the solstice it would be possible to observe the daily movement of the shadow, but during that period the readings would be unreliable or impossible between any two days. We now have a clue to the crosses on the Patolli board. If, as we have suggested, it was derived from a scale on the instrument representing thirteen day intervals, the crosses would indicate the part of the calendar when they were unable to distinguish the movement of the sun from day to day, though they would, of course, be able to observe the full thirteen-day period.

In conclusion there seems to be a very good case for equating the Patolli board with the trapeze and for believing that both were graduated in units of thirteen days. This does not necessarily imply that the primary basis for calendrical calculations was solar rather than lunar, but it does show an effective way of obtaining data for the correlation of the two. We may ask ourselves two questions. Did the possession of the instrument lead to the adoption of the enigmatic number 13, and the computing year of 364 days? The other question, rather more frivolous, is was the ban on the game of Patolli inspired by justifiable suspicions? Were the players really using the board as an abacus to compute their own calendar, and did they persuade the Spanish authorities that they were gambling as a cover for their forbidden activities?

Acknowledgments

The author is indebted to Mrs Doris Heyden and to Dr Otto Schondube for the photograph of Xochicalco; to B. Hellyer of the Science Museum, London for a formula for calculating azimuths and altitudes: to Professor Arthur Hopkins, who explained certain optical matters; to Dr Eric Thompson for valuable suggestions; to J. Kershaw for information on variations in the declination of the sun and on nutation, a phenomenon the author had never heard of before; and to Mr and Mrs Michael Glover and various friends and relations who acted as observers during the accuracy experiments.

REFERENCES

Caso, A. (1967) *Los calendarios prehispánicas* (a collected reprint of all Caso's calendrical papers). Universidad Autónoma de México.
Ditchburn, R.W. (1961) *Light.* London.
Girard, R. (1948) *El calendario Maya-Mexica.* Mexico.
Hoyle, F. (1967) *Astronomy.* London.
Herbert, A.P. (1963) *Sundials Old and New.* London.
H.M. Stationery Office (1961) *The American Ephemeris and Nautical Almanac;*

Explanatory Supplement to the Astronomical Ephemeris.

Joyce, T.A. (1913) *Mexican Archaeology.* London.

Marquina, I. (1951) *Arquitectura prehispánica.* Memorias del Instituto Nacional de Antropología y Historia, 1. Mexico.

Reed's Nautical Almanac (1972).

Sejourne, L. (1969) *Teotihuacan, metropole de l'Amérique.* Paris.

Solis, L.D. (1968) *La flor calendárica de los Mayas.* Merida, Yucatan.

Thompson, J.E.S. (1950) *Maya Hieroglyphic Writing: Introduction.* Carnegie Institute of Washington, Publication no. 589.

U.S. Hydrographic Office Tables of Computed Altitude and Azimuth (U.S. Hydrographic Office, publication no. H.O. 214. Also reproduced by H.M. Stationary Office as H.D. 486).

R.E.W. ADAMS

A trial estimation of Classic Maya palace populations at Uaxactun

The problem of estimating the sizes of the ancient populations of the Maya lowlands has several aspects: those of sample, technique, assumptions, and analogies. These are related to some degree to the social structural model one chooses to use, as well as to the period and the regional cultural variant selected. It has occurred to me that it might be useful to attempt an estimation of the size of the elite class population of one of the best excavated Maya ceremonial centres, using as a starting point the archaeological data as an independently derived, patterned piece of information.

The assumption of a Classic Maya social structure with a permanent, dynastically organized upper class is basic to this exercise. Justification of this assumption rests principally upon the evidence for hieroglyphic dynastic records developed by Proskouriakoff (1960), Kelley (1962), Berlin (1958), and others, in addition to the depictive data, indications of superior access to better nutrition (Haviland 1967), and of consistent, exclusive access to sumptuary goods by the same small group as reflected in graves (Rathje 1970).

The sample used is one derived from intensive excavation in the central Maya lowlands at the site of Uaxactun, where palace buildings have been excavated and/or mapped in detail. Supplemental information comes from sites well enough surveyed and preserved to provide patterns of architectural detail.

The sample involved is qualitatively best from the Late Classic period, especially from the latter part of it (*c*. A.D. 750-850); Rathje (1970) has argued that Classic period society changed from one in which authority was gained by those who accumulated wealth and open to all who did so, to one in which social status determined the access to both authority and wealth. This is a plausible interpretation of evidence from burial distribution and content. However, from the point of view of the dynastic records noted above, these clearly begin in the Early Classic period, that period during which, according to Rathje, there was a more open and achievement-oriented society. Further, palace residences also seem to be part of the Early Classic scene. Rathje reasonably argues that the appearance of special and sumptuous residences (palaces) signals a change in the nature of society in the Maya lowlands. My only quarrel is over the date at which this change takes place. Altar de Sacrificios, Tikal, and Uaxactun all have Early Classic palaces. The small site of Rio Azul has medium-sized palace structures which seem to be Early Classic. Holmul's palace-residential buildings may date to the Protoclassic. Thus the social change might well have taken place in the late Preclassic period. Whether or not the shift was of the sort that Rathje postulates, and whether or not it dates from A.D. 400 or A.D. 100, a pyramidal, elite-oriented social structure was undoubtedly in existence by A.D. 750.

I have argued elsewhere (1970) that Maya palaces are quite suitably arranged for elite class residence. Rooms which are fitted out with benches were designated as residential in function by Vaillant (Merwin and Vaillant 1931), but on an intuitive basis. Depictive evidence from several sites (e.g. the Bonampak murals) indicates that the benches were indeed living areas. The motor habits of the ancient Maya seem to have been well adapted to such physical arrangements, with a crosslegged 'tailor's' position being the favoured one for sitting. Confirmation of this interpretation comes from recent excavations at Becan, Campeche (Potter, in press), where palace rooms with benches in them are associated with such domestic features as built-in fireplaces, drains which serve tilted floors and which could have been baths, and many cupboards which might have served as storage places for portable furnishings. These cupboards seem to be correlated to a high degree with rooms with benches in them. This is also the case at Uaxactun (Smith, 1950: 78). Vaillant long ago noted that rooms with benches in them are consistently wider than other palace rooms. Finally, it should be noted that the rooms containing benches are grouped into clusters or what might be designated apartments of one or two rooms. These apartments tend to be together in clusters of from 2 to 8 rooms. They also, unlike palace rooms without benches, generally enjoy access to considerable outdoor paved area *on the same level.* For example, in the central acropolis palaces of Tikal, the upper floor rooms with benches open onto the stucco paved roofs of the first storey, providing accessory living space. The first storey rooms with benches, of course, have access to the paved courtyards and basal platforms on which the palace buildings are often set. In short, the argument for interpreting those clusters of palace rooms as living quarters which contain benches, and occasionally display other domestically functional features, seems strong.

The sizes of the domestic rooms, although they tend to be wider than rooms without benches, are still limited, usually not exceeding 19 square m. in the Uaxactun A-V palace. Taken together with the fact of the close association with outside space suitable for supplemental living area, the small spaces enclosed by the benched rooms suggests that they were mainly used for sleeping and associated purposes.

Negatively, one might also argue that given a dynastically organized permanent elite class, such a class should have had not only the extraordinary possessions that we find in their tombs and graves, but should also have lived in better housing. If we do not regard the palaces as select housing, the elite class must be relegated either to bush houses like those of the majority of population, or to perishable although sumptuous housing which has long since disappeared. Indeed, at sites such as Altar de Sacrificios where stone was scarce, there seems to have been a reliance on perishable housing for the upper class. However, even this was erected in the ceremonial centre and on quite large, stone-faced platforms. However, either of these alternatives seem less likely than alloting a certain amount of the palaces to elite residence. Referring to the accommodations of the elite of other early civilizations, it would be surprising if formal, community-built residences were not available to the Maya upper class. However, this is not a 'necessary condition' type of argument.

Granting that the above is convincing, then palace structures had at least a partial function as residential buildings. It is also undoubtedly true that they had additional functions as administrative, storage, and audience space, as has been suggested by many.

The above conclusions make it possible to apply some new techniques to the estimation of maximum numbers of elite class persons who might have been accommodated in Maya palaces.

One possible technique suggested by David Webster is to take a formula of about 10 square m. per person and apply it to the space available in any one palace building. Using the total floor space of the A-V palace at Uaxactun one arrives at about 214 persons in terms of maximum accommodation (Table 1). However, this seems much too high if one considers the A-V had functions other than residence, and if one considers that open paved area adjacent to the palace and on the roofs were probably living space also. The latter factor makes estimation by this means especially difficult since the open plazas have no clear architectural boundaries associating particular areas with particular buildings. Finally, it might be noted that Maya palace complexes are very individualistic and the amounts of space allotted to residence, administration, storage, court protocol, ritual and other functions are distinct in nearly every case. It may be that some such formula of space to person may be worked out, but as a start, this technique seems unlikely to reach any estimates of either the precision or order of magnitude that we need.

Another possibility suggests itself from the interpretation above of benches as the primary living space. The minimum function of housing is as protected sleeping space. An assumption must be made that benches served as the sleeping surfaces for elite class residents and that alternatives such as stick beds and hammocks were either not available or not used. The stick bed is not at all depicted in the art work that has survived from the Classic period, although it is mentioned in the historic sources. The origin of the hammock is a controversial matter and it is a device which may have been introduced from the circum-Caribbean area in the sixteenth-century. There is one possible depiction of the hammock on a piece of classic polychrome, the Pellicer Vase from Tabasco (Covarrubias 1957: 228). Even here, however, the swing or hammock in which a dignitary sits is made of jaguar skin, and not of woven material as was the case in South America or the Caribbean. The evidence for the Classic period use of the hammock seems fragile indeed. The most reasonable alternative seems to be the use of the benches.

Sleeping spaces can be measured on the benches and then a sex-age ratio of population derived from ethnographic or ethnohistoric sources and applied to arrive at some figure for the palace populations. This involves the final basic assumption that somewhere, historically or ethnographically, a population profile has been recorded that approximates that of the Classic period palace populations, and that we can recognize it.

An estimation of sleeping space available in the Uaxactun A-V palace requires the use of measured space on benches available during a single building phase, and therefore available for use at the same time. Phase IIh in the Late Classic period seems to have been the construction period during which maximum space was available in the palace. Based on stature figures, I am using 1.75 m. as a minimum adequate sleeping space for one adult. 1.50 m. is a generous space for width of sleeping space for two adults. Assuming that the nuclear family was represented most often as a residential unit, then pairs of adults and whatever children they may have had, probably occupied most of the apartment clusters in the palace. That such family units did occupy palace residential units is indicated by the scenes of elite class domesticity in the Bonampak murals. No doubt other residential social units did exist such as those including grandparents or other relatives. Such variations can probably be compensated for by using a general population age-sex profile from a conservative Maya village and imposing it on the total sleeping space of the palace.

Using the length/width figures, one arrives at 95 adult-sized sleeping spaces in Uaxactun structure A-V. Children up to the age of puberty (14) would take up only half the space necessary for an adult, and perhaps less. Assuming half spaces for children, then a maximum number of 190 children could be accommodated in the palace. However, with this number of children, no space for adults is available and perhaps no adult would wish to be present!

Obviously, the palace population was neither entirely adult nor entirely children, but a mix. Chan Kom has been a favourite source of demographic models for archaeologists. However, I am skeptical of the use of this village for the following reasons. In the matter of household size, it's average of 5.6 persons per house is probably much below the household size of most of its neighbouring villages. This is for the reason that Chan Kom was a first generation village of migrants at the time Redfield and his colleagues made their study and many of the old folks had been left in the parent village. Therefore, not only were the household sizes smaller than normal but the proportion of children in the total population was greater than normal (48%). I prefer to use the figures in Villa-Rojas' study of the X-Cacal subtribe of east-central Quintana Roo. In these conservative, more traditional villages, household sizes are larger (average 6.3), not crucial here, and children form about 33% of the population (Villa 1945: Table 4).

Using the X-Cacal population proportions, one arrives at a total Uaxactun A-V population of 114 people, of which 76 were adults and 38 were children. The data on A-V sleeping spaces is summarized in Table 1.

Table 2 summarizes room clustering and functional units in A-V, while Table 3 applies the percentiles derived from excavated zones to unexcavated palace buildings of Group B. It is estimated that 20 of the probable 34 rooms of the B palaces were residential. Accepting the estimate of 114 people in the A-V residential rooms, one arrives at an average of 2.53 persons of both sexes and all ages per room. Thus the B Group residential rooms represent a possible maximum capacity of 51 people.

Group C-H present relatively little problem in our estimates, even though they are unexcavated. C Group seems to consist of housemounds and the Early Classic pyramid (C-I). D Group contains but one building possibly large enough to be a formal palace structure, D-XX, which has exterior dimensions of only about 6 square m. A-V residential rooms are relatively large; up to 19 square m. It seems unlikely that more than 2 persons would be represented in this building. It may be that Group D was in disuse in Late Classic times in any case (Smith 1960: 63). E Group is seemingly non-residential, the only possible exception being E-X, which, however, lacks benches. Again, E Group may have been disused during Late Classic times. F Group has a possible palace building in Str. XIV, which about 10 square m. F Group is also Late Classic in date, but again it seems unlikely that a capacity of more than 3 or 4 people is represented by the building. G Group is another housemound cluster. H Group has two possible palaces, structures III and XI, measuring 30 and 60 square m. respectively. However they are so similar in conformation to other temple structures at Uaxactun, B-VIII for example, that I have deleted them from consideration. Structure A-IX probably contained nine rooms about the size of those in A-V, unit T. Fourteen persons might have been accommodated in A-IX.

Table 1 Available estimated sleeping spaces in Uaxactun

Building: A-V

Const: M	*Sleeping Spaces*	*Const: T*	*Sleeping Spaces*
		Room 75	2
Room No. 32	2	76	2
33	2	77	2
34	3 children	78	2
37	3 children	79	2
38	2	80	2
39	2	81	(10)
(8 adults & 6 children)	10 full spaces		

Const: N		*Const: W*	
		Room 82	2
Room 19 – (41)	2	84	4
42	2	85	2
	(4)	86	
		87	4
Const: Q		88	2
		89	4
Room 56	1		(18)
57	1		
58–59	2	*Const: L*	
91	4		
	8	Room 26	6
		30	2
Const: S		31	2
		29	2
Room 67	1	28	6
68	2	49	2
69	2	92	2
70	2	93	2
71	2	94	2
74	2		
	(11)	51	2
			(28)

Const: P			
Room 46	2	95 full	
47	2	spaces	
48	2		
	—		
	(6)		

Notes: 1. Phase IIh.
2. Room refs. to A.L. Smith 1950: Figs. 69-70.
3. All spaces are adult size unless otherwise specified.

Table 2a Room clustering and functional classification in Uaxactun A-V

Construction unit	Single rooms	2 Room clusters	3 Room clusters	4 (5) Room clusters	Non-residential
M	32/39	33-34, 37-38			
N	42	19-41			(general purpose)
P	48	46-47			
Q		56-57, 58-59			60/61
S	67/68/69/70				72/74
T	77/78/79	75-76, 80-81			
W	82/84/88-89		85-86-87		
L	26/28/29/31/49			30-92-93-94 (-29)	
C					5-6
G					13-14 (66)
H					15-16 (65)
I					17-18
R					62-63-64
Unit total:	21　+	8　+	1　+	1　　+	11 = 42
Total rooms:	21　+	16　+	3　+	4 (5?)　+	17 = 62

Table 2b Summary of A group room totals by functional category

Building	A-V		A-XVIII	A-IX	Cumulative Total	
Elite Residence	45	(73%)		9	53	56%
Religious ritual	10	(16%)			5	5%
Ceremonial	3	(5%)			16	17%
Unspecified (general purpose)	4	(6%)	15		21	22%
	62	(100%)			95	100%

Note:　Rooms 92-93-94 were closed after the Terminal Classic (ALS:43).

Table 3 Estimated residential rooms in Group B

Building	Number of Rooms
B-I	5
B-II	16 (est. 5 in missing 2nd story)
B-IX	5
B-XIII	4
B-XXV	4

Total of 34 unexcavated rooms. 56% are estimated as residential in use (see Table 2b), which is 19.

In sum, a maximum of 19 additional persons might be accommodated by the possible elite residential rooms of Group C to H. Thus a somewhat ephemeral 70 persons must be added to our estimates based on A-V, or 184 persons total.

Some implications of the above figures are particularly interesting. One of the aims of this paper is not to achieve a precise population profile, patently impossible at present, but an order of magnitude estimate. Such order of magnitude estimates have been made for the supporting population of centres like Uaxactun, but without reference to the elite class segments. The revision of the Uaxactun estimates given by Willey et al. (1965: 578) depend largely on ceilings established by the subsistence potential of maize-growing swidden cultivation utilizing about 114 square km. of arable land around the centre. Using Ursula Cowgill's median figure of about 76 persons per square arable kilometre (1962) as reasonable, then one comes to a total sustaining population of 8664. Adding the elite population (184), there were possibly 8849 persons involved in the life of this dispersed city. Of this number about 33 percent may have been below the age of puberty, leaving around 5894 adults to participate fully in the life of the community.

Possibilities of higher population which we have assumed to be placed on population growth are too limited. Importation of maize from outlying zones as far away as several hundred miles might be possible with use of favourable transportation facilities such as were available to sites on the rivers of the southern lowlands. Importation of dried fish from the coasts is a theoretical possibility that must be considered (Lange 1971). However, the data are strongly against this resource having been utilized (Ball & Eaton 1972). Root crops and ramon nuts are important supplements and dietary alternatives that might raise the population potential by factors of 2 or 3. Puleston's thesis is that *ramon* nuts were used as at least a supplemental crop and were possibly as important as maize. One of the stated advantages of the *ramon* nuts is that they are much more drought-resistant than maize. However, recent field observations made in 1970, 1971 and 1972 by J.W. Ball indicate that during the most severe droughts ramon nuts do not develop and that the crop is at least scarce and at worst non-existent. Ursula Cowgill has argued against the use of root crops as an important food source (1971). Even so, considering that during a run of good years, with supplementary foods from roots and nuts, population might have expanded beyond the limits set solely by the constraints of swidden-maize cultivation, then alternate total population figures might be double the figures given. On the other hand, Boserup has persuasively argued that population growth inspires intensification of agriculture rather than the other way around. Using the population solely dependent on maize and supplemental plants we have an interesting possibility of calculating the portion of the total population constituted by the elite class; 2

percent. Doubling the population figure (17,698), the elite class fraction drops to 1 percent. The adult males of the elite segment constituted an even smaller proportion of total population; under ½ or ¼ of one percent, dependent on whether one uses the lower or higher population estimates.

Judging by a reconstruction of southern lowland Classic social structure developed on the basis of depictive and artifactual evidence (Adams 1970) there must have been a considerable number of people in and around the ceremonial centres who catered to the needs of the elite and their political and economic organization. The question is, how many full-time, non-farming specialists were involved? Many specialities were presumably for maintenance of the centre as a whole and were part-time jobs. Construction specialities were probably of this nature. Small artifact manufacture, costume fabrication, sculpture, and personal service were probably full time occupations directly attached to elite class demand. Such civil servants as were present were probably attached to a single ruling family, with most of the leg-work done by non-specialists filling *cargo* obligations. Jade and jade-working skills were such scarce commodities that the precious stone was probably imported in finished form to a centre the size of Uaxactun. This is implied by the fact that jade pieces found at Uaxactun stylistically closely resemble other pieces from the central lowlands. Conversely, there is not enough jade at the site to argue that Uaxactun was the jade centre for the region. Neither did the centre fabricate its own obsidian artifacts. Tikal, 20 kms. to the south, has literally tons of debitage (W.R. Coe, personal communication), where Uaxactun produced a couple of sacks full during the 12 years of excavation. Tikal seems to have been the obsidian redistribution centre and also to have fabricated the incised obsidians found under stelae at Uaxactun. Both jade and obsidian were imports from the Guatemalan highlands and it seems that Tikal may have had the regional monopology on both. Thus we probably can conclude that Uaxactun had no lapidaries of its own.

The polychrome pottery produced in such quantities was possibly a different matter. Culbert (personal communication) and Rands have evidence for village craft specialization around the large lowland centres of Tikal and Palenque. It may well be that a community subject to Uaxactun, or even the ceremonial centre itself, acted as the regional factory. Stylistic studies suggest this at Uaxactun, Tikal, Altar de Sacrificios, and technological studies indicate it for the Palenque region; polychrome potters of sufficient sophistication to turn out the finest products at Uaxactun were probably not local. The evidence for funerary visitation by related elites from other ceramic regions (Adams 1971) would indicate that these items might be imported from outside the zone, brought to the centre as final gifts to the dead by relatives. Sculpture and stucco modelling were undoubtedly local specialities, judging from the amount of them at

Uaxactun. Perhaps a single sculptor, with an assistant, could have accounted for both types of art work of any single period.

Personal servants probably made up the bulk of the full-time, non-elite, non-farmers. I estimate the number of households at about 50 based on the number of apartment units of all sizes in the palaces. I can only suggest two servants per household as the minimum necessary to take care of domestic needs. Assuming that the elite class did nothing towards the domestic workload, then servants were needed to cook, serve, haul water, clean the apartment, care for children, and run errands. This gives a result of about 100 servants to care for the elite of Uaxactun. Domestic duties may well have been taken care of on a rotational basis by the general population, and therefore the 100 is not incremental to the population figures given before. Domestic service is well known to have been part of the tribute owed the upper classes by the lower in sixteenth-century native society of Mexico and Yucatan. As seen above, the number of craft specialists could have been relatively insignificant in numbers.

To return to our order of magnitude perspective, then, it seems that in the case of a centre the size of Uaxactun we are dealing with an elite class population certainly less than 200 in number, probably less than 150. These aristocrats constituted less than 2 percent of the population and quite possibly less than 1 percent of it. If only adult males had full participation in civil, military, and religious affairs in the Uaxactun zone (there are no detectable records of women in the texts there, and only one woman (burial B-1) was in a burial chamber) they were only a half or a quarter of one percent of the total population; about 30 in number.

Turning to other sites, Tikal and Becan offer some of the best possibilities for tests of the formulae and figures developed from the Uaxactun exercise. However, the Tikal data seem to vary significantly from those of Uaxactun, with a much lower percentage of the Central Acropolis palace area being residential than expected. This is subject to two alternative interpretations. One is that our figures and methods are wrong. Another is that excavation sampling at Tikal, where the only large palace exposure was in the Central Acropolis, has biased the results. This is the palace zone nearest to the major temple cluster of the North Acropolis and to the main plaza with its clustering of memorial stelae. It may well be that much more of the Central Acropolis was devoted to administration and ceremonial functions for this reason, and that the major elite residential areas were such palace clusters as old Group F (Str. 5E1/5F45-48, Carr and Hazard 1961), the South Acropolis, and the structures of the enclosed courts to the East of the Central Acropolis (Strs. 5E 55-60). Approaching Tikal with another set of figures, Haviland's most recent estimates of the total Tikal population as 40,000 (1970) might indicate a maximum elite class of 1 to 2 percent or 400 to 800 persons housed in the formal palace residences. Because of the difficulties of sample at such a large site as Tikal it is not certain at present whether the capacity to house such an elite population in formal palaces actually existed. Tikal, however, does represent a population contemporary with that of Uaxactun, the elite residences dating to the middle of the Late Classic. There is an order of magnitude of difference between elite class sizes, as might be expected. At Becan, although the rooms suitable for residence seem generally larger, the formulas seem to fit well. Larger room size in the Rio Bec area does not necessarily imply a larger elite class population, however, since it may be that there was simply a preference for more space per person in this cultural district. Uaxactun seems to have got along with minimum space.

If the above figures are approximately correct, then it becomes easier to understand how the socially disruptive and biologically catastrophic events of the late ninth century A.D. (Willey and Shimkin 1971) could have swept away the small directing elites, and left only leaderless remnants of population.

REFERENCES

Adams, R.E.W. (1970) Suggested Classic period occupational specialization in the southern Maya lowlands. In W.R. Bullard, Jr. (ed.), *Monographs and Papers in Maya Archaeology.* Papers of the Peabody Museum of Archaeology and Ethnology, vol. 61.

Adams, R.E.W. (1970) in press (ed.) *Preliminary Papers on the Archaeology of the Maya Lowland Intermediate Area.* Middle American Research Institute, Tulane University, New Orleans.

Ball, J.W., and J.D. Eaton (1972) Marine resources and the prehistoric lowland Maya: a comment. *American Anthropologist,* 74, 772-6.

Berlin, H. (1958) El glifo 'emblema' en las inscripciones Mayas. *Journal de la Societé des Americanistes de Paris,* n.s., 47, 111-19.

Boserup, E. (1965) *The Conditions of Agricultural Growth: The Economics of Agrarian Change under Population Pressure.* London.

Carr, R.F. and J.E. Hazard (1961) *Map of the Ruins of Tikal, El Peten, Guatemala.* Tikal Report no. 11, University Museum, University of Pennsylvania, Philadelphia.

Covarrubias, M. (1957) *Indian Art of Mexico and Central America.* New York.

Cowgill, U.M. (1962) An agricultural study of the southern Maya lowlands. *American Anthropologist,* 64, 273-86.

Cowgill, U.M. (1971) Some comments on *manihot* subsistence and the ancient Maya. *Southwestern Journal of Anthropology,* 27, 51-63.

Haviland, W.A. (1967) Stature at Tikal, Guatemala: implications for ancient Maya demography and social organization. *American Antiquity,* 32, 316-25.

Haviland, W.A. (1970) Tikal, Guatemala, and Mesoamerican urbanism. *World Archaeology,* 2, 186-98.

Kelley, D. (1962) Glyphic evidence for a dynastic sequence at Quirigua, Guatemala. *American Antiquity,* 27, 323-35.

Lange, F.W. (1971) Marine resources: a viable subsistence alternative for the pre-historic lowland Maya. *American Anthropologist,* 73, 619-39.

Merwin, R.E. and G.C. Vaillant (1932) *The Ruins of Holmul, Guatemala.* Memoirs of the Peabody Museum of Archaeology and Ethnology, Harvard University, vol. 3, no. 2.

Potter, D. (in press) *Civic Architecture at Becan, Campeche, Mexico.*

Proskouriakoff, T. (1960) Historical implications of a pattern of dates at Piedras Negras, Guatemala. *American Antiquity*, 25, 454-75.

Rathje, W.L. (1970) Socio-political implications of lowland Maya burials: methodology and tentative hypotheses. *World Archaeology*, 1, 359-74.

Smith, A.L. (1950) *Uaxactun, Guatemala: Excavations of 1931-1937.* Carnegie Institution of Washington, Publication no. 588.

Villa Rojas, Alfonso (1945) *The Maya of East Central Quintana Roo.* Carnegie Institution of Washington, Publication no. 559.

Willey, G.R., R. Bullard, Jr., J.B. Glass and J.C. Gifford (1965) *Prehistoric Maya Settlements in the Belize Valley.* Papers of the Peabody Museum of Archaeology and Ethnology, Harvard University, vol. 54.

Willey, G.R. and D.B. Shimkin (1971) The collapse of Classic Maya civilization in the southern lowlands: symposium summary statement. *Southwestern Journal of Anthropology*, 27, 1-18.

J. ERIC S. THOMPSON

'Canals' of the Rio Candelaria basin, Campeche, Mexico

In their highly important article on ridged fields in southern Campeche in the April 1972 issue of *American Antiquity*, Siemens and Puleston discuss the many apparent ancient waterways of the upper Candelaria which 'seem to be the marks of former access canals between rivers and settlements or *milpas*'; as well as others which roughly parallel the Candelaria river and which, they suggest, 'could have been built mainly to circumvent river bends'.

It is certain that the Maya constructed canals. The clearest case is the canal joining two lakes by the site of Muyil on the east coast of Quintana Roo (Mason 1927: 161). Quirigua produces less certain evidence. In discussing the transportation of stelae from quarry to that site, Hewett (1912: 166-67) wrote that 'traces of a series of canals are to be seen in and about the ruins', and he speculated that the stelae were rafted along these.

Nevertheless, the lines marking observed 'canals' on the Siemens and Puleston map of the upper Candelaria (reproduced here as Fig. 1) hardly bear out the view that the greater part of these could have served as access canals. Relatively few connect with the river; many instead appear to start and finish right in swampland, or they connect two areas of higher ground. Indeed, some in the flood plain are a mere 200 to 300 m. long and lead nowhere; others are so close together that one can only accept the reluctant conclusion that the Maya with great labour constructed these canals to serve as aquatic equivalents of eight-lane highways. Puleston informs me that these waterways close together are up to nearly 10 m. wide (in contrast to the long waterways which run from 1.50 to 3 m. wide).

The bypass explanation offered for those waterways which roughly parallel the river is hardly convincing. The long bypass canal seen in the centre of the map is scarcely shorter than the section of smooth-flowing river bypassed. If built as a bypass, it seems a singularly wasteful procedure; it circumvents no rapids, merely a glassy stream such as that in which Ophelia met her end. If not mainly for canoe traffic, what purpose can these waterways have served?

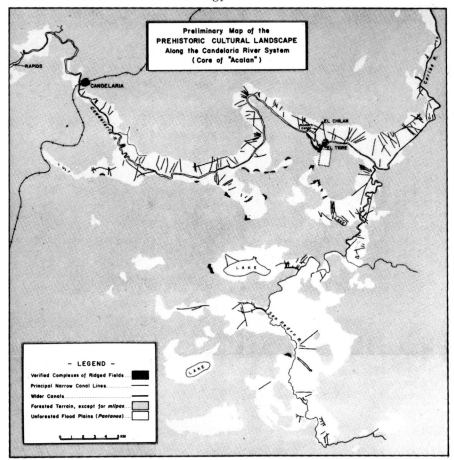

Figure 1   The upper Candelaria showing waterways and ridged fields. After Siemens and Puleston.

There is some evidence, not as strong as one might wish, which permits an alternative explanation, namely that many of them may have served as fisheries, for they lie in the low areas, under water during the rainy season and swampy at other times, bordering the river. During the rainy season, when 'the floods have lift up their voice', they bring fish downstream into the swamp. As the waters recede in the dry season many fish take refuge in natural or, in this case, artificial waterways in those swamps, where they can be easily caught.

The Putun *cacique* Pablo Paxbolon made a trip up the Candelaria in 1566 to round up apostate Indians near Itzamkanac, where the 'canals' are thick on the ground or, rather, in the swamp. He knew the area well, for he had lived there as a boy until the settlement was moved to Tixchel, on the coast, in 1557. In describing his trip, he told of how, after a troublesome passage of the rapids, he reached the sluggish upper reaches of the river where he and his party stopped to fish in the 'lagoons' (Scholes and Roys 1948: 188, 431). The last rapid is marked on the extreme left of the map. Accordingly, he was fishing the 'lagoons' in the area covered by the map, all of which, except for the short section of river (half of which is bordered by high ground) below Candelaria town, shows 'canals' in profusion crisscrossing the swamp land on either side of the river.

One should mark Paxbolon's use of the term which has come down to us as 'lagoons'. He specifically states that he was fishing, not in the river, but in lagoons, but there are no lagoons along that part of the Candelaria. Paxbolon was a Putun (Chontal) Maya and wrote his reports in Putun even in the 1560s. I have not access to the Spanish version but suppose that the term there used was *lagunas*. The Maya tended to use a general term applicable to swamp, marsh and lagoon; for example the Yucatec *ukum* was used for the above and even extended to cover rivers, apparently those flowing through swamps, and lagoons, for the river connecting Lake Bacalar with the Rio Hondo which passes through lagoons and stretches of swamp and, near its mouth, divides into many streams separated by a great number of small islands, was called Noh (Great) Ukum. Roys (1957: 159) identifies this with the Rio Hondo, but the description does not tally; the Hondo's mouth is without those many islands. The Noh Ukum surely takes its name from the lakes and swamps through which it sluggishly flows.

In view of the above, there is a strong possibility that Paxbolon, in his original description in Putun of the trip, used a term referable, not to the non-existent lakes, but to the semi-swamp with its artificial waterways found by Siemens and Puleston in this very region.

Swamps make poor fishing grounds. One may, therefore, reasonably suppose that Paxbolon and his men stopped to fish in that particular stretch of river above the rapids because they were well acquainted with its advantages. The party reached the upper Candelaria on April 30, at the close of the dry season, when the low semi-swamp would have dried, but there would be water in the 'canals', and, I submit, Paxbolon knew from the days of his youth that at that time those artificial waterways held much fish.

Perhaps these waterways were constructed, repaired or augmented in proto-historic times when the Putun group in question moved inland from the coast, where it had lived close to famous fishing grounds, to settle on the upper Candelaria, in the precise area covered by the Siemens and Puleston map. They would have met the newcomers' former dependence on a good fish supply and, with a little fencing, might have insured a constant stock of turtles, for the coastal Putun had developed a flourishing industry of worked tortoiseshell. One might speculate that the people of the upper Candelaria, perhaps at a far earlier horizon than the proto-historic, being well aware of the use of natural fish refuges, as described below, but lacking that geographical advantage in their own territory, constructed artificial ones.

Naturally, some artificial waterways in the area might have been used for canoe traffic — Siemens and Puleston note one access canoe in the area made by recent arrivals of non-Indian culture — and some may have served both as fish refuges and as canals, but very many, notably those of greatest width which are grouped close together in near parallel lines, which do not reach the river, are, I feel convinced, fish refuges. If many have that function, it is likely that all were constructed for the same reason.

There is evidence for fish refuges elsewhere in Middle America. Michael Coe informs me of the technique being used near the great Olmec site of San Lorenzo, in the Coatzacoalcos drainage. He writes: 'Dry-season fishing at San Lorenzo is predicated upon the existence of ox-bow lakes and small back-swamp ponds which are replenished when the rains come and all the low-lying land is flooded. As the dry season advances, the fish become increasingly concentrated, and seine- and throw-net fishing is intensified. In the wet season, tarpon and gar are harpooned or speared from dugouts over the now-flooded savannas. There are no artificial canals now, and I can detect none from the aerial photos.'

Fish refuges may have been used in the sixteenth century in the Grijalva-Usumacinta delta, which lies about midway between the upper Candelaria and San Lorenzo. The *relación* dated 1579 of Santa María de la Victoria, previously Potonchan, the ancient Putun Maya capital at the mouth of the Grijalva, informs us that the Indians fished in the rivers and *ciénagas*, and their catches were a very important food source (*Relaciones de Yucatan*, 1898, 1: 369). *Ciénaga* is marsh or swamp; as swamps do not themselves harbour large quantities of fish, this statement may refer to natural or perhaps even man-made fish refuges in the swamps.

Certainly, vast numbers of small lagoons, stretches of backwaters and waterways, all holding water, are visible to an observer flying over that huge semi-swamp and low savanna area in the dry season. In past flights, unaware of the problem, I had not looked for any that might have been artificial. In fact, with so many natural fish refuges in this delta land, there may have been little or no need for making them, although closer inspection may show sections where natural fish refuges are few or entirely absent. In any case, the same method of taking fish entrapped when the waters were dried up from the face of the earth would have been followed whether the refuges were natural or artificial.

Data on pre-Colombian fishing techniques in Middle America are rare. Carrasco (1950: 68) cites an entry in the Basalenque Spanish-Matlaltzinca vocabulary of 1641: *canal de pescado donde pescan, nicaxthoth*. This could mean an artificial fish refuge such as postulated for the upper Candelaria. Among towns of the Province of Tochtepec listed in the *Codex Mendoza* (p. 46) is Michapan, signifying fish canal; the glyph shows a fish in a canal presented in cross section. Peñafiel (1885: 141) read this *en el agua que tiene pesca* or *rio de pescados*, although noting that *apan* signifies canal. Indeed, river is *atoyatl*, and that term would have been incorporated, had the place name referred to a river with fish. *Michapan* could refer to an irrigation, or even a traffic, canal which chanced to have fish in it, but more probably it refers to an artificial fish refuge. The location of the site is uncertain; Barlow (1949, map) gives a queried position in southern Veracruz south of the great swamp between the San Juan and Tesechoacan rivers and some 60 km. WNW of San Lorenzo itself, of whose natural fish refuges we have already quoted Coe's account. Barlow gives no reason for his tentative position of Michapan; it may be mere coincidence that his location seems significant in terms of fish refuges.

The Molina vocabulary has *estanque de pescado, michacaxitl, michamanalli,* good evidence for fish-stocking, but hardly referable to fish refuges.

Outside Middle America there is evidence of water refuges and even more advanced forms of fish conservancy. Thomas S. Schorr, who has made a special study of this subject, has kindly allowed me to refer to certain material in his forthcoming report on channelled depressions — his preferred term for ridged fields — in Colombia. He has documentary evidence for pisciculture in one such formation in the central Cauca valley as early as the sixteenth century; and he has observed present-day fishing in channelled depressions in the same general region.

Gordon Willey (1966-71: vol. 2, Fig. 5.77) publishes a photograph after J.J. Parsons (1966) of the San Jorge basin of the lower Magdalena, Colombia, identified as of agricultural ridged fields. It seems possible that fish refuges are an alternative explanation of these channels.

In India and southeastern Asia, I am given to understand, fish refuges comparable to those deduced for the upper Candelaria are common.

The above interpretation of the 'canals' of the upper Candelaria, if generally accepted, contributes to the problem of Maya sustenance, and invites us to pay more attention to fish refuges, whether natural or artificial, as highly beneficial to local nutrition and perhaps commerce.

REFERENCES

Barlow, R.H. (1948) The extent of the empire of the Culhua Mexica. *Ibero-Americana*, 28.

Carrasco, P. (1950) *Los Otomies: Cultura e historia prehispánicas de los pueblos Mesoamericanos de habla Otomiana.* Universidad Nacional de México.

Hewett, E.L. (1912) The excavations at Quirigua in 1912. *Archaeological Institute of America Bulletin 3*, 163-71. Santa Fe.

Mason, G. (1927) *Silver Cities of Yucatan.* New York and London.

Parsons, J.J. (1966) Los campos de cultivos prehispánicos del Bajo San Jorge. Academia Colombiana de Ciencias Exactas, Físicas y Naturales, *Revista*, 12, 449-58. Bogotá.

Peñafiel, A. (1885) *Nombres geográficos de México . . . Estudio jeroglífico de la matrícula de los tributos del Códice Mendocino.* Mexico.

Relaciones de Yucatan (1898-1900) *Colección de documentos inéditos relativos al descubrimiento, conquista y organización de las antiguas posesiones españolas de ultramar.* vols. 11 and 13. Madrid.

Roys, R.L. (1957) *The Political Geography of the Yucatan Maya.* Carnegie Institution of Washington, Publication no. 613.

Scholes, F.V. and R.L. Roys (1948) *The Maya Chontal Indians of Acalan-Tixchel: a Contribution to the History and Ethnography of the Yucatan Peninsula.* Carnegie Institution of Washington, Publication no. 560.

Siemens, A.H. and D.E. Puleston (1972) Ridged fields and associated features in southern Campeche: new perspectives on the lowland Maya. *American Antiquity*, 37, 228-39.

Willey, G.R. (1966-71) *An Introduction to American Archaeology.* 2 vols. New York.

DENNIS E. PULESTON

Intersite areas in the vicinity of Tikal and Uaxactun

In spite of all the attention that has been focussed on the ancient Maya in recent years, an overwhelming bias towards the investigation and excavation of 'ceremonial centres' has made it very difficult to deal with overall questions regarding demography and subsistence. This in turn has placed serious limitations on our ability to reconstruct diachronic models of how this civilization functioned and grew. One of the important areas that has been neglected as a result of this bias is the space between sites, which I will refer to as 'intersite areas'. It is these areas which I wish to discuss here, in the light of the settlement pattern survey completed at Tikal in 1968.

What is an 'intersite area'? Clearly the definition rests on the definition of 'site'. Here I will attempt to follow Willey and Phillips (1958: 18) who write that 'about the only requirement ordinarily demanded of the site is that it be fairly continuously covered by remains of former occupation'. It follows that we must classify what is meant by 'continuously covered' and at this point I think that it is useful to recognize the applicability of the term to two discrete levels with respect to ancient Maya settlement. The first occurs at the level of the 'household'. As one of the basic units of Maya settlement, the plaza unit, consisting of one to four or more structures arranged around a paved plaza surface, represents the epitome of 'site' as Willey and Phillips define it. The second occurs at the level of 'community', as when we speak of the site of Tikal. Where then do we put 'site' limits? The settlement pattern survey I have referred to above reveals a well-marked drop in Classic period settlement density that coincides with the line of Tikal's apparently defensive earthworks system (Puleston and Callender 1967: Fig. 1) located 4.5 km. north and 8.8 km. southeast of the centre of Tikal (Fig. 1). I have accepted this combination of 'emic' (the earthworks) and 'etic' (the drop off in settlement density) boundaries as representing the limits of the site. Since the full extent of the earthworks is still not known and the entire area has not been mapped, the total area of Tikal is therefore estimated to be approximately 120 square km. The terrain

Figure 1 Overall map of the Tikal National Park and Uaxactun area covered by the Tikal survey. Mapped areas are indicated by the dot-dash line. The cruciform Ricketson survey at Uaxactun should be shifted slightly to the left.

outside this feature and outside possibly similar site limits for Uaxactun and other sites represents the 'intersite area'.

Recent interest in settlement patterns has produced much important new information on residential settlement (Haviland 1966). Almost invariably, however, such studies have been carried out in the immediate vicinity of a major centre, and undoubtedly within site limits, if Tikal presents a typical pattern. Bullard's (1960) trail survey of the northeast Peten presents an important exception to this, but before I refer to this study in particular I would like briefly to examine two factors which have contributed to the lack of information on intersite areas.

The first of these is the overall 'site orientation' of archaeology. Almost invariably archaeological investigations in the Maya lowlands, perhaps more frequently than elsewhere, have begun at the centre of some major or minor architectural complex and worked outwards as far as funding and available labour would permit. Because of the size and complexity of ancient Maya centres this has generally not been very far in proportion to the total area that seems to be covered by these sites. A second reason for this bias in this region is the density of southern lowlands vegetation, which does not permit free-ranging surveys with the aid of aerial photographs such as are presently being carried out in the valleys of Mexico and Oaxaca.

Despite the paucity of data, information regarding overall site and intersite settlement patterns and density has long been recognized as crucial for the resolution of problems such as whether the larger ancient Maya sites were 'ceremonial centres', without a significant residential populations or 'cities', and whether extensive or intensive food producing techniques formed the basis of Classic Maya subsistence (Willey 1956). Ricketson's (Ricketson and Ricketson 1937) Uaxactun house mound survey represents the first concerted effort to obtain residential settlement data in the southern Maya lowlands. On an area of 1.94 square km., 78 structures were located indicating a density of 40 structures/square km. Assuming his sample to be fairly representative of settlement all over the lowlands, Ricketson went on to estimate tentatively the population of the entire Yucatan peninsula. It now appears that the entire survey probably lies within the limits of what could fairly be called the 'site' of Uaxactun. For this reason the survey is representative only of more densely settled site areas. Careful remapping of the south arm of Ricketson's survey, however, reveals that his mappers overlooked more than 60 percent of the visible structures (Fig. 2). This can probably be attributed to over-caution in the designation of these features and the lack of previous knowledge as to what house ruins looked like. Thus if we eliminate Ricketson's survey, the only data on intersite settlement come from what are best referred to as trail surveys. Basically, these surveys have been carried out by taking notes on mounds and chultuns that are encountered along the mule trails that crisscross the

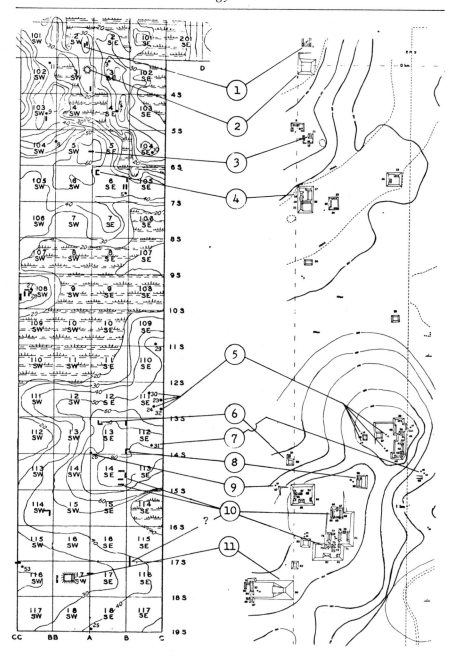

Figure 2 A group by group comparison of the Ricketson and Tikal-based surveys of settlement just south of Uaxactun. About 60 percent of structures mapped in the more recent survey were missed by the earlier survey.

Peten. Bullard's (1960) survey has been one of the most useful of these. Others have been carried out by Tozzer (1913 Pl. 31) and Graham (1967: 40). Unfortunately there are serious limitations to these data. The density of vegetation to the left and right of trails, particularly in the Peten, makes it virtually impossible to see enough of the countryside to obtain a sample that would allow one to characterize settlement density correctly for any particular area. The dispersed nature of Maya settlement makes it easy to pass right through settlements without seeing them. On one portion of the south survey strip at Tikal, between 3.5 and 4.6 km. south, it is possible to walk down the trail through one of the most heavily settled areas on the strip without seeing a single platform, simply because of the thickness of the undergrowth.

Bullard (1960: 370) on the basis of his survey concluded that settlement density was principally conditioned by the availability of water and large, level, well drained areas suitable for house sites. He did not feel that 'house mound' concentrations near ceremonial ruins were any greater than elsewhere. This view was sustained by Willey in his reviews of the Tikal maps, when he wrote that for the time being he would 'like to hold to the argument that the density of small mound structures is just as great in localities at some distance from the ceremonial centres as it is in close proximity to such centres — even in close proximity to Tikal' (Willey 1962: 118). In light of the Tikal survey, which I will now describe briefly, I feel that this view of ancient Maya settlement can be demonstrated to be incorrect.

For the Tikal survey we used a trail datum, much as Bullard did, though in our case it was a series of straight survey trails which we carefully measured and staked. All but the Uaxactun section of these trails were survey trails which were laid out, extending 12 km. north, south, east and west from the centre of Tikal, by the surveyors of the Tikal National Park. Thus we were unable to escape entirely from the site orientation of earlier projects. Mapping was accomplished by 5-man mapping teams, using a Brunton compass and pace technique, that went out 125 m. to either side of the survey trails. Tests of the technique on plane table mapped portions of Tikal revealed that while accuracy of group locations was inevitably less precise, coverage, with the exception of chultuns, was essentially just as complete as by slower methods.

In all a total of more than 25 square km. was mapped. If the strips are extended into the already well-mapped central 9 square km. of Tikal another 2.7 square km. can be added to the strip samples. In a more detailed analysis of these data I have separated architectural and settlement remains into four categories; (1) epicentral Tikal, a nucleus of ceremonial and what are probably elite residential structures (Harrison 1968), (2) residential Tikal, which extends out to the earth-works, (3) residential Uaxactun, which extends about 2 km. south from the centre of Ricketson's survey where settlement density declines sharply, and (4) intersite areas. We will now look at settlement density in the latter three categories. If we combine the residential portions of the site of Tikal from the four survey strips we can produce a sample area totalling 11.25 square km. on which 1347 structures were found. The total intersite portions of the survey strips comes to 15.12 square km. on which 596 structures were found. The sample of the Uaxactun residential area is quite small, 1.0 square km. 112 structures were found on it. Hereafter it will be included with the Tikal data so that we have only *two* basic categories, (1) site residential areas and (2) intersite areas.

Table 1 The calculation of upland settlement density

	Total area of sample (km²)	Total no. of structures	Total area* of available uplands (km²)	Upland settlement density structures (per km²)
site residential areas	12.25	1459	7.42	197
intersite areas	15.12	596	6.76	88

* Area taken up by structures and plazas has been subtracted.

In terms of raw densities this provides a contrasting 119 structures/square km. for the combined 'site residential areas' and 39 structures/square km. for intersite areas. On this basis, intersite settlement is roughly one third as dense as in 'site' areas. These figures should not be accepted at face value, however, for the terrain further from Tikal is interlaced with greater proportions of swamp or *bajo* than are found nearer the centre of the site. As the areas of three different kinds of *bajo*, as well as uplands, have been calculated individually for every quarter square km. of the mapped area, this variable can be controlled.

Thus, when 4.25 square km. and 8.08 square km. of *bajo* are subtracted respectively from the total 'site residential' and 'intersite' areas, a more meaningful comparison of settlement densities can be made. When this is done (see Table 1) we find 197 structures/square km. in the site residential areas and 88 structures/square km. in the combined intersite areas, indicating that uplands settlement is more than twice as dense in site areas as it is in intersite areas.

The fact that a ceramic test-pit survey was carried out in conjunction with the mapping project allows us to extend this disucssion a bit further. The survey carried out by Robert Fry (1969) combined a stratified sampling technique with randomized selection of about one third of all the plaza units on the north and south strips. Out of a total of 90 groups tested, 41 were located in what I have included as intersite areas here. Some important patterns are revealed. In comparison with areas within what later becomes the site residential area I have discussed above, Preclassic settlement is comparatively light. Sometime during Early Classic times there appears to have been a really substantial increase in population. While out of 41 tested groups only 7 showed even possible evidence of Preclassic occupation, all but 1 produced evidence of Early Classic occupation. This does not mean that all these structures were occupied contemporaneously. Carefully excavated Early Classic residential structures carried out both by William Haviland in the central 9 square km. of Tikal and others in intersite areas do not seem to show the degree of sequent construction that is so typical of Late Classic structures.

In Late Classic times a curious change takes place in certain parts of the intersite areas. Many plaza units which were occupied in Early Classic times are occupied sporadically or in some cases abandoned never to be occupied in Late Classic times at all. This is in direct contrast to the pattern revealed by the excavation of well over a hundred structures in the central 9 square km. of Tikal where all mapped groups were probably in use during at least one point of time within the Late Classic Period, roughly A.D. 770 (Haviland 1970: 192). It seems possible that this is evidence of 'centralization' as described by Flannery (1972). Elsewhere (Puleston 1968) I have suggested that these areas might have been taken over for slash-and-burn cultivation of maize by the elite. Another possibility is that increasing friction and the danger of raids may have made these peripheral areas less desirable for permanent kitchen gardens. Certainly important changes in intersite settlement patterns took place between Early and Late Classic times.

It is important to point out, however, that population density still appears to have been high in these areas. I include here some greatly simplified and preliminary calculations. Following Haviland (1970) I will assume that 16 percent of the structures occupied in Late Classic times were non-residential. If the remainder were occupied by an average of 5.4 persons, a figure derived from the measurement of structure floor areas by following Naroll's (1962) formula, overall population density on the intersite upland may have been as high as 300 persons/square km. This is still considerably lower than the figure of 900 persons/square km. which can be derived from the site residential area. Non-contemporaneity of occupation in intersite areas may reduce the intersite population density figure considerably. I would suspect, however, that it would still be much too high to have allowed this area to have served as a slash-and-burn agriculture 'sustaining area' for the more heavily settled 'site' area even if the higher bajos were under cultivation.

Moving on to Postclassic times we come to the most dramatic change of all. The discovery of only one definite locus of Caban ceramics in the test-pitting of both the north and south strips argues strongly against the possibility that in Postclassic times significant populations may have continued to occupy peripheral areas, even after the ceremonial and administrative centres were totally abandoned. All indications are that apart from very isolated instances, the Tikal area, in contrast to other parts of Peten, really was almost totally abandoned after the collapse.

I would like to summarize by emphasizing the following points: (1) important differentials exist between settlement densities inside and outside the Tikal earthworks: (2) this differential may be used to define what can be fairly considered 'site limits': (3) on the basis of these limits the site of Tikal may have covered an area of 120 square km. (4) at other Maya sites where earthworks have not been found sensitive mapping is going to be necessary in order to define site limits of the basis of density differentials: (5) settlement density in intersite areas around Tikal is high, probably too high to have allowed these areas to have served as maize producing sustaining areas for the site proper, forcing us back to the probability that the ancient Maya were depending on intensive cultivation of high yield crops, such as root crops and the *ramon* or breadnut: (6) there is no evidence for the existence of a significant Postclassic population in the peripheral intersite areas we have surveyed.

In conclusion I would like to say that I believe it would be well worth our while to devote considerably more energy to quantified study of intersite areas than we have to date. Comparative data are badly needed for other parts of the lowlands, and until such studies are carried out, our discussions of prehistoric demographic patterns will be significantly impaired.

REFERENCES

Bullard, W.R., Jr. (1960) Maya settlement pattern in northeastern Peten, Guatemala. *American Antiquity*, 25, 355-72.
Flannery, K.V. (1972) The cultural evolution of civilizations. *Annual Review of Ecology and Systematics*, 3.
Fry, R.E. (1969) *Ceramics and Settlement in the Periphery of Tikal, Guatemala.* Ph.D. dissertation, Department of Anthropology, University of Arizona. University Microfilms, Ann Arbor.
Graham, I. (1967) *Archaeological Exploration in El Peten, Guatemala.* Middle American Research Institute, Publication no. 33.
Harrison, P.D. (1968) Form and function in a Maya 'palace' group. *38th International Congress of Americanists* (Stuttgart, 1968), vol. 1, 165-72.
Haviland, W.A. (1966) *Maya Settlement Patterns: A Critical Review.* Middle American Research Institute, Publication no. 26, 21-47.
Haviland, W.A. (1970) Tikal, Guatemala and Mesoamerican urbanism. *World Archaeology*, 2, 186-98.
Naroll, R. (1962) Floor area and settlement pattern. *American Antiquity*, 27, 587-9.
Puleston, D.E. and D.W. Callender, Jr. (1967) Defensive earthworks at Tikal. *Expedition* 9, no. 3, 40-8.
Puleston, D.E. (1968) *Brosimum alicastrum* as a subsistence alternative for the Classic Maya of the central southern lowlands. M.A. Thesis, Department of Anthropology, University of Pennsylvania. University Microfilms, Ann Arbor.
Ricketson, O.G. and E.G. Ricketson (1937) *Uaxactun, Guatemala, Group E-1926-1931.* Carnegie Institution of Washington, Publication no. 477.
Tozzer, A.A. (1913) A preliminary study of the prehistoric ruins of Nakum, Guatemala. *Memoirs of the Peabody Museum of American Archaeology and Ethnology*, 5, 136-97.

Willey, G. (1956) Problems concerning prehistoric settlement patterns in the Maya lowlands. In G.R. Willey (ed.), *Prehistoric Settlement Patterns in the New World*, Viking Fund Publication in Anthropology no. 23, 107-14.

Willey, G.R. and P. Phillips (1958) *Method and Theory in American Archaeology*. Chicago.

Willey, G. (1962) A review of the map of the ruins of Tikal, El Peten, Guatemala. *American Antiquity*, 28, no. 1, 117-18.

NORMAN HAMMOND

The distribution of Late Classic Maya major ceremonial centres in the Central Area

The large sites of the lowlands, now generally covered by the term 'major ceremonial centres', have been the focus of Maya archaeology since its beginning. From the first excited account of Diego Garcia Palacio of the ruins of Copan in the sixteenth century, followed by Juan Galindo at the same site in 1833, and the expeditions of Antonio del Rio and Dupaix to Palenque at the beginning of the nineteenth century, attention has centred on the monumental architecture and sophisticated sculpture in stone and stucco that mark the culture of the Classic Maya as one of the great original creations of human society.

The later nineteenth-century explorers, Stephens and Maudslay, continued this emphasis upon the most obvious and striking aspects of Maya civilization, and from the recording of sculpture and the fortuitous survival of the Landa manuscript and the Dresden Codex sprang the study of Maya epigraphy, beginning with the work of Cyrus Thomas and Ernst Förstemann from 1880 onwards and culminating in the second quarter of this century with the vast accumulation of data published by Sylvanus G. Morley and elucidated by men such as John Teeple and Eric Thompson. Maya studies in the New World pursued much the same priorities as Classical Archaeology in the old, with a heavy emphasis on inscriptions and works of art, and in much the same way ignored the advances in scientific technique that were being made of necessity in investigating the less well-endowed cultures of prehistoric Europe and North America. The parallels between the history of Maya studies and that of Classical archaeology are many and strong, but must be considered elsewhere.

Because of this bias the religious and ceremonial cores of the major centres continued to occupy almost the entire attention of field-workers until well after the Second World War, with a few significant exceptions: the excavation and identification of residential structures outside the ceremonial centres began with the work of Edgar Hewett and Gerard Fowke at Quirigua in 1912 (Hewett 1913:

242-3), both, interestingly, brought into the Maya field from North American archaeology; the study of the distribution of residence by the use of explicit samples began at Uaxactun (Ricketson and Ricketson, 1937); and Thompson's 1931 excavations at San José were again explicitly conceived as an investigation of a small and hopefully 'average' site against which the major centres could be seen in proper perspective (Thompson 1939).

In practically all other cases the major sites were considered in isolation from their environments, and often each building or monument was similarly treated. Scant attention was paid to the articulation of a site, to the way in which it was planned, its dominance of or by the local microtopography, the range of resources available, or the multiplicity of other factors that had resulted in the existence of a large and complex focus of human activity at that particular location. In Morley's massive *The Inscriptions of Peten* (Morley 1937-8) the environment and resources of the region are described in seven introductory pages, with minimal further data for each site.

A major development occurred in the 1950s, when Willey brought the systematic study of settlement patterns into Maya archaeology, renewing and advancing the work begun at Quirigua and Uaxactun, and the University Museum of Pennsylvania began work at Tikal with a settlement study as part of the programme. In the Belize Valley (Willey et al. 1965) and at Tikal (Carr and Hazard 1961; Coe 1965, 1967) the contexts of sites and their relationships to other sites were considered.

The notion of a hierarchy of sites had been implicitly formulated by Ruppert (Ruppert and Denison, 1943), who had distinguished sites with stelae from those without, and major centres themselves had been arranged in four hierarchical classes by Morley (1946), but the first explicit statement of the structure of a site hierarchy within an area was made by William R. Bullard, Jr. (1960) on the basis of a survey in northeastern Peten which was itself originally inspired by the Belize Valley work in 1954-6. The work there had shown a linear hierarchy, the more important sites being more widely spaced along the valley than the less important, and Bullard expanded this notion along a second axis in his formulation of the territorial hierarchy of 'cluster', 'zone' and 'district', each territory centring on a site characterized as a 'hamlet', 'minor ceremonial centre' or 'major ceremonial centre'. The hierarchy was nested, the zone consisting of a number of clusters, the district of a number of zones. The possibility of an hierarchy within the class of major ceremonial centres, with a very large centre such as Tikal exercising suzerainty over a number of smaller centres, was also recognized. In a later paper Bullard (1962) estimated the population that could have been controlled by a major centre, on the basis of site distribution rather than the carrying capacity of the land, and came up with a figure of between 5000 and 9000, far below the 50,000 estimate for Uaxactun (Ricketson and Ricketson 1937: 21), but based upon a 'district' of only 100 square km. of usable upland. Bullard's notion of a nested hierarchy of sites restated in practical and archaeological terms (and clearly without direct knowledge) Christaller's (1933) model of central places. Recent application of this theory to the 'ceremonial centres' of Roman Britain, the walled towns (Hodder and Hassall 1971; Hodder 1972) shows that the model can and should be applied to the Classic Maya situation, although the level of data availability and reliability is much lower;[1] it has also shown that central-place theory has a definite predictive value in demonstrating the relative importance of a site from its position in the overall network, a point which will be considered further below.

The Belize Valley study was followed by other Peabody Museum projects under Gordon R. Willey and A. Ledyard Smith, at Altar de Sacrificios and then Seibal, in which major centres were studied within their matrix of settlement and outside contact: but still the site was seen as a focus of purely human factors — the introductory volume in the Altar de Sacrificios publication (Willey and Smith, 1969) disposed of the environment and its resources in eight pages. At the same period, however, the work of Sanders (1962-3) was much more ecologically and economically oriented, and the notion of 'cultural ecology' has been accepted in Maya studies for a decade now, combined with traditional archaeological preoccupations such as ceramics in the work of Rands (1969) at Palenque, and used to produce new archaeoeconomic explanations as in Puleston's (1971) work on *ramon* as a starch staple and its storage in *chultunes* at Tikal.

The investigation of long-distance trade, particularly between the lowlands and the Guatemalan highlands, was begun in 1964 by Thompson, who used ethnographic and ethnohistoric material to document Postclassic and post-conquest trade in perishables and demonstrate the probability of such a trade in the Classic period; I have used the same approach in adumbrating a model for the Classic obsidian trade (Hammond 1972*b*), using material identified as to source by X-ray fluorescence analysis. A similar use of source identification has been employed by Sabloff and others in documenting the manufacture and dispersal of fine paste ceramics, resulting in the delineation of ceramic trading units larger than that elucidated by Rands (1969) for Palenque and making the identification of an hierarchy of marketing areas and marketing systems with the aid of settlement pattern study (Smith 1972) an intriguing possibility.

Within the last few years, in fact, interest in the formal economic substructure of Classic Maya society and civilization has burgeoned, and in 1970 I attempted to develop one aspect of this at Lubaantun, a fairly small major ceremonial centre in the southern part of Belize (British Honduras) (Hammond 1970, 1972*a*). My aim was to define the 'region of control' or 'realm' ruled from that centre, and then to examine the range of resources available within that realm that could be exploited, and the ways in which their distribution governed site location and intra- and inter-realm trade.

By reference to the locations of adjacent and apparently coeval major centres, each presumably with its own region of control, the imposition of a simple network of Thiessen polygons indicated the territory closer to Lubaantun than to any other centre, and hence more likely to form part of its realm. These artificial boundaries were then compared with obvious natural ones, and the divide of the Maya Mountains at over 1100 m. and the Caribbean Sea taken as bounding the realm to northwest and southwest respectively. On the other axis, along the flanks of the Maya Mountains, the straight-line artificial boundaries suggested by the Thiessen polygons came close to the watershed of the Rio Grande basin, on a branch of which river the site of Lubaantun lies.

From this I concluded that the probable realm of Lubaantun during the latter part of the Late Classic — the only period when the site was occupied — comprised more or less the whole drainage basin of the Rio Grande, embracing a range of environmental zones from the high volcanic-metamorphic plateau of the southern Maya Mountains at 1100 m. above sea level, down through the high and low foothills of limestone and then banded sandstone and siltstone, and across the low-lying coastal plain to the Caribbean shore, backed with mangrove swamps and giving on to a shallow sea within the barrier reef, studded with small mangrove or coral islands. Within this realm, an area of some 1600 square km., the bulk of the 30 confirmed and reported sites are in the foothills between 50 m. and 300 m. elevation, an area of rolling topography and well-drained soils highly suitable for *milpa* cultivation and including the largest block of top-quality cacao soils in southern Belize (Hammond, in press, Chapter 7). Other sites lie on the coast and the offshore islands or cays, and seem to have had a fishing and trading economy integrated into the regional market system centred on Lubaantun.

The ceremonial centre itself lies where the foothills, coastal plain and river valley join (Fig. 1), controlling overland transport along the edge of the foothills from valley to valley and river transport at the head of canoe navigation; the site is defensible, and it and the surrounding settlement are on a series of well-drained, well-ventilated elevations with hillslope soils well suited to maize and especially to cacao, and with hunting, gathering and fishing territories all within less than 5 km. radius (Hammond 1972a: 786-90).

We have in Lubaantun, therefore, a site the location of which can be completely explained by reference to ecological and economic factors, with even the choice of the Rio Grande basin rather than, for instance, that of Middle River, or Golden Stream immediately northeast, explained by the presence of the rich cacao soils of the

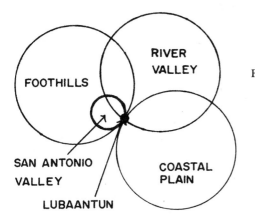

Figure 1. Environmental determinism in ceremonial centre location: the site of Lubaantun is in a highly advantageous position at the junction of foothills and plain, at the head of navigation on the river and adjacent to its protein, water and transport potential, and also close to the rich cacao soils of the San Antonio valley.

San Antonio valley around the ceremonial centre. If the locations and resources of all other major centres were to be examined in similar detail a vast amount of material would no doubt emerge to support this hypothesis — that the overall distribution of such sites is the sum of the individual site locations, each governed by purely local factors and subject only to each site having enough surrounding territory to support its tributary population. The disposition of major centres around the Maya Mountains massif, for example, shows each realm, as defined by Thiessen polygons, containing highland, foothill and lowland zones, cross-cut by the course of a major river on which the major centre stands (Hammond, 1972*a*, Figs. 20.25-6) and spaced at intervals of 24-34 km., with a median and mode of 31 km.

The more overwhelming this explanation seems in its completeness and neatness, the more it behoves us to examine its converse, that the overall distribution of major centres is in fact a function of the whole network with local factors determining only the actual siting — in other words that strategic location dominates tactical siting rather than otherwise. Hodder's application of central-place theory already cited, from the way in which predictions of site importance on the basis of position in the network are substantiated by archaeological evidence, shows that this is a tenable hypothesis. Thus a true explanation for the distribution, spacing and relationship of Classic Maya major ceremonial centres could lie at either extreme, or anywhere in between.

In tackling this problem the first consideration is clearly the distribution of major centres, and as a corollary, the definition of a 'major ceremonial centre'. No explicit definition has been enunciated, but the presence of large temple-pyramids, long range-like buildings termed 'palaces', ball-courts, sculptured and plain stelae and altars, a concentration and variety of monumental architecture have all been used as *ad hoc* criteria. One of the pressing needs of

Maya studies if we are to take the study of political and territorial relationships between centres further in archaeological as well as epigraphic terms (see Molloy and Rathje, this volume) is for a single archaeological definition of what a major ceremonial centre is, and some expression of the similarity or difference between centres on the basis of their size, architecture and monuments. The best method would seem to be a rank-ordering (Pounds 1969) on the basis of a large number of factors such as area of ceremonial structures, cubic volume of construction in the area, number and variety of structures, number of monuments and so on, each factor being appropriately weighted. Such an index would give us a boundary definition, perhaps obvious, perhaps arbitrary, but at least consistent, for the status of 'major ceremonial centre' and a means of investigating hierarchies within the class.

Although necessary, this will still be a flawed method because of the inadequacy of the data: we have only to compare Maler's map of Seibal, reproduced in Morley's *Inscriptions of Peten* as Fig. 199*b*, with the map made by Ian Graham for the Peabody Museum in 1964-8, and the 12 stelae described by Morley with the 21 now extant, to realize that even Morley's great compendium of data is a poor basis for this kind of work.

It is because of this lack of reliable comparison between sites that I have treated them all in the ensuing discussion as being of equal political status when examining their distribution in the southern lowlands; I am aware that this may not be so, indeed probably is not so, but the nature of the inequality and its permanence are factors at present only hinted at in the few large-scale site surveys and recent epigraphic work (for example Molloy and Rathje, this volume; Marcus 1973). Changes in political control may be swift; the focus of administrative, economic and religious government of a region may shift from one site to another, leaving behind the permanent architectural stock of the old order. Crowther and Echenique (1972) distinguish between 'stock', the physical facilities which form the concrete matrix of a society, and the 'activities' which occur both within and between places, and note that stock responds very slowly to the shifting demands of activities since it is fixed and expensive to alter, while activities may alter considerably in volume, kind and distribution over a short space of time. The system represented in fossil form by the ceremonial centre contained both demand and supply sectors, activities creating a demand for space and buildings which were supplied by the provision of stock in specific location of different activities within a site and the spatial relationships between them. I don't want to take the examination of the internal structure of the ceremonial centre any further here, except to note that analysis of activities from stock form and location may be another way of defining the major centre as a focus of particular activities, and that if we accept the reasonable equation made by Sjoberg

(1960) of the ceremonial centre as a pre-industrial city in function and in most aspects of form except population density, then we should also bear in mind the conclusion of Crowther and Echenique (1972) that 'A city can be regarded as a complex system of interrelated elements such that a single change can lead to repercussions throughout the city'. This reflects on an independent, practical and relatively small level the notion of tightly-coupled systems characterised by Rappaport (1969: 19-22) as 'hyperintegration' (and in a paper by Flannery (1972) published after the first presentation of this one as 'hypercoherence').

To return to our consideration of the distribution of major ceremonial centres: we have seen that no explicit definition of such exists, but that most workers in the Maya field have a fair idea of what is meant; sites such as Tikal, Palenque, Calakmul, El Mirador would be universally accepted as major centres without a precise recital of their structures and monuments. Even a small site such as Lubaantun, with only three large temples, the largest pyramid merely 12 m. high, and two ball courts, but entirely lacking stelae, would be fairly generally accepted, but a site such as El Encanto (Morley 1937-8: II, 2-7) with its single pyramid and stela might occasion some debate in spite of its acceptance as a major centre by Bullard (1960). In the discussion below I have listed as major centres all sites claimed as such on the basis of architecture, monuments, ball courts, E-group 'observatories' etc. and apparently functioning in the Late Classic; one or two doubtful examples may have crept in at the bottom, but are almost certainly balanced by the omission of sites such as Cenote, known but inadvertently left out of the list, and Ixtutz, only made public since this paper was first presented (Greene Robertson, 1972). The list is not perfect, but omissions and inclusions are unlikely to make any radical difference.

The same may be said of the area coverage: for northeast Peten we have Bullard's classic survey (1960) and for the adjacent region of southern Campeche and Quintana Roo that of Ruppert and Denison (1943), with Graham's (1967) more recent work filling a gap in north Peten. British Honduras is covered by the site map made by the soil survey under A.C.S. Wright in the 1950s, updating that of Thompson (1939). South Peten is less well covered, apart from the Pasión sites and those around the Maya Mountains, and west of Paso Caballos in northwest Peten information is so scanty that I have left the area out of consideration apart from the sites on the Usumacinta and the Rio San Pedro. In the area under consideration, most of Peten, British Honduras, and the adjacent parts of Campeche and Quintana Roo, I have listed 83 major ceremonial centres, ranging in size from sites with only a few plazas or stelae such as El Encanto, Pasión del Christo and San Jose up to the largest sites presently known, Tikal and El Mirador. Omissions which are probably culpable are Cenote, Ixtutz, La Amelia.

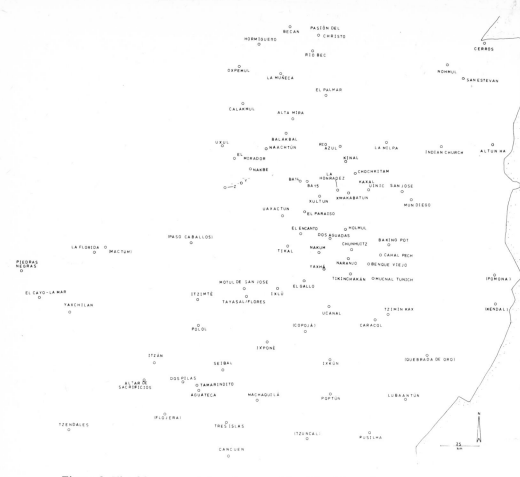

Figure 2 The 83 ceremonial centres considered in this study.

The distribution of these 83 sites (Fig. 2) seems to vary in density, with fairly wide spacing in south Peten and around the Maya Mountains, getting more closely spaced along the Pasión and up towards Lake Peten Itza, and in the northern part of the area considered in Campeche and Quintana Roo, and between these areas, in northeast Peten and the upper Belize Valley, most tightly packed of all. Here we have some of the largest and most noted sites in the southern lowlands — Tikal, Naranjo, Nakum, Yaxha and others — crammed into an area that is small by comparison with that enclosing a similar number of sites to north, south or west.

As recorded by Fig. 2 the distribution of major centres is clearly not uniform, ranging from a spacing of some 30 km. around the Maya Mountains through 20 km. or so in south Peten and south Campeche to 10 km. or less in northeast Peten; and the disuniformity seems to be non-random, with sites being progressively more tightly packed from north, south and west towards a 'core area' reaching from Tikal eastwards to the Belize border. This disuniformity is so striking and its trends are so regular that it is presumably of some importance in Late Classic Maya history, and particularly in the relationship between the ceremonial centres, their

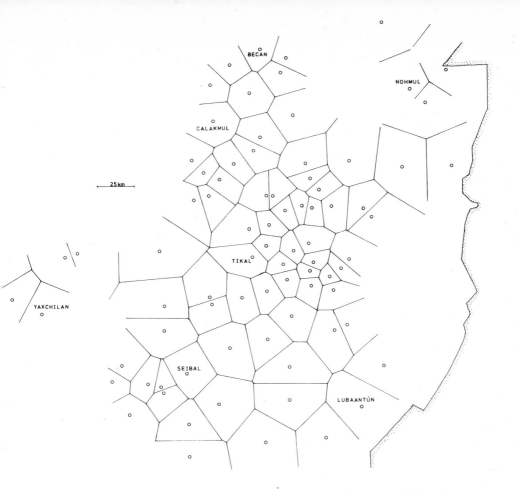

Figure 3 A network of Thiessen polygons imposed upon the ceremonial centre
distribution, delineating the territory closest to each site.

rulers and their subject populations; it certainly deserves examination
and if possible explanation.

The first possibility which must be considered is that the distribution recorded in Fig. 2 is hopelessly wrong, and that the distribution
of major centres is in fact completely different from that depicted.
This seems unlikely for most of the area considered, since northeast
Peten, Belize and the Pasión Valley have been fairly well explored,
and it seems unlikely that Ruppert and Denison would have missed a
substantial number of sites in Campeche. South Peten may well
acquire a few more sites, but the coverage on the whole is reasonable — a new site may be discovered here and there, as Itzan was in
1968 and Ixtutz in 1970, but the patterns will remain basically
stable.

If we accept that the distribution in Fig. 2 is essentially accurate
there are a number of factors that may help to explain it; but first
the phenomenon must be defined more exactly. Fig. 3 shows a
network of Thiessen polygons imposed upon the distribution of
Fig. 2, defining the territory closest to each centre, and its most
striking feature is the vast range in polygon sizes, from over 1600

square km. around Lubaantun down to just over 100 square km., less than a tenth of the area, around Benque Viejo and Naranjo; a number of 'territories' in south Peten are around 1000 square km. and even those in the areas immediately north and south of the 'core area' attain 600-800 square km. (Table 1.) Even if we reduce the territory of Lubaantun to the area of it known to be habitable by *milpa* farmers the territory is still in excess of 600 square km., and the mean territory for the 45 closed polygons obtainable is around 500 square km.; the discovery of several more sites would only reduce this slightly and would not affect the total range. By contrast the mean area for 10 territories in northeast Peten, of sites in Bullard's (1960) survey, is 253 square km. including areas of *bajo*. The polygon boundaries, imposed on Bullard's map, show that even in this relatively undifferentiated region each territory contains a range of environmental zones and a perennial water supply, and that in many cases the inter-territory boundaries cut across *bajos* or run along rivers which could form natural boundaries. Puleston's data on the Tikal-Uaxactun intersite area (Puleston, this volume) suggests that the diminution and rise of settlement density along a line between two centres may be used to determine boundaries more precisely. The use of Thiessen polygons in defining boundaries is a purely initial one, suggesting where evidence for natural or artificial frontiers may be sought, and their utility in delineating regions of control is also dependent on the assumption that the centres are in a coequal rather than hierarchical relationship; in either case, however, and no matter how small the territory, there is a strong probability that the area of the polygon includes the 'sustaining area' that provided the basic economic substructure for the ceremonial centre, and the analysis of this is in itself a useful task.

Another way of examining the disuniformities in ceremonial centre distribution is by measuring the distance to the nearest neighbour (Clark and Evans, 1954), a technique that considers the relationships of sites to each other rather than defining their putative regions of control. For the 83 sites in Fig. 2 the mean distance to the first nearest neighbour is 15.04 km., to the second nearest neighbour (mean of 78 sites) 22.84 km., and to the third nearest neighbour (mean of 75 sites) 27.07 km. (Table 1.) These distances again seem unlikely to shift more than a small amount in either direction with the addition of new sites.

As with the Thiessen polygons, the striking feature is the great range of distances, with first nearest neighbour distances from 5 km. to 33.5 km., second from 9 km. to 41.5 km. and third from 13.5 km. to 59.5 km. The true range of second and third nearest neighbour distances apply to sites on the edge of unsurveyed territory, and for this reason five such sites have been omitted from the second nearest neighbour distance mean and eight from the third. Only first nearest neighbour distances are considered further here.

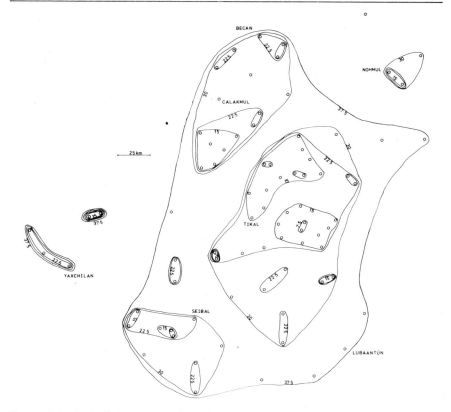

Figure 4 A single-link contour plan of nearest-neighbour distances between sites.

The disuniformity of distribution and the trend to shorter nearest neighbour distances in the 'core area' of northeast Peten and across north of Tikal into southeast Campeche can be seen in Fig. 4, where a single-link contouring method (devised by A.G. Sherratt) gives a surface with peaks (or troughs) in the areas of lowest first-neighbour distances. The contour interval of 7.5 km. is based on half the overall mean first-neighbour distance and its standard deviation (7.52, 7.59). There are a number of 'reflexive pairs' of sites within the 7.5 km. contour (Haggett, 1965, 232-3), but the most substantial blocs are those within the 15 km. contour. These cover most of northeastern Peten and adjacent western British Honduras, with a third bloc around El Mirador. These three major blocs occupy, but extend eastwards beyond, the 'core area' defined by Rathje (1971) as the region where Classic Maya civilization began in response to the stimuli of economic deprival, and where the earliest known lowland Maya stelae were raised from the third century A.D. onwards.

The significance of the variations in nearest-neighbour distance can be examined statistically, and a number of questions posed. Four subsets were extracted from the overall set of 83 sites, and their

Table 1 The 83 sites used in this study, with their nearest-neighbour distances and size of 'territory' as defined by Thiessen polygons, when computable

| Site | Source | Nearest neighbour distances (km) | | | Area of Thiessen polygon (km (* denotes 'E-group' present) |
		1st	2nd	3rd	
Becan	Ruppert & Denison 1943	19	21	23	
Pasion del Christo	"	10.5	19	34.5	
Hormiguero	"	19	23	23	
Rio Bec	"	10.5	21	25	*
Oxpemul	"	19	24.5	27	*
La Muñeca	"	23	25	27	612*
Calakmul	"	24.5	31	33	*
El Palmar	"	27	30	32.5	*
Alta Mira	"	10	25.5	27	
Balakbal	"	10	16	26	430*
Uxul	"	11.5	23	23	*
Naachtun	"	14.5	16	21	443*
El Mirador	Graham 1967	11.5	11.5	16	250
Nakbe	"	11	11.5	14.5	328
'Y'	"	10.5	11	16	395
'Z'	"	10.5	20	20.5	
Cerros	B.H. Map	26.5	27.5		
San Estevan	Bullard 1965	13.5	26.5		
Nohmul	Gann & Gann 1939	13.5	27.5		
Altun Ha	Pendergast 1967	33.5	46.5	59.5	
Indian Ch.	Thompson 1939	33.5	35.5	38	
La Milpa	Thompson 1939	28.5	29	29.5	
Kinal	Graham 1967	9.5	10.5	19	258
Chochkitam	Adams & Gatling 1964	9.5	13.5	13.5	236
La Honradez	Adams & Gatling 1964	7	12	16	200
Xmakabatun	Morley 1938	7	13	13.5	205
Xultun	"	12	13	14.5	235*
Kaxal Uinic	Thompson 1939	13	13.5	20	443
San Jose	Thompson 1939	8	21.5	32.5	500*
Mun Diego	Thompson 1939	8	28	32.5	
El Paraiso	Smith 1937	13.5	14.5	14.5	260*
Uaxactun	Smith 1950	13.5	16.5	19.5	679*
Tikal	Coe 1965	12	19.5	21	596*
El Encanto	Bullard 1960	12	14.5	16.5	224
Holmul	"	11.5	13.5	18.5	426
Dos Aguadas	"	11.5	11.5	15.5	236
Nakum	"	11	11.5	17	233*
Chunhuitz	"	6	13.5	14.5	180
Baking Pot	"	8	18	24	
Cahal Pech	"	8	9.5	16	
Naranjo	"	6	10	14	130
Benque Viejo	"	9.5	9.5	14	128*
Yaxha	"	11	15.5	17	223*
Tikinchakan	"	10	14	15	287
Mucnal Tunich	Thompson 1939	9.5	15	16	

El Gallo	Bullard 1960	15.5	17.5	21.5	393
Ixlu	"	17.5	20.5	21.5	600
Tayasal	Morley 1937-8	5	20.5	31.5	518
Motul de San Jose	"	5	21.5	31	740
Itzimte	"	16.5	31	31.5	
Polol	"	16.5	32.5	36.5	
Ucanal	"	22.5	24	25	647*
Caracol	Satterthwaite 1951	9.5	27	30.5	789
Tzimin Kax	Thompson 1931	9.5	25	36	*
Pomona	Kidder & Ekholm 1951	18.5			
Kendal	Thompson 1939	18.5			
Ixpone	Guatemala Map	26	32	33.5	1051
Copoja	"	22.5	24	26	672
Ixkun	Morley 1937-8	22.5	24	34.5	1009
Itzan	Willey & Smith 1969	12.5	21.5	30	
Altar d.S.	"	12.5	24.5	25	
Dos Pilas	"	9	12	21.5	388
Tamarindito	"	4.5	9	20	174
Aguateca	Graham 1967	4.5	12	20.5	379
Seibal	Willey & Smith 1969	20	27	30	789
Flojera	Morley 1937-8	24	25	27	
Tres Islas	Morley 1937-8	22	24.5	27	793
Machaquila	Graham 1967	24.5	30	38	1108
Cancuen	Morley 1937-8	22	40.5	46.5	
Tzuncal	"	33	40	40.5	
Poptun	Shook & Smith 1950	22.5	33	35.5	1129
Pusilha	Joyce et al. 1928	31.5	35.5	40.5	
Lubaantun	Hammond 1970	31.5	31.5	48.5	1665
Quebrada de Oro	B.H. Map	31.5	37	41	
Yaxchilan	Morley 1937-8	22.5	41.5	41.5	
El Cayo	"	21	22.5	45.5	
Piedras Negras	"	21	41.5	47.5	
La Florida	Graham 1970	9	41.5	45.5	
Mactum	Guatemala Map	9	48	54	
Tzibanche	Harrison 1972	3	12		
Rio Azul	Adams & Gatling 1964	10.5	20	28.5	696
BA-14	"	8	16	20	412
BA-15	"	8	13	20	311
		Mean of 83 sites: 15.04	Mean of 78 sites: 22.84	Mean of 75 sites: 27.07	Mean of 45 sites: 498 km²
	Reflexive pairs:	25	10	5	

first-neighbour distances compared in various ways (Table 1). Subset 1 consisted of 15 sites, all in the area of northeastern Peten surveyed by Bullard (1960) and all except El Paraiso (Smith 1937) marked on Bullard's map; their mean first-neighbour distance was 10.4 km. Subset 2 comprised 16 sites in north Peten and south Campeche in the area surveyed by Ruppert and Denison (1943) with a few additions at the southern end of the area from Graham's (1967) survey; the first-neighbour distance was 15.1 km. Subset 3 consisted of 25 sites in south Peten, the upper Pasión and around the Maya Mountains, taken from various sources and with a mean first-neighbour distance of 18.4 km. Subset 4 comprised 19 sites possessing 'E-group observatories',[2] geographically cross-cutting subsets 1-3 and including sites from all three; the mean first-neighbour distance was 14.76 km. Subsets 1-3 were each taken as being internally consistent coverage of an area, subset 4 as a group of sites of presumed equally high status on one level at least, the apparent possession and use of an observatory. Since this trait is one usually taken as denoting major ceremonial centre status, this subset was intended to act as a control on the overall set, where the status of some sites might be in question. The tests below were carried out by Dr Sophie Bowlby of Reading University.

The first question was to see if the variance of the nearest neighbour distances in any sample were significantly different from that in any other sample: using the F test at the 5 per cent confidence level one sample, subset 1, was found to be significantly different from all others, while the variances of the others were not.

The second question was whether the mean first-neighbour distance of any sample was significantly different from that in any other sample: using a t-test for the difference between means subset 1 was found to be different from all others, from the overall set and subset 3 at the 1 percent confidence level and from subsets 2 and 4 at the 5 percent confidence level; the other means were not significantly different from each other.

The third question was whether the pattern of points formed by the site distribution was clustered, regular or random in the overall set or any subset. Calculation of R values (overall: 1.3065; subset 1: 1.8595; subset 2: 1.9086; subset 3: 1.516) shows in all cases a pattern more regular than random; i.e. tending to a triangular lattice, with the difference between mean first-neighbour distance and that expected for a random distribution being significant at the 5 percent level in all cases. The value of R would be zero when all points are clustered in one location, 1.00 for a random distribution and 2.15 for a uniform triangular lattice. The values obtained suggest that the overall network is influential in determining strategic site location, although Hodder (personal communication) suggests that the values are higher than they should be because of the difficulty of defining precisely the size of the area within which any set or subset of points lies; it may be possible to resolve this by re-running the test on a set of points with closed Thiessen polygons, using the sum of the areas of these.[3]

The tendency towards a lattice in the areas covered by subsets 1 and 2 has also been detected by Flannery in work coeval with this paper (1972: 421), using subsets of slightly different composition

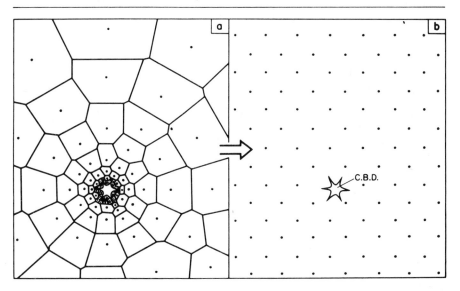

Figure 5 The Classic Maya situation in microcosm? The relationship between trade service centres and population density in a modern city: in (*a*) land is given proportional representation, i.e. the method of depiction is comparable with Fig. 3, while in (*b*) land is represented proportional to population. The spacing of service centres diminishes and the 'territory' of each shrinks with increasing population density, but each centre serves the same size population. (After Abler, Adams and Gould, 1971, Fig. 10-31; CBD--Central Business District.)

(only sites marked as 'major ceremonial centre ruins' by Bullard (1960), and only 'sites with stelae' as noted by Ruppert and Denison (1943). Flannery's nearest-neighbour mean distances for Bullard's sites are: 1st: 10.33 km.; 2nd: 13.33 km.; 3rd: 16.08 km.; only the first of these was calculated for subset 1 here, which contained the site of El Paraiso in addition to Bullard's 14 sites, but it is interesting that the figure of 10.4 km. obtained is close to Flannery's and reinforces the suggestion made earlier that the addition of further sites to the overall set will produce only minor variations in the figures given.

The formal measurement of 'territory' size and nearest-neighbour distance thus confirms the initial impression given by the distribution, that there is a marked packing of sites in northeast Peten and adjacent British Honduras, with a minor focus around the lower Pasión. These areas contain some of the largest and most complex ceremonial centres in the Maya Central Area, while the more widely-spaced centres seem to be also smaller and less complex, e.g. Lubaantun, Pusilha. Rathje's (1971) notion of a 'core area' and a 'buffer zone', or at least that of two concentric and differentiable zones, receives some support from the distribution on a graph of first-neighbour distances: it is strongly bimodal, with a major peak between 6-12 km. and a lesser one at 18-24 km.; subset 1 has a single peak at 6-12 km., subsets 2 and 4 are bimodal with the 6-12 km. peak stronger than the 18-24 km. one, and subset 3 is unimodal with an 18-24 km. peak. Of the 41 sites with first-neighbour distances between 6-12 km., 30 lie in an area bounded by Alta Mira, Uxul, Tikal, Mucnal Tunich and Mun Diego, containing only 4 other sites, with nearest-neighbour distances attaining only 14.5 km. at most. The other 11 sites with first-neighbour distances in the 6-12 km. range are scattered in 5 'reflexive pairs', each first-neighbour to the other, with Dos Pilas attached to the Tamarindito-Aguateca pair. Thus there would seem to be a 'core area' where all first nearest neighbours are within 14.5 km. and the bulk within 12 km. but a minimum of 6 km. away, and a peripheral zone where distances are greater, up to more than 30 km., except for a few reflexive pairs.

So far I have been concerned with the exposition of this problem, and I would hope that the data presented will remain firm enough to stimulate further theorising; the rest of this paper will discuss a few avenues along which explanation might be pursued.

Explanatory factors can be divided into several major categories: ecological, demographic, political *et sim.* An ecological explanation could likewise take several forms: one has been advanced already, that each site is strategically located purely by the tactical operation of local topographic and environmental factors; another would be that general topographic and climatic factors operating over the whole Central Area are responsible. Very few sites are at more than 200 m. elevation and almost none over 300 m., although such uplands do exist in the 'southern lowlands', so that altitude and the associated lower temperatures could be seen as a powerful limiting factor. Most sites are on or near a stream, river or lake, and those that are not have *bajo* or a waterhole nearby, so the year-round availability of drinking water can obviously be canvassed as another constraint. Climate does not vary significantly over the area except for total rainfall, and may be discounted as a general factor.

A second set of ecological factors are those concerned with the availability or otherwise of resources: the packing of centres in the 'core area' could be seen as a response to the superabundance of a particular resource or resources in general — particularly fertile soils giving high yields or multiple cropping, wild plant or wild animal protein, or an industrial resource such as flint or building stone. But northeast Peten does not appear to be particularly abundant in resources vis-à-vis the rest of the area: soils are not particularly different and where animal protein is present in lakes such as Yaxha or Peten Itza the ceremonial centres are no more closely spaced. Wild plant resources may be a different matter: Puleston's (1971) work has demonstrated the correlation of *ramon* with settlement, suggesting either deliberate planting or more probably selective culling, and the probability that it was gathered and stored; but ethnohistoric and ethnographic evidence suggests that it was a reserve staple that evened out some of the uncertainty of maize yields rather than a prime staple, or if the latter, one that was only brought into constant use under heavy demographic pressure. The importance of this sort of resource is the ability it gives to maintain population at a high density even if the prime staple fails (although in very dry seasons even *ramon* fails) — it raises the basic carrying capacity of an area, in the same way that river molluscs were used, at Lubaantun at least, as reserve animal protein, ensuring a supply when game was scarce and thus reducing the area needed to support any given population under adverse conditions.

The converse of resource abundance is resource depletion, and Rathje (1971) has shown that his 'core area', in large part coincident with that noted here, apparently lacks such necessities as salt, obsidian and metates and had to import them. His thesis is that the consequent necessity for long-distance exchange led to the rise of stratified society in the Central Area capable of sustaining such a mechanism; its weak points are that it holds good only for the area where early monuments are known, and does not explain why Classic civilization should begin in northeast Peten rather than the arid heart of the Yucatan Peninsula to the north; that a good supply of metate stone was available and exploited in the Maya Mountains, on the fringe of his 'core'; and that obsidian trade between the highlands of Guatemala and the Pasión Valley site of Seibal was established centuries earlier in the Escoba Mamon phase (Graham et al. 1972) of 600-300 B.C., if not in the preceding Real Xe phase of 800-600 B.C. The emergence of the stela cult seems likely to be as unrelated to the underlying origins of Classic Maya civilization as its cessation is to the collapse, except as one facet of a manifold phenomenon.

In sum, the range of resources in the 'core area' of closely-packed major centres does not seem to be vastly different from that of the periphery, although with a smaller range of environmental zones than sites near the coast or the Maya Mountains, and long-distance exchange to supply basic needs such as obsidian was apparently instituted by the Middle Preclassic.

A second major class of explanations may be called 'demographic-political', since the latter is often bound up inextricably with the former, and of course both are intimately connected with resource supply (see many of the papers in Spooner (ed.) 1972). The presence of a large number of major centres within a relatively restricted area is in itself evidence that a large population existed there, providing labour and skills for the construction and mainten-ance of the centres and being the *raison d'être* of the system of political, administrative, religious and economic control reflected by and exerted from them. A ceremonial centre is after all a service centre for a population in much the same way as a modern shopping/civic centre/church complex is. A map of such service centres in a modern city (Fig. 5) shows a similar packing of

Thiessen-polygon or hexagonal territories and a concomitant shortening of nearest-neighbour distances towards the centre; the controlling
variable there is population density — there is a critical ceiling level
of population which can be served by a single centre, and presumably
a critical floor level of population necessary to support a centre.
Similarly a theoretical model of disuniform rural population density
as envisaged by Christaller has the same appearance (e.g. Harvey
1919, Fig. 14.8); if this data is plotted to give uniform population
density the larger central polygons express larger overall populations
and perhaps greater political or economic importance.

It certainly seems possible that a major cause of the packing of
large sites in the 'core area' is high population density, both allowing
and needing a larger number of service centres; I have suggested
elsewhere (Hammond 1972: 788) adapting a notion of Warwick
Bray's, that a critical ceiling population of around 50,000 was the
largest that could be effectively controlled from a single centre with
the degree of population dispersal and political organisation existing
in the Late Classic.

If, for the sake of argument, we accept that the direct reason for
the packing of ceremonial centres in northeast Peten is that the Late
Classic population there was larger and denser than elsewhere in the
Central Area (and Puleston's data in his paper in this volume suggest
that population growth and agglomeration were both occurring at
Tikal), then we still have to find an explanation. There is no inducive
force in the way of increased resources, so we should perhaps seek
coercive forces. The most obvious of these is simply population
growth in itself, for any one of many biological, nutritional or social
reasons, and the inability to move away into areas of unoccupied or
sparsely occupied land. The results of excavation at a number of
Central Area sites over the last four decades have shown that almost
all parts of the Central Area except perhaps the southeastern flanks
of the Maya Mountains were settled by the Late Preclassic, and
although the hiatus described by Willey (this volume) marked a
dramatic decrease in ceremonial centre construction and stela erection, there is no evidence that there was a decline in population,
merely in its level of exploitation for non-subsistence activities. It
therefore seems probable that by the Late Classic all parts of the area
were at least as densely occupied as they were a millennium before,
and most likely that the population was in fact much higher. The
foundation of Lubaantun in the eighth century A.D. on a previously
unoccupied site suggests that at the southern end of the Maya
Mountains population was expanding into one of the few areas of
unoccupied territory, perhaps as the latter end of an expansion of
the Chol-Chorti south and west into the highland zone that apparently ended in the region of Asunción Mita (Thompson, 1970,
Chapter 3). Thompson's work on the Putun (Thompson, 1970,
Chapter 1) and that of Sabloff and Willey (1967) both suggest

population movement and growth in the lower Usumacinta, and although there is at present no evidence a similar phenomenon in the centre of Choloid territory across southern Peten would not be surprising.

If they were surrounded by similarly enlarging populations the inhabitants of northeast Peten would be unable to move outwards, they would be subjected to what Chagnon (1968) characterizes as 'social circumscription', a notion already applied to the Maya Area by Carneiro (1970) as a factor in the origins of Classic civilization, and noted as a possible process in the Late Classic by Flannery (1972, 421). Certainly Chagnon's description of the results of social circumscription at a lower developmental level on the Yanomamö of Venezuela contains some striking parallels with the Late Classic situation: the villages at the centre of the Yanomamö territory are larger, more nucleated, with a higher population density, defended and enmeshed in marriage alliances with their neighbours. The villages are always well-spaced, but the nearest-neighbour distances at the centre of the territory are much smaller than those at the periphery; at the periphery villages are more widely-spaced, more isolated, less in conflict or alliance, smaller and less nucleated. Ceremonial construction for feasting and formal reciprocal trading are much less. Thus the physical size of the central villages reflects the importance of contact and ceremonial display.

We have already seen that the 'core area' ceremonial centres are among the largest, that population size and density where it has been investigated (Tikal) is much greater than at a peripheral site (Lubaantun; Hammond 1972a), that interaction in the form of alliances seems to have occurred in the 'core' (Molloy and Rathje, this volume; Marcus, 1973). Ceremonial centres are well-spaced — very rarely less than 6 km. and even in the most tightly-packed part of the 'core' on average 10.4 km. apart — but much closer than in the periphery (average 16-18 km., range up to 33.5 km.). Evidence of defences or firm boundaries intended as a statement of territorial rights have been found at Tikal, the Bonampak frescoes and other depictions give evidence of warfare in the Late Classic, and in general Chagnon's and Carneiro's idea that increased population density leads to increased friction seems to be supported rather than otherwise. It is precisely this friction which Carneiro proposes as a prime mover in the formation of the state, and it may be that the collapse of Classic civilization, whatever its direct cause, interrupted the emergence of even larger political entities in the Central Area, based on more widely-spaced giant centres such as Tikal and El Mirador, as the political evolution of the Maya overbalanced on too narrow a socio-economic base.

NOTES

1 Since this volume went to press this challenge has been taken up by Marcus (1973), using a cosmographic model of four directional 'capitals' to which she links a nested hierarchy of ceremonial centres. The argument is vitiated by the failure to recognize that a proposed change of 'capitals' by A.D. 849 (on uncertain epigraphic evidence) must then logically involve a wholesale realignment of the entire Central Area settlement hierarchy — something for which there is little evidence. A second weakness is that nearest neighbour distances are taken direct from Flannery (1972), who bases them on Bullard's site hierarchy, while nevertheless altering the status of several sites (e.g. Chunhuitz, El Encanto, El Gallo) from that accepted by Flannery.

2 i.e. structures similar to that in Group E at Uaxactun (Ricketson and Ricketson, 1937); the use of these structures for categorizing sites was suggested by William L. Rathje.

3 Since this volume went to press I. Hodder and C. Orton have kindly pursued this matter further, using the sites in subsets 1-3 and nine others. They report: The boundary around the sites of each subset was assessed by drawing perpendiculars to the line between each peripheral site in the subset and its nearest outside neighbour. In all three cases the pattern of sites was not significantly different from random, but the tendency to significance increased with site density. This covariation between increasing density and increasing departure from randomness could be due to chance, but also competition increases with density and proximity and this could affect patterns.

To detect competition between sites at higher densities a method similar to Pielon's (1962) was used: nearest neighbour distances greater than 14 km. were ignored, so that a truncated sample of close neighbours only was considered. This included 15 of 16 sites in subset 1, 6 of 9 in subset 2 and 6 of 14 in subset 3 (the subsets having been previously reduced to sites where a complete Thiessen polygon was obtainable) and the 9 other sites. The distances were divided into equal cells and the number of sites falling into each cell was compared with that expected on a random distribution. The difference for the 36 sites considered (15 + 6 + 6 + 9) showed significant evidence for competition, as did that for subset 1; subset 2 showed much less significant evidence, even using sites up to 15 km. apart (n=7), and subset 3 showed none.

There was thus evidence of competition at high density (subset 1) and to a lesser extent at medium density (subset 2) but not at low density (subset 3); in sum, it would seem that localised competition between sites did occur, increasing in intensity with closer distance.

Hodder and Orton's conclusion (the mathematical section of which I have omitted from this note) thus supports the commonsense notion that increasing proximity enhances competition for resources and that this is expressed spatially by increased regularity in distribution, with nearest neighbour distances clustering just above a minimum acceptable degree of separation.

4 I would like to acknowledge the assistance of David L. Clarke, Sophie Bowlby, Ian Hodder, C.R. Orton and William L. Rathje in preparing this paper.

Fig. 6 is reprinted from Abler, Adams and Gould (1971) by kind permission of Prentice-Hall, Inc.

REFERENCES

Abler, R., J.S. Adams and P. Gould (1971) *Spatial Organisation.* London.

Adams, R.E.W. and J.L. Gatling (1964) Noreste del Petén: un nuevo sitio y una mapa arqueólogica regional. *Estudios de Cultura Maya,* 4, 99-118.

Bullard, W.R., Jr. (1960) Maya settlement pattern in northeastern Petén, Guatemala. *American Antiquity,* 25, 355-72.

Bullard, W.R., Jr. (1965) *Stratigraphic excavations at San Estevan, Northern British Honduras.* Royal Ontario Museum, Occasional Papers, no. 9.

Carneiro, R.L. (1970) A theory of the origins of the state. *Science,* 169, 733-8.

Carr, R.F. and J.E. Hazard (1961) *Map of the Ruins of Tikal, El Petén, Guatemala.* Museum Monographs, University Museum of Pennsylvania, Tikal Reports, no.11, 1-26.

Chagnon, N.A. (1968) Yanomamö social organisation and warfare. In M. Fried, M. Harris and R. Murphy (eds.), *War: The Anthropology of Armed Conflict and Aggression.* New York.

Christaller, W. (1933) *Die zentralen Orte in Süddeutschland*. Jena.

Clark, P.J. and C.E. Evans (1954) Distance to nearest neighbour as a measure of spatial relationships in populations. *Ecology*, 35, 445-53.

Coe, W.R. (1965) Tikal: ten years of study of a Maya ruin in the lowlands of Guatemala. *Expedition*, 8, 5-56.

Coe, W.R. (1967) *Tikal: A Handbook of the Ancient Maya Ruins*. Philadelphia.

Crowther, D. and M. Echenique (1972) Development of a model of urban spatial structure. In L. Martin and L. March (eds.), *Urban Space and Structures*, 175-218, Cambridge.

Flannery, K.V. (1972) The cultural evolution of civilisations. Annual Review of Ecology and Systematics, 3, 399-426.

Gann, T. and M. Gann (1939) *Archaeological Investigations in the Corozal District of British Honduras*. Bureau of American Ethnology, Bulletin no. 123, 1-57.

Graham, I. (1967) *Archaeological Explorations in El Petén, Guatemala*. Middle American Research Institute, Tulane University, Publication no. 33.

Graham, I. (1970) *The Ruins of La Florida, Petén, Guatemala*. Papers of the Peabody Museum, Harvard University, no. 61, 425-55.

Graham, J.A., T.R. Hester and R.N. Jack (1972) Sources for the obsidian at the ruins of Seibal, Guatemala. *Contributions of the University of California Archaeological Research Facility*, 16, 111-16.

Greene Robertson, M. (1972) Notes on the ruins of Ixtutz, southeastern Petén. *Contributions of the University of California Archaeological Research Facility*, 16, 89-104.

Haggett, P. (1965) *Locational Analysis in Human Geography*. London.

Hammond, N. (1970) Excavations at Lubaantun 1970. *Antiquity*, 44, 216-23.

Hammond, N. (1972a) Locational analysis and the site of Lubaantun: A Classic Maya centre. In D.L. Clarke (ed.), *Models in Archaeology*, 757-800. London.

Hammond, N. (1972b) Obsidian trade routes in the Mayan area. *Science*, 178, 1092-4.

Hammond, N. (in press) *Lubaantun: A Classic Maya Realm*. Papers of the Peabody Museum, Harvard University.

Harrison, P. (1972) *Precolumbian Settlement Distributions and External Relationships In Southern Quintana Roo*. MS.

Harvey, D. (1969) *Explanation in Geography*. London.

Hewett, E. (1913) The excavation of Quirigua, Guatemala, by the School of American Research. *Proceedings of the XVIII International Congress of Americanists*, Pt.II, 241-8.

Hodder, I. (1972) Locational models and Romano-British settlement. In D.L. Clarke (ed.), *Models in Archaeology*, 887-909. London.

Hodder, I. and M. Hassall (1971) The non-random spacing of Romano-British walled towns. *Man*, 6, 391-407.

Joyce, T.A., T. Gann, E.L. Gruning and R.C.E. Long (1928) Report on the British Museum Expedition to British Honduras, 1928. *Journal of the Royal Anthropological Institute*, 58, 323-50.

Kidder, A.V. and C.F. Ekholm (1951) *Some Archaeological Specimens from Pomona, British Honduras*. Carnegie Institution of Washington. Notes on Middle American Archaeology and Ethnology, no. 102.

Marcus, J. (1973) Territorial organisation of the Lowland Classic Maya. *Science*, 180, 911-16.

Morley, S.G. (1937-8) *The Inscriptions of Petén*. Carnegie Institution of Washington Publication no. 437.

Morley, S.G. (1946) *The Ancient Maya*. Palo Alto, California.

Pendergast, D.M. (1967) Altun Ha, Honduras Británica: Temporadas 1964 y 1965. *Estudios de Cultura Maya*, 6, 149-69.

Pielon, E.C. (1962) The use of plant to neighbour distances for the detection of competition. *Journal of Ecology*, 50, 357-68.

Pounds, N.J.G. (1969) The urbanisation of the classical world. *Annals of the Association of American Geographers*, 59, 135-57.

Puleston, D.E. (1971) An experimental approach to the function of Classic Maya Chultuns. *American Antiquity*, 36, 322-35.

Rands, R.L. (1967) Ceramic technology and trade in the Palenque Region, Mexico. In C.L. Riley and W.W. Taylor (eds.), *American Historical Anthropology: Essays in Honor of Leslie Spier*, 137-151. Carbondale and Edwardsville.

Rappaport, R.A. (1969) *Sanctity and Adaptation.* Paper presented at Wenner-Gren symposium, Burg Wartenstein.

Rathje, W.L. (1971) The origin and development of Lowland Classic Maya civilisation. *American Antiquity*, 36, 275-85.

Ricketson, O.G. and E.B. Ricketson (1937) *Uaxactun, Guatemala: Group E, 1926-31.* Carnegie Institution of Washington Publication no. 477.

Ruppert, I. and J.H. Dennison, Jr. (1943) *Archaeological Reconnaissance in Campeche, Quintana Roo and Petén.* Carnegie Institution of Washington Publication no. 543.

Sabloff, J.A. and G.R. Willey (1967) The collapse of Maya civilisation in the southern lowlands: a consideration of history and process. *Southwestern Journal of Anthropology*, 24, 311-36.

Sanders, W.T. (1962-3) Cultural Ecology of the Maya Lowlands. *Estudios de Cultura Maya*, 2-3, 79-122 and 203-41.

Satterthwaite, L. (1951) Reconnaissance in British Honduras. *University Museum Bulletin*, 16, no. 1.

Shook, E.M. and R.E. Smith (1950) Descubrimientos arqueológicos en Poptún. *Antropología e Historia de Guatemala*, 2, no. 2, 3-15.

Sjoberg, G. (1960) *The Pre-Industrial City.* Glencoe, Ill.

Smith, A.L. (1937) Ruins of El Paraiso and Juventud. In Ricketson, O.G. and E.B. Ricketson (1937), 295-296.

Smith, C.A. (1972) *Market conditions and stratification among peasants.* Paper presented at American Anthropological Association meeting, Toronto.

Spooner, B. (ed.) *Population Growth: Anthropological Implications.* Cambridge, Mass.

Thompson, J.E.S. (1939) *Excavations at San Jose, British Honduras.* Carnegie Institution of Washington Publication no. 506.

Thompson, J.E.S. (1964) Trade relations between the Maya Highlands and Lowlands. *Estudios de Cultura Maya*, 4, 13-50.

Thompson, J.E.S. (1970) *Maya History and Religion.* Norman, Oklahoma.

Willey, G.R., W.R. Bullard, Jr., J.B. Glass and J.C. Gifford (1965) *Prehistoric Maya Settlements in the Belize Valley.* Papers of the Peabody Museum, Harvard University, no. 54.

Willey, G.R. and A.L. Smith (1969) *The Ruins of Altar de Sacrificios, Department of Petén, Guatemala: An Introduction.* Papers of the Peabody Museum, Harvard University, no. 52, pt. 1.

RENÉ MILLON

The study of urbanism at Teotihuacan, Mexico

This article deals with the study of urbanization and urbanism at Teotihuacan, Mexico (Figs. 1-7) in which Bruce Drewitt, George Cowgill and I, as well as others, have been engaged for some years. The research we have been carrying on forms part of the Teotihuacan Mapping Project of the University of Rochester, largely supported by funds from the National Science Foundation. The research on this project began in 1962 and is still in progress.[1]

Our work at Teotihuacan has involved the preparation of a detailed map of all of the ancient city at its height (*c.* A.D. 600) (Fig. 3); narrative descriptions of visible structural remains and structurally related spaces for this area of *c.* 20 square km. or 8 square miles, and less detailed information on an additional 33 square km. or 13 square miles; surface collections from all of the sites (*c.* 5,000) in the 20 square km. of construction shown on Fig. 3; the encoding of data from all of these sites for computer analyses (Cowgill 1967, 1968); a programme of test excavations growing out of information obtained in the mapping and in part testing our interpretations from surface data; studies and analyses of workshops in obsidian, ceramics, figurines and other materials, including the work of lapidaries; studies of botanical and faunal remains found in kitchen deposits and in deposits of fill; analyses of human skeletal remains found in our excavations and in the excavations of others at Teotihuacan; and a comparative study of urbanism and urbanization in non-industrialized societies in other parts of the world.

There are many aspects of our work at Teotihuacan which have been duplicated by archaeologists studying other large sites. But what I think was different about our work at Teotihuacan, first of all, was our commitment to map *all* of the ancient city in detailed fashion, even though we knew that it covered many square miles. To map the 20 square km. shown on Fig. 3 it was necessary to make a surface reconnaissance covering a total area of 53 square km. (Millon 1964). Another distinctive aspect of our mapping survey was our

Figure 1 Ancient Teotihuacan. Aerial view of the pre-Hispanic city in the Valley of Teotihuacan, near Mexico City, showing the northern half of the city's principal avenue, the 'Street of the Dead', and many of the buildings on both sides of it. The Pyramid of the Moon is at the north end of the street, foreground; the Pyramid of the Sun is at centre, left, and the Ciudadela precinct, beyond the Sun Pyramid, left. Opposite the Ciudadela is the Great Compound, which is largely unexcavated. The city extended to the foothills in the distance (see Figs. 2 and 3). The Valley of Teotihuacan is part of the Valley of Mexico and it opens onto the central part of the Valley of Mexico at upper right. Mexico City is not visible but is at extreme upper right, 25 miles southwest of the ancient city.

decision to make written descriptions of each structural unit or structurally related space to accompany the data we recorded on map sheets that had been prepared photogrammetrically, even though this meant preparing more than 5,000 such site record sheets. Third, we made surface collections from all but a small number of these 5,000 sites, collections which were recorded in the field and brought to the laboratory for study and analyses, including encoding for computer analyses. Fourth, we tested some of the most important field interpretations we had made from surface evidence in test excavations. Larger sites than Teotihuacan have been mapped, but not completely. More extensive programmes of test excavations have been carried out at large sites, but without an intensive knowledge of each of thousands of sites. One of the results of all of this is that we do not have to extrapolate from our data to determine how large Teotihuacan was or how intensively it was occupied. We can make our estimates on the basis of a survey of the whole city.

We also know a great deal about many other aspects of city life at Teotihuacan. We have located hundreds of craft workshops in the city. We know that there were more than 400 obsidian workshops and more than 100 ceramic workshops when the city was at its height, as well as scores of workshops in other materials. Collections from each site make possible the preparation of distribution maps of all kinds. George Cowgill has prepared a number of these and will be preparing many more (see Cowgill, this volume).

Clearly, all of this has taken a great deal of time. But we believe that our results up to now, and the results we know will be emerging from analyses in progress, demonstrate the value of such intensive and extensive methods.

In addition, in the first volume of our project series, we decided to publish the evidence from our mapping survey in a way that in itself is not unusual, but is, I believe, unique on the scale at which we are doing it (Millon 1973). We divided the area we mapped into 500-metre squares, oriented not to astronomic north but to the north-south orientation of most Teotihuacan buildings (c.15°30' east of north). There are 147 such squares in the map of the ancient city c. A.D. 600 (Figs. 3-5). The area we surveyed by surface reconnaissance was mapped photogrammetrically at a scale of 1:2000, which is the scale of the map of ancient Tikal in Guatemala (Carr and Hazard 1961). Each of the 147 500-metre squares in Fig. 3 is being published at this same scale (1:2000), which permits the representation of a considerable amount of detail. Each 500-metre square at the 1:2000 scale is a square 25 cm. on a side (c.10 inches). These 147 sheets are labelled Field Data sheets (e.g., Figs. 4a and 5a). They show not only the topographic, vegetational and other detail prepared photogrammetrically, but also those data from our surface survey which could be recorded graphically on map sheets (boundaries of mounds, exposed walls and floors, site boundaries, special potsherd

Figure 2 Photogrammetric map of the region of ancient Teotihuacan, prepared from a reduced mosaic of the topographic map sheets used in the field to produce the map shown in Figure 3. The grid system of 500-metre squares is oriented to the 'Street of the Dead', the north-south axis of the ancient city (about 15°30′ east of north).

Figure 3 (below). Map of the ancient city of Teotihuacan at its height (c. A.D. 600). The city covered about 20 square km. (8 square miles). the map shows a number of partially or completely excavated structures, many of which appear in greater detail on the inset map. Most structures shown on the map are unexcavated, however. They are hypothetical reconstructions based on Teotihuacan Mapping Project surveys of surface remains of unexcavated and partially excavated structures. Most of the buildings shown were one-storey apartment compounds. Note the canalization of

K E Y

1 BARRANCA HUEXOLOCO	11
2 RIO SAN LORENZO	12
3 BARRANCA PATLACHIQUE	13
4 BARRANCA DE MANTANALES	14
5 BARRANCA MALINALCO	15
6 BARRANCA COROTLAN	16
7 SAN MARTIN DE LAS PIRAMIDES	17
8 SAN FRANCISCO MAZAPAN	18
9 SANTA MARIA COATLAN	19
10 SAN SEBASTIAN CHIMALPA	20

MOON PYRAMID
SUN PYRAMID
CIUDADELA
MUSEUM AND PARKING LOT
PERIFERICO, MODERN ROAD AROUND
ARCHAEOLOGICAL ZONE
TOLL ROAD TO MEXICO CITY
ROAD TO OTUMBA
BARRANCA, PIEDRAS NEGRAS
RIO SAN JUAN NORTH BRANCH
RIO SAN JUAN SOUTH BRANCH

BARRIOS OF TEOTIHUACAN
(TEOTIHUACAN DE ARISTA)

PURIFICACION TILMATLTLAN
SAN JUAN EVANGELISTA TLALOTLACAN
PUTLA
MAXUYOCO
COXOTLAN

RANCHO OZTOYOHUALCO
HACIENDA METEPEC
HACIENDA TLAJINGA
CERRO MALINALCO
CERRO COLORADO EL GRANDE
CERRO COLORADO EL CHICO

L E G E N D

EXCAVATED STRUCTURE
MOUND
LOW MOUND
DEPRESSION
MODERN BUILDING
VEGETATION
ROAD
PATH OR TRAIL
WATER COURSE
RAILROAD
HIGH VOLTAGE POWER LINE
POWER/TELEPHONE AND TELEGRAM LINES.

ELEVATION AT ZERO POINT OF GRID SYSTEM
CA. 2276 METERS ABOVE MEAN SEA LEVEL.

PHOTOGRAMMETRIC MANUSCRIPT MAP PREPARED BY
CIA. MEXICANA AEROFOTO, S.A., MEXICO., D.F.
AND HUNTING MAPPING, INC., ROCHESTER, N.Y.

THIS MAP IS A MOSAIC MADE FROM REDUCTIONS OF THE MACHINE DRAWN, PHOTOGRAMMETRIC PENCIL SHEETS WHICH WERE NOT ORIGINALLY INTENDED FOR PUBLICATION. SUCH OF THESE SHEETS SHOW A FEW MINOR DISCREPANCIES AND PROBLEMATIC REPRESENTATIONS, MOST OF WHICH ARE RESOLVED ON THE FINAL 1:2,000 DRAWINGS IN VOLUME 1 OF THE PROJECT REPORTS. IT IS PUBLISHED IN THIS FORM IN THE BELIEF THAT ITS USEFULNESS OUTWEIGHS ITS DEFICIENCIES AS A PUBLICATION AS THEY EXISTED IN MARCH, 1962, BEFORE MOST OF THE EXCAVATIONS OF MEXICO'S INSTITUTO NACIONAL DE ANTROPOLOGIA E HISTORIA (INAH). EXCEPTIONS ARE THE ROAD AROUND THE ARCHAEOLOGICAL ZONE AND THE HIGHWAYS CONSTRUCTED SINCE 1962.

TEOTIHUACAN MAPPING PROJECT
RENE MILLON, DIRECTOR
DEPARTMENT OF ANTHROPOLOGY
UNIVERSITY OF ROCHESTER
ROCHESTER, NEW YORK
PRINCIPAL CARTOGRAPHERS:
BRUCE DREWITT AND GEORGE COWGILL
AIDED BY GRANTS FROM THE

GRID IS ORIENTED
CA. 15°25′ EAST OF
ASTRONOMIC NORTH.

SUN PYRAMID
19°41′30″ N.LAT.
98°50′30″ W.LONG.

TEOTIHUACAN IS 40 KILOMETERS (25 MILES)

MILES

KILOMETERS

CONTOUR INTERVAL ONE METER

TEOTIHUACAN
ESTADO DE MEXICO
M E X I C O
TOPOGRAPHIC MAP

SEPTEMBER 1970
COPYRIGHT 1970 BY RENE MILLON

MEXICO

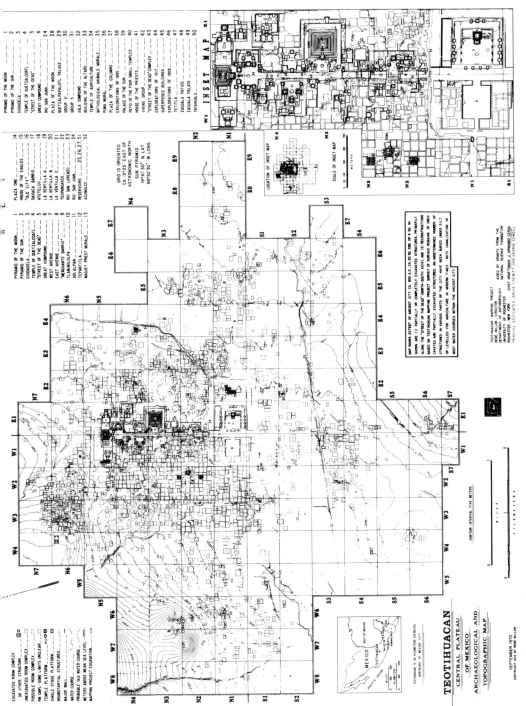

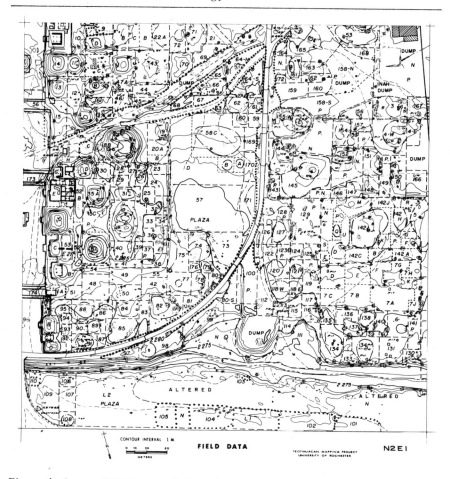

Figure 4a Square N2E1, one of the 500-metre squares on the Teotihuacan map. It is on the east side of the 'Street of the Dead', immediately to the north of the Ciudadela (see Figure 3). This is a topographic sheet showing field data collected in the preparation of the map. Contours are at one-metre intervals. Site boundaries are indicated by dashed lines. Each site is identified by a number (e.g. 48), or a number and a letter (e.g. 35 A). Numbers are normally shown only with the first of a series of sub-sites (e.g. 1 A; the other sub-sites of site 1 to the north — B, C, D, E, F, G, etc. — bear only identifying letters). Buildings along the 'Street of the Dead' have been reconstructed by the Mexican government. Elsewhere, exposed walls (W) and floors (F) are indicated, and, if necessary, numbered. The main datum for elevations on the map is at top, right centre. One of the triangulation points used in obtaining horizontal control for the map is shown at bottom left.

In the volume in which the map is published (Millon 1973) this, and the other 146 map squares comprising the map, are published at a scale of 1:2000 (which is considerably larger than the above). All map squares showing topographic and field data, such as above, bear overlays on which are printed the architectural interpretations which mapping project personnel have made of these data. Fig. 4b, right, is the overlay drawing for Fig. 4a.

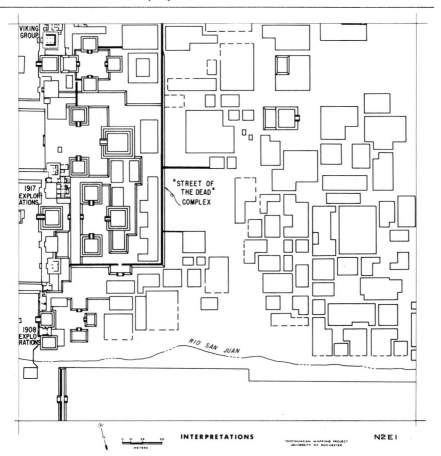

Figure 4*b* Architectural interpretations for Square N2E1, the overlay sheet for
    Fig. 4*a*, left. This drawing shows temples, platforms, apartment compounds
    and other buildings, as project personnel think they would have looked
    anciently, based on the data shown at left and on written descriptions and
    surface collections for each numbered site and sub-site at left. The 'Street of
    the Dead' Complex, part of which is shown above, is a large walled complex
    of temples, platforms and residences between the Sun Pyramid and the
    Ciudadela. It was found by mapping project personnel (Wallrath 1967).
    Buildings shown as open rectangles were either apartment compounds, or
    smaller residential compounds. In the latter case, room arrangements may
    have been similar to the excavated residential compound in site 1 F (left of
    site 52 B) (Fig. 4*a*, left centre).

concentrations, special concentrations of obsidian, stone, etc.). Each
of these 147 Field Data sheets is covered by an acetate overlay
printed in red, on which are presented our architectural interpretations of the archaeological evidence obtained in our survey and
noted on the Field Data sheets and on site records (e.g., Figs. 4*b* and
5*b*). This and the narrative data to be presented in volume 2 of our
reports will enable the reader to evaluate our architectural interpret-

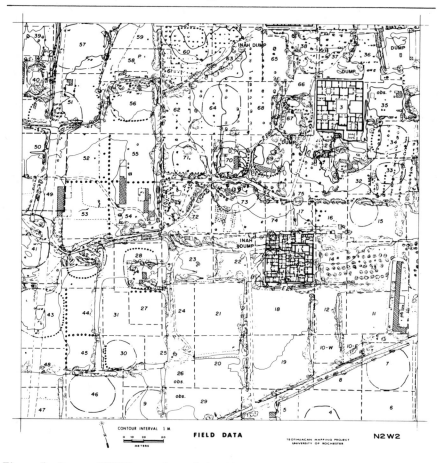

Figure 5*a* Square N2W2, another of the 500-metre squares on the Teotihuacan
map. It is northwest of the Great Compound and its east edge is 500 metres
west of the 'Street of the Dead'. Like Fig. 4*a*, this is a topographic sheet
showing field data collected in the preparation of the map. This square is
located in a neighbourhood of apartment compounds, two of which have
been completely excavated and one of which has been partially exposed.
Consult Fig. 4*a* for additional comments on field data sheets such as the
above. Fig. 5*b*, right, is the overlay drawing for Fig. 5*a*, above.

ations for himself. Figs. 4 and 5 represent two of the 147 pairs of
map sheets, with the Field Data on the left (Figs. 4*a*, 5*a*) and the
architectural interpretations on the right (Figs. 4*b*, 5*b*). The latter
sheets are printed on transparent overlays in the map volume (Millon
1973). The squares represented are N2E1 on the 'Street of
the Dead' and N2W2, a neighbourhood of apartment compounds.
(For location of these squares, see Fig. 3). Each of the open
rectangles drawn on the interpretations sheet represents an apartment compound, a great walled, windowless compound, composed
of rooms, porticoes, passageways, patios with underground drainage
systems, and walls often bearing mural paintings, like those of the

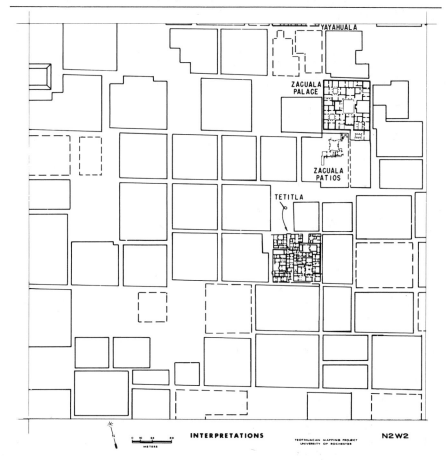

Figure 5*b* Architectural interpretations for square N2W2, the overlay sheet for Fig. 5*a*, left. This is a neighbourhood of apartment compounds. The rectangles shown on this square represent apartment compounds and, if excavated, the author believes they would reveal arrangements of rooms, porticos, patios and accessways similar to those in the excavated apartment compounds in this square (e.g., Tetitla, Zacuala Palace).

excavated apartment compounds in square N2W2 – Tetitla and Zacuala Palace, which are completely excavated, and Zacuala Patios, which is only partially excavated. These compounds are often 50 m. or more on a side and represent the basic residential unit.

In addition to the 147 individual Field Data sheets with interpretations overlays, there is a four-colour map of the entire city in the same volume at a scale of 1:10,000, with an inset of the major part of the 'Street of the Dead' area at 1:5,000. (Fig. 3 is a reduced version of that map.) In addition, there is a large 1:2,000 four-colour map of the north-central part of the city as we think it was *c*. A.D. 600. Finally, the volume includes a photogrammetric map of the area surveyed at a scale of 1:10,000. (Fig. 2 is a reduced version.)

The second volume, nearing completion, contains narrative sum-

TEOTIHUACAN APARTMENT COMPOUNDS

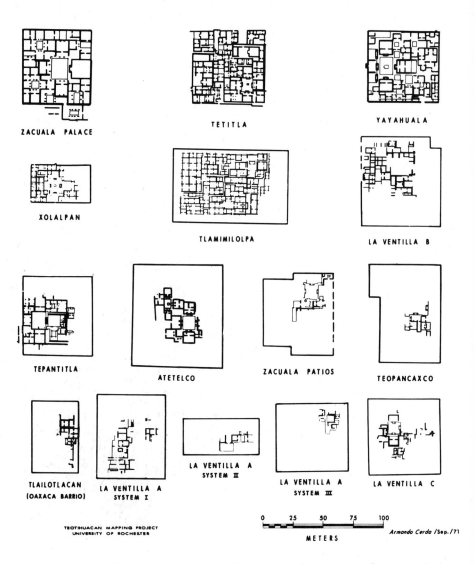

Figure 6 Plans of excavated or partially excavated apartment compounds in Teotihuacan drawn to the same scale. In the case of partially excavated compounds, the locations of most exterior walls are approximate.

maries of each of the 5,000 sites, including descriptions, comments and references on excavated buildings, as well as plans of the latter at a scale of 1:500. All completely or partially excavated residential compounds and other residential structures so far uncovered in the ancient city have also been brought together on two sheets for comparative purposes (Figs. 6, 7).

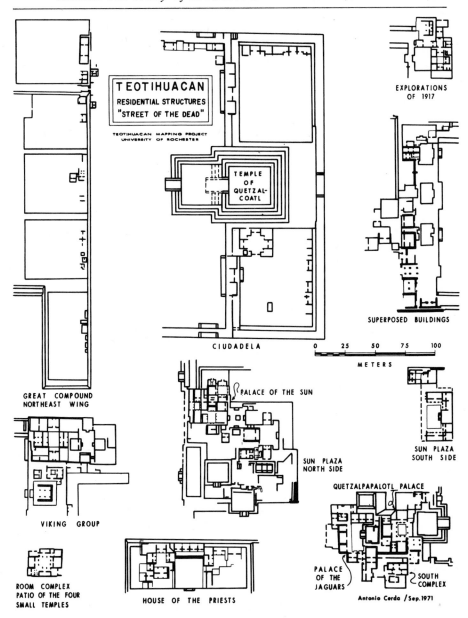

Figure 7 Plans of excavated or partially excavated residential structures on the 'Street of the Dead' drawn to the same scale as the apartment compounds in Fig. 6.

The Teotihuacan map

What are some of the things we have been learning about Teotihuacan as a pre-Hispanic Mexican urban centre that make all of this study worthwhile? The immense size and importance of Teotihuacan have been recognized for some time. But its extent, as well as the kind of place it was, have been the subject of widely varying views. How did Teotihuacan come into being? How large was its population? How densely was it settled? Who lived there? What was the social composition of the city's population? Did groups of kinsmen and people sharing occupations play significant roles in the city's life? How important was craft production in the economy of Teotihuacan? How important a role did planning play in the growth of Teotihuacan? Was the city as we see it on the map the result of the gradual fulfilment of a master plan? How important was the unparalleled attraction of Teotihuacan, the religious and pilgrimage centre, to the economic, social, cultural and political life of the city, and to the people within its orbit? What is the relation of the ecological approach to the study of Teotihuacan urbanism? What were the relations between the foreigners living in the enclave in the western part of the city which we call the 'Oaxaca *barrio*' (Fig. 3, no. 17) with other Teotihuacanos and with the Teotihuacan hierarchy? How did the Teotihuacan state come into being? What is the relation, if any, between irrigation and the rise of the Teotihuacan state? How was the city organized politically and administratively? How is the extraordinarily pervasive and extensive influence of Teotihuacan in so much of Middle America to be interpreted? How do its internal organization and the processes involved in its rise and expansion compare with what we know about non-industrialized cities in other parts of the world? What contributions can the study of Teotihuacan make to comparative studies of urbanism and urbanization?

These are some of the questions that our work and the work of others at Teotihuacan have helped to formulate and elucidate. It will be possible to touch on only a few of these questions in this short article. Some of them are dealt with in the text of the volume on which this article is based (Millon 1973). Others will be dealt with in subsequent volumes.

The ancient city was divided into quadrants (Fig. 3). The north-south axis is the 'Street of the Dead', the name given the then ruined city's main street by the Aztecs, long after the city as such had ceased to exist. The east-west axis is subordinate to the north-south axis. It is formed by two avenues we found in surface reconnaissance that terminate in the city's centre and that are interrupted by the city's two largest precincts, the Ciudadela and the Great Compound (Fig. 3, nos. 3 and 6). I have called these avenues West and East Avenues (Fig. 3, nos. 7 and 8). We found the Great Compound in our survey. We think its great central plaza was probably the city's main marketplace and that its two extensive wings may have housed state functionaries.

The density of settlement in the city's four quarters differs markedly. The northwest quadrant is by far the most densely settled and presumably, therefore, the most populous. It is also the quadrant with the greatest concentration of occupational specialists and is also one of the oldest sections of Teotihuacan. For various reasons I call the northwestern part of the later city's northwest quadrant the 'Old City' (Fig. 3, no. 16).

A striking feature of the northern and northwestern part of the city is the many major walls and great walled precincts that we found in our survey of this area (Fig. 3). The group of large walled compounds west of the Moon Pyramid may have been designed, at least in part, to close off these areas from the rest of the city, to provide precincts that could be entered at only one or two entry points.

The walls in these large precincts would have served defensive purposes, but it is not clear if they were designed with defence in mind. Walled compounds impede free access to the 'Street of the Dead' on the east for most of the distance between the Moon Plaza and the Ciudadela (Fig. 3, inset). It is also possible that the long north-south wall that ends in square N4W2 (Fig. 3) extended as far south as square N2W2 (Figs. 5a, b) and perhaps as far south as the north side of the river in N1W2. We did not find any continuation of the wall beyond the point where we show it ending when we surveyed this area in the field in preparing the map. But the contours south of the end of the wall from N4W2 to N1W2 suggest that a wall may in fact have existed for a major part of this distance. See, for example, the contours two blocks west of Tetitla (Figs. 5a, b). If the southern extension of the long west wall did exist, it would have closed off all of the northern half of the 'inner city' on the north and west.

The discovery in our survey of the network of massive walls and great walled precincts in the northwest and elsewhere significantly changes one's views on how these parts of the city looked, and raises new questions about what kind of a city Teotihuacan was. Certainly it is clear that Teotihuacan was not the defenceless open city that has often been described. In addition to the walls just discussed, there are natural barriers in the form of steep-sided stream beds on the west, the east, and a kilometre south of the city's centre (Figs. 2, 3). In addition, the maze of canals in the southwestern part of the city, where intensive *chinampa* cultivation (Lorenzo 1968) is practised today and may have been anciently (Sanders 1965), would have impeded easy access to the city. Teotihuacan would not then have been a 'pitiful helpless giant' if subjected to attack. In addition, the city's apartment compounds and other residential compounds (numbering some 2,200) are natural fortresses. An attacker would have had to pass through narrow streets while subject to attack by Teotihuacanos on the roofs of their compounds, as was the case in Tenochtitlan, the Aztec capital, when Cortés and his army were under attack from the rooftops of Aztec house compounds. Clearly,

Teotihuacan would not have been an easy city to take if its populace were determined to defend it. To think of it as an 'open city' is misleading.

Evidence from both surface survey and excavation indicates that Teotihuacan was divided into *barrios* or neighbourhoods. Some groups of compounds are so clearly set off from surrounding structures that they form easily definable spatial units (Fig. 3, the cluster of compounds in N4E2 of which Tepantitla, no.12, forms a part). Other groups of compounds are set apart by what we find on the surface beneath which they lie. There are clusters of compounds where the same crafts seem to have been practiced (obsidian working, pottery making), where foreigners from the same place lived (the Oaxaca *barrio*, Fig. 3, no. 17), where foreign pottery from many different parts of Middle America is found, and where we think merchants may have lived ('merchants' *barrio*', Fig. 3, no. 9).

The Oaxaca barrio

The Oaxaca *barrio* is a section of the city in which people from what is now the state of Oaxaca lived. The valley of Oaxaca lies some 200 miles southeast of Teotihuacan. The Oaxaca enclave was found in our surface survey. The first evidence of it was a concentration of fine wares from Oaxaca in our surface collections from an area in the western part of the ancient city. Because of this concentration we showed our pottery collections from this area to John Paddock of the University of the Americas, since he is a specialist in Oaxacan archaeology. He confirmed our findings, commenting not only on the presence of various fine wares from Oaxaca, but also on the apparent presence of domestic or utilitarian wares from that area. The latter was unexpected and obviously of the greatest importance. Because of our mutual interest in the discovery, Paddock directed a brief excavation in one of the compounds in the enclave in late 1966 under our permit from the Mexican government. We pursued the excavation in this same compound for some time thereafter on an intensive basis, as part of our Teotihuacan Mapping Project test excavations.

Two of Paddock's students, Peter Goodwin and Paul Morrissey, found a number of fragments of a Monte Alban funerary urn apparently associated with an extended burial near the surface. Extended burials are rare in Teotihuacan, but common in Oaxaca. The urn dates from a period in the Oaxaca sequence known as the Epoch of Transition, which is marked by the beginning of Teotihuacan influence at the great Valley of Oaxaca centre of Monte Alban. But the urn was evidently an heirloom if associated with the burial, for the other vessels found when the burial was excavated date towards the end of Teotihuacan's history as a city. A strati-

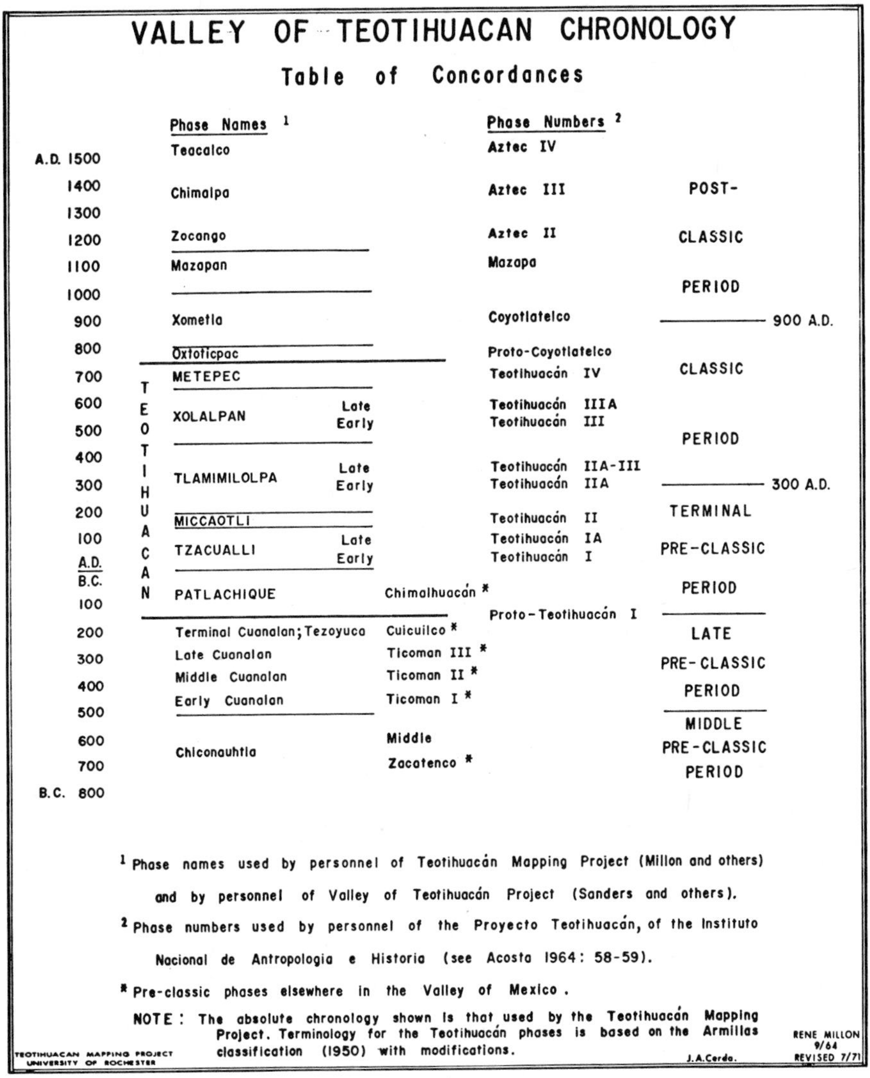

VALLEY OF TEOTIHUACAN CHRONOLOGY

Table of Concordances

	Phase Names [1]		Phase Numbers [2]	
A.D. 1500	Teacalco		Aztec IV	
1400	Chimalpa		Aztec III	POST-
1300				
1200	Zocango		Aztec II	CLASSIC
1100	Mazapan		Mazapa	
1000				PERIOD
900	Xometla		Coyotlatelco	———— 900 A.D.
800	Oxtoticpac		Proto-Coyotlatelco	
700	METEPEC		Teotihuacán IV	CLASSIC
600	XOLALPAN	Late	Teotihuacán IIIA	
500		Early	Teotihuacán III	
400				PERIOD
300	TLAMIMILOLPA	Late	Teotihuacán IIA-III	
		Early	Teotihuacán IIA	———— 300 A.D.
200	MICCAOTLI		Teotihuacán II	TERMINAL
100	TZACUALLI	Late	Teotihuacán IA	
A.D.		Early	Teotihuacán I	PRE-CLASSIC
B.C.				
100	PATLACHIQUE	Chimalhuacán *		PERIOD
			Proto-Teotihuacán I	
200	Terminal Cuanalan; Tezoyuca	Cuicuilco *		LATE
300	Late Cuanalan	Ticoman III *		PRE-CLASSIC
400	Middle Cuanalan	Ticoman II *		PERIOD
500	Early Cuanalan	Ticoman I *		
600	Chiconauhtla	Middle		MIDDLE PRE-CLASSIC
700		Zacatenco *		PERIOD
B.C. 800				

(Left margin vertical: TEOTIHUACAN)

[1] Phase names used by personnel of Teotihuacán Mapping Project (Millon and others) and by personnel of Valley of Teotihuacán Project (Sanders and others).

[2] Phase numbers used by personnel of the Proyecto Teotihuacán, of the Instituto Nacional de Antropologia e Historia (see Acosta 1964: 58-59).

* Pre-classic phases elsewhere in the Valley of Mexico.

NOTE: The absolute chronology shown is that used by the Teotihuacán Mapping Project. Terminology for the Teotihuacán phases is based on the Armillas classification (1950) with modifications.

TEOTIHUACAN MAPPING PROJECT
UNIVERSITY OF ROCHESTER

RENE MILLON
9/64
J.A.Cerda.   REVISED 7/71

Figure 8 Chronological chart for the Teotihuacan Valley. The absolute dates for Teotihuacan shown at left represent the author's views on how conflicting radiocarbon dates from the ancient city can best be reconciled.

graphic pit excavated in one of the rooms by Evelyn Rattray, then a University of the Americas staff member, disclosed that the earliest building level of the compound dated to the latter part of the Tlamimilolpa phase in the chronology of Teotihuacan (*c.* A.D. 400) (Fig. 8).

Our excavations in the compound uncovered part of the compound's principal temple, a large structure that faced west. The temple had the typical Teotihuacan temple facing — the *tablero-talud*, a rectangular recessed panel resting on a sloping lower wall. In all other respects as well, the compound was constructed like other apartment compounds at Teotihuacan (Fig. 6, bottom left), though not of the best building materials. There was a good deal of adobe construction in walls, for example. All excavated deposits contained both Teotihuacan pottery and pottery that was either from Oaxaca or locally-made versions of Oaxacan wares, including domestic wares.

As a matter of fact, our excavations in the Oaxaca *barrio*, which included single pits in three other compounds in the *barrio*, provided important support for one of the assumptions we had made in our surface survey. Teotihuacan compounds and other structures seem to have four or more successive building levels, each of which is built on successive deposits of mixed fill partly derived from the upper walls and roofs of earlier building levels. We had assumed that the fill in most cases must have been brought from nearby local dumps, supplemented by accumulated rubbish and the older fill from deliberately destroyed and/or collapsed upper walls and roofs of the compound under reconstruction. If this were true, then the ceramics found on the surface covering a compound or other structure would reflect reasonably accurately the actual architectural and occupational history of the building. The Oaxaca *barrio* provided an ideal test of this assumption, because of the foreign pottery we found on the surface of the mounds in this area. We found Oaxaca or Oaxaca-like pottery to be present from top to bottom in all of our excavations there. Our assumption of localized dumps received still further support from excavations we later carried out in the 'merchants' *barrio*' on the eastern edge of the city (Fig. 3, no. 9). There also surface survey yielded a high percentage of foreign pottery. In this case most of it was from Veracruz and the Maya area to the east and southeast of Teotihuacan. The same range of foreign wares found on the surface was found in our two excavations there. In both cases, in the 'merchants' *barrio*' and in the Oaxaca *barrio*, the foreign pottery present could not have been brought in as fill from other parts of the city in the quantities found, because it occurs rarely in the rest of the city.

Our excavations in the Oaxaca *barrio* uncovered another Oaxacan urn, apparently ritually smashed late in the city's history, in a small room attached to the south side of the temple previously mentioned (Millon 1967*a*; 1968*a*: Fig. 4; 1973, Figs. 58, 59). Excavated by Juan Vidarte, it dates to the beginning of the Monte Alban IIIA phase, according to Ignacio Bernal (personal communication). It is thus very little later than the Epoch of Transition urn found by Paddock.

Both urns belong, therefore, to the time period in Monte Alban when contacts between Teotihuacan and Monte Alban are traditionally thought to have become important. The excavations in the Oaxaca barrio suggest that these ties began in the latter part of the Tlamimilolpa phase (*c*. A.D. 400) (Fig. 8). Interestingly, the ceramic links to Teotihuacan at Monte Alban may begin slightly earlier. The Teotihuacan forms which appear in Monte Alban during the Epoch of Transition are either forms with a wide time span (*floreros*) or are forms that appear to co-exist only in the middle of the Tlamimilolpa phase at Teotihuacan (*c.* A.D. 350).

In many ways the most striking discovery in the Oaxaca *barrio* was a stone-lined tomb in Oaxaca style, complete with antechamber. The tomb had been looted at least twice. The only remains of the tomb offering were a few broken fragments of pottery vessels. Local Teotihuacan wares predominated. But between the tomb and its antechamber a stela had been set into the wall. On the stela, carved in Monte Alban style, was a Zapotec glyph ('L', the glyph for motion, counterpart of the Nahua glyph *olin*) and below it the number 9 (first a bar standing for five and below it four dots) (Millon 1968*a*: Fig. 5; 1973, Figs. 60*a*, 60*b*). The stela and the glyph carved on it appear to have been carved from a re-used Teotihuacan building stone. The stela is not portable (it weighs over 600 pounds) and must have been carved at Teotihuacan. The tomb is very late in Teotihuacan's history, surely dating to the seventh century A.D., whereas the Oaxaqueños had originally come to Teotihuacan in the late fourth or early fifth century. In form and in construction the tomb indicates that the people of the *barrio* still observed a funerary cult which was basically Oaxacan, hundreds of years after the establishment of the Oaxacan enclave in Teotihuacan. Teotihuacanos did not bury their dead in stone-lined tombs and did not erect carved stones to memorialize their dead. The use of the two funerary urn heirlooms also indicates continuity in tradition.

All of this indicates that the people who lived in the Oaxaca *barrio* preserved many of their customs and beliefs during the hundreds of years that the enclave existed in the city. At the same time, it is also important to realize that not only did they live in standard Teotihuacan apartment compounds, using standard Teotihuacan orientations (they may have had little choice in this), but that they also used the standard Teotihuacan architectural conventions for the main temple in one of their compounds. In addition, the offerings which they made consisted predominantly of locally made pottery vessels in Teotihuacan style. The continued existence in this *barrio* of domestic customs, burial practices, rituals and beliefs of Oaxacan origin may represent part of the process whereby the people of the *barrio* maintained their cultural identity as Oaxaqueños, within a metropolis where they were a tiny minority and not of high status.

We do not yet know what the Oaxaqueños were doing in Teotihuacan. Teotihuacan civilization had been flourishing for hundreds of years when the Oaxaqueños came to the city. It is possible that they were traders, but if they were we have no evidence for it. No doubt the presence of Oaxaqueños in Teotihuacan facilitated interchanges between the two societies, and the Teotihuacanos may well have adopted some Oaxacan ideas and practices, particularly in the fields of writing and calendrics.

I do not recall any representations of armed Teotihuacanos at Monte Alban. If there were any, they would be rare when compared to the representations of what appear to be armed Teotihuacanos in the Maya area. Altogether, the evidence suggests that the relationship between Teotihuacan and Monte Alban may have been closer and of a different kind than the relationship of Teotihuacan to other foreign centres. There may have been a kind of 'special relationship' between Teotihuacan and Monte Alban. This may explain why so far the only unmistakable foreign enclave at Teotihuacan is the barrio of Oaxaqueños. Perhaps some of the artistic links between Teotihuacan and Monte Alban are at least in part reflections of this 'special relationship'. Possibly this relationship was manifested and strengthened through marriage alliances at the highest level. One wonders if Tomb 105 at Monte Alban might be commemorating such ties.

The Teotihuacan apartment compound

As noted previously, the standard Teotihuacan residential building is a one-storey apartment or other residential compound, of which there are some 2,200 in the city. Most such buildings that have been excavated have at least one major patio, with one or more temples facing into it. The most prominent temple, if more than one is present, is usually on the east side of the patio and faces west. Apartment compounds appear to have been built with the plan of the entire compound in mind from the outset of construction or from the outset of a re-building of it. Most excavated compounds appear to have been re-built completely or largely so, three, four or more times. The planned layout of these compounds suggests that some of them and perhaps many of them were built and occupied by groups of a corporate character, whose members participated in common rituals in the compound's temple or temples (Fig. 6).

There seems to have been a tendency for people living in the same apartment compound to engage in the same occupation. There is evidence from the work of Michael Spence that related males lived in some apartment compounds (Spence 1971). In many *barrios* the same tendency for occupational clustering existed, as we have seen. A number of *barrios* have one or more temples within them, larger than and distinct from those within compounds, suggesting the existence of *barrio* temples in at least some parts of the city. *Barrio* temples and a tendency to grouping by occupation or place of origin suggest that some *barrios*, as well as some apartment compounds, may have had a degree of corporateness.

There is insufficient space in this article to discuss at any length the evidence for the internal composition of the populations living in apartment compounds at Teotihuacan. But it is useful to note what that research suggests at this point. Two critical aspects of the Teotihuacan apartment compound can be used to look at it in comparative perspective — the relative inflexibility of the apartment compound as a living unit and the fact that there were so many hundreds of these compounds in large clusters throughout the city (Figs. 3, 6).

What emerges first from an examination of comparative evidence from non-industrialized cities in various parts of the world is a realization of how very unusual a standard residential urban unit the Teotihuacan apartment compound is. What emerges next is a realization that it would be oversimplifying the evidence to postulate that those who lived in these compounds either were organized solely on the basis of strong kin ties or solely on the basis of relatively impersonal landlord-tenant relations. Much more likely is a more complex model involving individual or corporate ownership of compounds, combined with a variety of diffuse relationships of dependency that would be less than kinship yet more than landlord-tenant relations . . . perhaps something analogous to the social composition of the successive 'circles' of the 'family' in large landholdings in the traditional Japanese village in early Tokugawa Japan (Smith 1959: 6 and passim). The outermost 'circle' of people in a compound might have consisted of people linked to each other by patron-client ties in a framework of ritual kinship. This model will remain hypothetical until it can be tested in the controlled excavation of one or more apartment compounds, and at the outset it may be possible to test only some of its dimensions.

But it is worth noting that it was possible to arrive at such a model for the population of the Teotihuacan apartment compound from the study of comparative archaeological, ethnographic and historic evidence in which no configurations moderately closely resembling what we find at Teotihuacan were encountered. The comparative study itself helped to define and bound the problem and to suggest a model for the archaeological evidence not found in the comparative evidence itself. It was not found in the comparative evidence because the evidence from Teotihuacan stands out as so unusual in comparative perspective, a fact which was not apparent when I started the comparative study. Thus, what emerges is a model for the Teotihuacan evidence to be tested in excavation that rests on comparative study, but at the same time does not replicate any particular evidence from any specific non-industrialized urban setting elsewhere in the world (cf. Flannery 1967: 122).

A preliminary analysis by Richard I. Ford and Joel N. Elias of some of the plant material we recovered from the flotation of kitchen floors we excavated in Tetitla (Fig. 5a, E24) was reported on at the 1972 annual meeting of the Society for American Archaeology in Miami Beach (Ford and Elias 1972). I want to call attention to two aspects of this preliminary report — the great range of plant material represented, indicating an extremely intensive exploitation of the environment,[2] and also the possibility that at least some of the maize consumed was not ground in Tetitla, or at least that it was not ground in the kitchen area where we were digging. The possibility therefore exists that already prepared *masa* or maize dough could be obtained in the market-place. The fact that most of Tetitla appears to have been occupied by people of high status in Teotihuacan society, although by no means the highest, may be a factor here. Even so, should the possibility of this kind of market-place exchange of so basic a staple as maize dough receive further support, it would imply greater complexity of exchange, specialization and economic interdependence within the city than most investigators would have thought possible ten years ago.

Planning

Teotihuacan was clearly subject to planning (Drewitt 1967, 1969), but it is not clear whether it was built in accordance with a master plan established early in the city's history (Robertson 1963: 35). The cruciform layout probably was established early, around the time of Christ, and the basic orientations of most structures shortly thereafter. But whether the city was entirely laid out or intended to be entirely laid out in accordance with a single preconceived plan is the question.

The building of Teotihuacan over a period of several centuries may have been the result of the slow fulfilment of some kind of master plan. But it may also have been the result of a series of additions to a basic cruciform plan, additions of varying degrees of magnitude and complexity, which, when we see the completed whole, may give more of an impression of the realization of a master plan than actually was the case. Robertson has made this argument with respect to the build-up of the 'Street of the Dead' (1963: 35-6), but there it seems to be only partially applicable. The orderly way in which Teotihuacan structures are disposed argues that planning was involved when any part of the city was laid out. But it does not necessarily argue that there was a single, detailed, early master plan.

Population

Not long ago I estimated that Teotihuacan's population at its peak was probably around 125,000 (Millon 1970: 1079-80). This estimate was based on conservative assumptions about the number of people living in an apartment compound, using excavated apartment compounds as a guide. Estimated populations for unexcavated apartment compounds were made by measuring the area of each and arriving at a separate figure for each. I now think that my assumptions were too conservative, and that the population of Teotihuacan may have reached 150,000 to 200,000 or perhaps even higher.

Craft production

Whether or not these figures are correct, it is clear that Teotihuacan must have had a population that numbered at least 100,000. This in itself is impressively large for a pre-Hispanic city. But even more important, a significant proportion of the city's population was engaged in craft activities. To be sure, it is very likely that most of the people residing in the city lived from the cultivation of land outside it. But we have found more than 500 craft workshops in our archaeological surface survey of the city. Moreover, we have tested the validity of our surface interpretations in excavations and have found them to be sound. The vast majority of the workshops we have found are obsidian workshops, most of which appear to have been in use when the city was at its height. There are also some 200 other workshops, most of which were ceramic workshops; but there are also workshops where lapidaries worked, where figurines were made, where ground stone implements were made, where slate was worked, where basalt was worked and where shell was worked. In addition, there must also have been an unknown number of workshops where craftsmen worked in materials and with tools that left no traces or that we have not been able to recognize. Still other craftsmen must have been engaged in building the city's many structures — masons, plasterers, carpenters, and others.

Thus, a significant proportion of the population of Teotihuacan must have been involved in craft production and craft activities. In addition, a great deal of what was produced in the city must have been exported. This must certainly have been true of much of the obsidian worked in the city. Did the growth potential represented by the expanding craft of obsidian working play a significant role in the rise of Teotihuacan as a city (Jacobs 1969; Millon 1970)? I believe that it did and that it will be possible to establish this. In any event, it is clear that the quantitative importance of craft production would have had major consequences for the quality and nature of economic, social and political relationships, for the growth in importance of marketplace trade, and in these and many other ways would have contributed to the shaping of Teotihuacan as an urban centre.

No matter how important obsidian working may have been, however, it seems highly probable that it will have to be viewed in the context of a number of parallel and intertwined processes of change. The growing attraction of Teotihuacan, the ritual centre, and Teotihuacan, the craft and market centre, the predictably increasing attraction of the city as city, the changing social composition of a growing urban society, the apparently growing division of the society into classes and status groups of a markedly stratified character, the growing power of an expansionist state — all these, and other processes as well, must be taken into account, along with the powerful impetus for internal growth of the city's economy provided by obsidian working and, later, other crafts. It is such processes of change that transformed Teotihuacan into the greatest religious centre, the greatest craft centre and the greatest market centre of its time in Middle America.

The Valley of Teotihuacan has a rich agricultural potential (a small area of potential *chinampas* and an irrigable alluvial plain of some 36-40 square km. — *c.* 15 square miles). Others have singled this out as playing a decisive role in the rise of the city (Sanders 1965; Sanders and Price 1968). Instead, I see it as another variable. Given what we know now, I think it most likely that the valley's agricultural potential came to be developed as the requirements of a growing population of craftsmen and other specialists increased in the rapidly expanding early city (cf. Adams 1966: 43). In short, I do not see the valley's irrigable potential as crucial either to the centralization of authority at Teotihuacan or to the formation of the Teotihuacan state. The major sources of the transformation of Teotihuacan society seem to have lain in the city itself.

Urbanization at Teotihuacan

I have previously argued that the marketplace may have played an important role in the integration of Teotihuacan's complex urban society (Millon 1967*b*; 1968*b*: 114), taking off from suggestions made by Eric Wolf, Angel Palerm, and Julian Steward (Steward 1955: 62-3; Wolf 1959: 17-18, 82-3). The argument in essence is that, in an urban society as complex as Teotihuacan seems to have become, with so many outsiders attracted to the city by its market-place(s), temples, and shrines, the institution of the market-place would have provided a focal point for the competing and clashing interests of the various sectors of Teotihuacan society and of those outsiders attracted to it. Whatever may have been the differences among them, all would have had a stake in the maintenance of the 'peace of the market'. The institution of the market-place could have been sustained by the religion of Teotihuacan, by its prestige, by the meaning its rituals must have given to the world, and by the strength of the feelings of loyalty and devotion engendered by its all-pervasive symbols. The two institutions could have nourished and supported one another, supporting and supported by the Teotihuacan state.

This, of course, is at best a partial model for the integration of

Teotihuacan society. Until we know more about the relations between Teotihuacan's rulers, its bureaucracy, and its military on the one hand, and other classes, status groups, and sectors in Teotihuacan society on the other, and of the relations of the latter to each other, we shall have only an imperfect and partial view of what must have been some of the most critical social relations in Teotihuacan society. To take an obvious example, what were the relations between those who cultivated the soil and the Teotihuacan hierarchy? Who controlled cultivated land — those who cultivated it, large landowners, kin groups, the state, some combination of these, or still some other group or groups? These and similar questions are not easy to answer with archaeological evidence alone.

Teotihuacan unquestionably was the preeminent ritual centre of its time in Middle America. It seems to have been the most important centre of trade and to have had the most important market-place. It was the largest and most highly differentiated craft centre. In size, numbers, and density it was the greatest urban centre and perhaps the most complexly stratified society of its time in Middle America. It was the seat of an increasingly powerful state that appears to have extended its domination over wider and wider areas. It became the most influential centre in Middle America. It rose in an area of relatively rich ecological potential, astride the major trade and access route into and out of the Valley of Mexico. But the evidence argues that the impetus for the transformation of both city and countryside lay in the city, not in the countryside.

Occupational specialization, proliferating crafts, high urban density, and a large, markedly stratified population — these are all differing manifestations of the intense process of urbanization that went on in Teotihuacan early in the Christian era. Together with this was the unparalleled attraction that Teotihuacan's shrines and temples and market-place(s) must have exerted over peoples from an increasingly wide area. The intensity of urbanization at Teotihuacan appears to set it apart from other contemporary centres in Middle America. Indeed it appears to stand alone as the most highly urbanized centre of its time in the New World.

Teotihuacan and the ecological approach

The unique character of Teotihuacan has long demanded explanation, even before its great size and enormous complexity as a city were realized. The most popular recent 'explanation' is basically ecological, based primarily on the presumed importance of the managerial requirements of the Valley of Teotihuacan's irrigation system and its presumed relationship to the centralization of authority in the incipient Teotihuacan state.

The Teotihuacan Valley is semi-arid today. While it may have enjoyed a greater rainfall 2,000 years ago, it would still not have had a particularly rich agricultural potential were it not for the springs that come together in the southwestern part of the ancient city (S1W5 and adjacent squares to the west and south). These springs provide water both for the irrigation of the alluvial plain in the lower part of the Teotihuacan Valley and for the cultivation of *chinampas* in the high water-table area near the confluence of the springs. *Chinampas* are artificial islands in a swampy or shallow water area with a constantly available supply of moisture. They are extraordinarily productive when cultivated by labour-intensive means. They covered large sections of the shallow lakes in the southern Valley of Mexico at the time of the Aztecs, providing for their urban markets (West and Armillas 1950; Palerm 1955; Sanders and Price 1968: 148-9, 151; Armillas 1971). While the *chinampas* of the sixteenth century were much more extensive, labour-intensive *chinampa* cultivation may have been first exploited in the small *chinampa* area of Teotihuacan (see also Lorenzo 1968: 58, Fig. 13).

There is still no direct archaeological proof for irrigation in Teotihuacan times. No one has yet excavated any canal dating to the period when Teotihuacan flourished. However, there is clear evidence from our archaeological survey of canalization of ancient water-courses within and beyond the city, often in accord with Teotihuacan orientations (Figs. 2, 3) (Drewitt 1967: 80, 85-6, 88, Fig. 1), and archaeological evidence that irrigation in the Teotihuacan Valley goes back at least to Toltec times (*c.* A.D. 1000) (Millon 1957). Evidence for canal irrigation by Teotihuacan times or earlier exists in Puebla (MacNeish 1967; Johnson 1972) and Oaxaca (Flannery et al. 1967). In view of this and of the simple technology needed to use the present system, it would be surprising if the Teotihuacanos had not irrigated as large an area as the water flow permitted. This is our view, and that of others (Sanders 1965; Adams 1966; Lorenzo 1968; and Parsons 1968).

The produce from an expanding irrigation system in the Teotihuacan Valley may have contributed significantly to the support of the city when it began to grow to great size. As mentioned earlier, it seems to me more likely that the realization of its potential was stimulated by the increasing requirements of craftsmen and other specialists in the rapidly growing city, rather than the reverse. But in any case, it is little short of the absurd to see in the managerial requirements of so small an irrigation system a decisive factor in the phenomenal growth of the city, in its social, economic, or political organization, or in the rise of the Teotihuacan state (cf. Wittfogel 1957, 1967; Sanders 1965; Parsons 1968; Sanders 1968; Sanders and Price 1968).

The irrigated plain in the lower Teotihuacan Valley is not the Valley's only major resource. The Valley contains major deposits of obsidian, and we know that obsidian working was the city's principal craft from very early times. Two of its most important plants thrive under semi-arid conditions — maguey and the nopal cactus — and we have unmistakable evidence that both were grown in Teotihuacan times. Nopal is, among other things, the host for an insect producing cochineal dye. At the time of the Spanish Conquest, cochineal was an important dye source for the Aztecs.

In addition, the Teotihuacan Valley opened on the north shore of the Valley of Mexico's largest lake, Lake Texcoco. This location was of strategic importance not only because of the potentialities for communication and transportation provided by the five-lake system of the Valley of Mexico, but also because the lakes were major economic resources in themselves.

Given the geographical setting of Teotihuacan, the strategic importance of its location in manufacturing, commercial, and political terms may have become apparent quickly to the early Teotihuacanos. Whether the potential of Teotihuacan as a religious centre was viewed instrumentally early in the city's history remains to be explored.

One has only to look at the great size of Teotihuacan in relation to its valley very early in its history to realize that the rise of Teotihuacan, the economic centre, cannot be understood without reference to the simultaneous rise of Teotihuacan, the sacred centre. To try to 'explain' the rise of Teotihuacan solely or even largely in ecological terms is to fail to recognize the revolutionary quality of the growth of Teotihuacan. The 'urban revolution' culminating in the great metropolis that transformed and soon came to dominate much of central Mexico is the product of a complex network of closely intertwined circumstances that we are only just beginning to unravel.

The richness of urban civilization at Teotihuacan and the revolutionary qualities of city life in the great metropolis are grotesquely violated when viewed purely or mainly in ecological terms.[3] But even more important, if an ecological 'explanation' is accepted, the search for understanding of Teotihuacan society is largely ended, just when it should be beginning.

Without a social order responsive to change and a favoured ecological setting, Teotihuacan might have become an important pilgrimage centre. But there would be no reason to expect it to grow into an important economic and political centre or to develop the cultural magnetism of a metropolis. Similarly, Teotihuacan's strategic location, its access to resources of strategic potential, and an expanding market for its exports might provide the basis for an important market centre and a small city-state, but not necessarily for a sacred metropolis with an unparalleled attraction for other Middle American peoples.

Teotihuacan cannot be understood without understanding its ecological setting and the society whose members exploited that setting and grew to greatness in it. But it still remains an enigma if an attempt is made to understand it solely or mainly with reference to that setting. In the volume from which much of the foregoing has been taken (Millon 1973), there is a discussion on the rise of Teotihuacan and some comments are offered about what may have gone into the making of Teotihuacan. There is no space to go into these formulations and hypotheses here. Whether they survive is not important. What is important is that we have sufficient respect for the evidence to recognize that, after the ecological setting of Teotihuacan is analysed and evaluated, we are still faced with major interpretive problems and that ecological analyses are inadequate to handle them.

NOTES

1 This article draws on and partly summarizes sections of the text of the first volume on our researches at Teotihuacan (Millon 1973). Because of space limitations, it was not possible to include or summarize any of the discussion from that volume on the rise and fall of the ancient city. The article also includes two illustrations (Figs. 6 and 7) from the second volume on our researches, which is not yet completed. It also includes other material that does not appear in the first volume. The research was supported by NSF Grants G23800, GS207, GS641, GS1222, GS2204 and GS3137.

2 Preliminary analyses of faunal remains by David R. Starbuck in 1972 suggest similar intensive exploitation of the fauna of the region.

3 See Trigger (1971) for a critique of this kind of an ecological approach.

REFERENCES

Adams, R. McC. (1966) *The Evolution of Urban Society: Early Mesopotamia and Prehispanic Mexico.* Chicago.

Armillas, P. (1971) Gardens in swamps. *Science*, 174, no. 4010, 653-61.

Carr, R.F. and J.E. Hazard (1961) Map of the Ruins of Tikal, El Peten, Guatemala. Tikal Reports, no. 11. Museum Monographs, University Museum, University of Pennsylvania. Philadelphia.

Cowgill, G.L. (1967) Evaluación preliminar de la aplicación de métodos de máquinas computadoras a los datos del mapa de Teotihuacan. In Teotihuacan, *XI Mesa Redonda*, vol. 1, 95-112. Sociedad Mexicana de Antropología.

Cowgill, G.L. (1968) Computer analyses of archaeological data from Teotihuacan, Mexico. In S.R. and L.R. Binford (eds), *New Perspectives in Archaeology*, 143-150. Chicago.

Drewitt, B. (1967) Planeación en la antigua ciudad de Teotihuacan. In Teotihuacan, *XI Mesa Redonda*, vol. 1, 79-94. Sociedad Mexicana de Antropología.

Drewitt, B. (1969) *Data Bearing on Urban Planning at Teotihuacan.* Current Research Report presented at Annual Meeting of the American Anthropological Association, November 1969, New Orleans.

Flannery, K.V. (1967) Culture history v. cultural process: a debate in American archaeology (a review of G.R. Willey, *An Introduction to American Archaeology*, vol. 1, *North and Middle America*, 1966). *Scientific American*, 217, no. 2, 119-20, 122.

Flannery, K.V., et al. (1967) Farming systems and political growth in ancient Oaxaca. *Science*, 158, no. 3800, 445-54.

Ford, R.I., and J.N. Elias (1972) Teotihuacan paleoethnobotany. Paper read at Annual Meeting of the Society for American Archaeology, May 1972, Miami Beach.

Jacobs, J. (1969) *The Economy of Cities.* New York.

Johnson, F. (ed.) (1972) *The Prehistory of the Tehuacan Valley* (general editor R.S. MacNeish), vol. 4, *Chronology and Irrigation.* Austin, Texas.

Lorenzo, J.L. (1968) Clima y agricultura en Teotihuacan. In J.L. Lorenzo (ed.), *Materiales para la arqueología de Teotihuacan*, Serie Investigaciones, no. 17, 51-72, Instituto Nacional de Antropología e Historia.

MacNeish, R.S. (1967) A summary of the subsistence. In *The Prehistory of the Tehuacan Valley* (general editor R.S. MacNeish), vol. 1, *Environment and Subsistence*, ed. Douglas S. Byers, 290-309. Austin, Texas.

Millon, R. (1957) Irrigation systems in the valley of Teotihuacan. *American Antiquity*, 23, no. 2, 160-6.

Millon, R. (1964) The Teotihuacan mapping project. *American Antiquity*, 29, no. 3, 345-52.

Millon, R. (1967a) Urna de Monte Albán IIIA encontrada en Teotihuacan. *Boletín del Instituto Nacional de Antropología e Historia*, 29, 42-4.

Millon R. (1967b) El problema de integración en la sociedad teotihuacana. In Teotihuacan, *XI Mesa Redonda*, vol. 1, 149-55. Sociedad Mexicana de Antropologia.

Millon, R. (1968a) Teotihuacan: primera metrópoli prehispánica. *Gaceta Médica de México*, 98, no. 3, 339-50. Academia Nacional de Medicina.

Millon, R. (1968b) Urbanization at Teotihuacan: the Teotihuacan mapping project. 37th International Congress of Americanists, 1966, *Actas y memorias*, vol. 1, 105-20. Buenos Aires.

Millon, R. (1970) Teotihuacan: completion of map of giant ancient city in the valley of Mexico. *Science*, 170, no. 3962, 1077-82.

Millon, R. (ed.) (1973) *Urbanization at Teotihuacan, Mexico.* Vol. 1, *The Teotihuacan Map*: Part 1, *Text*, by R. Millon; part 2, *Maps*, by R. Millon, B. Drewitt and George L. Cowgill. Austin, Texas.

Palerm, A. (1955) The agricultural basis of urban civilization in Mesoamerica. In J.H. Steward et al., *Irrigation Civilizations: A Comparative Study. A Symposium on Method and Result in Cross-Cultural Regularities*, Social Science Monographs, no. 1, 28-42. Washington.

Parsons, J.R. (1968) Teotihuacan, Mexico and its impact on regional demography. *Science*, 162, 872-7.

Robertson, D. (1963) *Pre-Columbian Architecture.* New York.

Sanders, W.T. (1965) *The Cultural Ecology of the Teotihuacan Valley: A Preliminary Report of the Results of the Teotihuacan Valley Project.* Department of Sociology and Anthropology, Pennsylvania State University, University Park.

Sanders, W.T. (1968) Hydraulic agriculture, economic symbiosis and the evolution of states in central Mexico. In B. Meggers (ed.), *Anthropological Archaeology in the Americas*, 88-107. Washington.

Sanders, W.T. and B. Price (1968) *Mesoamerica: The Evolution of a Civilization.* New York.

Smith, T.C. (1959) *The Agrarian Origins of Modern Japan.* Palo Alto.

Spence, M.W. (1971) *Skeletal Morphology and Social Organization in Teotihuacan, Mexico.* Doctoral dissertation, Southern Illinois University.

Steward, J.H. (1955) Some implications of the symposium. In Julian Steward et al., *Irrigation Civilizations: A Comparative Study. A Symposium on Method and Result in Cross-Cultural Regularities*, Social Science Monographs, no. 1, 58-78. Washington.

Trigger, B. (1971) Archaeology and ecology. *World Archaeology*, 2, no. 3, 321-36.

Wallrath, M. (1967) The Calle de los Muertos complex: a possible macrocomplex of structures near the centre of Teotihuacan. In Teotihuacan, *XI Mesa Redonda*, vol. 1, 113-22. Sociedad Mexicana de Antropología.

West, R. and P. Armillas (1950) Las chinampas de México. *Cuadernos Americanos*, 50, año 9, no. 2, 165-82.

Wittfogel, K.A. (1957) *Oriental Despotism: A Comparative Study of Total Power*. New Haven.

Wittfogel, K.A. (1967) Review of *The Evolution of Urban Society: Early Mesopotamia and Prehispanic Mexico*, by R. McC. Adams. *American Anthropologist*, 69, no. 1, 90-2.

Wolf, E.R. (1959) *Sons of the Shaking Earth*. Chicago.

GEORGE L. COWGILL

Quantitive studies of urbanization at Teotihuacan

The Teotihuacan Mapping Project, initiated in 1962 under the direction of René Millon, involved preparation of a detailed topographic map which was then used for a comprehensive archaeological survey of the ancient city. This work yielded a detailed archaeological map of the entire city and a wealth of other information relevant for the study of urban society at Teotihuacan. The archaeological map itself and a summary of the entire project and preliminary conclusions are now in press (Millon, Drewitt and Cowgill, in press), and further volumes of a monograph series are in preparation. A number of shorter papers have also reported on this work; see especially Millon in this volume and Millon (1967a, 1967b, and 1970).

In the course of the project, detailed record forms were filled out and systematic surface collections of ceramics and other artifacts were made for more than 5000 separate tracts within the city. These tracts, of varying sizes and shapes, were designed to pertain as closely as possible to distinct architectural units, such as apartment compounds, temples, or other structures; or to culturally significant spaces between structures, such as plazas or streets. We refer generically to any such unit as a site. Sometimes a single site was divided into several tracts for collection purposes.

As part of my participation in the Teotihuacan Mapping Project, I have supervised creation of a computer data file which now stores some 281 items of information on each of the sites recorded by the survey, including data on over one and a quarter million sherds and other artifacts. It is among the largest, if not the largest, of any computer files of archaeological data so far created. The present working version of the file is now being checked, revised, and edited in order to produce a version suitable for distribution to other researchers, as well as for our own further studies.[1] My purpose here is to describe this file and our experiences with it and to present a small proportion of the results already obtained from it. In order to keep the paper within reasonable size, I will concentrate on results bearing on the overall growth and development of the city. This choice also stems from the desire to keep the paper at least relatively free of mathematical concepts which are still unfamiliar to most archaeologists. Results derived from a computer need not be abstruse, and I trust that what I have to say will be directly and obviously meaningful within the presently shared conceptual framework of studies of ancient urban societies.

The data file

In its present form our file contains, for each site, counts of total sherds collected, total sherds assigned to each major phase, totals for each of some 29 ceramic wares or categories, breakdowns by phase for many of these categories, counts of total obsidian and some 9 obsidian categories, manos, metates, and 24 other lithic categories, shell, worked shell, and worked bone fragments. Altogether, there are 147 different counts of ceramic and other artifact categories. The remaining 134 items include observations on visible traces of ancient floors and walls and other *in situ* architectural features, building debris of various kinds, information on the slope, setting, vegetation, cultivation or other present land use, present condition of the site, its size and the location of its centre relative to the base point of the Teotihuacan archaeological map; and field interpretations of the apparent architectural and functional character of the site.

Because computer work did not start until the field work was already very far along, we did not have a code sheet that could be filled out in the field. Transcribing the data from the site record forms onto code sheets, and checking and correcting this work, was a tedious business for all concerned, although it required only a fraction of the people-hours needed for the original field work. It would be preferable to have a field form that provides for directly recording observations in a coded format which can later be copied directly by a key-punch operator, or possibly even field forms that can be read by machine. However, the coding should receive considerable preliminary testing before a final version is selected, and there must always be plenty of open space left for uncoded remarks.

The code sheet data was in turn copied onto some 50 thousand IBM cards. This was a far more routine job than the coding itself, and was comparatively painless and inexpensive. Our experience was that bad keypunchers tended to be those who hated the job and did not stay with it long, while those who kept at it were fast and accurate, and spotted and corrected most of their own errors. My spot-checking of the work revealed a very low error rate in most of the work turned in.

A 'verifier' might next have been used for further error-checking. This is a machine on which a second operator recopies all the code sheet data. An error is indicated if there is any discrepancy between the recopied punching and the original punch card. We chose instead to write a computer program to check the data, partly because we thought it would be quicker and cheaper, and partly because the program could also check for certain code sheet errors and inconsistencies, which verification would not do, as well as check for errors in copying code sheets. Since the program could not recognize all possible errors, and since in fact some errors did survive all our checking procedures, it might well have been worth using a verifier as well as our error-checking program.

I designed and supervised the error-checking program and much of the writing and testing was done by Seth Reichlin. For each site it verified that all cards were present and in the correct sequence and that no punches were in places that should be blank, and it listed impossible or highly improbable data values and checked sums for internal consistency. For example, it checked that the sum of the ceramic category count was within 2 percent of the punched value for total sherds. In general, a tolerance of plus or minus 2 (in counts, not percentages) was set for other categories, which meant that attention could be focussed on correcting substantial errors, while some minor discrepancies were allowed to remain. These minor errors have negligible effect on the validity or reliability of the data (in comparison with other validity and reliability problems that will be discussed below), and to have corrected them all would have increased the work significantly without improving the data very much.

After being checked and corrected, all the punch cards, some 27 boxes full, were fed into a card reader and the information copied directly onto a single magnetic tape. Reichlin and I wrote another program which performed several editorial operations, including some revisions and simplifications of format and the automatic merging of data items into single site records for some of the cases where single sites had been divided into several collection tracts. This program, MERGE, read our first data tape as input, performed its operations, and produced a second tape as output.

This tape, which we call Data File 6, is our present working file. It still has some limitations and rough edges. The merging operation has only been completed for about half the city; there are still a few hundred cases where two or more tracts are represented for a single site, and for most purposes these should be merged (although, for checks on reliability, it is quite useful to have these multiple records). For various reasons some whole sites were omitted from Data File 6, and there are significant amounts of missing data for certain data categories. Also, a score or so more errors have manifested themselves or been located through further checking, which had eluded all our previous screening. Work is now in progress on correction of these errors and addition of missing sites and missing data in order to produce a fully edited file.

A more fundamental limitation of Data File 6 comes from the fact that since the data were coded there have been significant improvements in our understanding of the chronological positions of some ceramic categories and modes; mainly as a resuit of analyses by Evelyn Rattray of data from stratigraphic excavations which formed a small part of the overall program of the Teotihuacan Mapping Project. Related excavations and analyses by Darlena Blucher have also been very valuable. Recent restudy of about a hundred of the surface collections included in Data File 6 indicates that the original coding was satisfactorily accurate and reliable for most categories. Overall changes in these cases are all under 10 percent and are often far smaller. However, revisions in phase totals are substantial for the Miccaotli and Metepec phases, and, while assignment of material to the general Patlachique-Tzacualli time range is very accurate, a substantial proportion of Patlachique ceramics may have been incorrectly coded as Tzacualli. Restudy of a larger subsample of our collections, in the light of these new stratigraphic findings, is urgently needed.

Another shortcoming of Data File 6 is that the categories used in our code now prove to be too broad to answer some important questions which were not clearly formulated when the code was designed. This is partly because we neglected some things which in hindsight now seem obvious, but it is also because our ideas have changed and developed over the past few years. This is, of course, only one more example of the fact that all archaeological classification schemes are systems which are useful and relevant for certain problems at a certain stage in the study of a region, rather than 'the' unique or ultimate way to classify or describe the data (Hill and Evans 1972). Many of the new problems raised by our data call out for further field work, including excavation, for their study. Fortunately, many others can be dealt with by further study of a sample of our existing collections, which have been saved in their entirety, and we hope to incorporate such further studies with the chronological restudies previously mentioned.

Meanwhile, in spite of its limitations, Data File 6 has provided us a great deal of reliable and useful information. Before presenting some of the results from it, it is necessary to say something about some of the inherent problems and limitations of interpreting archaeological surface data, which are independent of any particular classification system or tape-editing procedures.

Inferences from quantitive surface data

Any archaeological work based on surface survey has to face certain problems about the validity and meaning of surface data. One problem is that what is found on the surface may not reflect particularly well what is below the surface or may even be quite misleading, either because material which is abundant some distance below the surface only reaches the surface in relatively small proportions; or because material is moved about by being incorporated in fill borrowed for later buildings, by water action, or by cultivation or other recent human activity, so that it occurs in substantial amounts at places some distance from where it was made or used. Masking of earlier material by later deposits may exist to some extent at Teotihuacan, but it is important to realize that the situation at Teotihuacan is very different from what it seems to be in the deeply stratified *tells* of the Near East. Except for platforms and pyramids, accumulations of cultural material at Teotihuacan are usually not very deep. Excavations in apartment compounds generally reveal stratified occupation levels spanning several centuries, but except perhaps near the 'Street of the Dead' the distance from present ground surface to sterile subsoil is rarely more than 2 to 5 metres. Few, if any, of these residential structures seem to have been established before early Tlamimilolpa times, and it looks as if the occupational debris of earlier periods was dug through in order to provide the Tlamimilolpa structures solid foundations in the hard subsoil of the region. Subsequently, a good deal of the fill for each new phase of a building was re-used fill from superseded building phases, which might belong to the same structure, or, presumably, might well be partly from refuse from other structures in the vicinity. All this means that a considerable proportion of the older artifacts and ceramics, incorporated originally in the fill of some early structure, has since been re-incorporated into fill for later structures, and given a good chance of finding its way to the surface.

One of the strongest arguments against there being much 'masking' of earlier material at Teotihuacan is the sheer quantity of early material collected by the project in regions where evidence for occupation in later periods was also abundant. If materials from early phases are at all under-represented in our surface collections, then the quantities originally produced must have been much higher than in later periods. This would imply either a drastically higher per capita consumption rate for ceramics in early times (which is not impossible but not suggested by any other evidence I am aware of), or a much larger population in Tzacualli times than later (which seems most unlikely).

It is not likely that percentages in surface collections and percentages in even the most superficial levels of excavations will agree closely, since the techniques of collection are so different. For the surface collections, rim and feature sherds (bases, handles, decorated body sherds) were collected and plain body sherds were not collected, and the chance of any sherd's being spotted probably drops sharply for sherds less than 2 or 3 cm. in maximum dimension. In our excavations, material was screened and everything above screen mesh size saved. Analyses of the material from these excavations are still in progress, and I have not yet compared excavated frequencies with surface collection frequencies in any detail.

For present purposes, what is important is that excavations have so far consistently corroborated our previous judgments about both the type of structure present and about major periods of occupation. We have not found unexpected concentrations of material in lower strata that were not represented on the surface. And, both in the 'Oaxaca *barrio*' (in square N1W6) and in the 'Merchants' quarter' district (in square N4E4), unusual quantities of foreign sherds that were manifest on the surface also proved to be present in the excavated materials.

As to the problem of material having been moved about since its original use, the sheer size of Teotihuacan is in our favour. For many of our studies of distributions we have found it convenient to aggregate site data into arbitrary blocks of 250 by 250 metres, each of which covers 6.25 hectares. It is unlikely that either re-use in building fill or other natural or human agencies of transport have carried much material more than a few hundred feet from where it was used. Watercourses may carry material much further, but they are few and localized at Teotihuacan, and material carried any distance by them will probably be noticeably water-worn, if not destroyed. Adjacent sites often show sharp and statistically highly significant differences, both in absolute counts of materials collected and in relative percentages of different categories. By aggregating data in 6.25 hectare blocks, we have selected a size considerably larger than would be needed to control for redeposition. It is clear that our surface data are often distinctive of much smaller areas.

There are problems about redeposition that remain, of course. For example, the Pyramid of the Sun contains roughly a million cubic metres of fill, which is fairly rich in Tzacualli and earlier ceramics wherever it has been tested by tunnels. If we suppose, for the sake of illustration, that this represents 2 million cubic metres of fill that was compressed to half its volume, this would correspond to a layer one metre thick covering an area of 200 hectares. While there is no reason to suppose that scraping the top metre off 200 hectares of land is even approximately how the fill for the pyramid was obtained, this kind of computation does at least suggest that building the pyramid would not seriously have depleted the supply of Tzacualli sherds in Teotihuacan, but might well have made a noticeable dent in the supply. It seems possible that the relatively low quantity of Tzacualli and Patlachique sherds in square N3W1, which was very rich in sherds for Miccaotli and later Teotihuacan phases, may reflect procurement of fill for the Pyramid of the Sun from this region (compare Figs. 3, 4, and 5).

There is also no doubt that present conditions of sites strongly affect the amount of material collected. Excavation and restoration of a structure, for example, often means that virtually nothing is left lying about on the surface for collection. Also, ceramics may be relatively scarce in places with heavy modern occupation, if there are sizable areas that are paved over or covered by buildings. Agricultural practices can affect ceramic abundances, partly by vegetation that makes collection difficult, and partly by recent plowing that brings material to the surface. When fields are cleared of rock, mano and metate fragments and other sizable stone fragments may be selectively accumulated in the stone rows which border many contemporary fields. Decades of collecting figurine heads for sale to tourists may have selectively depleted the supply in some regions. Sheet erosion on sloping ground may have exposed unusual quantities of material, or, if the erosion is too heavy, it may have removed nearly everything. In some flat regions, around square S2W1 for example, it is possible that silt accumulations conceal significant evidence. Where illicit excavators have recently been at work, there may be relatively copious pottery fragments uncovered and tossed aside in their work.

Because our data file includes information on slope, erosion, silting, and present condition and use of sites, much can be done to allow for all these effects. But for the distribution maps published here, the main thing is to be aware that counts of sherds collected per hectare, however nicely quantitative they look, cannot be relied on as more than very rough indicators of either population densities or intensities of ancient activity. Rather than focussing attention too strongly on any single map, it is far better to compare several, and note situations where a particular category is scarce in a region where material in general was abundant, or abundant in a region where material in general was fairly scarce. From this it is only a step to mapping percentages or ratios of one category to another, and such maps are a very useful complement to maps of absolute quantities. Site conditions which may have a strong effect on the absolute amount of material collected are likely to affect relative proportions much less.

Finally, amounts of material collected will depend on the specific collection techniques employed. Nearly all our material was collected by one or several individuals from among a group of 3 or 4 highly trained local workmen, who would cover a tract systematically, walking slowly a short distance apart and collecting all rim and feature sherds, obsidian and lithic artifacts and figurines that they saw. An effort was made to keep the practices uniform, and, judging by repeated collections from some sites in different years, I believe that the work was reliable, in the sense that for a given site, with given vegetation and surface conditions, different workmen in different years could be expected to collect approximately the same quantity of material, in approximately the same proportions. There are a few exceptions to this. Collections made in 1962, in the course of what was essentially exploratory work to locate the boundaries of the urban zone, are smaller than those made later. In squares N1W2 and N1E5 many collections were made under the direction of staff members who were unusually thorough, and several times the ordinary quantities of material were collected. In these cases correction factors have had to be estimated and applied. In general, however, variations in counts due to variations in collection practices are not likely to be large, relative to other sources of variation, including, of course, actual variations in intensity of ancient activity in different sites.

In detailing all these difficulties and possible difficulties, I have bent over backward to avoid giving the impression that because we have large and quite exact counts of sherds, we can make very exact estimates of population densities or activity intensities. It is also fair to say that our work has given us a far better basis for making such estimates than is the case for most archaeological projects (see Parsons 1972: 142) and that, when all is said and done, there is no doubt that our distribution maps do tell us a good deal about differences between phases and about regional differences within phases that is true in general terms. Although a sizable range of uncertainty remains in our quantitative estimates, they rest on a far better basis than is usual for survey data.

Bases for population estimates

Cook (1972) has used excavated data from several sites to estimate the total number of pots made and used in these sites, and has used assumptions about the average number of pots used per person per year to convert these into estimates of population. On the basis of our surface collections, there seems to be no way at present to guess the total number of pots made and used at Teotihuacan, although clearly it was very much larger than the total number of sherds we have collected. Our maps and tabulations of counts of sherds collected are roughly proportional, subject to the factors discussed above, to the total amount of pottery produced or used in each region, but we have no idea what the factor of proportionality is.

The key fact which makes any sort of conversion of sherd counts into population estimates possible is that Millon has estimated the Xolalpan phase population entirely on the basis of the size and number of architecturally substantial residential structures that were evidently occupied in Xolalpan times, without using sherd counts at all (except that he reasoned that substantial structures with no or very few Xolalpan sherds collected *may* have been abandoned prior to the Xolalpan phase, and he excluded these from his count of structures) (Millon 1970: 1079-80). He concluded that the population of the Xolalpan city was not less than 75,000; was more likely around 125,000; and might possibly have been considerably larger, perhaps exceeding 200,000. The ratios of these estimates to the total count of Xolalpan ceraamics in our collections can be used as a basis for estimating populations in other phases.

Unfortunately, there are several sources of substantial uncertainties in this procedure. First, there is the possibility that material from some phases is not very well represented on the surface. Evidence that this is not likely to be important for the earlier phases at Teotihuacan has been discussed previously. Paradoxically, it is possible that it could be a problem for the *latest* occupational phase of substantial structures. Millon (in Millon, Drewitt and Cowgill, in press: 28) argues that the latest occupation debris might be partially or perhaps completely obscured by the collapse of rubble-filled walls on it. If the walls were built significantly earlier, so that they incorporate only earlier ceramics, the surface evidence could be misleading. A larger number of careful excavations and analyses of material from the uppermost floors of relatively undisturbed structures should reveal whether or not this is in fact a serious problem. Second, I know of no reason to assume that the number of pots used (or, not quite the same thing, the creation of potsherds) per person per year was more than very roughly comparable in different periods of the city's history. Among other things, ceramic workshops are likely to produce unusually high numbers of sherds per person per year. This probably has some effect on distributions within phases, and it could affect between-phase comparisons. If pottery-making for export was more important in the Xolalpan phase than earlier, this could lead to underestimation of earlier populations. However, until more is known about this, for estimating populations in other periods one must assume that the pots per person per year did not change very much, but recognize that uncertainty about this greatly increases the margin of possible error in one's estimates. A third major source of uncertainty in demographic estimates is uncertainty about the duration of the ceramic phases. The durations shown in Millon's chronological chart (this volume, Fig. 8) should probably be thought of as plus or minus at least 50 years, and for some phases the estimates may be off by perhaps as much as a century. Since our reasoning is that a given amount of ceramic debris might reflect the activities of a population averaging 1000 people for 100 years, or of a population averaging 500 people for 200 years, these uncertainties about phase durations can have quite large effects on population estimates. Finally, for Miccaotli, Metepec and possibly Patlachique, revisions in the ceramic chronology mean that, for the time being, there are appreciable uncertainties about the sherd counts themselves.

Once again, lest it seem that I have so cogently pointed out all the difficulties that the only reasonable thing would be to avoid making any population estimates at all, I should remind the reader that the archaeological literature, both for Teotihuacan and for distant parts of the world, is full of population estimates and graphs which are based on far more slender evidence than we have.

Another problem which is brought into acute focus by our distribution maps is the question of converting evidence about areas covered by given densities of sherds into meaningful statements about sizes of settlements. Again a sort of calibration can be effected by looking at the Xolalpan evidence. The Teotihuacan archaeological map shows all sites which exhibited good evidence of substantial structures (apartment compounds, temples, etc.) and also enough Xolalpan phase pottery to attest occupation during that phase. The map also shows small insubstantial structures in regions where there were appreciable amounts of Xolalpan ceramics but no architectural evidence of substantial structures. Leaving aside these relatively small areas apparently occupied by insubstantial structures, a comparison of sherd density contours on Fig. 5 with the distribution of architectural evidence for substantial structures should give at least a general idea of the kinds of sherd densities that reflect occupation of the kind and intensity associated with substantial structures in Xolalpan times. It can be seen from Fig. 5 that no sizable areas without substantial structures have densities over 12 sherds per hectare, while many substantial structures occur in regions of lower sherd density. Few sizable areas in the 6 to 12 sherds per hectare range fail to show clear evidence for substantial structures, while relatively few substantial structures are in regions with densities below 6 sherds per hectare, and very few substantial structures are in regions where the sherd density is below 3 per hectare. In areas where the density is below 1.6 per hectare almost no evidence was found for substantial structures, and in the 1.6 to 3 per hectare fringe there begin to appear sizable areas in which there is no evidence for substantial structures, although sometimes the sherd quantities suggest an occupation with insubstantial buildings. On the basis of Fig. 5, I conclude that, in regions of Teotihuacan not subject to conditions that considerably increase or lower the average proportion of ceramics exposed for collection, a density of 12 or more sherds per hectare is very strong evidence for substantial occupation; a density in the 6 to 12 range is good evidence for at least fairly substantial occupation; the 3 to 6 range is reasonable evidence for occupation; and the 1.6 to 3 per hectare range is somewhat marginal and suggests either brief occupation during only a part of the phase, or scattered rather than closely-spaced occupation sites, or both. A density below about 1.6 per hectare suggests, unless reasons why sherd counts should be abnormally low are known, that there was little or no occupation or utilization for any activities which would have generated ceramic debris.

For interpreting sherd densities for phases other than Xolalpan, I know of no reasons for suggesting other guidelines except that, while we estimate the Xolalpan phase to have lasted about 2 centuries, there are other phases (including Patlachique, Miccaotli, and Metepec) which may have lasted only a century or so (or, for Miccaotli, possibly even less). For these shorter phases, one might perhaps promote each density level one step in significance, so that 0.8 to 1.6 per hectare would suggest brief or scattered or possibly shifting occupation; 1.6 to 3 per hectare would be reasonable evidence for occupation, and so on. However, in Figs. 2 through 5, I have consistently shown the 1.6 per hectare contour dashed, to suggest that it may be about at the fringes of meaningful occupation, while the 3 per hectare and higher contours are shown by solid lines.

Lest anyone be tempted to overgeneralize from these results, there are two points which deserve the strongest possible emphasis. First, it would be totally inappropriate to conclude that the interpretations I have suggested for specific density levels form the basis for any kind of general rules that would apply to other surveys or other sites. For other surveys conducted in the same region but using different collection practices, as well as for any work at all done in other regions, where surface conditions and ratios of pots per person per year may vary drastically, the minimal sherd densities that give good evidence for occupation may be very different. All I suggest is that, since the limits of architectural evidence for substantial Xolalpan occupation fit fairly well within the 3 to 6 per hectare sherd density contours, then these same contours can be used as a rough guide for evaluating sherd densities for other phases, in the context of our specific project.

The second point is that any attempt at all simply to estimate gross total area of appreciable occupation evidence is rather arbitrary and obscures very great differences in ceramic densities which may exist within the region where there was clearly *some* ancient activity. For example, simply to indicate the region where Xolalpan sherd densities of 6 to 12 or more per hectare give strong evidence of substantial occupation would be to obscure the fact that there are some regions where the Xolalpan sherd density was over 400 per hectare. Density contour maps provide much more information than do maps which simply suggest an estimated perimeter of settlement. Other techniques for summarizing areas of sherd cover and degrees of concentration within these areas are discussed below.

Maps

A good technique for using our data file to map the distribution of fairly rare categories, such as jade fragments, is to get a computer listing of all sites from which examples were collected, and then place one dot on the map for each example, on the site it came from. But for categories totalling more than abot 50 or 100 specimens the

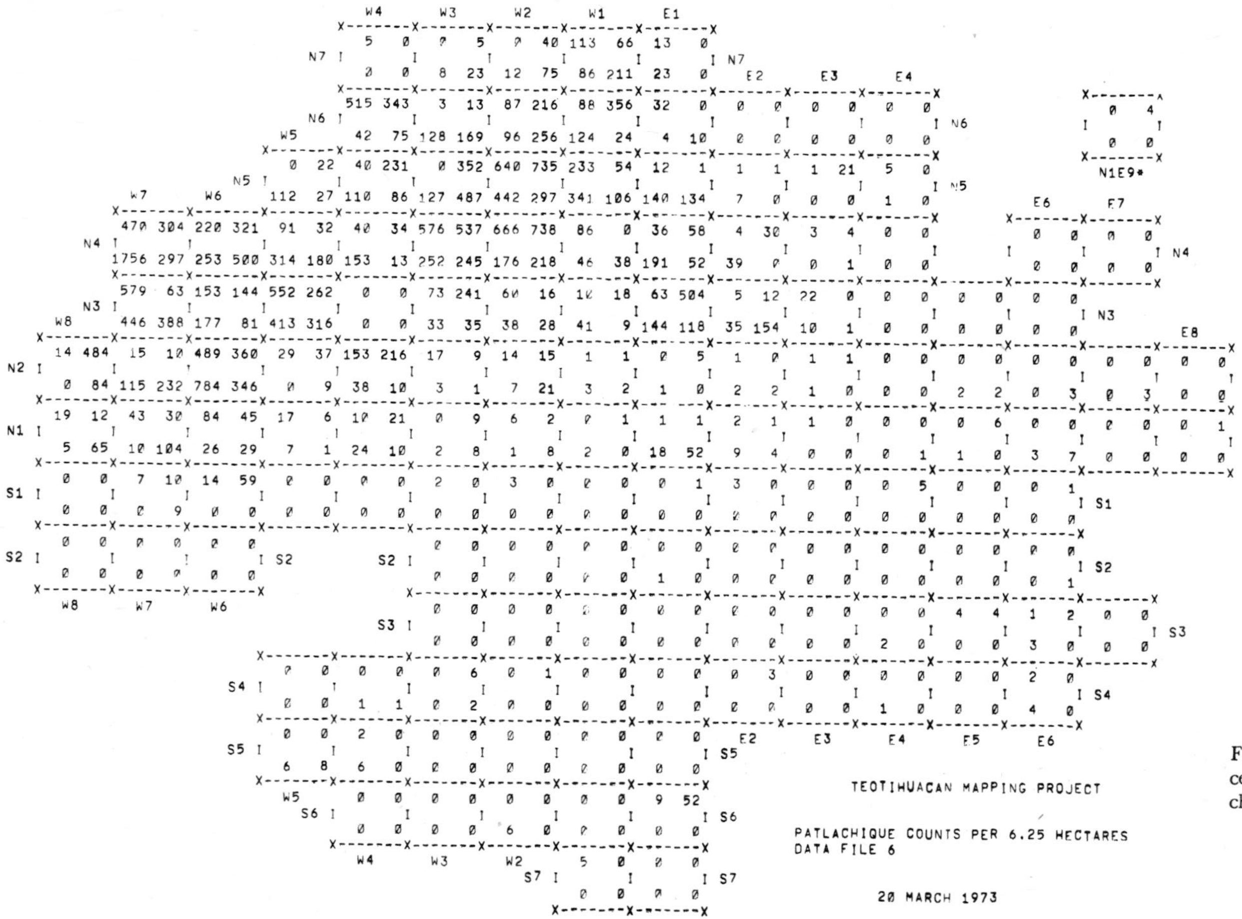

Figure 1 Computer printout of ceramic densities for the Patla-chique contour map, Fig. 3.

dots in some areas become so numerous that they blur into a solid mass, the eye has trouble in judging more than broad differences in concentration, and the mapping becomes quite laborious. For getting a good idea of general regional trends, but *not* of specific concentrations in single sites, it is useful to aggregate data within standardized arbitrary blocks and make 'contour' maps which show the approximate regions within which the number of specimens collected per hectare exceeds some given quantity.

A number of computer programs exist which will produce such maps as output, and earlier we experimented with some of these (Cowgill 1967). For some purposes they are quite useful. However, for the present, at least, we have found it preferable to write our own much more economical program, which takes advantage of the coded data on the location of the centre of each site, accumulates counts for a given category for all sites whose centres are within a given 250 by 250-metre quadrant of the arbitrary 500-metre squares of the archaeological map, and prints out the numbers in a format which resembles the map itself. This program was originally developed by me and Seth Reichlin; later I and Michael Ester modified it and developed the map printout feature. Fig. 1 is an example of the computer output from this program; it shows the data on which the Patlachique contour map (Fig. 3) was based. The grid pattern and labelling of the archaeological map is reproduced, except that, in order to make the print fit onto one standard page (limited to 131 characters per line), the far eastern square N1E9 has been moved into an unoccupied space in the northeast. Some squares which were included on the topographic map but not on the final archaeological map, such as N4W8, are omitted in the printout since no data for them was coded. Within each square in Fig. 1, four numbers are printed, one in each corner. These are the cumulated counts of Patlachique phase sherds in Data File 6 for all sites within each 6.25 hectare (250 by 250-metre) quadrant of the map square. These numbers, then, can be converted to *average* counts per hectare by dividing by 6.25. Thus the lowest density shown on the contour maps, 1.6 per hectare, corresponds to a 6.25 hectare block where 10 sherds were found. Dividing 10 by 6.25 gives 1.6. For higher densities, the contour maps show whole numbers which sometimes involve slightly rounding off some exact decimal ratio. For the computer printouts we have chosen to print the actual count of sherds in each 6.25 hectare block in order to help keep in mind the actual amounts of data on which the contour maps are based, as well as to avoid dealing with decimals in limited spaces. For the contour maps, the counts have been converted into counts per hectare for the sake of standardization.

The block size of 250 by 250-metres was chosen purely for convenience. Since all sites within a given 500-metre square of the archaeological map are located together in a single section of the data tape, it was convenient to use these map squares in summarizing regional data. Accumulating overall data from whole square seemed a needlessly drastic blurring of regional details. Dividing each square into 4 smaller squares gives considerably more detail, without introducing complications which would be unreadable on maps of the scale of Figs. 2 to 5. Arbitrary squares of this size are a good compromise between showing only forest and showing only trees, for some purposes, but for other purposes much smaller blocks, or even individual sites, can better be used as a basis for drawing contours. The surface areas of most individual sites range from about 400 square metres (0.04 hectares) to about 5000 square metres (0.5 hectares), and very few sites cover more than one hectare. The average site area is about 1/3 hectare. When the 141 500-metre map squares represented in the computer file were divided into 564 squares of 250 by 250 metres, some 489 proved to include one or more sites. In some cases, especially near the city margins, a single square may include one or two sites and a good deal of apparently unoccupied space. Elsewhere, 20 or more sites may be located within a single 6.25 hectare block. In either case, a good deal of significant internal variability may be averaged out by the block size we have used. The reader will find it instructive to compare the N2W6-N3W6 region in Fig. 5 here with the computer map of the Xolalpan distribution for just these two squares, based on individual site data, which we previously published (Cowgill 1967). Fig. 5 gives a good general idea of how N2W6-N3W6 fits into the overall Xolalpan distribution pattern for the whole city, but loses much of the meaningful detail of the earlier map. At present, it does not seem economically feasible to map distributions for the entire city in site-by-site detail, but perhaps this could be done for selected regions of the city. Needless to say, such detailed maps would, like our present maps, include the archaeological and topographic data which it was necessary to omit on the earlier maps (Cowgill 1967). In mapping data on an individual site basis, the possibility of some effects due to redeposition cannot be ignored, but all our evidence, from both survey and excavations in surveyed sites, is that such effects are small unless the site is unusually small or unusually heavily altered.

From computer printout like that of Fig. 1, it is relatively easy to locate the highest counts, identify them by circling in red, and draw a corresponding contour outline in pencil on a copy of the Teotihuacan archaeological map. The exact path of each contour line is determined by 'eyeball' interpolation between the numbers on the map. It is convenient to begin with the highest levels and work downward to the lowest levels. After the pencil version is done it can be copied in ink. Computer programs exist which will draw contour maps. While we do not feel completely satisfied with computer-drawn maps for our purposes so far, they are certainly a useful alternative in some situations, and they deserve serious consideration. There are also programs which will produce 'three-dimensional' perspective drawings of density surfaces. These are dramatic and give a strong sense of broad patterns, but for serious study they seem difficult to see.

In our contour maps, lines march with a certain grand indifference through and over buildings, pyramids, huge platforms and other large features. From the explanation of how the maps were made, it should be obvious that the lines reflect general regional trends rather than individual site data, and even though specific lines pass through specific buildings, it would be a complete misuse and misunderstanding of these maps to think that they tell one how much of a specific kind of material was collected from any specific site. That kind of question can be answered by printing out data on the specific site, or, for that matter, most easily by consulting the original site record in the non-computer files. In general, given the size of the blocks used for aggregating data, the simple interpolation technique used, and the possibilities of some redepositional movement, one would do well to think of most contour lines as subject to an uncertainty of at least 50 or 75 metres (that is, they could easily be shifted one way or the other by a tenth or a seventh of the dimensions of the 500-metre squares of the archaeological map).

After some experimentation I have chosen to use a logarithmic scale for contour intervals, in which each level is one-half the preceding level. For Fig. 2 to 5, the contours shown represent densities of 400, 200, 100, 50, 25, 12, 6, 3 and 1.6 sherds collected per hectare. This set of levels has the advantage that an enormous range can be shown without the need for an immense number of lines. However, since the intervals are not equal, it is important to emphasise that the contrasts in density represented really are very great.

In Fig. 2 regions with densities of 25 per hectare and above are emphasized by being lightly shaded. In figs. 3 to 5, regional densities of 100 per hectare and above are thus emphasized. In line with common topographic practice, 'basins' in which a lower density area is completely surrounded by areas of higher density are indicated by arrows pointing from higher densities to lower densities. Sometimes an arrow is used instead to show the region to which a high numerical value pertains, when there was not room to put the number within the region. In these cases, the tail of the arrow begins next to the number, and the two different uses of arrows should not cause serious confusion.

Growth and changes in the city

Our map program can be used to produce density contour maps of counts of any ceramic or artifact category included in our data file. Or it can be modified to compute percentages, ratios, or other functions of the original counts, and display the results on printouts similar to Fig. 1. For example, maps could be produced for counts of total censer fragments collected, or for counts of phased censer fragments by phases, or for phased censer fragments as percents of phase totals, for each phase. We have produced and examined many such maps and expect that production and interpretation of such maps will be one major aspect of research with the edited file we are now producing.

In order to illustrate some results and possibilities of these maps, I will concentrate on a few that show overall phase totals. Since these are based on our present working data file, it is possible that our present maps, Figs. 2 to 5, will differ in some details from versions based on the fully edited file, but it is unlikely that any substantial differences will emerge from the editing alone. It is possible that revisions in the chronological placement of some ceramic categories may alter the ceramic composition of some phases sufficiently to make for significant changes. Specific problems of this kind will be discussed below for individual phases.

The Cuanalan phase

The Cuanalan phase (the local variant of Ticoman, cf. Millon, this volume, Fig. 8) is the first phase for which there is any appreciable ceramic evidence for occupation at Teotihuacan. Fig. 2 shows 3 regions of fairly heavy sherd densities. One, in squares S1W6 and N1W6, is the site recorded as TF35 in Sanders' survey of the valley (Sanders 1965: Fig. 5). A second concentration, in N4W7 and running into N4W8, is Sanders's TF105. Unfortunately this and some other Preclassic concentrations run off the mapped area because research support was limited to that needed to map the area covered by the Classic Period city. The third Cuanalan concentration, in square S3E6, is a small settlement not located in Sanders' survey. Elsewhere in the urban zone of Teotihuacan a few Cuanalan sherds occurred in widely scattered spots, and in a thin but fairly continuous scatter around the slopes of Cerro Colorado (the hill with peaks in N2W7 and N3W7), which links the two concentrations in the west. There is also a fairly light but significant scatter of Cuanalan ceramics centering on N5W2. This last concentration is in the region which became an area of heavy ceramic cover in the later city. Otherwise the pattern of Cuanalan ceramic concentrations is notable mainly for its lack of correspondence to anything in the later city. It is probably not accidental that the settlement centred in S1W6, which, together with the Cuanalan site itself seems to have been one of the two largest Cuanalan settlements in the Teotihuacan

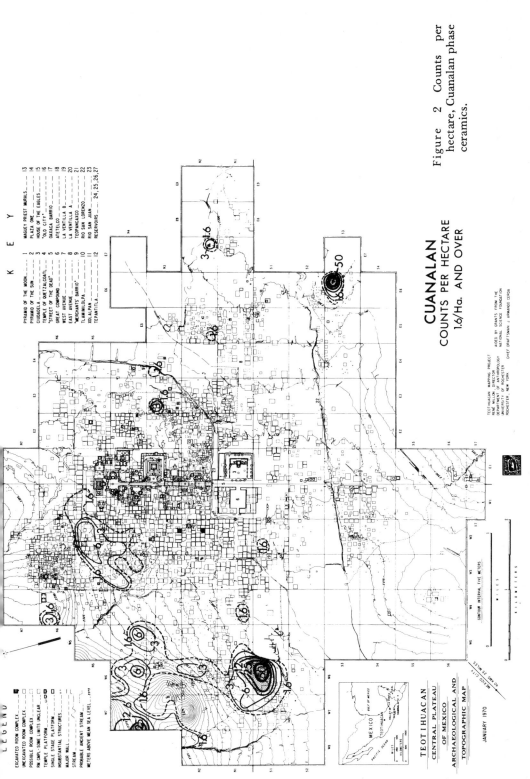

CUANALAN
COUNTS PER HECTARE
1.6/Ha. AND OVER

Figure 2 Counts per hectare, Cuanalan phase ceramics.

TEOTIHUACAN MAPPING PROJECT
RENÉ MILLON, DIRECTOR
DEPARTMENT OF ANTHROPOLOGY
UNIVERSITY OF ROCHESTER
ROCHESTER, NEW YORK

AIDED BY GRANTS FROM THE
NATIONAL SCIENCE FOUNDATION

CHIEF DRAFTSMAN J. ARMANDO CERDA

K E Y

PYRAMID OF THE MOON _____ 1
PYRAMID OF THE SUN _____ 2
CIUDADELA _____ 3
TEMPLE OF QUETZALCOATL ____ 4
"STREET OF THE DEAD" _____ 5
GREAT COMPOUND _____ 6
WEST AVENUE _____ 7
EAST AVENUE _____ 8
"MERCHANTS BARRIO" _____ 9
TLAMIMILOLPA _____ 10
XOLALPAN _____ 11
TEPANTITLA _____ 12

MAGUEY PRIEST MURALS _____ 13
PLAZA ONE _____ 14
HOUSE OF THE EAGLES _____ 15
"OLD CITY" _____ 16
"STREET OF THE DEAD" _____ 17
OAXACA BARRIO _____ 18
ATETELCO _____ 19
LA VENTILLA B _____ 20
LA VENTILLA A _____ 21
TEOPANCAXCO _____ 22
RIO SAN LORENZO _____ 23
RIO SAN JUAN _____ 24, 25, 26, 27
RESERVOIRS _____

LEGEND

EXCAVATED ROOM COMPLEX
UNEXCAVATED ROOM COMPLEX
POSSIBLE ROOM COMPLEX
RM CMPL: SOME LIMITS UNCLEAR
TEMPLE PLATFORM
SINGLE STAGE PLATFORM
INSUBSTANTIAL STRUCTURES
MAJOR WALL
STREAM
PROBABLE ANCIENT STREAM
METERS ABOVE MEAN SEA LEVEL

TEOTIHUACAN
CENTRAL PLATEAU
OF MEXICO
ARCHAEOLOGICAL AND
TOPOGRAPHIC MAP

JANUARY 1970

CONTOUR INTERVAL FIVE METERS

MILES

KILOMETERS

MEXICO CITY

MEXICO

CENTRAL PLATEAU OF MEXICO

Valley, should be in the general vicinity of the later city, but sherd density in this particular district drops off rapidly in later phases. It is also difficult for me, at least, to escape the suspicion that a sizable Cuanalan settlement was located so near the springs which provide much of the water for the modern irrigation system because this water supply was already an attractive and strategic agricultural resource. However, so far as I know there is still no hard evidence that irrigation in the Teotihuacan Valley had begun by this time. And, even if it had, there is a world of difference between suggesting that utilization of some of the water for irrigation would provide a good incentive for locating a sizable (for its time) settlement nearby, and suggesting that we might be seeing here a hydraulic 'prime mover' which accounts for the rise of the later city. A preoccupation with hydraulic agriculture as the decisive factor in the development of early cities or early states ignores, if nothing else, a multitude of other factors which seem more important. In this case, it also ignores the fact that the city which later developed was out of all proportion to the local system, which cannot have ever covered more than 4 or 5 thousand hectares or demanded any very elaborate controls.

Excluding the part of the settlement not covered by the map, there is a total area of about 35 hectares in which the density of Cuanalan sherds collected was 12 per hectare or higher, another 40 hectares in which they ranged from 6 to 12 per hectare, and roughly another 100 hectares in the 3 to 6 per hectare range. In all, this makes about 175 hectares in which the density was 3 or more per hectare. It may well be that not all this area was occupied at all at any one time, and sizable parts of it must have been occupied by fairly scattered dwellings. But, even with these allowances, the total area with considerable evidence for occupation seems much larger than the 5 or 10 hectares which Sanders (1965: 168) indirectly implies. Presumably the reason for the discrepancy is that Fig. 2 shows the results of a very detailed and thorough survey; while Sanders's was more rapid and only recorded areas with quite high sherd densities. If so, this raises problems about the comparability of our data with that from the surveys of the Teotihuacan Valley and the eastern and southeastern parts of the Basin of Mexico by Sanders (1965), Parsons (1971), and Blanton (1972a, 1972b). It may be that many of the rest of their sites would appear larger and more populous if they were surveyed as thoroughly as Teotihuacan.

Sanders estimated that the settlement in S1W6 probably consisted of fewer than 300 people and was certainly less than 500 people. Millon (in Millon, Drewitt, and Cowgill, in press: 50) estimates the entire population of all Cuanalan phase settlements within what was to become the urban zone of Teotihuacan as perhaps about a thousand. A comparison of the ratios of Cuanalan to Xolalpan sherd counts in Data File 6, allowing for the probably somewhat longer duration of the Cuanalan phase, suggests that the average Cuanalan population may have been around 1 to 1.5 percent of the average Xolalpan population. Using Millon's low estimate of 75,000 for the Xolalpan population, middle estimate of 125,000, and high estimate of 200,000; this suggests that possibly the Cuanalan population averaged somewhere between 750 and 3000, with 1500 a middling estimate. This is well in line with Millon's estimate, although it suggests that his may be just a little on the low side. The main thing about all estimates of the Cuanalan population is that they agree that it was very small relative to the later city.

The Patlachique phase

Patlachique-phase ceramics (Fig. 3) differ strikingly from Cuanalan both in total quantity and in distribution. Taking the figures in Data File 6 at face value, the total count of Patlachique phase ceramics is about 15 percent of the Xolalpan total. If the duration of the Patlachique phase was about ¾ that of Xolalpan (as estimated by Millon, this volume, Fig. 8), then the average Patlachique population may have been about 20 percent of the Xolalpan population; that is, between 15,000 and 40,000, perhaps about 25,000. These are unexpectedly large numbers; much larger than previous estimates for the Patlachique population. For example, Millon has recently suggested that 'perhaps it was between five and ten thousand, perhaps considerably more. This is a relatively low density for a settlement of such size' (Millon, in Millon, Drewitt and Cowgill, in press: 51). However, given the uncertainties of our chronological estimates, it is quite possible that the Patlachique and Xolalpan phases were of roughly equal duration, and this assumption would lower the Patlachique population estimates to the range of 11,000 to 30,000, with a best guess around 19,000.

An additional complication is introduced by the possibility that a significant proportion of the ceramics that actually date to Patlachique times have been counted as Tzacualli in the Data File 6 tabulations. If this possibility is confirmed, it will increase still further the estimate for the Patlachique population. Also, the area of highest Patlachique sherd density in the city (in square N4W7) runs off the map, and part of the Patlachique settlement is not included in our counts. Taking all these factors into account, a population estimate of 10,000 for Patlachique-phase Teotihuacan now appears to me to be conservative; 20,000 a reasonable guess; and 30,000 a definite possibility. These figures are, of course, *averages* for the whole phase; we have to imagine the population having been around 1 or 2 thousand at the beginning of the phase, then growing very rapidly (at a rate of perhaps 1% per year or even more), and reaching an amount well above the 'average' figure by the end of the phase.

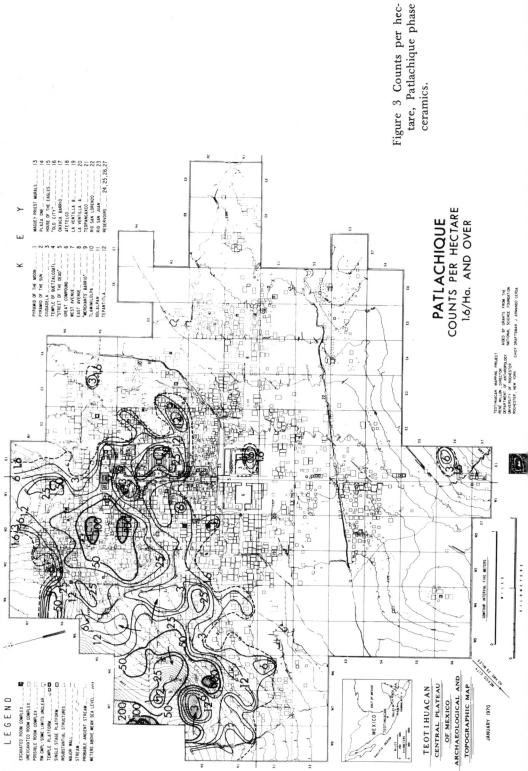

Figure 3 Counts per hectare, Patlachique phase ceramics.

Perhaps these high population estimates for the Patlachique phase should not be too surprising. Since it is clear that the Patlachique settlement at Teotihuacan covered a large area, what the sherd counts suggest is that the density of settlement within this large area may not, after all, have been unusually low. Within the area covered by the map, the density of Patlachique sherds is 12 per hectare or more over about 520 hectares, with several regions of over 100 per hectare and one region of over 200. Densities of sherds collected range from 6 to 12 in another 100 hectares, and from 3 to 6 in 155 hectares, making a total of some 825 hectares (8.25 square km.) in which there is evidence of more than slight Patlachique occupation. This is a little larger than Millon's estimate of more than 6 square km. for the Patlachique settlement. If we assume that there were 20,000 people living in about 800 hectares, the overall average population density would have been about 25 people per hectare, which is about half the probable overall average density of people of Xolalpan Teotihuacan. Presumably, of course, in both phases there were some regions of considerably higher population densities and other areas of much more scattered or even intermittent occupation.

Unfortunately, virtually nothing is known of Patlachique residential architecture. Almost certainly the substantial apartment compounds, which lend themselves to relatively high population densities, did not become widespread until the Tlamimilolpa phase. Nevertheless, even if Patlachique dwellings were architecturally much less substantial, an average population density of 25 per hectare seems feasible, both architecturally and socially. In terms of contemporary settlements in the Teotihuacan Valley, 25 per hectare is just on the borderline between what Sanders (1965: 50) defined as 'compact low-density village' and 'high-density compact village'.

The significance of these higher estimates for the Patlachique population is that they imply that a substantial part of the population growth formerly attributed to the Tzacualli phase actually occurred during the Patlachique phase, and this demographic growth in turn implies that there was already very considerable economic, and perhaps also political, development during this period. This adds further force to Millon's suggestions (in Millon, Drewitt and Cowgill, in press: 52) that the obsidian industry, and possibly other crafts, were already becoming important during this phase; that some of Teotihuacan's shrines were of growing 'international' importance; and that the effects of its strategic location as a market centre were already being felt. In some ways it makes the Tzacualli developments seem a little less explosive, but mainly what it does is to suggest that the period of explosive growth began somewhat earlier than had been thought. Excavations designed to learn more about the Patlachique city are urgently needed; in order to establish the character of the obsidian industry at that time, to test our suspicion that significant ceremonial architecture along the 'Street of the Dead' had its inception this early, and, if possible, to learn more about Patlachique residential structures. For a period when events were moving so quickly, a more refined ceramic chronology is also urgent. It is not enough to ask whether some things that have been called Tzacualli are truly Patlachique in date. We should try to define several subphases clearly and aim for chronological controls on the order of a century, or, if possible, even briefer periods.

From the perspective of the Basin of Mexico as a whole, the suggestion that Patlachique-phase Teotihuacan may have been larger and more complex than had been thought does not seem unreasonable. Developments in the Teotihuacan Valley have seemed rather late when compared to Cuicuilco and other settlements in the southern part of the basin. I am only suggesting that Teotihuacan may not have been as much later in getting started as had been thought.

In comparison with earlier published maps of the area of Patlachique settlement at Teotihuacan (e.g. Sanders 1965, Millon 1967a) Fig. 3 differs in that it indicates an essentially continuous settled region in the northwest. Although there are separate ceramic concentrations in the far west and in N4W2-N5W2 there is a light to moderate scatter of ceramics in the region connecting these centres. The N4W2-N5W2 concentration is in the region which appears to have become the major settlement focus of the Tzacualli city. Moderate to fairly high densities also cover the northern part of what was to become the 'Street of the Dead', the region around the Moon Pyramid and Groups 5-prime and 5, and notably around the Sun Pyramid. While no excavations in this region have yet seriously tested the possibility that some pyramid groups or other important later structures had Patlachique beginnings, the ceramic distributions do suggest that the city was beginning to take shape this early, or at least that the north-central and northwestern sections were. An isolated and weak concentration of sherds around the Ciudadela suggests that there may possibly have already been some special importance attached to this spot, but since at this time there was still no suggestion of the major east-west axis that later intersected the 'Street of the Dead' here, it is difficult to say why this region should have been important in Patlachique times, and this concentration remains enigmatic. Another minor concentration in S6E1 is perhaps related to a small separate Patlachique settlement in S8E1-S8E2 that is outside the mapped area.

In most of N3W1 and N4W1 Patlachique sherd densities are relatively low, forming a deep embayment in the contour patterns, even though in later times (cf. Fig. 5) ceramic densities in this region were high. Conceivably it was from this region that, in Tzacualli times, much of the fill for the Pyramid of the Sun was taken. However, if there were many important lesser temples or other structures in this region, then the last thing one would expect is that they would have been razed in order to provide fill for the great pyramid. Since Patlachique and Tzacualli densities are not too low on the Plaza of the Columns group or on the temple group facing the 'Columns' group in N4E1 (cf. Millon, this volume, Fig. 3), one can speculate that these groups were important enough in their own right to resist being destroyed to provide fill for the Sun Pyramid, but that other structures in N3W1-N4W1 were demolished for this purpose. All this remains, at best, a fragile speculation until it can be tested in the field. However, it does call attention to the possibility that Patlachique settlement may have been heavier and more continuous between N4W2 and N3E1 than is suggested by the sherd densities of Fig. 3.

The Tzacualli phase

The distribution map for the Tzacualli Phase (Fig. 4) indicates that by the end of this phase there was at least light occupation over practically the whole area ever covered by the city of Teotihuacan, as well as a substantial region beyond the northwestern margins of the mapped area. In comparison with Patlachique, the total area of substantial sherd cover expanded tremendously; the district of heavy Patlachique occupation in N4W7 and N4W8 dwindled considerably; sherd densities increased greatly in a large area centred around N5W2; and there are considerable sherd concentrations east of the 'Street of the Dead', especially around the Xala compound in N4E1, the Pyramid of the Sun, and the Ciudadela. The southern and eastern regions that seem to have had negligible Patlachique occupation now show light to moderate sherd cover. Densities of sherds collected were over 200 per hectare from a total area of about 80 hectares; over 12 per hectare in some 1680 hectares (16.8 square km.), between 6 and 12 in another 340 hectares, and between 3 and 6 in a further 340 hectares; making some 23.6 square km. over which 3 or more sherds per hectare were collected. This last figure should *not* be taken as a good estimate of the total area of the settlement. Because of the technique of grouping sites into 6.25 hectare blocks, the low density fringe includes a number of regions where a few scattered sites and fairly large areas with no evidence for occupation occur. Perhaps around 21 or 22 square km. would be a better estimate of the settlement area.

It turns out that corresponding total areas for corresponding sherd densities are remarkably similar for the Xolalpan phase, although the locations of the high density regions are strikingly different.

The total Tzacualli sherd count in Data File 6 is about 60 percent of the Xolalpan count (assuming that about 60 percent of the Thin Orange pottery collected should be included in the Xolalpan total). If the Tzacualli phase lasted only about ¾ as long as the Xolalpan phase

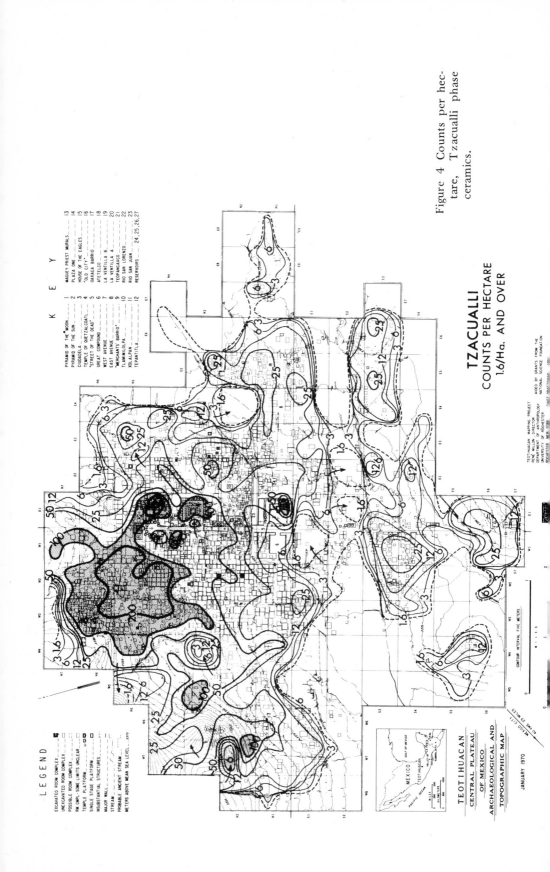

Figure 4 Counts per hectare, Tzacualli phase ceramics.

(Millon, this volume, Fig. 8), then an average population of about 80 percent of the Xolalpan average would be suggested. However, the duration of Tzacualli could easily have been as great as or even greater than the Xolalpan phase. Moreover, there is the possibility that some of the Tzacualli ceramics really belong to the Patlachique phase, although the more we invoke this supposition to lower Tazacualli estimates, the more we must raise those for Patlachique. All this leads to the suggestion that the Tzacualli phase population may have been somewhere between 30 and 70 percent of the Xolalpan population, provided the rates of creation of potsherds per person per year were at least roughly similar in two phases. This leads to estimates which are substantially higher than Millon's most recent suggestion (Millon, Drewitt and Cowgill, in press: 52) that the population may have been about 25,000 to 30,000, or may have been considerably more. Our evidence is more in line with earlier estimates of 30,000 to 50,000 or more, although it tends to raise these a little and suggests that 50,000 to 60,000 is more of a 'middle range' estimate than a probable upper limit. The upward revision is less drastic than for the Patlachique phase.

Fig. 4 shows that the southern part of the Tzacualli city is separated from the northern part by a strip about 400 metres wide in which sherd densities are below 3 per hectare, although at least a light scatter of Tzacualli pottery bridges this gap. Total quantities of all ceramics collected in this strip were low, and the low Tzacualli densities at least in part reflect conditions unfavourable for large surface collections. Preoccupation with whether this 'ought to be' two separate settlements or a single continuous settlement can lead to fruitless semantic quibbles unless the context of the question is made explicit. It seems probable that, throughout the city's history, the region south of the Rio San Lorenzo was a little bit isolated physically, and possibly also socially, from the central districts of the city. On the other hand, major features of the overall city plan, such as the 'Street of the Dead' and the standard directional orientations of building walls, clearly continued unchanged into this region in Xolalpan times, and the 'Street of the Dead' possibly was already laid out in this region by the Tzacualli phase (Millon, in Millon, Drewitt, and Cowgill, in press: 52). Although there was a small independent Patlachique settlement a short distance south of the mapped region, there is little that suggests that the Tzacualli map reflects the coalescence of two separate communities. A more probable interpretation is that we are seeing a sort of overflow from the northern nuclear part of the city, resulting in a light occupation of the southern districts in Tzacualli times.

A high Tzacualli sherd density around the Ciudadela suggests that there was already some important structure there, although nothing so far excavated appears to be that early. On the other hand, the rather moderate densities around the Great Compound, in N1W1, raise some doubts about its importance this early. Although the central plaza of this complex may have been cleared down to subsoil in later times, one would expect that if Tzacualli ceramics had been abundant there they would have been incorporated in quantity in the fill of the north and south platforms, and would now be available in some quantity on the surface.

Broadly, the computer data on ceramic densities and areas covered adds to the evidence that Tzacualli-phase Teotihuacan was already a very large and complex city. As Millon (Millon, Drewitt and Cowgill, in press: 52, 54) points out, by the end of the phase the Pyramid of the Sun was close to its present height and more than twenty 'three-temple' complexes had been built. Their disposition on both sides of the 'Street of the Dead' demonstrates that at least the northern half of that great avenue had already been laid out, and many other features of the later city's plan may also prove to date this early. The obsidian industry seems to have developed markedly.

In spite of the fact that there are fewer gross differences between Tzacualli-phase Teotihuacan and the Xolalpan city that had been thought until now, the remaining evidence for differences should not be minimized. For example, all indications are that Tzacualli residential architecture had not yet developed the large, often compactly grouped, apartment compounds that were so characteristic of the city in Tlamimilolpa and later phases. And, while Teotihuacan economic and perhaps political influence must have been already expanding rapidly beyond the Basin of Mexico, it had evidently achieved nothing like the areal extent or the supremacy of later times.

Still, the thrust of the data is to suggest that by late in the Tzacualli phase the city had already been relatively large, relatively important, and relatively complex for several centuries. From our own perspective, this may have been only the beginning of the great period for Teotihuacan. But it seems likely that, to its builders, the Pyramid of the Sun seemed to be the culmination of an already impressively long period of rapid development and social and political innovations.

The Miccaotli and Tlamimilolpa phases

Sherd density maps for these phases show patterns intermediate between those of Tzacualli and Xolalpan. The heaviest Miccaotli concentrations are from the eastern part of W3 to E1 and from N3 to N6. Relative to Tzacualli there is retraction on the north and west, great expansion in the south and east, and a shift of the 'centre of gravity' toward the 'Street of the Dead'. There is probably a higher proportion of ceramics within 1500 m. west or 500 m. east of the northern part of the 'Street of the Dead' than at any earlier or later time. It is conceivably significant that the western limit of heavy Miccaotli sherd cover is fairly close to the large north-south wall near the eastern edge of square N5W4. If this wall was partly for defence and not entirely for segregating neighbourhoods within the city, it most likely was built either early, before Teotihuacan was strong enough to prevent invasions which could pose any threat to the city itself, or late, when outer zones of defence were crumbling. There is a great deal of evidence for Miccaotli occupation outside this wall, but it may have protected the parts of the city considered most important. On present evidence, the wall might be either early or late.

Quantities of Miccaotli sherds are consistent with the notion that the population was greater than in the Tzacualli phase and less than in Xolalpan. Given uncertainties about the duration of the phase and recent changes in the ceramic chronology, nothing more specific can be said, for the moment.

Tlamimilolpa sherds are somewhat more numerous than Xolalpan in our collections. Possibly the Tlamimilolpa phase lasted a little longer, and this need not mean that the population density was actually higher then than in the Xolalpan phase. However, it does at least suggest that population growth had levelled off by Tlamimilolpa times, and that thereafter there was little or no demographic growth. Relative to Miccaotli, Tlamimilolpa shows little or no further retraction in the northwest. There is a substantial proportional increase around the Great Compound and the Ciudadela and in most of a strip roughly following East Avenue as far as N1E9. This reflects a significant southward and eastward extension of high sherd densities. A Miccaotli trend toward increases in N6W3-N7W3 and in S3W1-S4W1 continues further in Tlamimilolpa. In N5W2 densities decline from the Tzacualli peak.

The Xolalpan phase

Fig. 5 shows substantial decrease relative to Tzacualli in N5W2 and around the western and northern periphery. Increases are most pronounced in N3W1, N2E2, N6W3-N7W3, and S3W1-S3W2. All of these carry trends further that had appeared in the intervening phases. The cumulative effect is a striking difference in the locations of high sherd densities, while the city margins change relatively little (except in the northwest) and the gross overall areas at or above a given density also show little change. For Xolalpan, 200 or more per hectare were collected from about 90 hectares; 12 or more per hectare were collected from about 1650 hectares; there were 6 to 12 per hectare in an additional 450 hectares; and 3 to 6 in 250 hectares more; making some 23.5 square km. from which densities collected were 3 per hectare or higher. Compared to the Tzacualli figures,

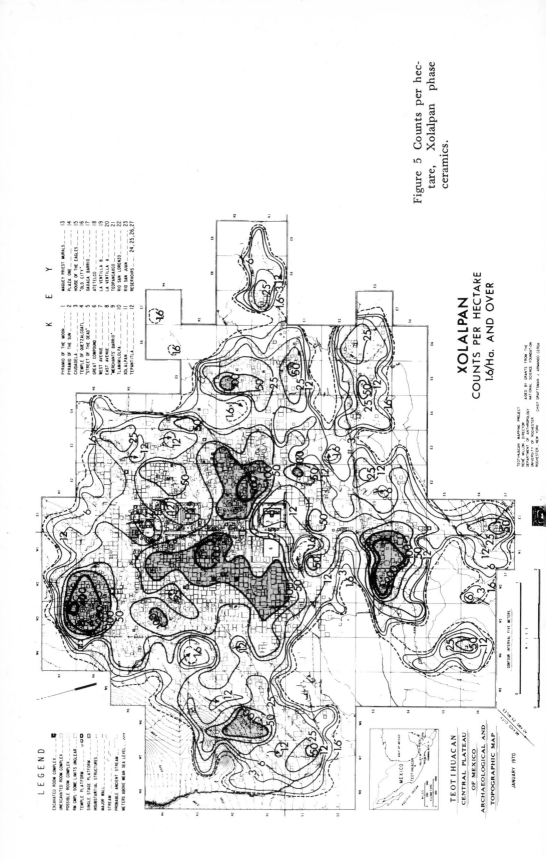

Figure 5 Counts per hectare, Xolalpan phase ceramics.

those for Xolalpan show a slightly larger total area of high sherd densities, but a somewhat smaller total area in which there is good evidence of some occupation.

It remains possible that the distribution pattern for one phase or the other is either more concentrated into a few high-density regions or more evenly spread out over the city. Figure 6 shows one way to investigate this kind of question. For Patlachique, Tzacualli, and Xolalpan, the 6.25 hectare blocks were ranked from highest to lowest density of sherds collected, and the cumulative sherd counts were computed and converted into cumulative percentages of phase totals. In Fig. 6 these cumulative percentages are plotted against a logarithmic scale of areas, so that one can read off the total percentage of sherds from a given phase that are from the most densely covered total area of a given size. Thus, Fig. 6 shows that the most heavily covered 500 hectares of the Tzacualli city yielded about 62 percent of all the Tzacualli sherds collected; that the most heavily covered 500 hectares of the Patlachique settlement yielded 90 percent of the Patlachique sherds; while no region smaller than about 1300 to 1400 hectares will include as much as 90 percent of the Tzacualli or Xolalpan sherds.

The approach represented by these cumulative curves may prove to be useful as a way of making judgments about site occupation areas more comparable between one research project and another, and also more meaningful, especially when there are multiple occupations on a single site. It does, however, require gridding the site in some way, and, for comparisons, making grid sizes equal or at least taking effects of grid size into account.

Cumulative sherd counts may correlate only very roughly with cumulative people counts, and I think it only approximately true that the area with 95 percent of the sherds contained 95 percent of the people, and perhaps not even roughly true that the area with 50 percent of the sherds also contained 50 percent of the people.

Fig. 6 shows that Patlachique ceramics are concentrated in a much smaller region than are those of Tzacualli or Xolalpan, a fact already apparent from the distribution maps. However, what is less obvious, the cumulative curves for Tzacualli and Xolalpan are almost identical.

Of course, the locations of high density regions are quite different for the two phases. The Xolalpan concentrations in N6W3-N7W3 and in S3W1-S3W2 are in districts where there is considerable evidence for a variety of craft activities, including pottery manufacture, and the growth of Teotihuacan industries may be the main reason for these concentrations, both because they employed many people and because pottery manufacture, if not the other crafts, by its nature produces quantities of ceramic debris.

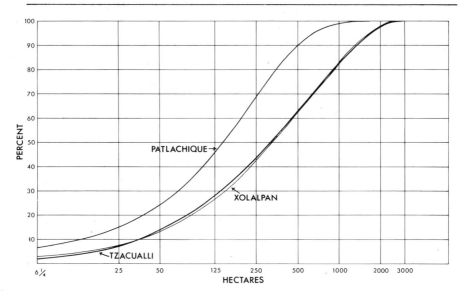

Figure 6 Maximal cumulative percentages of phase totals as functions of area for
the Patlachique, Tzacualli and Xolalpan phases.

The Metepec phase

In general the Metepec density distribution pattern does not differ
markedly from the Xolalpan pattern. It does not substantiate the
notion that there was any decline in the intensity of occupation in
the centre of the city. It suggests that, if anything, there may have
been relatively more intense activity along the 'Street of the Dead'.
This is illustrated by Fig. 7, which is an example of a somewhat more
complex kind of map than the density maps previously discussed.
Fig. 7 is intended to show regions where the proportion of Metepec
to Xolalpan is relatively high, and also regions where the proportion
is relatively low; that is, regions of relative increase or relative
decrease in ceramic densities. In order to do this, however, one
cannot simply use the raw counts, because the Metepec phase
probably only lasted about half as long as Xolalpan, so the Metepec
counts should be multiplied by 2. An additional rough correction has
been applied to allow for changes in ceramic chronology since Data
File 6 was created. The ratio of these adjusted Metepec counts,
relative to the sum of adjusted Metepec plus Xolalpan, was then
computed, results multiplied by 1000, and printed out as 3-digit
integers in a format similar to Fig. 1. This yields a value around 500
for a block where, in terms of the adjustment factors, the estimated
sherds per year are about the same for Metepec as for Xolalpan.
Numbers higher than 500 imply a higher proportion of Metepec
sherds, with 1000 meaning that there was only Metepec and no

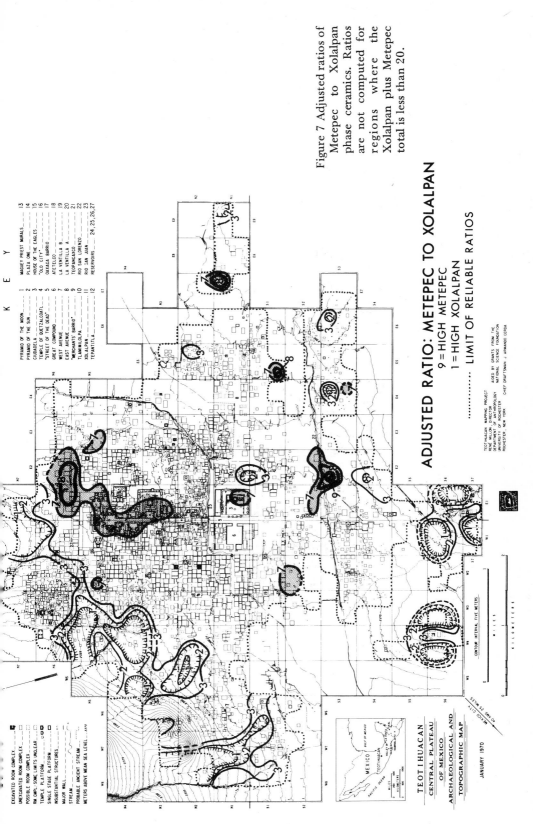

Figure 7 Adjusted ratios of Metepec to Xolalpan phase ceramics. Ratios are not computed for regions where the Xolalpan plus Metepec total is less than 20.

ADJUSTED RATIO: METEPEC TO XOLALPAN

9 = HIGH METEPEC
1 = HIGH XOLALPAN
········· LIMIT OF RELIABLE RATIOS

TEOTIHUACAN MAPPING PROJECT
RENE MILLON, DIRECTOR
DEPARTMENT OF ANTHROPOLOGY
UNIVERSITY OF ROCHESTER
ROCHESTER, NEW YORK

AIDED BY GRANTS FROM THE
NATIONAL SCIENCE FOUNDATION

CHIEF DRAFTSMAN J ARMANDO CERDA

TEOTIHUACAN
CENTRAL PLATEAU
OF MEXICO
ARCHAEOLOGICAL AND
TOPOGRAPHIC MAP

JANUARY 1970

CONTOUR INTERVAL FIVE METERS

K E Y

PYRAMID OF THE MOON	1
PYRAMID OF THE SUN	2
CIUDADELA	3
TEMPLE OF QUETZALCOATL	4
"STREET OF THE DEAD"	5
GREAT COMPOUND	6
WEST AVENUE	7
EAST AVENUE	8
"MERCHANTS' BARRIO"	9
XOLALPAN	10
TEPANTITLA	12
MAGUEY PRIEST MURALS	13
PLAZA ONE	14
HOUSE OF THE EAGLES	15
"OLD CITY"	16
OAXACA BARRIO	17
ATETELCO	18
LA VENTILLA B	19
LA VENTILLA A	20
TEOPANCAXCO	21
TLAMIMILOLPA	22
RIO SAN LORENZO	23
RIO SAN JUAN	
RESERVOIRS	24, 25, 26, 27

EXCAVATED ROOM COMPLEX
UNEXCAVATED ROOM COMPLEX
POSSIBLE ROOM COMPLEX
RM CMPL; SOME LIMITS UNCLEAR
TEMPLE PLATFORM
SINGLE STAGE PLATFORM
INSUBSTANTIAL STRUCTURES
MAJOR WALL
STREAM
PROBABLE ANCIENT STREAM
METERS ABOVE MEAN SEA LEVEL

MEXICO

GULF OF MEXICO
TEOTIHUACAN
MEXICO CITY
PACIFIC OCEAN

MILES
KILOMETERS

Xolalpan at all. Numbers lower than 500 imply a higher proportion of Xolalpan, and zero implies that there was only Xolalpan and no Metepec at all.

In producing the map, blocks were omitted if the total actual count of Xolalpan plus Metepec was less than 20, since samples smaller than this might easily show relatively meaningless extreme ratios which are mainly due to sampling fluctuations. The dotted line in Fig. 7 shows the boundaries of regions for which total counts per block were over 20. The line indicates regions within which samples were judged statistically adequate for this specific ratio computation, and does not indicate the limits of significant evidence for occupation in either the Xolalpan or Metepec phases, which often run beyond the limits of the dotted line.

Ratios are indicated on the map by a scale of 0 to 10, rather than 0 to 1000. The 9 contour line encloses areas of very high Metepec relative to Xolalpan, while the 8 and 7 contours enclose areas of less marked Metepec increase. These regions are also indicated by shading. The 1 contour encloses areas of very marked Metepec decrease, while the 2 and 3 contours enclose areas of less drastic Metepec decrease. The 1 and 2 contours are emphasised by hachure. In order to focus on areas where changes are pronounced, the neutral 5 contour and the 4 and 6 contours are not shown.

Fig. 7 shows several high Metepec peaks in the eastern and south central parts of the city, notably in the mound group in N1E7 where a concentration of Metepec material led to the recognition and naming of the phase in the 1960s. There is also an unexpected but sizable peak around S3E2, and a moderate rise around the Ciudadela. But the largest region of relative increase for Metepec runs irregularly from Square N6E2 southwest to the Moon Pyramid and from there along the 'Street of the Dead' to just south of the Sun Pyramid. Areas of sharp Metepec decline are most extensive on the northwestern periphery, with some irregular patches of low Metepec in the far south and southwest. The only non-peripheral district where sherd densities declined sharply from Xolalpan to Metepec is a small region just east of the Ciudadela. The N6W3-N7W3 region continues to have high absolute sherd densities, and the percentage shift from Xolalpan is not great.

It is quite possible that future work will change the specific adjustment factor represented in Fig. 7, but it is very unlikely that the basic pattern will be changed much.

The total Metepec ceramic count in Data File 6 suggests that the average Metepec population, during most of the phase at least, was not markedly lower than the Xolalpan population. This adds to the body of evidence that decline of the city was not drastic, in some aspects at least, until very close to the end.

Conclusions

While computers do not marvellously overcome all the difficult problems of archaeological inference, the combination of unusually detailed and thorough surface survey with computer techniques of data analysis does tell us far more about Teotihuacan than we knew before. Within the space limitations of this paper it has not been possible to say much about the statistical analyses which have been completed or planned (Cowgill 1967, 1968, 1970) or about results from mapping specific categories of ceramics and artifacts. I have concentrated on a discussion of important problems of interpreting surface survey data and the ways we are handling them, and on results bearing on the demographic history of the city and on overall ceramic distribution patterns for the successive phases from Cuanalan through Metepec. Comparable data have been mapped for the subsequent phases, from Oxtoticpac through Aztec, but cannot be discussed here.

The most important demographic finding is that the population of the city in the Patlachique phase was considerably greater than had been thought, and somewhat greater in the Tzacualli phase. The growth rate during these phases was clearly very high (perhaps 1 percent per year), but the rate of increase in subsequent phases must have been very much lower, and there is at least a possibility that the total population did not change drastically during most of the Tlamimilolpa, Xolalpan, and Metepec phases.

Our distribution maps give a far more detailed picture than has been available before of differences between phases in the regional distributions of ceramics, and these surely reflect at least broadly differences in regional population densities, intensities of ceramics-producing or ceramics-using activities, or both. Some interpretations of these patterns have been suggested. Much fuller interpretations will be possible when these results are integrated with distribution maps for specific ceramic categories, with examinations of our collections for evidences of ceramic workshops that are now only partly completed, and with various kinds of statistical analysis.

NOTES

1 Current work on the data file is supported by National Science Foundation grant GS36960 to Brandeis University. Support for the Teotihuacan Mapping Project came from a series of N.S.F. grants to the University of Rochester; G23800, GS207, GS641, GS1222, GS2204 and GS3137. I am indebted to other members of the project for many kinds of assistance with the computer work, and especially to René Millon, initiator and director of the project, who has encouraged the computer work and provided many very valuable and stimulating discussions of results at various stages. These discussions have undoubtedly improved the quality of the research described here, but I take personal responsibility for the conclusions and suggestions I have made.

REFERENCES

Blanton, R.E. (1972*a*) Prehispanic adaptation in the Ixtapalapa region, Mexico. *Science*, 175, 1317-26.

Blanton, R.E. (1972*b*) *Prehispanic Settlement Patterns of the Ixtapalapa Peninsula Region, Mexico.* Occasional Papers in Anthropology, Department of Anthropology, Pennsylvania State University.

Cook, S.F. (1972) Can pottery residues be used as an index to population? *Miscellaneous Papers on Archaeology*, Contributions of the University of California Archaeological Research Facility, 14, 17-39.

Cowgill, G.L. (1967) Evaluación preliminar de la aplicación de métodos de máquinas computadoras a los datos del Mapa de Teotihuacán. *Teotihuacán: XI Mesa Redonda*, México, 1966, 95-112, Sociedad Mexicana de Antropología.

Cowgill, G.L. (1968) Computer analysis of archaeological data from Teotihuacan, Mexico. In S.R. and L.R. Binford (eds), *New Perspectives in Archaeology*, 143-50. Chicago.

Cowgill, G.L. (1970) Some sampling and reliability problems in archaeology. In J.-C. Gardin (ed.), *Archéologie et calculateurs*, 161-75. Centre National de la Recherche Scientifique, Paris.

Hill, J.N. and R.K. Evans (1972) A model of classification and typology. In D.L. Clarke (ed.), *Models in Archaeology*, 351-73. London.

Millon, R. (1967*a*) Extension y población de la ciudad de Teotihuacán en sus diferentes periodos: un cálculo provisional. *Teotihuacán: XI Mesa Redonda*, México, 1966, 57-78. Sociedad Mexicana de Antropología.

Millon, R. (1967*b*) Teotihuacan. *Scientific American*, 216, 38-48.

Millon, R. (1970) Teotihuacan: completion of map of giant ancient city in the Valley of Mexico. *Science*, 170, 1077-82.

Millon, R., B. Drewitt and J.A. Bennyhoff (1965) The Pyramid of the Sun at Teotihuacan: 1959 excavations. *Transactions of the American Philosphical Society*, 55, part 6. Philadelphia.

Millon, R., B. Drewitt and G.L. Cowgill (in press), *Urbanization at Teotihuacan.* Vol. 1: *The Teotihuacan Map.* Austin Texas.

Parsons, J.R. (1971) *Prehistoric Settlement Patterns in the Texcoco Region, Mexico.* Memoirs of the Museum of Anthropology, University of Michigan, no. 3.

Parsons, J.R. (1972) Archaeological settlement patterns. *Annual Review of Anthropology*, 1, 127-50.

Sanders, W.T. (1965) *The Cultural Ecology of the Teotihuacan Valley.* Department of Sociology and Anthropology, Pennsylvania State University.

JEREMY A. SABLOFF, WILLIAM L. RATHJE, DAVID A. FRIEDL, JUDITH G. CONNOR and PAULA L. W. SABLOFF

Trade and power in Postclassic Yucatan: initial observations

Introduction

In the past few years, the study of trade has become crucial to the understanding of the development and maintenance of Mesoamerican civilization (among others, Flannery 1968; Parsons and Price 1971; Rathje 1971*a*, *b*, in press, 1973; Silva-Galdames 1971; Tourtellot and Sabloff 1972; Webb 1964). These studies have gone far beyond descriptions of items exchanged and have emphasized the role of trade in larger cultural systems. While anthropologists have now integrated trade and trading centres into their analysis of cultural systems, few scholars have focused on an analysis of the trading centres themselves. Yet such a focus can greatly contribute to the testing and refinement of hypotheses of culture change (see, for example, Rathje and Sabloff 1972), because trading centres are both sensitive indicators of change in economic and political structures and actual mechanisms of that change.

In February, 1972, the authors initiated an archaeological project in order to study the adaptation of cultural systems to changing stimuli and to test a number of specific hypotheses about the role of long-distance trade in the rise, maintenance, and fall of Meso-american civilizations. The island of Cozumel, Quintana Roo, Mexico (see Figs. 1 and 2) was chosen for detailed analysis for several reasons. First, we know from the rich ethnohistoric literature that the island was a pivotal trading centre between Honduras, Yucatan, and Tabasco in Late Postclassic times (Scholes and Roys 1948; Thompson 1970). Second, the archaeological remains have a time depth from at least the Late Preclassic period through the sixteenth century (post-Conquest) with large surface remains from the Post-classic period (see Fig. 3). Third, because of its position on a heavily used Postclassic trade route, the cultural system on Cozumel was constantly exposed to and constantly reacted to changing environmental stimuli.

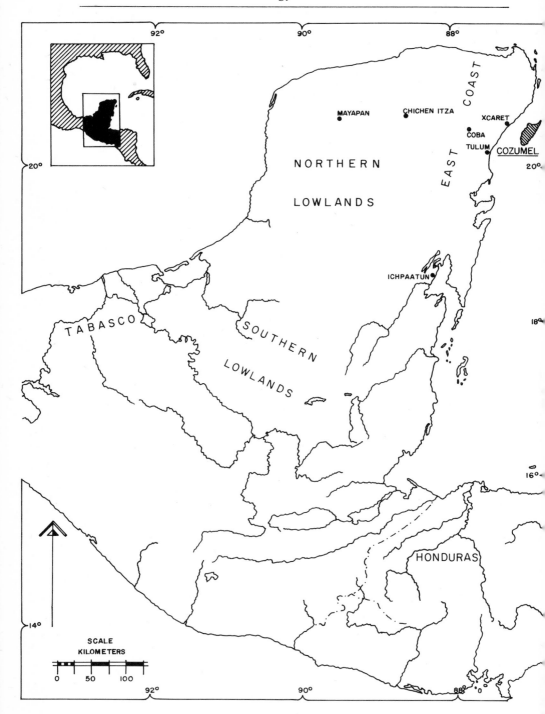

Figure 1 Map of Yucatan.

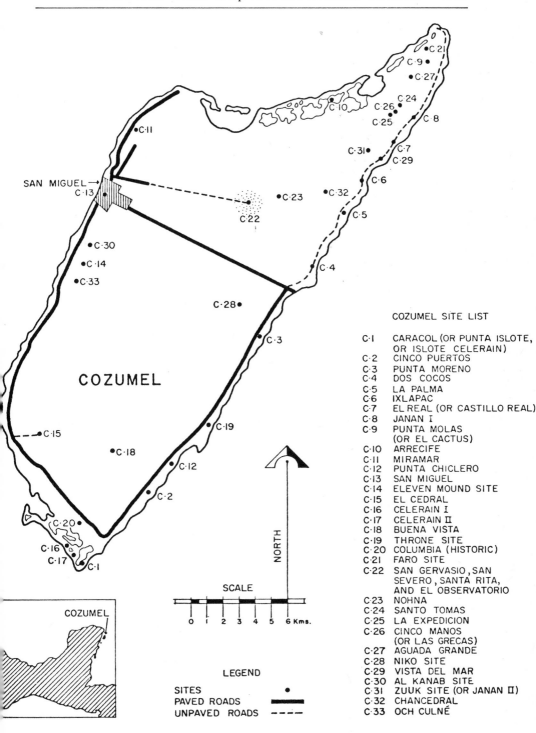

Figure 2 Map of Cozumel.

COZUMEL SITE LIST

C·1	CARACOL (OR PUNTA ISLOTE, OR ISLOTE CELERAIN)
C·2	CINCO PUERTOS
C·3	PUNTA MORENO
C·4	DOS COCOS
C·5	LA PALMA
C·6	IXLAPAC
C·7	EL REAL (OR CASTILLO REAL)
C·8	JANAN I
C·9	PUNTA MOLAS (OR EL CACTUS)
C·10	ARRECIFE
C·11	MIRAMAR
C·12	PUNTA CHICLERO
C·13	SAN MIGUEL
C·14	ELEVEN MOUND SITE
C·15	EL CEDRAL
C·16	CELERAIN I
C·17	CELERAIN II
C·18	BUENA VISTA
C·19	THRONE SITE
C·20	COLUMBIA (HISTORIC)
C·21	FARO SITE
C·22	SAN GERVASIO, SAN SEVERO, SANTA RITA, AND EL OBSERVATORIO
C·23	NOHNA
C·24	SANTO TOMAS
C·25	LA EXPEDICION
C·26	CINCO MANOS (OR LAS GRECAS)
C·27	AGUADA GRANDE
C·28	NIKO SITE
C·29	VISTA DEL MAR
C·30	AL KANAB SITE
C·31	ZUUK SITE (OR JANAN II)
C·32	CHANCEDRAL
C·33	OCH CULNÉ

NORTH

SCALE

0 1 2 3 4 5 6 Kms.

COZUMEL

LEGEND

SITES   •
PAVED ROADS   ▬▬▬
UNPAVED ROADS   - - - -

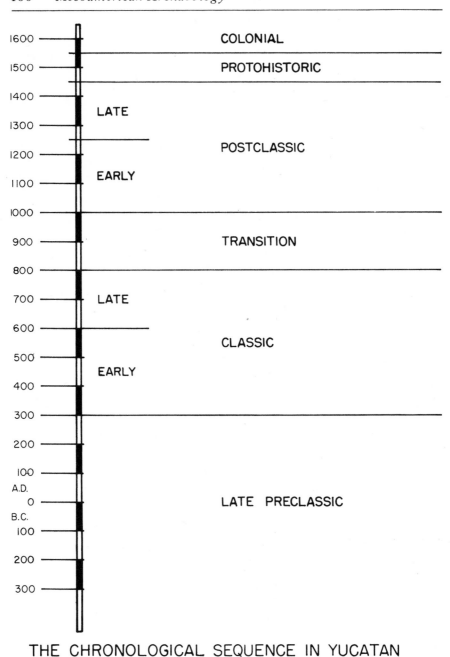

THE CHRONOLOGICAL SEQUENCE IN YUCATAN

Figure 3 Chronological chart for Yucatan.

Theoretical background

Based on cross-cultural data, it can be assumed that Cozumel could have been organized into one of two different types of structures at any one point in time: a trading port or a port-of-trade. *Trading ports* are autonomous units controlled by their own centralized organizations. The cost of running the port is paid by customs and other administrative fees levied on the uses of the facilities.

A *port-of-trade*, or free port, has a very different structure from a trading port (cf. Rathje and Sabloff 1972). It is a neutral area composed of a series of factories, or trade embassies, each independent of the others but dependent for direction upon a home base of trade resources supply. Ports-of-trade, like Delos or Whydah for example, are usually underwritten by a single or several major trading powers which guarantee neutrality and pay the cost of communal port facilities and administration. Few, if any, duties are charged. The powers are merely supporting a neutral zone where they can market goods in bulk to customers who transport the commodities home. The port-of-trade cuts distribution costs for the bulk trade items of large trading enterprises as long as the port attracts customers and the desired goods in return.

A port-of-trade is obviously dependent upon the large trading powers which guarantee its neutrality. What happens to a port-of-trade, however, when its controllers can no longer pay the money needed for maintenance and/or can no longer attract customers in volume? Does the port-of-trade collapse or does it change the nature of its operations? Does the structure of a port-of-trade allow it to adapt more readily to environmental changes than other culture types? If it does, as we have already suggested elsewhere (Rathje and Sabloff 1972), then how and why? These questions are one of the main areas of interest of the Cozumel Project's archaeological research.

In order to answer the question 'why do ports-of-trade appear to adapt more readily to external changes than other systemic types?' we plan to test the following general hypothesis: the more specialized the economic subsystem of a culture (i.e., the fewer the natural resources the economic subsystem has to draw upon), the more mobile and flexible (in decision-making) the politico-religious subsystems must be in order for the entire system to persist under external stress. In the case of a trading centre, persistence would be defined as the maintenance of population, cultural level, and its central position in the larger trading network (cf. Easton 1965). From this hypothesis we would deduce that at three crucial points of major culture historical change in Yucatan (Transition/Early Postclassic, Early Postclassic/Late Postclassic, Late Postclassic/Protohistoric), the island of Cozumel, although having a narrow and specialized economic subsystem based on a single resource (its relative location), was able to make the necessary adaptive responses in order to insure systemic persistence. The island was able to make such responses because of its mobile and flexible politico-religious subsystem. That is to say, it would have had a better chance (probability) of persistence than a system with a more rigid politico-religious subsystem, whether the economic subsystem was specialized or broad-based. From this, we propose that Cozumel was able to persist through the three transition periods while the other neighbouring centres (Coba, Chichen, then Mayapan) did not because Cozumel had a more mobile and flexible politico-religious subsystem while the latter had more rigid ones. If Cozumel had had a non-flexible politico-religious subsystem, then we would argue that it would not have persisted as a strategic node in the Yucatecan trading routes throughout the period c. A.D. 800 to the time of the Conquest. As can be seen in Protohistoric times, for which good ethnohistoric data are available, Cozumel was in constant danger of being cut out of the trading system by the equally viable Chetumal-Acalan route (see Chapman 1957). However, we are still engaged in tightening this hypothesis and clearly specifying and defining all its constituents and parameters. We plan to discuss this general hypothesis in detail in a later publication. In this paper, we will begin to examine a specific hypothesis concerning 'how' trading centres adapt to the situation outlined immediately above.

The specific hypothesis we will begin to examine in this paper is that an initial port-of-trade structure which loses major outside support must revert to a trading port structure in order to survive, by attempting to establish direct relationships with resource areas and centres of resource distribution. The port, in effect, establishes itself as a strategically placed middleman in long-distance exchange.

There is a good evidence that during the Early Postclassic period the Toltecs controlled the major trade routes in Yucatan. We would hypothesize that Cozumel was a port-of-trade under Toltec sponsorship. The problem of evaluating this hypothesis is now under study.

After the Toltec system collapsed, our hypothesis would predict that Cozumel's organization changed from that of a port-of-trade to a trading port. It follows from this that Cozumel would have set up ties with specific resource distribution centres. A test for this hypothesis is Mayapan, a site for which there is ample data (see Pollock, Roys, Proskouriakoff, and Smith 1962, and the Current Reports of the Carnegie Institution of Washington). Identifying the strength of relationship between Mayapan and Cozumel is the problem with which this paper will deal. It is a culture historical problem defined as relevant to the Project by a processual problem. Before the nature of Cozumel's reaction to change can be fully documented and understood, many more studies will be necessary. This paper represents a statement of one of the problems with which we are concerned and the methods we are employing to solve it.

Test case: Cozumel and Mayapan

It is our belief that there was a major socio-political shift at the beginning of the Late Postclassic period (c. A.D. 1250) in the greater Yucatan peninsula. With the ending of Toltec overlordship in the thirteenth century A.D., Yucatan witnessed what has sometimes been called a 'Maya resurgence'. But this 'resurgence' did not represent a revival of the old Classic religio-political order. Rather, it signified the triumph of a new merchant elite who rapidly rose to a position of economic and political ascendency from Tabasco to the East Coast.

This new elite had gained valuable lessons from their previous Toltec overlords. They were clearly able to see how the Toltec-run trading networks operated and the wealth that entered the local capital of Chichen Itza. It must also have been obvious to them how much more lucrative the trading routes would be if they were locally run without any drain to foreign controllers. With the fall of Chichen Itza and the end of Toltec ascendency (the reasons for which are an interesting problem in themselves), the newly emerging elite were able to follow the successful blueprints of their Toltec predecessors. First, they had to replace the central power node which had been lost with the fall of Chichen Itza. This was accomplished with the founding of Mayapan. In this regard, it is of more than passing interest to note that the founders of Mayapan were said to have come from Cozumel (Pollock, Roys, Proskouriakoff and Smith 1962: 32-3). Second, they had to insure the non-interruption and safety of the trading routes. This security was probably established through alliances between the merchant elites of all the trading centres on and near the peninsula and was reinforced religiously through the institution of a pilgrimage route which exactly paralleled the principal trading route. The shrine of Ix Chel was located on Cozumel and people, especially merchants (see Scholes and Roys 1968: 33, 57), came from as far away as Tabasco (where Ix Chel also became an important deity) to worship at her shrine.

Basically, we would hold that in the absence of a foreign power, trade in the greater Yucatan was insured through elite alliances and the spread of shared elite concepts and goods. On Cozumel, this shift would be reflected, we believe, in its change from a port-of-trade under Toltec aegis to a trading port with close elite ties which it forged with such power nodes as Mayapan in order to insure its continued strategic role in long-distance trade. Although there may have been major cultural differences between the populations of these two centres, as well as cultural and functional differences among these and other allied sites such as Tulum or the Campeche-Tabasco centres, there emerged, we would hold, a shared merchant elite culture.

It has already been noted in the literature that the city of

Mayapan shares a number of architectural and constructional features with contemporaneous sites on the East Coast of the peninsula (Pollock, Roys, Proskouriakoff and Smith 1962: 36, 231). Sites on Cozumel, conforming in many respects to what is already known of the Late Postclassic period on the East Coast, likewise share certain features with Mayapan. Very generally, our data broaden the range of shared attributes and strengthen the affiliation of Mayapan with Cozumel; but more intriguing is the possibility we now anticipate of clarifying the nature of this affiliation.

The people of Mayapan defined space in a manner unique in pre-Conquest Yucatan: they surrounded their city with a massive wall, and surrounded their residences with house lot walls. This first feature, found elsewhere at Tulum, Xcaret, and Ichpaatun on the East Coast (Sanders 1955: 260, Fig. 2; Andrews 1965: 323) can safely be considered a public community feature designed and executed by the ruling administration. On the other hand, the house lot walls at Mayapan are crude, often only a single course of large stones, and often demarcating a space around residences without connecting to the walls of neighbouring residence groups. Generally, they form a patchwork of occasionally connected circular or sub-rectangular enclosures. This second feature can be considered a private construction by individual family groups.

Our 1972 field investigations (also see Sabloff and Rathje 1972) have shown that massive walls are not found enclosing any of the settlements on Cozumel, but boundary walls are found. These walls are not limited to settlement zones, nor do they form a haphazard patchwork; instead they comprise a rectangular grid system oriented approximately 20° east of north that covers all but a fraction of the 186 square miles of the island. Outside of settlement zones, the enclosures range from 150 to 250 metres square. At the small settlement of Aguada Grande, the location of structures is closely oriented to the grid, so that the wall connecting these structures and forming houselots around them conform to it (Fig. 4). At other sites, the wall becomes idiosyncratic in settlement zones, diverging from the grid to connect structures and form houselots in relation to structures located to best advantage on high ground. However, this divergence is very precise: within a single enclosure layer away from any settlement the grid reasserts itself. The walls are much better made than those at Mayapan, probably standing to a height of a metre and a half.

Where they articulate with buildings that have been dated, the walls date to a construction period in the Late Postclassic. Although parts of the grid may have been laid down in earlier periods, the precision of orientation and uniformity of the construction technique all over the island argue for a single building period. In contrast to the private walls at Mayapan, the completely interconnecting, uniformly oriented walls of Cozumel must be considered at the very

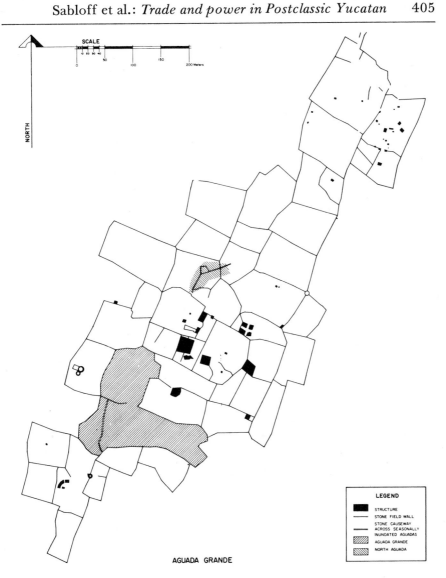

Figure 4 Aguada Grande, Cozumel.

least a carefully coordinated effort by elite family groups dispersed throughout the island. At most, it is a massive project by a civil administration able to impose its definition of all available land space on the island.

Cozumel's wall grid, like the nucleated and enclosed cities of Mayapan and Tulum, is in stark contrast with what is known of Maya concepts of space and land use in other periods and places. At the time of the conquest in Yucatan, land was communally owned as a rule (Roys 1943: 36) with farmers using land as they needed it. Roys quotes a native informant report (1943: 36): 'The lands were in

common and so between towns there were no boundaries or
landmarks except between one province and another because of
wars, and in the case of certain hollows and caves, plantations of
fruit trees and cacao trees, and certain lands which had been
purchased for the purpose of improving them in some respect.' At
the time of contact, boundary walls generally seem to imply private
ownership. It would certainly be unjustified to jump to the conclusion that all land on Cozumel was privately owned at the time of
the wall-grid's construction without other evidence. Certain deduc-
tions, however, can be made.

While it is possible that the wall-grid on Cozumel had some
ceremonial significance, it seems more plausible that a concept of
land as property was in operation at the time of its construction.
Such a concept would have necessarily entailed a much tighter
regulation of land use at the time on Cozumel than apparently
existed on the Peninsula at contact. Roys describes a class of
commoner farmers and fishermen who exploited communal resources and paid taxes to their lords (1943: Chapter 6). Given the
nature of the grid, this situation could have existed on Cozumel only
if lands were alloted to communities by some centralized authority,
the communities then assigning *milpa* lots of individual farmers. In
other words, all land would be property of the state as represented
by the elite ruling group.

More plausible is a situation in which the island was divided up
into great estates owned by elite families owing allegiance to a
centralized authority — the ruling merchant family or group of
families on Cozumel — but owning the land and operating as semi-
autonomous manor lords. This conception is tentatively supported
by our present data on settlement patterns.

In relation to the presence of house lot walls along with the
absence of field walls at Mayapan compared with the presence of the
latter on Cozumel, it should be noted that land pressure on Cozumel
may have been much greater than at Mayapan where plentiful *milpa*
land may have been available outside the great wall. Inside the wall,
where there was pressure, garden and house lot plots were divided by
walls in a manner which would be conceptually similar to that on
Cozumel. In addition, if the lot wall concept had developed first on
Cozumel, which at this point is pure speculation, our 'commonalty
of elite culture' hypothesis would predict that only the elite at
Mayapan (who lived within the great wall) would adopt such a
concept, while the commoners (who farmed plots outside the wall)
would retain their traditional concepts.

Pollock, Roys, Proskouriakoff and Smith (1962: 231) have noted
the strong resemblance of certain elite residence structures at Tulum
to those typical of Mayapan. On Cozumel, four elite dwellings that
can be positively identified as Mayapan type also have been located.
Other prominent residences apparently fall within the range of

variation found at Mayapan but diverge from the norm in that they are single-roomed. Detailed comparison of residence architecture at Mayapan and on Cozumel must await further investigation, but typical Mayapan elite residences are represented on the island (a good example is shown in Fig. 5); furthermore, they occur exclusively in residence assemblages.

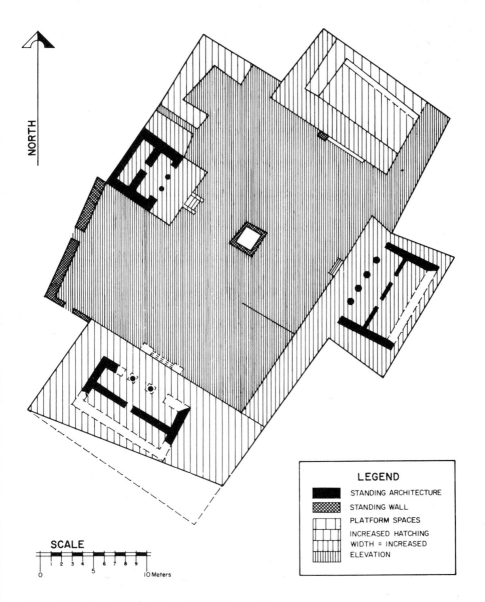

LEGEND

▰ STANDING ARCHITECTURE

▨ STANDING WALL

▤ PLATFORM SPACES

INCREASED HATCHING WIDTH = INCREASED ELEVATION

SCALE

0   1 2 3 4   5   6 7 8 9   10 Meters

Figure 5 La Expedición, Complex I, Cozumel.

Again, these residence assemblages conform in most respects to those considered typical at Mayapan. The typical Mayapan group consists of a major colonnaded residence, a smaller one-roomed colonnaded oratory situated at right angles or facing each other across a small plaza with a group altar or shrine in the centre of the plaza. Only one elite assemblage on Cozumel conforms precisely to this type, the other four so far located diverge in some respects; in one the oratory is not colonnaded, in another the main residence is not colonnaded. A third combined typical Mayapan civil-religious structures with residence structures on one large four-sided platform with a large colonnaded shrine in the centre. The significance of these contrasts in detail cannot be assessed at the present time, but one thing is clear: the elite residence assemblages of Cozumel closely resemble those of Mayapan, and the assemblages of Cozumel are the only ones to date on the peninsula that show such resemblance.

At the small settlement of Aguada Grande, no elite residence was found. This is the only settlement so far located on the island where a reasonable argument for planned location of structures can be made. Only a few residential structures could be positively identified at the site and only one construction period is represented at the site: Late Postclassic. Altogether, Aguada Grande gives the appearance of a planned centre built in one period for some specific function rather than a slowly developing community ceremonial centre. Its location on a road running north-south from the northern point of the island towards the medium-sized settlement of La Expedición, and the fact that it is the northernmost settlement on the island will ultimately contribute to its final characterization.

At La Expedición a single elite residence assemblage was found (Fig. 5) with a scattering of lesser residences (11 positively identified) located to the north, west and south, interspersed with large rubble platforms, some of which were isolated, others of which were agglutinated to form platform complexes covering up to 200 square m. It is more than likely that the elite assemblage functioned as the civil-religious centre of the settlement, but its primary characterization as a typically Mayapan elite residence allows the tentative identification of the settlement as the estate of a noble family.

La Expedición is located on a ridge of high ground running north-south about 500 m. inland from the northeast coast of the island. Aguada Grande is located four km. to the north on the ridge, and the medium-sized site of Zuuk (or Janan II) is located about four km. south of La Expedición on the ridge. At Zuuk, as at La Expedición, a single elite residence assemblage has been identified with several lesser residences in its immediate vicinity. South of this residential district is a group of large rubble platforms. These are not agglutinated as at La Expedición but are distributed over half a square km. Within this group are two small temples located side by side on a north-south axis. Two shrines are located on a single platform about 200 m. west of the elite residence group. These shrines face the residential district (east) and possibly mark its western perimeter. Again, the settlement pattern indicates that there was only one elite family in residence at Zuuk.

At the site of Buena Vista in the south-central part of Cozumel, elite residential structures are found together with colonnaded halls, identified at Mayapan as civil-religious structures, on a single large four-sided platform. Emanating off of this platform to the south and east is a complex of tightly agglutinated large rubble platforms covering at least half a square km. A few lesser residential structures on isolated platforms have been identified to the west of the main assemblage, and one residential structure on the rubble platform complex has been found. Undoubtedly further investigation will reveal more residences and clarify the nature of population structure at the site. However, it can be positively stated that there is only one elite residential assemblage in the settlement zone. Buena Vista is considerably larger than La Expedición and Zuuk, and the presence of civil-religious architecture combined with elite architecture on the main platform indicates that the situation is more complex than at the other two sites.

San Gervasio is the largest site so far discovered on the East Coast, covering at least 100 hectares and consisting of at least two hundred structures and complexes. It is a dispersed settlement formed of clusters of mounds with lesser residential units loosely interspersed among them. There were two civil-religious complexes at the site, located at its eastern and western extremities. The eastern assemblage comprises two colonnaded halls, a large colonnaded temple, two smaller temples and a long low platform that probably was the foundation for a perishable structure. These buildings are arranged on a four-sided plaza with a large altar or shrine in the centre. The main temple has been dated to the Late Postclassic by an offeratory cache located in front of its staircase. The westernmost complex will require excavation to identify its structures as it is comprised of tall, long, narrow rubble platforms in a plaza arrangement.

Preliminary exploration of San Gervasio has located three positively identified elite residential assemblages and three more that can be tentatively identified as such, subject to further investigation. These residences are located in the immediate vicinity of the two civil-religious complexes. San Gervasio was clearly an important centre, with a number of elite families in residence, and it probably functioned as the centre of political authority on the island. Its dispersed settlement pattern and lack of city walls contrast it with Mayapan and Tulum, indicating that defence was not necessary and coerced nucleation not a factor in its development.

Raised causeways or *sacbés* have been found extending from San

Gervasio to the east, north, and south. There is a *sacbé* running north-south at the Zuuk site which has an offshoot running directly to the residence district. *Sacbés* extend out from Buena Vista to the east and north. Causeways through seasonally inundated regions to the north and south of Aguada Grande indicate the presence of a north-south route there. These *sacbés* do not simply connect architectural groups but run for considerable distances away from settlements. A thorough survey of them will be carried out during the 1973 field season. The existence of a widespread network of such roads would be consistent with the tight spatial organization of the island.

On present evidence, it seems unlikely that a major seaside settlement that functioned as a port existed on Cozumel in the Late Postclassic period, at least nothing that might be compared with Tulum. There are lagoons at both ends of the island with shrines located in or near them and with causeways leading away from them to the interior. These areas would have been ideal as docking facilities for light draft canoes. The picture that is emerging then is of transportation routes from the coast serviced by elite estates that moved commodities to centralized locations on the island such as San Gervasio, while probably also supplying temporary warehouse and residence facilities. At the central locations, commodities would be recombined and sent on to other docking facilities, such as that which probably existed where the modern pueblo of San Miguel is located, to be shipped on. Such a conception would explain why a seaport such as Tulum would be heavily defended, while no such features are found on Cozumel. The centralized location of storage facilities would in itself be ample protection against marauders. The small shrines distributed along the east coast, often located directly in front of medium-sized settlements, could have functioned as a warning system against attack, and an elaborate internal communication and transportation network would have facilitated rapid mobilization for defence. In other words, the whole island may have constituted the port, with the functions usually nucleated in a single sea-side location dispersed throughout the island. The advantage of such an organization is greatly increased security for the commodities brought to the port. This would be an important advantage in light of the lack of a foreign power insuring Cozumel's safety during the Late Postclassic period. The disadvantage (if one wants to view it as such) is the tremendous amount of effort required to coordinate the facilities. Our data indicate a very tight socio-political and spatial organization of the island in the Late Postclassic, precisely the kind of organization needed to administer such a dispersed economic system.

Both the dispersed settlement pattern of Cozumel and the nucleated pattern of Mayapan reflect the power of the ruling merchant elite to impose radical concepts of spatial organization on their subject peoples. Both sites had the same kind of socio-political coordination, although results were probably achieved cooperatively on Cozumel, while coercively at Mayapan (as we know from ethnohistoric sources). We would argue that this similar quality of socio-political coordination reflects the close links between Cozumel's and Mayapan's elite.

It is known that members of the elite families of Mayapan personally supervised trading expeditions. Based on the socio-cultural link that can be established between the elites of Cozumel and Mayapan in terms of residence form, construction techniques, and other shared traits, the elite of Cozumel probably operated in the same manner — particularly when Cozumel's strategic location on a major trade route is considered. Based on the available evidence, we suggest that Cozumel functioned as a major trading port and storage facility on the East Coast, a place where large, logistically complex expeditions would be organized in complete security before being sent into relatively hostile territory. Tulum and Ichpaatun could have provided relay facilities and even some storage facilities, but the major task of commodity collection and expedition organization would have taken place on Cozumel.

Turning to the ceramic evidence linking Mayapan and Cozumel, similarities in the ceramic assemblages of Mayapan and the East Coast of Yucatan were first pointed out by Sanders (1960) and discussed in greater detail by Smith (1971). The occurrence of similar wares as well as the presence of traded types indicates a reasonable amount of contact between the two areas during the Late Postclassic. A meaningful evaluation of the degree and nature of this contact on Cozumel will require a careful comparative study of the ceramic assemblages and associations from both Cozumel and Mayapan. Such an analysis has recently been started.

Smith (1971) defines two major ceramic complexes at Mayapan. The Hocaba complex (A.D. 1250-1300), which marks the beginning of the construction stage at the site, is dominated by Mayapan Red ware (54.3 percent) with significant quantities of Mayapan Unslipped ware (19.8 percent) and Peto Cream ware (10 percent). Of these, Peto Cream ware, notably Xcanchakan Black-on-Cream, has been found to occur without Mayapan Red ware in deposits at Dzibilchaltun and on the surface at Chichen Itza, indicating a somewhat earlier context. It is Smith's feeling that this ware could have formed part of a complex associated with the traditional phase between the abandonment of Chichen Itza and the founding of Mayapan.

The Hocaba complex is followed by the Tases complex (A.D. 1300-1450) which is marked by a sharp decline in Mayapan Red ware (27.6 percent), an increase in Mayapan Unslipped ware (59.4 percent), a significant decrease in Peto Cream ware (.4 percent) and the appearance of San Joaquin Buff ware (.9 percent). The increase in Mayapan Unslipped ware is associated with the appearance of

Chen Mul Modelled type full-figured effigy censers, which have an almost identical East Coast counterpart, Sanders' Tulum Buff paste censers. It is also during the Tases phase that Tulum Red ware first occurs as a trade ware (.01 percent) at Mayapan.

Preliminary testing on Cozumel has yielded a body of data on the basis of which some general observations can be made. Although there is evidence on Cozumel of occupation extending back at least to Late Preclassic times, the major period of florescence can be assigned to the Late Postclassic or Mayapan period.

Test excavations at the site of La Expedición tentatively suggest two periods of construction associated with Late Postclassic ceramics. The earlier period is marked by a predominance of Peto Cream ware over Tulum Red ware and Mayapan Red ware, or possibly an absence of these latter altogether. The later construction period, on the other hand, is characterized by a much greater quantity of Tulum and Mayapan Red ware than Peto Cream ware. It is possible that the earlier period could be representative of the Early Postclassic/Late Postclassic transition phase, while the later period is clearly contemporary with Mayapan. Further excavations at La Expedición and other sites, plus the laboratory analysis of unslipped wares, as well as slipped wares, should clarify this preliminary organization of the data.

The reconstruction would certainly support our hypothesis, since if Cozumel's position as a port of trade were placed in jeopardy with the decline of Chichen Itza and the demise of the Toltec trade system, we would expect attempts to form new independent alliances to get under way very soon after the breakdown of the Early Postclassic system, i.e., during the transitional period. Such alliances would then have been extended to Mayapan as that site became the focus of economic and political power in northern Yucatan. It is of more than passing interest to our hypothesis that the Carnegie Institution of Washington was able to define two major periods at Mayapan as we noted above. During the former period, which is defined by the Hocaba ceramic complex, occupation was limited to the centre of the site. A number of buildings in this area, such as the Castillo, show much similarity to buildings at Chichen Itza which date to the preceeding period. A short time later, in the period defined by the Tases ceramic complex, Mayapan was expanded to its full size with a great increase in population and presumably in importance, too.

In evaluating the ceramic relationship between Cozumel and Mayapan, several different aspects of similarity can be considered. These will be based on certain assumptions about the difference between ports of trade and trading ports and will involve a comparison of similarities between Cozumel and other mainland sites during the Early Postclassic. According to the model, Cozumel should exhibit a closer relationship with Mayapan during the Late Postclassic than with any other mainland site during the Early Postclassic.

Similarity can be approached not only in terms of quantity of traded wares, but also in terms of the similarity of the percentage composition of these wares. We would expect, for example, to find significant similarities in the percentages of Peto Cream ware and Mayapan Red ware at both Mayapan and Cozumel. Another test expectation would predict an increase in local imitation of traded wares in the Late Postclassic due to the existence at that time of broader and stronger socio-cultural ties with an external power. How strong, for example, are the similarities between Tulum Red ware and Mayapan Red ware and between Tulum and Mayapan effigy censers? We would not expect to find the same degree of sharing in a port of trade where the neutrality of the port would set it apart culturally from other centres. And finally, we might expect to find a greater similarity in the distributional contexts of traded wares and closely related local wares in Late Postclassic elite residences due to similar patterns of use and discard which our hypothesis of a commonality of elite culture would predict.

The major problem that remains is that of objectively quantifying ceramic similarities (trade wares present, local imitations, and their discard contexts) between Cozumel and other sites.

The first difficulty to overcome is that of sampling bias in the excavations of sites throughout Yucatan and on Cozumel. For the sake of argument, however, we will proceed as if the samples are representative of the sites from which they are drawn. In relation to the Cozumel-Mayapan comparison, structures excavated and locations within structures pitted will have to be placed into categories which are comparable at both sites. In this way the debris found in a house bench at Mayapan will be compared with the debris found in a house chultun from Cozumel, rather than with a test pit in an open plaza or a total sherd count. In other words, comparable context categories must be constructed for both sites. Because of the general use of only three criteria in the Mayapan report, context categories may have to be limited to simply 'residential', 'ceremonial' and 'cenote', or the original data from Mayapan (now on file at the Peabody Museum, Harvard University) may have to be restudied in order to provide narrower units of comparison.

These parameters will organize the data for evaluation. The first step of the procedure will then be to run analyses of the range of variability with context categories at Mayapan and set up standard deviation units. Next, the range of variability within context units on Cozumel will be calculated and the difference in the variation between Mayapan and Cozumel will be derived. A simple X^2 test can be used to determine whether they are significantly similar. If they are, weight will be added to the prediction of strong interconnection during the Late Postclassic between Cozumel and Mayapan. It is only by comparing the results of this analysis with the results from an analysis on Early Postclassic material, however, that a meaningful test can be realized.

Ceramic analysis of the kind just mentioned will be undertaken in the 1973 season. It should also be noted that important similarities exist in non-ceramic artifactual assemblages between Cozumel and Mayapan. The laboratory study of the Cozumel assemblages, however, has only just begun and so we are not in a position to comment on it at the present moment.

Research design for future evaluations: brief comments

Our research plans for the 1973 field season will be oriented, in part, towards securing data which can be used to further test our hypothesis about the culture changes on Cozumel and its links with Mayapan. First, we plan to concentrate our attention upon the major site of San Gervasio, where we will excavate at least one Late Postclassic elite residence complex. We would predict that we should find a great similarity in plans, artifacts, and associations between this complex and complexes at Mayapan. In order to contrast this Late Postclassic situation on Cozumel with the hypothesized port-of-trade model for the Early Postclassic, we also hope to find a good stratigraphic situation at San Gervasio which will allow us to study the changes between the Early and Late Postclassic period. There are some preliminary indications that we may be fortunate enough to find such a field situation. We would predict that in the Early Postclassic period we should find a local Maya culture with a thin veneer of Toltec traits and goods and that the relationship between Cozumel and Chichen Itza differed significantly from the close Cozumel-Mayapan elite ties.

We will also continue our general survey of the whole island of Cozumel. In relation to the results of this survey, as they pertain to Early Postclassic remains, we might expect less evidence of a powerful central authority, as reflected in a settlement pattern, which would differ from that of the Late Postclassic period. Furthermore, the east coast shrines should pertain only to the Late Postclassic period, since their defensive function would have been fulfilled by the Toltecs in the Early Postclassic period. Finally, Cozumel's role as a pilgrimage shrine should also not date earlier than the Late Postclassic period. It is our hypothesis that Ix Chel's shrine was located at San Gervasio, and we are hopeful that our intensive investigation of this site in 1973 will enable us to test this hypothesis.

To conclude, in our coming field season, we plan to further test the working hypotheses suggested in this paper. Some will have to be revised and others discarded. Hopefully, though, our basic hypothesis will prove to be a strong and productive one. If it does receive additional support, we also plan to show how it fits into a more general hypothesis about the nature of culture change at trading centres as contrasted with major resource and administrative centres and show the relevance of this hypothesis to the development and maintenance of long-distance trading networks in Mesoamerica and the rise and fall of Mesoamerican civilizations.

Acknowledgments

The Cozumel Archaeological Project is being carried out under the auspices of the Peabody Museum, Harvard University and the University of Arizona, with the cooperation and authorization of the Instituto Nacional de Antropología e Historia of Mexico. The staff of the 1972 season included J. Sabloff and W. Rathje, co-directors, D. Freidel, J. Connor, P. Sabloff, A. Enriquez Bringas, L. Freidel, P. Urban, S. Burns, and H. Smelker. The first season of fieldwork was made possible through grants from the National Geographic Society, the Ford Foundation, and the Harvard Graduate Society, as well as the generosity of Mrs Charles Ayling and Mr Landon Clay. We are grateful to all the above institutions and individuals and to all the authorities and friends in Mexico City (at I.N.A.H.), Cozumel, Cambridge, and Tucson who made our work possible. We wish also to thank our crew members, Marcial Castro, Pastor Cocom, Edgardo Cocom, Amerigo Cocom, and Luis Rojas, for their enthusiastic labour throughout the field season. Lastly, we would like to thank Gordon R. Willey and Stephen Williams for their helpful comments on the paper.

REFERENCES

Andrews, E.W. IV (1965) Archaeology and prehistory in the northern Maya lowlands: an introduction. In Robert Wauchope (general ed.), *Handbook of Middle American Indians*; vol. 2, ed. C.R. Willey, 228-330.

Chapman, A.M. (1957) Port of trade enclaves in Aztec and Maya civilizations. In K. Polanyi, C.M. Arensberg, and H.W. Pearson (eds), *Trade and Market in the Early Empires*. Glencoe, Ill.

Easton, D. (1965) *A Systems Analysis of Political Life*. New York.

Flannery, K.V. (1968) The Olmec and the valley of Oaxaca: a model for interregional interaction in formative times. In E.P. Benson (ed.), *Dumbarton Oaks Conference on the Olmec*, 79-110. Washington.

Parsons, L.A. and B.J. Price (1971) Mesoamerican trade and its role in the emergence of civilization. *Contributions of the University of California Archaeological Research Facility*, no. 11, 169-95.

Pollock, H.E.D., R.L. Roys, T. Proskouriakoff, and A.L. Smith (1962) *Mayapan, Yucatan, Mexico*. Carnegie Institution of Washington, Publication no. 619.

Rathje, W.L. (1971a) *Lowland Classic Maya Socio-Political Organization: Degree and Form in Time and Space*. MS, doctoral dissertation, Harvard University.

Rathje, W.L. (1971*b*) The origin and development of the lowland Classic Maya civilization. *American Antiquity*, 36, no. 3, 275-85.

Rathje, W.L. (in press) Praise the gods and pass the metates: a hypothesis of the development of lowland rainforest civilizations in Mesoamerica. In M.P. Leone (ed.), *Contemporary Archaeology: An Introduction to Theory and Contributions*. Carbondale, Ill.

Rathje, W.L. (1973) Classic Maya development and denouement. In T.P. Culbert (ed.), *The Classic Maya Collapse*, Santa Fe and Albuquerque.

Rathje, W.L. and J.A. Sabloff (1972) Cozumel, Quintana Roo, Yucatan: one test of a model of cultural fluidity and ports-of-trade. Paper read at a Meeting of the Society for American Archaeology, Miami.

Roys, R.L. (1943) *The Indian Background of Colonial Yucatan*. Carnegie Institution of Washington, Publication no. 548.

Sabloff, J.A. and W.L. Rathje (1972) A study of changing Precolumbian commercial patterns on the island of Cozumel, Mexico. Paper read at the 40th International Congress of Americanists, Rome.

Sanders, W.T. (1955) An archaeological reconnaissance of Northern Quintana Roo. *Current Reports of the Carnegie Institution of Washington*, no. 24, 179-22.

Sanders, W.T. (1960) *Prehistoric Ceramics and Settlement Patterns in Quintana Roo, Mexico*. Carnegie Institution of Washington, Publication no. 606, Contribution 60, 155-264.

Scholes, F.V. and R.L. Roys (1968) *The Maya Chontal Indians of Acalan-Tixchel*. 1st ed. 1948. Norman, Oklahoma.

Silva-Galdames, O. (1971) Trade and the concepts of nuclear and marginal cultural areas in Mesoamerica. *Cerámica de Cultura Maya*, 7, Supplement.

Smith, R.E. (1971) *The Pottery of Mayapan*. 2 vols. Papers of the Peabody Museum of Archaeology and Ethnology, Harvard University, vol. 65.

Thompson, J.E.S. (1970) *Maya History and Religion*. Norman, Oklahoma.

Tourtellot, G. and J.A. Sabloff (1972) Exchange systems among the ancient Maya. *American Antiquity*, 37, 126-34.

Webb, M.C. (1964) *The Postclassic Decline of the Peten Maya: An Interpretation in Light of a General Theory of State Society*. 3 vols. University Microfilms.

GORDON R. WILLEY

The Classic Maya hiatus: a rehearsal for the collapse?

In the latter half of the sixth century A.D. the Classic Maya civilization of the lowlands underwent a marked slowing down in that most sensitive sphere of its high ritual activities, the carving and dedication of Initial Series stelae. This near-cessation of monumental commemoration followed upon almost three centuries of a vigorous preoccupation with what has been termed the 'stelae cult'; and when this slow-down was over, stelae dedication was resumed with intensity for almost another 300 years. This 'hesitation' or near-gap in Maya Initial Series monuments and dates has been referred to as the Classic Maya 'hiatus'. Archaeologists have puzzled over its significance; but, in contrast to the more spectacular ninth-century failure and general collapse of Maya lowland civilization, which was also first signalled by a decline in stelae activities, this hiatus has not received the consideration that it probably deserves, though it has been noted and remarked upon by a number of Mayanists, among them Morley (1938-9: vol. 4, 333), Proskouriakoff (1950: 111-12), Thompson (1954: 55-6), Willey (1964), and M.D. Coe (1966: 86). I would like now to right the balance somewhat by focusing attention on the hiatus and to do this by asking the question: to what extent did the hiatus foreshadow the eventual final collapse? Was it a kind of ominous and unconscious 'rehearsal' for the later disaster? For if Maya civilization of the lowlands carried within itself, from its beginnings, the seeds of its own destruction, as some have suggested, one might expect this to be true; and by examining the structure and dynamics of the 'little collapse' of the hiatus we may place ourselves in a better position to understand the later 'great collapse'. We are, of course, comparing one shadowy and imperfectly comprehended set of events with another; but, by the very nature of archaeology, where one fact seen in a certain context may help us recognize and confirm a comparable fact in another context, such an examination could clarify both sets of events.

The observed facts of the hiatus may be set down quite simply. The earliest known Maya Classic Initial Series monuments and dates appear in the latter part of the 8th *baktun*. They are in sites clustering in the northeastern Peten, in what might be considered the very heart, or 'core area', of the southern lowlands — at Uaxactun, Tikal, Uolantun, and Balakbal. At Uaxactun and Tikal, at least, these first monuments occur in the context of a rapidly rising ceremonial centre development, at the close and climax of the Terminal Late Preclassic or Protoclassic Period. In fact, their appearance is taken to mark the beginning of the Early Classic Period at about A.D. 250 to 300. In the next two and a half centuries the stelae cult spreads to other sites, in most cases probably being assimilated into the evolving politico-religious developments of other Terminal Late Preclassic centres. By the end of the 5th *katun* of the 9th *baktun* (9.5.0.0.0 or A.D. 534) the stelae cult was also found at Xultun and Naachtun, in the northeast Peten, and, much farther afield, at Altar de Sacrificios, Yaxchilan, and Piedras Negras, on the Usumacinta drainage, and at Copan in the far southeast of the lowlands. It is shortly after this that the hiatus begins. From 9.5.0.0.0 until 9.8.0.0.0, or from A.D. 534 to 593, there is a sharp drop-off in both the number of monuments dedicated and in the number of sites where these few occur. In the old original heartland of the stelae cult there are no monuments at all between 9.5.0.0.0 and 9.9.0.0.0 at either Uaxactun or Naachtun; Tikal has only one, questionably dated at 9.6.13.0.0; and Xultun has one — not an Initial Series — that may be read as 9.7.10.0.0. On the Usumacinta drainage, Altar de Sacrificios shows a hiatus from 9.4.10.0.0 to 9.9.5.0.0; Yaxchilan has a similar gap; and Piedras Negras has two somewhat controversial hiatus monuments. Copan does somewhat better; Morley read three monuments to the 6th *katun* and one to the 7th, although with some questionings; but even by accepting all of these there is a lessening in the record by comparison with earlier or later times. Most interestingly, some of the firmest hiatus dates are from peripheral regions or regions which, up until that time, had no dated stelae. Pusilha, in southern British Honduras, has solid dates at 9.7.0.0.0 and 9.8.0.0.0 and a possible one at 9.6.0.0.0. Tulum, in the northern lowlands, has a 9.6.10.0.0 date, and there is also a stela at Coba which may date to the hiatus. Turning to the west, and going beyond the Usumacinta drainage, there is a 9.6.0.0.0 date at Tonina, in the central Chiapas highlands, and there are *katun* 8 dates at Comitan and Chinkultic in the same general region. In sum, during the hiatus, whose nadir is marked at the 6th and 7th *katuns* of the 9th *baktun*, there is very little stelae activity in the northeast Peten heartland, minimal activity on the Usumacinta, somewhat more at Copan, but the first inception of the stelae cult at sites on the eastern, western, and northern peripheries of the southern lowlands. (The basic sources for these stelae dates are in Morley 1938-9, 1920. For Coba see Thompson, Pollock and Charlot 1932.)

So far, the hiatus has been defined solely in terms of stelae dedications and dates, but is there a corresponding decline in other aspects of culture? Here we are handicapped by limited information, but where we do have data there does seem to be a similar decline. Thus, at Uaxactun, in the great acropolis-like structure A-V, the last building subphase (I*h*) of the Early Classic or Vault I Period has an associated stela with a date of 9.3.10.0.0 (A.D. 504). The immediately overlying building is also dated by a stela, this one with a reading of 9.9.6.2.3 (A.D. 619). The implications are that the intervening era between these two dates, which spans the sixth century A.D., was a time of little or no constructional activity (A.L. Smith 1950: 24-5, 67-8, 86-7). At Altar de Sacrificios the constructional story is much the same. The hiatus there is represented by the late Ayn, Veremos, and early Chixoy phases, spanning the sixth century and during which there was little major building (Adams 1971: Willey 1973). For Tikal, detailed data on construction by phase have not yet been published, but the preliminary reports suggest that the time of the hiatus was a relatively slack architectural period (W.R. Coe 1965, 1967). These are also sites which manifest the stelae dedication hiatus; but it would be interesting to see what the architectural records at Tonina or Pusilha show for the same time. One would anticipate a positive co-variance between monuments and architecture at these sites, too, which would mean that they would show building activity in the last half of the sixth century A.D.

Aside from the declines, in stelae activity and, probably, in architecture, the hiatus must also be characterized as a time of culture change and cultural re-orientation; or at least this change and reorientation is revealed immediately after the hiatus. Proskouriakoff has referred to the hiatus as a 'dark period' in Maya sculpture, one which reflected a 'momentous historical event' that disturbed normal development; but, in her words, it was then followed by 'a restoration of order and a new pulse of creative activity' (1950: 111-12). And in ceramics there can be little doubt but that the re-orientation from Tzakol to Tepeu traditions occurred at some time during the hiatus. R.E. Smith has made this definition at Uaxactun (1955), and Adams' Altar de Sacrificios ceramic studies and those of Culbert at Tikal confirm it (Adams 1971; Culbert 1973). In architectural techniques, as has long been known, the hiatus also appears to mark the changeover from heavy block masonry to a veneer-like treatment. Indeed, following out of all this, the hiatus separates Early Classic from Late Classic in a very effective fashion, although whether one should draw the line nearer 9.8.0.0.0 (or about A.D. 600), as has been conventional, or at 9.6.0.0.0 (about A.D. 550), as W.R. Coe has suggested, is still undecided. (R.E. Smith (1955) was probably the first to specify 9.8.0.0.0 as the Early-Late Classic dividing line. See W.R. Coe 1965, and Willey, Culbert, and Adams 1967.) In brief, the archaeological record as we read it now shows that the last half of the sixth century A.D. was, to put it conservatively, a disturbed time in the southern Maya lowlands. Old patterns were being disrupted; new ones presumably were in formation; but for several decades there was a hiatus in what had been the normal courses of cultural activity.

How does this archaeological record compare with that of the ninth century when this southern lowland Maya civilization collapsed? (The circumstances of the collapse have been summarized by Willey and Shimkin 1971, 1973.) Obviously, the cessation or slowing down of the stelae cult during the hiatus is very reminiscent of what happened two to three centuries later, as is the slackening of major architectural activity in the ceremonial centres. These archaeological aspects almost certainly point to a weakening of the central socio-political structure of the culture in both instances. The differences here are largely those of degree and duration. The quiescence or semi-moribund condition of the centres in the sixth century stands in contrast to their complete death and abandonment at the close of the ninth century, and the approximate half-century of the hiatus is substantially less than the 100 years or more of the final decline. These differences, in turn, undoubtedly relate to others. Foremost among these is the matter of population. Here we need more and better information, especially on residence or house mound counts; but from the evidence that is now available there does not seem to have been anywhere near the same kind of population reduction in the hiatus as in the collapse. In the latter, the sustaining populations of many centres were truly decimated between 9.19.0.0.0 (A.D. 810) and 10.4.0.0.0 (A.D. 909), with virtual abandonment of the site region after that (as at Tikal; see Culbert 1973). This would not appear to have been the case for the hiatus. Certainly nothing as drastic as this occurred on a wide scale; however, there are some indications of population decline at some sites during the hiatus, such as at Altar de Sacrificios (see Willey 1973; for Seibal see A.L. Smith and Willey 1969; Sabloff 1973) and this is a matter that deserves close attention in settlement investigation at other sites.

Besides these above considerations, there were, of course, great differences in the outcome of the hiatus and the collapse — as the names themselves indicate. After the collapse there was no real sculptural or architectural revival, at least not in the southern sector of the lowlands; and in ceramics the break and tradition change of the end of the ninth century were much more profound than those of the sixth.

These comparisons between the hiatus and the collapse can be extended further by directing attention not so much to the immediate events of each as to their broader antecedent cultural settings. This has been done for the collapse in connection with a recent symposium on that theme (Culbert 1973, Willey and Shimkin 1973). The structure of Maya society and culture as it appeared just before the ninth century A.D. was analysed in some detail, insofar as this could be done from archaeological data, and an attempt was made to isolate the stress factors that were operating on and in it. Among other things, it was pointed out that at the climax of the Late Classic Period, in the eighth century A.D. and just before the collapse, Maya population of the southern lowlands was at an all-time peak. Both house mound tabulations, where these are available, and a survey of Late Classic ceremonial centres functioning at this time indicate this. Closely related to this demographic situation are subsistence prac- tices. While short-cycle swidden agriculture was undoubtedly practiced in many places in the southern lowlands in the Late Classic, there are also lines of evidence (Sanders 1973) to indicate that this was supplemented by long-cycle swidden cultivation in regions and on soils where this was possible. Also, riverine lowlands were known (Siemens and Puleston 1972) to have been cultivated in places, and perhaps *bajos* or swamps were similarly utilized. Food resources other than maize and beans appear to have played a large part in the diet at certain sites, such as the probable breadnut harvests at Tikal (Puleston 1968). In brief, the reconstructable picture of Maya lowland Late Classic life is one of the maximization of all available food resources, and of populations increasingly pressing on these resources. It is highly unlikely that this same demographic- subsistence relationship obtained —or obtained to such an intensified degree — in the Early Classic period.

There are also inferred differences in the socio-political contexts of Early Classic versus Late Classic Maya society. A number of trends can be plotted from Early to Late Classic which indicate these differences. For one thing, there is a steady change in the nature of hieroglyphic texts, and these changes are particularly pronounced between Early and Late Classic. The earlier texts are much shorter and would appear to be restricted largely to time-counting and other calendrical matters. The later texts are longer, and in some instances (Proskouriakoff 1963, 1964) have been demonstrated to pertain to historical events and to royal lineages. In ceremonial centre architec- ture the multi-roomed palace-type building becomes more important in the Late Classic than in the Early Classic (R. McAdams 1956). The burial customs of the Late Classic differ from those of the Early, especially as these customs involve grave contents, the ages and sexes of the occupants, and the ceremonial centre as opposed to domestic dwelling loci of the graves (Rathje 1970). These changes, together with those of the monuments and architecture, imply an ever- widening social gulf between Early and Late Classic. While it is possible that ancient Maya society was class-structured throughout its entire Classic period history, all the clues point to an increasing rigidity of this class-ordering in the Late Classic; and this, combined with other factors, including those of over-population and subsist- ence pressures, could have produced a stress in Late Classic society that had not been so critical in Early Classic times.

A related stress factor on the Late Classic socio-political scene was undoubtedly that of competition between the aristocratic elite of the different ceremonial centres (Robert Rands emphasized this particular point in the Santa Fe symposium discussions on the Maya Collapse, October 1970). In their efforts to outdo each other in size, splendour, hieroglyphic scholarship, and other hierarchial activities, the rival dynasties must have imposed great economic burdens on their sustaining peasant populations. While this may also have been the case in the Early Classic, the much greater number of such centres active in the Late Classic, together with the population pressures of the late period, suggest that stress of this sort was probably more pronounced in the Late Classic. This seems supported by the fact that all of the pictorial evidence of warfare in the Maya Classic — and judging from the representations this was a warfare of Maya against Maya — are of the Late period.

As a final comparison between the circumstances of the Early and Late Classic, let us take a look at foreign influences. Unlike the other comparisons, we are not so much concerned with trends or intensifications of processes as with simply different historical patterns. Both the Early and Late Classic Maya of the lowlands experienced Mexican contacts. In the Early Classic these contacts derived from Teotihuacan. The extent to which these contacts were carried out through trade, the actual presence of foreigners, or military and political involvements are undecided; however, at a minimum, trade must have been an important mechanism in the relationships. Although some of these Teotihuacan influences began to appear quite early, dating back to the Terminal Late Preclassic (Pendergast 1971), their concentration was later, falling in the century between A.D. 450 and 550. (W.R. Coe 1962, 1965, 1967; Willey 1971; Willey and Shimkin 1971. There is also an M.A. thesis by N.M. Hellmuth (1969) which is concerned with Mexican symbols in Early Classic Maya art.) This would be on a late Tzakol 2 — Tzakol 3 ceramic horizon and would be just before the hiatus. The influences are seen in ceramics, for the most part what appear to be locally-made imitations of the Teotihuacanoid lidded tripod jars. A cultural synthesis is seen in some pieces which combine lowland Maya and Teotihuacan decorative techniques and design motifs. At Tikal, which appears to have been the central focus of the Teotihuacan influences, there is, in addition, a stela with Teotihuacan iconography (W.R. Coe 1965). An important fact in this Teotihuacan-Early Classic Maya relationship is that the Guatemalan highland site of Kaminaljuyu also played a role, perhaps a mediating one, involving trade in obsidian. While some central Mexican green obsidian does occur in the Maya lowlands at this time, most of this highly useful stone (or glass) is of the black or grey varieties that probably originated in the Guatemalan highlands, some of it at no great distance from Kaminaljuyu (see especially Sanders and Price 1968;

Sanders 1973). But whatever the processes of the Teotihuacan-lowland Maya contacts, or by what routes or however mediated, what is certain is that they came to an end very abruptly with the hiatus. This, naturally, prompts questions as to the relationships between the Teotihuacan influence and the hiatus. Given the timing of the events, it does not seem likely that the Teotihuacan 'impact' on the lowland Maya brought about the hiatus — at least not in any direct way. On the contrary, The Teotihuacan influences appear concurrently with the most brilliant growth of the Early Classic culture. We are, instead, led to ask if the withdrawal of the Teotihuacan influences did not precipitate the hiatus?

The historical pattern of foreign involvement for the Maya of the Late Classic period is quite different from that of the Early Classic. This time the contacts seem to be derived from a source that is Toltec-like, but we cannot be more specific than this. They occurred along a broad front on the western side of the Maya lowlands. It is quite probable that the peoples immediately involved were Maya, although Maya of a Non-Classic cultural tradition. The foreign influences are seen in Fine Orange pottery and figurines and in the iconography of certain monuments at a few terminal Late Classic sites (for the Fine Orange pottery see Sabloff 1970, 1973; for the monument iconography, with particular reference to the site of Seibal, see J.A. Graham 1972). The timing of these Late Classic foreign influences is distinctly different from that of the Teotihuacan influences on Early Classic Maya culture. Whereas in the latter case the Teotihuacan elements are seen concomitant with — and perhaps stimulative to — the Early Classic climax and prior to the hiatus, the Mexicanoid intrusions into the Late Classic do not appear until well after the Late Classic apogee has passed and the decline toward the collapse has already set in. In fact, arguments have been advanced (Sabloff and Willey 1967; see also Adams 1973 and Sabloff 1973) that the bearers of the Fine Orange ware who invaded the Usumacinta and Pasion Valleys were the prime causal forces in the Late Classic collapse; however, these arguments tend to be invalidated by the fact that in many sites the decline was well-advanced before this alien pottery tradition is introduced. While there was very likely an invasion of Mexicanized foreigners into the Classic Maya realm in the ninth century A.D., it probably did not take place until the dissolution had begun.

In these comparisons of the hiatus and the collapse we have reviewed the structure and developmental background of each, but what of their causes or inferred causes? Very little has been written about the cause, or causes, of the hiatus. Most Mayanists have simply noted it and passed on (Proskouriakoff 1950: 111-12; Thompson 1954: 55-6). However, Morley, whose indefatigable searching out and recording of the stelae inscriptions first revealed the hiatus phenomenon, did speculate about it (1938-9: vol. 4, 333):

The great expansion of the monument-erecting complex to all parts of the Maya area, which we have seen took place in the second quarter of *baktun* 9 (9.5.0.0.0 to 9.10.0.0.0) and thus exactly coincides with this three-quarters of a century of decreased monumental activity, may explain this observed decrease. The Maya during these four *katuns* were devoting their energies to the extensive occupation of the Old Empire region; it was definitely a period of expansion, and only a few centres here and there found themselves in a position to erect sculptured stone monuments on the successive 10 *tun* period-endings, though all, so to speak, were accumulating reserves against the more abundant days that were to follow.

Morley delivers this in passing, with no particular insistence upon it being a very satisfactory explanation; but it is a very feeble statement of cause. If energies were used up in 'pioneering' new territories, one would expect these 'outposts' of Maya civilization to have been suffering the most of all from such exertions; yet it is exactly here, on these outermost peripheries of the old Maya lowlands, that we find most of the hiatus stelae dedications. Nor does it seem likely that the older, more established centres would have abandoned their stelae cult activities to divert their energies and wealth to the 'provinces'. Finally, the concept of hoarding up cultural energy, the accumulation of reserves for the great effort to come, is at best a poetic conceit; it is certainly not an explanation.

The only other attempt to explain the causes behind the hiatus has been developed, incidentally, in connection with what we might call the 'trade failure hypothesis' as this has been applied to the later Maya collapse. The hypothesis has been formulated by both Webb and Rathje (Webb 1973, but see also 1964; Rathje 1971, 1973), and to see it in proper perspective it is necessary to turn to the question of the final collapse. In contrast to the problem of the hiatus, a very great deal has been written about the Maya ninth-century collapse. I will not attempt to summarize it all here; this has been done in the recent symposium on the subject referred to above. No ultimate conclusions were drawn in this symposium, although a majority of the participants did agree upon the significance of those internal stress factors within Late Classic Maya society which made it vulnerable to dissolution. These have been referred to as: ecological limitations, over-population, the widening social gulf between aristocracy and peasantry, and expensive competition between ceremonial centres. To these may be added the external stress factors of military pressures, trade disruption, or both. Such pressures were seen as being applied by Non-Classic Maya peoples along the western and northwestern frontiers of the southern Maya lowlands. While the symposium summary statement (Willey and Shimkin 1973) did not go much beyond this in delineating these external stress factors,

Rathje's participant paper (Rathje 1973) spelled things out in much greater detail in the course of developing what might be considered a 'field theory' which explains the interactive processes between the institution of trade and the rise and maintenance of highly complex societies.

Very briefly, Rathje's hypothesis states that the Maya lowlands, and especially the northeast Peten 'core area' of these lowlands, were lacking in natural products necessary to support large complex societies, namely, such things as hard stone for corn-grinding implements, obsidian, and salt. In order to obtain these requisite raw materials the leadership of the 'core area' communities, for instance, Tikal or Uaxactun, developed long-distance trade with areas where such resources were to be obtained, as in the Chiapas and Guatemalan highlands. To carry out such trade meant organization and management above the household level; and, similarily, the redistribution of goods from such trade demanded an hierarchial governmental structure. Lowland Maya social and political complexity had its start in these beginnings in the Preclassic period, and this complexity was further elaborated in the succeeding Classic period. The centres of this earliest rise of civilization in the 'core area' had trading connections with other, and at that time lesser, centres in what Rathje has called the 'buffer zones'. These 'buffer zones' were the lowland regions surrounding the 'core area', and they were more advantageously placed, geographically, for highland and other Meso-american-wide trade than was the 'core area'. For a time, the lesser centres of the 'buffer zones' served an intermediate, relaying role in supplying needed raw materials to the sites of the 'core area'. In return for these services they received the benefits of the religious and status-defining esoterica and the manufactured luxury goods of the 'core area'. Eventually, however, with increasing sophistication, and profiting by their more favourable geographical locations, the 'buffer zones' centres usurped the trade control from the 'core area', precipitating the downfall of its cites.

While this highly compressed outline of Rathje's ideas does not do them full justice, his hypothesis, to this point, seems consistent with the facts as we know them. It also gives us an insight on the hiatus. We have already asked if the Teotihuacan withdrawal from the Maya area may not have brought on the hiatus. If Rathje is correct, if Early Classic 'core area' development was vitally related to the Teotihuacan supervised trade, then the relinquishing of that supervisory power and the loss of that trade could have had serious results in sites such as Tikal and Uaxactun. Another 'expectation' leading out of Rathje's hypothesis is met by the appearance of hiatus stelae in distant 'buffer zone' sites such as Tonina, Comitan, Chinkultic, and Tulum. While the 'core area' suffered these 'buffer zone' sites came to prominence. However, not all of the sites which Rathje defines as being in the 'buffer zones' enjoy a similar rise during the hiatus. Altar de

Sacrificios very definitely does not. It is marked by the stelae hiatus, by an architectural decline, and, probably, by a population drop. Nor is its recovery after the hiatus a prompt one. The Tepeu 1 horizon is weakly represented, and it is not until Tepeu 2 times that it returns to its old pre-hiatus vigour. For Yaxchilan, down the Usumacinta from Altar de Sacrificios, the situation may well be the same. At least the stelae dates there — which is all that we have to go on — suggest that it was.

It may be that this failure of Altar de Sacrificios, and perhaps Yaxchilan, to meet the 'expectations' of Rathje's hypothesis is a problem of 'buffer zone' definition. The lower Pasión-middle Usumacinta region may have been more closely allied to the 'core area' during the Early Classic than Rathje has conceded. But then the whole matter of the 'buffer zone' centres in the Late Classic is a little perplexing as one attempts to follow out Rathje's hypothesis. Many of them enjoy a great florescence after the hiatus, although in some cases, as at Altar de Sacrificios, it seems a little delayed. But then the 'core area' centres also experience this florescence; Tikal and Uaxactun go on to greater glories, as do other 'core area' sites. They are not choked off — at least not for another 200 years — by the giants of the 'buffer zone' such as Yaxchilan, Piedras Negras, or Palenque. In fact, they would appear to be sharing trade goods, prestige, and power with them. What we have before the hiatus is a centralization of trade and power in the northeastern Peten 'core area' zone; what we have after the hiatus are multiple centres of trade and power.

This leads me to wonder if we are not witnessing the results of a process which Blanton has outlined in an attempt (1972) to explain settlement changes in the Valley of Mexico. He notes that while Teotihuacan was at its height there were no rival extractive and tribute centres in the valley, and he suggests that the downfall of the great city may have been brought about by the fact that an increasingly greater part of its sustaining rural population could no longer participate in the symbiotic networks (or trade and other functions) that were focused on that centre. Subsequent to the fall of Teotihuacan, a number of moderately large centres did develope, before these were, again, reduced under the hegemony of Tula. In other words, there is a dialectic between centralization and decentralization, between leadership power and subject demands; and if we were to assume that Early Classic society of the Maya lowlands was a more centralized one than the conventional conception of it, with a controlling leadership at Tikal, then the springing up of new ceremonial centres in the Late Classic might be viewed as a 'balkanization' to meet the demands of the increasing populations. This would not deny a trade failure as the causal force behind the hiatus; but it would see, rather, the interval of the hiatus, when the capital power of Tikal was weakened, as the opportunity to break out of the old structure and to form new centres of power.

I would agree with Rathje that the final, ninth-century collapse of the Maya was also triggered by another trade failure. I will not attempt to detail his arguments for this except that I do not think that the interactions between 'core area' and 'buffer zones', as he has defined them, are as important as he does. For one thing, the 'core' sites and the 'buffer' sites go down together. I am inclined to believe that what happened here was that a new, outer 'buffer zone', of Non-Classic or Mexican-Maya states, formed along the western edge of the southern lowlands and strangled trade for both the older 'buffer zone' and the 'core area'. For it seems highly likely that the Late Classic centres, of both 'buffer' and 'core', were closely linked with each other in a network of economic, political, and religious relationships. But all of this leads on to other arguments and discussions beyond the range of this short paper.

Let us conclude by returning to the original question. Was the hiatus a 'rehearsal' for the collapse, a pre-enactment of similar responses to similar failures? I would say yes. The near-cessation of the stelae cult and the lag in ceremonial centre construction presaged the like events of the 'great collapse'. With the 'little collapse' of the hiatus there was recovery. In fact, as David Friedel (personal communication, 1972) has observed, one of the important points about the hiatus is not that the Maya survived it but that, in many ways at least, they appear to have come out of it stronger than before. This suggests that, along with the inherent weaknesses in the lowland Maya system, there were also some inherent adaptabilities. Just what all of these were, and what the balances were between them, is not yet clear. But with the 'great collapse' there was no recovery; and I would judge, from what we know now, that this was because the stresses within Maya lowland society — of ecological adjustment, of population pressure, and of socio-political divisiveness — were far greater in Late Classic times than they had been in the Early Classic. In the sixth century A.D. the danger of the compounding of disasters was much less than it was to become in the ninth century. Moreover, I would hazard the guess that recovery after the final collapse was made much more difficult because of external stresses, in the form of alien populations on the western borders of the Maya domain, that had not been such a factor three centuries earlier.

But more basically, I take the position that the hiatus and the collapse were phenomena with a similar cause. This cause was the severance of the symbiotic relationships between Maya civilization and the other Mesoamerican civilizations that were contemporaneous with it. The heights that Maya lowland civilization attained were made possible by this symbiosis, and the cutting of it initiated the hiatus and it initiated the collapse. I realize that this is debated ground for to hold it places Maya lowland civilization in a 'secondary' status in the developmental typology of civilizations. I would mitigate this by saying, further, that we still have much to learn about the relationships between 'primary' and 'secondary' civilizations. Why, for instance, do the latter often outdo the former in many fields of endeavour? Maya hieroglyphics and mathematics come immediately to mind in contrast to counterpart developments of the Mexican highlands. Webb, Rathje, and others have argued that the essence of the Maya symbiosis with the upland regions and civilizations of Mesoamerica was most significantly in the institution of trade. I think that this is a very productive hypothesis because it is susceptible to archaeological examination through the testing and counting of objects and the statistical manipulation of these. At the same time, let me, as an old or 'traditional' archaeologist, point out that the great emphasis on 'trade' in archaeological research is enjoying a current vogue. This is not undeserved. It is a theme that has much to offer. But we should not refrain from framing other hypotheses, from seeking out clues to other processes that may help us explain cultural growth and adaptation as it arises from contacts among human societies and cultures.

REFERENCES

Adams, R.E.W. (1971) *The Ceramics of Altar de Sacrificios.* Papers of the Peabody Museum of Archaeology and Ethnology, Harvard University, vol. 63, no. 1.
Adams, R.E.W. (1973) Transformation and termination in the ceramic sequence at Altar de Sacrificios. In T.P. Culbert (ed.) (1973).
Blanton, R.E. (1972) Prehispanic adaptation in the Ixtapalapa region, Mexico. *Science,* 175, 1317-26.
Coe, M.D. (1966) *The Maya.* New York.
Coe, W.R., Jr. (1962) A summary of excavation and research at Tikal, Guatemala: 1956-1961. *American Antiquity,* 27, 479-507.
Coe, W.R., Jr. (1965) Tikal: ten years of study of a Maya ruin in the lowlands of Guatemala. *Expedition,* 8, 5-56.
Coe, W.R., Jr. (1967) *Tikal, A Handbook of the Ancient Maya Ruins.* Philadelphia.
Culbert, T.P. (1973) The Maya downfall at Tikal, Guatemala. In T.P. Culbert (ed.) (1973), 63-92.
Culbert, T.P. (ed.) (1973) *The Classic Maya Collapse,* Santa Fe and Albuquerque.
Graham, J.A. (1972) Aspects of Non-Classic presences in the inscriptions and sculptural art of Seibal. In T.P. Culbert (ed.) (1973), 207-20.
Hellmuth, N.M. (1969) *Mexican Symbols in the Classic Art of the Southern Maya Lowlands.* M.A. thesis, Brown University, Providence, Rhode Island.
McAdams, R. (1956) Some hypotheses on the development of early civilizations. *American Antiquity,* 21, 227-32.
Morley, S.G. (1920) *The Inscriptions at Copan.* Carnegie Institution of Washington, Publication no. 219.
Morley, S.G. (1938-39) *The Inscriptions of Peten.* Carnegie Institution of Washington, Publication no. 437, 5 vols.
Pendergast, D.M. (1971) Evidence of Teotihuacan-lowland Maya contact at Altun Ha. *American Antiquity,* 36, 455-60.

Proskouriakoff, T. (1950) *A Study of Classic Maya Sculpture.* Carnegie Institution of Washington, Publication no. 593.

Proskouriakoff, T. (1963) Historical data in the inscriptions of Yaxchilan (Part I). *Estudios de Cultura Maya*, 3, 149-67. Seminario Cultura Maya, Universidad Nacional de México.

Proskouriakoff, T. (1964) Historical data in the inscriptions of Yaxchilan (Part II). *Estudios de Cultura Maya*, 4, 177-203. Seminario Cultura Maya, Universidad Nacional de México.

Puleston, D.E. (1968) *Brosimum alicastrum as a Subsistence Alternative for the Classic Maya of the Central Southern Lowlands.* Unpublished M.A. thesis, Department of Anthropology, University of Pennsylvania, Philadelphia.

Rathje, W.L. (1970) Socio-political implications of lowland Maya burials. *World Archaeology*, 1, 359-75, London.

Rathje, W.L. (1971) The origin and development of lowland Classic Maya civilization. *American Antiquity*, 36, 275-85.

Rathje, W.L. (1973) Classic Maya development and denouement: a research design. In T.P. Culbert (ed.) (1973), 405-56.

Sabloff, J.A. (1970) Type descriptions of the fine paste ceramics of the Bayal Boca complex, Seibal, Peten, Guatemala. In W.R. Bullard, Jr. (ed.), *Monographs and Papers in Maya Archaeology*, 357-404, Papers of the Peabody Museum of Archaeology and Ethnology, Harvard University, vol. 61.

Sabloff, J.A. (1973) Continuity and disruption during terminal Late Classic times at Seibal: ceramic and other evidence. In T.P. Culbert (ed.) (1973), 107-32.

Sabloff, J.A. and G.R. Willey (1967) The collapse of Maya civilization in the southern lowlands: a consideration of history and process. *Southwestern Journal of Anthropology*, 23, 311-36.

Sanders, W.T. (1973) The cultural ecology of the lowland Maya: a re-evaluation. In T.P. Culbert (ed.) (1973), 325-66.

Sanders, W.T. and B.J. Price (1968) *Mesoamerica, The Evolution of a Civilization.* New York.

Siemens, A.H. and D.E. Puleston (1972) Ridged fields and associated features in southern Campeche: new perspectives on the lowland Maya. *American Antiquity*, 37, 228-39.

Smith, A.L. (1950) *Uaxactun, Guatemala: Excavation of 1931-1937.* Carnegie Institution of Washington, Publication no. 588.

Smith, A.L. and G.R. Willey (1969) Seibal, Guatemala in 1968: a brief summary of archaeological results. *38th International Congress of Americanists*, vol. 1, 151-7. Stuttgart-Munich.

Smith, R.E. (1955) *Ceramic Sequence at Uaxactun, Guatemala.* 2 vols. Middle American Research Institute, Publication no. 20, Tulane University, New Orleans.

Thompson, J.E.S. (1954) *The Rise and Fall of Maya Civilization.* Norman, Oklahoma.

Thompson, J.E.S., H.E.D. Pollock, and J. Charlot (1932) *A Preliminary Study of the Ruins of Coba, Quintana Roo, Mexico.* Carnegie Institution of Washington, Publication no. 424.

Webb, M.C. (1964) *The Post-Classic Decline of the Peten Maya: An Interpretation in the Light of a General Theory of State Society.* Ph.D. dissertation in anthropology, University of Michigan, Ann Arbor.

Webb, M.C. (1973) The Maya Peten decline viewed in the perspective of state formation. In T.P. Culbert (ed.) (1973), 367-404.

Willey, G.R. (1964) An archaeological frame of reference for Maya culture history. In E.Z. Vogt and Alberto Ruz Lhuillier (eds), *Desarollo Cultural de Los Mayas*, 137-86. Universidad Nacional Autónoma de Mexico.

Willey, G.R. (1971) An *'Addendum'* to the second edition of above, 179-84.

Willey, G.R. (1973) *The Altar de Sacrificios Excavations: General Summary and Conclusions.* Papers of the Peabody Museum of Archaeology and Ethnology, Harvard University, vol. 64, no. 3.

Willey, G.R., T.P. Culbert, and R.E.W. Adams (1967) Maya lowland ceramics: a report from the 1965 Guatemala city conference. *American Antiquity*, 32, 289-315.

Willey, G.R. and D.B. Shimkin (1971) The collapse of Classic Maya civilization in the southern lowlands: a symposium summary statement. *Southwestern Journal of Anthropology*, 27, 1-18, University of New Mexico, Albuquerque.

Willey, G.R. and D.B. Shimkin (1973) The Maya collapse: a summary view. In T.P. Culbert (ed.) (1973), 457-502.

JOHN P. MOLLOY and
WILLIAM L. RATHJE

Sexploitation among the Late Classic Maya

One of the goals of archaeology is to develop processual models which describe and explain cultural patterns and to test these models against the remnants of extinct cultures. Kidder (1962) has observed that such studies are relatively easy for archaeologists who are not encumbered by the confusing panorama of recorded history. The minutiae of complex personalities, 'lucky breaks', and specific events often muddle models of neat general trends which can be supported by measuring, weighing, plotting, computerizing, or even subjectively describing, mute material objects. It is, therefore, no surprise that few archaeological models have been applied to make sense of the 'idiosyncratic' events of written history.

At present, Classic Maya archaeologists are being forced into a confrontation with this problem. The pioneering studies of inscriptions by Proskouriakoff (1950, 1960, 1963, 1964), Berlin (1958, 1968), Kelley (1962, 1965), Barthel (1968) and others, are pulling the Classic Maya from the murky depths of archaeology into what some might call the light of history. This transition is exciting because it will force models developed from, and tested by, material relationships to reaffirm their usefulness and validity by testing against the written word.

The core/buffer zone construct is an archaeological model (see Rathje 1971, 1973, in press). As applied by Willey (this volume) the model suggests that differential distribution of basic resources within the Maya area had an important effect upon the development of Classic Maya civilization. Willey's paper raises interesting questions about the utility of the core/buffer zone model and about the Classic Maya hiatus and subsequent reorientation.

This paper will use patterns in the exchange of women, as recorded in published texts and accompanying iconography, to test the usefulness of the core/buffer zone model and to answer partially one of the questions raised by Willey: how did the core re-establish and maintain itself after the hiatus?

The core / buffer zone model

The core/buffer zone model outlines two lowland areas useful to the study of Classic Maya cultural systems. Basic resources, the first component of the model, are defined as those commodities found through time in every household participating in a given subsistence strategy (cf. Fried 1967, Leone 1968). They may be absolute (i.e. salt) or culturally defined (i.e. sinks, stoves and indoor plumbing in the contemporary U.S.A.). These resources provide one useful avenue for material studies because they represent the articulation among ecology, subsistence activities and technology at the individual household level and because the procurement of basic resources is prerequisite to the efficient functioning of many critical organizations in cultural systems (see Rathje, in press).

Pre-Columbian Maya agriculturalists required three basic resources: mineral salt, obsidian for razor-sharp cutting tools, and hard rocks for grinding implements (for the rationale behind selecting these three resources, see Rathje 1971; in press). These three commodities are procurable throughout the Guatemalan highlands. In the southern Maya lowlands, however, there are few places where it is possible to procure these commodities efficiently (Fig. 1; see Rathje 1971: Fig. 1). The need to import goods into the southern lowlands indicates the potential utility of a division of the Maya area into zones on the basis of criteria relevant to exchange potential (for a detailed preliminary attempt to make the division totally objective see Rathje et al., in press).

In brief, three areas can be isolated (see Fig. 1). (1) The *high-land zone* is an area of great ecological diversity and close spacing of resource zones and contains most basic resources (see Sanders and Price 1968). (2) The *buffer zone*, the lowland periphery, contains some extractable basic resources and major bulk transport systems (rivers and the Caribbean Sea). The juxtaposition of tropical rainforest with several other ecozones creates general ecological variety and the potential for exchange of goods throughout the buffer zone. (3) The *core zone*, the centre of the lowlands, is landlocked and sequestered from basic resources by the buffer zone. Tropical rainforest is the only major ecozone in the core and ecological variety is minimal. The core area, as objectively defined on the basis of resource distribution, transport potential, and ecological variety corresponds almost perfectly to the area of tight packing independently described by Hammond (this volume).

Maya culture history and the model

The model argues that in the core area, basically the northeast Peten, complex administrative organizations were developed to facilitate the

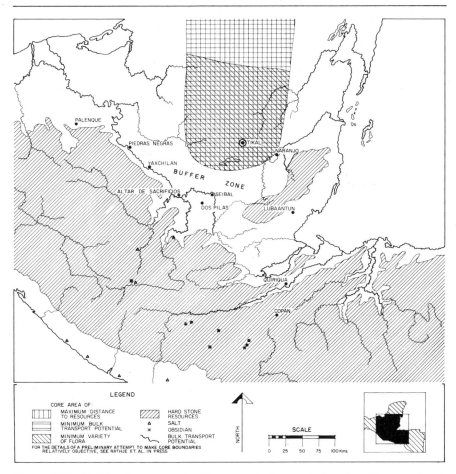

Figure 1 The highland, core and buffer zones in the central and southern parts of the Maya area.

collecting, production, transport and exchange involved in basic resource procurement over long distances (Rathje 1971). Although there were few natural resources with exchange potential in the centre of the lowlands, the core's procurement needs required a set of tradeable commodities. This set developed, as a result of the functional interaction between social stratification and its material correlates (the symbols which affirm the limited distribution of authority and other scarce attributes of status).

To work efficiently, Maya hierarchical organizations required the production of status items and the ideology behind their use. This complex of goods, ritual, and ideology became one major set of scarce 'artificial' resources available to the core (e.g. the stela-commemoration/ceremonial paraphernalia complex). In addition, the possibility exists that at some point in the Classic sequence at least one staple resource, perhaps manufactured textiles, was produced in large quantities by complex craft organizations in the core (if such were the case then raw cotton, possibly procured from the Alta Verapaz, would have become still another imported critical resource). These manufactured commodities were exported to the buffer zone which in turn relayed basic and other resources to the core (this process is outlined in more detail in Rathje, in press). By or before the beginning of the Early Classic the ceremonial complex was exported from the core to the buffer zone.

Between A.D. 400 and 500 Teotihuacan gained control of the Guatemalan highlands. The model proposes that Teotihuacan established direct contact with the core, the area in the lowlands with the most highly concentrated demand for highland resources and the major lowland loci of collection, production and movement of resources in bulk. Teotihuacan representatives may have regulated or partially regulated the core-Guatemalan exchange system. The linkage between the core and the huge Teotihuacan network exponentially increased the potential demand in the core for organizations to produce and transport goods and, therefore, expanded employment opportunities. The process of intensification of trade with Teotihuacan drained population from the buffer zone to staff growing core procurement-production and transport organizations. As a result, buffer zone population reached an extremely low level at several centres during the Early Classic (e.g. Palenque, Piedras Negras, Seibal).

When Teotihuacan control of the highlands dissolved in the sixth century A.D., the system of direct core-highland procurement transactions was disrupted. The withdrawal at the close of the Early Classic of half of the highland-lowland procurement and distribution system created a vacuum in the control of highland-core trade. One expectable response from the core is the movement of population into the buffer zone to re-establish, facilitate, and control the ruptured trade link. The evidence seems to support this construct. During Tepeu 1, a number of large centres developed in the buffer zone (e.g. Palenque, Yaxchilan, Piedras Negras, Copan, Lubaantun, Dos Pilas and Aguateca; Vinson 1960, Grieder 1960).

During the 120 years between 9.6.0.0.0 to 9.12.0.0.0 the buffer zone centres successfully made off with the core's entire repertory of scarce 'artificial' resource production know-how. Pretty polychrome pottery, astrological flummery, and the stela-commemoration complex, in a variety of regional styles, all became local properties of the buffer zone.

The full impact of Teotihuacan's withdrawal and subsequent buffer zone development led to the growth of large buffer zone centres capable of competing with core centres in the production of scarce 'artificial' resources. Once they had access to both core- and buffer-zone-produced scare 'artificial' resources, those buffer zone centres engaged in core/buffer zone exchange systems were able to manipulate exchange rates favourable to themselves. This led to decreased return on investment in production of scarce 'artificial' resources in the core. Indeed, buffer zone centres could potentially isolate the core from scarce basic resources.

Test expectations of the model : conflict

A principal expectation derived from the core/buffer zone model would be competition for basic and other scarce resources developing in the Late Classic between centres within the core and buffer zone centres. One example from archaeological data and stelae texts records core actions on a critical buffer zone trade route. About 9.9.0.0.0 (Grieder 1960), the southern buffer zone, specifically the Seibal-Petexbatun region, located at the crux of bulk transport systems leading to the highlands, was resettled. Re-establishment of direct core-highland transaction systems implied strong control of the southern buffer zone settlements by a single, centralized core administrative unit. Conflict and resolution were inevitable.

At 9.12.7.0.0 or perhaps 9.12.10.0.0 a Tikal (core) lord pro-claimed a victory on the steps of the hieroglyphic stairway at Dos Pilas on the shores of Lake Petexbatun. He wrote that he was Captor of Macaw. He wrote it 10 times (Graham 1973). As a result, Tikal is more often commemorated in Petexbatun than at home, which is a commentary on the importance of the victory. Winning once again put the core in the position of procuring its salt and obsidian and volcanic stone directly from the highlands. However as various organizations have recently pointed out, prolonged warfare, espec-ially when waged in a rain forest, is often counter-productive and colonialism is often expensive. Therefore, civilizations attempt to mini-max investment in war and often seek diplomatic alternatives. One such alternative is royal marriage.

Test implications of the model: sexploitation

Hostilities are harmful to the relationships between areas. The victor is usually forced to make capital expenditure on occupation forces and administrators. From the core/buffer zone model it is expectable that the core would use force primarily as a threat while attempting to exploit new scarce 'artificial' commodities to expand and maintain its resource procurement potential. Further relationships between core and buffer zone centres can be viewed from this perspective.

As recorded on stelae, the core metamorphosed status, in the person of the flower of womanhood, into a harem of scarce resources exchangeable for other critical commodities. There is no lack of precedent for this specific manoeuvre to regain and hold political and economic power. The Hapsburgs, in fact, publicly declared that they used their daughters' marriages to shore up their waning authority. Many other ethnohistoric and historic analyses from all over the world illustrate the use of women in cementing alliances and attaining status (for example, Lévi-Strauss 1968, Leach 1954, Fox 1967, Flannery 1968). There is abundant evidence, also, from pre-Conquest Mesoamerica that access to status was strongly associated with access to the genealogical attributes of women (Pollock et al. 1962, Caso 1966, Chadwick 1971). There were, for example, the Postclassic Valley of Mexico rulers who went to ridiculous lengths to obtain bonafide 'Toltec' wives.

In order to analyse the movement of women in relation to status in Mesoamerica, status must be defined in culturally relevant terms. Bishop Landa (in Pollock et al. 1962) stresses two criteria, a vassal's current power and capability to rule and the length of his royal genealogy, used by the folk hero Kukulcan to redistribute lands to his vassals after the revolution leading to the founding of Mayapan. This can be extrapolated to mean the dynasties of old and powerful cities would be likely to have critical status attributes generally missing for the elites in new centres. In the Maya Lowlands at the beginning of the Late Classic, most established dynasties were concentrated in the core while most buffer zone elites were only emerging. It seems likely that the young *nouveau riche* dynasties would have been willing to provide resources in exchange for the attributes of legitimacy. Thus, the core could have manipulated buffer zone demand for its women to transform competitors into allies. A core centre like Tikal, whose power and procurement ability were being challenged by new buffer zone centres, might well have realized a return on investment of women in buffer zone elite marriages in the form of basic resources or access routes from newly allied buffer zone lords.

The exchange of women for status or resources is nothing new. What is significant is that an archaeologically derived model potentially explains the direction in which the majority of women should have moved in the Late Classic — from core to buffer zone. This model will ultimately only be statistically validated when the majority of commemoration texts on stelae have been translated; however, some marriage records have already been read and can be used to evaluate this expectation at the level of a mechanical model.

Interaction between Tikal and Yaxchilan

Yaxchilan's geographic position in the Maya lowlands is critical in terms of the core/buffer zone model. The city is located just above the rapids that divide the upper and the middle Usumacinta River. All trade entering and leaving the highlands and buffer zone areas to the west and northwest of the Usumacinta had to pass through

Yaxchilan if traders were to take advantage of the bulk transport system provided by the upper Usumacinta and its major tributaries. Yaxchilan was thus a key node of trade in the core/buffer zone interaction system.

The texts relevant to Late Classic Yaxchilan/Tikal contacts revolve around the accession of Bird Jaguar to the throne of Yaxchilan in the Mayan year 9.16.1.0.0. At this time Yaxchilan was a relatively old, large and powerful ceremonial/civic centre exhibiting a stela-commemoration complex dating back to the Early Classic. The city was subordinate to Tikal in terms of formal status categories but the Jaguar Dynasty of Yaxchilan was widely held in high esteem. Proskouriakoff (1963; 1964) has conjectured that Bird Jaguar was only one of multiple claimants to the throne of Yaxchilan and that a 12 year hiatus between the death of Bird Jaguar's predecessor and probable father, Shield Jaguar, and the accession of Bird Jaguar to the throne of Yaxchilan was a period of kin strife. This conjecture was supported by the following evidence (Proskouriakoff 1964):

1. Bird Jaguar engaged in at least one major battle during the 12 year hiatus.
2. Bird Jaguar's mother, the last consort of Shield Jaguar, repeatedly appears in iconographic-epigraphic contexts with Bird Jaguar. Proskouriakoff implied that this repeated commemoration of his mother may have been a deliberate stratagem of Bird Jaguar.
3. After his accession to power Bird Jaguar preserved and re-used in temple construction a set of earlier lintels exhibiting close historical (or legendary) relationships between Sky-Tikal and Jaguar-Yaxchilan.

There is further evidence backing Proskouriakoff's induction:

1. Both Bird Jaguar's mother and his first consort exhibited Sky in their name strings (both were Sky women — many, thought not all, specialists in Classic Maya texts concede that the Sky Dynasty was a recognizable entity and the home dynasty of Tikal).
2. Proskouriakoff (1963; 1964) noted that a Bat Jaguar was associated epigraphically with Bird Jaguar. She speculated that Bat Jaguar was either an alternate title of Bird Jaguar or an ally and agent of Bird Jaguar. Bat Jaguar was commemorated in association with Bird Jaguar at both Yaxchilan and Piedras Negras. Recently, a named portrait of a Bat Jaguar was discovered on a commemorative burial vessel from Burial 116, the Temple I tomb at Tikal, where Bat Jaguar is given the appellative 'Captor of Yaxchilan' (Trik 1963: 9).
3. At Yaxchilan both Bat Jaguar and Bird Jaguar assumed the Tikal associated Sky God title.

4. Finally, Bird Jaguar took the 'Seating' power as well as the 'Accession' power. Prior to 9.16.1.0.0 the 'Seating' power had been held only by Tikal, Palenque, and Copan rulers (Berlin 1967). The 'Seating' power may have implications for differential function, status, and organizational principles separating these cities from most lowland Maya ceremonial-civic centres.[1]

It is tempting to construct an historical synthesis of this mass of data, but first Temple I, Tikal, must be dated. The date of Temple I is in question. The position of the crucial long-count date on Temple I, lintel 2 cannot be directly fixed. The two possible positions for the critical short-count dates are 9.13.13.0.0 and 9.15.15.13.0. Satterthwaite (in Coe et al. 1961) persuasively argues for the earlier date because a rare grapheme introduces two other texts associated with a *katun* 3. However, this grapheme Yax-double Cauac may simply read 'new 52 year cycle'.

Proskouriakoff's style dating of the Temple I lintels supports a 9.16+ date (Coe et al. 1961). Since the only Bat Jaguars known in the Classic texts are from Tikal and Yaxchilan and since both are explicitly reported as being implicated in Yaxchilan's internal affairs, it seems reasonable to suppose that they are one and the same individual. If this supposition is acceptable then both history and style dating would support later placement of Temple I, lintel 2 (9.15.13.13.0). For the purposes of argument only, this later date will be accepted as valid.

It may now be speculated that Tikal, or more correctly, the Sky Dynasty may have given Shield Jaguar a Sky Woman in a bid for power at Yaxchilan, hoping for a son of the Sky Woman who could claim the throne. After the death of Shield Jaguar, Tikal backed Bird Jaguar's claim to the throne with armed force. Bat Jaguar (who is also called Bat Sky at Tikal) was sent to aid Bird Jaguar in both war and diplomacy during Bird Jaguar's successful consolidation of power at Yaxchilan. A Sky Woman was sent to Yaxchilan as Bird Jaguar's first consort. 'Sky God', 'Seating' power and 'Accession' power status categories associated with the Tikal-Sky Dynasty were granted to Bird Jaguar to reinforce his claim to the throne and to cement the alliance between the Sky and Jaguar Dynasties.

If this admittedly speculative reconstruction is acceptable, it can be concluded that:

1. The flow of status categories (the Sky God title, the 'Seating' power, and the need to reassert earlier ties of kinship) was from Tikal to Yaxchilan.
2. The flow of the status categories 'Sky God' and 'Seating' power was tightly bound to the acquisition of a Sky Woman.
3. Reciprocity in woman exchange is at least indirectly suggested by texts from Tikal. (These are several Jaguars, some of them women, in the Tikal texts.)

4. These data suggest that the input of a mother and then a wife into a smaller lower-status buffer zone site from a large higher-status core site may have been a core strategy for formalizing political alliances.

Interactions between the Sky Dynasty and Quirigua - Copan

In terms of the core/buffer zone interaction system, Copan and, to a lesser extent, Quirigua occupied important positions with reference to highland resource procurement. Copan served as a centre of political and economic integration for parts of the Guatemalan highlands, most of El Salvador and the Ulua Valley. Quirigua was a principal resource area for obsidian (Longyear 1952).

Between 9.14.10.0.0 and 9.16.0.0.0 the Sky Dynasty achieved political control at Quirigua and Copan. Kelley (1962) has discussed in some detail the dynamics of this probable takeover. Above we have argued that the Sky Dynasty at Yaxchilan was related to that at Tikal. Kelley (personal communication) has considered the probable kinship relations of personages exhibiting the Sky Dynastic title at Etzna and other Classic centres to the Sky Dynasty at Tikal. This widespread relationship of the Classic Maya Sky Royal House to the Tikal polity supports the conjecture that the Sky Royal Houses at Copan and Quirigua were related by kinship to the Sky Royal House at Tikal. Further, there exists a class of conditional verbs with characteristic suffixes which are associated with personages bearing either the Sky Dynastic title or the Tikal emblems in their name strings (Thompson 1962). This class of verbs and characteristic suffixes occurs with Sky personages at Copan and Quirigua. It is felt that this evidence is sufficiently persuasive, at least for the sake of argument, that the Sky personages at Copan and Quirigua were related to and closely interacted with the Tikal Sky Dynasty. Further research on this problem will be required before a fully convincing demonstration can be made.

The Sky Dynasty appears to have established itself at Copan and Quirigua through the following, partially conjectural, mechanisms:

1. A Sky Woman may have been married to the local Copanec ruler or possibly to his brother. At present we have no certain evidence of a commemorated Sky Woman at Copan in *katun* 15 of *baktun* 9, but a number of lines of converging evidence suggest the possibility.
2. A Copanec royal person glossed by Kelley (1962) as 'Two-Legged-Sky' was established at Quirigua as the result of two events, the first occurring in 9.14.13.4.17 and the second in 9.15.6.14.6. Neither event is associated with a normal birth, accession, or seating verb.

3. Two-Legged-Sky, then a young boy, appears to be the protagonist in the first event while the local Copanec ruler, not a member of the Sky Dynasty, is the protagonist in the second event. Two-Legged-Sky sometimes exhibits the Copan emblem glyph in his name string; however, in inscriptions associated with the second and subsequent events, Two-Legged-Sky becomes invariably identified with the Quirigua emblem glyph.

4. Shortly thereafter, Two-Legged-Sky interacts intensely with a local Quirigua woman whom Kelley glosses as 'Black Bat Woman'. A state of marriage is probably, although nor surely, indicated.

5. In 9.16.12.5.17 the local Copanec ruler is succeeded in Copan by a member of the Sky Dynasty.

6. Thereafter, until the cessation of elite activity at Copan and Quirigua all but one ruler of these centres are members of the Sky Dynasty.

7. The last known leader of Copan and Quirigua, a Sky Dynasty member, appears to hold authority at both cities.

8. At Quirigua the normal birth, seating, and accession verbs are associated regularly with Copanec rulers.

The data summarized above suggest the following historical reconstruction: A Sky Woman was initially swapped to Copan in the 14th *katun* of *baktun* 9. Her son was invested with authority at Quirigua by the then-current Copanec ruler who was probably the putative father of Two-Legged-Sky. In 9.16.12.5.17 a brother, son or nephew of Two-Legged-Sky was invested with the ruling power at Copan and took both the 'Accession' and 'Seating' categories of authority. Thereafter Sky men were almost invariably rulers at both cities.

This whole process has striking parallels to events at Yaxchilan where Bird Jaguar assumed both the 'Seating' and 'Accession' powers. This nearly coeval reorganization of status-authority categories combined with the ubiquitous presence of the Sky Dynasty at both Copan and Yaxchilan is suspicious. Was there an attempt to reorganize the Lowland political structure under the direction of the Tikal (core) centred Sky Dynasty?

Interaction between Altar de Sacrificios, Yaxchilan and Tikal

Altar's status-may have been higher than the size of the site suggests. Its strategic location in relation to highland trade combined with venerability place Altar below Tikal, Yaxchilan and Copan but well above Quirigua and make it another useful example of female exchange patterns. Adams (1971) has inferred historical events surrounding a royal funeral on the basis of data from a double elite burial at Altar. The date of the interments is probably just after 9.16.1.0.0. The interpretation, with slight emendations, relates that a woman of the Jaguar Dynasty resided at, and died at, Altar *c.* 9.16.1.0.0. Bird Jaguar, Ruler of Yaxchilan, and an unknown Jaguar from Tikal journeyed to and participated in the funeral. They were accompanied by kinsmen, probably from the Chama region of the Alta Verapaz. Bird Jaguar assumed the Jaguar priest costume and appears to be the chief participant. A young lady of the local elite committed suicide as an auto-sacrifice and was buried with the older woman. The following inferences may be drawn from these events.

1. The emblem glyph of Altar is unknown, as is that of the older woman's home polity. The woman had closer kin ties with the Yaxchilan Dynasty (Yaxchilan) than the Tikal Dynasty (Sky). In the ceremony all participants had access to and used the Jaguar Dynastic title.
2. Tikal royalty and the ruler of Yaxchilan physically participated in an important ceremony at Altar de Sacrificios. Such activity has strong implications for the inter-city integrative function of a mobile royalty.

We may conclude that direct participation by core-higher status elites in ceremonies associated with females in buffer zone-lower status centres was an integral part of the woman-swapping complex and that such direct participation served to reinforce bonds and ties between core and buffer zone.

Conclusions

Between 9.12.0.0.0 and 9.16.0.0.0 there were textual indications, as expected, that:

1. Commemorated status categories radiated from Tikal (the core) to the buffer zone. Little reciprocity was commemorated.
2. The radiation of status categories was intimately associated with, and indeed may have been primarily a function of, patterned female exchange.
3. Reciprocity in female exchange was only apparent in Tikal's relations with the powerful and venerable city-dynasty of Yaxchilan-Jaguar, and there Tikal probably intervened directly to aid Bird Jaguar who was a claimant to power through a Sky female.
4. The female-swapping syndrome was an important mechanism linking and integrating Classic Maya inter-centre interaction. The core women and their genealogical attributes were another resource which carried the seeds of its disintegration as a scarce

core-controlled commodity. Genealogical attributes are additive, and unlike basic resources, do not maintain a high constant market potential. Once one buffer zone elite had core attributes, his/her descendents would become increasingly less enthusiastic customers for core women. This inevitable dissemination of a scarce core resource no doubt had an effect upon the timing and the nature of the Classic Maya collapse. The stress placed upon buffer zone polities by competition for resources within the traditional lowland core/buffer zone system may have led some buffer zone centres to seek alternative procurement strategies. Formal woman-swapping alliance patterns may have been involved in Classic Maya/non-Classic Maya interactions.

5. As an additional observation, it is interesting to note that two buffer zone polities attempted to by-pass core genealogical attributes in legitimizing their new status. Both Copan and Palenque (Kelley 1962; Berlin 1968) used mythological, cosmological and other contrived bits of data to legitimize their power publicity. That this strategy was only partially successful is demonstrated by Copan's acceptance of the postulated reorganization of status and authority categories *c.* 9.16.0.0.0.

In sum, one of several potential types of woman-swapping that linked great core centres to lesser buffer zone centres has been examined. This female exchange pattern confirms the expectation that status categories radiated from core to buffer zone and were direct mappings of core (polity-dynasty)/buffer zone (polity-dynasty) female exchange. Is it too much to conclude that they were also inverse mappings of basic resource flow? Perhaps the core didn't lose its daughters, but gained powerful son-in-laws and resources. To answer one of Willey's questions, this exchange pattern is one example of the way the core area developed new scarce resources to exchange for continued political and economic power and basic resources.

The archaeological model used seems to have picked out a trend in historically recorded patterns of female exchange. The history of each site studied, however, is unique and raises new questions that require more specific evaluation in relation to resource competition between core and buffer zone sites. In the Maya area there is a potential for a long and productive interplay between materialist models and historical inferences.

Acknowledgments

We are indebted to T. Patrick Culbert for merciless editing and criticism at each phase of this paper's preparation. Special thanks are also due to D.H. Kelley for his part in germinating some of the ideas presented here, to Gordon R. Willey for helpful comments, and to Norman Hammond. Fig. 1 was prepared by Charles Sternberg.

NOTES

1 Berlin (1967) has proposed a religious function for the 'Seating' power and a secular function for the 'Accession' power. We feel that the 'Seating'/'Accession' power categories may represent superordination/subordination.

REFERENCES

Adams, R.E.W. (1971) *The Ceramics of Altar de Sacrificios.* Papers of the Peabody Museum of Archaeology and Ethnology, Harvard, vol. 63, no. 1.

Barthel, T. (1968) El complejo 'emblema'. *Estudios de Cultura Maya*, 7, 159-93.

Berlin, H. (1958) El glifo 'emblema' en las inscripciones Mayas. *Journal de la Société des Américanistes, n.s.*, 47, 111-20.

Berlin, H. (1968) The tablet of the 96 glyphs at Palenque, Chiapas, Mexico. Middle American Research Institute, Publication no. 26, 135-49.

Caso, A. (1966) The lords of Yanhuitlan. In John Paddock (ed.), *Ancient Oaxaca*, 313-35, Stanford.

Chadwick, R. (1971) Native pre-Aztec history of central Mexico. In G.F. Ekholm and I. Bernal (eds), *Handbook of Middle American Indians*, vol. II. Austin, Texas.

Coe, W.R., E.M. Shook and L. Satterthwaite (1961) The carved wooden lintels of Tikal. *Tikal Reports*, 6, 15-112. Philadelphia, University Museum.

Culbert, T.P. and W.L. Rathje (1971) Procurement prerequisites and critical commodities. Paper read at the Annual Meeting of the American Anthropological Association, New York.

Flannery, K.V. (1968) The Olmec and the valley of Oaxaca: a model for inter-regional interaction in formative times. In E.P. Benson (ed.), *Dumbarton Oaks Conference on the Olmec*, 79-117. Washington.

Fox, R. (1967) *Kinship and Marriage.* Baltimore.

Fried, M.H. (1967) *The Evolution of Political Society: An Essay in Political Anthropology.* New York.

Graham, J. (1973) Aspects of non-Classic presences in the inscriptions and sculptural arts of Seibal. In T.P. Culbert (ed.), *The Classic Maya Collapse*, Santa Fe and Albuquerque.

Grieder, T. (1960) Manifestaciones de arte Maya en la región de Petexbatún. *Antropología e Historia de Guatemala*, 12, no. 2, 10-17.

Kelley, D.H. (1962) Glyphic evidence for a dynastic sequence at Quirigua. *American Antiquity*, 27, no. 3, 323-35.

Kelley, D.H. (1965) The birth of the gods at Palenque. *Estudios de Cultura Maya*, 5, 93-134.

Kidder, A.V. (1962) Wanted: more and better archaeologists. *Expedition*, 2, no. 2, 17-24.

Leach, E.R. (1954) *Political Systems of Highland Burma.* Boston.

Leone, M.P. (1968) *Economic Autonomy and Social Distance: Archaeological Evidence.* Unpublished Ph.D. dissertation, Department of Anthropology, University of Arizona.

Lévi-Strauss, C. (1968) *Elementary Structures of Kinship.* Boston.

Longyear, J.M. (1952) *Copan Ceramics: A Study of Southeastern Maya Pottery.* Carnegie Institution of Washington, Publication no. 597.

Pollock, H.E.D., R.L. Roys, T. Proskouriakoff, and A.L. Smith (1962) *Mayapan, Yucatan, Mexico.* Carnegie Institution of Washington, Publication no. 619.

Proskouriakoff, T. (1950) *A Study of Maya Sculpture.* Carnegie Institution of Washington, Publication no. 593.

Proskouriakoff, T. (1960) Historical implications of a pattern of dates at Piedras Negras. *American Antiquity*, 25, no. 4, 454-75.

Proskouriakoff, T. (1963) Historical data in the inscriptions of Yaxchilan (Part 1). *Estudios de Cultura Maya*, 3, 149-168.

Proskouriakoff, T. (1964) Historical data in the inscriptions of Yaxchilan (Part 2). *Estudios de Cultura Maya*, 4, 177-202.

Rathje, W.L. (1971) The origin and development of lowland Classic Maya civilization. *American Antiquity*, 36, no. 3, 275-85.

Rathje, W.L. (in press) Praise the gods and pass the metates: a hypothesis of the development of lowland rainforest civilizations in Mesoamerica. In M.P. Leone (ed.), *Contemporary Archaeology: An Introduction to Theory and Contributions*, Carbondale, Ill.

Rathje, W.L. (1973) Classic Maya development and dénouement: a research design. In T.P. Culbert (ed.), *The Classic Maya Collapse*, Santa Fe and Alberquerque.

Rathje, W.L. et al. (in press) Trade models and archaeological problems: the Classic Maya and their E-group complex. Paper read to the International Congress of Americanists, Rome, 1972.

Sanders, W.T. and B.J. Price (1968) *Mesoamerica: The Evolution of a Civilization.* New York.

Thompson, J.E.S. (1962) *Catalog of Maya Hieroglyphs.* Norman, Oklahoma.

Trik, A.S. (1963) The splendid tomb of Temple I at Tikal, Guatemala. *Expedition*, 6, no. 1, 2-18.

Vinson, G.L. (1960) Las ruinas Mayas de Petexbatun. *Antropología e Historia de Guatemala*, 12, no. 2, 3-12.

BARBARA J. PRICE

The burden of the cargo: *ethnographical models and archaeological inference*

Change or continuity will receive different emphasis according to whether we consider the structure, the form, or the function of a social institution. (Carrasco 1961: 494)

The existing ethnological literature is inadequate for the purposes of archaeological interpretation because it contains either ideal descriptions of technologies, detailed descriptions without behavioural correlates, or no descriptions of technologies. (Ascher 1961: 323)

The following speculations represent a preliminary examination of the development and changing function of a *cargo* system among the lowland Maya between the Early and Late Classic periods. However, the principal objectives of these remarks will be methodological, concerned in general with the broader problem of the application of ethnographic models to archaeology — especially with the question of deciding the relative merits of particular ethnographic models, the most suitable of a number of possibilities. Recent writings of the so-called New Archaeology have, with a quite laudable emphasis upon broad questions of cultural process, drawn heavily upon the use of ethnographic analogy (Binford 1962, 1967; Deetz 1968; Hill 1968, 1970; Longacre 1970), while other writers have tended to stress the limitations inherent in its use. In criticism, it has been noted that the ultimate test of any hypothesis, however derived, is ultimately and necessarily based upon strictly archaeological data. An emphasis upon process, however, rather than upon details of form, can be regarded as strengthening certain kinds of inferences from ethnographic data provided that some operationalizable basis for drawing such inferences be developed. Obviously the testing of the inferences must be carried out against archaeological data, since that is all that remains to us: yet a second problem in operationalization. But there need be no conflict in principle between an ethnological model and a processual one, even where inadequacies of data necessitate that parts of this be written in the conditional. This paper is in basic accord with the position that historical or palaeo-ethnographic reconstruction does not constitute explanation. But it is in the present that the behaviour responsible for the material remains we observe can be most fully and directly seen. The traces left by this behaviour upon objects and upon the environment would be directly measurable and directly correlatable with observed behaviour in the present — only indirectly and inferentially so for an archaeological context.

This leads us to state our first assumption: where the directly comparable material remains in two situations (archaeological, ethno-historic, ethnographic) resemble each other, to that degree and in those respects that they are similar, then the behaviour which can be tied to these resemblances was similar also. The term 'similarity' does not imply identity; there are no identities in nature. 'Similarity' may in this context be taken to refer to artifact distributions, to isolated or repetitive individual behaviours and their localization, and to institutions and associations of institutions. The advocacy of ethno-graphic models and their usefulness in Mesoamerican archaeology does not, additionally, imply the plugging-in of any ethnographic data in any archaeological context; the basis upon which this is to be done must first be carefully reasoned and fully specified. Failure to do this in the past, along with the uncritical acceptance of contem-porary data that may be irrelevant or misleading in archaeological applicability, may in part be responsible for the archaeological skepticism concerning this potentially fruitful approach, not only to generating hypotheses, but to explanation.

Mesoamerican, especially Maya, *cargo* systems have been described ethnographically in great detail (Tax 1937, 1953; Bunzel 1959; Vogt 1969; Cancian 1965, etc. etc.). The system has attracted such detailed ethnographic attention initially because of its picturesqueness, its blend of Indian and Colonial Spanish elements, its pervasiveness in modern Maya social organization. Because of this pervasiveness, the institution has been amenable to various analyses which themselves reflect the changing major currents in general ethnological theory and in Mesoamerican studies in particular — from the antiquarian search for 'survivals', through the development of the folk-culture theory (Redfield 1941) and its variants and critiques, approached from the social anthropology of peasantry (Foster 1953, 1965), and from economic anthropology (Tax 1953). The salient features of the institution are clear from these descriptions. It occurs almost exclus-ively in culturally 'Indian' communities (except where it is specifi-cally tied in with purposes of commerce or tourism, and here its structural characteristics are very different). The basis of the *cargo* system is itself hierarchical, with more positions of lesser, fewer positions of greater prestige and expense; often it is dual with civil and religious offices forming two parallel hierarchies and advance-ment dependent upon sequential progression through the offices of both. Assumption of office is by individual rotation for periods of one year, during which the individual is responsible for all expenses entailed by the office. Since, for higher offices, the incumbent not only incurs heavy expenses but may be for all practical purposes economically unproductive himself during his term, he frequently borrows heavily from real and fictive kin, or may rent, pawn, or sell land to finance his participation. The redistributive implications of these facts will be discussed in more detail below. After his year of service, a man may wait several years before assuming a higher position, to recoup losses; in some communities his immediate relatives will not be obliged to assume positions for at least part of this time. While in theory all persons of appropriate sex and age are eligible and ostensibly obliged to participate, communities differ in the actual incidence of participation. Tax (1953) found fuller participation in Panajachel than in the community of Chichi-castenango (Bunzel 1959), a difference attributable to the consider-ably larger population of the latter. Cancian (1965) has noted the stresses of population growth upon the ideally 'democratic' system of Zinacantan, where some offices have 20-year waiting lists. Because prestige depends in some measure upon participation, because office-holding is expensive, and particularly so where the ratio of total population to offices, particularly high ones, is large, incumbency in these larger communities tends to be confined to the wealthier members: thus, the *cargo* rotation is itself more stratified in larger communities.

While not all Mesoamerican peasants are culturally 'Indian', nearly all groups defined as Indian today (with perhaps the exception of the possibly unique Lacandon) are peasants. Their communities exist, by definition, within the overall socio-economic context of highly stratified, state-organized, primarily agrarian societies, of which they constitute the bottom level. Within this level, further inequalities of wealth occur (Lewis 1951; Tax 1953; Foster 1948, 1967). These too seem to be greater the larger the size of the community. If some of these differences of wealth are ephemeral from year to year or generation to generation, others are not. We define wealth as differential (in this case preferential) access to strategic resources, which in largely agrarian communities include land, water and capital equipment. This economic, material definition is used, not only for the obvious reason that this is what wealth is, but for the additional reason that a material definition will, unlike concepts such as 'prestige', be easily operationalized in both ethnographic and archae-ological contexts. In the present, we can measure actual land holdings, as Lewis did for Tepoztlan; while in an archaeological context this information would not be directly available in most cases. Lewis, however, notes the positive correlation between families owning large amounts of land and capital goods, and those which also own more other kinds of material possessions which they keep in their houses. They may live in more substantial housing: a rich man, behaviourally speaking, is one who lives like a rich man. Distinctions in size, quality of materials, type of construction, and location within the settlement of housing correlate well with wealth differences in Panajachel and in 'San Carlos' (Gillin, 1951). These are distinctions that are clearly visible without informants, the distinctions that overwhelmingly obtain between Sutton Place and Harlem. In spite of the ideology of inconspicuous consumption typical of peasant societies (Foster 1965; Wolf 1957), these differences exist in such communities, themselves at the bottom of a larger Eltonian pyramid. We shall return later to the consideration of archaeological indications of similar phenomena for the Classic lowland Maya. We observe in passing, however, that we have translated a sociological criterion into material terms, as applicable archaeologically as ethnographically.

The pervasiveness of the *cargo* system in Mesoamerica — its wide distribution and its deep and wide-ranging effects on the dynamics of community life — has led to considerable suspicion among various investigators that it may have pre-Conquest roots. Parsons (1936), in her study of Mitla, was specifically interested in the idols-behind-altars in various aspects of Zapotec life, including this one. Reliance on a simple age-area hypothesis alone would suggest the antiquity of the institution in this area (an illustration that data may support a limited or even erroneous theory). Tax et al. (1952) and Foster (1960) have noted the differences between the systems of Mesoamerica and of Spain; many of the differences are not attributable simply to differences between Iberian and overseas-Colonial manifestations of Spanish culture, thus implying that at least some of the residue represents native institutions or syncretisms. The idea of pre-Columbian origins has been explored by historians (Gibson 1964, 1967) and ethnohistorians (Carrasco 1961) in efforts to document the native precursors of Colonial and post-Colonial society. In general, these approaches have used a direct-historical model and have been productive of considerable new data on relative time depth of various of the component traits. In anthropology, there has been reliance on the genetic model, where data from all branches of anthropology are synthesized for historical reconstruction (Vogt 1964, Romney 1957).

A critical point governing the applicability of the genetic model is the demonstration of direct historical links between prehistoric and historic or modern populations. If this link is absent or doubtful, the legitimacy of inferences drawn on the basis of the comparison is rendered dubious. This broad condition is generally met in the case of the Maya, although closer examination reveals at least one outstanding historical question: how close must this historical link be? In the case of Classic Peten, most strikingly, who and where are the direct descendants of the occupants of, say, Tikal? Ethnographic and linguistic data give us a number of collateral 'descendants', and no reliable or valid way to distinguish grand-nephews from grand-sons. Hawkes (1954) in a generally pessimistic view of the potentials of archaeological inference using ethnographic data, nonetheless affirms the necessity of demonstration of this historical link if ethnographic observation is to be used to interpret prehistory.

One can make a number of criticisms of the historical-genetic model, in spite of the data which its use has generated, and in spite of the obvious fact that such data are themselves crucial in the interpretation of process. Knowledge that A precedes B leads us to infer one process — which would be quite different if B preceded A. Nonetheless, the genetic model is avowedly particularistic (see Harris 1968) and therefore of limited comparative or cross-cultural generalizability. Because it is essentially descriptive, it provides the necessary information on where and when, although it cannot necessarily deal with questions of how. Because the model itself cannot separate historical continuity from quite different processes of parallelism and convergence, it need not pose the question of why some historical lines undergo, in the course of time, marked changes in level of complexity, and how and why these changes of grade occur. The ultimate attempt is to document origins rather than to explain persistence or modification of traits. Origins, by their nature, cannot be explained in nomothetic terms, while differential survival or replacement can and must be. Ultimately, questions other than the purely historical must be asked of the data, however they may have been obtained. We shall return to the question of whether, even where demonstrable historical links exist, these are in fact the most relevant parameter of comparison in the formulation of an archaeologically testable model derived from ethnology.

Carrasco, for instance, in his study of the fiesta system, has no consistent basis for identifying and sorting out the pre-Columbian traits relevant to tracing the development of Colonial and post-Colonial social organization in central Mexico. His proposed antecedents from Aztec society constitute in large part simply the recruitment and weeding-out devices of any hierarchical social institution that one might expect to find in any stratified society. Paradoxically — given the specificity necessary to strictly historical reconstruction — his antecedents are so generalized that they are equally applicable to the description of corporate advancement at International Business Machines. He has no consistent way to demonstrate that some of his data might be more applicable, more relevant, than others; yet, on other grounds to be discussed below, many of his conclusions, and often not the ones he most emphasizes, appear to be valid, or at least potentially testable. These are problems that are common to many inductive formulations, not necessarily limited to historical ones.

Vogt himself (1964) contrasts the genetic model with what he calls the 'ecological model'. He does not develop the latter except to point out that its predictions may diverge from those of the genetic model, and that it offers an analytical alternative. A point that this paper will proceed to develop is that the alternative is one more productive of explanation, and at least potentially capable of a methodological sophistication lacking in historical models, precisely because the means of testing a conclusion are so different. The use of this model will, however, require a very different view of social institutions, one that provides a consistent basis for determining the nature and extent of cultural similarities and differences and their importance. This paper will demonstrate the significance of social organization as an integral part of an ecological model that can be used archaeologically.

The underlying premise of the ecological model is that human behaviour is acted upon by natural selection, which acts to perpetuate favourable variations and eliminate unfavourable ones. All cultural traits, regardless of their historical origins, are subjected to greater or lesser selective pressures, the major source of which is the environment, both natural and social. Behaviour, in turn, is capable of modifying these pressures, and any ecological model must accordingly be capable of dealing with the complex positive and negative feedbacks inherent in the system as a whole. In such a system, some components will be more important than others: i.e. they will be more consistently and strongly subject to selective pressure. These traits, for each system, must be empirically determined (see Steward's 1955 discussion of the culture core for a basically similar statement that not all aspects of behaviour may be of equal importance in terms of the system as a whole). The model developed here relies on White's concept (1949) of culture as an energy system, and the most significant features will be those most intimately involved with the conversion and utilization of energy. From an evolutionary viewpoint, it will largely be these on which selection will operate most strongly.

It is largely technology — although not all of technology — that is primarily responsible for the capture of energy from the environment; we can also stress the energy function of social organization as integral to an ecological model. What social organization is, in this perspective, is a flow chart of distribution and utilization of energy by a population. Social institutions do work; they move energy around a society in regular and systematic ways. They are therefore adaptive. This view of social organization may be considered somewhat unusual, largely in what it excludes from more traditional approaches to the subject; as it minimizes ideals, beliefs and mental templates that may exist in the mind of informant or investigator, it concentrates instead on actual behaviour, specifically that involving energy exchanges and transfers.

The advantage of this view is that it can be applied to archaeological contexts, at least in principle; the flow of energy in a society is necessarily involved with material parameters, and will be reflected in the numbers and distribution of people (the basic adaptive index in biology), their differential control of the total energy supply (stratification), their utilization of various types of material objects. Archaeological data are ultimately the remains of such objects and their associations. These, the results of behaviour, can in turn be used to reconstruct the behaviour responsible which, in prehistory, can no longer be directly observed. In a very real sense any statement of causality is an inference, and, furthermore, a deductive statement requiring proof. If a particular social institution or set of behaviours is closely involved with energy capture and/or flow, material evidence of its presence should be easily recoverable archaeologically, and hypotheses of its presence should be testable against data recovered. By contrast, that behaviour which leaves no potentially discoverable or testable impact upon the natural or social environment can legitimately be regarded as unimportant, subject perhaps to considerable free variation precisely because such variation makes little difference in energy or evolutionary terms.

This view of social organization necessitates comparison of institutions on the basis of the work they do, and of how well, comparatively speaking, they do it. It thus permits, where more formal emphases would not, consideration of functional alternatives — of the fact that observably different behaviours may have similar effects and, conversely, that formally similar behaviours may function quite differently in different contexts. On the explicit assumption of regularity of the relationship of behaviour and its visible material effects, one could use this approach equally for past or present data. Documentation and testing of the relationship postulated between behaviour and its results, however, can be done only in the present, where both halves of the posited equation can be directly observed. Ethnographic data provide, therefore, the testing of what archaeologically must be stated and assumed.

Thus far we have contrasted the genetic model with an ecological-energy-flow model, to indicate two differing approaches to the broad question of selecting and testing ethnographic analogies for archaeological use. Briefly, the use of such analogy, however derived, is based on the assumption that where, in two situations being compared, stated similarities occur, it is then legitimate to postulate the existence of additional similarities not directly observed. This process is on firmest ground when the relationship of what is only postulated to what is observed can itself be stated operationally. Given any problem in analogical inference, it remains to consider the parameters for choosing one analogue rather than another. This is the area that has so far seemed most tenuous to many writers on the subject.

Smith (1955) for instance states that analogical inference provides no way to decide among alternatives; Ascher (1961) notes the methodological difficulty in eliminating weak hypotheses. Thompson (1956) considers this process to be in large measure subjective, depending on the competence and experience of the investigator. Binford, although he has very successfully used ethnographic analogy, has nonetheless claimed that the investigator's broad familiarity with ethnographic data is what enables him to formulate an analogy and to choose among possible alternatives (1967). It is the claim of this paper, however, that it is possible to state explicit parameters that can be operationalized to formulate and to decide, given a particular problem, upon the relative probabilities when alternatives exist.

If our problem is a historical one, then the genetic model provides such a framework; the criterion is that of demonstrability of historical links. Often, however, we are asking different questions of the data, and this may be irrelevant or misleading. Reasoning from the ecological model sketched above provides an alternative, and the relevant parameters can be deduced from the model itself. First, our best comparisons will be between examples which share fundamental statable ecological similarities (see Meggers and Evans 1956). The more such similarities can be demonstrated, the higher the probability of discovering additional ones. Not only ought the natural environments to be similar in stated ways, but more importantly, the societies should demonstrably exploit these environments in similar ways. There is nearly always more than one way to exploit any given habitat, and environmental similarity need not entail ecological similarity.

Second, the different possible ways of exploiting a habitat will have predictable consequences for the size and distribution of its population. These therefore should be testable against observed ethnographic or archaeological data. When these are adjudged similar, the legitimacy of the comparison and of additional analogues is strengthened. Third, it follows that the probability is increased that societies exploiting similar habitats in stably similar ways will face similar problems in capturing and distributing energy. Given the operation of natural selection, it is likely that institutions to meet these needs will have to share certain kinds of functional similarities which in turn may determine structural or formal similarities as well. We may assume that in details of form a number of variations may exist at this level of analysis, not all of which may significantly affect the energy efficiency of the institution (potentially measurable) and not all of which may leave observable material consequences that would enable us to make these distinctions. In such cases, selection pressure is low if not absent, and the decision among possible alternatives can be regarded as trivial anyway (a conclusion which does not follow from most of the social organization literature, which seems largely preoccupied with just such functional triviality).

In illustration of the three stipulations stated above, we cite an example that is not legitimate and is misleading (Reina 1967). In his attempt to generalize contemporary production figures from Flores to extrapolate some conclusion about Classic Maya agricultural productivity in Peten, Reina ignores the fact that modern settlement at Flores and the Classic Maya ecosystem, although in the same general area and habitat, were very different. For the modern inhabitants of Flores, agriculture is an occasional 'insurance-policy' activity; the bulk of the community's food-stuffs arrive by plane from Guatemala City. Community residents are largely officials for the province of Peten, or *chicleros*, or workers for Aviateca. In addition, the entire demographic pattern is totally non-comparable: Flores is virtually the only settlement in this part of Peten today. If agricultural systems and population size exhibit the relationship postulated by Boserup (1965), the Classic period productivity/ carrying capacity of Peten is not inferable on the basis of Reina's data.

The parameters we have cited as underlying the formulation of a strong analogy are also those which direct the attention to choosing a situation in which to look for probable analogues. Drawing upon an ecological model, which assumes the regularity of process in human behaviour, it then becomes irrelevant to distinguish between analogy and homology. Analogy is necessarily a concept based on comparability of function, while homology is based on sharing of common origins, even regardless of differential function. We deal, in summary, with a last stated limitation of the use of ethnographic analogy: Binford's (1968) claim that its use will enable us to reconstruct, for the past, only those features which survive to be recorded in the ethnographic present, actually precluding discovery of alternative patterns that may be truly extinct. This seems unduly pessimistic, on the basis of Binford's own stated concern with process. Process, unlike details of form, can be regarded as regular, as capable of analysis following the uniformitarian principle. Processes can be reconstructed on the basis of the effects they regularly produce. If a total configuration reconstructed on this basis can be found to have no precise ethnographic analogue, this fact indeed is significant in the treatment of cultural evolution. Recall that we are dealing not with identities but with similarities, and that variability of this sort is the raw material on which selection operates. Since ethnographic analogy is by its nature systematically testable, any such situation should be apparent. Contrary to Binford's statement, analogy is capable methodologically of discovering such a condition; as suggested here, its use entails considerably more than extrapolation of present observations back into the past.

We return, accordingly, to a consideration of the ethnographic context of the contemporary Maya fiesta system; the analysis will be that suggested in the preceding paragraphs. The occurrence of the institution in the peasant sector of a stratified agrarian society is significant; the fact that this peasant sector is largely Indian may be interesting, but for the present model is largely irrelevant. The structural characteristics of peasantry have been described elsewhere (Wolf 1966, Wagley and Harris 1955, etc.). The nature of the relationship of this class to others, superordinate to it, determines much of the behaviour of peasant populations. Various aspects of this relationship have been emphasized by different writers concerned with the function of the *cargo* system. Redfield (1941) stressed its role in reinforcement of the community solidarity of the folk society, a solidarity that is contrasted with the individualism of the urban end of the continuum. Numerous writers have noted its role as a means of redistribution of wealth within the peasant group itself (Wolf 1966, Foster 1965, Tax 1953), a mechanism for assurance that inequities of wealth within the community will be ephemeral. We have previously noted, for instance, that a man must often sell or pawn land to pay the expenses of his office. In essentially static economies, where the size of the pie is indeed limited, periodic re-slicing does serve as an important means of minimizing internal conflicts that could jeopardize the competitive position of a community vis-à-vis other groups of equal or superordinate status (Wolf 1957, 1966; Steward 1950).

In terms of the material conditions of life, the access of peasants to the means of production is limited, contingent upon the payment of a fund of rent. Yet in agrarian societies, the labour of such a group is responsible for generating energy (=wealth) for the entire hierarchy. What the fund of rent does is to siphon this energy from the group that harnesses it to other groups in the population. Funds of rent may include taxes, rent, *corvée* labour services, sharecrop arrangements, etc. A significant point is that in the case of the Maya *cargo* system we have a partial congruence between the fund of rent and another of Wolf's basic funds of the peasant budget. In the *cargo* system the ceremonial fund constitutes one part of the fund of rent. As such it is, in effect, part of the government (Carrasco 1961). The analysis presented by Harris (1964), which has heavily influenced this one, notes the coercive and exploitative aspects of the system in his citation of the reluctance with which incumbents frequently assume office; service is often an obligation rather than a privilege. The ecosystemic functions are quite clear, in that economic stasis and shortage of resources are often the product of the class structure, not necessarily of overpopulation or limitation of carrying capacity. The system serves an elite by removing energy (i.e. wealth) from a producing class and diverting it elsewhere through the society. At the same time, this elite maintains its own position by preventing capital accumulation and therefore competition elsewhere in the society. The *cargo* system, by economically linking diverse parts of the society, acts in social integration, abetted by force. Force is also applied within the community to assure compliance. The prestige accruing to office-holders is illusory in that real power lies outside the *cargo* system entirely; the appeal of prestige to motivate participants is less relevant to the present analysis than the socio-ecological effects of the periodic land redistribution: it is on the latter than natural selection operates, regardless of ideals or of motivations. Any other institution that accomplished this end would be subject to selective pressures very similar to those operating on the *cargo* system — and to this extent we could deem the two similar and functional alternatives.

We summarize some salient features of the *cargo* system as described ethnographically, in exploration of some of the archaeologically discernible implications of these features.

1. The system occurs in the peasant sector of a stratified agrarian society. We should expect a higher probability of finding such a system archaeologically if we confine our attention to societies that are demonstrably of this type. Archaeological indicators of this kind of society are several. One of the more important is monumental civic architecture, because of the labour and organizational requisites of construction, and also because the pressure for housing for a given institution should be greater the bigger that institution and the greater the number of personnel involved. Monumentality of housing arrangements indicates the relative ability of that organization to divert energy to its own use: its housing is thus frozen, fossilized energy utilization. It is assumed that the size of such construction overall is in some sense proportional to the total energy content of the society. Further, we can take the size (= amount of energy expended) of structures related to particular institutions as a material indicator of their relative importance. A second, more inclusive material indicator of this type of society is site stratification (Sanders and Price 1968). Complexity of site stratification indicates a comparable degree of internal social differentiation and complexity of relationships among component institutions. Simple societies would not need, nor could they support, such institutions. These criteria provide an archaeologically testable method of distinguishing between egalitarian and non-egalitarian societies.

Non-egalitarian society appears in Peten before the end of the Late Formative, with the appearance of pyramid temples and a distinction in settlement pattern between centre and hinterland, where sites possessing civic architecture contrast with those lacking it (site stratification). Settlement evidence in general may be difficult to use for Peten, in that most data derive from the immediate areas of major centres and may thus be atypical. However, even such data do not seem inconsistent with Bullard's (1960; 1962) more general survey. The demographic picture appears throughout the Formative and Classic sequence to have been essentially one of filling in, but without major shifts in underlying economic base. Bullard observes that favoured areas for agricultural settlement lie along slopes on well-drained ground. As the area filled up demographically from initial population to the collapse, we have no shifts in settlement location — as we do in Teotihuacan Valley (Sanders 1965) — and such shifts would be major archaeological indicators of shifts in economy. In their absence, we may infer the intensification of production that would accompany a rising population to have taken the form of shortening of the fallow periods of swidden cycles, permitting increased densities. Civic centres may or may not be closely associated with areas of heavy rural settlement. Since, according to Bullard's data, areas favoured for construction of these sites were high, prominent ridges, there may be little consistency of association here — association may rather be fortuitous, depending on the proximity to each other within a local ecosystem of these two major niches. The preceding statements imply that civic centres draw upon a dispersed population base, and that their relative size will depend not on that of the population of the immediate situation, but on that of a far larger sustaining area comprising many settlement units.

A number of writers have pointed out that major organizational changes seem to occur between Early and Late Classic Maya (Culbert 1970; Adams, personal communication). These may represent a more or less gradual but marked shift, for whatever reasons, from ranked to stratified institutions. Differences between ranking and stratification may be clear in principle — they may be analysed, however, as quantitative changes rather than as quantum leaps. No systematic, explicit formulation exists to translate the sociological definition (Fried 1967) into material terms. Some suggestions, archaeologically testable, follow. Some are better than others, and this list is by no means exhaustive.

(*a*) All else being equal, the probability of stratification increases with increasing numbers and densities of people in the sustaining area. The comparative ethnography of the present cargo system certainly supports this. The period immediately preceding the collapse of major centres in Peten is one of population maximum. Haviland (1965, 1966) in his small mound investigations, reports that nearly all tested showed Late Classic occupation. Regardless of whether all were simultaneously occupied, the Late Classic distribution contrasts with that of preceding periods, and is much larger.

(*b*) Ranked systems tend to offer more social mobility than stratified ones — in ranked systems, the larger and more complex, the less mobility. Sahlins' ethnographic data from Polynesia (1958) and Fallers' African material (1965) suggest this for contemporary situations. A good deal of recent archaeological data from Peten offers evidence of the decreasing flexibility, increasing ascription, of class position from Early to Late Classic.

Haviland's conclusions (1967) from the statures of skeletons constitute one principal line of argument. Those individuals interred in contexts with elite associations are statistically taller and more robust than those recovered from ordinary housemounds. This distinction in stature within a total population is more apparent in Late than in Early Classic burials. Differential stature associated with the appurtenances of socio-economic distinctions imply that differential access to strategic resources occurred in the childhood of the individual, and would thus reflect the heritability of class membership. Some individuals, in other words, were better nourished as children (utilization of resources, dependent ultimately upon access to them) and these were more likely than other individuals to be elaborately interred upon their demise.

Rathje's evidence from burial locations (1970) is closely related to, and supports, the osteological data cited above. Interments in and close to the civic centre tended to contain more, and more elaborate artifactual associations, than those in outlying housemounds. Again, the differential is marked most in the Late Classic, in contrast with earlier periods. We therefore have evidence associating stature with artifact associations, and these associations with location of interment — and of contrast between Early and Late Classic.

(c) Stratification refers to differential access to strategic resources, i.e. to energy; ranking refers to prestige hierarchy. As implied in prior discussion of the skeletal materials, it is the differential utilization of resources that enables us to infer access. The differences noted ethnographically within communities — differences in quality of housing and quantity of material possessions — are taken as the evidence of differential access, on the assumption that a man spends what he has. If he does not do so, he does not, in terms of behaviour, have it. Palace structures (Coe 1965; 1967) are most common in Late Classic contexts; we are, for the present, assuming an at least partially residential function for these. Significantly, too, Proskouriakoff (1963) documents an example of an Early Classic temple complex at Uaxactun, rebuilt as a Late Classic palace — the diversion of space formerly utilized for civic, public purposes, to at least partly private use. It is suggested that the presence of truly elite housing, private residences, is a material, on-the-ground, indicator of social stratification (Copan is a problem here).

(d) Speculation: The function as nodes in a redistributive economy that underwrites prestige positions in ranked societies (Parsons and Price 1971) necessitates that incumbents of the positions draw heavily upon the support of their kin or non-kin subordinates. This is certainly the case in Oceania in the ethnographic present. We have a structural resemblance between this pattern and the ethnographic observation for the contemporary *cargo* system, that an incumbent's relatives and *compadres* are called upon to support the incumbent's expenditures. Because the total institutional settings are so radically — if quantitatively — different, this formal similarity cannot be regarded as an identity. But it may suggest a structural antecedent to the *cargo* system, and, in the Maya area, the critical transition period may be that between Early and Late Classic.

2. The contemporary *cargo* system is a method of rotation of civic responsibility and expense among participants at various hierarchical levels, each step more expensive and prestigious than the one preceding it. In effect, the incumbent is responsible for paying that part of the community's annual tax, since the expenses of the fiesta are spent primarily outside the community. There is an identity of ceremonial fund with part of the community's fund of rent, and this burden is circulated.

   (*a*) In the present, the system, while confined to the lowest class, acts to equalize access to resources within the community. Especially in demographically large communities, access to *cargo* positions tends to be restricted to those most able to afford it; those who are locally most well off economically. Archaeologically, the probability of existence of such a system would be strengthened by evidence of differential wealth within, as well as between, classes. Haviland, in his Tikal settlement data, has noted the presence of differences in size, materials and elaboration within his category of small-structures. These can be seen as comparable to Lewis' Tepoztlan or Gillin's San Carlos housing data.

   (*b*) Spatial patterning of the *cargo* system is variable today. Depending on the level of the position, and upon the community, the *carguero* may store the paraphernalia of office in his home, or in a special structure such as a town hall or church. The archaeological correlates here would be obvious, although available data on the necessary associations are scanty at best. In communities like Chichicastenango, where a pattern of effectively dual residence obtains, the incumbent must live in the town centre (and, incidentally, thus remove himself physically from the land on which he normally lives and from which he derives income) for the duration. One could note the high probability of continuity in settlement pattern in the Maya area in spite of the *congregación* policy of the Spanish, and speculate at least that dual residence may be an old pattern. The Spanish did not impose an elite upon the Maya, but replaced a native one, which would have found it advantageous to regulate many of the things the Spanish regulated. The increased site stratification of the Late Classic, including numbers of small, outlying civic centres which would have housed *cargueros*, may be taken as one indication. Miles' (1957; 1958) descriptions of what seem to resemble *municipio-* and province-level units comprising several physically distinct settlement units constitute the physical evidence of several levels of site stratification; the physical distances involved may render more probable the reconstruction of at least some instances of dual residence. Generalization here is admittedly difficult in that contemporary data necessarily derive from a different ecological zone than the now depopulated Peten. Much of this is thus admittedly speculative.

3. To continue and develop the preceding section, the ecosystemic function of the *cargo* system is the regulation of inter- and intra-class competition, and the transfer of energy from producers to consumers. Harris (1964) has noted that it tends to be most exploitative in areas where the fiesta cycle is not combined with periodic markets (and thus profit opportunities), or with local craft specialization in non-agricultural activities (a correlate of market systems, and itself in part a response to local land pressures).

(*a*) The pressure within a peasant community to equalize resources will increase as the ratio of population to resources becomes more unfavourable. An unfavourable ratio can result from a number of identifiable factors, some acting to reinforce each other in positive feedback. Among these, we note population growth without corresponding increase in intensification of production; and/or the pressure of an elite class draining off the capital formed (including the withholding of some lands from production to create an 'artificial' population pressure, to secure a labour supply more cheaply). Additional contributory factors include the lack of other local economic niches into which surplus population can move, and the synergistic effects of two or more of these factors in combination.

Archaeologically, Late Classic Maya, on evidence previously cited, was a period of both maximal population and — not unexpectedly — of maximal social stratification. Competitive pressures of the sort suggested should become more intense more quickly, and at a lower level of size and density, in swidden, contrasted with permanent, agriculture, because of the greater land needs per producer. In spite of Puleston's data (1968) on *ramon* as a probable infield crop, the remainder of Maya agriculture in the lowlands involved the shifting cultivation of annuals. With population growth, fresh or regenerated lands would have been at a premium. One function of the Maya elite class may have been the periodic reallocation of land — from the top. Intracommunity pressure among the peasantry, backed up by the kind of 'ritual' regulatory mechanisms we are postulating, could have reinforced this to a significant extent.

(b) There is evidence of craft specialization among the Classic Maya (Adams 1970), but not of the type or patterning found in contemporary highland Guatemala (McBryde 1947) or Aztec period central Mexico. One could maintain that Classic Maya craftsmen were always a small group whose production was largely consumed by the elite. This contrasts with the specialization by community in crafts consumed by a general population integrated economically by periodic markets. Although Rathje (1971) notes the importance of trade in basic commodities as a stimulus to social stratification in central Peten, there seems to be a dearth of convincing evidence that true markets were of great significance (Parsons and Price 1971). The geographic environment of Peten — open and relatively uniform — would have militated against development of intensive, small-scale local symbiosis (Sanders 1956), all else being equal.

(c) Drawing upon points raised in (a) and (b) above, it would seem that integrative problems for Classic Maya society would have been relatively severe. Lacking intensive economic symbiosis, and given a comparatively dispersed settlement pattern and an agricultural system that does not especially stimulate cooperative labour investment, both geographic and hierarchical integration would be more difficult. These are the conditions noted by Harris as leading to a hypertrophy of the contemporary fiesta system. It is interesting to note that today (as was not the case in Colonial times) the *cargo* system in many areas is virtually extra-governmental in its operation, and lacks power: municipal officials with whom the national government actually deals, and who do have local formal powers, have different credentials and are differently recruited. In Guatemala today, these real officials are usually Ladino, members of a superordinate group. Anyway, the para-officials of the *cargo* system are subordinate, responsible to an elite outside the peasant system itself. It is speculated that some of the residents of the small, outlying Late Classic civic centres may have come from the lower levels of the elite group, keeping an eye on a rotating lower officialdom. Given the increased social stratification in Late Classic times — and what various writers have called an increasing gulf between classes — this rotating of lower officials could have provided some functions of cultural brokerage (Wolf 1957) between peasantry and elite.

The present paper has attempted to develop an operationalizable, testable, deductive approach to the problem of formulating ethnographic analogy for archaeological use. It is clearly speculative in its choice of illustration, and of necessity programmatic in its suggestion of test implications which may admittedly not be borne out by either the comparative ethnography or the archaeological data. With reference to this particular example, it is obvious that many of the features observed in the contemporary Maya *cargo* system are, in terms of the genetic model, of Spanish origin. Many of the jobs these features perform, however, would have been necessary in Late Classic Maya times as well. The truth or falsity of the speculations advanced are ultimately less important than is the potential contribution to method: we have sketched a method of proof which can operate equally to disprove.

We have chosen to develop an adaptive model to define significant cultural similarities and differences, considering institutions as comparable insofar as they do similar work or solve similar problems in two instances. Variation of form in this kind of analysis is less important for the present. Thus Freeman's rejection (1968) of the use of an adaptive model on the basis that it cannot reveal cultural similarities strikes us as overly pessimistic, in many of the ways that Binford's (1968) critique of ethnographic analogy seems overly particularistic. For purposes of this paper, regularity is assumed to lie on the level of processes regulating and determining human behaviour. Variations in form of institutions are expectable when these do not significantly affect the efficiency of the institutions.

These remarks have been intended to stimulate a somewhat different approach to problems of social organization, an approach that may be productive of cross-cultural and diachronic regularities. Societies organized in given ways face certain integrative, and what for want of a better term might be called distributive, challenges. Whatever the formal differences, the significant aspects of these institutions — those demonstrably most closely linked to getting the work done — will leave traces which by their nature will be expressed in material form. Because ethnographers have until recently not emphasized these aspects of the institutions they describe (much of ethnography too is particularistic), much of the comparative data archaeologists could use is lacking.

Recent ethnographic literature, however, has come to recognize that ritual behaviour can, in many of its aspects, be regarded as producing ecosystemic consequences (Rappaport 1967, Meggers 1971). This view emphasizes regularity of process, often at the expense of the detail produced by other theoretical approaches to ritual. It must ultimately be asked which circumstances strengthen, and which minimize, the importance of ritual as a socio-economic and environmental regulator. So far, this seems never to have been done.

In order to develop usable and testable models of the isomorphisms of the relationships between energy flow and those institutions which regulate it in different types of societies, it does little good to emphasize the particularistic. For the kind of model we are proposing, for instance, it is irrelevant and methodologically illegitimate to retrodict an institution such as the *cargo* system back to Classic Maya times by extrapolating back, from the evidence of Maya art, how generally permeated with religion Maya culture was, and therefore, how correspondingly more probable the inference that ritual would have been a powerful regulator of behaviour. This may be true, but the question we have asked is different, which governs the appropriateness of various kinds of answers. What is most needed from ethnographers is a broader comparative picture of institutions from a range of peasant-organized societies which do the work of the Mesoamerican *cargo* system. The material effects of these variations could then be examined for degree of correspondence with archaeological observations, and the most suitable alternative from a number of potential analogies selected on this basis.

Acknowledgments

Although the speculations and conclusions advanced in this paper are entirely the responsibility of the author, sincere thanks for comments and criticisms, and for moral support are due to Richard S. White of the American Museum of National History; to Karen Kerner and David Feingold of Columbia University; and to William L. Rathje of the University of Arizona (whose facility in the matter of titles is truly unparalleled). Special appreciation, please, to William Rathje; to Gordon R. Willey of Harvard University; and to Andrew Sherratt, University of Cambridge, for their having provided a timely bridge over troubled waters.

REFERENCES

Adams, R.E.W. (1970) Suggested Classic period occupational specialization in the southern Maya Lowlands. In W.R. Bullard (ed.), *Monographs and Papers in Maya Archaeology*, Papers of the Peabody Museum of Archaeology and Ethnology, Harvard University, vol. 61, 487-502.

Ascher, R. (1961) Analogy in archaeological interpretation. *Southwestern Journal of Anthropology*, 17, no. 4, 317-24.

Binford, L.R. (1962) Archaeology as anthropology. *American Antiquity*, 28, 217-25.

Binford, L.R. (1967) Smudge pits and hide smoking: the use of analogy in archaeological reasoning. *American Antiquity*, 32, 1-12.

Binford, L.R. (1968) Archaeological perspectives. In S.R. and L.R. Binford (eds), *New Perspectives in Archaeology*. Chicago.

Boserup, E. (1965) *The Conditions of Agricultural Growth*. Chicago.

Bullard, W.R. (1960) Maya settlement pattern in northwestern Peten, Guatemala. *American Antiquity*, 25, 355-72.

Bullard, W.R. (1962) Settlement pattern and social structure in the southern Maya lowlands during the Classic period. 35th Congreso Internacional de Americanistas, *Actas y Memorias*, Mexico (1964), 279-87.

Bunzel, R. (1959) *Chichicastenango: A Guatemalan Village*. Seattle.

Cancian, F. (1965) *Economics and Prestige in a Maya Community*. Stanford.

Carrasco, P. (1961) The civil-religious hierarchy in Mesoamerican communities: pre-Spanish background and colonial development. *American Anthropologist*, 63, no. 3, 483-97.

Coe, W.R. (1965) Tikal, Guatemala, and emergent Maya civilization. *Science*, 147, 1401-19.

Coe, W.R. (1967) *Tikal: A Handbook of the Ancient Maya Ruins*. Philadelphia.

Culbert, T.P. (1970) *Sociocultural Integration and the Classic Maya*. Paper presented at 35th Annual Meeting of the Society for American Archaeology, Mexico.

Deetz, J. (1968) The inference of residence and descent rules from archaeological data. In S.R. and L.R. Binford (eds), *New Perspectives in Archaeology*, Chicago.

Fallers, L. (1965) *Bantu Bureaucracy*. Chicago.

Foster, G.M. (1948) *Empire's Children: The People of Tzintzuntzan*. Smithsonian Institution, Institute of Social Anthropology, Publication no. 6.

Foster, G.M. (1953) What is folk culture? *American Anthropologist*, 55, no. 1, 160-73.

Foster, G.M. (1960) *Culture and Conquest: America's Spanish Heritage*. Viking Fund Publications in Anthropology, no. 27, New York.

Foster, G.M. (1965) Peasant society and the image of limited good. *American Anthropologist*, 65, no. 2, 293-315.

Freeman, L.G., Jr. (1968) A theoretical framework for interpreting archaeological materials. In R.B. Lee and I. de Vore (eds), *Man the Hunter*, 262-7. Chicago.

Fried, M.H. (1967) *The Evolution of Political Society*. New York.

Gibson, C. (1964) *The Aztecs under Spanish Rule: A History of the Valley of Mexico 1519-1810*. Stanford.

Gibson, C. (1967) *Tlaxcala in the Sixteenth Century*. Stanford.

Gillin, J. (1951) *The Culture of Security in San Carlos*. Middle American Research Institute, Publication no. 16.

Harris, M. (1964) *Patterns of Race in the Americas*. New York.

Harris, M. (1968) *The Rise of Anthropological Theory*. New York.

Haviland, W.A. (1965) Prehistoric settlement at Tikal, Guatemala. *Expedition*, 7, no. 3.

Haviland, W.A. (1966) *Maya Settlement Patterns: A Critical Review*. Middle American Research Institute, Publication no. 26.

Haviland, W.A. (1967) Stature at Tikal, Guatemala: implications for ancient Maya demography and social organization. *American Antiquity*, 32, no. 3.

Hawkes, C. (1954) Archaeological theory and method: some suggestions from the Old World. *American Anthropologist*, 56, no. 1, 155-68.

Hill, J.N. (1968) Broken K Pueblo: patterns of form and function. In S.R. and L.R. Binford (eds), *New Perspectives in Archaeology*, 103-42. Chicago.

Hill, J.N. (1970) Prehistoric social organization in the American Southwest: theory and method. In W.A. Longacre (ed.), *Reconstructing Prehistoric Pueblo Society*, 11-58. Albuquerque.

Lewis, O. (1951) *Life in a Mexican Village: Tepoztlan Restudied*. Urbana, Ill.

Longacre, W.A. (1970) *Archaeology as Anthropology: A Case Study*. Anthropological Papers of the University of Arizona, no. 17.

McBryde, F.W. (1947) *Cultural and Historical Geography of Southwest Guatemala*. Smithsonian Institution of Washington, Institute of Social Anthropology, Publication no. 4.

Meggers, B.J. (1971) *Amazonia: Man and Culture in a Counterfeit Paradise*. Chicago.

Meggers, B.J., and C. Evans (1956) The reconstruction of settlement pattern in the South American tropical forest. In G.R. Willey (ed.), *Prehistoric Settlement Patterns in the New World*, Viking Fund Publications in Anthropology, no. 23, 156-64.

Miles, S.W. (1957) Maya settlement patterns: a problem for ethnology and archaeology. *Southwestern Journal of Anthropology*, 13, no. 3, 239-48.

Miles, S.W. (1958) An urban type: extended boundary towns. *Southwestern Journal of Anthropology*, 14, no. 4, 339-54.

Parsons, E.C. (1936) *Mitla: Town of Souls*. Chicago.

Parsons, L.A., and B.J. Price (1971) Mesoamerican trade and its role in the emergence of civilization. In R.F. Heizer and J.A. Graham (eds), *Observations on the Emergence of Civilization in Mesoamerica*, Contributions of the University of California Archaeological Research Facility, no. 11, 169-95.

Proskouriakoff, T. (1963) *An Album of Maya Architecture*. Norman, Oklahoma.

Puleston, D.E. (1968) *New Data from Tikal on Classic Maya Subsistence*. Presented at 33rd Annual Meeting of the Society for American Archaeology, Santa Fe.

Rappaport, R.A. (1967) *Pigs for the Ancestors*. New Haven.

Rathje, W.L. (1970) Socio-political implications of lowland Maya burials: methodology and tentative hypotheses. *World Archaeology*, 1, no. 3, 359-74.

Rathje, W.L. (1971) The origin and development of Lowland Classic Maya civilization. *American Antiquity*, 36, no. 3, 275-85.

Redfield, R. (1941) *The Folk Culture of Yucatan*. Chicago.

Reina, R.E. (1967) *Milpas* and *milperos*: implications for prehistoric times. *American Anthropologist*, 69, no. 1, 1-20.

Romney, A.K. (1957) The genetic model and Uto-Aztecan time perspective. *Davidson Journal of Anthropology*, 3, 35-41.

Sahlins, M.D. (1958) *Social Stratification in Polynesia*. Seattle.

Sanders, W.T. (1956) The Central Mexican symbiotic region. In G.R. Willey (ed.), *Prehistoric Settlement Patterns in the New World*, Viking Fund Publications in Anthropology, no. 23, 115-27. New York.

Sanders, W.T. (1965) *Cultural Ecology of the Teotihuacan Valley*. Pennsylvania State University, Department of Anthropology (multilith).

Sanders, W.T., and B.J. Price (1968) *Mesoamerica: The Evolution of a Civilization*. New York.

Smith, M.A. (1955) The limitations of inference in archaeology. *Archaeological Newsletter*, 6, 3-7.

Steward, J.H. (1950) *Area Research: Theory and Practice*. Social Science Research Council, Bulletin no. 63. New York.

Steward, J.H. (1955) *Theory of Culture Change*. Urbana, Ill.

Tax, S. (1937) The municipios of the midwestern highlands of Guatemala. *American Anthropologist*, 39, no. 2, 423-44.

Tax, S. (1952) *Heritage of Conquest: The Ethnology of Middle America.* Glencoe, Ill.

Tax, S. (1953) *Penny Capitalism: A Guatemalan Indian Economy.* Smithsonian Institution of Washington, Institute of Social Anthropology, Publication no. 16.

Thompson, R. (1956) The subjective element in archaeological inference. *Southwestern Journal of Anthropology*, 12, no. 3, 327-32.

Vogt, E.Z. (1961) Some aspects of Zinacantan settlement patterns and ceremonial organization. *Estudios de Cultura Maya*, 1, 131-46.

Vogt, E.Z. (1964) The genetic model and Maya cultural development. In E.Z. Vogt and A. Ruz Lhuillier (eds), *Desarrollo Cultural de los Maya.* Universidad Nacional Autónoma de México, Seminario de Cultura Maya.

Vogt, E.Z. (1969) *Zinacantan: A Maya Community in the Highlands of Chiapas.* Cambridge, Mass.

Wagley, C., and M. Harris (1955) A typology of Latin American subcultures. *American Anthropologist*, 57, 428-51.

White, L.A. (1949) *The Science of Culture.* New York.

Wolf, E.R. (1956) Aspects of group relations in a complex society: Mexico. *American Anthropologist*, 58, 165-78.

Wolf, E.R. (1957) Closed corporate peasant communities in Mesoamerica and Central Java. *Southwestern Journal of Anthropology*, 13, 1-18.

Wolf, E.R. (1959) *Sons of the Shaking Earth.* Chicago.

Wolf, E.R. (1966) *Peasants.* Englewood Cliffs, N.J.